MW00592386

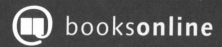

Read this book online today:

With SAP PRESS BooksOnline we offer you online access to knowledge from the leading SAP experts. Whether you use it as a beneficial supplement or as an alternative to the printed book, with SAP PRESS BooksOnline you can:

- Access your book anywhere, at any time. All you need is an Internet connection.
- Perform full text searches on your book and on the entire SAP PRESS library.
- Build your own personalized SAP library.

The SAP PRESS customer advantage:

Register this book today at *www.sap-press.com* and obtain exclusive free trial access to its online version. If you like it (and we think you will), you can choose to purchase permanent, unrestricted access to the online edition at a very special price!

Here's how to get started:

1. Visit *www.sap-press.com*.
2. Click on the link for SAP PRESS BooksOnline and login (or create an account).
3. Enter your free trial license key, shown below in the corner of the page.
4. Try out your online book with full, unrestricted access for a limited time!

Your personal free trial **license key**
for this online book is:

qck8-i423-xzfd-r9wn

Testing SAP® Solutions

 PRESS

SAP PRESS is a joint initiative of SAP and Galileo Press. The know-how offered by SAP specialists combined with the expertise of the Galileo Press publishing house offers the reader expert books in the field. SAP PRESS features first-hand information and expert advice, and provides useful skills for professional decision-making.

SAP PRESS offers a variety of books on technical and business related topics for the SAP user. For further information, please visit our website: *www.sap-press.com*.

Martina Kaplan, Christian Oehler
Implementing SAP Enhancement Packages
2010, 220 pp., hardcover
978-1-59229-351-3

Marc O. Schäfer, Matthias Melich
SAP Solution Manager Enterprise Edition
2nd edition, updated and revised
2009, 555 pp., hardcover
ISBN 978-1-59229-271-4

Matthias Friedrich, Torsten Sternberg
Change Request Management with
SAP Solution Manager
2009, 297 pp., hardcover
ISBN 978-1-59229-261-5

Michael Willinger, Johann Gradl
Migrating Your SAP Data
2nd edition, updated and revised
2008, 373 pp., hardcover
ISBN 978-1-59229-170-0

Markus Helfen and Hans Martin Trauthwein

Testing SAP® Solutions

Galileo Press

Bonn • Boston

Galileo Press is named after the Italian physicist, mathematician and philosopher Galileo Galilei (1564–1642). He is known as one of the founders of modern science and an advocate of our contemporary, heliocentric worldview. His words *Eppur si muove* (And yet it moves) have become legendary. The Galileo Press logo depicts Jupiter orbited by the four Galilean moons, which were discovered by Galileo in 1610.

Editor Florian Zimniak
Translation Lemoine International, Inc., Salt Lake City, UT
Copyeditor John Parker
Cover Design Silke Braun and Graham Geary
Photo Credit iStockphoto.com/Pali Rao
Layout Design Vera Brauner
Production Manager Kelly O'Callaghan
Production Editor Graham Geary
Typesetting Publishers' Design and Production Services, Inc.
Printed and bound in Canada

ISBN 978-1-59229-366-7

© 2011 by Galileo Press Inc., Boston (MA)

2nd edition, updated and expanded, 2011
2nd German edition published 2010 by Galileo Press, Bonn, Germany

Library of Congress Cataloging-in-Publication Data
Helfen, Markus.
   [SAP Lvsungenn testen. English]
   Testing SAP solutions / Markus Helfen, Hans Martin Trauthwein. — 2nd ed.
       p. cm.
   Includes bibliographical references and index.
   ISBN-13: 978-1-59229-366-7
   ISBN-10: 1-59229-366-2
   1. Computer software—Testing. 2. Management information systems—Testing. 3. SAP ERP. I. Trauthwein, Hans Martin. II. Title.
   QA76.76.T48H4513 2011
   650.0285'53—dc22
   2010046321

Contents at a Glance

Dear Reader,

"Therefore test, who wants to bind himself forever, Whether heart will find right heart. The elation is short, the remorse is long." It may seem a little over the top to appeal to German dramatist and poet Friedrich Schiller as witness for a book on software testing. However, the antagonism project teams are struggling with has probably never been phrased more precisely than in the second verse of the citation: Trapped in the notorious triangle of deadlines, costs, and quality, project leads receive the final bill only when the solution has gone live.

If you tested whether the new solution really does what it is supposed to do, which side-effects it has on other functionalities, and whether its performance complies with the end-users' expectations before go-live, then good for you! For your testing projects, SAP equips you with a rich set of powerful tools, and by reading this book you get to know them all.

We appreciate your business, and welcome your feedback. Your comments and suggestions are the most useful tools to help us improve our books for you, the reader. We encourage you to visit our website at *www.sap-press.com* and share your feedback about this work.

Thank you for purchasing a book from SAP PRESS!

Florian Zimniak
Publishing Director, SAP PRESS

Galileo Press
Boston, MA

florian.zimniak@galileo-press.com
www.sap-press.com

Contents

5   Project-Related Testing with SAP Solution Manager and SAP Quality Center by HP 275

Preface to the Second Edition

Today, the business environments in which our customers operate are characterized by increased use of enterprise networks, a trend toward globalization, and ever greater integration of business functions. Under these conditions, enterprises face a multitude of challenges. They must implement and operate innovative software without disrupting business processes, and they must provide users with reliable and effective solutions of an increasingly complex nature. At the same time, risk must be minimized and the total cost of operation reduced. Against this backdrop, testing remains one of the essential challenges that must be met if enterprises are to ensure end-to-end lifecycle management of applications and implement and operate business-critical processes.

With SAP Enterprise Support, SAP offers customers holistic, solution-oriented support that fosters both innovation and solution integration. This helps safeguard your investments, strengthens SAP's long-term commitment to its customers, and forges joint partnerships. SAP Enterprise Support provides a tried-and-tested procedure and a clear roadmap for implementing the SAP Standards for Solution Operations, which naturally include a standard for test management. Our Solution Operations Standards enable effective end-to-end operation and management of solutions by our customers. Consulting services, training, and certification are also provided as part of our Run SAP methodology.

Our mission-critical support includes ongoing quality checks to analyze technical risk and ensure continuous improvement. In addition, our Support Advisory Center offers a direct channel of communication to ensure 24/7 support for business-critical processes that are based on service-level agreements and agreed-upon initial response times.

SAP Solution Manager, including its Enterprise Edition, is an essential component of our Global Support Backbone, given that SAP Solution Manager contains all the methods, processes, and tools required for quality management and testing. The functions provided for test management in particular have now been significantly enhanced and supplemented, as is well documented in this book.

SAP also offers a strategic portfolio of testing services that includes tools for designing testing tasks, minimizing the duration of projects, reducing project costs by increasing methodological efficiency, and achieving transparency of results by using license-free and integrated test tools within SAP Solution Manager. These are supplemented by tools for the provision and anonymization of test data for the automation of functional tests and for performance tests. This book shows you exactly what SAP offers its customers in this regard, using real-world customer reports to emphasize practical aspects. The authors can take particular pride in the sustainability reports, which describe the long-term effects of their consulting activities.

In developing our service offering, we have paid particular attention to its scalability in order to ensure that it can handle all our customers' needs. One way we do this is consistently productizing our consulting services during every phase of the lifecycle, with the highest level of quality guaranteed. A productization approach also allows us to consistently evaluate customer experiences and makes cost controlling more transparent, as testing costs can be accurately calculated and forecasted in advance. Productization also allows us to transfer knowledge to our customers more efficiently.

The creation of a global service organization that takes account of integrated service delivery from the very start by working with our near and offshore service centers also guarantees non-stop availability of services.

In recent years, both the authors and their SAP Test Management Consulting team have made key contributions to these areas, many of which are vividly portrayed in this new edition using a successful blend of theory and practice.

You will see for yourself how SAP is ideally positioned to provide effective support to our customers in the testing environment. In this context, I would like to extend my sincere thanks to the authors for their commitment to providing our customers and partners with the benefit of their combined experience in the form of this book. As for you, dear readers, I hope that this book gives you plenty of useful information about our tools and practical tips for your own activities, and that you can then put this information successfully into practice.

Best regards,

Gerhard Oswald
Member of the Board of SAP AG

Foreword to the Revised and Extended Second English Edition

Dear readers,

While there was never any doubt that the second edition would be translated, it unfortunately took quite some time to tackle this task. However, once the project was scheduled and assigned, it began without delay, thanks to the preparations that already had been made.

In essence, the content was revised and expanded to meet the information requirements of non-German-speaking customers.

The translation project involved, above all, adding information about current product versions (such as SAP TAO) and key innovations such as those in the area of IT reporting with SAP Solution Manager.

In order to avoid further extending the scope of the book, no customer reports were updated or added, with one exception: Because the ROI study of automated regression testing at our reference customer INVISTA had already been updated in 2009, this new information was added to the relevant chapter.

Thanks to this approach, we believe that we have made good use of this opportunity for careful enhancement in order to provide our readers with a publication that is comprehensive and that contains up-to-the-minute information. The authors hope that you find this book an enjoyable and interesting read.

Acknowledgements

Many thanks—once again—to Gerhard Oswald, our member of the Executive Board at SAP, who made it possible for the new edition of *Testing SAP Solutions* to be expanded and translated.

René Allissat reprised his role as copy editor for the translation project. Thank you for the top-quality support, which allowed us to achieve the desired result within a short amount of time. We would be more than happy to work with you again on future projects—that's a promise!

We would like to thank many of our colleagues within the SAP Group for their valuable contributions, in particular:

▸ Marcus Wefers and Sonal Kumar, who provided us with information about the current version of SAP TAO

▸ Melanie Reinwarth for her help with the translation of the chapter on eCATT

▸ SAP ALM Business Development Managers Michael Schleier and Andreas Wentz for assisting with review activities

We have tried, at all times, to shed light on the many support options offered by SAP in the area of testing. We hope, dear readers, that you will also follow this guiding principle and that this book will help you prepare for the decisions that lie ahead. After all, testing is and always will be one of the most important elements of Application Lifecycle Management for SAP solutions.

St. Ingbert, Germany
Markus Helfen
Hans Martin Trauthwein

Foreword to the Second Edition

Dear readers,

You may be wondering what exactly has changed since the first edition of *Testing SAP Solutions* was published in 2006 and why we would go to the trouble of putting together a second edition just three years after the first. Well, clearly there was a good reason to do so, or you wouldn't be holding the new edition in your hands right now! Indeed, many innovations, changes, and events occurred in relation to the testing of SAP solutions in the short period between the publication of the German version in the first quarter of 2006 and the summer of 2008, when the publishers asked us to work on a revised edition. In addition, new developments and surprises came along as we were working on this project, some of the most important of which are listed below. The authors were involved to a greater or lesser degree in each of these events, which are listed in chronological order.

▶ The inclusion of the HP Quality Center product in SAP's product portfolio as SAP Quality Center by HP (reselling strategy)

▶ The availability of the SAP Solution Manager Adapter for SAP Quality Center by HP (what a name!) to give customers the best of both worlds: management of project-relevant and solution-relevant information, such as business processes, in SAP Solution Manager (central data pool, single source of truth), and use of the sophisticated test-management functions of the SAP Quality Center by HP

▶ Availability of SAP Test Acceleration and Optimization (TAO), a solution for accelerated generation of test components, which is based on the business-process testing approach of the SAP Quality Center and uses additional functions of the Quality Center to execute automatic test cases in the SAP GUI environment

▶ Stagnation in the ongoing development of functions for testing within SAP Solution Manager

Events since the first edition

21

▶ Development of an official SAP testing stool strategy, which gives our customers two choices: "Testing Option 1" and "Testing Option 2".

▶ Announcement of SAP Enterprise Support and an Enterprise Edition for SAP Solution Manager.

▶ The emergence of testing as one of the main areas of investment in SAP Solution Manager development. The main innovations are as follows: Sequence control for test execution with workflow and email notification, the Business Process Change Analyzer, and integrated BW reporting.

▶ Restoration of a Product Manager for Test Management in SAP Solution Manager, while the role of the eCATT Product Manager is being filled once again.

▶ SAP's establishment of a global test service organization with a unified service portfolio, which will collaborate closely with individual local partners and with nearby and offshore resources.

▶ Drinking your own champagne: Product Development at SAP AG plans to use individual components of SAP Solution Manager internally. One example is the planned migration of both test management systems (one for manual test cases and one for automatic test cases) to SAP Solution Manager.

▶ The possibility of bundling testing activities for project-related testing and regression tests in a single central approach, namely, a test center, is being discussed as part of a strategic project within SAP IT.

▶ As of 2009, SAP faced the task of proving that holistic support strategies—comprising methodology, tools, and services—can produce measurable benefits by reducing costs of operating SAP solutions. The key performance indicators that were developed in collaboration with the SAP Usergroup Executive Network (SUGEN) are closely related, in some main categories, to the topic of "efficient testing procedures."

Our current real-world consulting experience indicates that, from SAP's perspective, everything needed to achieve this is already in place. Customers are invited to achieve these results with us. All that we need are initiative and commitment.

Feedback on the first edition In addition to this purely technical requirement for completeness of content, the extremely positive feedback on the first edition that we received both from our customers and within SAP naturally inspired and motivated us to embark on a second edition. In response to readers' suggestions, we also wanted to provide information about tools and functions that were added to the portfolio of SAP test tools after the first edition went to press and to provide a comparison of different tools. Tool comparisons often become obsolete very quickly, in some cases even before they are published, due to the dynamics of development (just consider all of the development undertaken in one year in SAP Solution Manager), and so this was a serious decision for the authors. However, we provide other recommendations on tool selection in this book. At this point, we would like to express our thanks, yet again, to everyone who gave us their feedback. We've tried to take it into account in the planning and realization of the current work, and we look forward to your feedback on this edition also.

Run SAP is the new methodology developed by SAP and delivered to our customers for managing the operation of their SAP solutions. Of course, this also includes test-relevant suggestions. Notwithstanding the diverse range of methodological concepts and best practices available, we felt that it was also important to move outside of our own sphere and demonstrate the relationship with major market standards such as ITIL[1] or the professional training schema developed by the ISTQB.[2]

Methodology and best practices

The practical relevance of our book is ensured by the abundance of tips and recommendations that we've included on the basis of our many years of consulting experience, and by the many customer reports that have been added. As a result we have included a relevant report based on our real-world experience for each topic covered. In our opinion, the updates of some customer reports from the first edition represent specific highlights of this new edition because, in these cases, we were able to demonstrate the long-terms effects (over approximately five years) of implementing the relevant methods, tools, and services. And these effects speak for themselves: Customer reports highlight outcomes such as effectiveness, security, reusability, stability, availability, increased efficiency, reduced cost, and ROI.

Practical relevance

Unfortunately, we did not have a customer report on the new SAP TAO product to include before this edition went to press. In addition, two

---

1 IT Infrastructure Library: international de facto standard for implementing IT service management.

2 International Software Testing Qualifications Board; see *www.istqb.org*.

other customer reports on other topics had to be withdrawn for different reasons shortly before publication. However, we believe that the reports we have included cover the relevant spectrum of topics very well.

The prospect of updating our material for the current version did not cause any alarm. Even so, although we were given everything we needed to undertake this task (see our acknowledgements below), it was a mammoth undertaking to complete this project, in particular since most of it had to be done alongside our day-to-day work.

We were never bothered by the fact that publication of this edition coincided with the announcement of other publications on the same range of topics because we were and remain 100 percent confident in our experience, our concept, our core messages, and our strategic statements. Ultimately, we must allow reader demand to be the judge, but we are sure that our readers will, once again, become our customers!

We, Markus Helfen and Hans Martin Trauthwein, wish you an enjoyable and interesting read.

Acknowledgements

The authors of a book such as this expose themselves to risk and visibility and put themselves and their good names on the line, to be met with either praise or criticism. Behind the scenes, however, a large number of people contributed directly or indirectly to this work, and to them we wish to express our heartfelt thanks.

Sadly, Michael Lauer, our co-author on the first edition, was not part of the authoring team this time around. However, Michael readily made himself available at all times to help us patiently with our questions. Many thanks for your assistance, Michael.

Of course, this kind of undertaking would never have been possible without the support of our families. Many thanks to our partners and children for your indulgence of us and for the sacrifices you made for us. Thank you Geneviève, Ute, Nina, and Marco.

Our thanks are also due to Gerhard Oswald, our member of the Executive Board at SAP, who made it possible for this new edition of *Testing SAP Solutions* to be published. Gerhard Oswald had already lent his support to the first edition, and so having him on board again this time was a huge boost to our confidence.

We also wish to extend sincere thanks to our customers who made direct and valuable contributions by sharing their experience of implementing methods, tools, and SAP test-management consulting in their projects in the form of a customer report. These reports will benefit anyone interested in this subject. Some of our customers have done this for the second time by working together with the authors to update their original reports from the first edition. In these "sustainability reports," you will experience the long-term effects that can be achieved with SAP's holistic support strategy.

Thanks are also due to those customers with whom we have worked in recent years to test, refine, and enhance our best practices. We can now look back on nearly 1,000 instances of direct contact with our customers, and these form the backbone of our expertise. Many thanks for allowing us to work with you.

Our team colleague and copy editor René Allissat played a vital role in revising and extending *Testing SAP Solutions*. He needed little input, advice, and time to produce top-quality research, content elaboration, and results. A very special word of thanks to you René: We wish you all the best and every success on your career path!

Our collaboration with the publisher was coordinated once again by our editor Florian Zimniak, who always strives to make each publication look as good as it possibly can. Working with him was always a professional, purposeful, and successful experience.

In our own departments, we would like to thank, first and foremost, our managers: Peter Seidl, Markus Albrecht, and Michael Rehm, for their support.

We extend our thanks to Patrick Arendt, Bernd Borutta, Benjamin Oberste-Berghaus, Michael Schleier, Christian Schwaninger, and Andreas Wentz, all colleagues on our SAP Test Management Consulting team, who made valuable contributions in the form of ideas, content development, research, or corrections.

We would also like to thank many of our colleagues within the SAP Group for their valuable contributions, especially:

- Nilgün Atasoy and Ralf Debus for the chapter on SAP TDMS
- Frank Krause, Markus Dinkel, and Melanie Reinwarth for their contribution on eCATT
- Marcus Wefers for his ideas and for giving his stamp of approval to our work, in particular in relation to SAP TAO
- Marc Thier and Michael Klöffer for their input regarding the SAP Solution Manager diagnostics
- Annette Wicker and Marc Voss for their help in creating the customer report by Deutsche Telekom AG
- Eric Siegeris for his discussion of and ideas for the Test Center chapter
- Young dad Jewgeni Kravets for his suggestions in relation to testing in eSOA implementation projects

Our work on this book was both challenging and fascinating due to the vast range of new projects, topics, and customer scenarios we were required to cover. We hope that this book will provide our readers with a degree of transparency that will help them make sound decisions. After all, testing is and always will be one of the most important elements of the Application Lifecycle Management for SAP solutions.

St. Ingbert, Germany
Markus Helfen
Hans Martin Trauthwein

Foreword to the First Edition

"Welcome to the Jungle!" Welcome to the Jungle? What does this catchy lyric from Guns N'Roses have to do with a serious specialized book from SAP PRESS? It all started some years ago as we drove back from a customer meeting, chatting about how to optimize our presentation material. In particular, we spent a long time discussing the challenges that our customers face in the area of testing. We wanted to illustrate these challenges in a presentation slide in order to represent our proposed solutions in a way that would "speak to" the customer. Our spontaneous brainstorming session brought up several challenges that we categorized as follows:

▶ Customer processes had been mapped to span multiple systems in a solution landscape; at that point, SAP had already successfully passed the stage of the New Dimension products. The solution landscapes operated by SAP customers had many different levels of heterogeneity.

▶ The technology also posed challenges in terms of test execution and the test tools that were mainly used. Could the automation tools in particular handle SAP's user interfaces, solutions, and technologies in a sustainable, robust, and cost-effective way?

▶ Test projects should follow a minimum set of methodological principles, rules, and conditions. This applies to the various test types and stages.

▶ A wide range of tools from different providers are available on the market. At that time, companies were making purchasing decisions with financial consequences that went far beyond the licensing costs of the third-party tools in focus.

We wanted to represent these four different dimensions—solutions, technologies, methodology, and tools—in a presentation slide. After a few more miles of driving, the representation problem was solved, but the title for our slide came to us only when the above-mentioned song

Challenges

was played on the radio and gave us the inspiration we needed. The animated slide was entitled, "Testing seems to be a jungle," and it is still in use today, albeit in updated form.

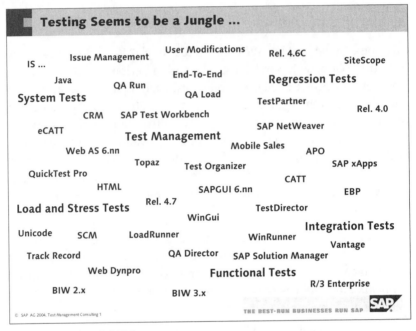

Figure 1 The "Jungle" Slide

Findings from approximately 380 customer projects

As you read this book, you will see that not only we have continued thinking about our customers since our fateful trip, but that the wide range of experience we've gained in our real-world consulting work has made it possible for us to undertake the writing of this book. Much of our experience comes from customer projects; we were in the fortunate position of having access to findings from approximately 380 customer engagements and projects, plus numerous other events and presentations on the subject of testing and quality assurance within the SAP customer base. Many of our observations and arguments arose from or were affirmed in discussions and collaborations with our customers.

We also realized that there still remains a significant need for information and reliable consulting in this area. Again and again, we encountered situations in which customers received poor consulting arising from lack of experience on the part of the consulting partner. In the eCATT area, in particular, we come across this situation several times a year; when, for example, the wrong drivers were recommended for the specific use in an automation activity. Ultimately, it is the customer who suffers the consequences of such misinformation if the topic falls out of favor and the motivation to continue working on it no longer exists.

We do not have exact figures for the usage levels of SAP test tools amongst the SAP customer base; we can say only that, based on the available evidence, the estimated level of unreported usage is undoubtedly much higher than may at first appear. Based on our monitoring of our customer base, we have seen that the level of traceable usage increases with the usage level of SAP Solution Manager. In particular, companies that are looking for a suitable initial use case of SAP Solution Manager quickly find what they are looking for in the area of testing and can immediately realize the potential benefits by finally dispensing with spreadsheet-based solutions.

SAP Solution Manager enables us to document projects and tests in a thoroughly reproducible manner in a central system. This represents a real step forward from earlier versions of the classic Test Workbench from SAP R/3 system releases, although the basic functionality of those systems is still alive and stable. Even customer requirements that are subject to compliance regulations can now be easily fulfilled. However, our customers still have a great need for information about SAP Solution Manager, which is why we have paid much attention to the topic of integrating the SAP test tools into SAP Solution Manager.

Central test documentation

Using proprietary SAP test tools is a natural consequence of using SAP NetWeaver as a strategic business process platform and of the associated increase in homogeneity of the solution landscape. It would be careless and even neglectful, to squander this advantage by using other tools without discovering and evaluating the alternative: the test tools from SAP.

Also, you may place your trust in the reputation of SAP Test Management Consulting as a trusted advisor in the testing environment. This reputation has been built on the basis of countless customer contacts, engagements, and projects. This book gives the reader access to the technical basics, our best practices, procedures, and arguments from the world of testing at SAP.

In designing this book, on the basis of more than 30 years of work and experience of best practices, we focused on the following areas of activity:

- Quality management, including creating, certifying, operating, and auditing quality management systems in different companies
- Quality assurance in developing, implementing, and operating software products
- Designing, planning, implementing, and executing numerous test projects with different goals and of different sizes

Decision-makers and managers in IT departments, as well as program and project managers of SAP customers, will find in this book tried-and-tested procedures for planning and realizing their own test projects.

In response to the initiative of Galileo Press, which at the start of 2005 began looking for a publication on the subject of testing SAP solutions, we took on the challenge of writing this book with a veteran team in order to find a path through and shed light into the above-mentioned jungle. This decision was based largely on our view that a book seemed to be the best way of sharing our experiences with customers.

St. Ingbert, January 2006
Markus Helfen
Hans Martin Trauthwein
Michael Lauer

1 Introduction

Widely varying levels of importance are still attached to the subject of "testing" among users of standard business software. For example, sophisticated testing processes are frequently employed in validated environments in the chemicals and pharmaceuticals industry, enabling a monitored, well-documented implementation or upgrade of SAP solutions. Equally, enterprises that have stringent requirements in terms of quality and system stability safeguard their critical business processes using change or release management, whereby changes are systematically documented, approved, tested, and implemented. At the heart of processes such as these, the testing of altered functions ensures that changes do not disrupt the production system.

Real-world testing of standard business software

In practice, however, we still also encounter some very pragmatic approaches, whereby testing activities are executed more implicitly and are often decentralized and not systematically recorded. As a result, it is virtually impossible to draw conclusions about the maturity and stability of an implementation or upgrade project, and project risks in terms of the quality of a solution can only be estimated to a very limited extent. In this kind of environment, live operation is frequently characterized by uncertainty about the effects of necessary changes. As a result, negative effects are accepted or efficiency-enhancing innovations and the use of new functions are put on hold.

The usual question that arises in this context is: "Why does standard software have to be tested?" This has been a moot point for quite some time. Naturally, it is the responsibility of a manufacturer of standard business software to ensure that its functions work without problems. SAP relies on extensive internal quality assurance processes and on strong industry support for this purpose. However, the customer must convert its enterprise-specific business processes into solutions based on SAP products. When implementing SAP solutions, this process is accelerated, for example by proposing core business processes or using industry-specific configurations (*industry solutions*). Industry solutions enable the

Testing the individual instance of a solution

implementation of specific processes such as those used by banks and insurance providers, the chemicals industry, the health care system, or the public sector.

Modifications and customer developments

In addition to a range of standardized processes, a customer-specific instance of a solution also comprises, above all, processes that make the enterprise unique and that give it a competitive edge. These processes are implemented using the existing functions in the standard software, which can be adapted to suit the enterprise's requirements using the customizing settings. Whenever this type of enterprise-specific adaptation of the standard functions is insufficient, enhancements or even modifications need to be made, and SAP systems provide a range of technologies for this purpose. If these modifications still do not suffice for certain areas within the enterprise, the option of a complete customer-specific development of specific functions within the SAP system is always available. Naturally, this option carries with it the possibilities, costs, and risks that go hand-in-hand with software development.

Service-oriented architecture

Service-oriented architecture (SOA) for business applications also provides methods for composing customer-specific processes from existing services. This enables a rapid implementation of small-scale projects at a manageable cost, for example, swift implementation of process innovations.

Standard business software is embedded in a largely heterogeneous and complex system landscape. Accordingly, interfaces such as those used with legacy systems, must be taken into account when creating customer-specific business processes.

Changes necessitate testing

In order to achieve an enterprise-specific instance of a solution, the customizing and additional development, including interfaces with other systems, must be validated by appropriate testing. This is the only way to ensure, at the level of business requirements, that the solution to be implemented meets the requirements that were originally documented and, above all, that it supports the enterprise's business processes as effectively as possible. From a technical perspective, it is also essential to ensure that the processes can be used at all times without errors and with an adequate level of performance. This also depends on customer-specific requirements, including the size of the system and the user load.

Thus, an enterprise-specific instance of standard business software must always be tested. In practice, this means that the customer must thoroughly test the business processes implemented in the software to ensure that they cover the specified requirements, verify their functional correctness, and assess their performance. The implementation of a new SAP solution or the upgrade of an existing system represents a more or less fundamental change to the system landscape. In this case, the necessity for and scope of the testing activities are obvious: all business processes, including any modifications and customer-specific developments, must be tested.

Testing activities will also continue after the system goes live, because a smooth flow of business-critical processes must be ensured at all times. Any change to the production system could impact negatively on business operations and therefore must be tested. These changes include IT-driven changes, such as imports of Support Packages and SAP Notes, as well as business-driven changes, such as upgrades or system consolidations following a merger.

The live system

The options for testing changes are as diverse as the range of events that might lead to these changes. Depending on the scale of the change and its criticality ("How critical is the process to the enterprise's routine operations?"), the scope of testing may range from the strategic validation of individual business processes to full-scale integration testing of all critical business processes. As part of this regression testing, significant savings can be made in both time and resources through the technical identification of the effects of changes and through test automation. Ideally, these already would have been taken into account during earlier project phases.

It is always useful to control and document testing activities as part of a testing process, regardless of the current phase of the solution within the application lifecycle. A systematic approach facilitates a high-quality implementation of new solutions or the implementation of changes without employing excessive resources. In addition, using test automation tools can significantly reduce the number of resources required to execute regression testing. Comprehensive reporting enables you to draw conclusions about the maturity of new solutions, upgrades, and changes, and perform fact-based, proactive decision-making. The documentation of testing activities, including all errors detected, ensures full traceability

Method

of the testing process, which is particularly useful given that supporting documentation may be required. This type of fundamental testing process requires the support of a tool.

With its proven methodology, namely SAP Solution Manager as a platform for managing SAP solutions throughout their entire lifecycles, and with a portfolio of integrated and third-party test tools, SAP offers end-to-end support for all testing activities for SAP solutions. This support is now available in the form of a global service portfolio and a global consulting organization.

Contents of this Book

This book provides a detailed insight into the range of testing methods and tools in the SAP environment. Theoretical descriptions are illustrated by a total of 13 real-world customer reports. In this new edition, seven brand new reports have been added in the various chapters. In addition, three of the customers represented in the first edition have now provided us with sustainability reports. These reports show how the methods and procedures described in the initial reports have been further developed and extended over a period of three years and how the use of test tools has continued during this time.

Part I:
Methodology

Part I, *Methodology*, describes in the following chapters the relevant concepts and methods used to test SAP solutions.

Chapter 2, *Theory of Software Testing*, explains the reasons for testing activities in the SAP environment and presents the various testing types and stages. The chapter also describes relevant aspects of current testing theory in the SAP environment. An example of a testing process is developed on the basis of the theoretical explanations. The chapter then closes with an overview of key considerations in the selection of test tools.

Chapter 3, *Test Methodology*, describes the procedure of preparing and executing a test project within the scope of an SAP rollout, using the established ASAP process. It includes fundamental methodological information and empirical best practices for the planning and implementation of testing activities.

Part II: Functional
Testing

Part II, *Functional Testing*, deals with the tools provided by SAP to support your test projects. Testing is managed using either the original functions in SAP Solution Manager (Testing Option 1) or via SAP Quality Center by

HP, which can be connected to SAP Solution Manager using an adapter (Testing Option 2). Both options allow SAP Solution Manager to fulfill its role as SAP's central application management solution and to act as a central data pool ("single source of truth"). The tools and procedures described in this part represent the practical steps and the corresponding technical implementation of a test project done as part of an implementation within SAP Solution Manager, as described in Chapter 3, *Test Methodology*.

Chapter 4, *Test Management with SAP Solution Manager*, gives you an in-depth insight into the SAP Solution Manager functions provided in Release 7.0 Enhancement Package 1, which you can use for test management activities.

This chapter describes test management using SAP Solution Manager and the Test Workbench (Testing Option 1) in the context of SAP Enterprise Support, Run SAP, and the SAP Standards for Solution Operations. It focuses, in particular, on the range of new functions provided with SAP Solution Manager 7.0 Enhancement Package 1.

Likewise, **Chapter 5**, *Project-Related Testing with SAP Solution Manager and SAP Quality Center by HP*, describes the procedure used for testing with SAP Quality Center by HP in conjunction with SAP Solution Manager (Testing Option 2). Here, the focus is on the procedure used for requirements-based testing based on an SAP Solution Manager project.

SAP Test Acceleration and Optimization (TAO) also provides a tool for component-based creation of automatic test cases as part of Testing Option 2. This tool is described in **Chapter 6**, *Supporting Test Automation with SAP TAO*.

Each of the chapters is fleshed out using practical reports that illustrate the complexity of testing and also show how enterprise-specific procedures can be mapped flexibly using the tools described.

SOKA-BAU, a reference customer for end-to-end test management, uses the full functional scope of SAP Solution Manager and the Test Workbench for test management of its projects. SOKA-BAU's customer report describes how the enterprise, as a participant in the customer valuation for SAP Solution Manager 7.0 Enhancement Package 1, was able to evaluate new SAP Solution Manager functions (such as the Business Process

Change Analyzer) at an early stage and integrate these into its testing process.

The Südwestfalen Energie und Wasser AG energy and water utility (SEWAG) used SAP Solution Manager for process documentation, configuration, and test management as part of an ERP upgrade.

The customer report by Bosch and Siemens Hausgeräte GmbH gives a detailed, practical account of the benefits of integrated test management using SAP Solution Manager within a groupwide program. The updated report shows how testing activities were continuously extended and optimized and, in particular, how the new functions in SAP Solution Manager and the Test Workbench were used for this purpose. It also shows how test automation was initiated successfully.

The report by Hamm-Reno-Group GmbH & Co. KG shows how a partially automated integration test provides greatly improved test coverage compared to manual tests, while at the same time reducing testing costs and achieving faster test cycle times. The updated report describes how the tried-and-tested procedure, which was optimized continuously, also succeeding in meeting customer expectations during testing activities in the context of a merger.

Endress+Hauser InfoServe GmbH & Co. KG opted for SAP Quality Center by HP and successfully used the tool to implement Business Process Testing, a method for component-based creation of test cases.

Meanwhile, DB Systel GmbH uses both testing options. While HP Quality Center is used as a test management tool and the HP Quality Center Dashboard is used for management reporting throughout the enterprise, SAP Solution Manager and the Test Workbench are used for SAP projects. A reporting interface that was developed as a consulting solution transferred the results of testing from the Test Workbench to HP Quality Center.

Automated testing activities provide an alternative to manual testing. **Chapter 7**, *Economic Aspects of Test Automation*, demonstrates the benefits of automating functional testing. It provides an overview of the main cost types for the automation of regression test sets. It also considers error costs, as you will need data on both cost types in order to create a business case.

The INVISTA Resins & Fibers GmbH report describes the creation of an automated regression test set using SAP's eCATT tool, and the benefits of this scenario. Together with SAP Test Management Consulting, the company created an ROI study, which has accompanied its testing activities for more than five years. The automated regression tests cover the company's critical regression tests and are used for all complex and extensive system changes. The overall result was a significant enhancement of system stability and quality for the implemented solutions, despite much-reduced testing costs. You can use the figures from this case study as reference values for your own estimates.

Following these economic considerations, we then move on to describe the tools themselves. **Chapter 8**, *Test Automation with eCATT*, describes SAP's test automation tool in SAP NetWeaver 7.02, the latest release as this publication was going to press. This chapter gives you an extensive overview of the basic functioning of eCATT and how to use its various test drivers. It equips you with the knowledge you need to take your first independent steps toward setting up test automation in your system.

The Zürcher Kantonalbank customer report describes the use of eCATT in a development project that was critical for this customer. Zürcher Kantonalbank uses automated tests for a wide range of application scenarios, and in this case was able to fulfill special technical requirements thanks to the flexibility, integration with SAP applications, and powerful capabilities of eCATT.

Chapter 9, *SAP Test Data Migration Server*, introduces you to an SAP tool that you can use to regularly transfer a subset of the data from your production system to your non-production systems. In addition to having low memory requirements and reducing the cost of a system copy or the providing of test data, SAP TDMS also enables encryption of production data. As well as describing various scenarios relating to the selection of production data, this chapter also describes the legal foundations and the technical options of data encryption, in particular in the area of SAP Human Capital Management solutions supported by SAP TDMS.

The customer report of Behr GmbH & Co. KG gives a practical account of the deployment and benefits of SAP TDMS as experienced by this reference customer.

Infineon Technologies AG also uses the SAP TDMS, in particular in the area of HCM, and its first-hand experiences are similarly related in a customer report.

Part III, *Performance Tests*, describes the methods and procedures used to test aspects of performance in the SAP environment.

Chapter 10, *Project Outline of a Performance Test*, introduces you to this third section of the book. This chapter presents a tried-and-tested procedure for executing performance tests, and deals with specific methodological aspects, such as determining a load profile and organizing the technical implementation.

After the methodological and organizational aspects, this section then illustrates the technical issues involved in performance tests. **Chapter 11**, *SAP LoadRunner by HP*, describes the powerful standard solution from SAP for executing load and stress tests. This chapter places particular emphasis on testing the SAP portal application. It also describes the SAP Performance Center by HP, which can be used for planning and executing performance tests across the enterprise.

HeidelbergCement AG used SAP LoadRunner by HP to implement a central consolidation system. Its customer report describes how the load test was implemented with the support of SAP Test Management Consulting.

The customer report from Sanofi Aventis describes the use of this tool in the context of quality assurance in a strategic portal implementation. This report goes into particular detail on the various technical challenges that arise from such tests and that often require consulting support.

Chapter 12, *Monitoring a Performance Test*, deals with various SAP transactions that have proved over time to be indispensable tools in every performance test. Alongside load generation, monitoring system behavior is one of the central challenges of a performance test.

Finally, in **Part IV**, *Test Center*, **Chapter 13**, also entitled *Test Center*, presents a holistic approach, which unites the activities described in the area of quality assurance for software in a separate organizational unit. In this way, for example, you can bundle all of an enterprise's testing activities in order to standardize them and thus achieve a higher level of quality in terms of testing activities while simultaneously reducing costs. This type of test center also lends itself perfectly to setup and operation by an external service provider.

The customer report by Deutsche Telekom AG describes how SAP Test Management Consulting established a test center as part of an extensive project. It shows how this test center initially implemented all testing activities for the project and since has also provided support for production systems, including cross-project IT reporting. This report demonstrates the spectrum of activities that can be covered by a test center and illustrates the testing procedure used in an SOA project.

Target Groups

One target group of readers for this book consists of decision-makers and managers in IT departments, program managers, and project managers who must tackle testing activities in order to ensure the integrity of their projects or the operation of their SAP solutions. Another target group includes customer employees who are involved in the technical implementation of testing activities.

Of course, we recommend that readers in both groups read the book in its entirety and in doing so, look "outside the box" of their own work. Nonetheless, certain chapters may be more relevant to one group than the other.

Part I, *Methodology*, is particularly relevant to the first target group. This group will also find Chapter 7, *Economic Aspects of Test Automation;* Chapter 10, *Project Outline of a Performance Test;* Chapter 13, *Test Center*, and, of course, all the customer reports, very relevant to their work.

For the second target group, all of Part II, *Functional Testing*, plus Chapter 8, *Test Management with eCATT*, are of particular interest, as these chapters contain the most information about tools. Chapter 9, which covers the SAP Test Data Migration Server, is also largely technical in terms of content, as is the whole of Part III, *Performance Testing*.

The customer reports serve as shared ground for both groups, as these sections deal with both methodological and tool-specific aspects, based on real-world customer situations.

PART I
Methodology

To make sure you gain the full benefit of the practice-oriented sections of this book, we first need to deal with theory. Despite our "testing seems to be a jungle" catchphrase, we want to make this subject approachable, and so we present in this chapter an easy-to-digest introduction to the basic principles of testing.

2 Theory of Software Testing

This chapter gives you an overview of the most important concepts of testing theory and the practical limits of these concepts. We start with a number of sections that are intended to help you understand basic concepts and to clarify the terminology. This is necessary because the terms and procedures used in the SAP environment are quite different at the detailed level from those used in the standard literature.

However, this chapter does not provide a complete treatment of the subject of software testing theory. Any readers who would like a thorough grounding in software testing theory should refer to, among other resources, the professional training schema developed by the ISTQB (*International Software Testing Qualifications Board, www.istqb.org*) and the publications based on this schema. The basic concepts relating to testing and test management are covered in detail in the internationally standardized curriculums ("syllabi") for the "Certified Tester" qualification.

2.1 System Changes Necessitate Testing

In the introduction to this book, we already looked at the question of why standard software needs to be tested. A customer-specific instance of an SAP solution, which is created through customizing, modifications, and enhancements, as well as its integration into a heterogeneous system landscape, always requires quality assurance to assess its suitability, functional correctness, and performance. This brings us immediately to a second question: When does a solution need to be tested? The answer to this question determines both the timing of testing activities, the fundamental nature of the testing, and the process model, as well as the structure, granularity, and content of test cases. In order to discuss the theoretical concepts and terminology, it is therefore essential to pursue this question in order to understand of these individual aspects.

Application lifecycle

Like all software products, an application in the SAP environment has a lifecycle, which starts with the implementation of a solution, includes ongoing maintenance, and finally leads to an upgrade of that solution. What distinguishes standard business software from other software products is its broad spectrum of applications. Because such a system acts as the "central nervous system" of the enterprise, many representatives from many different areas in the enterprise are involved in its implementation or upgrade in order to ensure that the software is adapted to meet the enterprise's requirements. This process can be viewed as an initial change of the standard software, involving customizing, modifications, and customer development in order to map enterprise-specific business processes in the system. Testing activities therefore need to determine whether the requirements made to the business processes—in other words, requirements made of the system—have been fulfilled. In this phase, testing is equally used to ensure the correctness of the mapped processes and the correct functioning of the system in subsequent live operation. The performance of the solution also plays a central role here. Depending on how important the processes are to the enterprise's business operations and the number of users involved, we can assess the criticality of any issues detected.

Maintenance

The maintenance of an SAP ERP system is uniquely important due to the extensive nature of the adjustments that can be made to it. SAP currently employs a 7-2 maintenance strategy. However, an SAP system may be operated for much longer than nine years. Many changes will be made to the system within this period. On the one hand, the software will be regularly optimized by SAP using Support Packages and Enhancement Packages; on the other, customer changes to business processes or the system will require immediate adjustment of the software.

The various change scenarios must all be taken into account in order to ensure systematic change management. Implementations and upgrades of SAP solutions require establishment of a structured process model for testing and for defining methods for test-case creation throughout the project. This is generally done on the basis of market and industry standards, and using established process models and best practices (see Chapter 3, *Test Methodology*).

Changes made to live solutions are the main reason for testing SAP solutions after the go-live phase. Essentially, each of these changes must be tested to ensure a smooth flow of business-critical operations. An appropriate testing strategy and suitable test cases must be chosen on the basis of the nature and extent of the change. For example, you can distinguish among changes made in the system by examining the reasons they are made, including:

Changes necessitate testing!

► **Business process-driven changes**

  ► *Company mergers and acquisitions* often require extensive changes to the system landscape and accordingly present challenges for the IT organization. These include the consolidation of systems, the addition of new systems in an existing environment, and the linking of entire system landscapes. Because critical business processes are usually impacted, tests must have sufficiently extensive scope.

  ► *Changes to business processes* may occur, for example, as part of ongoing optimization processes within an enterprise, or because the enterprise needs to innovate core business processes to ensure that it remains competitive or retains its market leadership. New legal requirements represent another reason for such changes. In these cases, testing must focus on the affected processes, and, where necessary, also take account of upstream and downstream processes.

  ► In the SAP environment, *functional upgrades* are delivered in the form of Enhancement Packages and provide new functions that can be implemented by customers if required. This category also includes customer-specific or partner solutions, as well as creation of composite applications based on enterprise services.

► **IT-driven changes**

  ► *Support Packages* and *SAP Notes* are delivered by SAP to correct errors and optimize functionality. One challenge associated with the testing of these objects is the identification of the business processes that are affected by the changes. SAP provides the Business

Process Change Analyzer tool to help with this task (see Section 4.4.5, *Extended Functionality for Creating Test Plans and Packages*).

▶ *Technical upgrades* refer to the upgrading of an SAP solution to a higher version. These always require functional testing of the system to determine whether the mapping of businesses processes still functions as required. The non-functional properties of the solution, such as performance, also need to be checked.

▶ *Changes to infrastructure* are changes to the system hardware. These include replacing the server hardware or changes to connected systems. These must be tested under realistic conditions in order to ensure satisfactory system performance; for example, in terms of agreed service levels.

Modifying existing test cases

In most cases, test cases from the solution's implementation phase already exist when these changes are made. It is essential to select the appropriate test cases from all cases that are available. It is also necessary to modify these test cases to suit the new conditions within the processes or within the system. In addition, new test cases need to be created, such as those needed for large-scale changes or inadequate documentation of existing tests.

Figure 2.1 shows the relative time and effort involved in testing each of the change events described above.

The change events shown here differ in terms of both the scope of testing required and the amount of time and effort associated with that testing. Accordingly, they require different test types, methods, and tools. The basic principles used to classify these elements are explained below in order to provide you with the theoretical foundation required to appreciate the practice-oriented sections of this book. This chapter also explains the terminology that will be used throughout subsequent chapters. These terms are based on market standards and on SAP-specific terminology.

In the next section, we begin by differentiating between basic text types and describing the typical test stages used in the SAP environment, which provide a basis for various procedures used during testing. Later chapters are devoted to the subject of test case creation and the basic principles used to select a test tool.

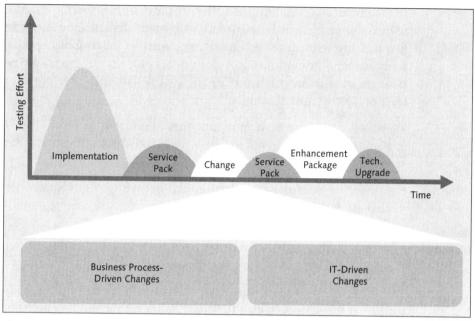

Figure 2.1 Change Events and Their Associated Testing Efforts

2.2 Test Types

The objective of software testing is to verify or enhance software quality to ensure that a solution complies with customer requirements. Specific requirements and the test cases based on these requirements are formulated on the basis of defined quality characteristics. Norms and market standards, such as norm ISO/IEC 25000, are used to define corresponding criteria. These norms distinguish between the following characteristics:

The objective of software testing

▸ Functionality

▸ Reliability

▸ Usability

▸ Efficiency

▸ Changeability

▸ Transferability

In the case of standard business software, the customer-specific instance of the solution must be tested. In this case, particular attention is paid to functionality; in other words, determining whether the customer-specific solution maps the customer-specific business processes as expected. The criterion of efficiency is also relevant, as it describes the performance level of the customized solution.

Therefore, one of the most important questions that arise in the context of a software test is whether the test should take runtime behavior into account.

Functional testing

▸ A test that does not take the runtime behavior of a program into account, but instead tests the *functional correctness* of the program, is referred to as a *functional test*.

Performance testing

▸ If, on the other hand, the runtime behavior is included in the test, we refer to this kind of test as a *performance test*.

Performance tests that are run as part of implementation projects usually test the entire system, taking the complete infrastructure into account. Performance tests are among the most important tests in technical system testing.

Test Type	Test Goal	Software characteristic
Functional testing	The expected result is returned.	Correctness
Performance testing	The result is returned in the expected time.	Efficiency

Table 2.1 Differences Between Functional Testing and Performance Testing

As you can see from Table 2.1, the two test types differ in more than their theoretical aspects; the different test requirements also affect the practical aspects of the tests. The procedures, methods, and tools used for performance testing are different from those used for functional testing, and so we will deal with these topics in separate chapters of this book.

2.3   Test Stages

Implementation, upgrade, and development projects all comprise several test stages. These stages can be sorted by the level of integration on which the software is tested. The test stages usually originate in the general V-model of software development. We'll first explore the SAP-specific test stages, which are based on this generic process model for the development and, in particular, the testing of software. This discussion also provides an opportunity to directly compare the terminology used in this book with the standard terms using in testing in general.

2.3.1   Test Stages in the General V-Model

The general V-model represents a straightforward software development process. The model, originally presented by Boehm[1] back in 1979, appears in various guises in the literature, differing in terms of the number of project steps involved, the level of detail, and the terms used to describe the individual elements. Rather than being a fully-fledged process model, the V-model instead serves to illustrate how specification and development phases relate to testing activities.

General V-model

The basic principle underlying all variations of this model is the V-shaped structure (see Figure 2.2). The design and development phases, shown on the left of the diagram, are borrowed from the iterative waterfall model. A testing activity appears opposite each of these phases, with each activity being of equal importance. The activities serve to verify the results of the corresponding development phases.

The development activities represented in the model describe the process that starts with the definition of requirements and ends with the implementation of the software development.

Development activities

▸ **Requirements definition**
All requirements (functional requirements, performance, user interface, and so on) of a piece of software to be developed are defined and approved in this step.

---

1 Boehm, B. W.: *Guidelines for Verifying and Validating Software Requirements and Design Specification*; Proceedings of Euro IFIP 1979, pp. 711–719.

▶ **Functional system design**
The requirements documents created in the first phase generally do not specify how the requirements are to be implemented in the system in practice. In this design phase, they are defined in the form of a software product, for example, with user interfaces and reports.

▶ **Technical system design**
This phase describes the technical architecture of the system, for example, by defining individual software modules, as well as their interfaces and dependencies.

▶ **Component specification**
Each module defined in the previous phase is then described in more detail and, if necessary, divided into further components, which are documented in such a way that programmers can immediately begin to develop them.

▶ **Programming**
This phase represents the actual implementation of the software in a system.

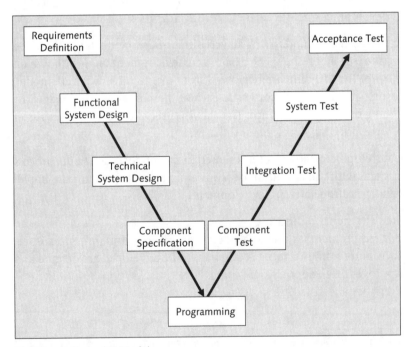

Figure 2.2 General V-Model

Starting with the smallest elements that can be tested (for example, function modules), a testing activity is assigned to each development phase.
The requirements defined in the individual phases are tested as soon as
the software or its constituent parts reach the required level of maturity.
This results in the following test stages in connection with the development activities.

▶ **Component test**
In this phase, individual function modules are checked against the
component specification. This activity is closely related to development and generally requires knowledge of the internal structure of
each module.

▶ **Integration test**
The integration test checks whether integrated components are working together successfully in accordance with the specifications.

▶ **System test**
This testing activity tests the entire system in terms of function
requirements and performance.

▶ **Acceptance test**
The acceptance test serves to verify whether the system fulfills the
formulated requirements from the point of view of the customer or
end user.

Although the V-model, in its basic form, no longer adequately meets the
requirements of today's development and implementation processes, it
is still an ideal construct for illustrating the various test phases. It shows
how various test phases are required within a development project, each
of them intertwined with the project's progress. A division into various
test stages is useful because each stage requires a different approach to
test-case creation, test planning, and test execution, and this must be
taken into account in the context of the project as a whole. This also has
a direct effect on the choice of testing tools used.

The structure of the V-model is universally applicable, and not limited to
new software development. It is equally relevant for an implementation
or upgrade project in the SAP environment.

SAP process models

A fundamental difference in the SAP environment is the underlying process model used. The ASAP Implementation Roadmaps (see Chapter 3, *Test Methodology*), for example, provide a comprehensive methodology for implementing and upgrading SAP systems. These roadmaps each consist of five phases, which cover the entire project, and go above and beyond the implementation and testing of system changes. Chapter 3 describes the ASAP methodology in detail, with a focus on testing. Here, the programming phase is replaced by the implementation phase, in which the customer-specific instance of the system (customizing and modifications or enhancements) is implemented. The upstream design phases correspond to the functional and technical documentation of the business processes that are to be implemented.

The test stages of the V-model must be adjusted accordingly. Depending on the scope of the project, the development of a new function may play a role in an implementation project, in which case the relevant testing must be executed. However, the focus is usually on the validation of the business processes that are mapped in the system. These are not to be considered in isolation when designing the tests. Rather, they must also be tested in the context of upstream and downstream processes and, if necessary, take account of connected systems. While acceptance testing is usually implemented in the SAP environment by involving the end users in the integration test, performance testing is considered very important in the context of SAP projects. It tests the system's response times and also provides a direct indication of the solution's acceptance.

The generic V-model ends with a successful acceptance test, and does not take account of the changes described above that are made during the lifecycle of the software. In the SAP environment, by contrast, an appropriate strategy for executing tests during live operation is a critical success factor. A separate process for testing following changes must therefore be defined.

Figure 2.3 shows the synthesis between the test stages of the V-model and SAP project methodology. The individual test stages in SAP projects are explained below.

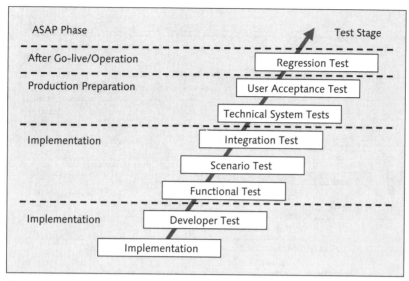

Figure 2.3 Test Stages in SAP Projects

2.3.2 Test Stages in SAP Projects

As in the V-model, a bottom-up strategy—that is, working from the part to the whole—is used without exception for functional testing in the SAP environment. Thus, integration level-based sorting is not only theoretical; it can also be roughly applied to the different phases of a project. The depiction of test stages is distinct from the description of a process model. The individual stages merely describe the nature of the testing and test cases that correspond to a specific project phase (see Figure 2.4). The process of executing an implementation project with its embedded test phases and the description of a testing process are discussed in Chapter 3, *Test Methodology*.

The first tests executed are *developer tests*. As the name suggests, this type of testing is carried out in the development phase by the developer. Developer tests are carried out at the lowest technical level and can encompass a wide range of testing activities, such as formal executability tests, tests of interim results between individual lines of code, and tests of individual function modules or transactions. In the SAP project methodology, developer tests are usually regarded as part of development activity and thus do not come under the heading of *functional tests* in the more restricted sense.

Developer test

53

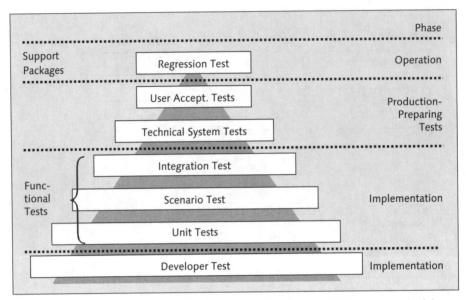

Figure 2.4 Bottom-Up Model of the Integration Stages in SAP Project Methodology

Unit test   *Unit tests*, also known as module tests, usually represent the lowest level of functional testing in the SAP environment. A unit test checks an individual transaction or function module. It focuses mainly on internal functions rather than on interfaces and integration.

Scenario test   *Scenario tests* test several related transactions. The subject of this type of testing is either a series of transactions within a business area or a business process that spans multiple areas. Scenario tests focus on the interaction between individual transactions and their interfaces, and can be run iteratively in order to build up larger end-to-end scenarios from smaller partial scenarios. Based on our experience, scenario tests are often run as an extension of unit testing in SAP projects.

Integration test   *The integration test* represents the final step in ensuring functional correctness. It tests the integration of SAP solutions with non-SAP applications and system interfaces. Customer business processes are mapped in the form of end-to-end scenarios, and the software is tested in accordance with these cross-module and cross-system scenarios.

Technical system test   System tests are known in the SAP environment as *technical system tests*, and they bring more components, such as infrastructure components, under the scrutiny of the testing process. Instead of looking at the functionality of the software in isolation, technical system testing checks the entire system, consisting of the database, application servers, front ends, networks, printers, and so on.

Performance tests are one of the most important types of technical system testing, which measures the throughput and response times of the system. Performance tests add an additional, crucial dimension to functional testing: the processing response times of multiple, simultaneously executed business transactions. The application to be tested must be functionally correct before performance testing can be carried out.

Performance tests

In addition to response times, another very important element must be included in testing before a system goes live: acceptance by future users of the solution. For obvious reasons, *user acceptance tests* cannot be automated and thus, like integration testing, require considerable investment of time and effort. The primary goal of user acceptance testing is to detect usability problems, mainly in the areas of dialog design and system response times.

User acceptance test

Based on our observations, user acceptance tests are seldom used in SAP projects, although future users are often taken into account in the functional testing described above. If this is the case, a performance test is essential; otherwise, the lack of a user acceptance test means that no conclusions can be drawn regarding the solution's response times in dialog-based user interaction.

The purpose of a *regression test* is to ensure that no unplanned or unexpected effects on the mapped functionality and business processes follow a process-related or technical change. In the SAP environment, regression tests are usually required after IT-driven changes, such as corrections or Enhancement/Support Packages.

Regression test

Regression testing is also required after business-driven changes, such as the remodeling of a business process in the system, or a change to the customizing settings. Therefore, a regression test does not represent a further level of integration. In practice, this kind of testing is usually restricted to a repetition of integration testing, based either on samples or on the full scope. A reduced test scope is often used in this case, as no deterioration is normally expected in terms of user acceptance and performance. Therefore, the scope of a sample test should always consciously be defined in accordance with the criticality of the changes and the risks associated with the occurrence of an error, or on the basis of technical criteria.

Selection of regression test cases

Test cases should ideally be selected with the assistance of a tool and on a technical basis in order to ensure that regression tests achieve the highest possible degree of validity and produce the most useful information. With the Business Process Change Analyzer, SAP Solution Manager provides functions that can be used to pinpoint which technical modules (such as programs or tables) have been affected by a change and to identify the relevant test cases (see Section 4.4.5, *Extended Functionality for Creating Test Plans and Packages*).

Regression test set

Without technically safeguarding the sample, a sound regression test set should at least cover the critical business processes and, if necessary, additional test cases that help to verify critical processes steps (for example, sales price calculation).

2.4   Black-Box Testing and White-Box Testing

Black-box testing

Another criterion for choosing the form of testing is the information used in relation to the structure of the system to be tested. If the system is regarded from the outside only, without the use of any information about its internal structure, we call this *black-box testing*. A user interface is not essential to execute black-box tests.

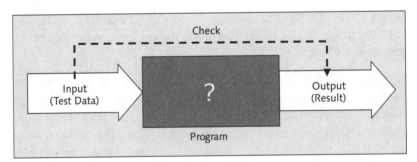

Figure 2.5 Black-Box Testing—Excludes Knowledge of the Internal Structure of the Tested Program

Because black-box testing does not use internal program information, it focuses on input data and results. The quality of these tests therefore depends wholly on the quality of the test data.

If information about the internal structure of the software — source code or internal interfaces, for example — is used, this is called *white-box testing*. White-box testing is used mainly in the software development process.

White-box testing

The advantage of these tests is that the additional information can be applied in a more targeted way to areas where errors are expected. At the same time, this targeted approach is also the biggest disadvantage of white-box testing. This is because the search for defects focuses on program parts that are known to be error-prone. White-box tests thus run the risk of ignoring errors in parts of the software that are usually robust and less error-prone.

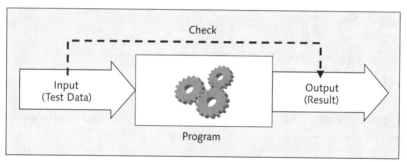

Figure 2.6 White-Box Testing — Includes Knowledge of the Internal Structure of the Tested Program

Black-box tests tend to be used for verification purposes and for final acceptance, while white-box tests are used more as developer tests and in the error elimination and debugging processes.

Data-driven black-box testing is most commonly used in the SAP environment, while white-box testing is less frequent in this context. Exceptions are made in very large development projects only.

Relevance in the SAP environment

2.5 Test Case Design for Black-Box Testing

Different input-data combinations produce different system responses. That is why your choice of test data is particularly significant in black-box testing. In principle, you can create artificial or synthetic data, or use real data from your production system.

Besides the input data to be used, it is also important to specify the expected result in a test-case description. The tester can then use this description for comparative purposes during the manual testing process. The result description can consist of the appearance of an event on the user interface (such as the system message "Material created"), checks behind the user interface (such as a test to determine whether worklist tables have been filled), or even semantic checks (such as a verification to determine that the correct increase in stock or value update has been made). The same principle applies here as before: The criticality of the application determines the scope and level of detail of the result description.

We will now describe some methods for designing test cases for black-box testing.

2.5.1 Equivalence Class Partitioning

Based on the observation that there are too many possible inputs and input combinations to take them *all* into account in a test, our aim is to help you to create a set of input data that is as representative as possible and that covers *all* the cases that occur in a transaction.

To do this, you first have to identify the values of an input or combinations of inputs that trigger different software behavior. An equivalence class is formed by all the input values, or combinations of these, that are intended to trigger the same software behavior.

The following simple example, based on an invoice-calculation program, illustrates the process of working with equivalence classes. First, the program determines the total number of input items. If the net invoice amount is less than €100, additional delivery costs of €6.20 are added to the invoice. If the net invoice amount is less than €25, an additional handling charge of €3.80 for short quantities is also added. Finally, the appropriate value-added tax (VAT) rate is applied to the net invoice amount, in accordance with the delivery destination. The equivalence classes for various input values can be represented as shown in the table below.

These equivalence classes relate to the net invoice amount. Because amounts of €100 or more do not incur delivery charges, it is easy to identify the class. Other classes will have to be created for the delivery charge and the short-quantity charge.

Class	Net Invoice Amount	Additional Charge
A	€0.01 – 24.99	€3.80 + €6.20 = €10.–
B	€25.00 – 99.99	€6.20
C	€100.–	–

Table 2.2   Example of Equivalence Classes (Net Amount)

The next equivalence classes, shown below, are those for the delivery destination. The relevant VAT rate is applied here. For the sake of simplicity, our example uses domestic (German) and foreign VAT rates only.[2]

Class	Delivery Destination	VAT Rate
1	Germany (D)	19%
2	Abroad (<>D)	0%

Table 2.3   Example of Equivalence Classes (VAT)

Once the equivalence classes have been defined for all input values, all the meaningful combinations are created from these. A test data set is therefore a meaningful combination of the equivalence classes that have been determined. Now you can create the actual test data sets by selecting a (random) value from every equivalence class.

Our example here contains six meaningful input combinations that can be regarded as representative of each of their equivalence classes.

One possible difficulty in creating and using equivalence classes in practice is that errors that occur in the process of determining the classes can cause the test quality to deteriorate to a considerable extent.

---

2   Due to circumstances that are unfortunately beyond our control, the value shown in the example may have risen again after this book went to press.

Equivalence Class Combination	Line Item Net Value	Delivery Destination	Expected Result (Gross Invoice Amount)
A1	€3.60 €2.48	Germany	(€3.60 + €2.48 + €10.00) * 1.19 = **€19.14**
A2	€11.30 €1.48 €2.00	Ireland	€11.30 + €1.48 + €2.00 + €10.00 = **€24.78**
B1	€34.30	Germany	(€34.30 + €6.20) * 1.19 = **€48.20**
B2	€69.50 €2.48	Ireland	(€69.50 + €2.48) + €6.20 = **€78.18**
C1	€179.50 €2.48	Germany	(€179.50 + €2.48) * 1.19 = **€216.56**
C2	€119.50 €119.50 €119.50 €119.50	Ireland	€119.50 + €119.50 + €119.50 + €119.50 = **€478.00**

Table 2.4 Example of Input Value Combinations Identified Using Equivalence Class Partitioning

2.5.2 Boundary Value Analysis

Extending the equivalence class procedure

A boundary value analysis is an extension of the equivalence class procedure. When identifying test data using a boundary value analysis, data sets that are closest to the limits of the permitted value ranges are always tested.

Boundary value analyses are based on the observation that errors occur most frequently in those special cases, which is why it is worthwhile to focus the search there.

To analyze the test data, you first determine the related areas of the same test data type. This is broadly the same as an equivalence class analysis. However, instead of selecting a random value from the class, this kind of analysis selects two representative values: the highest and the lowest. Obviously, a boundary value analysis can be used only if there is a specific order in the test data.

In the example above, the values €0.01 and €24.99 would be selected for the net invoice amount equivalence class A, €25.00 and €99.99 for class B, and €100.00 for class C.

Example of boundary value analysis

Because the delivery destination consists of discrete values, it functions as a variable within the input combinations. Therefore, only the following boundary values need to be taken into account:

Net Value Line Items	Delivery Destination	Expected Result (Gross Invoice Amount)
€00.01	Germany	€11.91
€24.99	Germany	€41.64
€25.00	Germany	€37.13
€99.99	Germany	€126.37
€100.00	Germany	€119.00
€00.01	Ireland	€10.01
€24.99	Ireland	€34.99
€25.00	Ireland	€31.20
€99.99	Ireland	€106.19
€100.00	Ireland	€100.00

Table 2.5   Example of Input Value Combinations Identified Using Boundary Value Analysis

2.5.3   Error Guessing

Departments design test cases based on the viewpoint of the user; the technical perspective of a developer supplements this. With the method known as *error guessing*, the developer creates test cases that enable him to select the inspection instructions and test data that will provoke as many errors as possible. In other words, he deliberately tests input, input combinations, and special cases that he believes will cause the system to return errors. Conversely, with this method, he avoids test cases that simply prove that the software functions correctly.

Provoking errors

The developer uses his own experience to get the best results from this kind of testing. He starts out by assuming that the software contains a particular, typical error, and creates input values or input value combina-

Experience

tions that bring this error to light. The advantage of error guessing is that it leverages the experience of the developer to find errors in a specific, targeted manner. A possible disadvantage is that this approach can be regarded as somewhat unstructured.

2.6   Test Data

Synthetic test data

Among other things, the procedures explained above describe how to identify test data that then has to be made available with the required specification in test systems. Synthetic test data can be created for specific purposes, either manually or by various tools, such as automation tools like SAP's Extended Computer Aided Test Tool (eCATT). The advantage of synthetic data obtained by means of the procedures described above is its excellent quality thanks to the use of application logic. On the other hand, the time and effort required identifying and creating the data—either manually creating the data or writing scripts—can be a disadvantage.

Production data

A different approach is often used in the SAP environment. Data is copied or migrated from the production system(s) to the test system. This data is highly familiar to the testers of the departments, and this makes their testing work considerably easier. Also, data from production systems is usually of high quality and consistency and should be made available in sufficient quantities, particularly in the case of transaction data.

2.7   Basic Procedures for Planning and Execution

Awareness of the various test stages and test types provides a foundation for implementing effective software tests. However, the basic principles outlined above have not yet indicated how testing is implemented at an organizational level. The main procedures used for this purpose are briefly discussed below.

Testing in the context of projects

Testing activities are usually embedded within a project implementation. This was illustrated above in the V-model, which shows the relevant test stages that correspond to each individual specification or development tasks in a project. Therefore, testing must always fit into a higher-level project methodology, which usually also determines an initial testing scheduling, specifying in what order and within which time frames the various types of testing can be executed. Established process models, which often are used in conventional software development projects, include the V-model XT and the Rational Unified Process. In the context of SAP projects, ASAP Roadmaps and Run SAP methodology similarly provide extensive methodological frameworks for implementing and operating SAP solutions (see Chapter 3, *Test Methodology*). Process models like these usually also include activities for software quality assurance. A testing process, at the very least, should be embedded in the project procedure, which describes the essential steps taken to implement testing for the specific project. Regardless of the project type and the specific nature of the testing, this type of project should contain at least the steps outlined below.

2.7.1 Test Preparation

The relevant testing activities should, if possible, be planned and drafted as part of project preparation. The first step in this process involves determining all aspects of the tests that are to be executed and documenting these in a structured way. This can be done in the form of a test concept document, which remains valid for the entire duration of the project, serving as a set of rules and guidelines for all testing activities. This concept document contains essential information relating to all testing to be executed within a project, as well as details of the individual test types and test stages. This information includes:

Test concept

- A classification of the test in the project context
- Associated documents (such as the project plan, overall quality assurance strategy)
- Test systems and objects to be tested; system landscape
- Contents of the tests (which characteristics are to be tested and which are not)
- Criteria for interrupting and terminating testing, as well as acceptance criteria
- Documentation standards (document templates, reporting)
- Testing roles and responsibilities
- Test tools used

Testing strategy   The testing strategy represents another key element of test planning and thus also of the test concept. This strategy defines the objectives of testing and the activities that will serve to meet these objectives. One element of the testing strategy is a risk analysis, which determines the scope of testing, priorities, and the granularity of the individual test type and test stages and of their testing methods. The potential risks are identified, and the test cases that are to be executed are weighted accordingly. In the case of business-process test execution, evaluations based on such criteria as criticality, frequency of execution, and numbers of users have proven useful. As a next step, the results of this evaluation provide a basis for scheduling and resource management for the testing activities at each test stage, enable the selection of suitable testing methods, and ensure that test cases have an appropriate level of granularity and are prioritized correctly. It is also useful to incorporate risk management into the project as a whole, so that project risks are taken into account in the specification of the test cases. Approaches to risk analysis for test cases range from pragmatic approaches to models that require a quantified risk evaluation or that take account of the complexity of the test objects.

Effort estimation   The testing strategy also incorporates the allocation of available resources or calculation of required resources. This implies an estimate of the required testing effort. Models with varying degrees of complexity exist for estimating the required testing effort, from experience-based estimated values to complex mathematical models based on the underlying parameters of the testing activities, such as number of test cases or average number of errors (for more information about estimating testing effort in the SAP environment, see Chapter 3, *Test Methodology*).

Templates for test concepts   The specifics of each individual project determine the degree of detail provided in the various areas within the test concept. It would not be useful at this point to provide an exhaustive discussion of the possible contents of a test concept. Guidelines for creating a test concept are provided by the test documentation standard IEEE 829[3]. If a project process model is available as a framework—consisting of methodology, tools, and document templates—templates may also be required for the implementation of this test concept. In any case, the objective of creating such a document is to provide a detailed description of all testing

---

3 IEEE Std 829–1998: *IEEE Standard for Software Test Documentation;* IEEE, New York, 1998.

activities. Depending on process maturity and on the size of the project, this information may also be divided among several standardized documents.

2.7.2 Test Case Creation

The testing strategy assesses which test objects (which in this context usually consist of transactions, transaction chains, and business processes) are to be tested, how they are to be tested, and the intensity of testing in each case. On this basis, individual test cases can be specified, with different test cases being allocated to various test phases, if necessary. In this case, manual test cases can be formulated using the methods for creating test cases and test data presented above. The manual descriptions should ideally provide a level of detail that will provide a basis for a subsequent automation of the test cases.

2.7.3 Test Planning and Execution

Within each test type, the individual test stages must be examined in detail, as the actual tests are executed within each test stage or—if stages are repeated—within each test cycle. The first step is to plan a test stage, whereby relevant test cases are selected for the stage from the complete set of test cases available. If the full range of tests is not to be executed, risk analysis can be used to select a subset. The risk analysis can also be used to prioritize test cases to ensure that critical test cases are executed first. Once the test cases have been selected, they can be assigned to the individual testers. The testers execute the test cases, document the test results in accordance with the specifications, and confirm the status of the tests ("OK", "ERRORS. RETEST REQUIRED"). If the testers detect any discrepancies, these are to be documented in the form of an error message. A corresponding process must also be established for the forwarding and processing of the error message and subsequent retesting. Within extensive projects, the use of a test management tools is virtually indispensible when it comes to the planning and execution of tests and the processing of error messages.

2.7.4 Test Evaluation

During the test phase, it is essential to ensure that everyone involved in testing is kept informed at all times about the status of the test results and the progress of testing in a way that is appropriate to each target group.

Reporting   Reporting represents a key element of test control for test managers and project managers in particular. Test evaluations allow them to check on a regular basis whether testing is on track to meet the test end criteria within the allotted time. Commonly used reports include an overview of the current processing status of the test cases and of error messages posted by testers. It is also useful to coordinate the processing of test cases and the information for message processing with the scheduling of the test phase. Test management tools can provide support for this purpose with appropriate charts and detailed reports. Reporting also serves to document the entire test cycle after testing has ended. In addition to an evaluation based on the test end criteria, a final test report is useful in order to fulfill documentation requirements or to provide a basis for optimizing a testing process in the sense of "continuous improvement."

2.8 Selecting Test Tools

Selecting appropriate test tools is a key aspect of implementing a testing strategy. You may certainly perform tests based on spreadsheet programs, but take care to select this methodology in connection with small test projects only (for example, a developer test executed by a manageable development team). For large test projects, in contrast, appropriate tools can enhance the efficiency of testing and create transparency throughout the entire testing progress. Which types of tools can be used with beneficial effects in a project and which functions are essential to these tools therefore rank among the most important considerations to be made in connection with testing projects.

2.8.1 Types of Test Tools

In essence, practically all of the processes and methods described in this chapter are supported by corresponding tools. In testing SAP solutions, the most appropriate tools are those for:

- Test management
- Change analysis
- Test automation
- Test specification and test case creation
- Provision of test data
- Performance testing
- Development-oriented testing

Test management

Test management tools help you to plan, execute, and evaluate tests. These tools provide the foundations that are essential for a structured testing process, and often offer a wide range of features that cover and unite a vast spectrum of application areas. Because of this functional diversity, the products available from the various manufacturers often differ markedly in terms of their functional focal focus and functional scope. This makes it all the more important to select the right tool for your project.

Planning execution, evaluation

Test management tools usually support the following fields of application:

- **Management of test cases**
  The structured storage of manual and automated test cases is a fundamental component of test management tools. Regardless of the subsequent test execution, test cases can be stored centrally, so that they can be located easily during test planning on the basis of their attribute assignment (for example, assignment to a test stage) and can be grouped together in individual test runs. Test cases usually can be managed in a structure (for example, thematically or based on the sequence in which they are executed), and indexing of the individual test cases is also useful. In the SAP environment in particular, it is also beneficial to store test cases based on the corresponding business processes. Some tools enable the use of document templates and combine the storage of test cases with document management functions, such as versioning and document release. In conjunction with digital signatures, this can ensure extensive traceability, which is required, for example, in order to comply with audit requirements. Additional

meta-information about each test case, such as its criticality, enables a risk-based approach to testing. Another option is requirements-based testing, where test cases can be linked to business requirements. Appropriate evaluations create transparency, by indicating which software requirements already have been implemented successfully.

▶ **Test planning and execution**
Tool-supported test planning includes the selection of test cases for a specific test stage, and the assignment of packages of tasks or test cases to individual testers. Many tools also support rules-based sequence control (for example, "Test case 2 may only be executed if test case 1 has been tested successfully"). Testers must always be able to process the test cases assigned to them, record the relevant status ("test successful" or "test failed"), and document the progression of the test (for example, the data used and generated). If automation tools can be integrated, these should likewise set the status and record execution logs automatically. In addition, some tools offer project management or other useful features, such as access to test systems, or the recording of details relating to test case execution.

▶ **Defect management**
There must be a way to directly record error messages during testing, with no integration gaps. Test management tools either provide a dedicated function for this purpose or enable the integration of a Service Desk. The function provided should enable the mapping of an individual error elimination process, starting with the recording and processing of the error message and ending with successful retesting. It is also useful if all persons involved in error elimination are automatically informed (for example, by email) about new tasks as they arise. Sophisticated service desk applications include an extensive range of functions that extends beyond the boundaries of the testing context. These functions may include support for error elimination processes, the integration of Change Request Management, or a connection to an external service desk.

▶ **Reporting**
The tool must allow all data generated by the testers, including test statuses and error messages, to be depicted in the form of graphics and reports in accordance with the test plan and project. Ideally, this should enable real-time checking of test progress, which in turn can be used for strategic control and ongoing monitoring of test progress.

Effective reporting functionality simultaneously creates a data basis for analysis and enables continuous enhancement of the testing process. For example, consistent checking of the expected and actual effort required for manual test execution supports realistic testing resource planning and better scheduling of the overall testing timeframe.

Various test management tools offer additional functions to supplement these basic elements. With development projects in particular, you can integrate release and configuration management tools that are capable of managing software versions and—if necessary—their source code and can also manage documentation objects. The integration of test management into the overall context of a project or of a live solution is equally useful and is particularly relevant in the context of SAP projects, for example in order to document the implementation of changes using Change Request Management.

Integration of other tools

The testing approach that is pursued by a tool must also be considered when selecting an appropriate tool for test management. Many tools supplement the functions outlined above with an overall methodological concept, which is frequently manufacturer-specific and with specific functions that support the concept. These may involve embedding test management in the broader context of application management, or specific testing processes, such as requirements coverage or risk analysis.

Test methodology

Change Analysis

Change analysis is of particular relevance in relation to the testing of SAP solutions. As explained earlier, any change to the software of a system, including changes to the customizing or the importing of Support Packages, may affect the correct functioning of business processes. A regression test is essential to ensuring that such a change does not harm core business processes. Change analysis tools can provide support for the selection of the test cases required for this purpose, by allowing you to determine a minimum scope for regression tests that makes the best sense for your project, and, in this way, assist with risk analysis.

Analysis of the effects of software changes

Test Automation

Test automation tools enable the execution of test cases without user interaction. Automated test cases are typically created using the capture-and-replay process. In other words, the automation tool records

Capture and replay

or "captures" the tasks of the user and saves these as an executable test script. The parameters of the script can subsequently be changed; for example, in order to assign different test data to it. Current tools go far beyond mere capture and replay, and also provide a range of commands, usually in script language, which enable the development of more detailed testing instructions or processing logic. Manufacturer-specific tools frequently offer added value in this regard by providing a range of commands that allows you to query system-specific data or to access data tables directly. Scripts are generally captured and replayed at the user interface level, with manufacturer-specific and integrated auto-mation tools occasionally also enabling the execution of scripts on the application server.

In addition to the functions offered by the automation tool, you also need to check whether it can be integrated into your test management tool or if the test results can at least be forwarded. In an integrated approach, which takes account of the system landscape to be tested, scripts can be stored centrally and executed in various systems. Another factor to consider is user management. Test automation scripts can help with the testing of roles and authorizations. Security aspects must always be taken into account in this respect. For example, you need to ensure that information for logging on to a target system is stored securely and is not visible in the plain text of the automation script.

Object-based test case creation
In addition to this established process, tools for object-based creation of test cases are gaining in importance. These tools allow you to put together automated test cases from individual components (usually input masks and user interaction) using the drag-and-drop principle. Individual components can be generated through an analysis of the target system. With this processes, some of the main tasks involved in test case creation are taken off the shoulders of the case's creator.

Test Specification and Test Case Creation

Tools can also provide support for the test design methods presented above for black-box testing (equivalence class partitioning, boundary value analysis). For example, such tools can determine equivalence classes and create test cases automatically using synthetic testing data.

Documentation tools
Documentation tools can help you to create test-case descriptions for extensive process testing. As in the capture-and-replay process for test

automation, these capture user interactions and simultaneously convert them into a document with screenshots and textual descriptions. This feature can accelerate the initial documentation of business processes and of the test cases based on these. Note, however, that you still need to add test instructions, test data, and expected results in order to test cases created in this way.

Provision of Test Data

Most customers focus on process-oriented and data-driven black-box testing for quality assurance in the area of software testing. Accordingly, the availability of test data of an appropriate quality and sufficient quantity is therefore or major importance. One way of ensuring that this is so is to use a copy of the production dataset in the SAP Environment. However, it may not be possible to implement this approach in certain cases or it may necessarily involve high costs due to the extensive follow-up work required, large quantities of data (frequently in the terabyte range), and in some cases data protection requirements. Tools for the creation of test systems simplify the process of setting up these systems in accordance with requirements, while taking account of the challenges specified above.

Testing with production data

Performance Testing

Performance testing checks the efficiency of a system by generating simulated system load. While this load can be generated by simulating dialog users in the system to be tested, the background load created by jobs must also be taken into account. The objective of performance testing is to ensure that a system can withstand various pressures; for example, handling the maximum number of users expected, periods of peak load (for example, end-of-year closings), or service level agreements. In addition, performance—directly expressed by a system's response times—represents a key criterion for user acceptance. The system load that is generated synthetically using automated user interactions, such as the execution of frequently used business transactions, is designed to provide the most representative profile of the real system load that can be expected subsequently. During load testing, the number of simultaneous users can be increased gradually in order to test the scalability of the application. Monitors are used to measure the response times of the individual components, and issues like locking problem can be

Dialog users and background jobs

detected. The objective here is to pinpoint bottlenecks, which can then be evaluated and eliminated. Informative, detailed reporting allows you to interpret the test results and optimize the systems accordingly. Your load testing tools should help you to provide the appropriate technical data to the monitors.

Development-Oriented Testing

Development tools   In a separate category is the development-oriented tool, which tends to play a subordinate role in the testing of standard software, or is limited to use in customer developments at the level of developer tests. Development-oriented tools including debuggers and tools for analyzing program code in a white-box approach or testing framework help you to access and check test objects at the function module level.

2.8.2   Tool Selection and Implementation

Benefits of
using tools   The application cases described above indicate that test tools can potentially yield significant benefits because of their functional diversity. When their use is optimized, considerable savings can also be achieved through reusability, transparency, and the bridging of integration gaps.

Costs of
implementation   At the same time, the costs of implementing and maintaining (licensing costs) the tools must also be considered, as well as the effort involved in adapting your existing testing process. Moreover, it is important to have realistic expectations for what can be achieved with a testing tool. Test automation can only be implemented to the benefit of your testing process if a suitable basis for testing is already in place; in other words, if manual test cases have been documented adequately. It is also essential to make the right selection in terms of a regression test set.

Key aspects of tool selection are described below. The selection process described here is based on the process outlined by the ISTQB.

Tool Selection

Maturity of the
testing process   When selecting test tools, the first thing to look at is the maturity of the current testing process. A critical analysis of the existing processing for executing software testing is essential. The identified strengths and weaknesses of the testing process (for example, in relation to test documentation, test execution, or the error elimination process) provide the

basis for selecting test tools. You need to examine the degree to which specific weaknesses in the process, such as documentation or reporting, can potentially be optimized with tools. In all cases, however, a defined and well-managed testing process is essential before you implement a new tool. In an environment in which tests are executed on an irregular basis without test-case descriptions and without the selection of suitable test cases, simply implementing a test management tool is of little benefit, while subsequent steps such as test automation also have little relevance. In cases like this, the testing process itself must first be defined in precise terms before any decisions can be made in terms of tool use.

As a next step, information about the current project situation can be used to supplement the estimation of the potential support and optimization that can be provided by a tool. The test management tool should also be able to map specific requirements for the testing process, such as documentation requirements or approval workflows. **Project-specific requirements**

Process maturity and project-specific requirements not only provide a basis for defining requirements for test tools. They also determine which tool types are selected. In cases where a test management tool is implemented for the first time, the reason for doing so is usually to provide a basis for the entire testing process and the associated functions. Our experience indicates that it is useful to initially use a test management tool to support basic requirements, such as test case documentation, test planning and execution, and error elimination, before attempting to take efficiency to the next level with test automation. **Steps in the implementation**

Next, all of the information gathered thus far is put together in a specification, which contains all requirements in the form of objective criteria. Additional aspects should also be taken into account at this point, in particular: **Tool specification**

▸ Existing tools and the integration options offered by these

▸ Options for embedding the new tools in the overall context of application management

▸ Current expertise among members of the software quality assurance team

▸ Learning curve and the costs involved in using the tool

▸ Licensing and maintenance costs of the tool

▸ Service offered by the manufacturer and the manufacturer's market position

Profitability analysis
A profitability analysis will also prove useful in this context. In addition to the obvious costs of acquisition and maintenance, you also need to consider the costs involved in creating test cases or migrating existing test cases, as well as the expenses associated with training and with adapting your existing testing process. Potential savings can be achieved, for example, through the reusability of test cases and the transparency of test results. Particularly significant savings can be made in terms of time and resources in cases where test automation is implemented (for more information, see Chapter 7, *Economic Aspects of Test Automation*). While they may be difficult to quantify, implicit criteria, such as enhanced quality of the solution with a structured testing process, should also be taken into account in the analysis.

Proof of concept
Next, a market study can be conducted to identify potential candidates. It is useful to assign a weighting to indicate the relevance of the criteria identified and to check selected tools on the basis of these criteria. For the products on your shortlist, you should then conduct a *proof of concept* study in addition to organizing a demonstration by the manufacturer. It is particularly important to check how the products can be integrated into your existing solution and tool landscape. Depending on your selection criteria, you may need to choose between a fully integrated tool and a less integrated, specialized tool that offers a best-of-breed solution. A final review of results will then allow you to make a solid choice of test tool.

Tool Piloting and Implementation

Pilot project
A pilot project is a suitable method for evaluating the chosen tool in the context of a real project. The purpose of a pilot project is to provide an objective way to check whether the selected product meets the requirements (so far only theoretically confirmed) when used in practice. A key element of such a project is the use of the tool in the company-specific testing process. It is essential to check whether the tool can support all unique features of the testing process, such as documentation requirements. However, the process may also need to be adjusted in order to leverage the full added value offered by the tool. Piloting the tool also

allows you to gather empirical values and to realistically estimate the capabilities of the tool. You can also update your cost-benefit analysis on the basis of your practical experience using the tool. In addition, you can start to document organizational and technical aspects of using the tool, for example, procedures, roles, authorizations, and naming conventions. You can also now be more precise in your estimation of effort that will be required in relation to training and coaching. Finally, do not underestimate the "commitment": the degree to which users of the new tool are prepared to start using it.

If the results of the pilot project are successful, the tool can be implemented in your organization as a whole. This should be done gradually and in coordination with any changes made to processes. Training and coaching must also be planned as part of the rollout phase and should be provided as soon as possible, as they may play a crucial role in acceptance of the tool right from the start of its implementation. In addition, it is useful to establish a review cycle, whereby the use of the tool in practice is evaluated on a regular basis and continually optimized.

Rollout of the tool

2.9 Conclusion

The core theoretical basis for test methodology, test case creation, and the selection of tools for testing, can be summarized as follows.

▶ Every change necessitates testing, from the implementation of an SAP solution to process-driven, technical changes during live operation.

▶ Test cases are designed differently at the different test stages. Dividing test cases in accordance with *integration levels* enables them to be designed in a targeted way (functional correctness versus runtime behavior).

▶ Either black-box testing or white-box testing can be used, depending on whether information about the system's internal structure is used.

▶ There are different test case design methods for black-box tests. In practice, a targeted combination of these methods is usually used.

▶ The test data is of central importance for test quality. You should therefore devote particular attention to the process of creating this data and making it available.

► In addition to specifying which input data is to be used, a good test case also describes the expected result and the relevant inspection instructions.

► The use of appropriate test tools is essential in large projects. A wide range of tools is available to support all aspect of testing. A methodical selection of the right tools is a basic prerequisite for realizing the potential benefits of using these tools.

This chapter provides basic methodological suggestions and experience-based best practices for planning and implementing tests in the context of SAP Roadmaps. It covers the entire project lifecycle. When discussing the individual phases, we refer to the relevant support options provided by SAP Solution Manager.

3 Test Methodology

Having discussed in the last chapter the available test methods and basic procedures used in testing projects, we now turn to the specific procedures that can be used in a testing project in the SAP environment.

The test methodology presented here is based on the roadmaps developed by SAP, which represent a standardized methodological framework for executing implementation, upgrade, and operation projects, and which can be integrated into SAP Solution Manager.

Roadmaps

The phases of a testing project that are discussed in this chapter correspond to the various phases outlined in the ASAP (Accelerated SAP) Roadmaps for implementing or upgrading SAP applications.

> **Note**
>
> These roadmaps are primarily intended as a guide to executing a new project and, as such, represent the thread holding the individual phases together. ASAP Roadmaps therefore cannot replace a testing manager's knowledge of testing standards and practical experience.

SAP Solution Manager provides both methodology and content, the latter in the form of best-practice documents and a library of process structures for implementation (Business Process Repository).

The information is presented in the context of each task. Using this information significantly improves speed within a test project.

The following sections provide an overview of the individual phases of a test project, based on the ASAP phases, and also indicate special, phase-specific considerations and how these are handled in the system. Established procedures and experiences from real-world projects are also discussed.

Please note that organizational considerations such as the availability of appropriate office space, travel planning, and so on, are outside the scope of this book. This section primarily covers project procedures along with the use of appropriate SAP functionalities for project management. The tools used in operational implementation are then discussed in detail in Chapter 4, *Functional Testing*.

3.1 Roadmaps in SAP Solution Manager

SAP provides its customers with roadmaps, which comprise detailed descriptions of proven methods, and serve as process models to support the implementation, upgrade, and operation of SAP solutions. These roadmaps also contain tasks for the planning and execution of software quality assurance, which are embedded in an overall methodology based on extensive and varied project experience.

ASAP Roadmaps The ASAP Roadmaps describe the key phases, work packages, and tasks that need to be taken into account in connection with the implementation or upgrade of an SAP solution. These roadmaps pursue a unified approach, combining the various process models with the relevant content and tools within SAP Solution Manager. They allow you to access document templates and best practices in the context of individual project phases and activities. SAP Solution Manager provides support for project control and the implementation of individual tasks.

The ASAP Roadmaps are available as standard offerings for a wide range of project types (including upgrade and rollout projects), and can be enhanced with solution-specific activities and tasks, depending on the solution to be implemented. You also can create a customer-specific roadmap (for example, as a modified copy of an ASAP Roadmap), integrate it into SAP Solution Manager, and use it like the standard roadmaps.

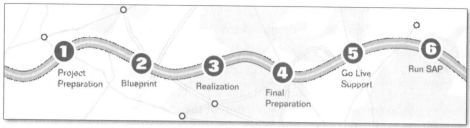

Figure 3.1 Phases in the ASAP Roadmaps

The Run SAP Roadmap offers a process model for the setup, implementation, and execution of standardized operating processes ("end-to-end solution operation") and can also be used via SAP Solution Manager. In addition to such procedures as user support, administration, or monitoring, this roadmap outlines how to set up test management along with the implementation of change management. The roadmap is part of the Run SAP methodology, which has as its primary objective the safeguarding of the smooth operation of SAP solutions. This objective can be realized using standards-based procedures. These include the methodology delivered with the roadmap, as well as documents describing standardized procedures and best practices (SAP Standards for Solution Operations), training courses and certifications, and services from SAP. A key component of this methodology is SAP Solution Manager, which provides all of the tools, contents, and service offerings required to implement the E2E Solution Operation Standards.

Run SAP Roadmap

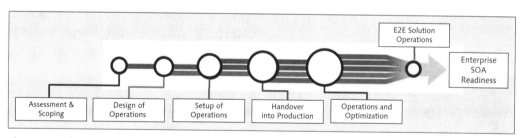

Figure 3.2 Phases in the Run SAP Roadmap

Against this backdrop, SAP Solution Manager represents an end-to-end application management platform that covers the implementation, operation, and optimization of solutions using a unified methodology. Relevant projects or project tasks can be implemented directly with the

Application management platform

tools in SAP Solution Manager, which provide solutions for applications throughout the entire lifecycle.

The sections that follow illustrate how SAP Solution Manager can be used to control and implement a project using roadmaps. Essential activities within a testing project are then described using the phases in an ASAP Roadmap. A detailed description of the test tools in SAP Solution Manager is provided in Chapter 4, *Functional Testing*.

3.1.1 Project Phases

ASAP process model

The ASAP process model can be divided into phases. In accordance with the approach presented earlier, SAP Solution Manager provides specific tools for each phase, and these enable the implementation of each step in the relevant phase. SAP Solution Manager's integrated approach supports cooperation between all parties involved in the project across all of the individual phases and areas of responsibility. Project information can be analyzed for the entire duration of the project, and extensive reporting functions are provided for reporting across several projects.

"Implementation/ Upgrade" work center

The tools you need to use the roadmaps and to process the individual project tasks are provided in the *Implementation/Upgrade* work center of SAP Solution Manager (see Figure 3.3) A detailed description of the underlying work center concept is provided in Chapter 4. This work center offers an overview of all projects that are currently implemented, and allows you to implement these projects using typical activities in each project phase, such as evaluating, planning, creating, and testing. With SAP Solution Manager 7.0 EhP 1 version, a separate work center is also provided for test management, which includes additional functions (such as the Business Process Change Analyzer).

Phases in the ASAP Roadmap

The core activities within the five phases of an ASAP Roadmap can be outlined as follows, along with descriptions of the corresponding tools in the work center.

▸ **Project Preparation**
The content-related objectives of the project (a testing project, for example) are planned and scheduled in this phase. The implementation strategy is also selected in the form of a specific roadmap. In addition, the project team is assembled, and basic project standards are defined. During this phase, SAP Solution Manager gives you the

option of starting or editing a new project with the basic parameters using the *Implementation/Upgrade* work center. These include the specific project parameters, including the associated project process, as well as the technical perspective in the form of the systems to be used by the project.

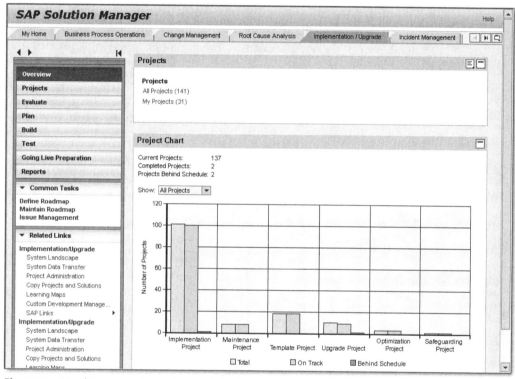

Figure 3.3 "Implementation/Upgrade" Work Center

▶ **Business Blueprint**
This phase defines the enterprise's requirements for the SAP application that is to be implemented, or for the implementation of its processes in the solution. At the end of this phase, the requirements documents are summarized in a business blueprint document and formally accepted.

Within SAP Solution Manager, an enterprise's business processes can be mapped in a defined storage structure in the project. This structure allows you to describe business processes at the hierarchically arranged levels of scenario, business process, and process step. The structure can be created by the customer using these structure elements or with the help of templates (Business Process Repository) and a technical usage analysis (Solution Documentation Assistant). These are described fully in (see Chapter 4, *Functional Testing*. The relevant information (such as requirements documents) can be managed using integrated document management functions. Later, the structure and the documents it contains can be added to a central business blueprint document. The functions for creating projects and creating the business blueprint are available in the PLAN area in the *Implementation/Upgrade* work center (see Figure 3.4). In addition, the EVALUATE area provides an initial overview of the contents delivered by SAP, such as the business processes provided in the Business Process Repository.

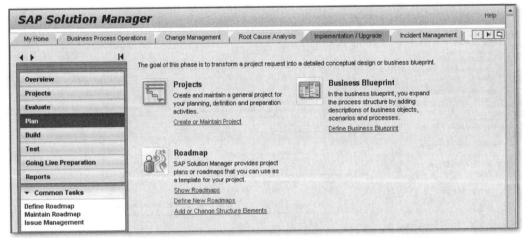

Figure 3.4 "Implementation/Upgrade" Work Center—the "Plan" Area

▶ **Realization**

This phase implements the requirements defined in the business blueprint (for example, by means of customizing or development), as well as the planning and execution of the related testing activities. In SAP Solution Manager, you can, integrate jumps to the relevant customizing and development objects into the process hierarchy in a structured form, among other tasks. Test cases can also be stored in the project structure. These test cases form the basis for setting up and implementing future testing activities.

These activities of the Realization phase can be accessed in the BUILD area of the work center (see Figure 3.5). This area also contains the functions that provide support for the distribution of customizing settings (BC SETS and CUSTOMIZING DISTRIBUTION/SYNCHRONIZATION).

The functions used in the test environment are located in the TEST area of this work center (see Figure 3.6) Here you can create test cases, manage test plans and packages, and execute the relevant reporting functions. Additional test functions (including the Business Process Change Analyzer) are provided in the *Test Management* work center in SAP Solution Manager 7.0 EhP 1.

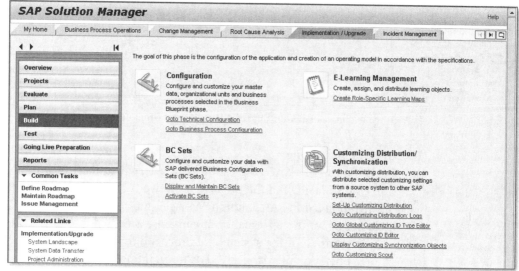

Figure 3.5 "Implementation/Upgrade" Work Center—the "Build" Area

▶ **Final Preparation**

In this phase, the project is prepared for the go-live phase, end users are trained, and final system tests (for example, performance tests) are executed. Ideally, this phase also includes preparation for automatic execution of regression tests to guarantee that no interruptions of live operations occur later on.

You can manage regression test cases, including, for example, eCATT test configurations (see Section 8.1.1., *Architecture of the Testing Landscape and eCATT Fundamentals*) within the process structure of the project. In addition, you can define training materials and make these available to end users via web pages (known as Learning Maps) as part of the Final Preparation phase. The functions for these two activities are provided in the BUILD and TEST areas of the *Implementation/ Upgrade* work center.

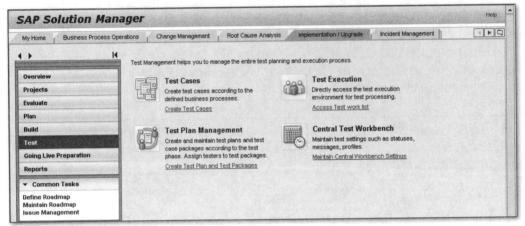

Figure 3.6 "Implementation/Upgrade" Work Center—the "Test" Area

▶ **Go-Live and Support**
In this phase, the SAP application is transferred to the live production environment, and the project is reviewed. The project is accordingly completed in SAP Solution Manager and the process structure, including all of the information it contains, is copied into a *solution*. This contains all of the system and process information required for the live operation of systems. To enable an immediate analysis of any issues that may arise, the solution and the process structure it contains, including the documentation, should reflect the current status of the production systems. Any testing activities that are to be executed during live operation are also based on the test cases defined in the solution as of this point (see Section 4.6, *Solution-Related Testing*).

A function for transferring the process structures is provided in the GOING LIVE PREPARATION area of the *Implementation/Upgrade* work center (see Figure 3.7) Here you can access relevant services that facilitate the go-live phase (SAP GoingLive Check) and are then available for periodic use as a "health check" once the solution goes live (SAP EarlyWatch Alert).

Project-relevant reviews can be conducted in the REPORTS area, which contains reports that may also be useful during the course of the project. The data that is collected as part of a project review allows you to verify project-relevant quality objectives and to initiate quality enhancement measures.

▶ **Run**

This phase is devoted to the operation of the successfully implemented solution. The contents provided for this phase represent the Run SAP methodology, and describe in particular the implementation and optimization of processes used for operation, such as business process operation, end user support, and change management.

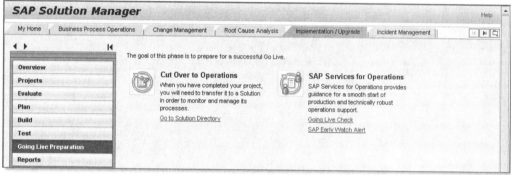

Figure 3.7 "Implementation/Upgrade" Work Center—the "Going Live Preparation" Area

3.1.2 Roadmaps

During all these phases, you can use the roadmaps stored for each project in SAP Solution Manager to help you plan and execute the related project activities. The roadmaps are available in the standard configuration with various characteristics for different types of projects. If necessary, you can also define enterprise-specific roadmaps or modify existing roadmaps as required. The relevant functions are also provided in the *Implementation/Upgrade* work center in the PLAN area (see Figure 3.4 above).

You can link a roadmap with an SAP Solution Manager project in the "Project Preparation" phase (see Section 4.4.1, *Creating a Project*). As part of project execution, the relevant roadmap can then be accessed for editing either in the project overview in the work center or in Transaction RMMAIN directly, with optional restriction of access authorization.

Getting started
with the Roadmap To start using the relevant roadmap for your project, you begin by selecting the project. Figure 3.8 shows an example of a roadmap (ASAP Implementation Roadmap 7.0). As well as using roadmaps in project, you can display roadmaps and their contents without reference to a specific project.

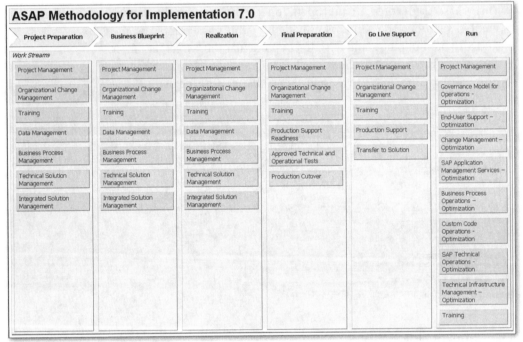

Figure 3.8 ASAP Implementation Roadmap in SAP Solution Manager

Download as an
HTML or Microsoft
Project file
You can download roadmaps from SAP Solution Manager as HTML or Microsoft Project files. You can use an HTML file as an offline version to view the documents and their contents independently of an SAP system. The Microsoft Project version can be used as part of project management.

The structure of the roadmap corresponds to the ASAP phase model (see Figure 3.1 at the start of this chapter). You can use filter functions to restrict the display of each work package. For example, you can use the filter SUBJECT AREA • BUSINESS PROCESS REQUIREMENTS, DESIGN, CONFIGURATION AND TESTING to display the activities that are relevant for testing. Combinations of filter criteria can also be used.

In the standard configuration, you access a roadmap from an overview screen showing the key project phases and packages of tasks in a roadmap (see Figure 3.9). When a project-specific roadmap is selected, the current processing status of the relevant packages is displayed in the overview.

If you select a phase or a task package, the display switches to a detailed view, where you can display all elements in the roadmap and edit these for a specific project. You can also use the filter function mentioned above in this view. The following elements can be used to structure a roadmap, and these are reflected in the tree display in the detailed view.

▶ **Phases**

The project phases described earlier in Section 3.1, *Roadmaps in SAP Solution Manager,* are shown as the highest level in the roadmap. A phase typically ends with a milestone, at which point it is necessary to verify whether the results required up to this point have been achieved. You can check which milestones belong to which project phases on the relevant view in project administration, where you can also define a date for the objective in each case. With Service Pack 18 or Enhancement Package 1 of SAP Solution Manager 7.0, a feature called Quality Gates is also provided as an additional option. You can use it to formally document the achievement of milestones or "quality gates" and link the software logistics of the project with the individual project phases (see Section 4.5.3, *Test and Quality Gate Management*).

▶ **Work packages**

Each phase contains a range of work packages. These are also shown in the Roadmap overview.

▶ **Activities**

Each work package comprises several activities, each of which contributes to the implementation of that package.

▶ **Tasks**

The fourth level in a roadmap represents the individual tasks, which consist of the individual steps taken to implement an activity.

> **Note**
>
> In the ASAP 7 methodology and all roadmaps based on this methodology, the structure of the project structure plan has been simplified, and now comprises the elements "Phases," "Work Streams," "Deliverables," and "Sub-Deliverables."

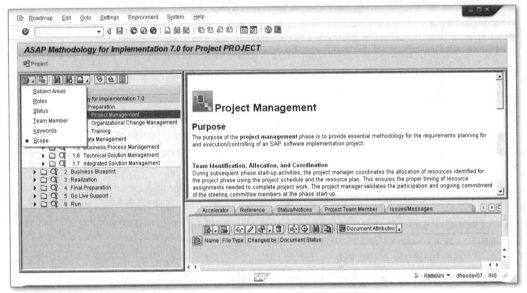

Figure 3.9 Filter Options in a Project-Specific Roadmap

In addition to these elements, you can also view the milestones and available SAP services (such as the SAP Feasibility Check) for each phase of the project in the roadmap. If needed, you can request the services with SAP Solution Manager via the SAP Service Marketplace.

Accelerators   When you select a node in a roadmap, a description of the corresponding element is displayed. In the context of selected elements, you can also use *accelerators* (such as checklists and templates), which have proven effective in many SAP projects. These can be used over the course of your project to speed up work. Based on recommendations and best practices from SAP project experience, the roadmaps have also been developed in accordance with internationally recognized industry standards, in particular ITIL (IT Infrastructure Library) and PMI PMBOK (Project Management Institute Project Management Body of Knowledge).

The project manager can assign the structure elements of a roadmap to individual members of the project team. You can control which employees are available for this purpose in project administration on the EMPLOYEES tab (see Section 4.4.1, *Creating a Project*).

The structure can then also be filtered by specific employees. This function can be used, for example, to select a personal worklist or to allow the project manager to keep track of who is doing what.

Later, during project execution, team members will open the tasks assigned to them and document the progress of their project activities here. A corresponding status and Notes function is provided for each structure element. The status is then displayed in the roadmap with an appropriate icon (see Figure 3.10).

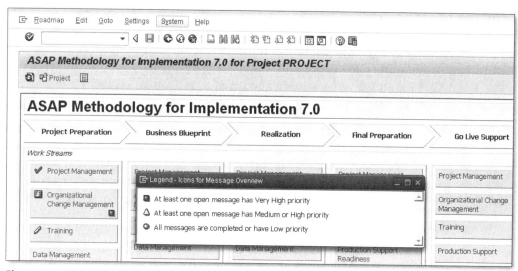

Figure 3.10 Status Display in a Project-Specific Roadmap

During the course of the project, project team members can also create problem messages here. These messages are transmitted to the Service Desk, where they can be processed by in-house support. The Roadmap overview allows you to view their processing status and also indicates whether prioritized messages have been closed or are still open. The messages created can be displayed in a list with the relevant icons to provide a quick overview of the processing statuses of the messages.

Project-related problem messages

3.2 Project Preparation

The Project Preparation phase in ASAP plays a decisive role in the Testing subproject of an SAP implementation or upgrade project. Even during this early phase, relevant testing activities can be set up in order to avoid development errors.

In this phase, you define a process for your testing project—just as you did when defining the overall project framework—and document the process in an appropriate test concept. The basic contents of this document were described earlier in Section 2.7.1, *Test Preparation*. In order to create a test concept, you can use both general standards for test documentation (in particular, IEEE 829) and content from SAP Solution Manager as your template. For example, the accelerators relating to the topic of test management in the Run SAP Roadmap also provide useful tips on the content of a test concept (see Figure 3.11).

It is the responsibility of project management to define the general test strategy and the essential underlying parameters, with the involvement of all subprojects. It's a good idea to get formal acceptance of the test strategy paper by all areas and subprojects.

Availability · It is useful to store the test concept in a central location, so that all project team members can refer to it at any time. Experience shows that, when using SAP Solution Manager, it helps to define the document on the PROJECT DOCUMENTATION tab at scenario level in the project structure of the current project. Using this approach, all members of the project team have access to the current version of the strategy paper.

Documentation of test types · The various test stages (among them developer testing, integration testing, and system testing) are also detailed in the test concept. The stages described in Section 2.3, *Test Stages*, can be used as a basis for these descriptions. For each test type, you should at a minimum specify information about the relevant project phase in which the tests are to be executed, the employee groups that are to be involved, and the relevant systems.

Quality objectives · The quality objectives of the testing project are also defined in the test strategy. These objectives include the desired level of testing coverage (see Section 3.4, *Realization*) that each test phase should achieve. You can also define the desired response times for processing errors with a service level agreement that you create in collaboration with the support unit.

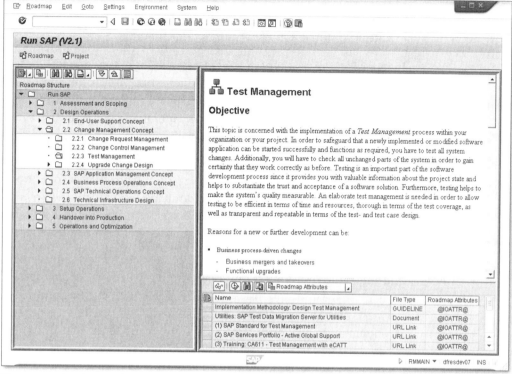

Figure 3.11 Accelerators for Test Management in the Run SAP Roadmap

As discussed in Section 2.8, *Selecting Test Tools*, test tool selection is a key   Test tools
component of a test strategy. Using the selection criteria provided in this
chapter, you can select suitable test tools for this project and even for
other projects or for the operational phase.

In large testing projects, such as the implementation of an SAP solution described here, the use of a test management tool is practically
indispensable for test planning, execution, and evaluation. This is also
true in terms of reusability. By using test management software, you
ensure that all test cases, test plans, and other components of testing are
permanently saved in a transparent manner and can also be reused for
subsequent tests.

All the work you do at this stage, including initial maintenance and structured administration of test case descriptions, will significantly simplify
the process of setting up the required testing activities in later project

phases. It helps, for example, to copy a test plan for follow-up testing, including the assignment to individual testers. Use of an appropriate tool can also simplify the documentation of test results.

In reporting, the results of individual test runs or of the complete project can be aggregated or displayed over the entire project timeline. With SAP Solution Manager 7.0 EhP 1, web-based reports of the same type can be executed using an integrated version of SAP NetWeaver BW. An external BW can also be used, provided that it is used for central data storage, for example.

For these reasons, selecting and piloting a test management tool, if one has not been used previously, should ideally occur in the Project Preparation phase. Similar considerations are equally valid for other tools, such as tools for test automation, test migration, or performance testing.

SAP test tool options
SAP offers a portfolio of various tools. In the areas of test management and automation, customers can choose from a wide range of approaches. In both of the test options outlined in this book, SAP Solution Manager acts as the central tool for documentation, configuration, and development in a project. Testing Option 1 refers to the use of the Test Workbench for test management and eCATT for test automation, the test tools that are integrated into SAP Solution Manager, and can be used without additional licensing costs. When it comes to the automation of testing activities, tools (for example, for the automation of HTML-based applications) that do require payment of an additional license fee can be integrated using a certified interface.

In Testing Option 2, an adapter is used to integrate SAP Quality Center by HP into SAP Solution Manager (integration of test and defect management), as a third-party test management tool that is subject to a license fee. The tools HP QuickTest Pro and, where relevant, SAP Test Acceleration and Optimization (SAP TAO) are used for test automation in this option.

Both options are described in detail in Section 4.1, *Test Management with SAP Solution Manager*. The criteria for tool selection specified in the last chapter (see Section 2.8, *Selecting Test Tools*) can be used to evaluate both solutions in the context of a project.

The competencies and responsibilities for testing activities should be clarified during the Project Preparation phase. This process involves defining roles for individual activities in the test environment, as well as formulating the corresponding tasks, responsibilities, and qualification profiles.

First, you need to appoint a test project manager who is primarily responsible for the creation of an appropriate framework for the Testing subproject (including norms and standards, testing process, knowledge transfer) and who will handle communication and coordination with other subprojects.

Depending on the complexity of the testing project, the project manager should be supported by one or more test coordinators. During the course of the project, the holders of these positions are responsible for implementing the preparation and execution of the defined testing activities. They also provide status information for reporting within the testing project as well as in the context of the overall project.

It also helps to devote time in the Project Preparation phase to the definition of roles and requirements profiles for other key activities in test case creation and test execution during subsequent project phases. If necessary, you may also select suitable candidates within the project at this point. You also need to decide whether to recruit persons for these positions from the user departments (for example, key users) or to set up a dedicated team. These roles include, in particular, test case designers, testers, users who will be responsible for message processing, and test automation experts.

The (overall) project leads should formally accept the test strategy at the end of the Project Preparation phase. The agreed-upon test concept must then be communicated to the entire project team and, stored in a central location.

The diverse considerations that arise in relation to project preparation clearly demonstrate just how wide-ranging the requirements of a testing project can be. In addition to the support provided by accelerators and Best Practices, help is also on-hand from SAP Consulting experts.

Competencies and responsibilities

Formal acceptance of the test concept

Support from
SAP Consulting With its global portfolio of services, SAP Consulting supports all phases of a testing project. It provides consulting services for the planning and preparation of testing activities, as well as for test implementation and execution. Services range from individual workshops to the transfer of expert knowledge (test methodology, tools, automation, or performance testing, among other subjects), to the outtasking of individual tasks (such as realization of a performance test or creation of automated test cases), or the complete outsourcing of testing activities (for example, by establishing a "test factory"). The consultants provide expertise in project methodology (such as planning and realization of testing activities as part of global rollout projects), technical issues (such as the implementation and configuration of test tools), and coaching in automation and other projects. Figure 3.12 provides an overview of the various consulting services provided. For a detailed description of individual services, visit *www.sap.com/services/testing*.

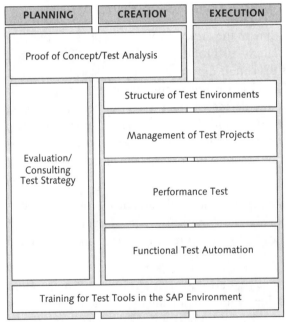

Figure 3.12 Overview of Global Test Service Offerings from SAP Consulting

To supplement the descriptions of these global services, the SAP Service Marketplace provides information about the SAP Test Management Consulting unit, including customer reports, presentations of tools and services, and useful links (see *www.service.sap.com/tmc*).

3.3 Business Blueprint

The enterprise's business and technical requirements for the SAP solution that is to be implemented are defined in the Business Blueprint ASAP phase. Because the requirements profile forms the basis of the testing activities to be performed in the Realization phase, all user departments should be involved in creating the requirements catalog. Ideally, the user departments should also undertake a planned/actual comparison of the requirements.

Business and technical requirements

3.3.1 Mapping Business Process Structure

You can use SAP Solution Manager to map the business process structures that will be implemented in a project. The structure of a project can be broken down into scenarios, processes, and process steps, with process steps generally representing transactions in the target system (at the transaction level).

These business process structures are set up in the Business Blueprint phase. The Business Process Repository can be used for this purpose. This is a collection of standard processes delivered in SAP Solution Manager, to be used as a template for defining enterprise-specific business processes. In addition to the structure itself, the Business Process Repository also contains textual descriptions for many processes, as well as contents such as transactions or configuration objects. Figure 3.13 shows an example of a process selected from the Business Process Repository. Customer-specific adjustments usually need to be made to these standard structures, and the Solution Documentation Assistant provides support for this purpose. This SAP Solution Manager function allows you to identify the structures used in the standard and the subsequent enhancement of these structures with customer-specific details (see Section 4.1, *Test Management with SAP Solution Manager*).

Structure of the Business Blueprint

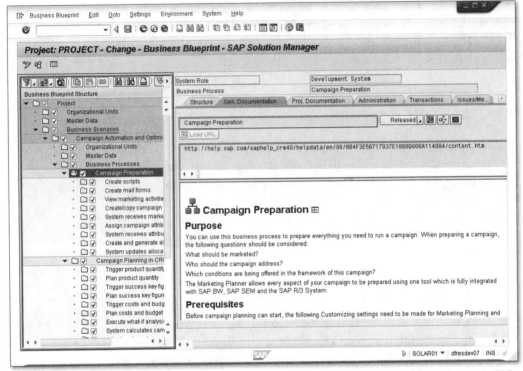

Figure 3.13 Example of Business Process Documentation Available as Content in SAP Solution Manager

Project documentation

You can store the project documentation, including requirements documents, in the Business Blueprint. It is also possible to define navigation jumps to the relevant transactions in the relevant target systems of the business processes. The process documentation is integrated at the same level referred to in the individual description. Requirements that apply to more than one process step can be stored at process level, while documents that apply to more than one process are stored at scenario level (see Figure 3.14). Documents defined in this structure can be indicated as relevant to the Business Blueprint and then grouped together automatically with SAP Solution Manager in the form of a central document describing the project creating, in fact, a "business blueprint." You can use filters to limit the scope of the document.

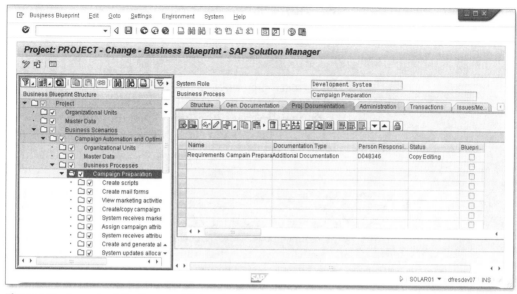

Figure 3.14 Example of the Storage of Enterprise-Specific Project Documentation

If you use Testing Option 2 (involving the use of SAP Quality Center by HP at an additional licensing cost), the documents defined in the blueprint can be assigned as business requirements on tab TRANSFER TO SAP QC BY HP, and the transactions and configuration and development objects can be assigned on that tab as test objects. The selected objects are transferred to SAP Quality Center by HP using the adapter that is part of this approach. There, test cases can then be created on the basis of the requirements and test objects that are documented in this way. During the testing activities, the "Requirement for test case" relationship allows you to use corresponding reports to determine whether the defined requirements are fully covered. In this way, Testing Option 2 supports requirements-based testing in the standard procedure. If you use Testing Option 1 (use of SAP test tools without any additional license feel), this type of process can be implemented in principle; for example, using naming conventions. With this method, such items as requirements documents and the test cases based on these are assigned the same name or the same prefix.

Requirements-based testing

When you create business process structures, you should always remember that these are primarily intended to facilitate the process-oriented

Sequential transactions

97

storage of project-specific information. The structures represent a meta-level that should enable the technical identification of connections.

3.3.2 Test Standards

As part of the testing project, test standards can be defined in the Business Blueprint phase. Test coordinators usually perform this task in consultation with the leaders of subprojects. Based on the test strategy, you can define how to document the descriptions of your test cases. Your choices range from purely textual descriptions to recordings of dialog user behavior, both of which can be generated with a documentation tool and enhanced with test steps. Once a corresponding document template has been created for the test case descriptions, it can be defined as the "project standard" in the SAP Solution Manager project.

Test case template
The content of SAP Solution Manager provides an appropriate template for test cases, which you can modify as needed to meet the requirements of your company or project. All test case descriptions should cover the following minimum requirements.

▶ **Test case title**
The title of the test case description should describe the test case as concisely as possible. Along with the attributes of a test document, the title is an important filter criterion when searching for a test case. You should therefore use appropriate naming conventions—for example,

prefixes for subprojects and scenarios—before you begin defining the test case.

▶ **Short description**

The short description of the test case provides a summary of the functions that are to be tested. Here you can also refer to such factors as existing documentation of the functions that are to be tested, which place the test case in the context of the relevant business process.

▶ **Preparation**

Here you specify the preparations that must be made before the test can be executed. These may include instructions on the use of specific master data and transaction data. For the purpose of reusability, it helps to keep the descriptions of the data to be used as generic as possible.

▶ **Execution**

Here you describe the steps required to test the functionality. Experience shows that it's a good idea to include appropriate screenshots here. The test case description should enable the tester to perform the test in a way that makes sense. The level of detail of these descriptions should be appropriate to the assigned tester's level of knowledge. In practice, the detail and quality of the instructions sometimes vary widely. It is useful to review the instructions critically to verify that the steps can be reproduced, especially during regression testing and subsequent test automation. This step is also particularly important if global integration of external test resources is being considered (for example, in the context of out-tasking).

▶ **Check/Expected result**

As with test execution, you specify here how the tester can determine whether the test was successful from a business and/or technical point of view. The descriptions should provide unambiguous information for evaluating the results of the test.

As part of the test standard, you should define appropriate test case attributes in addition to the naming convention of the test case title. Country IDs or technical filter criteria simplify the identification of the relevant descriptions, particularly for larger test projects. SAP Solution Manager also provides an option to define keywords that you can later use as additional selection criteria. You could, for example, flag test cases

Test case attributes

for specific test stages or for subsequent regression testing when you are storing the corresponding test case descriptions.

Try to design the creation and release processes in the test case descriptions as early as possible; for example, in the Business Blueprint phase. With Testing Option 1, simply define the relevant responsibilities and corresponding status options in the test case description. You can save the document status in SAP Solution Manager and, if necessary, use a digital signature to protect it from unauthorized changes.

It is also a good idea to specify during this phase which tests are to be documented and how. For example, with very little effort you can document development tests within a team, without using a test management tool. No matter how you decide to do it, the test results should be reproducible and stored in SAP Solution Manager.

Test reporting | In the Business Blueprint phase, you should also define how reporting is to proceed, and how the information requirements of the stakeholders can be covered at a minimum cost. In an ideal scenario, reporting has already been discussed as part of the process of tool selection. The test management tool you select must be capable of generating all graphs, reports, and detailed reports that are specified during this phase. You may also need to use the configuration to modify the reports of the test management tool with standard data.

Defect management process | Be sure to pay attention to error management and error correction. For this, you can define the groups of employees involved (including the support structures), the communication paths, error classes, and the related response times. It is particularly important note when the error corrections were imported into the test system during the test phase. It is helpful to schedule general transport periods (Friday afternoon, for example) and define the required exceptions, such as urgent corrections of very serious errors. Here, once again, all of the processes and escalation levels defined should be supported by the test management tool. In addition, transport control can be integrated for transport management.

Test-end criteria | Finally, the test ending criteria should be defined. It is necessary, in particular, to determine what to do with errors that are not corrected by the end of the test. When designing testing activities, you can schedule a defined follow-up testing phase to test the delivered solutions. This should also be defined from the point of view of the tools used; for example, by means of a corresponding test plan.

All information that is relevant for testing—including the test concept, manual test case descriptions, test plans, test results, and reporting—should be made available in a central location, so that the entire testing process can be tracked at all times.

3.4 Realization

The realization phase involves the implementation of the requirements documented in the business blueprint in the system. Realization is implemented using appropriate customizing settings and development activities (modifications and enhancements), all of which you can also store in the project structure in SAP Solution Manager (see Section 4.1, *Test Management with SAP Solution Manager*). Realization is verified across various test phases and ultimately prepares the way for acceptance of the solution.

In this phase, the required test cases are also created and stored in the test management tool.

Test case creation in SAP Solution Manager

If you use Testing Option 1, the test cases are assigned to the individual structure elements of the business blueprint as part of process documentation. This means that you can, for example, store test cases for individual transactions at test-step level and store test cases for integration tests at process or scenario level. You can also include descriptions of test cases as references to documents that are already attached to the structures (see Figure 3.15).

If you use an external test management tool, this is where the test cases are stored. You should check the degree to which references can be made to the business process structures and documents. If you use SAP Quality Center by HP as a test tool (Testing Option 2), you can use an adapter solution (at an additional licensing cost) to transfer the business blueprint and selected documents into SAP Quality Center by HP. In this way, you

Test case creation in external test management tools

can transfer requirements documents and test objects from SAP Solution Manager to SAP Quality Center by HP. This provides a basis for creating test cases in accordance with requirements-based testing methodology (see Section 5.2, *SAP Solution Manager Adapter for SAP Quality Center by HP*).

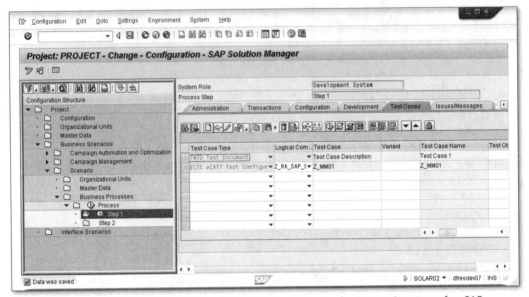

Figure 3.15 Adding a Test Case Description to the Process Structure of an SAP Solution Manager Project

Chapter 2, *Methodology*, describes the test stages (developer testing, functional testing, scenario testing, and integration testing) that are relevant during the Realization phase. Because each test stage has a unique focus, the content and level of detail of each test case description differs accordingly. For example, a developer's test case primarily covers formal and technical aspects, while functional descriptions of test cases are primarily treated from the user's point of view.

Test case descriptions You should consider the reusability of test cases, in particular in relation to functional descriptions of test cases. You can reuse module-specific test cases for scenario or integration tests because they are usually part of a business process. Ideally, integration test scenarios consist of module-specific descriptions of test cases. This is why you should start to think in terms of business process even during module testing, as module tests can also be split into individual business transactions. That approach simplifies later reuse of the test case descriptions that you have created. Above all, it offers an excellent starting point for test automation at a later stage because of its modularity.

The test case description for a development test is generally based on an IT concept and is written by developers for developers. Additional functional descriptions of test cases, however, should be created by the related user departments. User departments bring their day-to-day knowledge of business processes to bear on the test case. Because they are involved in the creation of requirements documents, they are already familiar with any functional enhancements that must be contained in the software being implemented. User departments should therefore be involved, especially in defining the degree of test coverage.

Because of the limited availability of resources for a project, a test is always a random one that you define in accordance with the principle of efficiency. User departments determine the importance of a business transaction in the context of a business process and thus indirectly determine the priority of a test case based on that transaction. You must consider the frequency of a business transaction and the possible effects of unavailable or error-prone functionality for daily operations when defining a test case. Experience in many projects has shown that the answer to a simple question, such as "What makes money for the company?" can help you identify the (critical) business transactions to be tested. This procedure can be supplemented by a technical approach, for example, a statistical analysis of the frequency with which the relevant transactions and reports are executed. Starting with Service Pack 16, SAP Solution Manager 7.0 provides a *Solution Documentation Assistant* to help with this (see Figure 3.16). This tool can calculate, for example, the frequency with which the transactions and reports defined in the business blueprint are executed. This allows you to select the most frequently used business processes, and to identify those that are rarely used and may be obsolete (see Section 4.5.2, *Test and Change Request Management*).

Degree of test coverage

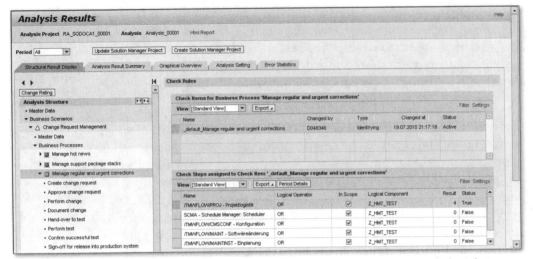

Figure 3.16 Analysis of the Execution Frequency of Transactions with the Solution Documentation Assistant

Defining random tests

You can follow one of two approaches to defining the scope of a random test.

▶ A degree of test coverage that you define should reach a quality goal with minimum effort. The goal might be to cover n % of Priority 1 business transactions and m % of Priority 2 business transactions.

▶ Given the maximum level of resources the project plan assigns to testing (time, money, and employees), as many test cases of Priority 1 to Priority x as possible should be covered.

Of course, the first alternative is more desirable. But in the real world, the second alternative is becoming more and more relevant because of the increasingly tight schedules. That's why you should keep an eye on the reusability of test case descriptions when you create them, even in early phases of the project. That will save you unnecessary additional work when trying to meet your quality goals in later phases.

The random tests you define and the descriptions of test cases available to you provide an overview of the preconditions that must be satisfied for the upcoming tests. This means that you now know how many tests you will need and what their qualifications should be, as well as the test systems required for testing, the authorizations needed, and the relevant test data (master data and transaction data).

If possible, the testing activities of the Realization phase should be executed in collaboration with and with the approval of the user departments. Because the upcoming testing is to occur in parallel with daily operations, it won't help, for example, to ask the accounting department for help with testing during month-end or year-end closing periods.

The involvement of the user departments should increase gradually in each testing phase. In a module test, the test team primarily consists of external application consultants and key users from the user departments. In other words, the test team is primarily made up of members of the project team. Module tests are often an internal testing activity in the project.

The presence of user departments should increase even during scenario tests to obtain early acceptance of the new software in the company. Here you should increasingly nominate and involve employees outside of the project team (determining who tests what) to give the user departments a first impression of the new functionality. The suitable employees should therefore be consciously prepared for their multiple functions in addition to receiving any training they may need in relation to how testing is to be conducted.

The integration test should be performed exclusively by employees of user departments, with key users and application consultants from the project team available as direct contact persons (as test team leads, for example). Because the integration tests involve a significant disruption of daily work, scheduling of training and testing should be done early in the project in consultation with the user departments.

Test preparation also involves deciding which systems are to be used for testing. You might have to set up new systems and incorporate them into the system landscape.

It makes sense to create users with the same name for each tester in the test systems and in SAP Solution Manager, and assign the necessary authorizations to these users. If generic users are used (TESTER01, TESTER02, and so on), an overview showing the assignment of testers and users for each test project must be available, in particular if any documentation requirements apply. This overview serves to clarify who has tested what, when, and with what results. It is particularly essential

Testers

Test systems

to maintain an overview of this type when test management tools are used without integration into SAP user administration.

IT support It is also particularly important to agree on the support needed with your SAP Basis staff in order to guarantee resolution of problems in near real-time during the test phases. Examples of this include manual starting of a background job, setting up missing authorizations for testers, and imports of urgent corrections. This approach can significantly reduce unnecessary wait time for user departments that are simultaneously performing their normal daily tasks.

Authorizations Authorizations are a potential source of error in testing activities. Checking authorizations is generally a testing goal in its own right, and is often done separately. If an error occurs, it may be the result of incorrect functionality or it may indicate a missing authorization. The resulting search can then involve several possible causes.

At the start of testing, the focus should be on detecting functional errors, and so testing should be performed by users with authorizations that are unrestricted as far as possible. Testers with defined roles and authorization profiles should only begin testing if a relatively stable degree of functionality is available. This approach can accelerate the search for errors.

It is always essential to ensure that at least one user (perhaps the test team lead) with relatively unrestricted authorization is available during testing. To accelerate test execution, this user can help avoid long wait times and access specific functions if necessary. Missing authorizations are then captured in an error message in parallel and retested at a later time.

Test data Attention should be devoted to the definition and availability of test data at an early stage during test preparation because a significant amount of coordination is required between all business areas involved. A sufficiently large time period must be scheduled for each test.

The creation of a central table has proven valuable in defining of test data. This table documents the required data that is specific to business processes. In the table, the financial department—which is usually at the end of a process chain—can make its needs known ("We can perform a meaningful test only when the following data is available."). Based on this information, upstream organizational units can define their needs and document the data that they can make available.

There are different ways to create the test data in the test systems. In addition to the functionality introduced in Chapter 9, *SAP Test Data Migration Server*, other options are available, including creation with eCATT, system copies, and client copies.

The issue of data protection must be considered when making test data available. In some cases, critical functions may only be tested by the employee groups for which they are intended and only by users with the required authorizations, especially when personal data is involved. Alternatively, test data can be anonymized (see Chapter 9, *SAP Test Data Migration Server*).

Data protection

Information about the test data can also be added to the test case descriptions for the testers. While the test case description can describe the classification of the required data (such as material of characteristic XY), a test data sheet can contain each characteristic. You might also consider linking to a central data pool from within the test case description. That way you can use the table created during the definition of the test data. The tester can then access the relevant test data along with the test case description. Because the tests must be reproducible, testers should document the actual data used when they perform a test.

Relevant test cases can be linked to individual test runs for each test stage, one the essential preconditions are in place. Depending on the tool used, these collections of test cases may be referred to as *test plans* or *test sets*. If you use the test tools available from SAP, these can be created on the basis of the business process structures of the Business Blueprint, which greatly simplifies execution of business process-oriented tests. In the next step, the individual test cases can be assigned to specific testers, for example, to the key users nominated by the user departments (see Chapter 4, *Functional Testing*).

In the SAP Test Workbench (Testing Option 1), you can use the "test package" construct, which allows you to create an individual worklist for one or more testers within the test plan. Using this approach, you can, for example, generate a test package for each business process and make this package available to one or more testers for the purpose of test execution. To ensure consistent process tests, experience has shown that it's also useful to assign a test package to everyone involved in the process. All testers then have access to the results of all test steps and can use the data in their own test activities; for example: document number = output of step n = input for step $n + m$.

In SAP Quality Center by HP, the test cases in a test set are assigned to individual users directly, and these users can then begin to execute testing.

Test case sequences

In addition, both test management tools allow you to map test case sequences, which enable automatic test control (for example, with the mapping of a control rule such as "Test case B cannot be tested until test case A has been tested successfully"). Both tools also provide email notification function for informing users as soon as testing begins.

Tester handouts

A tester should always be provided with documentation briefly outlining how to proceed. This tester handout can serve as a guide and a reference for test execution. Use of the selected tool should also ideally be documented with screenshots. The handout should answer the following questions.

- Where and how do I access my test cases?
- How do I access a test case description and the related test data?
- How do I access the relevant transactions of the test systems?
- How do I document test results?
- Which status is to be defined for the various possible results?
- How do I document errors?
- Who's available as a contact person if any problems occur?

This information should also be provided to the testers in the form of a short presentation; for example, as part of a central kick-off event. The handout can also be distributed among the testers at this event.

Test execution

Test execution begins after the test cases have been assigned to the testers. The testers can be informed about the start of testing by email, if this is facilitated by the selected tool or its configuration. Role-based and user-specific access to the test management tool helps testers to locate the test cases and work packages assigned to them. Based on the descriptions and the test data provided to them, the testers perform the testing activities and document their results. If testing also includes automatic test cases, these can also be started by the testers. If the Test Workbench in SAP Solution Manager is used, testers can access the transaction to be tested in the test system directly, provided that the relevant system data has been defined in advance.

During test execution, the test coordinator performs the related status analyses and reports results. The contents and structure of the reports and graphics are defined in the test concept, and ideally can be created by the test management tool directly. The reports are communicated to the relevant persons using the address data defined in the test concept. At the end of a test, the test coordinator blocks access to the test cases or test packages for the testers. In order to meet the related documentation requirements, test management tools usually also offer a function for "freezing" the final status of the test plan.

Status analysis and reporting

3.5   Final Preparation

In the Final Preparation phase, the company prepares for production with the software to be implemented. The company trains users and performs the final technical tests (performance tests). The software is tested in conditions as close to real life as possible. In particular, the tests verify technical issues and error-free transfer of data from legacy systems.

The Final Preparation phase also provides a good opportunity to conduct a review of the testing process that has been established up to this point. This type of review allows you to identify the strengths and, above all, the weaknesses of the established testing process and to promptly make any improvements required.

Review of the testing process

All documents describing the testing process and procedures relating to test planning and execution (in particular, the test concept) provide a starting point for the review. It is also critically important to check whether the testing process described in these documents was reflected in reality, or whether the actual process deviated from the process described so that the documentation needs to be adjusted.

A tried and trusted approach to the review is to compare the actual testing process with the desired target situation and, where relevant, with market standards or best practices. A pragmatic approach would involve listing all aspects of the process that are to be evaluated (such as the test strategy, reporting, or time and cost planning), and then performing a quantitative evaluation of the level of maturity determined in the comparison. Using this approach, you can easily detect where action needs to be taken first. On the basis of these initial estimations, a detailed analysis of the individual areas can be performed and the implementation of appropriate measures can be planned.

Methods for continuous improvement

The review should be conducted on a regular basis as part of the continuous improvement of the testing process. You also need to ensure that identification of areas for potential optimization is followed up by implementation of appropriate measures. The following tasks should therefore be established as an ongoing cycle.

► Conduct the review

► Identify optimization measures

► Prioritize and plan the implementation of these measures

► Implement measures

► Confirm and evaluate implementation of the measures

Elements of market and industry standards for general process enhancement (for example, Kaizen or Six Sigma) can be used when implementing a procedure for continuous improvement of the testing process. Specialized models for evaluating and improving testing processes also exist. One example of these is the *Testing Maturity Model* (TMM) developed by the Illinois Institute of Technology. With these types of models, you must always make sure that they fully cover the key aspects of your enterprise-specific testing process, in particular in relation to SAP-specific procedures.

In the Final Preparation phase, preparations are also made for the operation and maintenance of the production systems and the testing activities that will be used to safeguard live operation. Preparation for and possible automation of regression tests are important issues. Addressing them carefully will help you significantly reduce the manual effort involved.

We'll now describe one procedure for the selection and automation of regression tests. Regarding the preparation for and execution of system testing (including the system administration test), please refer to the related work packages of the ASAP Roadmap and the documentation provided there. The complex subject of performance testing is discussed in detail in Part III of this book (Chapters 10 to 13).

Regression tests help uncover errors that affect the functions of software after it has been changed. Making changes to previously stable software might mean that it no longer runs as intended. As described in Chapter 2, *Methodology*, this type of behavior may occur after any changes to the system in a complex system landscape. This applies equally to technically motivated changes (such as the importing of Support Packages or SAP Notes to eliminate errors) and process changes (such as the redesigning of business processes).

Regression testing

A regression test focuses on integration scenarios and is primarily an activity that protects the production system against unwanted effects of changes. Changes are tested in a QA system before they are transferred to the production system. You can import changes into the production landscape in a controlled manner only after the tests run without errors.

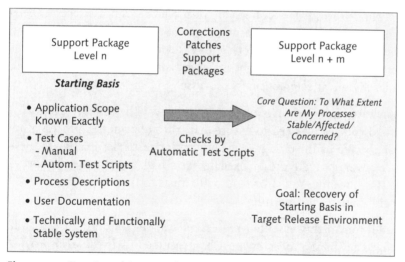

Figure 3.17 Overview of Automated Regression Tests

The regression test typically involves a subset of the test case descriptions processed during the integration test, and it covers the critical business processes of the company. The descriptions of the relevant integration test cases may be reused here. Figure 3.17 shows relevant aspects of an automated regression test.

Scope of testing

The test cases to be executed in the context of a change must be chosen with care. In an ideal scenario, a relevant test selection process has already been developed and subjected to a review as part of the continuous improvement of the testing process.

If a test is too limited in its scope, it may not cover all of the business processes that are affected by the change, and there is an increased risk of unwanted application responses going undetected and being transferred to the production system. If, on the other hand, a test has an excessively broad scope (admittedly a rare scenario in practice), the consumption of resources will be very high due to the execution of irrelevant tests, particularly in a manual testing context.

Risk analysis

In order to achieve risk minimization, it is necessary to select an appropriate subset of test cases when planning a regression test. As well as testing the core business processes, a regression test must test the processes that are actually affected by the change. In the case of process-oriented changes initiated by the enterprise itself (for example, the enhancement of existing processes), it is often very clear which business processes need to be tested again. The corresponding test cases can then be grouped together in a regression test set. In the case of technical changes (such as a Support Package import), on the other hand, it is sometimes difficult to identify the affected business processes.

In any case, the selection of test cases must always be based on risk analysis, and you always need to ensure that critical businesses processes are not impacted by the changes. The integration test cases relating to these processes must therefore be executed as a high-priority task as part of regression testing. You also want to minimize testing effort and carefully assign resources for retesting.

Business Process Change Analyzer

In addition to this essential regression test set, the test cases of the changed business processes must be executed. Tools can also provide support for this type of test case selection. The Business Process Change Analyzer in SAP Solution Manager 7.0 EhP 1 is a tool for change analysis, one that actively supports the identification of changes to technical objects, and thus also risk-based test case selection.

If you use the Business Process Change Analyzer (BPCA), system traces can be assigned to the business processes that are documented in the Business Blueprint. These system traces record the technical objects used by the processes. This step is ideally executed after testing is completed in the Final Preparation phase. If these traces are available, the BPCA can compare them with system changes in the form of transport requests (see Figure 3.18). The results of this comparison show all business processes that have technical objects that were changed by the selected requests. The Test Workbench uses this information to create a test plan containing all test cases assigned to the affected business processes. This proposal provides the foundation for a change-oriented test plan, which can be edited in the next step.

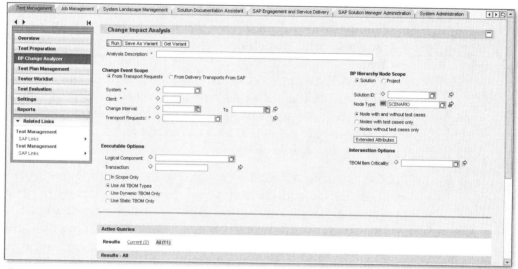

Figure 3.18 Change Analysis with the Business Process Change Analyzer

Because of the manual effort involved in regression testing, and in order to follow the principle of "never change a running system," many companies avoid maintaining their production landscape. Regression testing is usually the responsibility of user departments, and employees in those departments prefer to avoid testing because it piles up on top of their daily work. If changes are made at all (urgent corrections, for example), the required regression test is generally superficial.

Manual effort

Normally, the appropriate automation of the test execution can reduce the amount of manual work involved; by simulating a dialog user behavior, for example.

Automation of regression tests

As of SAP Web Application Server 6.20, eCATT provides a suitable test automation tool for this purpose without an additional license fee. Provided that the processes covered by the integration test run in the SAP GUI for Windows or Web Dynpro user interfaces, they are completely covered by eCATT, and web services can also be tested. The scripts generated by eCATT are defined in SAP Solution Manager, while the integrated Test Workbench is used for test execution and reporting. An interface that can be connected to eCATT via external automation tools is available for the testing of user interfaces that are not covered by eCATT (for example, HTML-based applications). The implementation of the BC-eCATT interface by external test tools can be certified by SAP at the request of the manufacturer. A list of tools that have proven successful in this interaction scenario is available at *http://www.sap.com/ecosystem/customers/directories/SearchSolution.epx* (select the fields BC-ECATT 6.2HTM or BC-ECATT 6.2WIN). In the context of Testing Option 2, HP QuickTest Pro is available as an automation tool and can cover automation of various user interfaces (such as SAP GUI and web interfaces) thanks to add-ins. In this case, storage of the automated test cases and reporting are integrated into SAP Quality Center by HP.

Because automatic test cases do not have to be started by a user department, and can be started as an internal service by a central tester group or SAP Basis, the user department only needs to be contacted only when an error occurs so that it can interpret the situation. You can also schedule the start as a period activity, so that manual effort is normally only required in the event of an error.

Test focus At the beginning of a test automation project, the user departments define the business processes that are to be covered by regression testing. A risk analysis is also useful in this case in order to identify the critical business processes. If appropriate key words have already been used to identify the test cases for module or integration testing, the relevant test case descriptions can now simply be selected.

If no relevant test case descriptions exist, user departments must describe the relevant processes. The use of documentation tools such as the SAP ProductivityPak by RWD has proven useful in this context. Such tools can record the behavior of the individual dialog user. These recordings can then be used as a template for test automation.

Regardless of the automation tool being used, test automation involves a task very close to development. Even if automation tools seem easy to use at first glance, some programming knowledge is still essential in order to set up sound, effective test automation. This applies, in particular, to the use of test data (setting parameters for input and output variables) and the creation of complex conditions for testing. While today's automation tools offer diverse, easy-to-use functions, practice shows that test automation can only be implemented by a user department in exceptional cases.

Automation team

Experience indicates that the best approach is to ask user departments only to provide the automation template, specify the test data, accept the scripts that have been generated, and be involved in error analysis. In this approach, a manageable team of experts (three to five persons) handles the actual automation. This team also creates and maintains the scripts as an internal service.

In the context of test tool selection (see Section 2.8, *Selecting Test Tools*), the test automation team decides on the automation tool it will use and confirms its decision with the management team of the overall project. Because this issue involves discussions of the budget, it's a good idea for the initial approach to the topic to involve a tool without licensing costs, such as eCATT. The right tool can be chosen on the basis of the information gathered in a proof-of-concept study.

Test standards

For such a proof-of-concept study, it is useful to begin by defining and automating a manageable scenario such as Create purchase order based on a released purchase requisition. It may be helpful to involve an external consultant in the first automated steps. The automatic scripts can be started with various users (authorizations) and varied test data in the proof of concept. The procedure should also be repeated with alternative tools, and the results evaluated and compared.

Training of the expert team should be planned in accordance with the tool selected. Experience shows the value of a customer-specific workshop that conveys the concepts of the test automation tool and creates the first automated test cases for customer-specific processes in the customer systems. This workshop should be scheduled to take place immediately prior to an actual testing project, because experience also shows that the lifespan of the knowledge gained in such a workshop is limited. A coach

Qualification and coaching

should work on the project during the first five to 10 days. The coach can act as a direct contact person for the test automation team to help it over the initial hurdles. Additional questions can then be discussed using email or telephone communication (*remote coaching*).

Defining
process flows

Process flows are also defined for the test automation project as part of the test standards. Doing so involves an activity closely related to development. The definition of these process flows begins with a request from the user department and ends with the acceptance by the user department. You also must define a start time for the automatic test cases. Along with periodic starts in the quality assurance system, it's a good idea to start test scripts there after importing software modifications.

The definition of defect management is especially important here, and reporting structures must also be defined. Because scripts can produce errors based on consciously and unconsciously modified functionality, you should regulate collaboration between the user department and the expert team. The expert team might have to adjust the scripts, which corresponds to a change request from the user department.

Naming
conventions for
test objects

A naming convention similar to that used for manual test cases should also be defined for the objects that are to be created as part of the automation project. If you use eCATT, these objects include objects of the SAP Repository that were created in the customer namespace; for example, system data containers, scripts, test data containers, and test configurations (see also Section 8.1.1, *Architecture of the Test Landscape and eCATT Fundamentals*). You can transfer any attributes and keywords from earlier test phases. The use of an appropriate naming scheme is also useful if are you are using HP QuickTest Pro as part of Testing Option 2.

In the selected test management tool, all relevant information should be available for the creation and execution of automated tests. This applies to the business process perspective (which process is to be tested with which test cases), the test project perspective (which test cases belong to a test stage or test run), and the technical level. If you use SAP Solution Manager, this is ensured by the mapping of the system landscape. This mapping not only incorporates textual references to the relevant target systems, but also connects these target systems to SAP Solution Manager using RFC connections. This means that if you use eCATT, test scripts can be stored centrally in SAP Solution Manager and executed in the relevant connected systems. The use of trusted RFC connections also allows you to realize a high degree of security because passwords for logging on to the target system are never defined in plain text (see Section 8.1.3, *Technical Requirements*). In any case, the results returned by the automation tool, including automatically generated logs and status information (see Figure 3.19) should be stored in the test management tool.

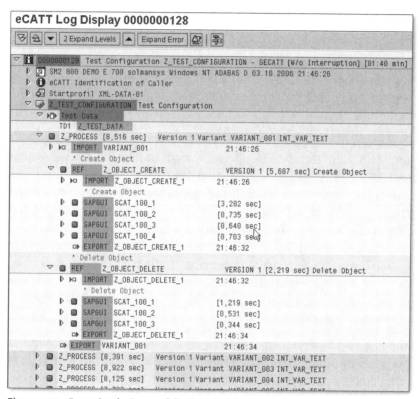

Figure 3.19 Example of a Successfully Executed Automatic Test Case (eCATT)

The regression test typically covers the critical business processes. In an automation project, you should therefore begin with a manageable number of such business processes. The coaching phase focuses on teaching the relevant users how to use the selected test automation tool. Automation can then be expanded to cover additional business processes: that are less critical or that are simply variants of previously automated processes. You can also ensure that automation focuses on covering particularly critical business functions.

Reusability The reusability of scripts should always be considered when they are being recorded. It makes sense to begin with the automation of individual test steps (one transaction per test script) and then, if necessary, link them with each other in various processes. Experience shows that you don't really want to map all possible variations of a transaction with a test script. The re-recording of a transaction is often much less time-consuming than the programming of complex flow controls in the test script (for example, conditional flow control with IF queries).

The reusability of test scripts increases with the parameterization of the entry fields. Values can also be transferred to these input parameters from systems containing the relevant date. The document numbers generated at runtime are transferred to output parameters to enable a continuous flow of entire business process chains.

Test scripts and test data are also to be defined in the test management tool. If eCATT is used in SAP Solution Manager (Testing Option 1), test scripts and information about their target system (system data container) can be linked to test configurations stored in the structure of a SAP Solution Manager project. Test configurations represent executable test cases because you already know what is being tested (the test script), where testing is to be executed (the system data container), and the data to be used for testing (default values). Specific test data can also be added to the test data containers, and the defined test data can naturally be reused across multiple scripts.

The Business Blueprint structure can also be used in order to group test cases in a meaningful way when storing the automation scripts. Tests of individual transactions can be stored at process step level, while integration tests comprising entire process chains can be stored at the level of business scenarios. Appropriate attributes can also help with the subsequent selection of test configuration objects.

If you use SAP Quality Center by HP (Testing Option 2), you can use HP QuickTest Pro to store generated scripts in the folder structure of SAP Quality Center. Note that a separation of test script, test data, and target system is not supported in this case

Business Process *Business Process Testing* is an additional function in SAP Quality Center by
Testing HP that allows you to build test cases from individual components. These individual test components can be created manually or using automation

tools. SAP TAO also uses this principle by compiling automated tests from individual components. As a next step, these components can be put together to create test cases. The reuse of components in various test cases enables a swift modification of test cases, as a change to one component is immediately detected in all test cases that refer to that component (see Chapter 6, *Supporting Test Automation Using SAP TAO*).

As when preparing for test execution for module and integration testing, the test cases for regression testing are compiled in a test plan and assigned to the relevant testers; for example, members of the expert team. If manual test descriptions are also to be used in this context, these are assigned to the user departments.

3.6 Go-Live & Support and Run

The SAP solution is transferred to the production environment in the "Go-Live & Support" ASAP phase. The completed project can be transferred at this point into a solution in SAP Solution Manager. Solutions refer to groups of systems that are generally production systems, which are managed as a unit. An example would be all systems belonging to an enterprise's subsidiary.

Going live

Using solutions means that your live system can access all of SAP Solution Manager's functions for system operation, some of which are based on the results of the implementation phase; for example, in the Business Blueprint. As a result, you can set up functions such as business process monitoring for cross-system monitoring of the systems mapped in the Business Blueprint (see Figure 3.20). This enables rapid identification of issues and their impact on business operations.

Maintenance of the production landscape also involves change request management, with changes occurring either as a consciously planned activity (for example, importing Support Packages) or as a matter of urgent necessity (error correction). In accordance with the ITIL standard processes, all changes are documented before they are transferred to the production system, confirmed using an appropriate workflow, and tested in the relevant systems in the QA landscape. Changes can only be imported into the production systems in a controlled manner after the corresponding regression tests have been completed without errors.

Change request management

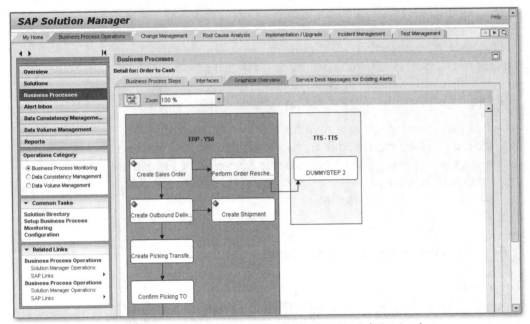

Figure 3.20 Business Process Monitoring in a Live Solution Landscape

The regression test has already been methodically prepared in the Final Preparation phase of ASAP. Tests required for critical business processes are identified and ideally are already available as test plans or test sets. Where applicable, a standard regression test set can be optimized by means of a change analysis with tool support, in particular, with the assistance of the Business Process Change Analyzer. By combining a risk-based change analysis with a large proportion of automated test cases, you can greatly reduce the effort involved in regression testing.

Execution   The actual execution of the test may occur periodically or in connection with a change. The results are made available to the relevant persons on the basis of the reporting structures that were previously defined. If errors occur, you must analyze and correct them in consultation with the user department. If you have to modify the test scripts, the user department generates an appropriate change request that will require acceptance by the user department after it has been approved and implemented. If correction of the error requires additional modification, a follow-up test is also required. If the regression test is highly automated, it can be repeated in its entirety.

The Run SAP methodology provides a considerable amount of support for the setup and continuous optimization of an effective support organization. Standards, procedures, Best Practices, and references to service offerings are available in SAP Solution Manager in the "Run" phase or the Run SAP Roadmap.

3.7 Conclusion

The roadmaps provided in the content of SAP Solution Manager can be used to map project management activities. The roadmaps for implementation and upgrade projects are based on the tried and trusted ASAP methodology. In addition, the Run SAP Roadmap provides project methodology for implementing and optimizing standardized processes for system operation. Roadmaps can also be adjusted to suit the specific requirements of an enterprise. A download function makes the roadmaps available offline so that you can edit them with external project management tools.

The "Project Preparation" phase is extremely important for a test project. In this phase, the test strategy is defined and documented in a test concept, together with the basic parameters. To help with the definition of a test strategy, SAP provides support for tool selection by providing relevant information and consulting services.

The "Business Blueprint" phase involves the definition of requirements for the solution to be implemented, and thus is also the basis for testing. In addition, the defined test strategy is developed as far as possible, and test standards are formulated. The drafting of the template that will be used for test descriptions is of particular importance during this phase, in addition to the definition of test reports, the defect management process, and the definition of test end criteria.

The "Realization" phase involves the implementation of the requirements documented in the business blueprint. Preparation for and execution of the testing activities are based on test standards. You should pay particular attention to the reusability of the test case descriptions, in order to avoid unnecessary work in meeting your quality goals. Test management tools offer significant support for the assignment of tests to individual test runs and to the testers who will be executing the tests. The same applies to monitoring and final reporting on the test progression and test results.

In the "Final Preparation" phase, the company prepares for the go-live dates for the software to be implemented. It trains end users and performs the final tests. Preparation of the regression test is an important issue here. Automating tests helps to minimize manual effort over the long term. In the context of test automation, the reusability of the automated test cases must also be considered.

In the "Go-Live & Support" phase, the go-live of the implemented solution is supported and carefully overseen. The "Run" phase safeguards the live systems against unintentional changes and any associated disturbances of live operation. The integrated approach of SAP Solution Manager enables the use of results of the implementation phase for live operation, and covers all requirements for the live operation of a system landscape. Documents and changes subjected to regression testing in the QA systems are transferred to the production systems in a controlled manner. You will find it helpful to consider using a tool-supported change analysis and automation of the regression test set (see Chapter 4, *Functional Testing* or Chapter 8, *Test Automation with eCATT*).

While this chapter primarily examined the methodology of a test project based on SAP Solution Manager, the following chapters focus on the implementation and mapping of testing activities in SAP Solution Manager or in integrated third-party products (Testing Options 1 and 2).

PART II
Functional Testing

The following chapter gives a detailed introduction to test management using the functionality provided in SAP Solution Manager Release 7.0 EhP 1. With the publication of Enhancement Package 1, the functions for test management have been expanded greatly. Therefore, we will focus on innovations in test management and on the versatile new functionality.

4 Test Management with SAP Solution Manager

This chapter gives you a comprehensive introduction to the range of functions provided by SAP using SAP Solution Manager Release 7.0 EhP 1 for your activities in test management. The use of the relevant tools is always based on your specific situation within Application Lifecycle Management (ALM). This chapter shows you how the available tools can be used in various stages of the application lifecycle, such as during an implementation project or in operation.

SAP provides its customers with two options for test management: Testing options

1. Option 1 involves use of the original SAP Solution Manager functions provided through integration of the basic functionality of SAP Test Workbench, among other methods.

2. In Option 2, SAP Quality Center by HP distributed by SAP in the framework of a reseller agreement is integrated via an adapter in SAP Solution Manager.

The central data pool (Single Source of Truth) operates in both scenarios of SAP Solution Manager. This data pool ensures that all relevant information for the Application Management Lifecycle is centrally available.

The chapter describes the first of the options offered by SAP that are provided to SAP customers within test management, namely *Testing Option 1*. We describe the use of the original SAP Solution Manager functionality that is provided, among other methods, via integration of the basic functionality of SAP Test Workbench. The following two chapters (Chapter 5, *Project-Related Testing with SAP Solution Manager and SAP Quality Center by HP*, and Chapter 6, *Supporting Test Automation with SAP TAO*) describe *Testing Option 2* with the scope of functions of SAP Quality Center by HP and the optional use of SAP Test Acceleration and Optimization (SAP TAO) for test automation.

Structure of the chapter

SAP Solution Manager is outlined in the context of SAP Enterprise Support in the first part of this chapter. SAP Solution Manager plays a major role for the SAP support infrastructure in SAP Enterprise Support. This infrastructure already begins with the customer in the sense that the customer-support structures are integrated into structures of SAP Active Global Support via the connection of SAP Solution Manager to SAP Service Marketplace. Moreover, SAP Solution Manager forms the basis of the end-to-end solution operations standards provided by SAP (including test management; see also *http://service.sap.com/supportstandards*) and the basis for Run SAP, the implementation method for these standards ("ASAP for Operations").

You can gain an overview on the scope of functions of SAP Solution Manager Enterprise Edition in Section 4.2.1, *Application Management Lifecycle*. The functions are explained as they relate to stages of Application Management Lifecycle.

The work center provides a central working environment for the relevant team member roles. This role-based concept is described in more detail in Section 4.2.2, *Work Center*.

Section 4.2.3, *Adapter and Functional Enhancements*, describes the integration scenarios provided for third-party products that effectively supplement the portfolio of functions already provided via the standard.

Section 4.2.4, *Projects and Solutions*, describes the key concepts for projects and solutions within SAP Solution Manager. The emphasis here is on the classification of these constructs within Application Lifecycle Management (what I use and when).

The reader can obtain an overview of the settings options after the fundamental classification of SAP Solution Manager and an introduction to the functions and concepts. Automating the basic configuration of SAP Solution Manager is dealt with here (Section 4.3, *SAP Solution Manager—Basic*

Settings) Insight is also given into cross-scenario and scenario-specific customizing (Section 4.4, *Project-Related Testing with SAP Solution Manager*). The overview concludes with a description of the connection options that exist in SAP Solution Manager with regard to the system landscape (Section 4.5, *Integration Scenarios*).

The (basic) configuration and connection of the system landscape to SAP Solution Manager are key prerequisites for developing individual use cases. This especially applies to the *test* use case. Once the reader has obtained an overview of these steps, the test procedure is then described in the next sections. We distinguish between project-related and solution-related tests, emphasizing the test-related use of SAP Solution Manager within Application Lifecycle Management (for instance, test use in implementation projects or operation).

The chapter also describes diverse integration scenarios that exist among various use cases of SAP Solution Manager. We discuss options for reusing documents already created, and show how effort can be reduced through the integration and reusability options within application management.

4.1 Testing in the Context of SAP Enterprise Support, Run SAP, and SAP Standards for Solution Operations

SAP provides its customers with three central maintenance offers that address different requirements and complement each other. The support offer is primarily used to achieve the following critical goals: handling of complexity, minimization of risks, and—last but not least—cost control.

The offer of SAP Active Global Support is documented in detail in SAP Service Marketplace (*http://service.sap.com*). The three central support offers are outlined as follows.

▶ **SAP MaxAttention**
This support offer has been designed for major customers with complex system environments. It provides customized support when implementing the continuous business processes of SAP solutions.

The offer focuses on core business processes, system landscapes, scalability and high availability, automation, and the safeguarding of IT investments.

▶ **SAP Safeguarding**
These important, project-based services support the customers during implementation, upgrade, and operation. They help to manage risks and to ensure the technical robustness of SAP solutions for customers, and are provided by a Technical Quality Manager (TQM) in situ.

▶ **SAP Enterprise Support** (see Figure 4.1)
This holistic support offer and its related services have been structured in such a way that SAP customers are supported across the entire lifecycle of their applications, from implementation to operation. The offer covers both SAP standard solutions, custom developments, and partner solutions.

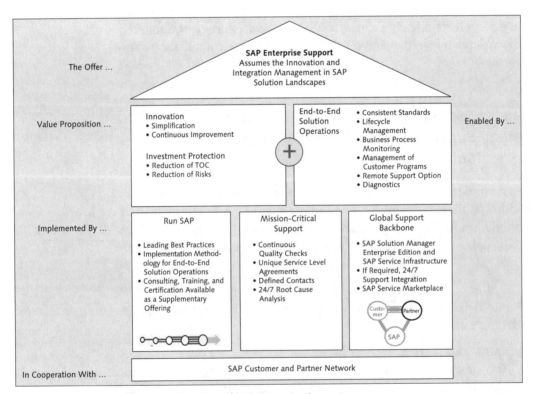

Figure 4.1 Overview of SAP Enterprise Support

In order to fulfill service agreements based on support offers against the background of increasingly complex system landscapes, SAP provides its customers with a solution using SAP Solution Manager that standardizes the interface between SAP and the customers. Using this solution, customers can also optimize internal processes (for example, internal support processes) in conjunction with the operation of the solution landscape.

SAP Customer Best Practices and standardized procedures are provided with the Run SAP method ("ASAP for Operations"), as well as standards related to and based on SAP Solution Manager for end-to-end solution operations that address known challenges within Application Lifecycle Management. This approach is briefly presented in the context of end-to-end integration testing.

Operational solution landscapes that map and support business processes of customers are subject to numerous changes. There are changes that result from the business operation itself, such as mergers and process-related changes. Other changes are initiated and implemented in conjunction with the maintenance of systems, including technical upgrades and support-package implementations.

Because each change to the IT systems requires an appropriate test, customers face the following challenges in mastering the preparation and performance of such activities.

Challenges

- ▶ **Tests in heterogeneous system landscapes**
  The execution and documentation of complex integration tests require the application of test management tools, particularly with regard to distributed locations. In some cases, only when tools are used can organizations build appropriate communication structures and enable reporting to error management.

- ▶ **Specification of test focus**
  When changes are copied to the production landscape, this always entails the question: What must be tested beforehand to ensure that the production processes function well? Where possible, this assessment shouldn't be based on gut instinct. Instead, the use of respective tools makes much more sense.

- ▶ **Appropriate test data**
  In order to make a convincing answer to the question previously

asked, appropriate test systems must be provided that are supplied with needed test data. Logical test data records are indispensable and should be provided in test systems using the least amount of time and effort and at the lowest cost possible. If necessary, they should be reproducible.

▶ **Minimization of manual testing through test automation**
Because tests are generally carried out parallel to business operations, the integration of appropriate testers from the user departments always burdens the daily business. In order to reduce manual efforts and related adverse effects to a minimum, appropriate test automation tools should be used.

▶ **Revision security and traceability**
Fulfilling demands to trace changes and to execute and document testing activities as a result of legal and regulatory provisions places additional demands on the tools used. To deal with these requirements and additional efforts and costs for implementation and configuration, you should carefully check issues such as authorizations, release mechanisms, versioning, or digital signatures beforehand.

E2E solution operation standards

The challenges listed here are addressed via one of SAP Standards for E2E solution operations, the description of which SAP provides its customers in SAP Service Marketplace (*http://service.sap.com/supportstandards*). These standards are based on SAP's huge wealth of experience with regard to operations of solution landscapes. The standards define in a generalized organizational model (see Figure 4.2) how Change Request Management, Incident Management, and in particular Test Management can be mapped using SAP Solution Manager. Versatile functions for application management in SAP Solution Manager are directly implemented at the interface between business and IT.

E2E test management shows how the listed challenges can be mapped using SAP Solution Manager. An extensive range of functions are available here that answer key questions in the test environment. The topic of test management is dealt with in the same way that we describe the specification of the test focus, the provision of test data, and the test automation. This range of functions is presented in more detail in later chapters.

Run SAP

With the Run SAP methodology, SAP provides a standardized procedure through which the E2E solution operation standards available in the enterprise can be implemented. This is similar to the standardized ASAP process model in terms of implementation, upgrade, and rollout projects, best practices, services, and basic training for customers provided.

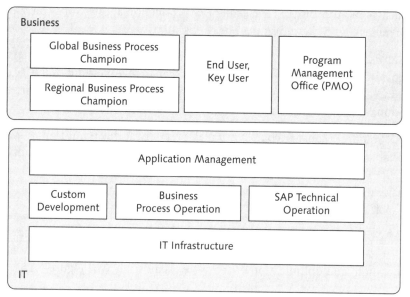

Figure 4.2 Generalized Organizational Model of E2E Solution Operation Standards

4.2 SAP Solution Manager Enterprise Edition

As described in the previous section, SAP Solution Manager Enterprise Edition (referred to as such since Release 7.0/SP15) is a central module of SAP Enterprise Support. This solution represents consistent further development of the functional scope of SAP Solution Manager.

There are a number of publicly accessible sources of information with regard to SAP Solution Manager Enterprise Edition. Some of these are listed in Appendix C, *Recommended Reading*.

4.2.1 Application Management Lifecycle

Because of the growing complexity of business processes, the mapping of these processes across different SAP and non-SAP applications—along with the ability of system-landscape companies to manage them—

131

increasingly relies on the support of tools to implement and operate these solution landscapes. These tools are supposed to help users handle various tasks during the entire lifecycle of the system landscape, from implementation tasks (such as project management) to operation (such as monitoring) to replacement of production applications (such as upgrades), with the minimum effort possible.

Many different tools are already used, and all of them support customers separately in specific tasks for application scenarios. As a result of the lack of integration among these tools, however, a lot of information is often redundantly stored and maintained.

Application management solution SAP Solution Manager comes into play precisely at this point to provide suitable functionality and the option to integrate an existing functionality in the form of a central data pool. SAP Solution Manager allows you to make use of synergy effects in various ways and therefore reduces the associated costs.

SAP Solution Manager provides numerous application scenarios that customers can use such as a control loop during the implementation, operation, and optimization of the system landscape (see Figure 4.3).

The following sections offer a general overview of representative use cases. You can find further details in the next few sections and in SAP Service Marketplace (*http://service.sap.com/solutionmanager*).

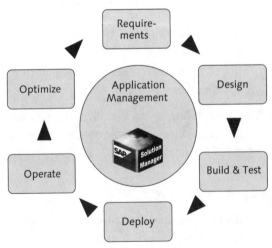

Figure 4.3 Lifecycle Within Application Management

The application scenarios of SAP Solution Manager are particularly useful because they are integrated within existing SAP Active Global Support structures and therefore allow a closer and more efficient collaboration between customers and SAP (collaboration platform).

The implementation of new business processes and the associated implementation of new applications need first of all to be transferred in a regulated and documented way throughout all the necessary project phases. Then the business processes to be mapped — including the settings and developments for non-SAP solutions (such as partner solutions) — need to be permanently described.

Requirements and design phase

SAP Solution Manager provides both the project procedure (including ASAP roadmaps) and the standard process structures to be implemented (some of them including test case descriptions) via implementation content. You can download the current release of this content in SAP Service Marketplace via the ST-ICO software components. You can significantly accelerate the project work by using this information.

The Solution Documentation Assistant can be used for documenting business processes to be implemented. It reads business process structures using an analysis project from a target system and then identifies it respectively in SAP Solution Manager. The user can specify the set of rules to be considered in a customer-specific way. An appropriate implementation project is then created based on the results of the analysis.

The process structures of the implementation project now provided can be customized and supplemented if required (for example, process steps in a third-party application). The relevant business processes are gradually documented from beginning to end in this way. Further information can now be stored in this project or in the process structures stored in the project (requirements, interfaces, and so on).

The user is provided with a Business Blueprint at the end of the Build & Test phase. Implementation can subsequently follow based on this blueprint. With the documentation of this blueprint, a central document can be generated in the system from SAP Solution Manager and submitted for acceptance if required. If desired, the process structures can now be locked in case of any subsequent changes.

Build &Test phase and Deploy phase

The planned status documented in the business blueprint is now implemented via customizing and development activities. The relevant IMG activities and development objects can be documented in the process structures, including responsibilities, and the implementation status can be stored there as well. If required, the current status of the implementation can be appropriately reported.

Further documents are linked in the process structures for each project phase. Test case descriptions and basic training documents, for example, can be specified here as representative types of documentation. These documents can then be further used by other use cases of SAP Solution Manager; for example, to generate test plans and learning maps.

All types of results are ultimately provided via the process structures in the form of central project storage and can be further used in subsequent phases of the Application Management Lifecycle. One example is the further use of a global rollout project. For this type of project, you have the option to define central, customer-specific process templates that can be used for locally customized implementation projects. You can automatically compare further developments of the central template with local implementation projects. These developments can then be copied if required.

With SAP Solution Manager 7.0 EhP1, Quality Gate Management functionality supports the user when copying project-relevant changes from the development environment to production. Underlying transport activities can be controlled depending on customer-specifiable quality gates (see Section 4.5.3, *Test and Quality Gate Management*). Because organizations need to copy changes synchronously across the limits of the system, especially in complex projects (for instance, changes in the portal including changes to the back-end system), Quality Gate Management supports this scenario for all development environments supported by SAP (ABAP, Java, .NET, C/C++).

Operate phase   The user is supported by a wide range of functions when the implemented end-to-end business processes are in operation. You can use SAP Solution Manager to set up the central monitoring of the system landscape by integrating CCMS functions already available in SAP Basis. The system-specific information collected can be linked to the business process structures mapped in SAP Solution Manager. You can therefore set up a business process monitoring that meets the information requirements of the people responsible for the respective business process.

Moreover, SAP Solution Manager EarlyWatch data can be collected from the connected systems, based on which EarlyWatch Alert reports can automatically be generated (see for instance, *http://service.sap.com/ewa*). These reports are evaluated and, depending on the results, forwarded immediately or at intervals to SAP Active Global Support. This enables a prompt reaction by SAP team members to any problems.

The collaboration between the IT and the user departments is regulated via service level agreements, such as those governing approvals on system availability and response times. These agreements can be stored as planned values in SAP Solution Manager where they can be automatically compared with the actual values collected by EarlyWatch. Based on results, SAP Solution Manager generates a detailed report designed to provide confirmation on adherence to the service level agreements.

Matters relating to system administration can also be handled centrally using SAP Solution Manager. The relevant activities for system maintenance are stored as a checklist for each system connected, and these are then processed by team members of the IT department, in decentralized fashion if necessary. As a result of their documentation character, these checklists complete the overview of all relevant activities and make it easier for new employees or external service providers to get started with the system.

In addition to these benefits within the enterprise, SAP Solution Manager also facilitates the interaction with SAP Active Global Support. For example, internal customer error messages can be entered in decentralized fashion in the connected systems and then processed centrally in SAP Solution Manager using SAP Service Desk. All the necessary system information relevant for processing the message is automatically appended to the message, which immediately accelerates the company-internal communication and processing. Employees can use the Service Desk function to search directly for appropriate solutions in SAP Service Marketplace or in a customer-specific solutions database. The solutions that have been discovered can then be directly imported into the relevant system by using the Note Assistant. If the company-internal search for a solution fails, the messages can be forwarded to SAP Active Global Support; the last current processing status on SAP's side is replicated in SAP Solution Manager. In the meantime, the Service Desk scenario described here is also provided in the form of a partner scenario.

SAP Solution Manager Diagnostics

If required, SAP Active Global Support employees can use SAP Solution Manager Diagnostics to immediately begin causal research in the customer's Java environment (for example, in SAP NetWeaver Portal). Solutions can therefore be promptly provided.

Extensive reporting functionality enables a wide range of evaluations and a prompt overview on the current status of the customer-specific solution landscape. Evaluations, for example can be executed with regard to key performance indicators (such as system availability) or for the processing status of Service Desk tickets. This information can be transferred if necessary to SAP NetWeaver BW for more detailed analyses.

To safeguard critical business processes implemented across the system, automated distribution scenarios for customizing settings can be configured using Customizing Synchronization. Settings can be synchronized in such a way that all target systems are automatically customized when there is a change in the source system. This guarantees the functioning of processes (also those processes across the system, such as comparison of CRM with ERP).

Optimize phase

SAP Solution Manager provides customers with direct access to SAP Active Global Support, where appropriate services can be ordered directly. Depending on the service, delivery can occur remotely. If applicable, it can also be initialized via the results of an EarlyWatch Alert.

Another scenario, based on the application scenarios assigned to operations, is represented by Change Request Management, which is based on the quasi-standard of the ITIL process. A change requests are created as a CRM transaction in SAP Solution Manager (for example, as a follow-on document of a Service Desk message). Once this change request has been approved, it generates in turn a follow-on document (change document) that is processed by the involved employees (roles) via an appropriate workflow and enables consistent traceability of changes to your processes. Maintenance scenarios, as well as large development and implementation projects, can be mapped via the Change Request Management application scenario.

With the Maintenance Optimizer, organizations have functionality that guides them through the planning, downloading, and implementation of support package stacks (composition of relevant support packages) and enhancement packages. Using a standard procedure, the user is guided through all stages and all information is compiled centrally. Furthermore, all open and completed maintenance procedures can be formatted in an overview so that they can be evaluated using a report function.

Last but not least, SAP Solution Manager has on hand a custom project type for upgrade projects, including an appropriate ASAP Upgrade Roadmap. Upgrade-relevant IMG activities can be identified, configured, and tested using this project type. The Custom Development Management Cockpit supports the user in identifying upgrade-relevant development objects and enables the user to initially calculate the effort required to customize an upgrade.

4.2.2 Work Center

SAP Solution Manager comprises a variety of functions that support the user within the Application Management Lifecycle. The scope of functions has been increasing since the first release, as is reflected in the number of relevant transactions in SAP Solution Manager. SAP Solution Manager has satisfied its users with functional enhancements; however, an ever-increasing number of complex functions have grown up alongside these enhancements.

An increasing number of user groups have been addressed via SAP Solution Manager as a result of the growing scope of functions. Attention has increasingly applied to employee groups that previously had no direct contact to SAP applications, particularly those involved in managing E2E-business processes (including testing activities). The SAP GUI-based image of SAP Solution Manager had resulted in current SAP users managing directly in SAP Solution Manager. However, non-SAP users experienced some problems in getting started.

In the light of this customer feedback, SAP created a user interface that addresses both complexity and user-friendliness. Since Release 7.0 SP15, a central transaction (SOLMAN_WORKCENTER) provides a user interface via SAP GUI with work centers that allow role-specific access to all relevant transactions and that can be defined in a customer-specific way

Transaction SOLMAN_ WORKCENTER

(see *http://service.sap.com/solutionmanager* • MEDIA LIBRARY • TECHNICAL PAPERS • *How To Adapt a Work Center View.pdf*).

Web Dynpro Application AGS_ WORKCENTER

Furthermore, the work centers are provided via the Web Dynpro application AGS_WORKCENTER. Using this application allows you to directly access the work center of SAP Solution Manager via a browser.

SAP NetWeaver Business Client (NWBC)

Alternatively, you can access the work center via SAP NetWeaver Business Client (NWBC). The user here has the same navigation options as in the browser, but the system arranges the interface elements in a slightly different way.

Work centers represent central work environments customized to customer requirements with access to role-specific functions. However, the structure of a work center focuses on the role or roles of an employee. The employee has access to all relevant information via various tabs relating to the work center and can process this information centrally (including documents, messages, alerts, and analyses). Access can be controlled via authorizations.

The work center concept supports an additional aggregation level via the *MyHome* work center. Here, the user can obtain an overview of all work centers assigned to him or her. The most important information at meta level is provided here in a type of cockpit. However, you can navigate to the role-specific work centers via links if necessary.

The underlying concept of this user interface is illustrated in the following example using the *Test Management* work center (see Figure 4.4).

Structure of a work center

A work center is fundamentally divided into three areas:

▶ **Navigation bar**
The user can here choose between the work centers assigned to him or her.

▶ **Navigation area**
Here the user navigates within a selected work center and selects the relevant content area.

▶ **Content area**
The information of interest to the user within the work center for each selection is displayed here.

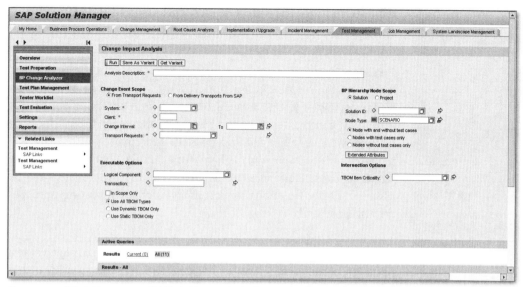

Figure 4.4 "Test Management" Work Center—"BP Change Analyzer" Navigation Area

The navigation area of the *Test Management* work center is divided into the following content areas.

"Test Management" work center

▶ **Overview**
The most important information in the content areas listed in the following is summarized at meta level.

▶ **Test Preparation**
The user obtains an overview of projects or solutions within SAP Solution Manager depending on the selection of the test preparation view. You can restrict the displayed result using specific filters.

You can start an analysis for a selected project. As a result, the user obtains a list that specifies which information is already available for those structure elements of the project which he or she needs to use for test-relevant functions (including transactions and test case descriptions). The prerequisites for using Business Process Change Analyzer can particularly be checked here (see also Section 4.4.4, *Creating Test Plans and Test Packages*).

▶ **Business Process Change Analyzer**
Here the user has the option to analyze projects and solutions to learn whether and to what extent a planned change (for example, transport

requests and delivery orders of SAP) has impacted the mapped business processes. Test plans are then automatically generated based on the result of this analysis.

▶ **Test Plan Management**
Parallel to the current Transaction STWB_2, the user gains a customized overview of test plans available using filter criteria, if applicable. Here, you can create other test plans, among other things. Existing test plans can be changed and deleted. Moreover, you can manage the attributes of the test plans here (for example, allocation of release scenarios). Test sequences can be created and relevant testers can be assigned. Other functions for test analysis or for reporting purposes are also provided.

▶ **Tester Worklist**
Here the user can access the test cases assigned to him or her via test packages in the form of work packages. The user can start his or her activities for test implementation here and subsequently document them (parallel to Transaction STWB_WORK). These documentation options also comprise the creation of error messages, among other things.

▶ **Test Analysis**
As with Transaction STWB_INFO, the user is provided with an extensive range of evaluation options for projects and individual test plans (including BW reporting).

▶ **Settings**
Here you can access the configuration options provided via Transaction STWB_SET. Moreover, the user can also implement the settings for integrated BW reporting and for Business Process Change Analyzer.

▶ **Evaluations**
Here the user can access all evaluation options provided. This also includes the analysis options enabled via the BW connection.

▶ **Associated Links**
The user is provided with relevant links to SAP Service Marketplace and to SAP Help Portal in the standard configuration. Further information sources can be integrated on the user role via a link if required.

In the *MyHome* work center, the aforementioned content areas are listed once again at meta level in the TEST MANAGEMENT area. From here, the user can directly navigate to the relevant content area of the *Test Management* work center.

4.2.3   Adapter and Functional Enhancements

With SAP Solution Manager, the user has an extensive range of support functions within Application Lifecycle Management (ALM). The scope of functions is defined by the integration of individual use cases within SAP Solution Manager and therefore allows a very effective reusability of information as well as central access to it.

SAP Solution Manager provides a wide range of options for maximizing reusability and integration, including ALM tools already used. Document management tools of third parties can be integrated so that documents managed there can be accessed via a link in SAP Solution Manager. You could, for example, manage test case descriptions externally. However, these descriptions are already available via a link in the test management functionality within SAP Solution Manager.

Integration via linking

Functionality of third-party tools is to some extent integrated into SAP Solution Manager via synchronization scenarios. One example here would be the integration of ARIS for SAP NetWeaver that is enabled by importing special transports to SAP Solution Manager. The user can model business processes in ARIS using this scenario as he or she has done so far. Using SAP Solution Manager only synchronizes the three hierarchy levels of the business process structures stored in ARIS that are required for effectively storing ALM-relevant information. The synchronization scenario can be initiated from both sides; namely, from SAP Solution Manager and from ARIS.

Integration through synchronization

Another integration scenario is provided via standard interfaces of SAP Solution Manager that can enable integration of the Service Desk in Incident Management. Message tickets are exchanged via a service-based interface, and the information required is provided to the relevant user groups based on requirements. It would therefore be possible to enter a ticket in a third-party tool, for example, and then process it there as first-level support. If required, the message is forwarded via the interface to the second-level support that processes its SAP-related tickets

Integration via standard interfaces

in the Service Desk. This includes execution of the root-cause analysis with Diagnostics and also communication with SAP Service Marketplace, including access to the SAP Notes database and forwarding of the ticket to SAP Active Global Support.

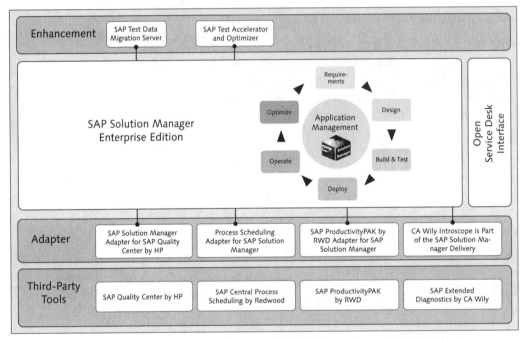

Figure 4.5 Integration Options of SAP Solution Manager Enterprise Edition

eCATT   Another standard interface is provided in conjunction with test automation. External test automation tools can be connected here to eCATT, already available via SAP NetWeaver Application Server ABAP. The external tool is called via eCATT and implements the desired simulations of the dialog-user behavior in the applications that aren't directly addressed via the driver concept of eCATT. The same concept is followed here as with all other integration scenarios in which SAP Solution Manager remains the central data pool (Single Source of Truth). The protocols generated from the external tool are integrated into the eCATT protocol and are therefore available centrally. The successful interaction between third-party tools and eCATT via this interface is certified by SAP. However, the third-party tool itself isn't certified (see Chapter 8, *Test Automation with eCATT*).

Third-party functionality can be accessed via adapters that are installed as a type of add-on in SAP Solution Manager. Here SAP provides adapters to integrate the following products.

Integration via adapter

▸ **SAP Quality Center by HP**
   Structure elements and requirements and test objects are transferred to the Quality Center by SAP Solution Manager via SAP Solution Manager Adapter for SAP Quality Center by HP, and are then available to use in preparing and implementing test management. The test results are then transferred again to SAP Solution Manager as a central data basis. Error messages can also now be exchanged via this adapter. However, these are then provided if necessary in SAP Solution Manager Service Desk for processing.

▸ **SAP Central Process Scheduling (SAP CPS) by Redwood**
   Necessary background jobs can be requested—for example, via the process scheduling adapter for SAP Solution Manager in a web form— and are approved via the Change Request Management in SAP Solution Manager. Background jobs are scheduled and documented in a process-oriented way that enables these jobs to be monitored centrally. Information is automatically exchanged between the tools involved.

▸ **SAP ProductivityPak by RWD**
   With SAP Solution Manager Adapter for SAP ProductivityPak by RWD, documents created on the basis of recording using the ProductivityPak (including manual test case descriptions) are automatically provided in the business process structure of SAP Solution Manager.

4.2.4 Projects and Solutions

Projects represent a central element for SAP Solution Manager. These projects can contain a number of functions, and different project types are provided. The selected project type affects the respective processing options in the individual project phases (such as Business Blueprint and Realization).

Because of the great importance of projects, users must have specific authorizations to be able to create and change them. The specifications of user roles provided standard SAP Solution Manager are described in the respective Security Guide (see *http://service.sap.com/instguides*).

The following sections describe the most important project types used in testing.

- **Implementation project**
  Implementation projects are set up and implemented here in SAP Solution Manager. Appropriate implementation roadmaps and process structures facilitate and accelerate the achievement of project results.

  Implementation projects can be activated in the same way as the project types listed specifically for using the Change Request Management functionality of SAP Solution Manager. As a result, even more complex projects can be handled in a technically controlled way.

- **Template project**
  Project structures including relevant documentation (for example, transactions and test case descriptions) can be encapsulated in templates. These templates can be reused to create an implementation project.

  The provided functions effectively support rollout projects. However, a versioning option that includes the associated automated comparison function (implementation project versus template used) facilitates the further development of templates (roll in).

- **Upgrade project**
  Based on this project type, customers obtain support with the implementation of technical and/or functional upgrade projects. A specific upgrade roadmap and the respective comparison functions enable companies, for instance, to precisely identify the customizing settings relevant to their release change.

- **Maintenance project**
  This type is primarily used to support maintenance of the system. Maintenance projects are assigned to maintenance cycles that are particularly important to Change Request Management. This project type enables you to carry out urgent corrections and planned changes (such as the importing of support packages) in a controlled way.

Projects are primarily used to document project results in the form of a central storage. They are primarily used for implementation-related use cases. Solutions, however, support the operation of the solution landscape. They can contain activities relating to monitoring and system administration, for example.

To enable the smoothest possible phase transition of application management, information from projects can be copied from projects to solutions and vice versa. The user is provided with a powerful transfer function that is used, for instance, once an implementation project has been completed (Go-live).

Business processes used in production are documented in solutions and, among other things, are used to provide relevant information in a support case or as a basis for the setup of Business Process Monitoring. Because of the huge importance of this documentation, changes should undergo an appropriate approval procedure so that they can be safeguarded. The check in/check out function can therefore provide valuable support. A maintenance project is therefore assigned to a solution and the aforementioned function is subsequently activated (see Figure 4.6).

Check in/check out of business processes

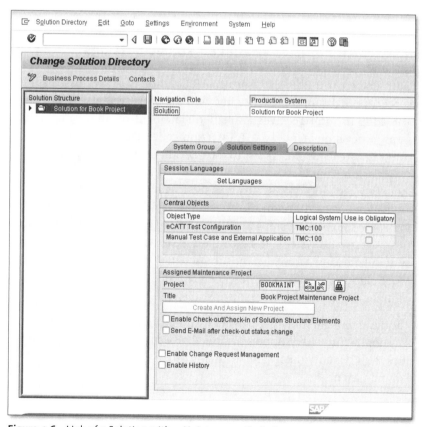

Figure 4.6 Link of a Solution with a Maintenance Project

The respective scenario then occurs as follows.

- The relevant structure elements are highlighted in the solution and their checkout is requested.

- Once the request has been approved, the respective structures are highlighted as checked out in the solution and are then transferred to the maintenance project assigned to the solution.

- Changes to the structures (for example, an additional process step) are implemented in the maintenance project. After the change activities have been completed, the check-in is requested to the solution (button REQUEST)

- Once the check-in has been approved, the changed structures are provided again in the solution and they are no longer marked as checked out.

4.3 SAP Solution Manager—Basic Settings

SOLMAN_SETUP   With Release 7.0 EhP, the user of SAP Solution Manager has a guided procedure that supports him or her with the basic system configuration. The administrator receives a detailed statement on the configuration steps to be implemented via Transaction code SOLMAN_SETUP. Moreover, he also has central access to the relevant documentation (see Figure 4.7). Customizing is to some extent executed and logged automatically, including activation of BC sets and services of the Internet Connection Framework. In addition to the relevant steps for SAP Solution Manager System, configuration steps are also provided via the guided procedure that refer to the systems to be connected; for example, mapping of the system landscape. Among other things, RFC destinations from and to SAP Solution Manager can be generated and then integrated with the central system into the system landscape.

The basic configuration of SAP Solution Manager still can be implemented as before without the support of guided procedures. The associated activities must be individually and manually processed in customizing of SAP Solution Manager.

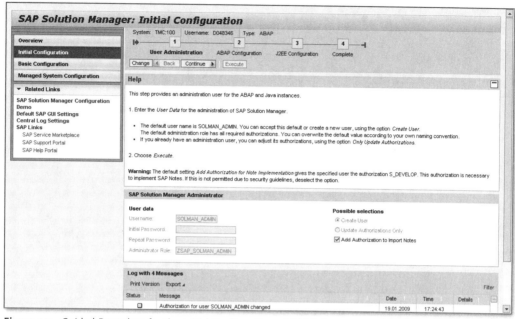

Figure 4.7 Guided Procedure for the Initial Configuration of SAP Solution Manager

Besides the steps of the basic configuration, cross-scenario and scenario-specific steps are provided via the Reference IMG. Scenario-specific configuration steps require to some extent both the steps of basic customizing and cross-scenario configuration. In such cases, the administrator obtains a respective note regarding dependencies.

To enable SAP Solution Manager to access the relevant systems of the solution landscape in the context of the different application scenarios, the solution landscape must be maintained in SAP Solution Manager and linked to it via RFC connections. These activities primarily involve tasks related to SAP Basis support.

Solution landscape

The procedure is described in detail in Transaction SPRO in SAP Reference IMG. For this reason, an overview is given at this point and reference is made to the documentation of the SAP Reference IMG. To do this, choose SAP SOLUTION MANAGER • BASIC SETTINGS • SYSTEM LANDSCAPE in the Reference-IMG of Solution Manager (see Figure 4.8). Naturally, the respective SOLMAN_SETUP functions are also provided.

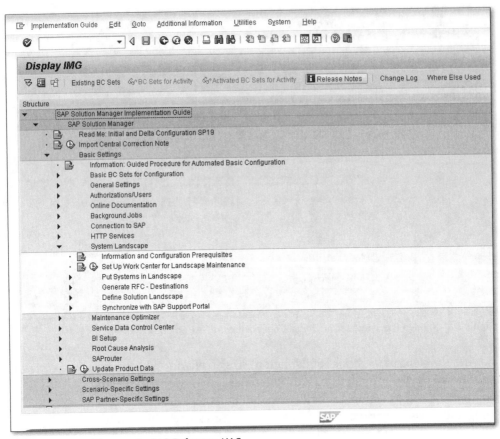

Figure 4.8 SAP Reference IMG

System/product assignment The mapping of the system landscape involves, among other things, assigning the systems to the different SAP products. The products are already provided in the standard version. If non-SAP systems are to be connected to SAP Solution Manager, the respective products also can be defined and assigned to the system to be created (see Figure 4.9).

With the System Landscape Directory and the Landscape Infrastructure Server, data related to the system landscape can be retrieved in an automated manner. In this way, SAP Solution Manager can automatically determine information on servers, databases, and systems from each customer landscape.

In early project phases, not all systems may yet be available in the system landscape. In such cases, you can create appropriate dummy systems in

SAP Solution Manager. These dummy systems are used as placeholders and can be subsequently enhanced with information relevant to the system and then promptly connected to SAP Solution Manager.

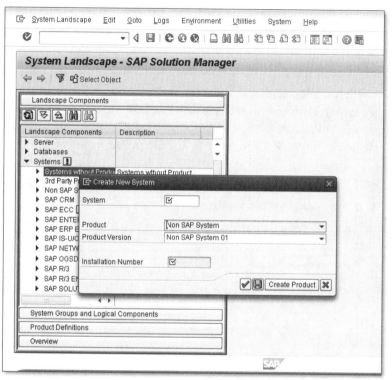

Figure 4.9 Creating a Non-SAP System in Transaction SMSY

Once the test-relevant systems have been made known to SAP Solution Manager and are available, they can then be connected to it via RFC connections. When SAP systems are connected, the user is supported by a wizard and the relevant RFC connections are automatically generated. Because it is necessary to generate trusted RFC connections, the user needs to have the necessary authorizations in SAP Solution Manager and in the SAP system to be connected.[1]

RFC connections

---

1 Via Trusted RFC, a user can navigate from SAP Solution Manager to a connected system without having to log on to the target system in the dialog. In the current context, this functionality depends on technical prerequisites (authorizations, for example), which are detailed in SAP Note 128447.

Logical
components

The systems within the solution landscape are divided into logical components according to their system roles: development system, quality assurance system, and production system, for example. Logical components represent a product-specific network of systems. Similar to the landscape systems, logical components are assigned to individual products. This way, selection of the respective systems is controlled. Thus, for example, you can only assign to the logical component SAP CRM those systems that are provided for this product in the respective release.

You may have to take into account certain conditions. For example, a logical component could contain the SAP CRM solution of an enterprise for Europe, while another logical component could contain the solution for Asia (for example, Z_CRM_EU and Z_CRM_ASIA).

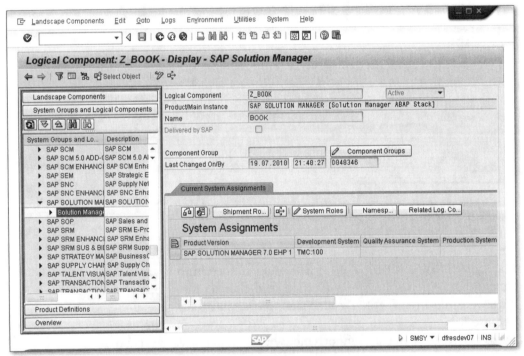

Figure 4.10 Creating a Logical Component in Transaction SMSY

Products and
system roles

The required SAP products, as well as appropriate system roles are provided standard for the classification and maintenance of logical components (see Figure 4.11). These products and system roles can be enhanced according to the project situation. Those that are not used can be deactivated if necessary.

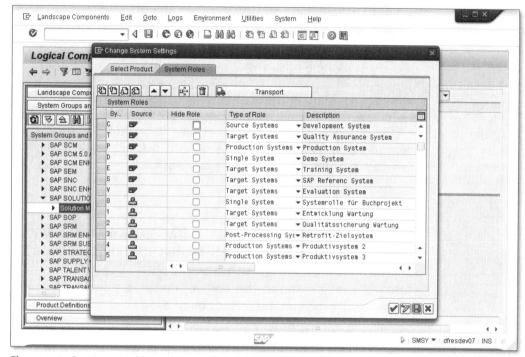

Figure 4.11 Creating an Additional System Role in Transaction SMSY

Correct mapping of the system landscape is a basic prerequisite for using SAP Solution Manager effectively in individual application scenarios. The complete system landscape (SAP and non-SAP systems) can be mapped and connected to SAP Solution Manager. The user is supported by various automated functions and default values.

Mapping the system landscape is primarily the responsibility of SAP Basis support. The necessary authorizations are usually provided only to these personnel.

4.4 Project-Related Testing with SAP Solution Manager

The following sections describe the test management procedure using original functions of SAP Solution Manager (Testing Option 1). All relevant activities relating to test management are fundamentally provided via the *Test Management* work center. The project is only created in a separate work center (*Implementation/ Upgrade*).

It is assumed in the next sections that the relevant system landscape is known in SAP Solution Manager and is connected to the central system via RFC destinations. Moreover, we assume that appropriate logical components are available. You can obtain further details on these steps in Section 4.3, *SAP Solution Manager—Basic Settings*.

4.4.1 Creating a Project

Projects can be created and changed in SAP Solution Manager via the *Implementation/Upgrade* (SOLMAN_WORKCENTER) work center or directly in SAP GUI via Transaction SOLAR_PROJECT_ADMIN. A web-based assistant provides another option, in which enables a project to be created clearly and quickly (Transaction AI_SPS).

The descriptions given in the following section are limited to creating projects via the work center (see Figure 4.12) because this user interface has now become the standard user interface of SAP Solution Manager. Some newly developed functions are only provided via this UI.

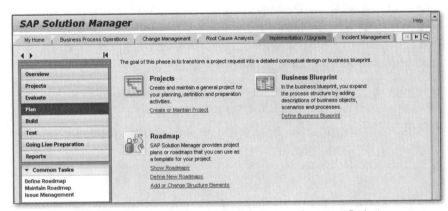

Figure 4.12 "Implementation/Upgrade" Work Center—Creating a Project

After calling the work center (see Section 4.2.2, *Work Center*), the user navigates to the respective functionality, for example via RELATED LINKS • PROJECT ADMINISTRATION. Once an appropriate project name has been assigned, the relevant project type is selected (see also Section 4.2.4, *Projects and Solutions*).

If you already use SAP Solution Manager in your solution landscape operations, you can now link the project with the systems provided for this purpose in the solution landscape.[2] Alternatively, you can also do that in a later phase of the project creation; for example, by manually assigning a logical component in the SYSTEM LANDSCAPE tab.

Once you have confirmed the entries, the system displays several tabs that can be used for maintenance purposes. All project-specific information (project framework data) can be documented in the ASAP phase Project Preparation via these tabs. The following sections primarily describe the mandatory entries that are relevant for the test.

The GENERAL DATA tab (see Figure 4.13) must be used to assign a meaningful title to the project. Furthermore, you can also enter information on project management data in this tab. You can also store a general project description here and document information on the project status and the relevant project data (both target and actual data).

"General data" tab

It's particularly important to specify the project language, as you won't be able to change the language retroactively. Among other things, the language is used to manage the project documents (including test case descriptions) assigned during the course of the project. These include test case descriptions, separated by language in SAP Knowledge Warehouse of SAP Solution Manager. Further important information on this topic, such as information on extensions and releases used, is queried when the project is saved. This information enables you to control access to project-specific documents (authorization object S_IWB). You can obtain

Project language

---

2 Solution landscapes consist of logical components that were created during the mapping of the system landscape (see Section 4.3, *SAP Solution Manager—Basic Settings*). In this way you can present complex system landscapes rather clearly and flexibly (for example, you could map all European systems across all applications). You can find further information on this topic in SAP Service Marketplace and in the SAP Help Portal.

further information in Appendix B of this book, *SAP NetWeaver Knowledge Warehouse—Functionality in SAP Solution Manager*.

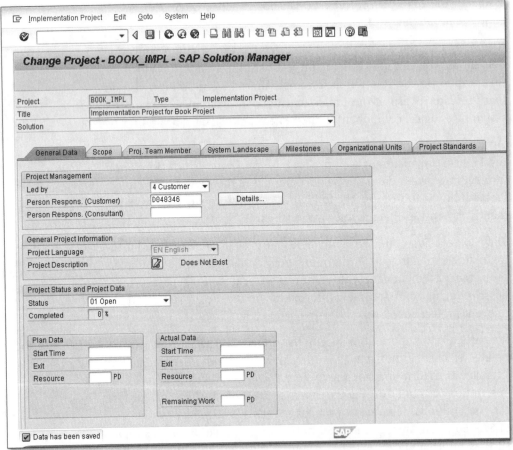

Figure 4.13 Creating a Project—"General Data" Tab

"Scope" tab   The SCOPE tab allows you to transfer project structures that are encapsulated in customer-specific templates. The system can provide standardized project structures including transactions and test case descriptions particularly in the case of rollout projects.

Roadmap   In this tab, you must also connect the roadmap that is relevant for the project (project procedure). In the ROADMAP SELECT subtab (see Figure

4.14), a roadmap is selected that suits the project type (for example, ASAP IMPLEMENTATION ROADMAP). These project-specific phase models contain SAP's standard implementation methodology and cover the most important aspects, phases, and milestones of an SAP implementation or upgrade project. In addition, the system provides links to accelerators that have proved themselves as best practices.[3]

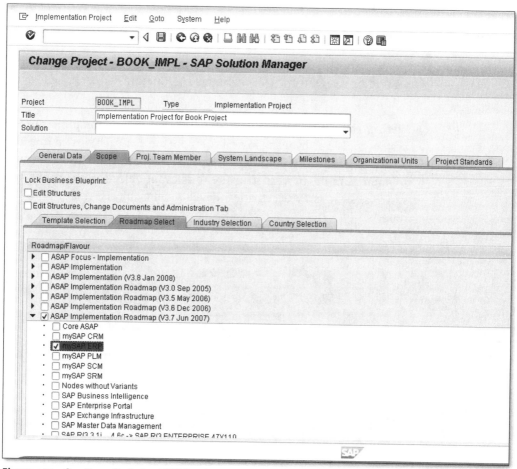

Figure 4.14 Creating a Project—ASAP Roadmap Selection

---

3 There is the option to define customer-specific roadmaps. Existing roadmaps can be complemented with additional phases and information. Customized project procedures (for example, group standard) can be mapped.

You can also establish relationships that refer to projects for countries and industries. However, this data is primarily for information purposes only.

Project team members

The PROJECT TEAM MEMBER tab can be used to maintain all project-relevant team members in the roles assigned to them. The RESTRICT CHANGES TO NODES IN PROJECT TO ASSIGNED TEAM MEMBERS flag can play a very important role in this context. This setting allows you, for instance, to control who is subsequently allowed to process test case descriptions for a certain node in the process structure.

System landscape

The SYSTEM LANDSCAPE tab is divided into four different subtabs: SYSTEMS, CENTRAL OBJECTS, IMG PROJECTS and CHANGE REQUESTS (see Figure 4.15).

The SYSTEMS subtab allows you to link the implementation project to the system landscape by using logical components. For each system role, the logical components reference the respective systems and thus enable you to jump from the process structure to relevant objects in the connected systems, such as IMG activities, development objects, transactions, or reports.

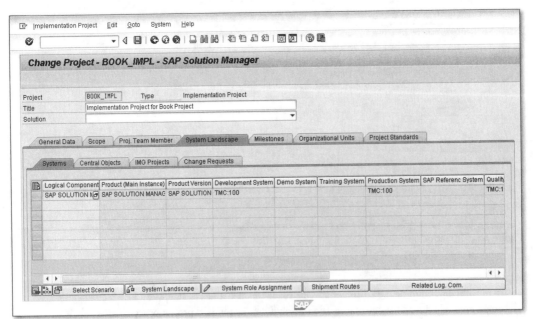

Figure 4.15 Creating a Project—"System Landscape" Tab

This assignment can be carried out via the referenced solution landscape when a project is created. However, this solution landscape subsequently supplies information to the logical components. In this case, the components are entered in the SYSTEM LANDSCAPE tab. You can, however, also insert logical components manually.

If you create the process structures of the project using Business Process Repository, SAP Solution Manager compares the logical components maintained in the SYSTEM LANDSCAPE tab with the products required for the mapped processes. If the desired entry in the SYSTEM LANDSCAPE tab doesn't exist, SAP Solution Manager automatically suggests an entry to the user and enters it after the user has confirmed it.

At an early stage of a project, specific systems may not yet be available and therefore cannot be assigned to logical components. In these cases, you can connect logical components to the project even if they are not yet assigned to any systems. Instead, they can be linked subsequently to the relevant systems.

Dummy systems

The CENTRAL OBJECTS tab allows you to specify which test objects (manual test cases and external applications, as well as eCATT test configurations[4]) can be referenced from those systems of the system landscape within the project. In this context, the use of SAP Solution Manager has proven effective as a central test management system that stores all test objects in this system. Consequently, you should select the SAP Solution Manager system in both cases and set the USE IS OBLIGATORY flags.

An implementation project also involves making customizing settings in order to map customer-specific processes in the system landscape. You must therefore create an IMG project including views in the IMG PROJECTS tab for each product in the respective development or customizing system.

IMG projects

With SAP Solution Manager 7.0, you can specifically activate projects for Change Request Management. You can activate a project via the ACTIVATE CHANGE REQUEST MANAGEMENT flag within the CHANGE REQUESTS tab and also create an appropriate project cycle.

---

4 These types of test cases are stored as objects in the repository. Test case descriptions based on SAP KW are not affected here.

Milestones When you create a project in SAP Solution Manager, the phases/milestones for using *Quality Gate Management* use cases are automatically assigned in the MILESTONES tab (see also Section 4.5.3, *Test and Quality Gate Management*).

Depending on the roadmap being used (see SCOPE tab), the milestones stored in the phase model are automatically maintained in this tab. You can manually add other milestones and assign concrete dates to them.

Organizational units The ORGANIZATIONAL UNITS tab allows you to maintain information on the organizational units that you use in your project. You can, for example, store data on the function, country, and time zone in this tab. This data is used for purely information purposes.

Project standards Each project contains numerous standards that are applied during the project work. The values specified in the PROJECT STANDARDS tab are used as default values in project management, in the roadmap, in the business blueprint, and in the configuration to create and document project results.

Appropriate standards, such as status values and document templates, are also provided in SAP Solution Manager. You can change these standards and add customer-specific attributes to them in the respective subtabs of the PROJECT STANDARDS tab (see Figure 4.16).

In the STATUS tab, you can store values that document processing status with regard to the creation and release of test case descriptions.

Keywords can be defined and assigned to test case descriptions, for instance. Those keywords can later be used as filters during the generation of test plans and packages. Moreover, the subtabs enable you to extend the evaluation options for test projects.

Templates You can create project-specific documents using templates. These templates can be stored in the DOCUMENTATION TYPES tab. Here it's possible to provide templates so that test case descriptions and test notices can be created.

The TABS tab allows you to hide those SAP Solution Manager functions if required that are not used in the Business Blueprint and Realization project phases.

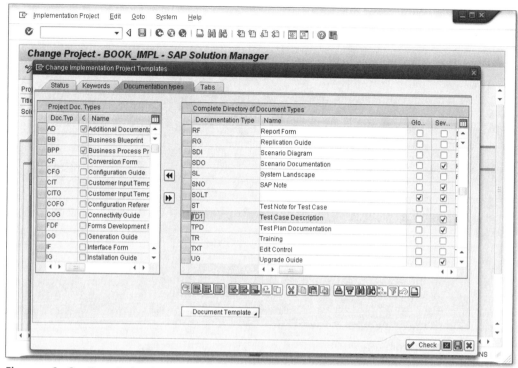

Figure 4.16 Creating a Project/Maintenance of Project Standards—"Documentation Types" Tab

Because of the huge importance of a standardized procedure for test management, we describe the following representative mapping options. Methods are also defined here that must be mapped at tool level.

Test standards

The standards in the SAP Solution Manager project primarily focus on creation and management of test case descriptions. Here you can primarily specify test case templates, document attributes, and release status and strategies. The test case descriptions created on the basis of the template are stored in the business process structure that is mapped in the project.

Test case descriptions

You can access standards in SAP Reference IMG via Transaction SPRO that primarily refer to the execution of tests (SAP Solution Manager • Scenario-Specific Settings • Test Management; see also Figure 4.17). Standards can also be maintained via Transaction STWB_SET.

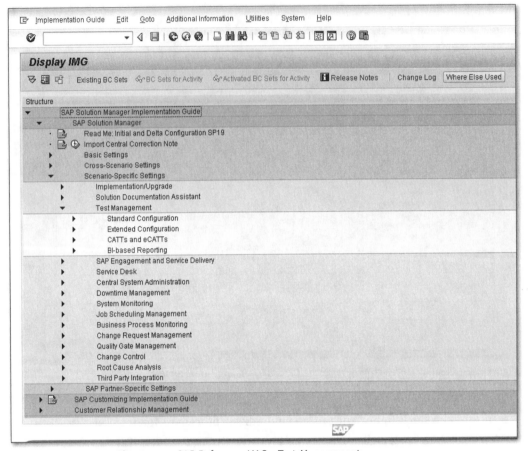

Figure 4.17   SAP Reference IMG—Test Management

You can, for example, maintain email options so that you can directly send information from the test packages. Moreover, you can define additional values in order to complement the default values. You can also create templates for the messaging system in order to automatically complement error messages from the tests with additional information (for example, about the test plan and test package from which a message has been sent). In particular, the basic settings for setting up release and workflow scenarios are implemented here.

Test notes   For result documentation, you can define with which functions the test notes that are to be created by the testers should be stored. Here, it is useful to create the test notes as KW documents. If you do this, you can benefit from the features of a document management system and you can define a template based on which test notes can be created (by reusing an existing template, for example).

Test series are attributes for test plans that enable you to group the test plans logically. You can define customer-specific test series which can contain several test plans. This assignment enables you to execute status analyses.

Custom attributes constitute another useful function. These attributes can be assigned, for example, to test case descriptions in order to appropriately categorize these descriptions. Attributes have an advantage over keywords in that the maintenance of these can be restricted by authorization objects (for example, locking versus subsequent changes). Digital signatures can also be used. The setting options are provided in Transaction SPRO via the path SAP SOLUTION MANAGER • SCENARIO-SPECIFIC SETTINGS • IMPLEMENTATION/UPGRADE • BLUEPRINT AND CONFIGURATION • OBJECT ATTRIBUTES.

4.4.2 Creating the Process Structure

The business process structures within a project are primarily used to store project-relevant information in a process-oriented way. In this structure, the result types can be stored and managed continuously during a project until they are required later on during the operation of the implemented business processes. The subsequent production operation is already prepared when the implementation project is implemented so that it can then quickly access all relevant information should any errors occur.

SAP Solution Manager provides three hierarchical levels so that it can map business process structures in the form of a storage structure: Scenarios, processes, process steps (see Figure 4.18). A project consequently consists of one or several scenarios (such as procurement processes) that are divided into one or several processes (such as purchase-order processing in ERP). A process consists of one or several process steps (for example, purchase order). However, the logical components of a project are assigned at this level and cross-system business process chains can also be mapped. The scenario structure you created is provided in the next phases of Application Lifecycle Management. Test plans are also generated on the basis of this structure.

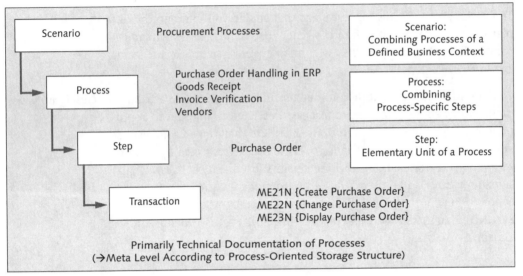

Figure 4.18 Granularity of the Business Processes to be Mapped

Options for creating a structure

Business process structures are mapped within a project in the STRUCTURE tab. You can navigate to the creation of structures via *Implementation/Upgrade* work center, for example, via PLAN • BUSINESS BLUEPRINT. When these structures are created, the user is supported by the functionality described in the following.

▶ **Manual Creation**
Business project structures can fundamentally be created and maintained manually. This option is particularly helpful for subsequently customizing copied structures.

▶ **Business Process Repository**
SAP Solution Manager content supports the user in creating the project structures. As part of the content, Business Process Repository provides a collection of predefined business process scenarios that can be selectively copied to the project.

Among other things, the business process structures contain scenario documentation, transaction assignments, IMG assignments, configuration guidelines, and BC sets. Some of them even contain predefined test cases. By providing this standardized information, SAP Solution Manager enables you to quickly establish basic characteristics for your business scenarios that can be adapted to your specific requirements.

▶ **Copy of Structures**
Business process structures can be copied between projects and solutions. This functionality is used to transfer structures, including information stored in them, to a solution after the operation has been completed. You can choose whether you copy the appended documentation as a real copy or as a reference.

▶ **Transfer from Templates**
Templates can be created using the "Template Project" project type (see Section 4.2.4, *Projects and Solutions*). Templates contain business process structures, including documentation stored there. Using these templates, these structures can be copied to implementation projects; in order to support global rollout projects, for example. This function is also used to some extent by consulting enterprises to document their consulting solutions. They provide added value and a strong sales argument (consulting solution, including documentation, to enable efficient and cost-effective implementation).

▶ **Concatenation of Structures**
Depending on their complexity, projects and the business process structures mapped for them can become unclear and therefore only manageable to a limited extent. To be able to map complex elements effectively, SAP Solution Manager introduced the option to concatenate process structures. The idea is to map subprojects, including relevant structures, which are then concatenated in a meta project for end-to-end process structures. You can navigate from the meta project to the subprojects if required. If required, concatenated process structures can be copied to the project to be concatenated (resolving a concatenation).

Important Note

In the current release of SAP Solution Manager 7.0 EhP 1, concatenated process structures aren't resolved when test plans are generated (see Section 4.4.4, *Creating Test Plans and Test Packages*).

▶ **Solution Documentation Assistant (SoDocA)**
The Solution Documentation Assistant analyzes existing business

Scenario

process structures for relevance and the result can be transferred to a particular project. The set of rules used for an analysis can therefore be defined in a customer-specific way.

The following scenario is therefore possible. A user creates a process structure based on the Business Process Repository. An analysis project is created for this project using the *Assistant for Solution Documentation* work center. An evaluation is then executed for this project. This means that the structures, including the transactions stored there, are analyzed with regard to their use in the target system based on system statistics. According to the rules stored in the rules database, structure elements are highlighted as used. The result of the analysis is transferred either in the underlying implementation project or in a new project to be created.

> **Note**
>
> In order to obtain the most meaningful results, the relevant workload data should be available to the target system in SAP Solution Manager for at least three months.

▶ **ARIS Synchronization**
With ARIS for SAP NetWeaver, you have the option of synchronizing relevant process structure elements into a project of SAP Solution Manager. The modeling of business processes is therefore carried out in the same way as in ARIS. Only the relevant structure elements for process-oriented storage are synchronized in SAP Solution Manager.

Please note that only three relevant hierarchy levels can be synchronized in ARIS. The actual synchronization can be initiated from ARIS and from SAP Solution Manager.

4.4.3 Integrating Test Cases

Result types can be stored in an existing business process structure of a project. In addition to jumps to customizing settings (such as IMG objects) and development objects (such as function modules), you can store test cases (manual test case descriptions and eCATT test configurations) and training materials (such as SAP Tutor notes) in this transaction. Depending on its relevance, this information is referenced to the scenario, process, or process step level (such as step or process-relevant or integrative test cases). References between individual pieces of information are possible within one project but also to other projects of SAP Solution Manager and can be reproduced via appropriate where-used list functions.

Manual and automated test cases can be integrated, for example, via the work center using the path: TEST PREPARATION • PROJECTS VIEW • SELECT PROJECT • GOTO • CONFIGURATION. Here you can select a tab within the structure of the relevant accounts and navigate to TEST CASES.

You should ideally integrate manual test case descriptions as objects of SAP Knowledge Warehouse into the process structure of the SAP Manager project (see Figure 4.19). The functionality of a document management system is provided for this.

Integrating manual test cases

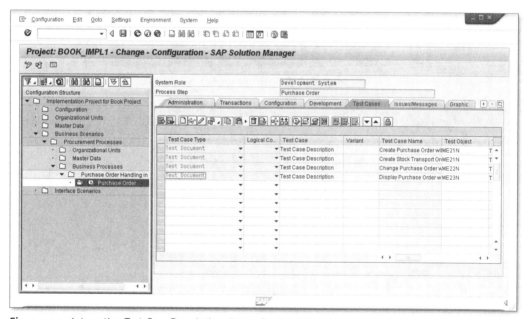

Figure 4.19 Integrating Test Case Descriptions into a Project Structure

You can, for instance, integrate a manual test case description as an SAP KW document on the basis of a test case template. To do this, you must use the document template that was stored as a test standard during the project preparation. Alternatively, you can upload existing test case descriptions into SAP KW or create references to other test case descriptions of the same process structure or from other SAP Solution Manager projects. A copying function facilitates these activities.

You also can use a link to reference test case descriptions from an external document management system in SAP Solution Manager. With this procedure you can continue to use tried-and-trusted structures that can be linked to additional SAP Solution Manager functions (synergy effects).

Test case attributes Test case attributes are either directly maintained when a test case is created directly or retroactively if necessary (see Figure 4.20). Not only do they contain important organizational information (for example, on the component or transaction to be tested), but also technical information (for example, on the test case type). Furthermore, you can store information on the release status, the priority, and the responsible person, and you can maintain comments and cross-references.

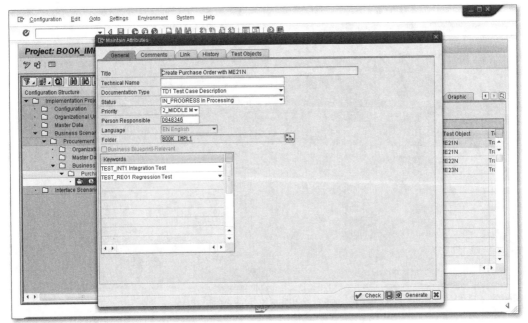

Figure 4.20 Attribute View of a Test Case Description

The maintenance of the search terms already enables you during the creation of a test case to establish the prerequisites that will later open up options that go beyond the SAP standard; for example, when generating test plans or evaluating test projects. Those search terms are defined in accordance with project standards and represent additional selection criteria that allow you to specify the desired results even more accurately.

The Test Cases tab enables you to link the manual test case descriptions to test objects. The test objects can be maintained on the basis of the objects that have been stored at the same level of the process structure in the Transactions tab. These objects can, for instance, be used by testers during the test execution in order to directly jump from their test package into the relevant transaction of the test system. The test is executed in the system provided for the specific test (user guidance).

Test objects

In addition to the manual test case, you can also integrate automated test cases that have been created with eCATT. To do this, you must reference test configurations and specify the relevant test case variants.

Integrating automated test cases

If automated test cases have been created using a third-party tool, you can integrate them into eCATT scripts and then reference them in the structures of SAP Solution Manager via test configurations. For this, you need to integrate the third-party tool via the official interface (BC-eCATT) of SAP NetWeaver Application Server.

4.4.4 Creating Test Plans and Test Packages

You can generate test plans based on the test cases integrated in the structure of an SAP Solution Manager project. These test plans contain all the manual test case descriptions and automated test cases relevant to a defined period and specified test purpose.

Test plans are managed in SAP Solution Manager via the *Test Management* work center in the Test Plan Management navigation area (see Figure 4.21). Here the user has access to the complete range of functions he or she requires to create and process test plans. All relevant test plans can be displayed at a glance in a list using filter criteria.

Test plan management

The user initially selects the underlying project when creating a test plan. When the project is selected, the total number of test cases to be integrated is limited to those that are managed in the process structure of the project. A test plan always exactly matches a project. Simultaneous assignment to several projects isn't possible.

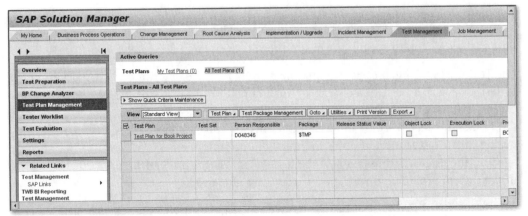

Figure 4.21 "Test Management" Work Center—Test Plan Management Navigation Area

Once the test cases have been selected, the test plan is saved as a repository object and assigned to an appropriate package. The test plan can then be further processed. The test plan is divided into work packages for testers.

Maintenance of test plan attributes

When a test plan is created, attributes need to be maintained that classify the test plan (for example, filter criteria) and help control test execution. The attributes also determine to which system the tester navigates when he or she activates an assigned test object while the test is executed.

The following paragraphs briefly deal with the most important test plan attributes that are also provided automatically to some extent when the test plan is created by the system. Further information can be directly found via the SAP online help in the application.

▶ **"General data" tab**

The underlying project is automatically added as an attribute by the system and cannot be subsequently changed. This project is linked with logical components, and via the SYSTEM ROLE attribute you can control to which system type the test plan refers and where the test objects stored in the test plan are activated (standard: quality assurance system).

The user can classify test plans associated with the same topic via the TEST SET attribute in such a way that several test plans such as cross-project plans can be evaluated. The field PERSON RESPONSIBLE is automatically assigned by the system. This assignment can however be changed subsequently.

Via the STATUS SCHEMA, you can activate a function that has been available since SP15 in SAP Solution Manager (see also Section 4.4.5, *Extended Functionality for Creating Test Plans and Test Packages*). A workflow can be triggered via the status values of a status schema; for example, a workflow that automatically informs the testers assigned to a test plan per email about the release and the start of a test. This status schema can be saved, among other methods, via a digital signature and can lock a test plan against any subsequent changes.

▶ **"Defaults" tab**
The user can control via the ONLY RELEASED TEST DOCUMENTS attribute whether only test case descriptions with a specific document status are considered when the test plan is created.

You can use the WITH TRANSACTIONS flag to control the scope of all test elements (including test case descriptions, test objects, and transactions) that you want to include in a test plan. If an SAP Solution Manager project contains entries in the TRANSACTIONS tab, you can include those entries in the group of test elements by checking the above flag. If you integrate transactions or reports as independent test elements in a test plan, testers can later assign a test status that refers to a transaction or report, irrespective of test case descriptions and test objects.

The TEST NOTE controls which document template tests subsequently document their test results when they run the test.

▶ **Automatic Test**
If automated test cases are assigned to the test plan, the user can specify the target system using the ECATT attribute by activating the test cases. The information on this system is provided via eCATT system data container and not via a logical component of SAP Solution Manager. Logical components distinguish systems from the product point of view and sometimes also from a geographical point of view (for example, all European SAP CRM systems). In contrast, system data containers typically aggregate all systems that are assigned a specific system role across different products (for example, all European quality assurance systems).

Selection of test cases

Once you have maintained the test plan attributes, you can select the test elements from the collection that are relevant to the target system. Appropriate filter functions (for example, search terms) help you with this. The system only provides test case descriptions here that are integrated into the process structure via the TEST CASES tab.

Business Process Change Analyzer

With Business Process Change Analyzer, SAP Solution Manager 7.0 EhP 1 provides a functionality that supports the user in his selection of test case descriptions. Transports and process structures are therefore compared at a technical level and the processes to be tested as a result of the change are identified (see Section 4.4.5, *Extended Functionality for Creating Test Plans and Test Packages*).

Generation of test plan

Once you have highlighted all the relevant test elements, you can start generating the test plan. To do this, an object to be transported is created in the SAP Repository. This object can be assigned to a package (development class). Because transport requirements are not typical in a central test management system, you can select the $TMP package here. The package can be subsequently changed if required (ATTRIBUTE VIEW • GOTO • OBJECT DIRECTORY ENTRY).

The generated test plan consists of the process structure of the SAP Solution Manager project and it contains the test elements that have been stored and selected in that structure. You can use SAP Solution Manager 7.0 to protect test plans against retroactive changes once they have been generated. You can do that via the following menu: GOTO • ATTRIBUTES. You can remove this protection at any time.

Generation of test packages

A test package represents a person-related and period-related view of a test plan. Test packages provide testers with the test case descriptions of a test plan that are assigned to them as a personalized work package. One or several testers can be assigned to a test package at the same time.

Similar to the generation of test plans, the selection of test elements is supported by the filter function. The generation of test packages also involves the creation of objects in the SAP Repository that can then be assigned to a package (development class).

Assignment of testers

The generation of a test package is followed by the assignment of testers. This is executed using the respective SAP users in the SAP Solution Manager system. Assigned test packages then appear in the testers' worklist that can be accessed via the *Test Management* work center in the TES-TER WORKLIST navigation area. You can release and lock test packages to enable time-based control of the processing of test packages. Locked test packages aren't displayed in the worklists of the assigned testers. The test package is released at the same time as the initial assignment of a tester.

Test sequences can be created within a test package already using SAP Solution Manager 7.0 SP15. Test cases within a test package can be directly assigned to a tester via this function. The system informs the testers per email when the previous test case is completed and the custom test can be started (see also the next Section 4.4.5, *Extended Functionality for Creating Test Plans and Test Packages*).

Test sequences

4.4.5 Extended Functionality for Creating Test Plans and Packages

The requirements for the use of a test management tool are becoming more extensive in an increasingly complex system landscape and in end-to-end business-process mapping.

For one thing, the number of relevant test case descriptions is significantly increasing because of longer business process chains. For another, the involved organizational units are distributed worldwide, which is resulting in an ever greater need for communication in the implementation of integration test scenarios.

For this reason, a test coordinator is primarily available for the following key questions.

▶ How can the scope of testing be sensibly restricted, and what needs to be tested when a change has been implemented in the system landscape (for example, once a support package has been imported)?

▶ How can communication within a required test be organized if the testers to be integrated work at various sites and the enterprise only has a limited travel budget at its disposal?

These questions are addressed in SAP Solution Manager using the following functionality.

▶ **Business Process Change Analyzer**
This function enables a technically based identification of the scope of testing.

▶ **Workflow**
Testers are automatically informed about required testing activities via this functionality.

▶ **Test sequences**
Comprehensive integration test scenarios can therefore be mapped and reproduced even more specifically in the system.

Business Process Change Analyzer (BPCA)

Changes to a system are usually imported via transports. However, these workbench and/or customizing requests consist, among other things, of lists of changeable objects. These changes—be they provided by SAP Support Packages, custom developments, or add-ons developed by SAP partners—may have an impact on the (partial) business processes mapped in the system, owing to their high degree of integration with SAP systems.

Because each change requires an appropriate test, it is challenging to identify the relevant scope of testing and the business processes to be tested. This frequently occurs more or less from gut instinct based on experience, which often results in an incorrect or at least over-dimensioned definition of the spot test. Many customers avoid the accompanying costs: costs for testing in the quality assurance environment or costs for troubleshooting in the production systems. This avoidance often causes the implementation of necessary innovations to be deferred.

This is where Business Process Change Analyzer (BPCA) comes in. Using BPCA, the scope of testing can be specified with solid technical grounding and the information value of relevant testing activities can be significantly increased. The test preparation and implementation costs are optimized using BPCA, and the frequency of errors in the production environment and accompanying troubleshooting costs are reduced.

BPCA—use phases

The use of BPCA can be divided into the following phases.

▶ **Analysis Phase**
In the analysis phase, BPCA compares the list on the changeable objects (object list of the relevant transports) with the technical objects that are assigned to the business process structures of a SAP

Solution Manager project. The user has an overview of all business processes changed as a result of this analysis phase.

▶ **Test Plan Generation**
Because test cases can also be managed in the business process structures mapped in SAP Solution Manager, an appropriate test plan can be generated based on the analysis result. The test plan can be customized if required (for example, adding additional test cases).

The following prerequisites are specified for the correct use of Business Process Change Analyzer.

BPCA prerequisites

▶ **Mapping of Business Process Structures including Assignment of Test Case Descriptions**
The respective activities including the connection of process structures via logical components have already been dealt with in the previous sections (see Section 4.4.2, *Creating the Process Structure*, among others).

▶ **Assignment of Relevant Technical Objects for Business Process Structures**
The relevant technical objects for the business process structures are assigned via technical bills of material (TBOMs) that are assigned to the transactions in the process structure in the form of an attribute.

The attribute view of a transaction in the process structure of an SAP Solution Manager project is called via the *Implementation/Upgrade* work center or directly via Transactions SOLAR01 and SOLAR02. Here the relevant transaction is selected in the TRANSACTIONS tab and the attribute view is activated.

The user is then provided with the TBOM tab within the attribute view. Either a static or dynamic TBOM list can be assigned to a selected transaction. The static list consists of all technical objects that have been assigned to the transaction (relevant tables, programs, and so on).

Static and dynamic TBOMs

The dynamic list is recorded by the user. The user then navigates from the attribute view to the transaction in the connected system, executes his dialog user activities, and records only the appropriate technical objects. Other recordings can be added if necessary in order to include all relevant objects in the dynamic TBOM list (also referred to as child TBOM). Transaction ME21N would be an example, in which standard purchase orders, as well as stock transport requests can be created. Figure 4.22 gives an example of the content of a TBOM list for this transaction.

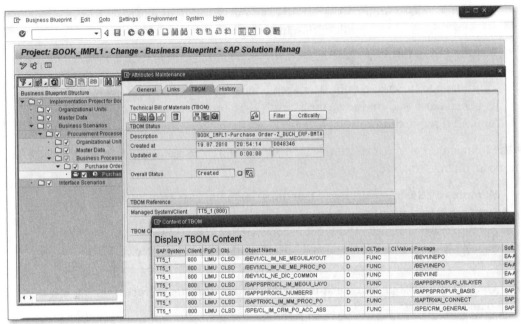

Figure 4.22 TBOM List of a Transaction

The static TBOM list can be connected very quickly as an attribute. With the dynamic TBOM, significantly more accurate results can be expected if a subsequent analysis is run to consider only the technical objects important to the customer. In practice, a multi-level approach is wise, in which static TBOMs are run first and these TBOMs are then successively replaced by dynamic TBOMs.

The subsequent analysis result can be affected when filter criteria and/or weighting characteristics are used. It is possible, for example, that only objects of a specific software component (such as SAP_BASIS) or a specific custom package are considered and objects of the chosen category are given a defined weighting (for example, if changes to objects of a custom package are possibly very critical).

Work center "Test Management—Test Preparation"

The *Test Management* work center verifies whether all the prerequisites for a purposeful use of Business Process Change Analyzer have been fulfilled. In the TEST PREPARATION area, the user can select the relevant project to execute a particular analysis. This analysis can be limited using respective filter criteria if necessary (see Figure 4.23).

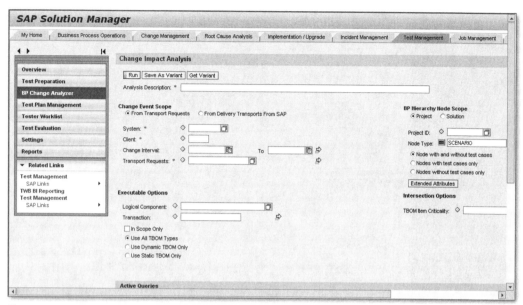

Figure 4.23 BPCA—Filter Options

As a result, the user obtains an overview of the selected process structure elements of the project and can view whether TBOMs exist for the transactions stored there (static or dynamic). Moreover, test cases possibly stored in the structure are also displayed here. By double-clicking, you can navigate from the overview to the structure element in the project for further analyses.

When all the necessary prerequisites have been fulfilled, the user runs a change impact analysis in the *Test Management* work center via the BP CHANGE ANALYZER navigation area (see Figure 4.23). The user gives an analysis description in the form of a title, selects the transports and process structures of the project or the predefined selection variant, and then directly starts the analysis or schedules it respectively.

Change impact analysis

The run or scheduled analyses are displayed in an overview in the BP CHANGE ANALYZER navigation area in the *Test Management* work center. If the analysis result already exists, it can be displayed via selection. The user then can gain on the detailed results attained from the analysis via DISPLAY DETAILS (including process step, transaction; see Figure 4.24).

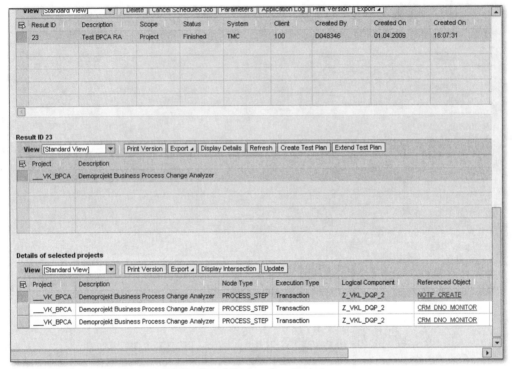

Figure 4.24 BPCA—Detail Screen of an Analysis

A test plan can now be generated based on the analysis results (RESULT OVERVIEW • CREATE TEST PLAN). The generated test plan can be adapted if required and then split into appropriate test packages (see Section 4.4.4, *Creating Test Plans and Test Packages*).

Restrictions Business Process Change Analyzer is available in its first version with SAP Solution Manager 7.0 EhP 1. (See SAP Note 1316524 for a list of Frequently Asked Questions.) Considerable savings in test preparation can be achieved using this version, as well as in subsequent test execution. The following central functional restrictions should be considered, however, when you use the current version of BPCA so that you can sensibly use the achieved analysis results.

▶ Only ABAP-based transactions in the analysis can currently be considered.

▶ When the dynamic TBOMs are recorded, only the system-internal objects are considered (no cross-system trace).

These points have already been included in the development plan of BCPA.

Communication plays an extremely important role, depending on the size of the test plans, the number of relevant test packets, the number of testers to be integrated, and their local distribution. If this aspect is not sufficiently considered, additional effort results as well as completely avoidable costs in such areas as central coordination.

Workflow

These efforts and costs can be reduced to reasonable levels using the workflow functionality. This functionality is already provided with SAP Solution Manager 7.0 SP15 and enables specified system operations to be automatically triggered in advance for defined test project situations (for example, information to all testers when a test plan is released).

From a technical point of view, the workflow functionality is based on a CRM transaction created in SAP Solution Manager (standard transaction type: TWTP), the assigned operations of which are triggered on a defined status. In the standard configuration, an email is sent, depending on the test plan status.

The technical configuration of the workflow functionality is described in great detail in the Reference IMG of SAP Solution Manager (SAP SOLUTION MANAGER • SCENARIO-SPECIFIC SETTINGS • TEST MANAGEMENT • EXTENDED CONFIGURATION • WORKFLOW). Besides the assignment of relevant authorizations and the activation of necessary BC sets, the transaction type including the action profile must be configured and assigned to the workflow scenario. Additional customizing settings are necessary depending on the use case (for example, setup of SAP Connect when external mail systems are used).

Technical prerequisites

When these primarily technical prerequisites have been fulfilled, the workflow functionality can be used for the following tasks:

▸ Assignment of a status schema on the test plan in the form of a test plan attribute

▸ Activation of the workflow functionality in the attribute view of the test plan

▸ Change of the test plan status in the attribute view of the test plan and the triggering of defined actions

Status schemata Two status schemas can be selected via the standard that differ in their scope. The DEFAULT status schema (see Figure 4.25) consists of nine status values, while the DEFAULT status schema however consists only of five status values. Customer-specific customizations should definitely be carried out in the customer namespace and require further customizing settings. That includes the assignment of the status schema for the transaction type and the scheduling of operations depending on the chosen status schema.

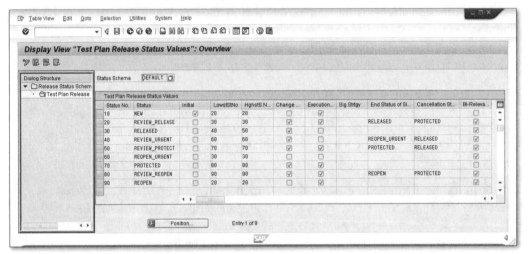

Figure 4.25 "Default" Status Schema

The stored status values, including the values on the following dimensions, can be specified in the selected status schema.

▶ **Change Lock**
This flag controls the changeability of the test plan, including the associated test packages. Released test plans cannot therefore be subsequently changed in this status.

▶ **Execution Lock**
This flag controls the executability of the test plan, including the associated test packages. Depending on the status, the testers are not able to access the test cases assigned to them and set the status.

▶ **Signature Strategy**

The status values can be secured via digital signatures. The respective signature strategy is assigned here. The status values maintained in the END STATUS OF SIGNATURE and CANCELLATION STATUS fields are automatically defined depending on this strategy.

▶ **BI Relevant**

This flag controls whether the underlying test plan in BW reporting is to be considered.

If the workflow functionality has been activated, the actions defined in the action schema are triggered depending on the test plan status. The respective dependencies are defined in this context via Post Processing Framework (Transaction: SPPFCADM, application: CRM_ORDER). Among other things, all testers are notified on the release of the test plan in the standard and the start of the actual test (see Figure 4.26).

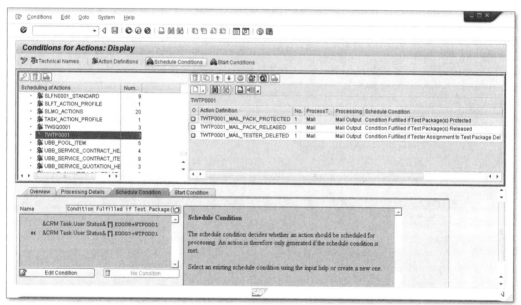

Figure 4.26 Action Profile TWTP0001—Schedule Condition for Action TWTP0001_MAIL_PACK_PROTECTED

The workflow functionality supports the test coordinator mainly with regard to communication at meta level (for example, start of a test or   **Test sequences** completion of a test). With regard to implementation, this scenario can be supplemented with test sequences. The following goals can be achieved using test sequences.

▸ Setup of test case sequences within a test package (for example, definition of integration scenarios)

▸ Direct assignment of testers for test cases within a test package

▸ Automated information of a tester on the completion of the directly previous test case within a test sequence

If a test plan including test packages and tester assignment has been created (see Section 4.4.4, *Creating Test Plans and Test Packages*), the user can select this test plan in the *Test Management* work center via the TEST PLAN MANAGEMENT navigation area and can then navigate from here via GOTO • SEQUENCES to the test sequence view (see Figure 4.27).

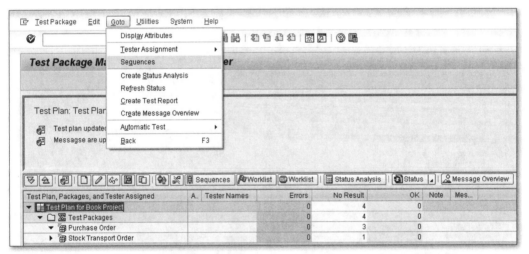

Figure 4.27 Test Sequences

Creating a sequence — In order to create a new test sequence for a test package, the relevant test package must be highlighted and the change modus needs to be activated. The user is provided with the desired functionality SEQUENCES • CREATE SEQUENCE. However, the test cases relevant to the test sequence of the test package must be highlighted (see Figure 4.28).

Figure 4.28 Creating a Test Sequence

Once a known name has been assigned to the test sequence, all selected test cases of the test package are assigned to this sequence and the system automatically provides a sequence within the sequence. Both the sequence name (SEQUENCES • RENAME SEQUENCE) and the sequence can be subsequently changed (MOVE TEST CASE • MOVE TEST CASE UP IN SEQUENCE OR DOWN).

The relevant testers can now be assigned to the test sequence or the associated test cases. The selection is limited to the test plan of test package of assigned testers. If a business partner has been assigned to the SAP user of the tester, this business partner can also be assigned to the test case.

Once all test sequences have been created and saved, the user should run a final automated test plan check (CHECK button). The system checks whether the necessary information has been maintained for a tester notification (including the email address of the SAP user and of the business partner). This check can also be run for individual test packages.

This functionality is mainly based on a technical point of view (similar to Workflow), the transaction type (standard: TWSQ), and a status schema, as well as an action profile (standard: TWSQ0001). If a test sequence within a test package is created, the system then automatically generates a relevant CRM transaction. A predefined action is now triggered via this transaction depending on the respective status (standard: email notification of the following tester).

4.4.6 Test Execution

When a test is executed, the testers access the test case descriptions via the test packages assigned to their SAP users in the central test management system. The assigned test packages are provided via the *Test Management* work center in the TESTER WORKLIST navigation area (see Figure 4.29).

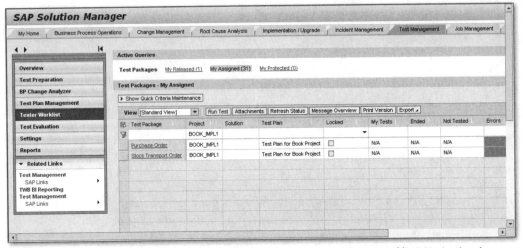

Figure 4.29 "Test Management" Work Center—"Tester Worklist" Navigation Area

When executing the test, the tester highlights the test package assigned to him or her and then navigates to the test case view via EXECUTE TEST. He can now access the test case description and finally document the respective test result using the status maintenance and the test note, as well as via an addition error message if applicable. Test notes have proved themselves particularly useful for documenting tests that have been executed without any errors. However, in the case of an error you should record an error message.

If the test plans and packages have been created on the basis of an SAP Solution Manager project, the tester can use the test objects stored in that project; for example to jump to the relevant transactions in the respective test system. Experience has shown that it is useful to integrate SAP Solution Manager into the system landscape via trusted RFC connections. This way, testers do not need to log on to each test system through a dialog. In addition, it is made sure that each tester works in the right system.

The tester defines the test status of manual tests using traffic light icons. By clicking on the icon, the tester can navigate to a corresponding maintenance dialog. The possible status options available for this are already defined via the test standards prior to the start of the testing activities.

Assigning statuses

If a customer wants to reproduce the testing activities involved in a manual test, you can maintain time data at this stage. These time efforts can be graphically formatted at a later stage in the status analysis (see Section 4.4.7, *Status Analysis*).

If automated test cases are started from the test package, eCATT documents the test results in a test log automatically and also automatically sets a traffic light icon with a corresponding status text. As a prerequisite for this status assignment, the COPY STATUS TO TWB flag must be set in the start options of eCATT.

The test standards also define, among other things, the detail in which test results must be documented. If a company has decided not only to record test results via the traffic light status, but also to document specific intermediate and final results for error-free tests (for example, document numbers), SAP Solution Manager provides the user with various options for this purpose. The alternative procedures must be considered in light of the individual obligations of the enterprise.

Test documentation

It may make sense for testers to enter specific values only in the SHORT TEXT field in the STATUS tab. These results can then be displayed in the status analysis (see Section 4.4.7, *Status Analysis*).

If you need to document additional information however, the test note function is particularly useful. When specifying the test standards, the technique to be used to create test notes is defined.

You can create test notes using SAP Editor. This information can be directly displayed at a later stage in the hierarchy view during the status analysis. If you want to include screenshots to support the documentation of the test results, you need to create the test note on the basis of an SAP KW template. Test notes created in this way are not displayed in the hierarchy view. They can however be integrated in a test report.

Test notes

When creating a test note based on a KW template, the user has the following options to choose from.

- **Creating a new document**
  When creating a test plan, the relevant KW template is specified for recording test notes (see Section 4.4.4, *Creating Test Plans and Test Packages*). The tester can create a test note based on this document template.

- **Uploading a file**
  Using this option, a tester can document his test result without the need of a specific document template. When the test note of the test documentation is uploaded, the uploaded document is automatically assigned to the selected document template when it is created.

> **Note**
>
> This option is provided if the test execution has been documented using a recording (for example, using SAP ProductivityPak by RWD).

- **Transferring a Test Document**
  The test case description in the test documentation is copied and assigned to the relevant document template (test note). If the test case description has already been defined in great detail, the tester can focus on the supplementation of the test data used and the generation of document numbers.

The selection of creation options based on a KW template can be restricted customer-specific way (see Figure 4.30). In the *Test Management* work center in the SETTINGS navigation area via TEST ORGANIZER SETTINGS, the relevant options under NOTES can be accessed.

If you create test notes as documents in SAP KW, you can safeguard the document status using a digital signature. This function is particularly applicable to enterprises that are required to produce supporting documents.

Error recording Should any errors occur, the tester defines the (default) status as ERRORS, RETEST REQUIRED (red traffic light icon) by way of a manual test and if necessary categorizes the found errors (including functionality, documentation, and translation) via the RESTRICTION field. The restrictions maintained in this field can later be statistically evaluated in the status analysis using a graph (see Section 4.4.7, *Status Analysis*).

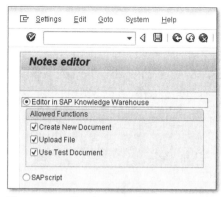

Figure 4.30 Test Note Configuration Options

When saving the entries, the SAP system prompts the tester to enter an error message. With SAP Solution Manager, the user has the option to enter error messages using SAP Service Desk (see Section 4.5.1, *Test and Service Desk*).

In order to guarantee complete transparency of testing activities, each change to the test status is documented in the HISTORY tab (see Figure 4.31). The status changes are formatted with time stamps and the relevant SAP users.

History

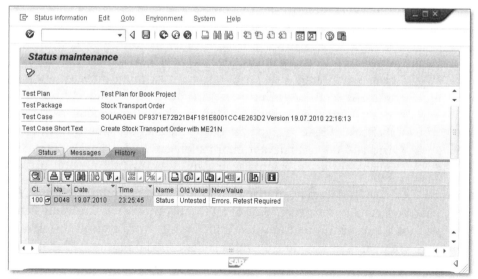

Figure 4.31 Change History Test Case Documentation

4.4.7 Status Analysis

While test execution involves several systems and is sometimes even carried out decentrally across multiple locations, the status analysis is executed centrally via SAP Solution Manager. Besides the test reports, SAP standard provides the user with a comprehensive Reporting functionality. The user can access these analysis options via the *Test Management* work center in the REPORTS navigation area.

Formatting options

There are fundamentally three formatting options:

▸ **Test report**
Test results can be summarized in a central report using an MS Word macro. The scope of a test report can become large, which is why this type of formatting should generally occur for defined project milestones (for example, creation after completion of a test).

▸ **Status analyses (standard reports)**
Test plan-specific and cross test-plan analyses can be executed on the basis of these reports. The results of these standard reports are formatted in a very structured and clear way (also graphically) and support the test coordinator with his ad-hoc reporting (where I am currently). The results can be exported and can then be further processed using MS Excel, for example.

▸ **BW reporting**
Using SAP Solution Manager 7.0 EhP 1, the user also has the option to execute BW-based analyses of test plans, with which the current analysis options of standard reports, as well as ad-hoc reporting have been significantly extended. You can run comprehensive analyses with SAP NetWeaver Business Warehouse (BW) using SAP on-board means, and then graphically format them (for example, progress analyses). If required, you can define the analysis options of the standard and the test-relevant information can be provided in attractive suitable-for-management dashboards.

Test report

A function is already provided with the test report in Basis-Release SAP Web Application Server 6.20/SP50 that allows the current result status of a test plan to be formatted using an MS Word macro. All relevant information is therefore downloaded to a local directory (including test case descriptions, test notes, and test documentation history) and then it is summarized in a central document using an MS Word macro. The classification of the document is based on the underlying business process structure of the project.

The user is provided with the functionality of the test result generation in the *Test Management* work center in the TEST PLAN MANAGEMENT navigation area. Once the user has highlighted the relevant test plan, he can navigate to the function via GOTO • CREATE TEST REPORT. The content of the test report to be generated can be further restricted using a filter function (see Figure 4.32).

The test report is created on the basis of a template. You can customize this template to customer-specific requirements using SAP Reference IMG. The field in the SAP Reference IMG is as follows: SAP SOLUTION MANAGER • CROSS-SCENARIO SETTINGS • DOCUMENT MANAGEMENT • GENERATION OF DOCUMENTS • ADJUST TEMPLATE FILES FOR GENERATION OF TEST REPORT.

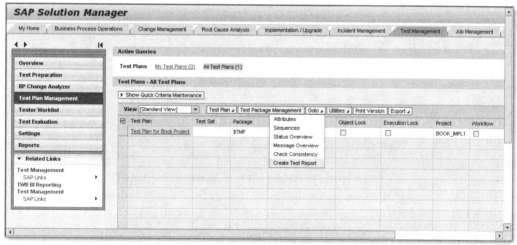

Figure 4.32 "Test Management" Work Center—Creating a Test Report

This way of processing test results is particularly suited for companies that are obliged to produce supporting documents. In this context, the test report represents a frozen status view of the testing activities at a given point in time.

If necessary, you can also print out and sign the documentation. It is also possible to upload the file as an SAP KW document, and you could protect it against any changes by using a digital signature.

Standard reports In the *Test Management* work center the user can obtain a very quick overview of the current status of the test plan in the Test Plan Management navigation area for a selected test plan via Goto • Status Overview (see Figure 4.33).

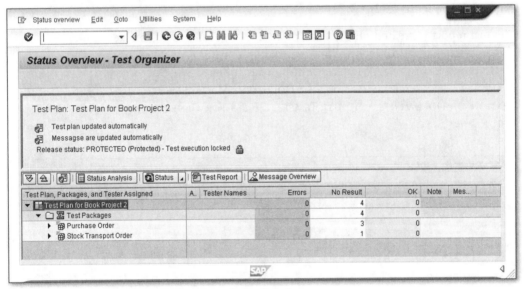

Figure 4.33 Test Plan—Status Overview

For test plans and test packages the system displays the status of the process and information on the quality, indicating whether it is OK or not. The values can be displayed as percentages or as absolute numbers (Utilities • Settings • Status...).

You can obtain a detailed display of the results by clicking on the Status Analysis button here. The results for each test plan or package are then displayed separately by test case. The layout of the display itself depends on the process structures of the underlying SAP Solution Manager project (see Figure 4.34).

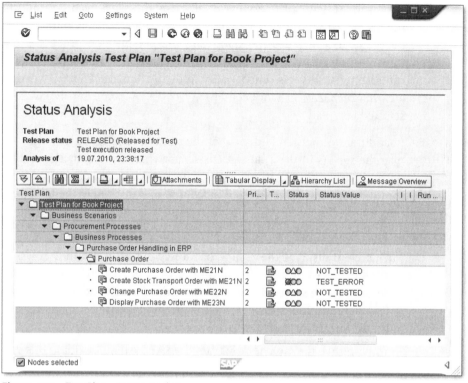

Figure 4.34 Test Plan—Status Analysis

Test cases can be contained in several test packages and therefore can be assigned different statuses for each test package. The overall status of a test case results from the consolidation of the individual statuses of its test packages. Note that the overall status is not the total of all individual statuses. Instead, the most problematic status is displayed. You can navigate to the individual results by clicking on the traffic light icon.

Overall status of a test case

In addition to accessing the test case description and test status, the test coordinator can also directly access the respective test notes and short texts that have been recorded by the testers for each test package. Error messages are displayed here for each test case. You can customize the display according to individual requirements via the layout function.

The user can gain an overview of all error messages recorded during the testing activities by clicking on the MESSAGE OVERVIEW button. This overview also includes the status and the person who processed the message. You can navigate to each message from the overview. The user can directly access this functionality in the test management navigation area *Test Management* work center via GOTO • MESSAGE OVERVIEW for a selected test plan.

Extended view options

In addition to the standard view of the status analysis, you can also display the results in the TABULAR DISPLAY or HIERARCHY LIST. Depending on the specific information requirements, both types of display have some advantages. Some selected functions are described in the following paragraphs.

▶ **Tabular View**
This view displays the results of the testing activities in a table. In addition to using the filtering options provided here, you can also customize the layout of the table according to specific requirements. For example, you can view the time period that has been maintained by the testers for each test (see Section 4.4.6, *Test Execution*).

You can save the table locally from the SAP system. By doing this you can further analyze the results statistically. For example, you can use external spreadsheet applications via the additional functions available and even format them graphically.

▶ **Hierarchy List**
If the test case descriptions and/or the test notes have been created using SAP Editor, these can be displayed in the view. For one thing, you can display the history of status changes via the following menu: SETTINGS • ADDITIONAL INFORMATION ...

Cross-test-plan results

In addition to the test-plan-related options of standard reporting already described, cross-test-plan results can be formatted in the REPORTS navigation area of the *Test Management* work center (see Figure 4.35). Here, for example, project-related analyses (results of all test plans of a project) can be executed or all test plans of a test set can be analyzed (cross-project analyses; see also Section 4.4.4, *Creating Test Plans and Test Packages*).

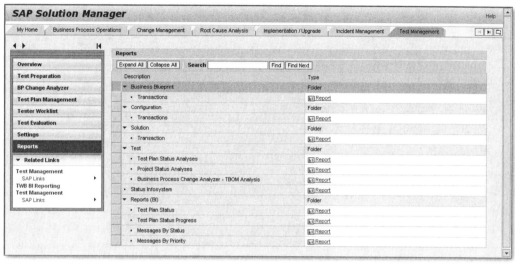

Figure 4.35 "Test Management" Work Center—"Reports" Navigation Area

Filter options allow the user to further limit the results in a customer-specific way. These results can be downloaded to a local directory for further processing if required. If the results of the displayed test plans are not up-to-date, the system notifies the user. If necessary, you can start a test-plan-specific evaluation from this transaction in order to update the individual results and hence the overall result.

There are additional options for evaluating testing activities in the navigation area. Projects can be evaluated during test case creation and storage to establish whether a test case exists for each node of the selected test structure. You can determine whether all prerequisites have been fulfilled for the use of Business Process Change Analyzer (see Section 4.4.5, *Extended Functionality for Creating Test Plan and Test Packages*).

With SAP Solution Manager 7.0 EhP 1, you can take advantage of analysis options available in the REPORTS navigation area of the *Test Management* work center. These are based on the functionality of SAP NetWeaver BW and create Business Warehouse content that is especially useful for executing period-related analyses (see Figure 4.36).

BW reporting

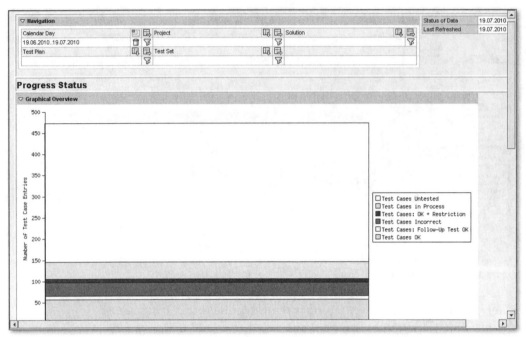

Figure 4.36 BW Reporting—Test Plan Status Progress

In order to be able to use this functionality, the following configuration steps must first be carried out.

- **General BW configuration in SAP Solution Manager**
  The nodes relating to BW reporting are provided in SAP Reference IMG via SAP SOLUTION MANAGER • BASIC SETTINGS • BW CONFIGURA-TION. The settings can also be implemented via the Guided Procedure (SOLMAN_SETUP).

- **Configuration of BW-based analyses in Test Management**
  The nodes are provided in SAP Reference IMG via SAP SOLUTION MANAGER • SCENARIO-SPECIFIC SETTINGS • TEST MANAGEMENT • BW-BASED REPORTING. Relevant data sources are activated and replicated here, and the required BW objects are created.

The relevant settings are then traced in the *Test Management* work center. The control activation log and the period of the daily data extractor operation, among other things, can be viewed in the SETTINGS navigation area (see Figure 4.37).

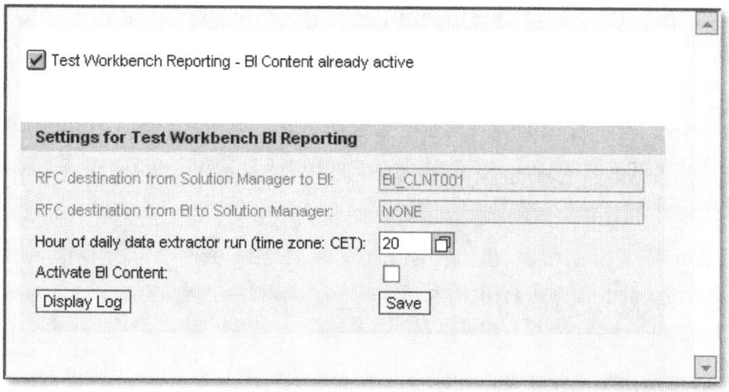

Figure 4.37 "Test Management" Work Center— Settings for BW Analyses of the Test Workbench

Because the data in BW is only updated once a day, the analysis options provided here are only suitable for ad-hoc reporting (target group: test coordinators). Given the extensive range of analysis and formatting options already available via the standard, this functionality is especially suitable for management reporting as a function of comprehensive IT reporting.

4.5   Integration Scenarios

▶ Within Application Lifecycle Management, SAP Solution Manager is characterized by the high level of integration of available application scenarios. The *Test Management* use case also provides various integration scenarios. The errors found during tests must be documented and processed. This is followed by a suitable subsequent test (via integration with Service Desk).

▶ The test results immediately impact transport of the tested changes; for instance, no transport of erroneous changes to production systems or implementation of correction transports. It's obviously necessary to integrate this use case with the *Change Request Management* and *Quality Gate Management* use cases.

▶ By using SAP Solution Manager Diagnostics along with the root-cause analysis for already found errors, scenarios are possible that check a system in terms of periodic checks (integration with End User Experience Monitoring).

The scenarios mentioned give you an idea of the integration required for SAP Solution Manager use cases. SAP Solution Manager 7.0 EhP 1 does not yet cover all application scenarios for the mapping of this technical integration; SAP strives to implement functional requirements gradually in continuous coordination with the customer (for instance, in DSAG workshops).

The following sections provide an overview of all current options and also indicate possible workarounds.

4.5.1 Test and Service Desk

SAP Service Desk is a functionality of SAP Solution Manager that supports users in mapping their Incident Management process. According to the de-facto standard for IT service management, ITIL (see *www.itil. org*), this process comprises the implementation of requests, customer requirements, or messages on service incidents in documented support requirements. To remedy these incidents as fast and economically as possible, it is advisable to implement a Service Desk, which represents one of the most critical connections between business departments and the IT organization.

The functionality of SAP Service Desk in SAP Solution Manager is based on SAP CRM service functions and represents a separate use case of SAP Solution Manager. It ranges from the recording of error messages up to escalation mechanisms such as those that apply if service-level agreements—such as those for response times—are exceeded. The tool also enables you to forward error messages to SAP Active Global Support (see Figure 4.38).

The functionality of the SAP Service Desk described here focuses on the recording of error messages within the scope of test result documentation. However, you can obtain further detailed information of its functionality from SAP Service Marketplace (*http://service.sap.com/solutionmanager*) and in the SAP Help Portal (*http://help.sap.com*). Moreover, SAP Solution Manager 7.0 contains a bidirectional interface that allows you to integrate external help desk functionality with SAP Service Desk.

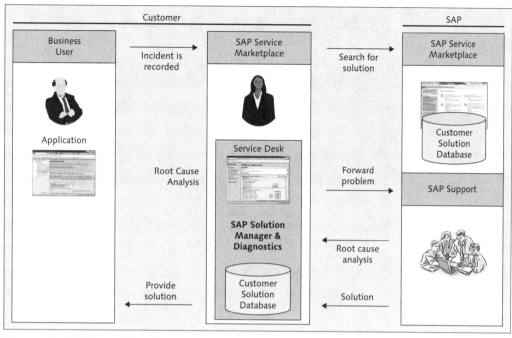

Figure 4.38 SAP Service Desk Overview

The following methods have proved effective in the context of recording error messages during test documentation.

Recording method

1. By double-clicking on the SAP logo within the transaction to be tested in the test system, you can directly navigate to a recording dialog (see Figure 4.39). In this case, system information is automatically appended to the message (such as information on the relevant component of the SAP application history). In addition to a title, the message is assigned a long text and attachments, such as screenshots.

   Once the message has been sent to the SAP Service Desk within SAP Solution Manager, the tester is informed about the message ID. The tester then has to store this ID in the MESSAGES tab of the status maintenance screen for the test case that has been carried out (see Section 4.4.6, *Test Execution*).

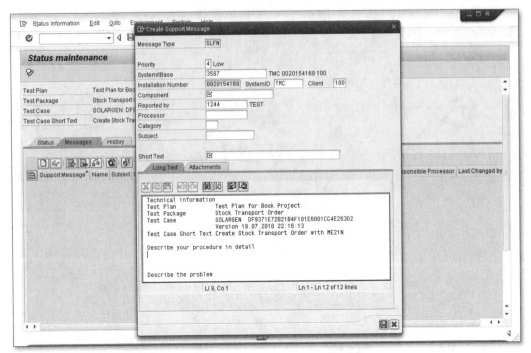

Figure 4.39 Message Recording via Test Status Maintenance

2. The message is created via the status maintenance of the respective test case within the central test management system (SAP Solution Manager). Here, the tester must first specify the respective test system, including the client, in order to include the system-relevant information in the message.

In this process, the message is created based on an SAP script template, in which test-specific information is automatically integrated with the long text (for instance, test plan, test package). The template (TEMPLATE_TWB_MSG) provided via the standard can be replaced by a customer-specific template. The relevant information is available in the Reference IMG under SAP SOLUTION MANAGER • SCENARIO-SPECIFIC SETTINGS • TEST MANAGEMENT • EXTENDED CONFIGURATION • MESSAGES.

After the message has been sent, the tester is informed about the message number. The message number is automatically copied to the MESSAGES tab.

The error messages that are entered in the test documentation are processed in SAP Solution Manager via the *Incident Management* work center. Here, the users can access the error messages assigned to them and communicate with the tester or person who sent the message via the service transaction if required.

The following describes some best practices that have worked in real life with regard to this integration scenario.

Best practices

▸ Many customers already use external help-desk tools for the production support of their system landscape. In order not to impact this production operation, SAP Service Desk can be used in parallel for the entry and processing of project-relevant incidents. Particularly for the implementation of the latest SAP functions (for instance, participation in a ramp-up), the communication with SAP AGS or the SAP development department is facilitated considerably through the comprehensive integration of SAP Service Desk with the SAP support infrastructure.

▸ Provided that SAP Service Desk is already used for the production support of the system landscape, you should think about using your own transaction type to document and process project-internal error messages (test messages). In this context, you assign the newly created transaction type via Transaction DNO_CUST04 in the PROCESS_TYPE field.

If the Service Desk partner scenario that is provided with SAP Solution Manager 7.0 EhP 1 is used, the user can select the relevant transaction type for creating the error message. Additional information on the partner scenario mentioned is available in the SAP Service Marketplace (*http://service.sap.com/solutionmanager* • SAP SOLUTION MANAGER FOR PARTNERS).

▸ Because a project organization usually exists only for a fixed term, you should still do without a rule-based routing of error messages entered (for instance one in which messages of the BC-ABA SAP component are automatically assigned to support team xyz). Here, a member of the project team (for instance, the test coordinator) should be assigned as the dispatcher who checks the messages entered for plausibility and completeness and assumes responsibility for assigning them to the relevant support team, on the other hand.

▶ The usage of the action-based mail dispatch (for instance, mail to the reporting person if status is PROPOSED SOLUTION) significantly accelerates the project-internal cooperation. Basic SAP CRM knowledge is beneficial for setup.

▶ Provided that the test case description was created on the basis of an SAP KW template, a URL to this document can be copied to the clipboard via the document's attribute view. This link can then be integrated with the DOCUMENTS tab in the service transaction. Then, the test case description is directly available to the user at the click of the mouse.

4.5.2   Test and Change Request Management

Changes to a system landscape are an integral part of Application Management Lifecycle. The changes to be implemented result both from the maintenance work on existing applications and from the implementation of new applications or the replacement and upgrades of existing solutions. The task of change management is to ensure the controlled planning and implementation of upcoming changes.

Functional scope The *Change Request Management* use case (ChaRM) already provided in SAP Solution Manager 3.2 SP 8 is a very comprehensive functionality which has been developed with reference to the relevant ITIL scenario and is based on SAP CRM processes, among others. The functional scope of this use case has been enhanced successively; in the meantime, a separate *Change Management* work center is now available (see Figure 4.40). The standard version of change management in SAP Solution Manager already is characterized by the following aspects. However, you can obtain further detailed information about its functionality from SAP Service Marketplace (*http://service.sap.com/solutionmanager*) and in the SAP Help Portal (*http://help.sap.com*).

▶ **Mapping of all change scenarios**
By means of Change Request Management you can implement both planned and unplanned changes in maintenance (for instance, urgent corrections for troubleshooting) and complex implementation projects (for instance, customer-specific development projects). Moreover, administration tasks can also be mapped via this use case.

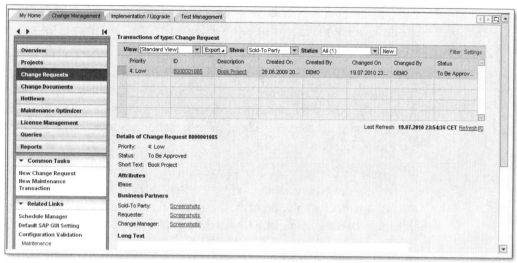

Figure 4.40 "Change Management" Work Center—"Change Requests" Navigation Area

▶ **Integration with transport system**

With Change Request Management in SAP Solution Manager, you can control the underlying transports (workbench and customizing) and improve or technically ensure the project-relevant transport logistics. Using CTS+, you can also transport Java objects via Change Request Management and thus also support SAP NetWeaver Portal projects.

The functional scope provides technical support for restricting the overshooting problem. By using CTS projects, the transport sequence is automatically calculated; the cross-system locking of objects also considerably limits the risk of overshooters.

▶ **Comprehensive reporting options**

Thanks to the close integration with the transport system, you can run comprehensive analyses up to BW reporting. If required, the reporting also works at the transport object level and enables a consistent traceability of all change-relevant activities at the touch of a button (for instance, in connection with corresponding verification forms).

Change scenarios are mapped via separate transaction types in SAP CRM. The definition of transaction types is based on the respective underlying scenario and also covers test-relevant aspects. These transaction types can also be created particularly in terms of a follow-up document. For example, based on a Service Desk process, this enables consistent integration with incident management (see Section 4.5.1, *Test and Service Desk*).

"Urgent correction" scenario

The "urgent correction" scenario covers the requirements for removing error situations in the production environment (unplanned changes) and is therefore directly connected with the maintenance of existing applications. The goal of the relevant processes is to provide the system changes mapped as quickly as possible in the production environment to remedy possible functional incidents.

The test of the relevant changes is run both by the developer in the development environment and by a tester in the quality assurance systems. The documentation of this test, however, is performed directly in the service transaction and not via the status maintenance dialog already presented (see Section 4.4.6, *Test Execution*) to minimize delays.

"Regular correction" scenario

The "regular correction" scenario covers all planned changes and is therefore available in maintenance as well as in complex implementation projects such as upgrades. The relevant tests in the development and quality assurance systems are performed in accordance with a particular project phase; these dependencies are technically ensured via suitable functions. The project-relevant transports are only possible in the intended project phase, which requires error-free implementation of tests.

Tests for regular corrections

By default, the following tests are applicable for regular corrections.

▶ **Developer test**
The developer test is implemented by the developer in the relevant development systems. If these tests don't produce any errors, the developer transfers his work results to the quality assurance system via a transport copy. These tests are documented in the respective service transactions (for example, status change of the transaction) and not via the status maintenance dialog of the test management functionality.

▶ **Module test**
The module test is run based on the development results that were transferred using transport copies. If errors are found here, the tester documents his result in the respective service transactions. The correction is made in the original transport until the module test was run without any errors. Only then does the developer release his trans-

ports. Import to the quality assurance systems can then take place. Here as well, these tests are documented in the respective service transactions (for example, status change of the transaction) and not via the status maintenance dialog of the test management functionality.

▶ **Integration test**
Because the integration test is both complex and important, it should be planned, implemented, and documented on the basis of the test management functionality (*Test Management* use case). The status change of the underlying service transaction that is necessary after an error-free test is not automatically copied; instead, this can then be done via an appropriate workaround (selection of the service transactions and status change via Report CRM_SOCM_SERVICE_REPORT).

If errors are found in the integration test, these must be remedied using test messages. These service transactions do not pass any approval process because they refer to already approved changes. They can be used to map the transports required for the correction.

These test messages cannot be created directly from the test management functionality in the standard version (*Test Management* use case). Only an organizational solution is available as a workaround here (for instance, assignment via a dispatcher).

4.5.3 Test and Quality Gate Management

Whereas the *Change Request Management* use case is intended to ensure consistent traceability and is therefore primarily aimed at enterprises that are obliged to produce supporting documentation, this scenario is possibly too complex for other enterprises. Nevertheless, these enterprises are interested in permitting and technically protecting the underlying transports, depending on the respective project phase ("ChaRM light").

In SAP Solution Manager 7.0 EhP 1, an initial version of the *Quality Gate Management* use case is available to these customers via the *Change Management* work center (see Figure 4.41). With this function, the user obtains a phase-based overview of the status of his projects. For predefined and customer-defined quality gates, a phase change and thus a transport of the relevant changes can only be made if the prerequisites defined in the quality gate are met. However, you can obtain further detailed information of its functionality from SAP Service Marketplace

"Change Management" work center— Projects

(*http://service.sap.com/solutionmanager*) and in the SAP Help Portal (*http://help.sap.com*).

Quality gates In the standard version, a total of four quality gates are available for each project: project start, scope-to-build, build-to-test, and test-to-deploy. The quality gates build-to-test and test-to-deploy are especially relevant for the testing activities within a project because they are used to start or complete the test phase.

Figure 4.41 "Change Management" Work Center—"Projects" Navigation Area—"Quality Gate Management" List View

There is no technical integration between Test Management and Quality Gate Management so far. The test results documented by a tester via the *Test Management* work center therefore have no direct impact on the quality gates defined. Here, the user must set the status and define the associated prerequisites for each quality gate. In this context, this definition can be as follows.

▶ **Build-to-test**

Standard reports can be used to verify that the prerequisites relevant for a test are met (see Section 4.4.7, *Status Analysis*). The result of a corresponding analysis run can be downloaded and attached to the quality gate in the meaning of a document. Thus, you can prove that the defined test-end criteria (for instance, no message with priority 1 is open), are met.

▶ **Test-to-deploy**

The test report created at the end of a test (see Section 4.4.7, *Status Analysis*) can be attached to the quality gate in the meaning of a document.

4.5.4 Test and Diagnostics

Due to the growing complexity of the installed system landscape, root-cause analysis becomes more and more comprehensive in the case of error. Without suitable tool support, this analysis quickly resembles the proverbial search for the needle in the haystack, consuming valuable time. Particularly in the production environment, the associated downtimes may incur high costs.

With SAP Solution Manager 7.0 EhP 1, users are provided with four navigation areas in the *Root Cause Analysis* work center, which provides support in case of an error (see Figure 4.42).

"Root Cause Analysis" work center

▶ **End-to-End Analysis**

Here, the user can navigate to different complementary analysis tools; for example, to run a change analysis or an analysis of the exceptions, trace, or workload. The change analysis provides an overview of the changes made to the managed systems. The exception analysis is the starting point for the analysis of functional problems within a solution landscape. The trace analysis executes component traces and evaluates these to determine user requests with long execution times within a complex system landscape. The workload analysis gives an overview of the performance parameters within the entire solution.

▶ **System Analysis**

Here, the users are provided with analysis functions that allow for a change analysis of selected systems (among others, system comparisons). If required, the users can navigate to the expert tools of SAP NetWeaver from here and analyze systems.

▶ **Host Analysis**
The various host analysis applications enable the analysis of historical performance data as well as Windows Explorer-like navigation within the directory structure. Via the OS Command Console, the user can send specific operating system commands to connected hosts.

▶ **Database Analysis**
Here, the users can navigate to the Database Administration Cockpit (DBA Cockpit) for a selected database. The DBA Cockpit provides a central access point for monitoring and managing databases for all database platforms supported.

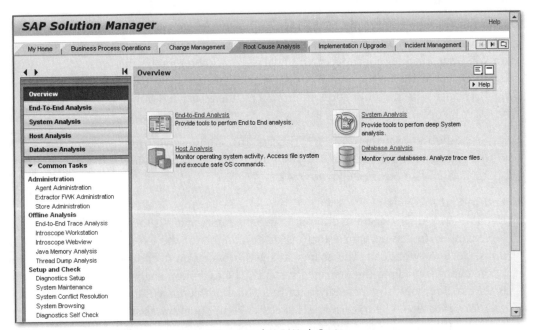

Figure 4.42 "Root Cause Analysis" Work Center

The analysis options listed are available to the users also within a test project. The following presents some sample scenarios.

E2E change analysis The E2E change analysis displays all changes to the configuration parameters of the systems in a solution in a top-down view. These include information on the number, type, and time of changes. The information is formatted via BW reporting of SAP Solution Manager.

Within the test process, the E2E change analysis can be used to specify the scope of the testing activities; for instance, a regression test. For this purpose, change events—such as maintenance, parameter changes, transport requests, or implemented SAP notes—can be displayed for a defined period of time. This information can then be used to select the test cases that are required for the validation of the changes displayed. Business Process Change Analyzer can also be used for SAP maintenance objects as well as for transport requests to identify their impact on the business processes of a project or a solution.

The E2E trace comprises functions for the evaluation of execution times in the entire solution landscape. You can analyze, for example, runtimes of user requests to identify system components that are responsible for long runtimes and thus performance losses. For this purpose, the E2E trace displays the query together with the response times of all components involved in the execution of a query.

E2E trace

Within a test phase, the E2E trace can be used to detect performance problems during a test execution. Because the trace is always based on the execution of business processes and considers the entire system landscape, it can—particularly within the framework of integration tests—identify system components that cause long runtimes when they are called by a single user.

A performance problem that occurs during the test execution is documented via an error message in SAP Solution Manager's Service Desk. The person who processes the error message can now execute the trace together with the respective tester by reproducing the business process test case used in the test systems. As a result, the person processing the error message receives detailed information on the response times of the individual components beyond system boundaries and can thus isolate the error or the erroneous component. After the error has been corrected or the optimization recommendations have been implemented, the trace can be re-executed to document the correct system behavior and thus the successful troubleshooting.

During load tests, it makes sense to use the comprehensive monitoring and alerting functions of SAP Solution Manager in addition to the analy-

E2E monitoring, E2E alerting

sis functions provided by the load test tool used, such as SAP LoadRunner by HP).

End User
Experience
Monitoring The End User Experience Monitoring planned for the next SAP Solution Manager release is intended to enable continuous monitoring of the availability of business scenarios from the end user's perspective. At the same time, the response times of the respective components are measured across all systems addressed within the scenario.

The planned functionality is based the periodic execution of recorded test scripts that simulate the user interactions for the business processes to be checked. This would enable you to record a typical process flow from the user's perspective and execute it regularly within the scope of End User Experience Monitoring. This functionality would also enable you to evaluate the performance of the same business process at different enterprise locations. The monitoring results can be displayed as real-time information and also in the form of a history within SAP Solution Manager BW Reporting.

4.5.5 Test and IT Reporting

Test Management
Cockpit Through the integration of SAP NetWeaver Business Warehouse, comprehensive evaluation options are available in SAP Solution Manager 7.0 EhP 1. As described in Section 4.4.7, *Status Analysis*, the standard configuration already provides numerous additional graphical evaluations for test management. Moreover, the data available in Business Warehouse can be formatted customer-specifically using the known BW tools, so that a project-specific or enterprise-specific reporting is possible. You can use these tools, for example, to create cockpits that display all relevant evaluations of the testing activities (for instance, test status, test flow, or overview of error messages) in a format suitable for the target group (such as test management or project manager). The scope and content of evaluations can be freely defined using the data available; cross-project reporting is also possible. The evaluations can be accessed via a web site, which can also be integrated with a portal. This enables project stakeholders to call up the contents without having to access SAP Solution Manager. Such a Test Management Cockpit has been developed by SAP Test Management Consulting as a consulting solution within the framework of a project, which was subsequently implemented for other

customers too (see Section 13.4, *Customer Report from Deutsche Telekom AG*).

Another consulting solution also supports the entry and evaluation of test efforts. The results, particularly the cost-benefit comparison of various tester groups (business departments, dedicated in-house test teams, external consultants, outsourcing in the nearshore/offshore area), offer excellent controlling options and can also be displayed in the Test Management Cockpit.

However, SAP NetWeaver Business Warehouse integrated with SAP Solution Manager can be used for more than reporting of testing activities. Because SAP Solution Manager provides integrated tools for the entire application lifecycle of the solutions and system landscapes, which are managed using SAP Solution Manager, it is a natural extension to provide a comprehensive reporting also for other phases or IT processes. The data required here is already provided centrally in SAP Solution Manager. In the standard configuration, work environments for project management, incident management, change management, and for system and business process monitoring are provided via the work centers that each include corresponding graphical evaluations or reports. Furthermore, the integrated Business Warehouse is used in system monitoring to graphically evaluate performance key figures, such as system availability, system load, or database utilization, over a selectable period.

Reporting in other application scenarios

In this context, reporting is not limited to the SAP world. The application scenarios presented also involve non-SAP systems so that central IT reporting can consider the entire system landscape. Project management, test management, and incident and change management can refer to non-SAP systems; the monitoring functions of SAP Solution Manager also allow for the technical monitoring of non-SAP systems.

All data available in SAP Solution Manager can be processed for comprehensive IT reporting. If you use Business Warehouse, you can set up other cockpits in addition to the Test Management Cockpit; these cockpits can process data relating to change management or business process monitoring in a central web-based interface, for example. The respective stakeholders (management, change manager, project management office, or process owner) receive information and evaluations customized for their target group which are therefore always meaningful.

IT reporting

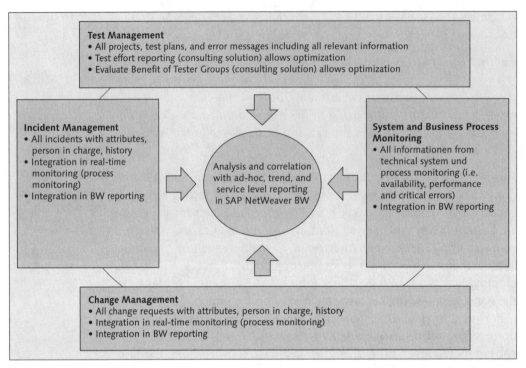

Figure 4.43 IT Reporting Creates Transparency Across All Processes and Systems (SAP and Non-SAP)

Strategic reporting BW reporting also enables the display of trends through historical values (for instance, incidents or changes per month or system load of the past year), correlation of data across application scenarios (for instance, change requests resulting from incidents or ratio of test effort to incidents from production systems), as well as the monitoring of service levels based on defined key performance indicators. The dataset can be presented flexibly and in an appealing format so that the evaluations support a fact-based decision as the organization prepares for concrete development of optimization measures.

Complex KPIs Corresponding KPIs can be aggregated or correlated from existing information; as a result, complex metrics can be utilized for evaluations, comparisons, and trend analyses. SAP itself uses such metrics for Application Lifecycle Management assessment workshops and to identify the maturity level, performance, and optimization potentials in the different phases of application management. This includes key figures for business continuity (for instance, planned and unplanned downtimes and incident solution time), process optimization (for instance, impact of system changes and their relation to planned and urgent change requests), and total cost of ownership (change efforts within the framework of support package implementations, CPU load, and database growth).

Thanks to these technical options, SAP creates a high level of transparency for the effectiveness and efficiency of IT processes implemented using SAP Solution Manager. IT managers can better control their service management processes, monitor workload and response times such as those for processing incidents and change requests, and determine compliance with defined service levels. IT services can therefore be improved continuously in the manner defined by the ITIL v3 library. Furthermore, IT reporting can support the implementation of IT organizational goals with regard to time, cost, and quality through continuous monitoring of defined key figures.

Transparency for continuous improvement

4.6 Solution-Related Testing

Projects and solutions are central objects that you can use to map the entire application management lifecycle in SAP Solution Manager. As Section 4.2.4, *Projects and Solutions*, already discussed, projects are primarily used to map implementation phases, whereas solutions are deployed in the operation of the business processes implemented.

Projects and solutions

During implementation, the business processes that should be implemented are mapped in an SAP Solution Manager project that serves as a storage structure, and central project results are stored in this structure or made available via markers. After the project has been completed, these process structures, including the documentation stored therein, are transferred to a solution. For this purpose, the user is supported by powerful copying functionality.

The operation of the business processes that should be implemented is already prepared during execution of the implementation project. After the transfer, the documentation provided then assists the internal support effort in processing possibly-occurring errors in the production environment. This is possible because the requirements as well as their implementation are documented in the process structures (for instance, navigations to IMG and/or development objects). Figure 4.44 shows test cases stored in a solution. Furthermore, the process structures mapped are also used to set up business process monitoring in the solution.

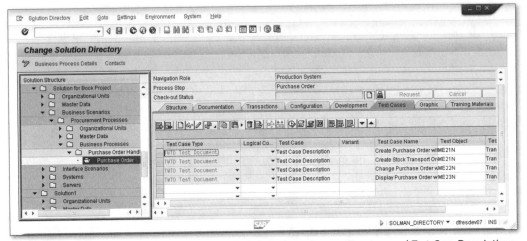

Figure 4.44 Solution Including Business Process Structure and Test Case Descriptions

Tests during operation

Because maintenance activities and thus changes to the processes used in production are run during business process operation (for instance, troubleshooting and import of support packages), testing activities also need to be performed then. Here, you must be sure to test the effects on the functionality already used (regression test) in addition to the changes made in this process.

For the preparation, implementation, and documentation of upcoming tests, the users basically have the same technical functionality at hand that they can use via the *Test Management* work center in connection with the project-relevant tests. Test case descriptions can be stored in the process structure; here especially the test case descriptions of the underlying implementation project can be reused. Based on this construct, you can create solution-specific test plans. These are split into test packages and then assigned to the testers using the test sequence functionality. The testers use the *Test Management* work center to access the work package assigned to them, run their tests from here, and then document their results.

Because the procedure is analogous to the descriptions of Sections 4.4.4, *Creating Test Plans and Test Packages*, and 4.4.6, *Test Execution*, this section primarily explains those aspects that must be considered in light of the current functional scope of SAP Solution Manager 7.0 EhP 1.

Specific features

▶ The test case descriptions stored in a project-specific process structure receive a document status (for instance, RELEASED) during the execution of an implementation project. If these process structures are transferred to a solution after a project has been completed and if you select the COPY DOCUMENTS option, the system simultaneously generates copies of the defined test case descriptions. The copied documents then receive the initial status of the relevant document status schema and must be released again, if necessary.

▶ When you transfer process structures to a solution, the project-specific test plans and packages are not taken into account. Because these objects are created with direct reference to the solution, they must be newly created after the transfer of the process structures.

▶ Business Process Change Analyzer can also be used for solutions to evaluate the effects of a change to the processes mapped. When you transfer process structures of a project to a solution, the TBOMs created in the project are not yet transferred in SAP Solution Manager 7.0 EhP 1 and must be generated anew after the transfer.

▶ In the TEST PREPARATION navigation area in the *Test Management* work center, you can run an evaluation for projects with regard to the defined transactions and TBOMs in order to evaluate, for example, the prerequisites for the use of Business Process Change Analyzer. In SAP Solution Manager 7.0 EhP 1, this evaluation is only available for transactions; an evaluation of TBOMs does not take place yet.

▶ The current version of SAP Solution Manager Adapter for SAP Quality Center by HP (see Section 2.2, *Test Types*) supports users in the implementation of project-relevant tests. The support of solution-specific tests is not intended currently.

4.7 Summary

Testing in the Context of SAP Enterprise Support, Run SAP, and SAP Standards for Solution Operations

In the environment of ever more complex system landscapes, SAP provides support offerings and supplies a process model that address known customer problems by means of E2E Solution Operation Standards. In this context, SAP Solution Manager is used on the basis of a generalized organization model. SAP Solution Manager supports customers in their daily tasks in the application management area. The E2E Solution Operation Standards can be implemented by means of the Run SAP method.

Application Management Lifecycle

SAP Solution Manager provides users with an application management solution that makes information on the system landscape available in a business process-oriented manner. The available integration options yield many synergy effects that facilitate and accelerate company-internal activities as well as the interaction with SAP Active Global Support as a collaboration platform. All application scenarios as well as the complete functionality are provided via uniform web interfaces, also referred to as work centers.

The application scenarios of SAP Solution Manager presented demonstrate that the entire lifecycle of an SAP system landscape can be mapped. In addition, SAP Solution Manager also provides options for integrating a company's existing solutions and complementing these solutions with additional functionality aimed at managing a system landscape. Investments that have already been made are protected and provided with significant added value.

Adapter and Functional Enhancements

The use of SAP Solution Manager within Application Lifecycle Management enables the integration of existing solutions. Tried-and-trusted procedures can be used by the users, and these processes are integrated with other usage scenarios of Application Lifecycle Management (ALM) at a central location.

Project-Related Testing with SAP Solution Manager

Via the *Implementation/Upgrade* work center, SAP Solution Manager offers comprehensive functionality to support project-preparing activities or to create a project scope and map project standards. This project context is particularly relevant for the preparation and implementation of test projects. Here, supplementing setting options are available via the reference IMG, via Transaction STWB_SET or via the *Test Management* work center. Within the scope of a project, a Business Blueprint is created that presents a description of the business processes used. For this purpose, besides the manual creation of the business process structure, different variants are available. These included the use of predefined processes from the Business Process Repository and use analysis with the Solution Documentation Assistant. The Business Blueprint then serves as a storage structure for project documentation, configuration, and development objects, as well as test cases.

Based on the test cases integrated in an SAP Solution Manager project, you can generate test plans that contain all manual test case descriptions and automated test cases that are relevant for a defined period and test purpose. Based on the test plans, test packages are created as work packages and assigned to testers. To generate these SAP Repository objects, users can employ filter functions. Since SP15 or EhP 1, additional functionality is available.

SAP Solution Manager 7.0 EhP 1 significantly enhances the scope of its test-relevant functionality and addresses the known cost drivers, definition of the test scope, and the associated follow-up costs due to an incorrect test case selection, as well as the communication within a test project. The complete functionality is made available at a central location via the *Test Management* work center.

Particularly in the workflow scenarios, proven functionality is used; namely integration of CRM processes, including actions. The knowledge gained in setting up the Service Desk or the Change Request Management can be leveraged here. At least basic CRM knowledge is advantageous for the customer-specific adaptation.

The test execution is done via the *Test Management* work center; here, testers can access the test packages assigned to them as work packages and document their results after the test. Test notes are available for the users for the documentation of error-free tests, and they can be created customer-specifically. Ideally, error messages are recorded using SAP Service Desk.

During the test evaluation and the status analysis, you can use a powerful functionality that is especially valuable when you are required to produce documentation. SAP Solution Manager complements the analysis options that are already provided by SAP NetWeaver Application Server. BW reporting, in particular, now provides manifold options for customer-specific analyses and processing.

Integration Scenarios

Linking the individual application scenarios by applying Application Lifecycle Management enables integration of the test management with other application scenarios and the functionality of SAP Solution Manager.

The "Test Management and Service Desk" integration scenario is already very mature. Error messages can be entered in the test documentation via the status maintenance. These error messages are processed in a separate *Incident Management* work center (if required, with forwarding to SAP Service Marketplace). The proposed solution is then available to the tester in his or her usual environment in the *Test Management* work center. From there, the test coordinator can run a central reporting on the error messages entered if required (see Section 4.4.7, *Status Analysis*).

SAP Solution Manager 7.0 EhP 1 does not yet provide full technical support for the "Test Management and Change Request Management" integration scenario. These gaps can be closed with suitable workarounds, and consistent traceability of all changes including the relevant testing activities can be achieved.

The Quality Gate Management functionality is used for the documentation of project milestones as well as for the transport control of entire projects. Direct technical integration between Quality *Gate Management* and *Test Management* use cases does not yet exist. Even so, the relevant quality gates can be designed in such a way that you can define result types of the status analysis as the prerequisite for the successful run of a quality gate, and can included these as attachments.

The integration scenario between the *Root Cause Analysis* and *Test Management* use cases particularly focuses on the analysis of the errors found during tests. Provided that testing in the operation environment is also understood as a continuous system monitoring, this test scenario will be supported by the planned functionality of the End User Experience Monitoring.

Solution-Related Testing with SAP Solution Manager

The preparation, execution, and documentation of solution-specific tests are similar to the procedure in project-specific tests. Consequently, the knowledge gained in the handling of project-specific testing activities can be reused.

For the transfer of project-specific process structures to a solution, some aspects must be taken into account against the background of the tests to be run in operation. Some of these aspects are concept-related (for instance, direct reference of a test plan to a project or a solution). Because an initial version of the functionality of Business Process Change Analyzer is available in SAP Solution Manager 7.0 EhP 1, and the primary focus is on the support of project-specific tests, post-processing work can result when the process structures are transferred so that this functionality can also be used in a solution environment.

4.8   Customer Report by SOKA-BAU

"Thanks to the enhancement package, test management obtained numerous new functions that support the user in test execution. The frequently criticized user interface has been considerably improved by SAP."

Roland Krüger
Head of SAP CCoE at SOKA-BAU

SOKA-BAU is the joint name of Urlaubs- und Lohnausgleichskasse der Bauwirtschaft (ULAK; the German vacation and wage compensation fund of the construction trade) and Zusatzversorgungskasse des Baugewerbes AG (ZVK; supplementary pension fund of the construction trade). Both are joint institutions of Zentralverband des Deutschen Baugewerbes e.V. (central association of the German construction trade), Hauptverband

SOKA-BAU

der Deutschen Bauindustrie e.V. (main association of the German construction industry), and Industriegewerkschaft Bauen-Agrar-Umwelt (German union of construction, agriculture, and environment). SOKA-BAU renders a myriad of services for enterprises and employees of the construction industry. These include safeguarding of vacation entitlement, financing of job training, additional pension plans for employees and proprietors, securing of value credits, and checking of industry-wide valid minimum wages. The focus of the procedures that are implemented by SOKA-BAU is to compensate for industry-specific disadvantages facing employees in the construction industry. SOKA-BAU works for more than 69,000 national and international organizations with more than 620,000 employees, as well as for approximately 424,000 pensioners. The total assets of the enterprise with approximately 1,200 employees amounted to a total of €4.8 billion in 2008.

SOKA-IT

The independent SOKA-IT division manages all IT services of SOKA-BAU and has offered its services to other enterprises since April 2007. The services of SOKA-IT include the planning, administration, and maintenance of the IT infrastructure as well as application development, hosting, storage, and archiving. The implementation of customer-specific and insurance-specific solutions is also one of the services rendered by SOKA-IT; for instance, the creation of software in the environment of pension payment determinations and obligation to provide pension documentation. Moreover, SOKA-IT processes the mass printout of SOKA-BAU with more than eight million pages each year; it is the largest mail dispatcher in the Rhine-Main area of Germany.

Customer Center of Expertise

The core tasks of SOKA-IT include conceptual design, administration, and operation of SAP systems for SOKA-BAU. The support organization responsible for these tasks has been certified as an SAP Customer Competence Center (CCC) since 2002.

Certification of CCoE

Within the scope of certification, the SAP support organization of SOKA-IT was comprehensively analyzed by SAP Business Transformation Consulting. For this purpose, the spheres of activity relevant for a support organization were identified and evaluated with regard to their strengths, weaknesses, opportunities, and risks, using SWOT analysis. Optimization potentials were identified and concrete measures were developed for categories such as vision and strategy, processes, and tools. The analysis revealed that the support organization of SOKA-IT is already very well organized in many areas, including governance, tools used, and—given top scores—culture and skills. In total, the CCoE has therefore been re-certified with a total score of 83 out of 100, an exceptionally good result.

The result of the certification documents the high quality requirement of SOKA-IT with regard to the operation of SAP solution landscapes, where SAP Solution Manager plays a central role. Roland Krüger, head of SAP CCoE at SOKA-IT, considers the high motivation and qualification of his employees as one of the major keys to its success. A comprehensive training concept and a program for the smooth initial training of new employees ensure fast buildup of expertise. There are also regular knowhow transfers on innovations and topics in the SAP environment. An active exchange of experience with SAP and also the German-speaking SAP User Group (DSAG) allows for a practical discussion of current developments. This feedback culture, the openness towards new functions and technologies, and good enterprise-internal flow of information ensure that SOKA-IT adapts new application scenarios and functions in good time. The enterprise plays a leading role, for instance, in the use of SAP Solution Manager.

Success factors

In this role, SOKA-BAU or its service provider, SOKA-IT, is available as a reference customer for various SAP technologies. One core aspect of this reference customer task is the end-to-end test management with SAP Solution Manager. This has been an important task for many years, and the company has built up profound know-how and a wealth of experience.

End-to-end test management

SOKA-BAU used SAP Solution Manager for test management in 2007 for the first time. Back then, for the release change from SAP R/3 to SAP ECC 6.0, SAP Test Management Consulting provided support to establish a new test process to implement in a standardized and structured manner testing activities within the scope of the release change and for future projects. Until then, test cases and test flows were described and documented in Microsoft Excel tables. This resulted in a non-uniform testing process within the various projects and business departments; the creation of a central reporting for running testing activities was only possible with great effort. Error messages were exchanged informally by email.

Project history

Project goals The following goals were primarily pursued with the implementation of a test management on the basis of the functional scope of SAP Solution Manager.

- Standardization of test management
- Centralization of storing test-relevant results
- Implementation of existing revision requirements
- Efficient test control including reporting
- Extensive test coverage with flexibly definable test depth per process and test phase

Beyond these, additional relevant goals were defined for the testing process. These included classification and structured description of the internal business fields as well as consistent documentation of business processes within SAP Solution Manager. Naturally, the goals initially determined also influenced the subsequent selection of the tool. For example, it was specified right from the start that an acceptance and release procedure was supposed to be considered in all project phases for revision purposes.

Test concept These requirements and their implementation were then documented in the form of a test concept in parallel to the project. For this purpose, the entire subject of test management was subdivided into individual areas in the early phases of the project. These areas were then processed and implemented systematically. This involved organizational aspects, such as the development of the basic test process, the test implementation, reporting, and the integration of the test phases with the existing procedure model of SOKA-BAU. Technical implementation was also planned; for instance, the authorization concept, the formatting of test data, and the configuration steps required. Another issue was how to include employees by preparing the necessary documentations and training.

Decision on SAP Solution Manager The basic requirements for a test management tool were determined based on the initially defined goals as well as the concept of the testing procedure. The goal was to structure a test process in accordance with the specifications planned. This requirement included test planning and execution as well as the integrated management of error messages. Furthermore, information on the status and progress of the test execution was supposed to be available at any time. Reporting was also to be processed for various stakeholders (for instance, project leads). The revision-proof documentation of testing activities (consistent traceability: Who has tested what and with which result), including the acceptance and release procedure, was another requirement.

Back then, the enterprise had an SAP Solution Manager system in Version 3.2. But the system was used only rudimentarily to meet technical requirements (for instance, license key generation). Now, additional functions were to be explored to generate additional benefits for the enterprise.

In Peter Hartmann (former test manager in project R3RW_2007), an employee was available who had already gathered experience with the Test Workbench. With the understanding that most basic requirements were already covered with the Test Workbench, its use within SAP Solution Manager was evaluated. Starting with the product release of SAP Solution Manager available at SOKA-BAU, the Test Workbench was integrated with the implementation methodology of SAP Solution Manager. For the first time, users could store project-relevant documents, including test cases with a business-process orientation using a document management system (SAP Knowledge Warehouse). As a result, it was possible to use SAP Solution Manager to also implement the required business process documentation, including the revision security and the acceptance procedure. The facts that SAP Solution Manager was available without additional license costs and that implementation and test management functionality could be used more or less out of the box supported the decision to use SAP Solution Manager as the documentation and test management tool within the scope of the release change.

To implement the test process using SAP Solution Manager and the Test Workbench, a procedure concept was developed which entailed an implementation in three steps. In the first step, the use of tools was piloted for the first time in release-change project R3RW_2007. In the second step, the Test Workbench was used in another project, the replacement of BS2000 with UNIX. Using the experience gathered this way and the continuous optimization of the test process, the Test Workbench was then comprehensively used for testing all relevant IT requests in the third step. Each of these steps involves the use of document management in SAP Solution Manager for managing test cases. In the area of insur-

Gradual implementation of the test management tool

ance solutions, SAP Solution Manager has additionally been deployed for documenting IT requests since April 2008.

Piloting

Within the framework of the R3RW_2007 project, the test process which had been designed based on those objectives was transferred to selected tools. The individual steps for test preparation, test execution, and reporting were initially mapped with the relevant functions of SAP Solution Manager and the Test Workbench.

This entailed the creation of a project and the description and subsequent documentation of business processes for a process-oriented storage structure. The deployment of the document management for describing business processes involved the use of status schemas. The test cases for the project were also created in accordance with the respective processes or process steps in the Business Blueprint on the basis of standardized document templates. This way, test cases were created for these test stages:

▶ Module/component test

▶ Migration test

▶ Interface test

▶ Integration test

Basic project standards, standardized templates, and some test cases were created anew during the project. This ensured a very high quality for the documents. These initial activities required the immediate support from business departments. The quite significant project efforts were reconciled with the steering committee.

Test planning

This formed the basis for creating the test plans necessary within the release change for the test steps mentioned. The subdivision of test plans into test packages enabled SOKA-BAU to flexibly assign test cases to the individual business departments and therefore allowed for precise control of the test execution. The continuous status check, as well as the final assessment of the testing activities, was run via the status information system of the Test Workbench. The test progress could be traced at different levels of detail (test stage or business department) and in real time, thanks to the use of test plans for different test stages as well as the use of test packages for business departments. The test report generated automatically at the end of a test stage allowed for revision-proof documentation on the execution and completion of testing activities.

Special attention was given to the messaging system in the testing environment right from the start. Figure 4.45 shows the troubleshooting process at SOKA-BAU that was mapped using SAP Service Desk within SAP Solution Manager.

Managing error messages

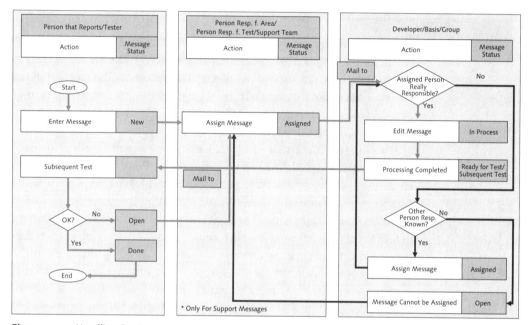

Figure 4.45 Handling Service Messages in the Test Management

An essential requirement for the management of error messages was to immediately notify the participating target groups about the status of messages. For example, developers were supposed to be informed immediately that a message was available for processing. Testers were supposed to be informed when the error they documented was ready for subsequent testing. For this purpose, the SAP Service Desk in SAP Solution Manager was configured accordingly with the support of SAP Consulting. An email notification was set up for the previously mentioned events, "New Error Message" and "Ready for Subsequent Test," as well as for the information that a message is being processed. The target groups of developers and testers or the creators of a message are thus

Email notification

immediately informed about the current message status. In the mean-time, the messages contain hyperlinks via which the relevant message can be called directly.

Training concept

Besides the technical implementation, the training concept established by SOKA-BAU was an essential factor in the successful implementation and consistent use of SAP Solution Manager in the test environment. An important goal was to familiarize the employees with the new process and the tools at an early stage.

For the R3RW project, typical roles were determined in the testing environment (for instance, project lead, test manager, test lead, and tester) in the design phase. Tasks, competences, and responsibilities were defined for these roles. The individual roles were related to the actual project roles or assigned to project team members. The training was developed based on the project roles defined. Trainings with specific scope were prepared, and training documents and system exercises were compiled for each role in cooperation with SAP Test Management Consulting. For example, an all-day training session was prepared for test leads that presented the complete test planning and execution, including the preceding creation of the Business Blueprint, as well as use of the document management in SAP Solution Manager. Testers received a half-day training session that focused on the procedure of executing and evaluating test cases in the Test Workbench. All training sessions were run on a demo system so that the users could immediately reproduce the work steps they had learned in exercises. For the R3RW project, approximately 120 employees were trained for the test manager role and 130 employees for the tester role; an average of 15 persons participated in one training. In-house employees and consultants of SAP Test Management Consulting were lecturers for the trainings. Within a very short period of time, all employees were familiarized with the newly implemented tool for documentation and test management. Peter Hartmann notes that this step considerably contributed to the acceptance of SAP Solution Manager at SOKA-BAU.

By using SAP Solution Manager and the Test Workbench, it was possible for the first time within the R3RW project to centrally control the testing process and implement it in a standardized form. Many of the initially defined goals were achieved already in the pilot phase of the test management.

After the R3RW_2007 project had been completed, the test management was reviewed in-house. For this purpose, about 220 project participants with different roles in using SAP Solution Manager were interviewed about test preparation, test organization, and troubleshooting. The review certified a high acceptance of the procedure selected. Feedback was especially positive regarding document management, the flexible assignment options by using test packages, and the option to navigate to SAP transactions in the target system during test execution. This also applied to reporting; here the creation of test reports was mentioned in particular. The handling of the Service Desk was identified as an optimization opportunity. Consequently, the Service Desk configuration was supplemented, and the email notifications were equipped with the previously mentioned hyperlinks. On average, the cost-benefit ratio for using the Test Workbench was evaluated as "reasonable." Peter Hartmann emphasizes that, compared with the previous procedure, the use of a tool for structured documentation requires extra time and effort initially but definitely pays off in better quality of the processes tested and in the meeting of revision requirements.

Reviewing the test management

During the R3RW_2007 project, an enterprise-internal proof of concept was performed with regard to the test automation using eCATT. Here, selected test cases of different test stages were automated and evaluated with regard to different criteria; for instance, creation effort and reduction of test effort.

Test automation

In particular, it was discovered that the runtime of multi-variant functional tests could be reduced considerably. For the test case "Account Statement Employee," for example, 40 variants to be tested are defined as test data in an eCATT test data container; the total runtime of the test case is less than 12 minutes. Compared with the manual test execution, which kept the tester busy for more than five hours, this reduces the time by a factor of 28.5.

The clear reduction of test effort for IT and the business departments was considered an essential criterion for using automated test cases. Another positive aspect was that eCATT saves the system and test data independent of the test script, which ensures maximum flexibility in test execution particularly in combination with the option to run tests in different systems and clients. Furthermore, all test runs are documented using an execution log and stored for the respective test case in

Benefit potentials of eCATT

accordance with the revision security requested. Harnessing the required expertise and particularly knowledge in the script language used were considered challenges for the further procedure. Relatively high initial training efforts were expected for the implementation of an internal test automation team. The same applied to the adaptation and maintenance of scripts; the customer thinks that a dedicated automation team must be available to adapt scripts after system changes so that executability is ensured at all times.

Overall, the proof of concept for automated testing using eCATT has projected a high value of benefit for SOKA-BAU projects. Selected scripts are being implemented successfully within regression tests. The further use of eCATT is currently planned.

Optimization and rollout of the test procedure The findings gained in the R3RW_2007 project and in the subsequent review were used for further optimization, so that the established process has also been used in other projects. The replacement of the previous BS2000 systems with UNIX was also implemented using SAP Solution Manager and the Test Workbench.

Since April 2008, the test management in SAP Solution Manager has been used not only for projects, but also for the documentation and testing of IT requests. In the medium term, the company plans to also deploy the Change Request Management functionality of SAP Solution Manager.

Support by SAP Consulting Thanks to the active exchange with SAP and DSAG, the test management at SOKA-BAU could always respond quickly to new developments and integrate them with the internal test process at an early stage. This way, additional functions and convenience characteristics have gradually been opened up in the test management environment. This openness has proven itself in the opinion of Peter Hartmann, and it is one of the reasons why SAP Solution Manager is used in its current version and with its latest functionality at SOKA-BAU.

Validating SAP Solution Manager 7.0 EhP 1 SOKA-BAU's participation in the customer validation of SAP Solution Manager 7.0 EhP 1 was a significant step in this development. When SAP asked SOKA-IT in September 2008 whether it was interested in participating in the upcoming customer validation, SOKA-IT took the opportunity was taken to build contemporary know-how with regard to new functions. This allowed SOKA-IT to use new key technologies of

SAP Solution Manager in the application scenarios, "Implementation" and "Test Management," as one of the first customers worldwide in real life. After consultation with Roland Krüger, an appropriate project was built in cooperation with SAP.

The validation project involved an upgrade of a system copy of the previous SAP Solution Manager system of SOKA-BAU from SP15 to EhP 1. Subsequently, a regression test of the already used functionality was run in this system. Then the new functions of Enhancement Package 1 were validated. After the successful validation, the SAP Solution Manager production system was upgraded to EhP 1, and the new functions were used in the production environment.

Scope of the validation

The customer validation at SOKA-IT focused on the following functionality:

- ▶ Basic/delta configuration on the basis of guided procedure (SOLMAN_SETUP)
- ▶ Work center (among others, *Test Management*)
- ▶ Using the Solution Documentation Assistant to support the creation of business process structures
- ▶ Using Business Process Change Analyzer to optimize the preparation of tests

Besides these central aspects, additional functions of EhP 1 were considered; however, these were not actually validated at SOKA-IT (for instance, Quality Gate Management). Furthermore, all innovations since SP15 were tested in the test management area. These included the release workflow for test plans and test sequences.

A copy of the existing SAP Solution Manager production system was used as the validation system. It was linked with SAP ERP and SAP BW systems to enable the test and the evaluation of new functions of EhP 1 (see Figure 4.46).

Validation system

Two SAP ERP systems, of which one was equipped with Enhancement Package 3, were used as the development and test environment to test the technical determination of regression test cases using Business Process Change Analyzer. Furthermore, three SAP NetWeaver BW systems (development, acceptance, and production) were connected.

The customer validation was based on the proven test procedure of SOKA-IT. Here, suitable test cases were created (if necessary) and uploaded to the live SAP Solution Manager. A test plan including test packages was set up, and the test was then processed and documented as usual. Both the internal reporting and the reporting to SAP were implemented using the standard functionality of SAP Solution Manager. Error messages were sent via the SAP support infrastructure, where they were processed and prioritized.

SOKA-IT presented the results of the customer validation in a final presentation, which also addressed the SAP development requirements that are relevant from the customer's perspective.

SOKA-IT concluded that the basic configuration of SAP Solution Manager using the guided procedure as very helpful. Thanks to the experience gained during the validation it was possible to complete the basic configuration of the live SAP Solution Manager within three hours.

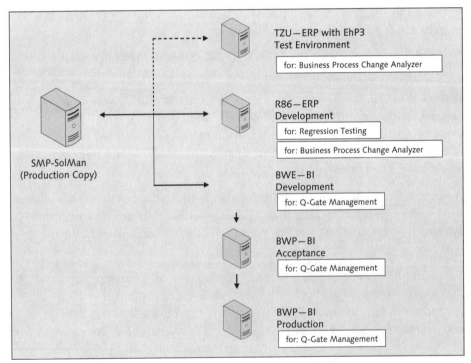

Figure 4.46 System Landscape for the Validation of SAP Solution Manager 7.0 EhP 1

SOKA-IT certified a high and immediate value from work centers because they significantly contribute to user-friendliness and thus to the acceptance of SAP Solution Manager. Particularly the test planning and execution, as well as the incident management, benefit from the clear web interfaces. The option to grant users access to their relevant work centers reduces the perceived complexity of the system considerably. It is also very beneficial that the users can personalize their work centers, for instance by creating their own layout or by setting filters. Because work centers are still used in some cases to call GUI-based transactions, SOKA-IT suggested improvements in this area to the SAP development department.

Work center

SOKA-IT also described as a clear relief the support provided by the Solution Documentation Assistant for creating business process structures. In particular, the available analysis options of an SAP system, including the derivation of the business process structures used, left a positive impression.

Solution Documentation Assistant (SoDocA)

SOKA-IT assessed the functional scope of the Business Process Change Analyzer (BPCA) as a significant step forward. Test efforts that build up during operation can be considerably decreased using the functionality that is already available today.

Business Process Change Analyzer

The information on the attribution of a transaction, including the technical bill of material (TBOM) created, is used as the basis of comparison for the relevant analyses after the implementation.

The project prepared in such a way was then compared with the transport requests or delivery objects of SAP (in this case, service packs) to identify business processes affected by the changes. Because test cases were also managed within the Business Blueprint in the selected project, one of the next steps involved the creation of test plans based on the change event.

Peter Hartmann said that the technical change analysis implemented using BPCA was an innovative and very helpful function that could yield valuable findings about the system changes, and these findings immediately affected the test scope. He also pointed out that the available functions could be supplemented. Here, he suggested optimization potentials with regard to handling (for instance, improved support for creating TBOMs). Overall, BPCA was evaluated positively, and SOKA-IT has used it in production since the second quarter of 2009.

Test case sequences

One function that has been requested by the test participants of SOKA-BAU since the initial test phases of the R3RW_2007 project is the option to specify the sequence for the processing of test cases. Within the scope of validation, the use of the new function "Test Case Sequences" was piloted in the Test Workbench. In particular, the automatic email notification for testers informing them when they can start with the execution of their test cases can significantly simplify the control of future testing activities, in the opinion of Peter Hartmann.

Status schemata for test plans

This same conclusion applies to enhancements in the area of test plan management. Because status schemata for documents and test cases have already been used in SOKA-BAU's projects, it was a logical consequence to use appropriate schemata for test plans. At SOKA-BAU, these will be used in future to lock active and closed test plans against changes and disable further test executions for closed test plans.

Reference customer for end-to-end test management

Today, SOKA-BAU and SOKA-IT are available as SAP reference customers for end-to-end test management. Thanks to the many years of experience in using SAP Solution Manager and the Test Workbench, as well as the findings gained in the customer validation with regard to SAP Solution Manager 7.0, the employees of SOKA-IT's CCoE have gathered comprehensive experience in the use of the test tools within SAP Solution Manager and can realistically point out the benefit potential of the new tools.

Conclusion

The example of SOKA-BAU shows how to gradually implement comprehensive test management using an already available SAP Solution Manager system. Current developments show how the proven procedure in the test management area can be supplemented reasonably by using the new functions of SAP Solution Manager 7.0 Enhancement Package 1.

Lessons learned

What can you learn from the experience of SOKA-BAU?

► First create a procedure model for the test process. It can be used to derive the requirements for the test tools to be used.

▶ The selection of a test management tool should also include the consideration of the upstream steps; for instance, the process documentation. Make sure that the individual functions can be integrated.

▶ A comprehensive training concept greatly contributes to the acceptance of implementing a test management tool.

▶ An open innovation-friendly enterprise culture, internal information events, and use of information (for instance, DSAG, SAP) ensure early awareness and adoption of new developments.

▶ The test tools in SAP Solution Manager have continuously been developed. New functions can be piloted with little effort within the optimization of test processes. Their value can thus be evaluated for your own test process.

▶ Using the test tools within SAP Solution Manager enables you to easily meet the requirements of in-house revision.

4.9   Customer Report by SEWAG

"SAP Solution Manager is the most helpful tool that could have been deployed in our upgrade project."

Detlev Voss,
Head Test Management SEWAG

Südwestfalen Energie und Wasser AG—SEWAG for short—is the regional energy group of three electricity providers in Southern North Rhine-Westphalia: Mark-E Aktiengesellschaft, Stadtwerke Lüdenscheid GmbH, and SEWAG Netze GmbH. The group's registered office is located in Hagen, Germany. More than 80 percent of the shares are held by the cities and towns of the region; the largest shareholders include the cities of Hagen (42.66%) and Lüdenscheid (24.12%), as well as the energy supplier RWE Westfalen-Weser-Ems Aktiengesellschaft (19.06%).

Südwestfalen
Energie und
Wasser AG

In 2007, the SEWAG subsidiaries provided approximately 8.1 billion kilowatt hours of electricity, 3.4 billion kilowatt hours of gas, 720 million kilowatt hours of heat, and 19.2 million cubic meters of drinkable water to about 280,000 customers in the region. About half of the energy is generated in group-owned power plants with a total output of more than 1,300 megawatts. The supply network for electricity, gas, and water managed by the grid company SEWAG Netze GmbH includes all output levels with a total length of more than 7,750 miles. With approximately 1,750 employees, SEWAG generated revenues of €820.9 million in 2007.

Upgrade to SAP ERP 6.0

In early 2008, SEWAG started to implement an upgrade of its previous SAP R/3 4.6C system to SAP ERP 6.0. One important goal of the upgrade was to consolidate the organically grown structures and heterogeneous system landscape as much as possible by implementing SAP ERP 6.0. The EU directives on the deregulation of the electricity and gas market were another criterion for the release change. These directives stipulate that European energy companies must keep a separate organization for the energy supply and grid use. This unbundling poses great challenges for the public utility companies because it must be implemented in processes and in the system. The associated requirements of the German Federal Network Agency are mapped in SAP ERP 6.0 via standardized processes. Within the framework of unbundling, it was determined that the tool that performs the data exchange with the Federal Network Agency requires a more current SAP ERP system than the currently installed release. The impending discontinuation of maintenance for SAP R/3 4.6C was a motive for the upgrade, in addition to the goal of meeting legal requirements and achieving a higher degree of centralization at the same time. SEWAG was a long-standing SAP customer since SAP R/2 times, and the decision to implement the release change was primarily based on technical aspects.

The project for the implementation of the upgrade commenced in January 2008 and was successfully concluded in June 2008. The business departments were involved in the upgrade via their managers within a steering committee as well as via the "SAP competence team" of SEWAG, which comprised the persons responsible for the individual modules.

One essential requirement of the upgrade was to maintain business operation. The complete functionality, which used to be run in the 4.6C system, had to be available in stable fashion in the SAP ERP 6.0 system. Another task was to implement the requirements to enable communication with the Federal Network Agency.

Using SAP Solution Manager

Against this background, SAP Solution Manager was selected in the upgrade project as the tool for documenting the business processes and for planning and implementing tests. The benefit of SAP Solution Manager for the upcoming project was determined together with SAP Consulting prior to the upgrade. Project planners studied which individual applica-

230

tion scenarios or which functionality of SAP Solution Manager could be used at SEWAG in the upgrade project. The results of this check were used to create a roadmap for using document and test management in the project. Another important part of this roadmap involved a concept for the functional use and for the training of the SAP Solution Manager users. Together with SAP Consulting, workshops were developed for all target groups that would work with SAP Solution Manager to familiarize themselves with the relevant functionality.

The training effort for using SAP Solution Manager turned out to be very low: A one-day workshop was sufficient for project and test management to communicate the procedures and basic operation. After a two-hour overview training, the employees of the individual business departments were able to store their processes in SAP Solution Manager in a structured manner and then add the relevant transactions and documents. Detlev Voss, head of test management, emphasizes that this led to high acceptance despite the initial reservations of having to use an additional SAP system. The users' feedback was positive in every respect, due also to the straightforward handling of the tool and the known look and feel.

Training effort

"Nevertheless, the simultaneous implementation of SAP Solution Manager during the upgrade project was first perceived as an additional challenge for the project management, test management, and the persons responsible for the modules," says Detlev Voss. Those responsible for modules had to deal with the new SAP ERP system as well as store their documentation and test cases—which used to be available in decentralized fashion in Excel tables or other documents—in SAP Solution Manager in a structured manner.

The Business Blueprint functionality was used at the project start to map business processes of SEWAG in SAP Solution Manager. Presenting corporate processes—ideally based on business process repositories within SAP Solution Manager—in the defined increment of scenarios, business processes, and process steps enables a process-oriented storage of all project data and results, including process documentation, configuration objects, and test cases.

Business Blueprint

To develop this structure along with contents, workshops were held for the competence team members' responsible for modules and other project team members. These workshops took place in a period of four to six weeks. The individual modules were handled in half-day workshops. Mapping the functions of the respective module in SAP Solution Manager was a direct element of the workshop. After the processes—referred to as "core activities" and "main functions" in SEWAG terminology—had been mapped, the respective transactions could be assigned to these via the TEST OBJECT field in the target system. Because the entire system landscape of SEWAG was mapped within SAP Solution Manager and was linked with SAP Solution Manager via RFC connections, the assignment enabled immediate navigation to the respective target system. This significantly facilitated both the evaluation of changes within the scope of the upgrade and the tests.

Business Process Repository

This step was also coordinated in several sessions as required. Where possible, processes of the Business Process Repository of SAP Solution Manager were used as templates to accelerate the definition of custom processes. The Business Process Repository is a collection of standard processes that are provided within the scope of the implementation content of SAP Solution Manager. The benefit consists of access to the contents that are already available in SAP Solution Manager; process descriptions, transactions, configuration objects, and instructions, as well as test cases are defined for many business processes. SEWAG was thus able to build on already existing templates or use these as templates for customizing its own processes. Within the scope of the upgrade, it was therefore possible to compare the previous, custom processes with the changes in SAP ERP 6.0.

In addition to the processes of the individual business departments, structures were created in the Business Blueprint that accommodate the interfaces between systems. Special importance was attached to those because experience showed that is where errors occur during an upgrade. The interfaces were mapped in the scenarios "SAP to SAP" as well as "SAP to non-SAP," each of which contain all system connections of the relevant category.

The result of these activities was that all project participants could work within the structure of SAP Solution Manager. "Transferring the company structures in the predefined 'process orientation' of SAP Solution Manager requires openness and rethinking if required," says Detlev Voss. Nevertheless, the development of the business blueprint was not as complex as initially assumed.

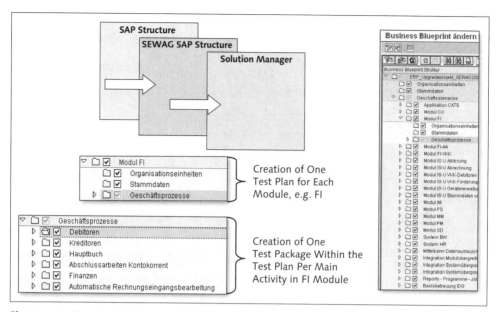

Figure 4.47 Creating the Business Blueprint

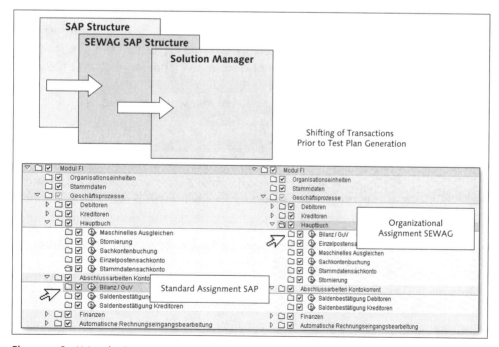

Figure 4.48 Using the Business Process Repository as a Template

In general, it's important to note that the creation of a Business Blueprint doesn't present a one-time investment for a single project. The blueprint can be reused in future for a multitude of changes; for instance, separation and consolidation of systems, or also for future upgrades. It is also possible to use the process structures in other use cases of SAP Solution Manager.

Creating process
transparency

Martin Menzel, project lead of the upgrade project at SEWAG, describes another benefit in this phase:

"One effect of defining a business blueprint that shouldn't be underestimated is the fact that SEWAG was able to use the business process structure at an early stage to make the complexity of the technical upgrade transparent for all participants."

This particularly involved both the persons responsible for the modules and the management team that acted as the project sponsor. Thanks to the structured presentation in SAP Solution Manager, it was possible to present the processes affected by the upgrade in their entirety to the management. This involved not only the various modules, but the interfaces to non-SAP systems. In addition to illustrating the project scope, this structure was also used as the basis to plan further work in the upgrade project. Simultaneously, the creation of the blueprint also involved the identification of custom developments that were no longer required after the upgrade to SAP ERP 6.0. SEWAG was able to estimate the project scope within a period of four weeks and map its total of business processes and interfaces.

Compiling the business blueprint along with all interfaces belonging to the SAP ERP system enabled a structured check of all interfaces involved in the upgrade. As a result, an add-on SAP system that was not compatible with SAP ERP 6.0 was identified even before the actual test implementation. An appropriate update of the product was triggered in time.

This involved a special version of a third-party product. Incompatibilities were detected for the access within the test plan of FI.

Central document
storage

The immediate benefit of using SAP Solution Manager in the upgrade project involved document management used within the scope of the Business Blueprint. This document management was deployed for the process documentation and for the storage and versioning of test cases.

Using the document management enabled SEWAG to set up a central documentation basis for the upgrade project as well as for other ongoing SAP projects in which all relevant information is saved. This included requirement documents, process descriptions, and change documentations at the business process level. The implementation of the upgrade project that was based on these documents was also mapped, particularly in the form of navigation to customizing and development objects in the SAP ERP system and the test cases already mentioned. Thanks to the process-related storage of all project information, users can interpret test results in the context of the existing documentation and evaluate and process error effects in the test on the basis of existing information. SAP Solution Manager uses the functionality of the integrated SAP Knowledge Warehouse so that functions such as release schemes and documentation history are available within document management. SEWAG used the latter for versioning and logging documents and test cases to ensure consistent traceability of changes that also meets the requirements of external auditors.

Tests within the scope of comparable projects used to be run without a particular structure at SEWAG. The test process for the upgrade project (see Figure 4.49) was therefore optimized using the SAP Test Workbench. For this purpose, SEWAG and a consultant of SAP Test Management Consulting created a procedure model that is based on the various roles in the test flow.

Test process in the upgrade project

Based on the business process structure and the test cases stored there, the next step involved the creation of test plans. A test plan includes any number of test cases for a specific purpose; for instance, for an integration test of a business department. When a test plan is created, the individual test cases previously created in the document management of the Business Blueprint can be selected on the basis of the previously created business process structure. This allowed SEWAG to use a process-oriented test procedure that considers real, cross-system business processes.

Test planning

A separate test plan was created for each SAP module. In parallel, test plans were developed for cross-module tests, and interfaces between SAP systems or from the SAP ERP system to non-SAP systems were also taken into account. In a subsequent step, the test plans were subdivided into personal work packages for individual testers. The personalization of worklists occurs when test packages are formed. These are assigned in SAP Solution Manager using the user of the appropriate tester which allows for a detailed reporting and exact documentation.

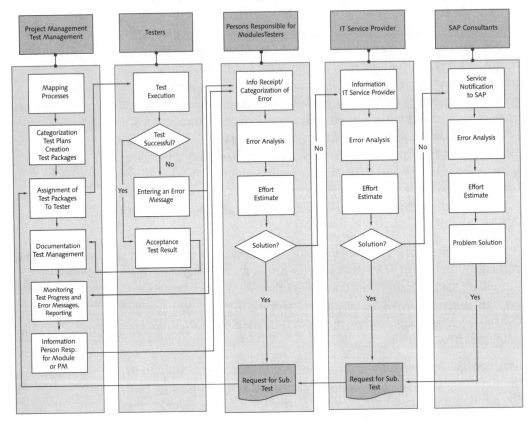

Figure 4.49 Test Process

The subdivision into and assignment to personal work packages effectively enabled coordinated implementation of tests. Testers of the respective business departments could access their test cases via a separate transaction for the role of the tester: the tester worklist. To implement the tests, they were supported by the respectively defined test case descriptions and the appropriate transaction. Moreover, the Test Workbench enabled the standardization of previously heterogeneous test documentation by providing uniform document templates.

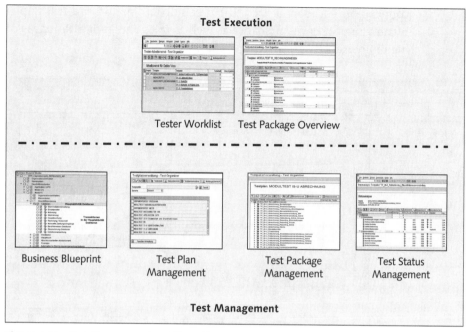

Figure 4.50 Test Management and Execution

Execution of tests was considerably simplified by transactions defined in the run-up. Testers could access the systems to be tested at the click of the mouse. Thanks to the trusted RFC connections, testers no longer needed to log on to the system again. With this integration option, SAP Solution Manager reinforces its position not only as a central application management platform, but also as a test management platform that calls the test objects defined in test execution and manages the subsequent result or error documentation.

Besides the planning and execution of tests, the new test process of SEWAG also involves the entry, forwarding, and deletion of error messages with a subsequent test. This process was mapped via the SAP Service Desk integrated with SAP Solution Manager. Here, the IT service providers of SEWAG and the relevant consultants benefit from the flexible configuration options of error management and from the option to forward directly to SAP messages that are sent in the course of the test.

At SEWAG, the system administration of SAP Solution Manager is performed by in-house IT service providers. Detlev Voss praises the close

Test execution

Problem messages

System administration

cooperation and emphasizes that precise coordination and fast implementation of user maintenance as well as roles and authorizations is of high importance during the test phases.

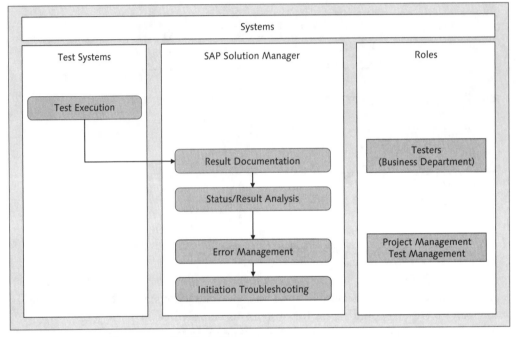

Figure 4.51 Test Execution

Prepared for future regression tests
The test procedure outlined here is implemented in running operation also after the successful go-live. The Business Blueprint is used for the documentation of system changes by assigning the relevant change documents to the appropriate processes. The associated test cases are mapped in regression test plans and implemented by the respective business departments. SEWAG plans to automate the regression tests in the medium term.

Reporting test results
Thanks to the new test procedure, it was possible to check approximately 1,490 transactions and reports in structured test cycles. Test coverage of about 95% could be achieved for the entire solution landscape of SEWAG, including non-SAP systems. In particular, the final test before the go-live showed a respectable result: 1,194 transactions were checked, of which 94% were evaluated as "OK" by the testers. Such a piece of information could not be determined prior to the use of the Test Work-

bench, or at least not without great effort. Previously, project leads had to gather information from every single business department that was available in a variety of formats. Within the Test Workbench, however, both management summaries and detailed reports on individual tests or on the entire project history can be created using the monitoring and reporting functionality. The status analysis happens in real time and reflects the current test progress. A comprehensive report about all test results achieved and error messages occurred is possible after the test phase has been completed. Detlev Voss:

> *"This enables us to provide statements to the management and project management at any time. The control, execution, and acceptance have become extremely transparent and considerably faster."*

Besides the apparent benefits of a structured, tool-based test, Detlev Voss also points out the organizational benefits of using the SAP Test Workbench:

Organizational benefits

> *"The clear assignment of users to test packages results in concrete task packages that are to be processed by the respective tester."*

While some tests often used to be forgotten in daily operation, "positive pressure" has emerged to process the tests with a clear focus and on time. Consequently, errors are detected much sooner.

Detlev Voss offers a positive overall summary: "SAP Solution Manager is the most helpful tool that could have been deployed in our upgrade project." He confirms that the upgrade project of SEWAG without SAP Solution Manager would have involved considerably more time and greater expense. Moreover, SAP Solution Manager made relations between processes and systems transparent and therefore reduced the complexity of the project. Detlev Voss advises all decision-makers for similar projects not to spare the initial efforts for defining the Business Blueprint. "It pays off to invest some time, even if you are pressed for time, to map clear structures. You can then use these as the basis." Martin Menzel confirms this evaluation:

Using SAP Solution Manager — conclusion

> *"With SAP Solution Manager, we've invested in the future. We've documented our structures permanently in SAP Solution Manager and can access all relevant documents at any time. We can also provide the processes mapped for other projects."*

Decision to use
SAP Consulting The deployment of SAP Consulting was also evaluated as very positive. The project team mastered more than 90% of the system-related tasks independently and was only supported by consultants of SAP Test Management Consulting in the initial phase and in some parts of the workshops. The consultants also provided support if the team members had to master challenges in the course of the project. "It would hardly be possible to receive such a high degree of competence from other service providers," says Detlev Voss, describing implementation of SAP Solution Manager. He also adds that the consultant of SAP Test Management Consulting came equipped with comprehensive process, method, and tool know-how. Detlev Voss affirms that the 10-day support of SAP Consulting was performed very cost-efficiently and that the consulting prices quotations from competitors were significantly higher.

Conclusion

The upgrade project was implemented successfully within the intended period of three months. Project lead Martin Menzel, attributes a large part of the smooth implementation to SAP Solution Manager:

> "We've successfully completed the project within the given time frame and budget with a high level of quality thanks to usage of SAP Solution Manager."

SAP Solution Manager served as a tool for process documentation and the planning and implementation of tests within the scope of the upgrade project. The development of the Business Blueprint and the subsequent business process-oriented, central storage of project-relevant information and all test cases made the project scope transparent. The tool-based test process enabled the monitoring of the test progress in real time.

Overall, the increased transparency and the flexible reporting revealed the complexity of the upgrade project. Risks, such as interface problems, were identified in good time. Martin Menzel:

> "SAP Solution Manager was a valuable tool in this project because it enabled us to control the technical risks of the upgrade."

All project documents and the results of all tests performed during the upgrade project are stored audit-proof over the entire project lifecycle.

The Business Blueprint and the process descriptions can be reused in future projects and in other application scenarios. Consequently, the one-time efforts in the context of the upgrade project present a long-term investment.

In addition to use of SAP Solution Manager, a proven process model for test management was particularly decisive in the project's success. This was provided by SAP Test Management Consulting on the basis of the ASAP methodology and international standards.

The committed project team was able to incorporate both default and custom transactions, functions, and processes into the structures within SAP Solution Manager and thereby make a major contribution toward achieving the project goals.

What can you learn from the experience of SEWAG?

Lessons learned

▶ The creation of a Business Blueprint raises awareness for the complexity of a project and reveals risks with regard to process relationships and interfaces between systems.

▶ The process structures developed and their relevant documentation can be reused versatility beyond the initial project, for instance in business process monitoring.

▶ A central, tool-based test implementation enables the monitoring of the test process as well as a meaningful reporting to identify project risks in good time.

▶ It's important to first compile a process model for test planning and execution, and then select a suitable test tool.

4.10 Customer Report by BSH Bosch und Siemens Hausgeräte GmbH

> **Note**
>
> This customer report originates from the first edition of this book. Following the original chapter is a sustainability report that describes the long-term effects of methods, tool use, and consulting support, as well as current developments or projects of the customer.

"SAP Solution Manager is a monolithic test management solution. From the terminology it uses to its operational concept to its look and feel, the entire solution complies with SAP standards."

Otto Geiger
Test Manager, BSH

Bosch und Siemens Hausgeräte GmbH

BSH Bosch und Siemens Hausgeräte GmbH, a joint venture of Robert Bosch GmbH, Stuttgart, and Siemens AG, Munich, is a globally operating group of companies with an annual turnover of more than €6.8 billion (as of 2005).

The range of products from these companies includes large and small appliances as well as a collection of Internet-enabled household appliances. With its main brands, Bosch and Siemens, BSH serves the household appliances market in the product areas of "cooling," "dishwashing," "cooking," and "laundry care." The two main brands are complemented with six special brands and several regional brands.

BSH has experienced rapid growth in the past 20 years. During that period the company has expanded its operations to 42 factories in 15 countries in Europe, the United States, Latin America, and Asia. Those factories and a global network of sales and customer service operations add up to a total of more than 70 companies in 40 countries with more than 34,500 employees under the umbrella of BSH.

The IT infrastructure of BSH is characterized by strong in-house competencies in many areas. BSH uses a wide range of SAP solutions that are divided into companywide and regional solutions (see Figure 4.52).

weBSH.net program and rollout

Bosch und Siemens Hausgeräte introduced the program weBSH.net in order to globally renew, harmonize, and improve the business processes on the basis of SAP R/3 Enterprise. The program contains the definition of a template that is rolled out from Germany into all sales operations. For the definition, administration, and rollout, BSH opted to use template projects in SAP Solution Manager.

Country-specific rollouts are carried out on the basis of the current template, as was the case with the sales operations in Spain in 2005. The country-specific functionality is transferred into the template during the project as it becomes possible and necessary. Thus the central template project is consistently revised or extended.

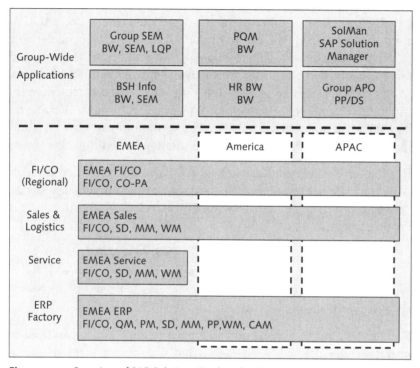

Figure 4.52 Overview of SAP Solutions Deployed at BSH

In the context of the rollout for the sales operations in Spain, a decision was made in favor of implementing SAP Solution Manager, in particular the testing functionality for the testing organization. Suggested alternatives to the use of SAP's application management platform were quickly ruled out. Because the testing scope consisted of hundreds of test processes, a manual test management was out of the question. Given this wide scope, organizing the testing activities on the basis of spreadsheet applications would simply have been impossible. Even documenting the test execution in a word processor would have been a real challenge.

At first, the use of a third-party tool was considered, but the implementation of a proprietary test tool was rejected because of its lack of integration with the SAP solution landscape.

Otto Geiger, the coordinator of the test project and test manager at BSH, considers integration with the SAP solution landscape to be the decisive factor. Although he sees slight technological advantages in the specialized test tools provided by third parties when compared with SAP Solution Manager, Otto Geiger believes that this advantage will constantly diminish due to ongoing development of SAP Solution Manager. Finally, he decided not to carry out a detailed evaluation of third-party test tools and instead opted for the integrated overall solution by SAP.

Avoiding license costs — In addition to the technical aspects, another clear restriction existed. Using a third-party test tool would have required investment in software licenses for the entire enterprise. Otto Geiger had a critical opinion about the related costs:

> *"The investment of a six-figure sum for a third-party tool generates a considerable need for justification. The question arises: Why do I suddenly need a six-figure sum for a tool that does something I have been doing for the past 20 years?"*

Organization of the test project — The organization of the test project for the rollout of the Spanish sales operation was defined at an early stage. The testers formed testing teams, each of which was coordinated by a test manager. A core testing team provided support for the individual teams. A test coordinator was responsible for organizing the entire project.

On the developers' side, a core development team was available as a central point of contact and as an interface to the development teams of the individual modules.

Additional developers provided further support. This testing support consisted primarily of employees of the headquarters. Testing support for employees in the regional offices was offered by providing systems, office space, users, and authorizations.

The entire support team consisted mainly of employees from the German headquarters. They provided support for the test execution and for triggering messages, and were always available to answer questions raised by the testers.

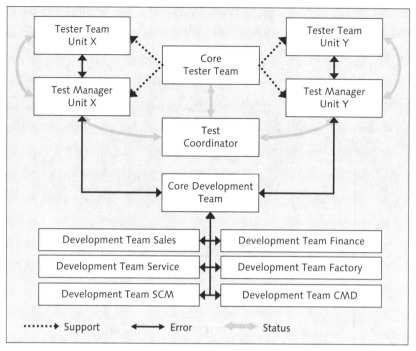

Figure 4.53 Organization of the Test Management

According to Otto Geiger, an appropriate overall organization is an essential factor for the success of test management. The scope of testing has a considerable influence on the design of the organization. Only if the test manager can obtain a realistic picture of the expected test effort at an early stage of the project can he select an appropriate organization for the test project. For this reason, external consultants supported cost estimates for the customer, particularly with regard to the costs incurred by a specific tool.

The following interrelationships were the basis for the sequence of preparatory actions.

Preparatory activities

- ▶ Relevant end-to-end business processes were identified and described by the user departments.
- ▶ Based on the process documentation the support team provided an estimate of the testing work to be expected.
- ▶ Based on the cost estimate the test manager defined an appropriate project organization.

Integration of SAP
Service Desk In addition to the test management functions of SAP solution Manager, BSH also integrated issue management functions provided by SAP Service Desk. Figure 4.54 illustrates the recording, forwarding, and solution-finding process for error messages that originate from the test cases.

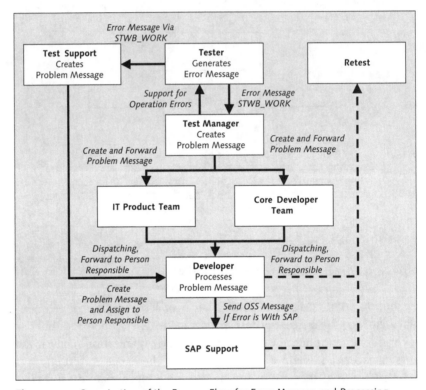

Figure 4.54 Organization of the Process Flow for Error Message and Processing

Organization of
the workflow The organization of the workflow was structured as follows: The testers were assigned personal, detailed worklists to process their tasks; then they carried out tests more or less independently and guided by the tool. Once they had completed the tests, they maintained the status of the test cases assigned to them. In addition, each test result was described in detail using the Test Notes function. In the case of an error, the Service Desk function was used to record an error message that was then administrated using SAP Solution Manager. This way, the solution process was triggered and monitored.

Because the testers in the regional companies were not always familiar with the test transaction, especially with regard to cross-module tests, the error message was first sent to the test manager. The test manager examined and assessed the message. If the error message was caused by an incorrect user interaction, the test manager supported the testers; if the error message signaled a real error, he converted the error message into a problem message. This way the developer resources were treated with care.

Depending on the type of the message or its assignment to a specific subject in the stored application area, the problem message was sent automatically to the core development team or to the IT product team. The responsible development team was then identified and the problem message was assigned correspondingly.

Problem message

The development team then attempted to provide a solution. However, if the error was categorized as being relevant to an SAP product, the team forwarded the message as an OSS message to SAP Support.

This process could be shortened by using the test support. The test support consisted of employees from the BSH headquarters who knew the members of the development teams and were thus able to assess their areas of responsibility. As a result, support team members were able to generate problem messages and assign them to the responsible developer team.

From the customer's point of view, this way of organizing the project was very useful. The use of SAP Solution Manager ensured a seamless integration of the test management and issue management processes.

The scope of the testing activities involved in the implementation project for the Spanish subsidiary was considerable. A total of 802 business processes were distributed to 598 test packages in the SAP Test Workbench. To cover the processes, a total of 3,877 individual test cases were required.

Scope of the test project

Compared to the overall project volume for the Spanish subsidiary, the scope of testing activities was substantial. Four of the 13 months of project duration were dedicated to developing; two of them to testing. Note, however, that those two months only comprised integration tests. All module tests were already carried out as developer tests during the development phase. These developer tests were not mapped in the SAP Test Workbench.

Sequence of actions A constantly recurring subject is the availability of knowledge transfer in the context of test projects. The integration tests were generally carried out by key users prior to their participation in the trainings. This was useful because the trainings were not disturbed by functional errors in the system. However, this method also raised the problem that key users were not yet sufficiently familiar with the system.

Process orientation of developers The people at Bosch und Siemens Hausgeräte addressed this problem by involving the developers directly in the test process after the developer tests were completed. The developers provided support to key users and error detection was accelerated.

However, the use of additional developers during the test project required a somewhat higher degree of organization. Developers often have a strongly component-based view that is oriented towards individual functions of the software. This rather technical viewpoint places the individual component as the focus, while the consistency of the tests with regard to a cross-component business process is not ensured.

Against this background, Otto Geiger regards the use of test management software oriented towards the business process as being very positive:

> *"Developers are always very technology-focused. This is absolutely valuable regarding the design and implementation, but not when it comes to testing. Using SAP Solution Manager, we are able to gear the developers more towards the business processes. This way we can focus their attention on the consistency of the test."*

Support by consulting Before the collaboration of BSH and SAP Test Management Consulting began, the test management activities of BSH were supported by a different quality assurance service provider. Eventually, this service provider was completely replaced by SAP Consulting. Otto Geiger gives the reasons:

> *"Those consultants were too focused on tools. We couldn't identify any method or process model. They structured the organization around the tool but managed to reach only a user level using SAP Solution Manager. This is not enough if you want to design a test structure and test*

process organization in the given framework. In total, I was not happy at all."

After SAP Test Management Consulting had taken over, the design and organization of the testing activities developed increasingly well, and the project finally got going.

SAP Consulting Deutschland supported the test project in the following areas:

▶ Test design and development of a process model

▶ Qualification for using the tools

▶ Usage support for SAP Solution Manager with a focus on the SAP Test Workbench

▶ Integration of SAP Test Organizer

▶ eCATT qualification

▶ SAP Service Desk

Due to the numerous pending rollout projects still waiting to be carried out in the different subsidiaries, a number of comparable projects needed to be done. This creates the potential for considerable cost savings if existing test cases, methods, and processes are reused. This potential is only limited by the relatively low level of standardization in the individual companies of Bosch und Siemens Hausgeräte GmbH.

Reuse and cost saving potentials

This situation is accounted for by isolating country-specific peculiarities of the rollout projects in the context of a continuous consolidation and improvement in process. The results of completed rollout projects are then examined in recurring workshops where existing materials are analyzed and reviewed. In those workshops, reusable material is separated from the country-specific material and consistently extended.

Based on his experience, Otto Geiger places high expectations into this method:

"Even though the level of standardization at BSH is comparatively low, there will be options for the reuse of certain elements. We strive to improve both the learning curve and the degree of reusability. By using iterative processes we will make sure that results that have been achieved once, such as test cases and concepts, can be used as often as possible."

Potential

Because of those learning effects, the expectations for the test management tool have risen considerably. Further development potential was identified with regard to the reporting options of SAP Solution Manager. A prioritization of business processes and issues would be desirable in several project situations.

Differentiation of the degree of progress by structural levels would be helpful in order to make it easier to determine in which modules the test process has progressed how far.

A look ahead

Because of the large number of rollout projects to be carried out in the near future, BSH will need to handle a considerable number of testing activities. The reuse of test cases that have already been prepared raises questions regarding the automation of functional tests and regression tests. Although the rollout project in Spain focused on the test organization, the possible implementation of test automation was already demonstrated by the SAP consultants on the basis of a prototype. BSH now intends to implement a test automation using eCATT in future projects.

Conclusion

The rollout project for the Spanish subsidiary was almost completed in the provided timeframe. The organization of the test was efficiently supported by the integration of the SAP Test Workbench in SAP Solution Manager. Thanks to the progress status analysis in real time and the automatically created test reports that were already organized according to process structures, the test process could be efficiently monitored.

However, what was even more important than the tool for the success of the project was the use of a solid process model during the test. This process model was designed as a template project in SAP Solution Manager in collaboration with SAP Consulting and is now being permanently developed further by Bosch und Siemens Hausgeräte. The project template supports the organization with predefined processes and test cases that can be quickly adapted to the specifics of the respective subsidiaries. This way, the investments into the test organization can be ultimately protected.

Lessons learned

What are the lessons can you learn from the experience of BSH?

▸ You should clarify the scope of your test project at an early stage.

▸ You should determine an organizational structure at an early stage.

▸ You should first consider a process model before thinking of tools.

▸ You should choose a test tool that can provide optimal support for your requirements.

▸ You should make sure that the tools you use can be integrated.

4.11 Update of the Customer Report by BSH Bosch und Siemens Hausgeräte GmbH

"We've used SAP Solution Manager for five years. The functionality initially provided has already helped us to improve our test processes and automate test cases. Acceptance of the tool in our business departments has grown with the new functions and with our experience of the benefits, acceleration, and security that SAP Solution Manager provides when used in a project. In our recent very large projects, SAP Solution Manager has definitely been our absolutely key element to ensure the quality of our projects."

Norbert Liss,
Head Application Architecture and Quality Management

The rapid growth of BSH Bosch und Siemens Hausgeräte GmbH has continued in recent years. Since our customer report in 2005, the number of BSH employees has increased to more than 40,000. Company sales have increased to approximately €8.76 billion (as of 2008). | Company growth

BSH documents its sustainability strategy in its report "Environmental and Corporate Responsibility," which has been published annually since 1992. In May 2006, Dr. Kurt-Ludwig Gutberlet, Chairman and Chief Executive Officer of BSH, was presented the international B.A.U.M. special award 2006. The Bundesdeutsche Arbeitskreis für umweltbewusstes Management e.V. (B.A.U.M., German Environmental Management Association) honored Mr. Gutberlet for BSH's pioneering role in the area of sustainable development and corporate citizenship. | Sustainability

In December 2008, BSH received the first German sustainability award as "Germany's Most Sustainable Company." It was acknowledged that one of BSH's essential strengths can be found the continuous improvement of its products' environmental properties. As a manufacturer of energy-efficient household appliances, BSH safeguards its competitiveness and jobs and makes a considerable contribution to saving resources and protecting climate. Another aspect that was considered involved social sustainability, which is implemented through a wide range of measures ranging from high health and safety standards to comprehensive training and further training programs.

Changes in the IT organization
Continuous enterprise growth and constant process innovation call for a high degree of flexibility and operational readiness also in the IT organization. Against the background of these requirements, the enterprise's IT organizational structure has fundamentally changed in some areas. An essential aspect to ensure the agility required is to focus more strongly on regional concerns. The Europe, Asia, and Americas regions, for example, were each bundled in a separate responsibility area; the global IT product development was streamlined to achieve a higher degree of standardization. Clear cross-departmental functions were defined for governance topics. One of these functions includes the architecture and quality management area. The task area led by Otto Geiger was converted into a separate department under the supervision of Norbert Liss. This ensures that the standardization of quality assurance can be advanced from a central point and across the company.

weBSH.net
The SAP solution landscape was mainly shaped by the *weBSH.net* project. The template project strives for optimization and harmonization of business processes on the basis of SAP solutions. The original report described the rollout of the template for Spain; in the meantime, the project has been fully implemented in Central Europe (Germany, Benelux, Austria) and in Turkey. A rollout is planned for the systems in Northern Europe (Scandinavia, Baltic countries) and Great Britain for 2009/2010.

Additional SAP projects
Furthermore, SAP NetWeaver BW 7.0 was implemented. The enterprise also started to use SAP NetWeaver Portal. Initially, selected business scenarios were provided via the portal; the focus was on processes from the SAP HCM environment. The implementation of SAP CRM is currently in the planning phase.

Optimizing the test process
The test process which was implemented during the rollout of the *weBSH.net* processes in Spain was further optimized and successfully used in other rollouts. The procedure for planning and implementing tests was

continuously optimized with regard to both processes and technology and adapted to new requirements. Besides the adaptation of organizational workflows, this primarily involves the more extensive use of SAP Solution Manager as well as the use of new functions in the test management area.

Otto Geiger, coordinator of the test project in 2005, considered integration of the test management tool with the SAP solution landscape as well as the availability provided free of licensing costs to be the decisive factor. Even though he believed that third-party solutions provided a technology edge for specialized functions, he confirmed that SAP Solution Manager has been continuously further developed, which reduced this edge constantly. This estimate proved to be true, in the opinion of Norbert Liss. Today, SAP Solution Manager provides numerous new functions and improvements particularly in the test management area. Some essential innovations have been adapted by BSH at an early stage; the usage of additional functions is currently being evaluated.

Using new functions of SAP Solution Manager

At BSH, SAP Solution Manager continues to be the core application in the test management and test automation area. The usage of the functionality provided has been extended as part of the continuous improvement of the test process. Technically, SAP Solution Manager has been upgraded to Service Pack 15 in the meantime. One of the main reasons was to utilize the new functions in the test management area, which are available with this service pack.

The work centers represent an important innovation. They provide role-based access to the tools and functions provided in SAP Solution Manager. Thanks to the introduction of work centers, it was possible to considerably improve the acceptance of SAP Solution Manager among business departments. For example, the user interface is also available via a web browser. Access via SAP GUI is not required. The enhanced user-friendliness of the web interface structured by tasks has an especially positive effect. Norbert Liss comments on this:

Work center

> *"For testers, the work center presents a more user-friendly user interface than the classic transactions in the test management environment."*

The sequence control of test cases is one of the functions that have been demanded by BSH's testers and test leads for a long time. This sequence control has been available as a new function since Service Pack 15. Users

Test case sequences

can define execution sequences via the TEST CASE SEQUENCES function that is available within the test package management; additionally, testers can be assigned to individual test cases directly. The sequence for processing test cases can be linked with a workflow, which can be used, for example, to implement an email notification of testers. Because end-to-end business processes are tested at BSH, the sequence control and gradual assignment of testers with email notification have been readily accepted.

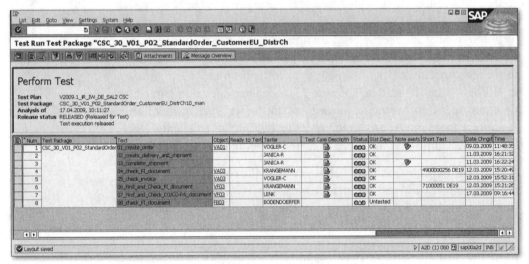

Figure 4.55 Test Implementation with Sequence Control

Evaluating
additional
functions

Currently, Enhancement Package 1 of SAP Solution Manager 7.0 is being implemented in a suitable test system to evaluate the use of Business Process Change Analyzer. The technical support for selecting the relevant regression test cases is supposed to be used to verify the associated options to accelerate the test preparation phase.

Optimizing the
error management
in the Service Desk

The test planning and preparation procedures, which already have been established and were presented in the first customer report, as well as the workflow organization of error management, are still used successfully. The latter have been optimized via further customizing of the Service Desk. For example, users who process the message and testers are now notified by email as soon as they need to process an error message or the retest. The email also contains a link to the appropriate work center so that users can quickly access the relevant tools and functions in SAP Solution Manager.

The test methodology has also been optimized continuously. The present approach has been enhanced by joint process tests. These are integration tests that are implemented jointly with local contacts at an early stage in the project workflow. The tests don't constitute a final acceptance, but are particularly used to trigger the change process in the countries in good time. The goal is to include all parties involved in the rollout in a timely manner.

Joint process tests

The tests that are thus implemented in the countries are run based on the test cases defined up to this point—comprising a total of up to 10,000 individual test steps—as well as on the basis of the results of the first migration tests.

Because all test cases required are already available within an SAP Solution Manager project in the context of a business blueprint and with the corresponding tagging, the joint process tests for a country can be prepared quickly, despite their scope. Moreover, the test status of the running process tests is available anytime.

It is possible to considerably raise the awareness of the end users of the new processes, thanks to the high number of employees that are involved in the tests. The early contact with the new system and the feedback from the countries immediately lead to a higher quality of rollout. Another important fact is that the acceptance of the new processes can be assessed at an early point in time. The participants in the country and the rollout team can therefore evaluate to which extent the new processes deviate from the previous procedure. Besides the initially implemented analysis of country-specific procedures, this also enables the enterprise to detect country-specific processes that have not been identified so far. These tests also generate the awareness in the country operation to help users adapt to the new processes. The actions needed (such as training sessions) and the effort required can be determined depending on the degree of change identified in this phase.

Thus, the joint process tests, whose implementation is only possible with a suitable test management tool, significantly contribute to the acceptance of the new business processes and thereby directly to the success of a rollout. The end users are introduced to the changed processes at an early stage of the project. Ralph Beer, test coordinator and responsible for SAP Solution Manager Test Workbench, emphasizes:

"In the past, this 'awakening'—that is, the awareness of the new processes—often did not take place until six or eight weeks prior to the go-live during the final integration test. Thanks to the joint process tests, the feedback of the future end users is now already available six months before the go-live."

The high quality of the template project's Business Blueprint that was created during the project preparation was helpful in this context. The test cases that are available for the various test stages up to the joint process test were assigned to the respective business processes. Moreover, customer-specific attributes and keywords were used for the blueprint and the documents it contained. These enable the direct selection of test cases with regard to test stage and rollout country. Moreover, this procedure allowed for the identification of core business processes. They were used to generate a *business process master list* in the form of an Excel document. If projects are transferred to the transition phase to prepare a country rollout, the contact partners concerned can use this list to evaluate whether the listed processes are relevant, adaptations must be made, or whether the defined business requirements apply. The business process master list is used to further advance standardization. This list ensures transparency about which standard processes can be used directly in a country and which processes must be validated.

The test automation that was targeted in the first report in the environment of the *weBSH.net* project was implemented with great success. The automation of test cases using eCATT was presented by SAP Consulting in 2005, and its feasibility was confirmed using a prototype. These were the first steps toward automation of existing test cases. Subsequently, an employee of BSH started to create eCATT scripts, initially for the service area. The activities were expanded continuously. The test effort could be reduced by 40% for the entire project using eCATT.

Currently, the individual business areas are responsible for the use and scope of test automation. The implementation is done by a team of internal employees that was formed for test automation. This team includes three automation experts who create and maintain test scripts. The employees that currently advance the test automation in the factory environment do not work full time on this task. Nevertheless, the deployment of a dedicated automation team ensures the build-up of expert knowledge on test automation and automation tools; the small size of the team also enables effective sharing of experience.

Today, the focus of the existing test automation is on factories. The *weBSH.net* template project has been rolled out at 25 factories already. Primarily, eCATT scripts are used there for regression tests. In some cases, automation of up to 90% has been achieved already. Even at factories where test automation is still being developed, automation of 20% to 30% has been achieved, with an upward trend.

Degree of automation

An annual meeting of all test managers has proven to be successful as a control event to increase the efficiency of testing activities. During this meeting, the test automation strategy in particular is evaluated with regard to effort and cost savings. The results determined or successes presented at the meeting are essential for continuing the automation strategy and thus expanding the test automation. The results shown in the meeting also have the effect of convincing other business units of the benefit of test automation.

Determining the test and automation strategy

Currently, major changes are in the works for the system landscape of BSH also in the non-SAP environment: The entire development landscape and the associated IT systems are restructured. This engineering landscape is strongly concatenated with the SAP landscape on the process side. Therefore, there is keen interest in mapping the holistic processes coherently within a tool and testing them in this environment.

Tests in the non-SAP environment

Compared with the *weBSH.net* project, this plan seems to be less complex initially. Nevertheless, the total scope of the program is in the tens of millions of test steps.

In this environment, BSH wants to implement a consistent and holistic test process and achieve a high degree of test coverage. Both the SAP environment and the non-SAP environment are supposed to be covered optimally within the tests. Here as well, SAP Solution Manager is used as the central tool for supporting testing activities.

The established test process that is implemented with the Test Workbench can be deployed to map test cases for non-SAP systems or record their status and documentation. Outside the SAP environment, only some convenience functions, such as the automatic navigation to the target systems, are not available or available to a limited extent. This is not a problem, in the opinion of Norbert Liss:

"For us, the added value of test management in SAP Solution Manager is not to be found in the navigation to the target systems. This is a really nice feature, but the essential added value is in the complete test organization and in the evaluation, particularly in the immediately available feedback on where we are. This way, we have everything under control via a central system."

Test automation in the non-SAP environment

The deployment of eCATT with the integrated use of a third-party automation tool is being evaluated for the test automation of non-SAP applications and the web interfaces beyond Web Dynpro. This approach enables test automation in the portal and Windows environment, while keeping the fundamental benefits of eCATT, particularly the full integration with SAP Solution Manager (administration) as well as the use of system and test data containers. Moreover, for the current three-member test automation team, only three single user licenses are required for the external tool used in the procedure described.

Convincing the business departments

According to Norbert Liss, one fundamental challenge is to convince the business departments to use SAP Solution Manager also for processes that are not supported by SAP. But people need to be convinced in every new project, says Ralph Beer. Irrespective of the tool used, the implementation of a new procedure must be explained to the business departments. Matters are complicated further by the fact that contacts change with every project, and the new ones need to be convinced yet again. Here as well, the access via the work center is considered a strong acceptance criterion for SAP Solution Manager.

Standardization of the test process

Another key criterion for using SAP Solution Manager in other projects is the higher transparency that has been achieved in previous projects. Thanks to the consistent use of SAP Solution Manager in the environment of country rollouts, it was possible to significantly increase the degree of standardization of test processes at BSH. This leads to a high quality of test implementation and reporting. The consolidation process mentioned in the first report has thus been effectively advanced.

Regression tests

The regression testing of systems that are already used in production provide evidence of the success of standardizing the test procedure via a central control of the software quality assurance. BSH's system landscape that is used in production has a high change frequency, which requires comprehensive regression tests. BSH uses a release management solution to implement system changes in a controlled manner. A full release has a size of approximately 15,000 transports, of which 10,000 to 12,000 transports are transferred to the target system at the time of the release. Within the scope of release cycles, regression tests are implemented three times a year at 36 locations (test units) of BSH in Europe. The tests each have a scope of approximately 16,000 individual test steps, which cover 700 standard processes and additional country-specific processes. Corresponding test plans can be created with little effort via the already existing process structures and test cases within SAP Solution Manager. For each release, three weeks are scheduled for the regression test phase. About 300 testers are involved at 36 locations during this period.

Conclusion

Norbert Liss believes that the structured test procedure within the scope of *weBSH.net* and the projects based on *weBSH.net* will ensure the success of BSH's biggest SAP rollout project so far. This success model has been continuously optimized, standardized, and provided in this advanced form to other SAP projects within the enterprise. Preparation of the various process tests can be implemented quickly via the convenience functions of the Test Workbench (test plan generation along the business processes and/or use of filters) as was true for the many test cases mentioned earlier. The assignment of testers to test cases and the process-oriented control of the test sequence enable reproducible and efficient work within the test implementation. The test flow can be monitored in real time via status monitoring, so the architecture and quality management of BSH are always important. Furthermore, the reporting of SAP Solution Manager fully meets the requirements of external auditors; the automatically generated test report provides a comprehensive status of all test results.

What additional lessons can you learn from the experience of BSH?   Lessons learned

▸ The deployment of SAP Solution Manager within rollout projects can effectively support the cross-country standardization via special template functionality.

▸ If the basic functionality of test management within SAP Solution Manager has been used, new functions (for instance, work center, test case sequences, or Business Process Change Analyzer) can be evaluated within projects and often be implemented with little effort.

- The deployment of work centers of SAP Solution Manager increases acceptance among software testers also in the non-SAP environment.

- Using user-specific attributes and keywords makes in simple to group test cases purposefully and thus accelerate the creation of test plans by using filters.

- Regular feedback loops can improve the effectiveness and the efficiency of test processes or the use of tools based on experience.

- The continuous evaluation of saving effects of test automation shows stakeholders on a fact basis which benefit the automated test approach has.

- A manageable, dedicated test-automation team enables learning about automation procedure and test automation tools within the company and allows for efficient implementation of test automation.

- Documentation and reporting functions of SAP Solution Manager meet the requirements of external auditors.

4.12 Customer Report by Reno Fashion & Shoes GmbH

> **Note**
>
> This customer report originates from the first edition of this book. Following the original chapter, you can find a sustainability report that describes the long-term effects of methods, tool use, and consulting support, as well as current developments or projects of the customer.

"To us, SAP Solution Manager represents a milestone in test management. The storage of test cases in the project and process structures essentially facilitates the preparation of a test project."

Roland Gartzky
Head of SAP Service Reno Fashion & Shoes GmbH

Reno Fashion & Shoes GmbH — With an annual turnover of approximately 20 million pairs of shoes, Reno Fashion & Shoes GmbH is a big player in the shoe industry. Since its founding as Reno Versandhandel GmbH in 1977, the company has undergone continuous development. In its early years, the company positioned itself in the market based on price. Since 1999, the company has focused on a strategic redirection towards becoming a fashion trend-setter.

The result of this change in strategies was rapid growth. Today, Reno's annual revenues add up to approximately €400 million, and the company has more than 5,000 employees in about 700 branch stores. New stores have recently been opened in the Baltic countries, the Ukraine, and Iran.

The company uses a central IT structure with in-house consultants and in-house developers working together. In this structure, knowledge is bundled and people can collaborate without the obstacle of long distances.

IT organization

As a retailer, Reno increasingly uses the SAP for Retail application. The current version of this SAP system handles daily processes of approximately 120,000 deliveries, 280,000 material movements, and 110,000 data records in invoicing. Reno's entire IT area employs approximately 50 employees: 30 in the basic IT area (hardware/cash balancing) and 20 in the SAP service area.

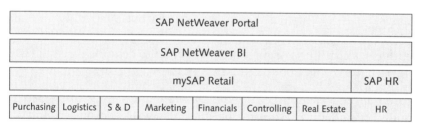

Figure 4.56 The Future Structure of the SAP Applications in the Reno Solution Landscape

The analysis of sales data provided by the SAP system is of strategic importance at Reno. Data is available for each Reno article, for example at what price and how often it has been sold in a given period. These details provide information on the prices that are possible in the market.

The SAP Test Workbench was used for the first time in 2001 in the context of an implementation project for SAP R/3 Retail 4.6C. At that time, the focus was on two aspects. The testing activities were carried out manually

Implementation project

and were managed within the Test Organizer. CATT scripts were used to migrate datasets, but not for testing purposes. The implementation of the SAP Test Workbench including CATT was already supported by SAP Test Management Consulting.

Roland Gartzky, Head of SAP Service, explains the reasons for implementing the Test Workbench:

> *"In the past, the test structure was managed in different tools: Access, Excel, MS Project, and various printouts in-between. This method contained several disadvantages; for instance it wasn't possible to carry out a search across different media. That's why we were looking for a consistent and central platform."*

eCATT implementation

The decision to use eCATT for the automation of regression tests at Reno was made during a workshop with SAP Test Management Consulting. During the course of this workshop, the functions, application scenarios, and benefit potentials were discussed. eCATT was implemented in the context of a support-package implementation. The building up of knowledge and the creation of scripts were defined as a separate subproject. After that, the implementation of a partly automated test process began. The test automation that was used for the first time in the context of a support package implementation was carried out internally by Reno. SAP Consulting provided support only with regard to specific issues. For example, a coaching session was held in order to describe the use of the SAPGUI driver and of the MESSAGE ... ENDMESSAGE command.

Cost-saving effects

Based on his experience with previous support package implementations, Roland Gartzky estimates the effort involved in a manual execution of this regression test to be approximately 200 full-time equivalents (person days). Due to the use of the new, partly automated test process, the entire test could be executed with approximately 95 full-time equivalents, a reduction which corresponds to cost savings of more than 50%. At the same time, the original project duration of three months could be reduced to approximately eight weeks. This was possible despite the simultaneous enhancement of the coverage and an increase in the complexity of the tests.

The migration to SAP Solution Manager was carried out in the context of a BI upgrade project after Roland Gartzky had visited a DSAG workshop on testing initiated by SAP Test Management Consulting in September 2005:

> *"During the course of this workshop I got a clear inspiration from the different speeches and system demos."*

The use of this integrated application management platform made it possible to organize central management of all business process-oriented test processes as the handling of the test case management was once again improved. The core of the new test management with SAP Solution Manager is the integration of all relevant project documents in the central project structure. In contrast to way test catalogs are used in the classical SAP Test Organizer, the storage of the test cases is not sorted by modules. Instead, the test cases are directly assigned to the individual process steps.

SAP Solution Manager

In practice, this new test case management philosophy provides several advantages. The most obvious aspect is that the generation of test plans takes much less time. Because integration tests are intended to check business processes as completely as possible, the test plans must reflect the process structures. For example, a regression test checks all business processes that may have been affected by a change. Because of the process-oriented storage of the test cases, one merely has to select the affected processes in order to generate the test plan. Thus the labor-intensive selection and combination of the relevant test cases from the test catalog is a matter of the past.

One of the current problems of managing test cases is the mapping of dependencies. If the integration test of a business process runs across several modules or solutions, the responsible processor or tester usually changes as well. Roland Gartzky:

Mapping dependencies between test cases

> *"In general, the support of integration tests works well. However, at this point it would be desirable to include dependencies between the test cases when compiling the test plans."*

Note by the Authors

The support of test sequences and mail notifications based on these have been implemented in the meantime and have been available as of SAP Solution Manager 7.0 SP15 (see Section 4.4.4, *Creating Test Plans and Test Packages*).

As this option has not been available up to this point, Reno decided to use the following method: The processes were not divided into person-specific test packages; a test package was created for each process, and all testers involved in the process were assigned to the test package. This way, the testers had an overview of the entire process and were able to monitor its progress. The assignment of the individual test cases to the testers was carried out outside of SAP Solution Manager. Although this method does not represent the SAP Best Practice, it has proven successful for Reno. The testers were primarily in-house consultants. Only for process changes were the test and the approval carried out by the user departments.

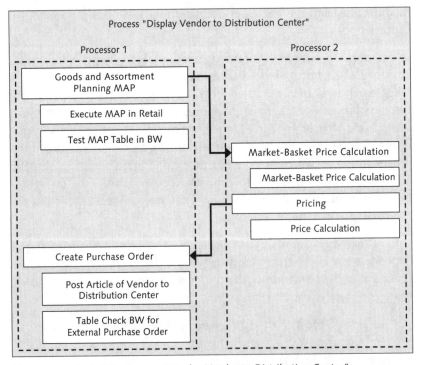

Figure 4.57 Part of the Process "Display Vendor to Distribution Center"

Integration with
SAP Service Desk

In addition to using the Test Organizer in SAP Solution Manager, Reno also used the Service Desk. The most important argument in favor of using SAP Service Desk during the tests was its fast and easy application by the user departments and the IT department. This user-friendliness enabled a swift and straightforward return of problem messages and thus provides immediate test results. Due to the structured recording of problem messages, these messages could be further processed with less effort despite a significant total number of messages that had to be processed.

The Service Desk implementation was supported by a consultant of SAP Test Management Consulting. A mixture of learning-by-doing, specific involvement of the consultants, and access to information provided by SAP Service Marketplace enabled the team to generate considerable benefits from the use of Service Desk with relatively little effort.

The approach of implementing different use cases of SAP Solution Manager one after the other and thus exploiting the benefit potentials step-by-step has proven itself. It is likely to be continued in the future.

Step-by-step realization of benefits

This gradual implementation smooths out the training requirements for users for a specific functionality and increases the acceptance of the tool, as users are not overstrained at the start by the new processes and organizational models of the tool. Roland Gartzky recommends this method to all customers:

> *"SAP Solution Manager is a platform with an extensive range of options, from test management and solution monitoring to change management and support desk, to knowledge management and service delivery. It is the nature of such an application management solution to touch many different subject areas. To implement such a broad range of functionalities all at once does not seem to me to be the right way. I would recommend that each customer first focus on those subject areas that provide the biggest short-term benefits to them. If success becomes obvious, the willingness to perform additional steps will definitely rise."*

That's exactly what Reno does. For the near future, the company plans a complete rollout to extend the Service Desk with the functions that haven't been used until now. Subsequent steps will then integrate change management and completely map the transport landscape. Moreover, they plan to use Business Process Monitoring in the future as well.

In the context of the implementation project for SAP Retail in 2001, Reno could already gather experience in using CATT. However, at that time the Computer Aided Test Tool was not used for testing purposes, but as a tool for migrating datasets as well as for data maintenance purposes.

eCATT and migration of CATT scripts

During implementation of SAP Solution Manager, Reno also intended to automate test cases. Again, Roland Gartzky decided to use the tried-and-trusted iterative method. Instead of implementing the complete automation of all business processes right away, Reno uses SAP Solution Manager in order to seamlessly link automated test cases with manual tests. For this purpose, the company also decided to use eCATT, which is available in SAP Solution Manager, as the automation tool. Existing CATT scripts that could be used in the context of automation were processed by the migration function of eCATT so that they could be used in higher releases. Based on the existing manual test cases suitable process steps were selected for the automation project, and individual business transactions were used by eCATT scripts in the context of those processes.

Transition from manual to automated testing
This method enabled Reno to carry out the transition from manual to automated testing step by step. While doing this, the company always kept an eye on the financial side of the test project, in that the initial costs of the automation were always weighed against the constant costs of manual tests. The result was a partly automated test process that enables an end-to-end coverage at considerably decreased costs. The eligible candidates for automation were primarily test cases that involved a high degree of manual testing effort and comprehensive requirements regarding the accuracy of the tests. The automation was not implemented just for the sake of it.

Roland Gartzky considers the greatest advantage of using eCATT to be the ability to automatically test a large number of variants. Today it is possible to test many different combinations by combining test data and scripts into variants. The testing of all defined variants of the different kinds and types of articles in conjunction with all sales structures improved test coverage significantly. Roland Gartzky regards the influence on the application stability as absolutely positive:

> *"The automated tests make me feel safe so that I can sleep much better at night even if complex changes have been made. Due to the automation via eCATT, we are able to cover many different combinations: all different product variants in all conceivable combinations. You cannot achieve this coverage with manual tests unless you are willing to accept a huge amount of effort."*

In addition, tests were carried out in the BW environment, in which eCATT scripts were used to perform comparisons at document level and to check the data transfer for correctness.

Conclusion

By using SAP Solution Manager, test management was successfully migrated to a central, process-oriented administration that was also integrated with other functions. In contrast to manual tests, a partly automated integration test enables much more comprehensive test coverage with reduced testing efforts and improved monitoring options. Reno also considers an increase in application stability to be the result of this established test process. Because of the seamless combination of manual and automated test cases in SAP Solution Manager, the test management of this mixed approach is smooth and efficient.

From the point of view of IT, Reno is not concerned about a further expansion of the company and it plans to further extend its use of SAP Solution Manager to the Service Desk, change request management, and transport management areas. SAP Solution Manager can support the roll out of established solutions to other enterprise divisions in many ways.

What can you learn from the experience of Reno?   Lessons learned

► An iterative approach smooths out problems and creates acceptance. Start with small steps, and exploit the benefit potentials step-by-step.

► When implementing new tools, you must also check, adapt, and once again roll out processes and organizational models.

► The automation of tests need not always be comprehensive and shouldn't be done just for the sake of it. The automated test cases must be able to either reduce short-term testing costs or to increase the application stability. You should use the option to store and manage manual and automated test cases in a process-oriented way in SAP Solution Manager in order to implement a partly automated process of integration and regression tests.

► Introduce new tools in real projects that can be considered pilot projects. This facilitates budgeting and boosts acceptance for later use in the operation.

4.13 Update of the Customer Report by Hamm-Reno-Group GmbH & Co. KG

Hamm-Reno-Group

The year 2005 presented a practical test for the established test management processes of the enterprise: Reno Fashion & Shoes GmbH merged with Wilhelm Hamm GmbH & Co. KG to form Hamm-Reno-Group GmbH & Co. KG. Today, the two enterprises operate in the Hamm-Reno-Group (HR Group). The holding looks back on about 120 years of tradition and has comprehensive expertise in the shoe industry. HR Group is one of the leading shoe enterprises in Europe.

Today, the group has a workforce of approximately 6,000 and sells about 40 million pairs of shoes, textiles, and accessories in more than 20 countries. The sales channels range from retail to specialized trade to wholesale. In addition to Reno stores, the products of Hamm-Reno-Group are also available in selected department stores.

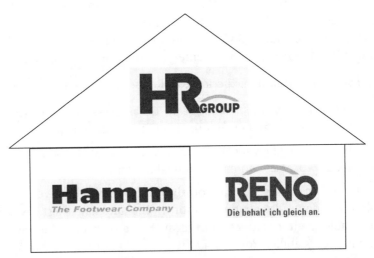

Figure 4.58 Hamm-Reno-Group (HR Group)

IT organization

The merger of the two enterprises presented major challenges for the IT organization. Their basic structure hasn't changed; furthermore the group relies on a central IT area to bundle the know-how of developers and in-house consultants and enable an efficient exchange of information.

To continue to ensure Reno's known flexibility to quickly and versatilely respond to market and customer requirements, the processes of the two companies had to be harmonized as fast as possible. The former Wilhelm Hamm GmbH & Co. KG changed from Microsoft Navision to the SAP solutions which were already used at Reno Fashion & Shoes GmbH. It was therefore necessary to map all goods processes of the company in the existing SAP systems of Reno Fashion & Shoes GmbH. For this purpose, both companies used a client. The transfer or adaptation of the processes involved a considerable growth of the process and system complexity. In October 2008, the SAP solution, Global Trade Services, was implemented in a parallel project within the scope of the merger in addition to the already existing retail processes. Overall, the following business models were updated or mapped completely anew in the SAP for Retail application used.

Mapping of new goods processes

- ▶ Retail based on stores
- ▶ Concession
- ▶ Wholesale
- ▶ Online retailing
- ▶ Franchising

The procedure presented in the first customer report for the test environment using SAP Solution Manager in combination with the Test Workbench—deployed in an SAP NetWeaver BW upgrade project for the first time—has proven itself. Like the use of eCATT for automating test cases, this procedure for using the tools for document and test management of SAP Solution Manager has continuously been optimized. The tools are now also used in other projects. The basic test process has proven as very reliable and therefore required only minor adaptations.

Proven procedure

In the environment of project implementation and test management, projects are used in SAP Solution Manager that define the process structure of the enterprise as a Business Blueprint. The current version of the Business Blueprint maps all new goods processes that must be considered within the scope of the merger. The Business Blueprint also includes the subdivision of the different business models.

SAP Solution Manager

Moreover, the IT projects rely on saving all project documentations, including the process descriptions and test cases, in SAP Solution Manager using the integrated document management. Roland Gartzky, Head of SAP Service Hamm-Reno-Group, emphasizes that using SAP Solution Manager for project documentation and implementation significantly contributes to the process safety and project success. Moreover, the structure of the Business Blueprint allows for a simple mapping of complex processes and thus creates an overview of all processes in a project including the relevant documents. The business process structure is maintained by the respective project lead; more extensive changes to the business blueprint are developed in workshops. This procedure ensures high stability of the structures mapped in SAP Solution Manager.

Test Process Under these conditions, the process-oriented implementation of regression tests has become a securely established procedure for any system changes. The Business Blueprint, which is always kept up-to-date, as well as the use of corresponding document attributes enable the selection of tests based on the business model, process, and test level. Roland Gartzky regards the test plans that are created this way as valuable constructs because they allow for the implementation of test measures in the context of the respective process chains and enable readily available progress control on the basis of the actually executed business processes.

Provided that test plans with such a structure are used consistently and holistically, these contribute to the structuring of testing activities and thus clarity. This particularly applies to the status monitoring of running test measures and reporting. At Hamm-Reno-Group, the test plans are used as the smallest units of test reporting, which can be analyzed individually or through multiple selection for individual projects.

End-to-end integration test The present procedure for assigning testers to test cases was kept: All participating employees are still assigned to an end-to-end business process, even if the process occasionally involves different business departments. But because in-house consultants of the IT organization are primarily used as testers, this variant is easy to implement in real life. The immediate assignment of testers to individual test cases is made organizationally. Thanks to the short distances within the central IT organization, the respective testers usually cooperate closely. As soon as a tester has completed the test cases within a business process, he or she notifies his or her successor. Consistent documentation of test cases, particularly the reproducibility of the information "which user has tested which test case with which result," can already be reproduced with the on-board means of the Test Workbench and can be called in the form of various reports.

Even though the procedure presented has proven itself and has been used successfully for four years, Roland Gartzky still sees optimization potential and has therefore instructed his team to evaluate the new Test Case Sequences function. The functionality which is frequently requested by customers is available as of Service Pack 15 of SAP Solution Manager 7.0.

The functioning of the sequence control works very well with the previously described scenario and also enables the implementation of the dependencies between test cases required in the first customer report. The customer can now specify the execution sequence of test cases within a test package. Moreover, a separate tester can be assigned to every test case, depending on the respective business department. Combined with the selection of specific test statuses, this also enables the definition of dependencies. As a result, the test team of Hamm-Reno-Group can clearly control responsibilities: A test case downstream in the process chain can only be executed if all previous test cases have been run with a positive result. Particularly the option to notify testers via email as soon as they can start executing their test cases is a highly valuable option for Roland Gartzky for optimizing coordination of testing activities and further accelerating the test implementation.

Test case sequences and dependencies

An initial pilot test for using the sequence control had positive results. In accordance with the proven policy of implementing new functions iteratively, the group currently plans the implementation of test case sequences for the next regression tests.

The automation of test cases has continuously advanced. The previous procedure was intended to focus on partial automation, in which manual and automatic test cases were linked within the scope of the test execution. Taking into account the cost-benefit ratio, the most promising test cases were successively automated. As a result, completely automated executable integration test cases were developed gradually. The benefit of this procedure is that the test automation could be advanced with low effort and without involving external consultants or automation experts. After the initial coaching by SAP Test Management Consulting, the group performed all subsequent steps independently and without external support.

Test automation

This procedure also revealed its strengths in the merger with Wilhelm Hamm GmbH & Co. KG. In the course of the merger, numerous new manual test cases emerged that were developed for new as well as for adapted existing processes. The new manual test cases were gradually converted into automated test cases according to the already established procedure using eCATT. As a result, the test automation could be expanded, and the degree of automation was continuously increased. A total of 393 process test cases were run for the merger of the two companies; about 10% of the test cases, which usually contain multiple variants and varying test data, are completely automated. Some of the approximately 40 test cases originate from the already established regression test set of the former Reno Fashion & Shoes GmbH and these check its critical core business processes, including the integration of SAP NetWeaver Business Warehouse. These test scripts were adapted non-recurrently for the testing activities related to the company merger.

The newly implemented business processes of the former Wilhelm Hamm GmbH & Co. KG used to be tested mainly manually; by contrast, the execution of the automated test cases allowed for a quick statement whether the previous processes were impaired by the system changes. Because both parts of the company work in one client, this check was particularly valuable within the testing activities. Thanks to the existing automation, this non-negative impact test could be run quickly and with little effort for the processes of former Reno Fashion & Shoes GmbH. Overall, the test phase for the project took about four weeks; the automatic test cases were executed in parallel to the manual test cases within one week.

In future, it is planned to expand the test automation and use the test cases for the implementation of support packages that used to be run once a year. Due to the lower test effort, it is intended to increase the frequency of implementations.

Conclusion

The procedures implemented in 2004 in the areas of test administration and test automation also supported the merger of Hamm-Reno-Group. Using the proven procedures for process documentation, test planning and implementation, the test management was able to successfully ensure the implementation of new business models and thus numerous new business processes. The tried-and-trusted principle of partly automating individual business cases based on economic aspects was also deployed for the new processes.

What can you learn from the experience of Hamm-Reno-Group? | Lessons learned

- ▶ Proven procedures and process models offer planning and implementation security also for comprehensive change events, such as a company merger.

- ▶ A stable test process and iterative optimizations enable the realization of benefit potentials in daily operation with low risk.

- ▶ The pragmatic approach to advanced automation of test cases gradually enables users to get familiar with test automation. The selection of suitable test cases leads to a quick ROI for test automation within the framework of this procedure; such an approach can basically also be implemented without external consultants.

This chapter provides an overview of how to use SAP Quality Center by HP as a tool for planning, managing, and executing testing in projects that are documented and implemented using SAP Solution Manager. The SAP Solution Manager Adapter for SAP Quality Center by HP is used in this context. The description of the functions presented here is based on the typical progression of a project implementation.

5 Project-Related Testing with SAP Solution Manager and SAP Quality Center by HP

The use of the SAP Quality Center by HP quality assurance suite is referred to here as "Testing Option 2" in accordance with the classification described in Chapter 4, *Test Management with SAP Solution Manager*. Once again, the Business Blueprint of SAP Solution Manager and selected documents contained in that Business Blueprint provide the foundation for test planning and execution. In this scenario, SAP Quality Center by HP is used for test management. It receives the relevant requirements documents and test objects from SAP Solution Manager via the SAP Solution Manager Adapter for SAP Quality Center. In Testing Option 2, SAP Quality Center by HP is used for test case creation, test execution, reporting, and defect management as components of the testing process. The adapter also transfers test results to SAP Solution Manager and synchronizes selected error messages.

Testing Option 2

Beyond test management and the planning and execution of manual functional test cases, Testing Option 2 also enables the use of HP QuickTest Professional as a test automation tool. Based on the methodology of "Business Process Testing," which is implemented in SAP Quality Center by HP and on the use of HP QuickTest Professional, SAP Test Acceleration and Optimization (SAP TAO) can also be used as an innovative tool for component-based creation of automated test cases.

Following an overview of SAP Quality Center by HP and its connection to SAP Solution Manager, which uses the adapter provided by SAP as a price-list component, this section discusses project-based testing using SAP Quality Center by HP as a test management tool. The focus here is on explaining the basic procedure used and highlighting the differences that arise when this tool is used. When discussing the testing procedure, we distinguish between the specific functions that correspond to those of the Test Workbench and those that differ essentially from its functional scope. Particular attention is paid to functional scope, technology, and the concept of requirements-based testing. We avoid entering into a detailed discussion of all functions and, in particular, of those that go beyond the testing process described here. Instead, we refer you to the extensive documentation provided by the manufacturers of the relevant products.

5.1   SAP Quality Center by HP

SAP Quality Center by HP is a web-based application that enables vendor-independent planning, management, and execution of the testing of key activities as part of quality assurance. For SAP projects, the most relevant functions of the application are the management of requirements, central storage of test cases, planning and execution of test cycles, defect management, and reporting.

HP Quality Center editions

HP Quality Center is essentially based on the Test Director for Quality Center, originally developed by the software provider Mercury, which was taken over by HP in November 2006. HP offers the current version of the Quality Center (Version 10.0) as Starter Edition, Enterprise Edition, and Premier Edition, each of which is aimed at a different target group.

HP Quality Center Starter Edition is aimed at relatively small teams and quality assurance projects. The Starter Edition has a reduced functional scope and can be used by no more than five users simultaneously.

The Enterprise Edition is geared towards enterprises with medium-sized or large quality assurance projects. This edition has by far the largest target group and is available from SAP as a price-list component called *SAP Quality Center by HP Enterprise Edition* under the terms of a reseller agreement.

The Premier Edition is aimed primarily at large corporations. It offers extended functions for cross-project and cross-initiative tasks for software quality assurance. Its distinguishing features include options to import, synchronize, and compare objects (for example, requirements and test cases) across several projects. In addition, error messages can be shared across projects and synchronized between different projects. The Premier Edition also allows cross-project reporting, which enables the combination and comparison of values from various projects. In addition, template projects allow you to distribute configuration settings among projects based on templates. HP Quality Center Premier Edition is also available from SAP as the price-list component *SAP Quality Center by HP Premier Edition*.

For the last two versions specified above, SAP offers Business Process Testing functionality, which is required in order to support test automation projects with SAP TAO. This functionality, which is subject to a license fee, enables component-based creation of test cases.

SAP Quality Center by HP includes a range of integrated modules for essential quality assurance tasks (note: the discussion below is largely based on the Enterprise Edition):

Functional Scope of SAP Quality Center by HP

▶ **Management**
Definition and management of releases and development cycles; creation of libraries and "baselines" in order to bring together test-relevant elements and compare these over the course of the project

▶ **Requirements Management**
Specification and management of requirements

▶ **Business Components**
Methodology for creating reusable test components for business process testing

▶ **Test Plan**
Creation and management of manual and automated test cases

▶ **Test Resources**
Central administration of additional resources such as those used by test automation tools

▶ **Test Lab**
Creation of test cycles, test planning and execution

▶ **Defect Management**
Management of error messages

▶ **Dashboard**
Library of user-defined analyses; creation of reports, including graphics, based on user-defined analyses

In the Requirements, Business Components, Test Plan, Test Lab, and Defects modules, a wide range of standard analyses are available in the form of graphics and detailed reports. User-defined reports can be created in the individual modules or from the Dashboard module. New charts and reports also can be created manually in the Dashboard.

Integration of HP QuickTest Professional
HP QuickTest Professional also can be integrated as a tool for automated functional testing, whereby automatic test scripts can be linked directly with the relevant test cases. HP QuickTest Professional has various plug-ins to support diverse protocols and user interfaces.

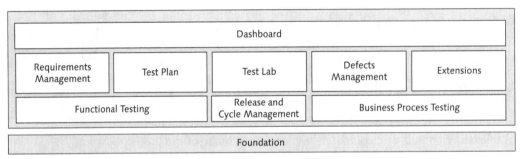

Figure 5.1 Structure of SAP Quality Center by HP

Requirements-based and risk-based testing
The design of SAP Quality Center by HP supports requirements-based and risk-based testing. The software can map the linking and comparison of business requirements to test results. These elements are of central importance when using the adapter in conjunction with SAP Quality Center within the application lifecycle that is managed in SAP Solution Manager. SAP Quality Center by HP also supports risk analyses of test cycles and effort estimates based on these.

Technical platform
Technically speaking, SAP Quality Center by HP is based on a web server with Java technology. Administrative and project-specific data are stored in an Oracle or Microsoft SQL Server database. Users access the application with a web browser. An authorization concept is available at project level.

5.2 SAP Solution Manager Adapter for SAP Quality Center by HP

The integration of SAP Solution Manager and SAP Quality Center by HP requires an adapter, which is provided by SAP as a price-list component. The SAP Solution Manager Adapter for SAP Quality Center by HP enables the use of SAP Quality Center by HP in place of the integrated test tools in SAP Solution Manager (see Figure 5.2). Data that is relevant for testing is sent to the Quality Center, while test results and error messages are returned to SAP Solution Manager.

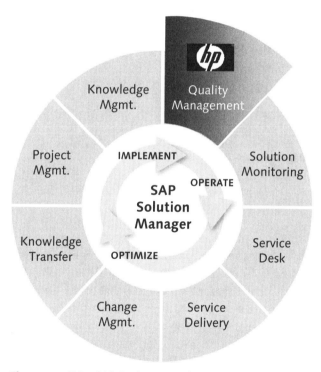

Figure 5.2 Using SAP Quality Center by HP in the Application Lifecycle

The core element of the adapter is the ability to transfer the Business Blueprint structure of an SAP Solution Manager project, together with requirements documents and test objects that are relevant for testing, to SAP Quality Center by HP. There, all test cases can be developed and the

Basic functioning of the adapter

corresponding testing activities planned, executed, and evaluated. The results of testing are sent back to SAP Solution Manager, as are selected error messages. Figure 5.3 provides an overview of the elements that are transferred by the adapter. The data transfer can be started manually from both tools or can be executed on a regular basis using background processing. In the standard configuration, the data in SAP Quality Center by HP is updated and selected test results returned on an hourly basis.

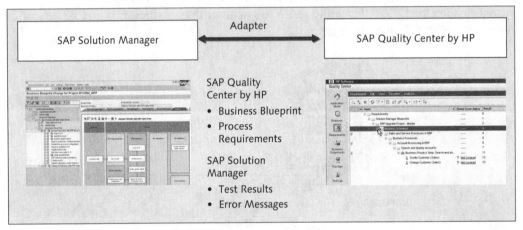

Figure 5.3 Data Exchange Using the SAP Solution Manager Adapter for SAP Quality Center by HP

Separation of project and test management

Using different tools to separate project management from test management also can help you divide the organization of these two management areas. This may be useful, for example, if a QA team is already using HP Quality Center and wants to continue using the tool that is familiar to its members for SAP projects. In terms of requirements-based testing, this feature of the design also separates the definition and management of requirements from the creation of test cases based on these requirements. Requirements can be defined in SAP Solution Manager. In addition, further requirements also can be created on the basis of the documents sent to SAP Quality Center by HP. However, thanks to the tests results that are transferred to SAP Solution Manager, project managers always have a clear overview of the status of testing as it relates to business-process requirements.

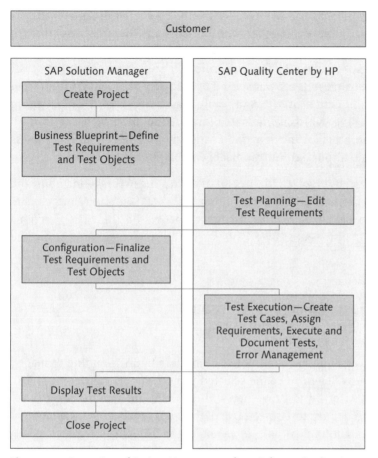

Figure 5.4 Separation of Project Management from Software Quality Assurance

Figure 5.4 shows a typical scenario, where SAP Quality Center by HP is used as a test management tool within an SAP Solution Manager project. The current version of the adapter supports implementation projects. SAP Solution Manager is used, for example, to document business processes in the form of a Business Blueprint as part of an implementation or upgrade project, as well as in live solutions. The (delta) configurations of the relevant systems continue to be documented and executed in the Business Blueprint. Using the adapter gives you the additional option within the Business Blueprint of defining objects already saved in a project (for example, process documentation, configuration objects, or development objects) as requirements documents and descriptions of the test objects for SAP Quality Center by HP. The adapter transfers the selected objects, together with the Business Blueprint structure, to SAP Quality Center by HP, where they can then be used to create test cases, thereby laying the foundation for the subsequent testing process. Similarly, test results are transferred back to SAP Solution Manager from SAP Quality Center by HP. As a result, a customer who is already using BW Reporting, which is integrated into SAP Solution Manager, to track project progress for incident and change management and for business KPIs, could also use it for test management reporting.

The main steps involved in this part of the testing process—including the essential preparations and integration with SAP Solution Manager—are described below. Here, the discussion focuses on the basic functions of SAP Quality Center by HP, its strengths, and integration using the adapter.

5.3   Test Management in the SAP Quality Center by HP

Once the essential preconditions are in place in SAP Solution Manager, the Business Blueprint of the selected project can be transferred to SAP Quality Center by HP, together with the relevant requirements documents and defined test objects. All of the steps involved in test planning, execution, and evaluation then take place in SAP Quality Center by HP. Members of the software QA team can use Internet Explorer to access the Quality Center and the relevant projects. Within SAP Quality Center by HP, users have access to modules covering a range of tasks that arise during testing. These are described below as they would work in a project-based testing process.

5.3.1   Creating a Project and Process Structure in SAP Solution Manager

If you want to use the SAP Solution Manager Adapter for SAP Quality Center by HP, a project with a Business Blueprint must first exist in SAP Solution Manager. This may be an existing project (for example, a project previously used to document the business processes and to customize the target systems as part of an implementation project) or a project that you create with the relevant business process structure as part of the preparations for testing. In both cases, the procedure follows the same steps outlined in Section 4.4.1, *Creating a Project*, and Section 4.4.2, *Creating the Process Structure*. As described in those sections, you can use all of the functions available in SAP Solution Manager for creating the Business Blueprint structure and the documents and objects within that structure. These functions also include an option to create the Business Blueprint using the Business Process Repository or the Solution Documentation Assistant. Over the course of the project, you also can store all project-relevant documents and objects in the Business Blueprint; for example, documentation for business processes, configuration objects, or references to development objects.

If SAP TAO is used for test automation, you can also use the Business Process Change Analyzer in SAP Solution Manager to identify which test cases are affected by a change. In this situation, the technical bills of material (T-BOM) for the transactions or business processes that are to be analyzed must already have been generated in the Business Blueprint.

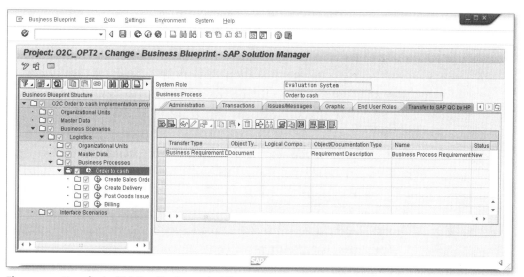

Figure 5.5 Transfer to SAP Quality Center by HP

The main difference between this option and Testing Option 1 in this phase is the use of the new TRANSFER TO SAP QC BY HP tab (see Figure 5.5). In order to implement the requirements-based testing con-

"Transfer to SAP QC by HP" tab

cept we described earlier, requirements and test objects can be added to the selected structure element of the Business Blueprint here (scenarios, business processes, and process steps). These refer to existing documents on the PROJECT DOCUMENTATION tab and objects that are to be tested (for example, transactions). New elements can be added in one of the following ways:

► **Assign objects as a test object**
This option allows you to add transactions and configuration/development objects as test objects on the relevant tab.

► **Assign documents as a business requirements document**
With this option, you add documents from the PROJECT DOCUMENTA- TION tab as requirements documents. In attribute maintenance for the individual documents, you subsequently can define test objects that are referenced in the document, for example.

These objects and documents provide the essential data required to create test cases in SAP Quality Center by HP. The TEST CASES tab is normally not used in Testing Option 2 and can be hidden in the project administration settings in SAP Solution Manager.

Once you have added the requirements documents and test objects to the Business Blueprint, it can be transferred to SAP Quality Center by HP. The relevant communication data can be defined for each project in project administration (Transaction SOLAR_PROJECT_ADMIN) under EDIT • CONNECTION TO HP QUALITY CENTER (see Figure 5.6). This data includes:

► A URL, which you select as a reference to a specific SAP Quality Center by HP installation; here, this is referred to as a logical port, and can be set up using the basic configuration of the adapter in customizing

► A communication user, which is a user of SAP Quality Center by HP that is to be used to execute changes; you can this specify this user in the customizing settings for the adapter or define it individually for each project

► The Quality Center project that is to be used to exchange the data, as well as the project domain in which the project was created

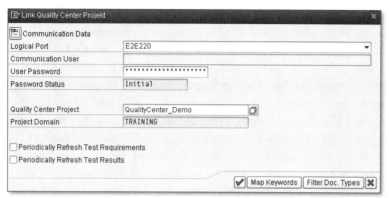

Figure 5.6 Linking an SAP Solution Manager Project with an SAP Quality Center by HP Project

You also can transfer the keywords defined in the project to SAP Quality Center by HP. To do this, use the MAP KEYWORDS option to import keywords from SAP Solution Manager into user-defined fields in SAP Quality Center by HP. You also can use the FILTER DOC. TYPES button to send selected document types to the Quality Center; if for example, you want to prevent the transfer of all documents to the structure nodes in SAP Quality Center by HP.

Data is synchronized either manually or on a regular automated basis using background jobs defined in the configuration. The above settings can be used to activate or deactivate periodic data updates. To start the manual transfer of the Business Blueprint, select the menu option BUSINESS BLUEPRINT • TRANSFER DATA TO QUALITY CENTER in the Business Blueprint transaction (SOLAR01) or the Configuration transaction (SOLAR02).

Data synchronization

5.3.2 Managing Requirements

In the REQUIREMENTS module of SAP Quality Center by HP, you begin by saving all of the requirements relating to the current project or the individual business processes. When you use the SAP Solution Manager Adapter for SAP Quality Center by HP, the Business Blueprint that is transferred from the linked SAP Solution Manager project is received by the REQUIREMENTS module. This module contains the documents and objects that were previously stored in the relevant structure element on the TRANSFER TO SAP QC BY HP tab (see Figure 5.7). Requirements documents are displayed here as "business requirements," while test objects are shown as "test requirements." It is also possible to create additional test requirements in SAP Quality Center by HP. This could mean, for example, that members of the software QA team could also formulate requirements for testing based on functional process requirements. These test requirements that are created directly in SAP Quality Center by HP are not taken into account during synchronization between the two test management tools in the adapter version described here.

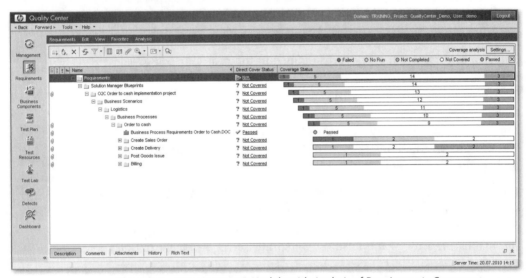

Figure 5.7 "Requirements" Module with Analysis of Requirements Coverage

In the next step, the test requirements are linked with test cases in order to implement the concept of requirements-based testing. You then can use reporting functionality to determine the coverage of requirements by individual tests in real time. The assignment of a requirement to a test case can be mapped as an *m:n* relationship. In other words, one test case may fulfill several requirements, while several test cases may be needed to fulfill a single requirement.

Evaluation of test coverage An option is provided for displaying test coverage next to each requirement. You can also view a detailed report of test coverage by selecting

ANALYSIS in the menu. Here you can view both the requirements coverage and the priority of each requirement (provided that this has been maintained) or the development of this coverage over time. In addition to graphical analyses, a selection of reports is also available; for example, requirements may be listed together with the corresponding test cases.

In the REQUIREMENTS module, you can also create empty test cases based on the requirements, which take account of the linkage specified above. A wizard is provided for this option in the context menu (see Figure 5.8).

Requirements-based creation of test cases

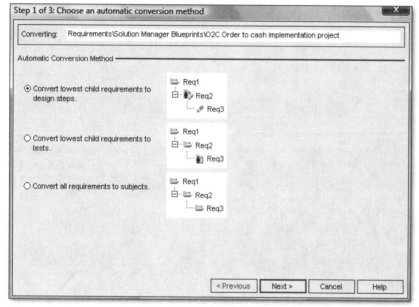

Figure 5.8   Creating Requirements-Based Empty Test Cases

In this module, you can double-click on a requirement to display its details and attributes and, in particular, references to the documents defined in SAP Solution Manager. You can then open the relevant document by clicking on the link provided. The following options for using additional functions of SAP Quality Center by HP are also provided:

Detailed display of requirements

▶ Add additional documents, URLs, screenshots or system information

▶ Assign releases or release cycles (note: you must be using the RELEASE MANAGEMENT module in Quality Center)

▶ Define dependencies between requirements
("requirements traceability")

▶ Assess the risks associated with requirements in the sense of
risk-based testing

Risk assessment
for requirements

If you use the risk assessment function (see Figure 5.9), you can define
risk information (criticality or failure probability) for each requirement.
Once this information is entered, the test level (full, partial, or basic tests
only) can be proposed on the basis of predefined rules. In addition, to
help you estimate the effort, the total testing time is calculated on the
basis of previously defined times for each level of criticality. You can also
have the results of this risk assessment process delivered in a report in
Microsoft Word format. You can edit the criteria, weightings, and estimated times on which the risk assessment is based in the configuration
of SAP Quality Center by HP.

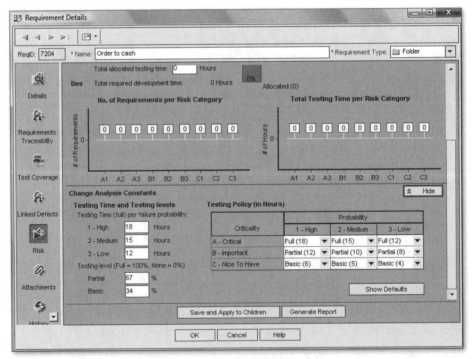

Figure 5.9 Risk Analysis in the "Requirements" Module

5.3.3 Creating Test Cases

Test cases can be created in a user-defined folder structure in the TEST PLAN module (see Figure 5.10), which is not to be confused with the test plan from the SAP Test Workbench in SAP Solution Manager. If the test cases were created using the wizard in the REQUIREMENTS module, the folder structure corresponds to the transferred Business Blueprint. As a result, the process structures created in the SAP Solution Manager project can be accessed here to facilitate the business process-oriented creation of test cases. Alternatively, you can maintain a separate folder structure or use existing structures. This has no effect on the linking of test cases with requirements.

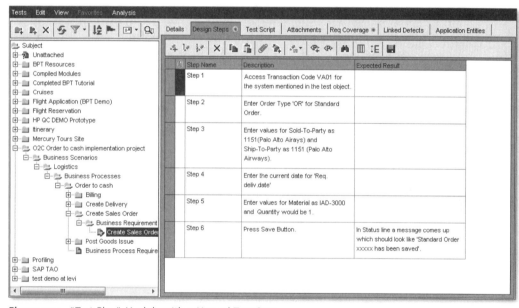

Figure 5.10 "Test Plan" Module with a Manual Test Case

A typical manual test case (DESIGN STEPS tab) in SAP Quality Center by HP is displayed as a list, comprising the individual test steps, each with a description of the activity involved and a description of the expected result. It is also possible to attach documents, such as detailed descriptions, screenshots, or test data, to the test or to individual test steps. As

Test case design

well as manual test cases, you can also create and manage automated test cases (for example, QuickTest Pro scripts or scenarios for SAP LoadRunner by HP). The test scripts of the automation tools that can be integrated are displayed on the TEST SCRIPT tab.

As in the REQUIREMENTS module, you also have the option here of linking requirements and test cases on the REQ COVERAGE tab.

Alternatively, you have the option of creating test cases based on components, using the Business Process Testing approach of SAP Quality Center by HP. The BUSINESS COMPONENTS module is used for this purpose in order to initially create individual modules, which subsequently serve to build a complete test case in the TEST PLAN module. By working with these reusable units, you can avoid the redundant description of actions that are used in more than one test case, such as system logon or material creation. This can speed up the creation of test cases because test case designers can access a library of existing components to use for the current project. This option also simplifies the maintenance of test cases, as changes are made to the modules directly and are copied to all test cases that use these components. Chapter 6 describes this method of test optimization for automated test cases using SAP TAO.

5.3.4 Test Planning and Execution

Test planning   Next, the TEST LAB module (see Figure 5.11) allows you to assemble test cases for individual test runs, assign these to testers, and execute them. Test runs are represented by a *test set*, which can contain any test cases from the TEST PLAN module. Test sets are put together using Drag & Drop, and are stored in a user-defined folder structure. The tests that are grouped together in this way are itemized on a list (EXECUTION GRID), where you can define additional information, such as the tester who is to execute the test and the date on which it is scheduled to be executed.

Test case sequences   On the EXECUTION FLOW tab, you can define the sequence in which tests are to be executed using a graphical editor. You can also define conditions (for example, test B must only be executed if test A is successful) and the time at which the test is to be executed.

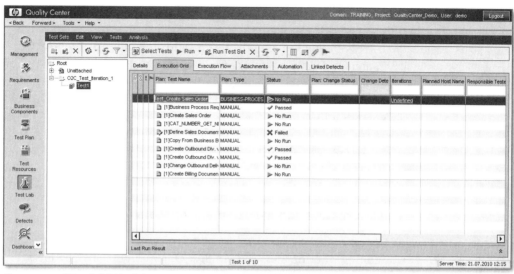

Figure 5.11 "Test Lab" Module

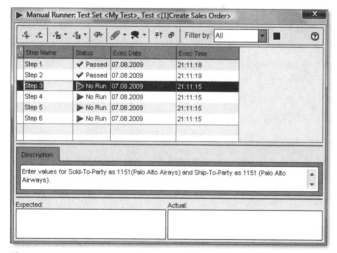

Figure 5.12 Executing a Manual Test

The testers are notified by email about when the testing activities are to start and can then begin to execute their assigned test cases. In a popup window called the MANUAL RUNNER, testers can display the individual steps in a manual test (see Figure 5.12), document the test steps, and evaluate the test result, for example by using document attachments and

Test execution

screenshots. Testers also can post error messages in the context of the current test case. Similarly, test automation scripts are executed using the corresponding tool and the test result is then returned to SAP Quality Center by HP. The information relating to all test runs is saved as documentation for test execution and provides a basis for reporting. The functions for manual test execution provide support for viewing and documenting test cases. However, support for test execution by means of a direct call-up of the test objects in the SAP environment (as has been implemented in the Test Workbench in SAP Solution Manager) is not currently possible.

5.3.5 Creating and Managing Error Messages

Defect
management

Another essential element of the testing process is the structured creation and editing of error messages. In SAP Quality Center by HP, messages for a module can be created in that module and linked with the relevant element, such as a requirement or test case. Error messages that are documented during the tests are displayed in the DEFECTS module (see Figure 5.13), and can be viewed by users with the relevant roles, such as developers. Status values can be used to map a troubleshooting process. Changes to an error message are saved in a history to ensure traceability. Other user-friendly functions include various filters, a search function for searching for texts in selected fields, a function for locating similar errors within a project (text search), and email notification.

Integration with
SAP Service Desk

As of SAP Solution Manager 7.0 EhP 1, you can use the SAP Solution Manager Adapter for SAP Quality Center by HP to synchronize messages between defect management in SAP Quality Center by HP and incident management in the Service Desk in SAP Solution Manager. As a result, error messages from SAP Quality Center by HP can be transferred to the Service Desk in order to benefit from its SAP-specific support options (for example, forwarding of the notification to SAP). You can also work in reverse and use the *Incident Management* work center, for example, to transfer messages that were originally created in SAP Solution Manager into SAP Quality Center by HP. This is important in cases where the central administration of all error messages in a project is to be managed centrally in the Quality Center.

In order to use this functionality, a one-off configuration in the customizing settings of SAP Solution Manager and SAP Quality Center is required.

In addition, you must use a function of the adapter in SAP Quality Center to synchronize the error messages of both systems (FIELD MAPPING).

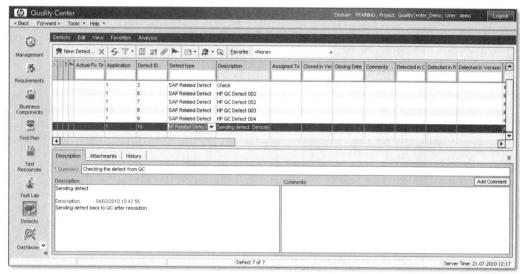

Figure 5.13 "Defects" Module

Error messages that are to be sent to the Service Desk can be classified as "SAP related defect" in SAP Quality Center. This classification controls the synchronization of selected messages with the Service Desk. Messages that are identified in this way have additional input fields, in which you can enter SAP-specific information, such as application component, system ID, and client.

Similarly, messages in the Service Desk of SAP Solution Manager can be sent to SAP Quality Center. This is achieved using the SEND SOLUTION TO EXTERNAL SERVICE DESK function (see Figure 5.14).

To prevent simultaneous editing of messages in both systems, one of the two message systems is identified as the "responsible system" for each message, so that this message can only be modified in this system. Responsibility for an error ticket can be actively requested or assigned. Messages that were deleted in SAP Quality Center are classified as "Deleted in HPQC" in SAP Solution Manager. Closed messages are displayed in both systems with the appropriate status.

Responsible system

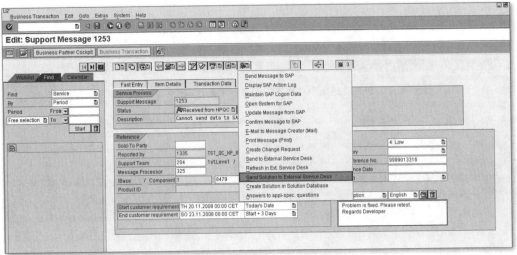

Figure 5.14 Forwarding a Service Desk Message to an External Service Desk

5.3.6 Versioning and Traceability

With Version 10.0 of SAP Quality Center by HP, various methods for object versioning and for ensuring the traceability of changes are available for the first time in the standard system.

Management Libraries can be created as collections of related objects (requirements, test cases, test resources, business components) in the MANAGEMENT module. A baseline can then be created from one of these libraries at a user-defined point in time, for example, to coincide with project milestones. A baseline represents a type of snapshot of the objects in the library. Baselines can be compared with one another or with the current version of the library, which allows you to keep track of changes to the objects in the library.

Versioning (version control) can be activated as an alternative or as an addition to this option. Versioning similarly applies to requirements, test cases, test resources, and business components. If versioning is activated, these objects must be checked in and checked out, and these actions are logged in a version history.

Both of these mechanisms are briefly described below, and can be used in combination with the testing procedure described in this chapter. This ensures that when SAP Solution Manager is used in combination with SAP Quality Center by HP, changes made in the Quality Center to objects that are relevant for testing can be traced and are transparent to users. The change and document history features in SAP Solution Manager can be used independently of these mechanisms.

The MANAGEMENT module contains two basic functions. The "Releases" function allows you to create releases and cycles for the applications that are to be tested. A release is defined as a group of changes to one or more applications, which are to be made available at the same time. A cycle is defined as a grouping of development and quality assurance tasks with a common objective within a release. Metadata, such as start and end dates, can be assigned to both elements. Requirements and test sets can be assigned to the individual releases and cycles. Similarly, error messages may contain information about the releases and cycles in which the error was found or in which the error is to be eliminated. Thanks to the concept of releases and cycles, you have many evaluation and checking options. This is true especially when it comes to testing and error elimination.

Release management

You can also call the LIBRARIES function from the MANAGEMENT module. Libraries and baselines can be created in a folder here, following the same principle. Libraries comprise objects, their contents, and the relationships between objects. The objects that can be grouped together in a library include the following:

Libraries

▶ Requirements

▶ Test cases

▶ Test resources

▶ Business components

When you create a library, you can select these objects from the relevant folder in the individual modules.

With HP Quality Center Premier Edition, you can also import libraries from the current project and other projects, which means that you can reuse existing elements.

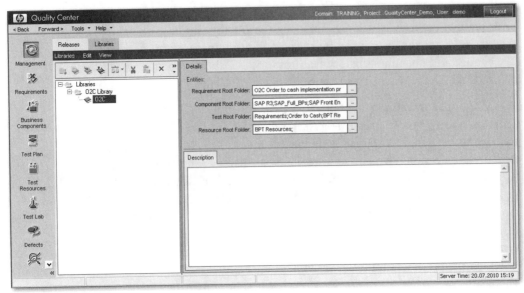

Figure 5.15 Creating a Library

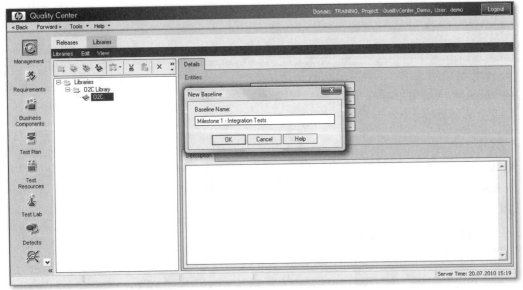

Figure 5.16 Creating a New Baseline

A baseline for the library can then be created at any point in time. This baseline contains the versions of the objects previously selected in the library that were valid at the time the baseline was created. This gives you a snapshot of the objects in the library, their field contents, and any relationships that may exist between the various objects. A baseline is typically created to coincide with a project milestone.

Baselines

When a new baseline is created, the system begins by checking whether all referenced objects are in the library.

It may take some time to create a baseline, depending on its scope. The status is displayed in the baseline overview, from which you can also access a progress log.

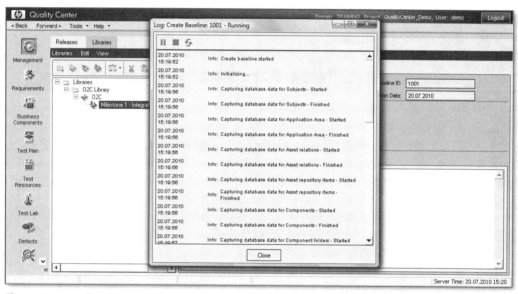

Figure 5.17 Baseline Creation Log

Baselines can be compared with one another or with the current project status. As with the compare function of the Business Blueprint in SAP Solution Manager, the corresponding function in SAP Quality Center by HP displays both versions of the library side by side. The comparison tool shows the individual objects in the hierarchy view of the relevant module. This view shows elements that have been added, moved, deleted,

Comparing
baselines

and changed. You can also display a detailed view of changed elements that compares both versions of an object and shows the changes at field level (see Figure 5.18).

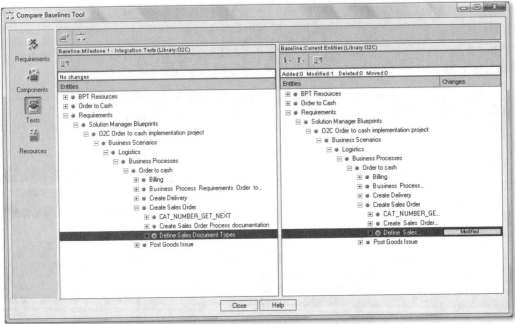

Figure 5.18 Comparing a Baseline with the Current Project Status

It is also possible to link a test set to a baseline. This action ensures that the version of the test cases defined in the baseline is used when testing is executed.

Baselines that you create also appear in the history of the relevant object. This feature enables manual versioning of objects; for example, in connection with project milestones. Once you create the baseline when a project milestone has been reached, it can also be used as documentation for the milestone or serve as the basis for acceptance. Thanks to the compare function, libraries and baselines provide support for the verification of changes over the course of the project and help you to estimate and verify the scope of the changes made.

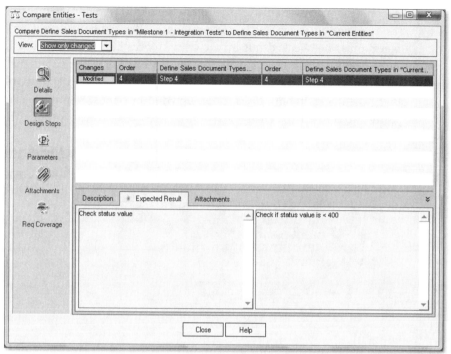

Figure 5.19 Comparison of a Changed Object (Test Step Within a Test Case) with its Previous Version

Another option for controlling and tracking changes is offered by versioning (version control). Versioning can be activated and deactivated for individual projects using the administrator environment of SAP Quality Center by HP.

Versioning (version control)

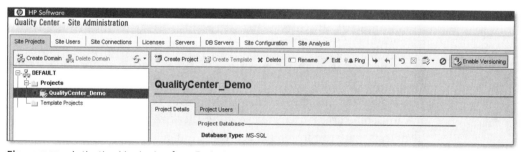

Figure 5.20 Activating Versioning for a Project

Versioning is also available for the following objects: requirements, test cases, test resources, and business components. If versioning is activated, objects must be checked out by the user before they can be changed. Checkout occurs automatically as soon as a user changes an object that is subject to version control. In addition, you can check out one or more objects manually. In both cases, a pop-up window opens, where you can specify a reason for the change.

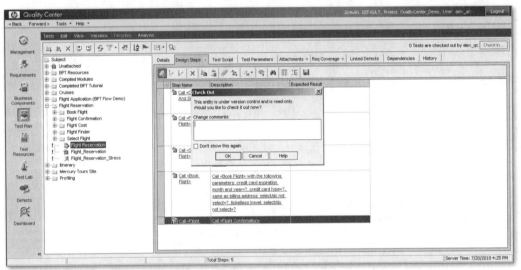

Figure 5.21 Document Check-Out Specifying a Reason for the Change

After a document has been checked out, it can only be changed by the current user. The version that is currently checked out cannot be displayed by other users. There are also options for undoing a checkout, checking out older versions of an object, and comparing different versions of the same object.

A new version is created when you check in a document for the first time and each time you check it in subsequently. This means that all changes are recorded in a change history, from which older versions of an object can also be accessed. Objects can be checked in individually, or a list of objects that are currently checked out can be displayed, from which you can then check in the objects currently in process.

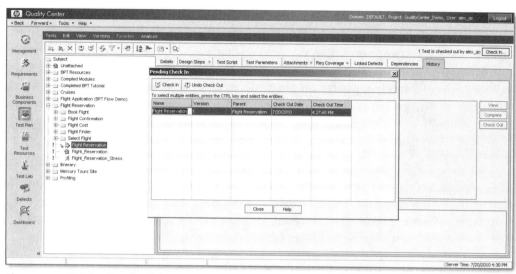

Figure 5.22 Outstanding Check-Ins

In the history, you can display the versions that are created in this way and compare them with one another. You use the compare function (described above in relation to baselines) for this purpose.

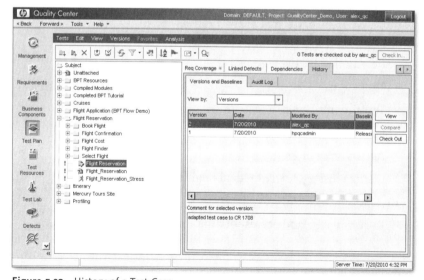

Figure 5.23 History of a Test Case

Versioning can be used in the same way as baselines to monitor changes to test-relevant objects managed in the Quality Center and to track change events, in essence creating an audit trail. Implementing versioning in the form of a check-in/check-out procedure with an option for specifying a reason for the change is particularly suited to cases where greater traceability is a priority. In addition, the check-out function can be used to lock objects that are currently in process against changes by other users.

If you use versioning, note that some data fields and some relationships between objects are not taken into account. From a technical perspective, it is important to note that both functions (baselines and versioning) play an important role in determining the size of the database. For more information about sizing and other technical aspects, check the HP documentation.

5.3.7 Status Analysis

The reporting function of SAP Quality Center by HP is provided in the REQUIREMENTS, BUSINESS COMPONENTS, TEST PLAN, TEST LAB, and DEFECTS modules. Context-specific standard graphics and reports can be accessed by selecting the ANALYSIS menu item.

Standard analyses   Analyses available in the standard system include:

- **Graphical analyses**
    - Requirements coverage
    - Test status
    - Test progress over time
    - Status of error messages
    - Age of error messages
    - Change history for individual fields (TREND)
- **Reports**
    - Requirements and corresponding test cases
    - Test cases with individual steps
    - Failed tests in the current test set
    - Error messages with their assigned tests and their execution status
    - Open error messages to be processed by the current user

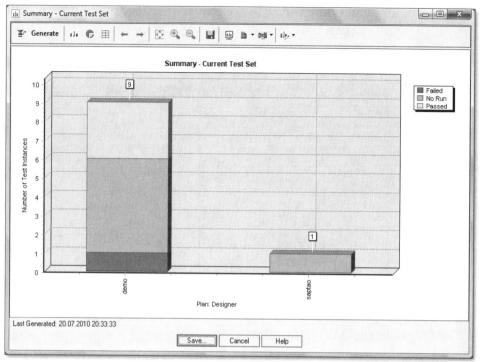

Figure 5.24 Graphical Analysis in the "Test Lab" Module

You can execute these analyses for individual objects (such as test sets) or for various objects simultaneously. Depending on the values that are to be depicted, you can display graphical analyses as bar charts, line charts, or pie charts. A drill-down function also allows you to display the individual elements that have been aggregated. In addition, you can adjust the display of graphical analyses or export them in various graphical formats. Meanwhile, reports can be exported into text or HTML files.

The REQUIREMENTS module also offers an analysis of test coverage with its COVERAGE ANALYSIS view, which is integrated into the requirements overview (see Figure 5.7).

Coverage analysis

It is also possible to create a "live analysis" for the folders in the BUSINESS COMPONENTS, TEST PLAN, and TEST LAB modules. These folders have a LIVE ANALYSIS tab, where a wizard is provided to help you generate graphical analyses. These are based on the contents of the relevant folder

Live analysis

and can only be displayed by the current user. The Live Analysis feature provides a quick overview of the elements in a folder.

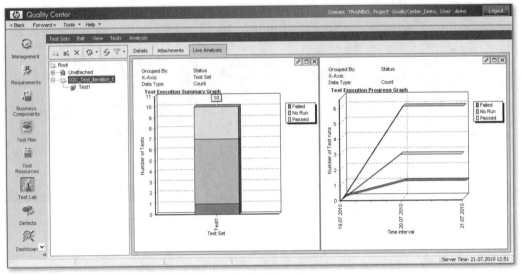

Figure 5.25 Live Analysis in Test Execution

Document
generator

The Document Generator in SAP Quality Center by HP provides a tool for preparing user-specific textual reports or documents based on the project contents (requirements, business components, test cases, test sets, and defects) in Microsoft Word format.

Dashboard

With Version 10.0 of SAP Quality Center by HP, the Dashboard functionality, which previously required a separate license, was integrated into the Quality Center as a module in its own right. The new Dashboard module in Version 10.0 offers two core functions. First, user-defined analyses can be stored in a folder structure in the Analysis View. Second, the Dashboard View brings all user-defined charts together in a single overview (dashboard).

Analysis View

User-defined analyses can be stored in the Analysis View. Two main folders, Public and Private are provided, in which you can then create various additional subfolders. These two folders control the visibility of the elements you create. Public analyses can be displayed by all projects users who have sufficient authorization, while analyses stored in the Private folder are only visible to the user who created them.

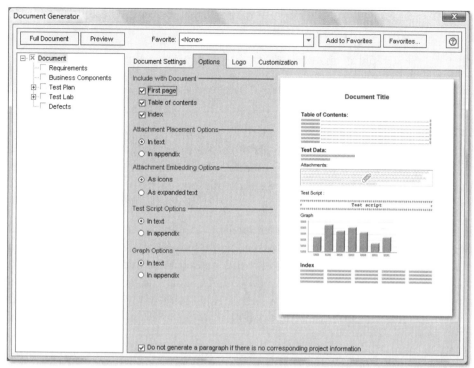

Figure 5.26 Document Generator for Creating Reports in Microsoft Word

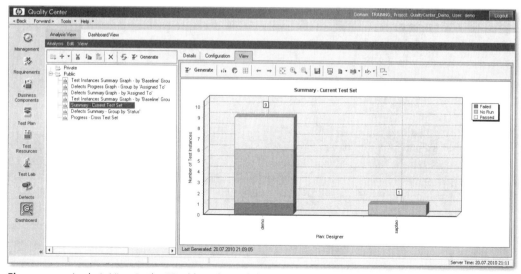

Figure 5.27 Analysis View in the "Dashboard" Module with User-Defined Analyses

SAP Quality Center by HP distinguishes between the following basic types of analysis:

- Graphical analyses
- Reports
- Excel reports

You can access these standard reports under ANALYSIS in the menu, and you can add them to the list of user-defined analyses at any time. In the ANALYSIS VIEW, you can modify the relevant documents and charts as required, for example by defining filters, an analysis period, or display options.

Graph Wizard · In addition to the graphics available in the standard configuration, you can use the GRAPH WIZARD to format your own analyses. This wizard guides you through a series of five steps, in which you define the required chart type, scope, filter options, and the data fields to be used. As a final step, you can also save a chart created with the wizard in the ANALYSIS VIEW of the DASHBOARD module.

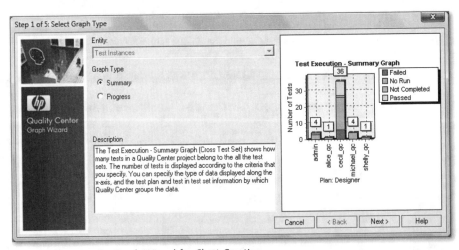

Figure 5.28 Graph Wizard for Chart Creation

Alternatively, you also have the option of creating charts and reports manually. In this case, you must first specify the objects that are to be analyzed (for example, error messages, requirements, or test cases), the basic chart type or report type, and a description for the new analysis. You then can define additional parameters on the CONFIGURATION tab of the newly created analysis.

Excel reports represent another type of user-specific analysis. In this case, you can create an SQL query, and the relevant data can then be output in Microsoft Excel. The REPORTS QUERY BUILDER is provided for this purpose. Among other things, you can use this tool to display the database fields that are available for a query. You also have the option of writing post-processing scripts, which are executed in Microsoft Excel. You can use this function to execute further calculations or generate charts, for example.

Excel reports

The graphical analyses saved in the ANALYSIS VIEW can be assigned to overview pages called dashboards in the DASHBOARD VIEW. You can use Drag & Drop to assign the analyses to a dashboard, and you can also adjust the size of each element. After you create a dashboard in this way, you can display it within SAP Quality Center or in full-screen mode and use a drill-down function to find element details.

Dashboard View

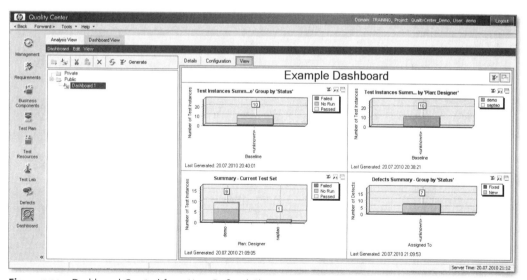

Figure 5.29 Dashboard Created from User-Defined Charts

5.3.8 Transferring the Test Results to SAP Solution Manager

You can use the Adapter to transfer the test results documented in SAP Quality Center by HP to the Business Blueprint of the linked SAP Solution Manager project. This enables basic reporting there in relation to the test results and requirements coverage. In the Quality Center, select the menu option Tools • SAP Tools • Update Solution Manager to update the Business Blueprint of the relevant project in SAP Solution Manager with the latest test results.

Link to requirements documentation
The test results are linked to the requirements documents or test objects that were defined at the start of the process. You can view the results in the implementation and configuration transactions (Transactions SOLAR01 and SOLAR02) on the Transfer to SAP QC by HP tab. If test results exist for individual objects, these are listed in the attributes of these objects. In addition, you can call up a detailed overview of all test results of projects that have been transferred from SAP Quality Center using the project evaluation (Transaction SOLAR_EVAL) and the Tests with SAP Quality Center by HP report provided there.

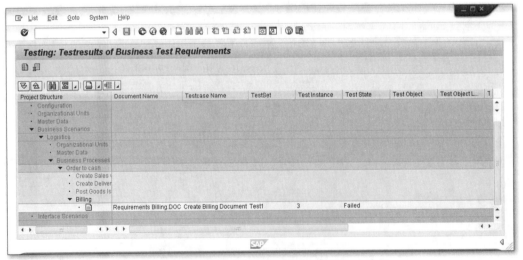

Figure 5.30 Test Evaluation in SAP Solution Manager

5.4   Summary

Integrating external tools using adapters gives you a way to meet the needs of the heterogeneous tool landscapes that are frequently found in practice. Adapters enable the use of various tools for specific tasks that arise during the project life cycle, without compromising the overall approach of the central application management solution. As a result, customers can choose the most suitable test management platform.

For the area of test management as part of Testing Option 2, SAP Quality Center by HP provides a manufacturer-independent, established tools suite for quality assurance, with particular strengths in generic usability and extensive reporting. In Version 10.0 of SAP Quality Center by HP, the use of baselines or versioning allows a revision history to be established for test-relevant objects, so that an audit trail is also available if the external test tool is used.

The connection to SAP Solution Manager using the SAP Solution Manager Adapter for SAP Quality Center by HP implements a requirements-based test methodology that uses an existing Business Blueprint and the requirements documents and test objects defined there.

5.5   Customer Report by Endress+Hauser Group

"SAP Quality Center by HP is intuitive to use, and its basic functions are quickly learned. The tool meets all of our requirements in terms of central access to test-case creation and execution, as well as defect management."

Ortrud Deutscher,
Head of Department, Quality, Security, Organization; Endress+Hauser InfoServe GmbH & Co. KG

The Endress+Hauser Group is a leading global supplier of process- measurement instruments and automation solutions for industrial process engineering. The group consists of a network of 86 companies based in 40 countries worldwide. It produces sensors and measurement instrumentation for practically all areas of industrial measurement within process technology. Endress+Hauser also supplies systems for measuring, monitoring, and automating manufacturing, logistics, and maintenance

Endress+Hauser

processes. Its portfolio is completed by consulting and support services provided in 97 countries across the globe, as well as lifecycle management for industrial plants. The group is headquartered in Switzerland. As of 2008, it employed 8,434 people and reported net sales of €1,211 million and consolidated operating earnings of €104 million.

IT organization

Endress+Hauser InfoServe GmbH & Co. KG is the Endress+Hauser Group's dedicated IT service provider, which became an independent organization in 1997. E+H InfoServe has around 250 employees deployed between Germany, the U.S. and Asia. The company's SAP Customer Competence Center was certified in 2001. It is also a certified SAP Hosting Partner since 2003.

Endress+Hauser has been a customer of SAP for many years. As far back as 1985, SAP R/2 was implemented at the group's production site in Maulburg. In 1993, SAP R/3 was implemented in its sales centers and sites worldwide. Today, the group has a diverse system landscape. For example, a range of SAP products is used within the group, including SAP solutions for Customer Relationship Management, Supplier Relationship Management, Product Lifecycle Management, SAP Business One, and SAP Business Information Warehouse.

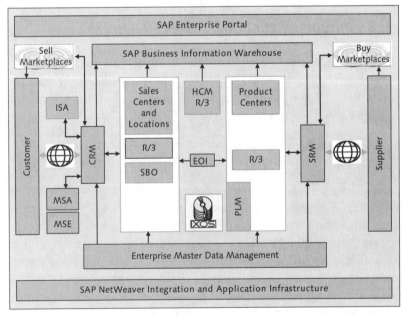

Figure 5.31 System Landscape of the Endress+Hauser Group

As part of the company's pursuit of continuous process optimization and with the maintenance cycle for SAP R/3 4.6C nearing its end, plans were made to upgrade the SAP systems to SAP ERP 6.0. The upgrade was implemented for a total of 10 SAP R/3 production systems at various sites worldwide. The project was brought to completion within the 2008 calendar year. The objective was to upgrade all of these systems, with approximately 4,500 SAP users, to the new release within one year.

Upgrade to SAP ERP 6.0

Sound testing management is essential to such a large-scale upgrade project. This requirement necessitated a critical examination of the testing process then in place and its alteration to suit the needs associated with the upgrade. An additional challenge was posed by the ambitious project schedule, which called for implementing the technical upgrade in parallel with the testing activities for various systems within 12 months. The aim, overall, was to harmonize the testing procedure to allow all testing activities to be carried out efficiently during the upgrade.

Before the project got underway, the existing testing procedure was evaluated. The test cases that had been created for the existing SAP R/3 systems were available as documents in Microsoft Word or Excel formats. Approximately 2,500 test cases had been documented in this way. In addition, CATT scripts were available for individual test steps. Overall, however, the company had not pursued a structured approach to test automation.

Review of the testing procedure

The existing test case library was only partly suited to use in the upgrade project. For example, most of the test cases described functional checks. The verification of end-to-end processes, which is essential to integration testing in particular, had not been documented consistently. Similarly, many of the test cases were obsolete and did not reflect the current functions in the R/3 production system. Moreover, the complete collection of test cases contained many redundant documents.

The existing testing activities were controlled at a purely organizational level, with test statuses and error messages also being managed decentrally. To enhance efficiency, the company planned to introduce a test management tool. The requirements for this tool were drawn up at the start of the upgrade project. In relation to the structured creation and administration of test cases, the initial objectives were to avoid creating the same problems described above when creating a new set of test cases, and to ensure a high level of quality for the test cases. The plan was to

Requirements for a test management tool

put a system in place that would be centrally available for the definition and administration of all test cases. This system was to be suitable not only for use in the SAP environment, but also for the management of test cases for parallel and future projects, for example, in a web environment or for software developed by the customer. Ortrud Deutscher, Head of the Quality, Security, Organization department at Endress+Hauser Info-Serve GmbH & Co. KG, explains the customer's requirements for the test management tool as follows:

> *"From our perspective, it was a fundamental prerequisite that the test management tool be accessible to the entire group, as testing is executed both by E+H InfoServe and at a local level by the individual companies all over the world. It was also important for us to be able to test all of our systems with this tool—not just SAP R/3, but also the software that we have developed ourselves and web applications outside of the SAP environment."*

The company also envisioned centralized test planning and execution for all project types. The main objective was a central system, with particular importance attached to using the tool throughout the group as a whole. To boost the efficiency of testing in the future, the company needed an option for creating automatic test cases or integrating a test automation tool. In accordance with the concept of central test documentation, the customer also required an option for referencing load test scripts.

Furthermore, the company lacked a central defect management system for the recording of error messages during testing activities. Therefore, the test management tool it chose would had to offer the functional scope required to enable the structured recording and processing of messages in terms of a troubleshooting workflow.

It was essential for the monitoring and reporting of testing activities to enable flexible evaluations based on the requirements of the project stakeholders.

Selection of
SAP Quality
Center by HP

At the start of the planning phase of the upgrade project, HP Quality Center was already in use at several companies within the Endress+Hauser Group. This meant that some areas of the company had already had hands-on experience of using this tool. In particular, the Product Development division of the group had been using HP Quality Center for years for such tasks as quality assurance in relation to software development for measurement instrumentation. As a result, it was possible to demonstrate the key functions of the tool to the stakeholders in the upgrade project, and this played an important role in the customer's decision in its favor. The tool fully met all of the criteria for a test management tool for the upgrade project. The use of this tool across the company also allows it to set standards for reporting as part of software quality assurance, as the relevant reports and analyses can be implemented consistently using HP Quality Center. For all these reasons, the customer chose HP Quality Center for this project. SAP issued the customer a new license to use the tool as part of the upgrade project. The SAP Quality Center by HP package provided by SAP contains the Quality Center, as well as standard functions for planning and executing testing activities, such as the BUSINESS PROCESS module, which was used in this project to create modular test cases. Because the licensing model for the software is based on the number of users working in the system at the same time, 55 licenses were provided for approximately 600 users who worked with SAP Quality Center by HP in connection with the upgrade.

Consultants from our implementation partner, HP, were responsible for server installation and initial setup of SAP Quality Center by HP, which were completed within two days. End users were able to access SAP Quality Center by HP from a web interface. Users needed a browser enhancement installed on their local computers in order to use this web application. This step was carried out internally by employees of E+H InfoServe. In addition, three Citrix servers were used to allow all users involved in testing activities in all countries to access SAP Quality Center by HP. This simplified the rollout of the application and, indeed, made it possible in cases where security settings did not allow for a direct local installation.

Installation of the SAP Quality Center by HP

As part of a package of approximately 25 full-time equivalents, the consultants also provided support to the E+H users as they took their first steps in the new tool. This began with a kick-off workshop with around 15 employees of E+H InfoServe, in which the overall concept of SAP Quality Center by HP and its functions were presented. Additional role-specific training was provided as part of a consulting package for future administrators of SAP Quality Center by HP and for test-case developers. Ortrud Deutscher was heavily involved in decision-making as regards

Training and coaching

the implementation and introduction of SAP Quality Center by HP, and points out that most of the consulting provided was in relation to methodology and design issues. Users, regardless of their role, were able to grasp the basics of using SAP Quality Center by HP in just a few hours. Use of the key functions for creating test cases and for planning and executing testing activities was taught within one day. Further consulting support primarily had to do with organizational aspects. These included the process-oriented storage of test components and test cases in the tool.

Following the initial workshops, the employees of E+H InfoServe began to implement the testing procedure for the upgrade project in the tool. In this task, they were assisted by the HP consultants, who provided regular coaching and further workshops over a period of four months.

Objectives of testing activities
The basic objective underlying the testing activities in the upgrade was to safeguard the system functions that were available before the upgrade so that they would continue to be available afterwards. Therefore, the goal that was defined for testing implementation was 100% coverage of the processes and functions that were to be tested. The execution of the individual testing activities included all companies of the Endress+Hauser Group that were involved in the project, and all of the required interfaces were to be tested. Another defined objective was that the testing activities were to be executed using the available resources.

Use of SAP Quality Center by HP
The functions that support the testing process are assigned to a set of integrated modules in the Quality Center. During the upgrade project, the TEST PLAN and TEST LAB modules were used for test-plan creation and administration and for planning and executing testing activities. DEFECT MANAGEMENT was also used for the administration of error messages. In addition to these essential functions, the BUSINESS COMPONENTS module was used for the creation of manual or automated components, from which test cases can be put together. In addition, the RELEASES module was used to group the test cases of the individual upgrades in the individual countries and to enable reporting for each system and each test phase.

However, the REQUIREMENTS module for the administration of requirements in SAP Quality Center by HP was not used. The functions in this module allow you to enter requirements relating to the test object, which can subsequently be linked with test cases. This allows you to implement a requirements-based testing process, where test cases are designed on the basis of business or technical requirements. This enables the evaluation of requirements coverage, which also can be linked to a criticality analysis or risk analysis.

Requirements-based testing was considered before the project began and was identified as being too time-consuming given the tight schedule. Since SAP Solution Manager was not used to document the upgrade, the option of using the SAP Solution Manager Adapter for SAP Quality Center by HP to transfer the relevant requirements documents and objects was irrelevant in this case.

Requirements management is currently used for in-house development, in particular in the area of web applications. In this context, the functions help the customer to achieve the required test coverage by checking that each of the requirements entered is covered by corresponding test cases.

In terms of administration and tools, implementation of the test organization for the upgrade project comprised four steps. First, the business components were created in SAP Quality Center by HP. Next, functional tests and process tests were created from these components. The structure and organization of Defect Management then were defined in parallel. In the fourth step, the newly created test cases were grouped together to form test cycles and were executed; this step also involved assigning test cases to testers, continuous monitoring, and final reporting on the progress and status of testing.

Test organization

By adopting the Business Process Testing approach of SAP Quality Center by HP, InfoServe opted for a tool-based approach to the creation of test cases. This concept is based on the modularization of test cases. While a complete testing process is usually created as a single, static document when test cases are formulated, Business Process Testing involves constructing test cases on the basis of components such as transactions, input masks, or workflow steps. These business components represent small, reusable units, from which entire test cases can be built. This approach avoids redundant descriptions of actions that are used in more

Business Process Testing

than one test case; for example, system logon. In addition, a change to one component is immediately applied to all test cases that use this component. This has the potential to reduce the cost of maintaining test cases following system changes.

Creating test components

Certain organizational issues required clarification when the project team began to apply the component-based testing approach to the upgrade project. Particular consideration was given to fundamental questions, such as the issue of who exactly was to create and maintain the components. Because component creation required expert technical knowledge of the functions in the transactions in the ERP system described earlier, the components were created by the IT employees of E+H InfoServe. It was also necessary to define a unified structure for the storage of components. Because the folder structure within which the components are to be grouped together is user-defined, this structure had to be drafted and defined in advance. Corresponding specifications make it easier to locate the created components and facilitates collaboration in the component library. After various options were teased out, the test-case developers favored the use of a structure similar to the SAP menu structure from SAP ERP 6.0 when organizing and creating this structure. The folder structure of the menu was modeled on the structure of component management in SAP Quality Center by HP structure (see Figure 5.32). The individual test components could then be created for each individual transaction. As a result, the components can be quickly found using a search based on functional criteria. According to Ortrud Deutscher, the process of defining a corresponding structure and adhering to it consistently is not a task to be underestimated and one that is essential to the use and acceptance of the solution.

In addition to other organizational tasks, such as defining useful naming conventions, particular attention was paid to the granularity of the test components. The project team defined the components as the smallest reusable units within a test case (see Figure 5.33), and decided to create these on the basis of SAP transactions, so that, depending on its complexity, a component corresponded to an SAP transaction or a screen. Components were also created for interfaces and for upstream and downstream steps in the workflow. Approximately 8,700 components were created in this way, from which approximately 5,756 test cases were built.

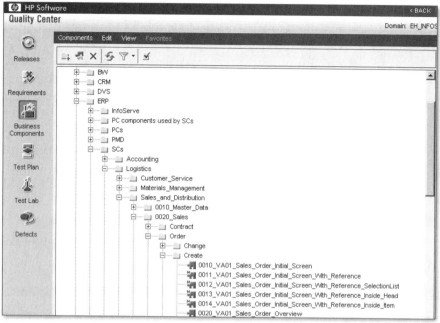

Figure 5.32 "Business Components" Module with Components from the Upgrade Project

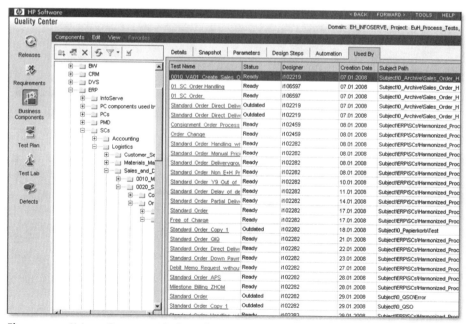

Figure 5.33 Using a Component in Several Test Cases

Test case design
Similar consideration was given to the creation of test cases. The project team took a business process-oriented approach to the organization of test cases. The user-defined folder structure in the TEST PLAN module reflects all business processes that are mapped in the SAP ERP system. This folder contains test cases for all variants of the relevant processes. Because the test cases were built entirely from the business components created in the previous step, it is a straightforward task to create test cases for process variants that differ only slightly in their process flows. In addition, system transitions and interfaces were mapped in the test cases and taken into account during their creation; these were also encapsulated in components and put together as test cases as part of the integration test (see Figure 5.34). The function tests and process tests were put together by E+H InfoServe's test-case designers in collaboration with the module experts and business department employees who were involved in the process.

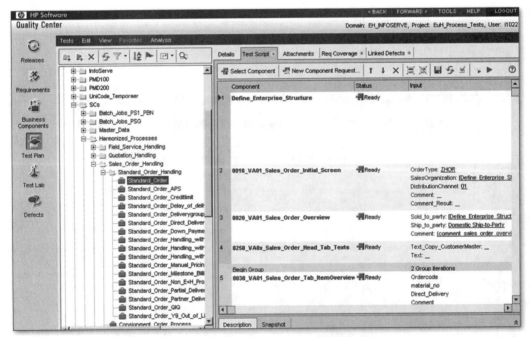

Figure 5.34 A Test Case Constructed from Components

When test case creation was completed, the individual test cases could be grouped together into *test sets*. Test sets can contain any number of test cases for a specific test execution purpose; for example, all process tests within an integration test for the upgrade project. In addition, test cases were grouped together using Release Management within SAP Quality Center by HP. In the standard system, this allows you to define release versions and release cycles for software, to which testing activities can be assigned in order to enable an evaluation of a specific version of the software. In the upgrade project, this function was used to enable an evaluation of the testing activities in relation to the updated systems and their clients. For this purpose, each production system and each client within each system was created as a release cycle, to which the relevant test sets were then assigned. As a result, it was possible to analyze the progress of the testing activities for the systems or individual clients at any time.

Test planning and execution

The test cases within the test sets were then transferred to test execution through assignment to individual testers. The integrated wizard for executing manual tests allowed the testers to process the test cases step-by-step and to assess and document the result of each test step. The testers were specifically instructed to enter the master data and transaction data created as a document to record successful test execution.

With manual test execution, testers can post an error message during the current test step. A workflow sends this to a dispatcher and then on to the relevant developers, so that the detected error can be identified and its cause eliminated before retesting is executed. This workflow had been mapped with various error status and criticalities in the Defect Management area of SAP Quality Center by HP. In addition, the integrated email notification function also allowed the employees involved in troubleshooting to be informed immediately. Approximately 1,000 error messages were recorded with Defect Management over the entire course of the upgrade project.

Defect Management

The Reporting functions of SAP Quality Center by HP were used to obtain information about the current status and progress of testing in real time. The evaluations were based on the tests sets; in other words, on the systems and clients created in Release Management.

Reporting

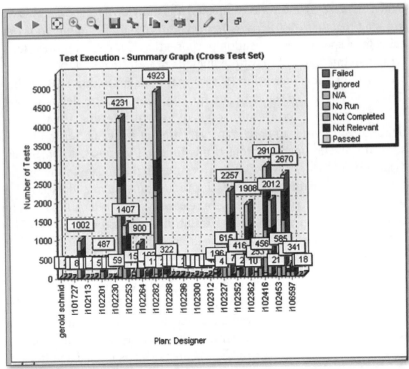

Figure 5.35 Graphical Analysis of Test Execution

Testing costs All testing activities for the upgrade project were executed successfully using the process outlined above. For each system upgrade, approximately 100 full-time equivalents were invested in the execution of the various test stages for each system. This included a preliminary test by employees of E+H InfoServe, an extensive integration test, and a final acceptance test.

Potential benefits of the testing procedure Ortrud Deutscher emphasizes that the initial costs of implementing a new test management approach with SAP Quality Center by HP were considerable because the test components, and therefore also the test cases based on these components, had to be created from scratch. However, the efficient construction of test sets, fast analysis of test results, and the management of error messages has already created a high degree of transparency. This fact is also documented in the system audit that accompanied the project, which was conducted by the auditing company PricewaterhouseCoopers. Its report confirmed that test management using Quality Center by HP supports a controlled and documented system upgrade.

Looking ahead, Ortrud Deutscher believes that the project will prove to have been worth the initial investment, as the company will be able to execute future testing activities at a much lower cost. For example, a Unicode migration is scheduled for this year, and the company plans to use the test cases from the upgrade project for this purpose. The same applies to regression tests executed after system changes. A corresponding set of regression testing—for example, to safeguard the implementation of SAP Notes—can be selected with a minimum of effort and transferred to test execution. As a prerequisite, the library of test components and test cases must be kept up-to-date at all times and adjusted following system changes. For this reason, the whole area of test organization and setup is managed centrally by an employee at E+H InfoServe. This includes administration of SAP Quality Center by HP, as well as coordination of maintenance for projects and storage structures within the tool and methodological support for projects that begin with the use of SAP Quality Center by HP.

The use of Business Process Testing simultaneously serves as a basis for component-based test automation. Ortrud Deutscher believes that the future holds great potential for this approach. Components that have been created manually can gradually be enhanced using test automation scripts. Using components for test automation also avoids redundancy in the creation of test cases. Automation scripts are not newly recorded or developed for each complete test case, but rather for each individual module.

Outlook for the automation of test components

In the medium-term, the use of SAP Test Acceleration and Optimization (SAP TAO) for this purpose is also conceivable. This tool builds on the functions of Business Process Testing. These components are generated by a system analysis, and can then be uploaded and used in the BUSINESS COMPONENTS module of SAP Quality Center by HP. The components generated by SAP TAO can be linked with action components, such as system navigation, in order to create automated test cases.

Conclusion

With the implementation of SAP Quality Center by HP, Endress+Hauser gained a central test management tool that ensured an efficient testing process as part of the upgrade project. All manual testing activities in the upgrade project were executed using this tool. SAP Quality Center by HP enabled central storage of test cases, as well as the planning, execution, and evaluation of all test runs, including the integrated recording and management of error messages. E+H InfoServe uses Business Process Testing, which represents a tool-supported method for creating test cases from individual components. It makes the process of creating test-case descriptions more efficient, as it is no longer necessary to repeat the description of the same steps in different test cases. In the medium term, the group plans to automate selected components to boost efficiency even further.

Lessons learned What can be learned from the experiences of Endress+Hauser?

▸ Test management tools increase the efficiency of an existing testing process by providing central access to all documents and results in the testing environment; these tools also serve to standardize individual steps.

▸ While tool-specific approaches may enhance efficiency even further (for example, in relation to test case creation), they often require an adjustment of the existing testing process and initially entail considerable efforts.

▸ The construction of manual test cases from BUSINESS COMPONENTS can reduce the costs that arise in relation to the maintenance of changed test cases. If a changed component is used in several test cases, you only need to make a single, central modification.

▸ Dedicating a staff role entirely to the optimization of the testing process, administration of the test tool, and maintenance of existing test cases, ensures compliance with the testing process and creates awareness of the importance of software quality assurance.

5.6 Customer Report by DB Systel GmbH

DB Systel GmbH is a leading provider of IT and telecommunications services for the mobility, transportation, and logistics market, as well as for cross-industry business processes. As a systems partner of Deutsche Bahn, one of DB Systel's main areas of focus is the provision of support to customers within DB AG. In addition, it provides its services to mobile and fixed network carriers, DSL providers, and cable network providers. DB Systel, which has a workforce of 5,000 employees, has its headquarters in Frankfurt am Main. DB Systel has many sites throughout Germany, which are grouped together in four regions.

DB Systel GmbH

The company operates many IT and TC platforms for Deutsche Bahn AG and, based on these platforms, offers services created by the bundling of individual technical components. These then form the basis for an ICT solution offering, in which the various offerings and services are brought together as an integrated solution. DB Systel strives to provide optimal support for its customers' business processes as a reliable partner for IT and TC solutions. Towards this end, DB Systel covers the entire lifecycle of these solutions. The company's service offering comprises all phases of the project lifecycle: from strategic planning, through development and implementation, to the operation and optimization of IT systems, TC systems, networks, and ITC landscapes. This wide range of services are united under the company's core competencies of consulting, planning, implementation, operations, and service, which support customers from all industries throughout the entire project lifecycle.

ICT Lifecycle Management

The company's management of IT and TC solutions and its execution of individual projects are based on the implementation of ITIL processes. To ensure the continuous improvement of software development and the service organization, the reference models of the Capability Maturity Model Integration (CMMI) approach are used. Figure 5.36 provides an overview of the procedures and processes used, and how they relate to one another.

Various tools support the implementation of the individual ITIL processes throughout the entire project lifecycle. Based on the process model shown above, tools from various manufacturers are used in a "best-of-breed" approach. Figure 5.37 shows part of the tool landscape in the area of software quality assurance.

Tool landscape

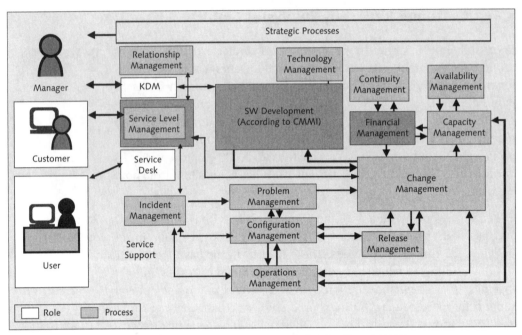

Figure 5.36 IT Management at DB Systel with ITIL and CMMI

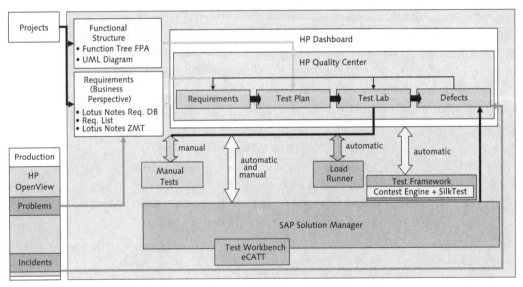

Figure 5.37 Tool Landscape for Software Quality Assurance

Across the organization as a whole, HP Quality Center is used for software quality assurance to support the testing activities relating to development, implementation, and the ongoing operation of applications within the project lifecycle. In this case, HP Quality Center is used primarily as a tool for test management and defect management within the enterprise. The business perspective describing business processes is largely documented in Lotus Notes. The function structure of the implemented software is mapped in standard notation, in particular UML.

Use of HP Quality Center across the organization

The full functional scope of HP Quality Center may be used, depending on the project. In addition to the essential functions such as creating and storing test cases, test execution, and reporting, the DEFECT MANAGEMENT module is also used for projects. HP Quality Center is also used for software development projects. In these instances, the functions relevant for development are used; for example, the administration of software releases. Such projects frequently also use the functions for documenting and assigning test requirements.

An SAP project, such as the one detailed below, represents an exception. For SAP projects, Solution Manager is used for documentation and test management. In this case, the integrated Service Desk is used for the administration of error messages.

One important reason why HP Quality Center is used across the enterprise for all other projects is its reporting functions. In addition to the tool's integrated reporting functions, DB Systel uses HP Quality Center Dashboard. This add-on component, which requires a separate license, allows you to query, analyze, and depict test results and test-based KPIs across several projects. DB Systel uses these functions to establish centralized management reporting for all of its current projects. In this scenario, the Dashboard allows the results from a wide range of projects to be brought together in a single interface. KPIs and test results from HP Quality Center (for example, test progress based on the number of completed/failed test cases or the number and criticality of errors detected) are united, aggregated, and formatted in a web interface.

HP Quality Center Dashboard

HP Quality Center Dashboard is based on the use of portlets, each one representing an individual piece of project information. For example, a portlet might represent the graphical formatting of project-specific KPIs (test progress, or errors detected in each test phase), which generally originate in the dataset of the testing activities in HP Quality Center.

Portlets can be configured individually, and can be grouped together as required in the tool's web interface.

At DB Systel, reporting based on HP Quality Center Dashboard is an enterprise standard in the area of software quality assurance. This tool is used to keep management and the project stakeholders continually informed about the quality and status of all ongoing projects. As a result, management always has an extensive and up-to-date overview of the status and progress of all projects, and can identify deviations from plans and risks at an early stage. Using the Dashboard, you can also tell how the quality of a project increases over a period of time, for example, a release cycle or a quarter.

In addition to project-specific analyses, each project supplies HP Quality Center Dashboard with the following data, in accordance with the specifications:

▶ Status and progress of test execution

▶ Status and progress of troubleshooting

▶ Test coverage (the ratio of successful to failed tests over time)

▶ Efficiency of troubleshooting (processing time for processing error messages, broken down by test phase and test class)

▶ Analysis of the cause of errors (errors per project and their cause, shown as a percentage)

▶ Quality of text execution (for example, the number of errors identified in each test phase)

Christian Pfaff, who has responsibility for SAP Solution Manager in the Standard Software Development Center within the Customer Competence Center, explains how HP Quality Center and enterprisewide reporting with the Dashboard proved to be a successful combination: The test process developed by DB Systel was implemented using the manufacturer-independent HP Quality Center, whereby the execution of manual tests in particular benefited from the web interface and wizard support for test execution and documentation. Within HP Quality Center, the areas of requirements management, test management, and defect management are integrated and can be used equally well for development and implementation projects.

Christian Pfaff points out how new projects can be set up in approximately two to three days. With approximately three new projects starting each month, the administrative effort involved is considerable. Around 3,350 users are currently working on DB Systel's ongoing projects in HP Quality Center, of whom 195 use the tool on a daily basis.

The extensive reporting functions in the Dashboard can therefore be fully used because of this consistent use of HP Quality Center. According to Christian Pfaff, the Dashboard enables monitoring and analysis, especially for strategic projects with high management visibility. Overall, the high level of transparency encourages communication across project areas and also leads to positive critical response.

The use of HP Quality Center throughout the enterprise is seen as a de facto standard that ensures that the basic data relating to all projects is made available for unified reporting with the HP Quality Center Dashboard. This requirement has a direct effect on the choice of a test tool.

However, as Christian Pfaff explains, the use of SAP Solution Manager and the Test Workbench was essential when it came to DB Systel's SAP projects. The reasons for this are many and complex. First, SAP Solution Manager was already in use at DB Systel's SAP Customer Competence Center (CCC); for example, for central administration, service desk functions, and monitoring of the SAP solution landscape. Further, the company already had experience of using the Test Workbench in SAP implementations in the context of software quality assurance. A pilot project to evaluate the use of eCATT was implemented in 2006, using both SAP Solution Manager and the Test Workbench. The use of these tools demonstrated several benefits for the SAP procedures used at DB Systel that could not be replicated in HP Quality Center. These benefits included versatile document management and user-friendly functions in test-case creation and test documentation, as well as SAP-specific functions in test automation (eCATT) and message processing (Service Desk), which are described in detail below.

SAP Solution Manager and the Test Workbench

Above and beyond these aspects of tool selection, the migration of existing test cases provided additional motivation for using SAP Solution Manager. Several hundred test cases already existed in the classic Test Workbench in the company's various R/3 4.6C systems, which had be created as part of two extensive implementation projects. These test cases were created and managed without SAP Solution Manager, using the

Use of existing test cases

Test Organizer available in all SAP systems. Migrating the test cases, including all existing documented test executions, into HP Quality Center would have involved considerable time and effort and therefore was not feasible. Just as important, the Test Workbench could only have been replaced at the expense of traceability, as all statuses and the accumulated documentation of all tests were stored there. In contrast, a migration or linking of test cases to SAP Solution Manager is supported directly by Solution Manager, and the existing test cases can be reused immediately within the context of a SAP Solution Manager project. This approach also meant that the existing test results could be preserved.

Test automation with eCATT

Test automation with eCATT in the SAP environment was evaluated in a pilot project as part of the company's "LVS/Lagerverwaltung" ("WMS/Warehouse Management") project. In this pilot project, SAP Solution Manager was used to map and document the business processes in a Business Blueprint and to define manual test cases for the project. Critical processes were then identified and end-to-end process chains were automated with eCATT on this basis. Meanwhile, the Test Workbench was used for text execution and scheduling and to evaluate the test cases. The objective of this project was to demonstrate a significant reduction in the costs incurred by testing with the use of test automation. In addition, at least 50% of the subsequent regression test scenarios in the project rollout were to be covered by test scripts. These objectives were successfully fulfilled. Using the central Business Blueprint as a basis, the project was rolled out to three additional company sites, involving the creation of local blueprints.

Benefits of using eCATT for SAP projects

Andreas Rückardt, the Project Manager for this project, already had many years of project-based experience with eCATT and was quick to realize the potential benefits of using the tool. Test planning and execution in the context of the process hierarchy proved to be particularly beneficial when it came to creating automatic test cases, which could begin with the partial automation of individual processes and process steps. In addition, SAP-specific functions could be implemented by using eCATT as an automation tool. For example, the use of the eCATT TCD driver helped to save a significant amount of time, as selected scripts could be executed on the server and without a front end. Furthermore, SAP Solution Manager and therefore also eCATT were available without an additional license fee, which meant that no investment in software licenses for a test automation tool was required during the pilot project.

Thanks to the project team's existing experience with the integrated SAP test tools, as well as the expertise acquired during the pilot project, the company identified additional benefits of integrating SAP Solution Manager and the Test Workbench that could not be replicated using HP Quality Center.

Process-oriented test planning and execution

On the basis of a Business Blueprint and the business process descriptions contained in that Business Blueprint, test cases were created in previously implemented projects in the context of each relevant process. These test cases were then put together as test plans for each test stage (for example, an integration test). One of the unique features of the integrated application management platform of SAP Solution Manager is the option for "out-of-the-box" mapping of process-oriented tests in terms of end-to-end processes, which also reflects the process flow that is actually documented.

Using the SAP Solution Manager Adapter for SAP Quality Center by HP makes it possible to transfer this approach (that is, the Blueprint structure and relevant documents) to HP Quality Center, where it can be used as a basis for creating test cases. By using the adapter, you can create test cases based on the documents that are transferred, and link these test cases with requirements documents or test objects that were defined in the Business Blueprint. This approach enables you to implement a requirements-based testing procedure, which allows you to evaluate test coverage based on the fulfillment of test requirements. However, because a large number of test cases already existed in many of the projects in this case, a data migration would also have been required.

The decision to use SAP Solution Manager and the Test Workbench was also based on criteria relating to test execution and documentation.

Test execution and documentation

Within SAP Solution Manager, you can define SAP transactions as test objects for test cases. As long as the required RFC connections are maintained, testers can navigate from test execution to the relevant test systems. Using Trusted RFC connections, this can be done without having to logon again. This function significantly reduces the effort and perceived complexity involved in test execution for the testers and avoids access errors. A reference to SAP transactions cannot be implemented in HP Quality Center, which means that in this case testers have to log on to the relevant system and call up the relevant transactions manually for each test case.

Documentation
standards and test
documentation Furthermore, SAP Solution Manager offers powerful document management functionality (integrated SAP Knowledge Warehouse), which enables flexible and, above all, traceable and audit-compliant documentation of test results in the context of test execution. In Solution Manager, test cases can be documented with a copy of a test case, with a document upload, or using a standard template. At DB Systel, standard templates were predominantly used, which ensured consistent documentation of the test results.

HP Quality Center also allows you to upload documents, while compliance with unified documentation standards is implemented at an organizational level.

Service Desk Yet another argument in favor of using SAP Solution Manager for SAP projects was provided by the option of using its integrated Service Desk. Even in the standard configuration, this allows error messages to be posted during testing activities and to be managed along a structured error elimination process. The relevant messages can be posted using SAP Solution Manager or from the individual SAP system, which is connected to SAP Solution Manager. In particular, this option of posting from the SAP systems themselves offered clear added value for DB Systel's project, as it meant that the relevant information could be communicated and transferred from the connected system, making the troubleshooting process much simpler and faster to complete. DB Systel also uses the option of forwarding messages recorded in the Service Desk to SAP Support directly, thereby avoiding any integration gaps that could arise here (for example, by opening an OSS message in the Service Marketplace).

Although Christian Pfaff regards Defect Management in HP Quality Center as easy to configure and intuitive in its usability, it nevertheless lacks the integration functions specified above for the SAP environment. However, the SAP Solution Manager Adapter now has a bidirectional interface for the exchange of selected messages between Defect Management in HP Quality Center and SAP Solution Manager.

Because of the benefits outlined above, DB Systel currently uses SAP Solution Manager and the Test Workbench as the main documentation management and test management tool for 11 SAP projects. Three projects use eCATT for test automation.

This means that the fundamental testing process for these projects, which includes test case creation, test planning, execution, monitoring, and analysis, is executed in SAP Solution Manager. However, it was necessary to comply with the specifications and implement central project reporting with HP Quality Center Dashboard. This involved transferring the aggregated test results for each test plan, as well as itemizing the error messages, including status and criticality, in accordance with the requirements described earlier. For this reason it was essential that the reference to the relevant SAP Solution Manager project remain clear at all times to enable project-based reporting.

Fulfillment of reporting requirements

As a potential solution, the project team initially considered using the SAP Solution Manager Adapter for SAP Quality Center by HP, which is provided by SAP as a price-list component. However, this tool uses a different approach: Using the adapter allows you to execute the entire testing process, including reporting, as well as test planning and execution, with HP Quality Center. In this approach, which corresponds to Testing Option 2, the test cases are based on requirements that have been defined as requirements documents and test objects in a Business Blueprint in SAP Solution Manager. However, the test cases themselves are created and managed in their entirety in HP Quality Center. Test results are sent back to SAP Solution Manager in the context of the business requirements defined in the Business Blueprint. In contrast, DB Systel's requirements envisioned this process working almost in reverse: DB Systel wanted test management with SAP Solution Manager and the Test Workbench, including all easy-to-use functions, to remain unchanged, and only wanted the information that was relevant for central reporting to be transferred to HP Quality Center.

SAP Solution Manager Adapter for SAP Quality Center by HP

In September 2007, a customized solution was therefore developed in collaboration with SAP Test Management Consulting. This solution enabled the transfer of test results from the Test Workbench in SAP Solution Manager to HP Quality Center. The key requirement for this solution was to enable the reuse of data in HP Quality Center Dashboard in accordance with the requirements for enterprisewide reporting. These requirements involved transfer of selected information about test statuses and error messages within the context of a project. In short, the following data fields were to be transferred for each SAP Solution Manager project:

Customized solution: reporting interface

Area	HP Quality Center Dashboard	SAP Solution Manager
Defect Management	Cause of error	CRM message SDTM → Subject
	Status	CRM message SDTM → Status (possibly System Status)
	Error class	CRM message SDTM → Priority
	Test phase	CRM message SDTM → Additional status (possibly "Test series" field in the test plan)
Test execution	Execution status	Test Workbench → Test status
	Project name	Project name (SOLAR_PROJECT_ADMIN) (or Test Plan Attributes)
	Release	Name of test plan for project
	Number of test cases	Test cases assigned to the test plan
	Duration of troubleshooting	Time recording for system status changes

Table 5.1 Fields for Reporting in the HP Quality Center Dashboard

In order to create a suitable interface, a design was developed to differentiate the solution to be created from the SAP Solution Manager Adapter and to outline various approaches for implementing the requirements. The basic procedure for transferring the required contents from SAP Solution Manager to HP Quality Center comprises the following steps:

▸ Export the relevant data from SAP Solution Manager

▸ Format the exported data

▸ Import the data into HP Quality Center

Data export from SAP Solution Manager

Two options for exporting the data were considered. In the first of these, an eCATT script would be used to read or export the required data from SAP Solution Manager. The data could then be formatted in the next step and then finally imported into HP Quality Center. The second option would use an ABAP application to export the data. In this case, an ABAP program would access the relevant system tables directly, read the required data, and write the data to files at operating system level. While this option required greater investment in terms of development, it offered a number of benefits. For example, it eliminated further processing steps at operating system level, as the format and content of the target files would be defined by the ABAP program itself. In addition, the program could be scheduled using SAP-internal job control, which would enable a regular export of the data using technology already available in the SAP system, and could also be planned, started, and monitored from each front end. Moreover, the ABAP implementation would enable the provision of a user interface for configuring the data export, where the required projects or test plans could be selected and stored as variants. The simplicity of the installation and configuration of this solution offered yet another advantage. This second option was ultimately selected on the basis of all of the benefits it had to offer.

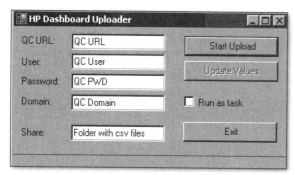

Figure 5.38 Configuration of the Data Import into HP Quality Center

The files generated by the data export can then be imported into HP Quality Center. The data import is executed using the Open Test Architecture Application Programming Interface (OTA API) of HP Quality Center. The interface can be called by any program (for example, programs developed with Visual Basic) and enables the enhancement of HP Quality Center and therefore also the integration of external applications. Using this approach, a tool was implemented at operating system level, which loads the data exported from SAP Solution Manager into an HP Quality Center project. As a result, the data required for test cases, test results, and error messages can be transferred to enable reporting in HP Quality Center Dashboard (see Figure 5.39).

Data import into the HP Quality Center

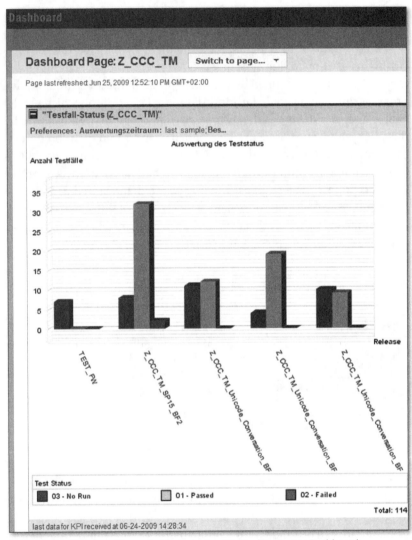

Figure 5.39 Display of Imported Data in the HP Quality Center Dashboard

Conclusion

The reporting functions in HP Quality Center Dashboard provide DB Systel, its management team, and its customers with an extensive overview of project progress, status and possible risks, which can be accessed at any time. The data required for reporting originates in the HP Quality Center quality assurance suite. The company's need for the relevant data to be made available for reporting means that HP Quality Center has in effect become the standard tool for test management at DB Systel. However, in order to allow SAP projects to benefit from the integrated approach of the SAP Solution Manager application management platform, user-friendly functions in the SAP environment, and test automation with eCATT, a solution was developed to allow the key results of test management and defect management to be transferred from SAP Solution Manager into the HP Quality Center. In this way, DB Systel's SAP projects can use the application management solution offered by SAP Solution Manager, while still fulfilling the company's requirements in terms of project reporting in HP Quality Center Dashboard.

What can be learned from the experiences of DB Systel GmbH?   Lessons learned

▶ The most suitable tools should be selected on a project-specific basis. The requirements of SAP implementation projects differ considerably from the requirements of any type of development project, for example.

▶ An integrated solution is always preferable to creation of additional interfaces. However, company-specific requirements may necessitate the use of a heterogeneous tool landscape.

▶ Tools like SAP Solution Manager and HP Quality Center have documented interfaces, which enable connections to external tools, although expertise in the relevant programming languages is required. Pragmatic or professional solutions can be implemented, depending on how much time and effort is to be invested.

▶ Using a justifiable investment, pilot test automation projects demonstrate the possibilities, opportunities, and risks associated with the automation of test cases and the use of new tools. They provide a starting point for discussing the next steps to be taken.

SAP Test Acceleration and Optimization supports you in auto-mating test cases that are oriented towards business processes. It does this by automatically generating test components for SAP GUI-based SAP transactions. Together with SAP Quality Center by HP and HP QuickTest Professional, you can compose and execute automatic business process tests for SAP systems.[1]

6   Supporting Test Automation with SAP TAO

Within Testing Option 2, the SAP Test Acceleration and Optimization tool (SAP TAO 2.0; price-list component) provides a new way to create automated test scripts. The development of SAP TAO was based on the following principles:

Functionality

▶ Simplifying creation of automated tests so that even employees without deep knowledge of automation tools and their script languages can create test components and compose automatic test cases

▶ Reducing the maintenance effort associated with automatic tests

Conceptually, SAP TAO builds on the use of the Business Process Testing approach of SAP Quality Center by HP. Here, test cases are composed from individual components within a graphical user interface for test cases (in the case of SAP TAO, these components are the required screen templates and actions). The SAP TAO application itself provides support during creation of these components. It does this by reading the transactions and screen templates to be tested from an SAP system and then automatically generating the corresponding components. You can achieve this either manually or by using the PROCESS FLOW ANALYZER function. The latter records user interactions (for example, a business process) in the test system and uses this information to generate the

---

1 See *https://service.sap.com/saptao*.

required components and a test-case design that contains the recorded components and user inputs.

The current release is SAP TAO 2.0.02, which supports SAP GUI-based applications. The test automation tool HP QuickTest Professional is used to execute the test cases composed in SAP Quality Center by HP.

Below, we will outline the basic idea behind SAP TAO. We will also describe the technical prerequisites as well as the tools required for the test automation procedure with SAP TAO. Finally, we will explain the basic procedure for using SAP TAO to automate and maintain test cases.

6.1 Basic Principle: Automation Through Composition

Significant savings can be achieved if you use automated test cases in regression tests. The tests themselves are executed with practically no need for staff involvement, thus reducing execution time considerably. The resources and time that become available can then be used in the testing environment to increase test coverage; for example, by executing additional test cases manually or by automating or refining additional tests.

Automation costs Irrespective of the automation tool used, you must compare the initial investment in automation (licensing costs as well as the installation, training and creation effort) and the ongoing maintenance of automatic tests with these benefits. Chapter 7 will provide detailed information about the financial aspects of test automation. Here, we will discuss not only the selection of suitable test cases but the extent of the associated effort and the responsibility for creating and maintaining the test cases (for example, an in-house quality assurance team versus outsourcing models). Depending on the quality of the existing manual test cases, coordination between user departments or those responsible for processes and the quality assurance experts dedicated to automating test cases often requires a great effort in practice.

Maintenance When maintaining automatic test scripts, the maintenance effort may be invalidated by changes to the system, user interface or process flow.

Consequently, scripts that are no longer executable must be revised after a test run so that a current, executable regression test set is available. The effort involved must also be considered from a financial perspective. The number of scripts to be modified and the complexity of the changes needed determine the maintenance effort involved. Other factors that affect the maintenance effort include the scope of the change to be tested, the test automation tool used, the experience of the test automation experts, and therefore the level of maturity associated with the automation scripts.

With this in mind, the goal of the SAP TAO concept is to accelerate the initial creation of test cases and to reduce the ongoing maintenance effort associated with automation scripts.

The Business Process Testing approach of SAP Quality Center by HP is used for this purpose. Here, test cases are built using individual reusable components. Such a component can be regarded as a module that executes a specific work step (for example, logging on to a system or creating a purchase order). You can then assign input and output values to these components so that they can be dynamically filled with values in different contexts. SAP TAO creates these components for SAP GUI applications by analyzing the repository in an SAP system. Here, SAP TAO generates components that are based on the screen definitions. The components to be created are selected manually (on the basis of the transaction and screen number) or automatically (by recording the business process to be automated). In addition to the components that are generated, each of which corresponds to a screen in an SAP system, SAP TAO makes available predefined components that implement user inputs, system interactions, and checks, among other things.

Business Process Testing

Thanks to the modular structure, you can reuse the individual modules not only in different test cases but in different contexts within these test cases. When maintaining test scripts created in this way, it is not necessary to modify the content of all affected test scripts after a change (in contrast to recording the test cases). Depending on the scope of the change, it may suffice to adjust only the changed components and test data.

Modular structure

6.2 Components of and Prerequisites for SAP TAO Technology

Tools used The SAP TAO approach is based on the tools and methods associated with Testing Option 2, which we introduced at the start of Chapter 4, *Test Management with SAP Solution Manager*. SAP TAO is an application that automatically creates test components, while SAP Quality Center by HP with Business Process Testing is used to compose or edit test scripts from the components created using SAP TAO. The HP QuickTest Professional tool is used to execute automated test scripts. All in all, the following systems and tools are used:

▸ *SAP Solution Manager* is used to document a project from start to finish. During a project, the requirements for your solution and the associated test objects are recorded in document management and can be transferred to SAP Quality Center by HP via SAP Solution Manager Adapter for SAP Quality Center by HP. With the Business Process Change Analyzer, you can identify changes to a project's business processes in order to determine the scope of the test. SAP TAO can also use the analysis results of the Business Process Change Analyzer to identify test cases or components that might be affected by a change. In addition, SAP Solution Manager with Service Pack 20 or higher is used as an SAP TAO license server.

▸ When testing is integrated into the entire application and project management, *SAP Solution Manager Adapter for SAP Quality Center by HP* is used to exchange data from the Business Blueprint, test-relevant documents, test results, and error messages between SAP Solution Manager and SAP Quality Center by HP. You can use SAP TAO without the adapter. In this case, however, the testing process is decoupled from the remaining application management life cycle. If you need requirements documents, these must be retained redundantly in both systems. Furthermore, test results cannot be analyzed in the context of the SAP Solution Manager project. Also in this case, error messages can only be processed in SAP Quality Center by HP.

▸ As mentioned at the beginning of this chapter, you use *SAP Quality Center by HP* to create and edit test cases and to plan and analyze tests. In addition to the parts of the application already introduced in Chapter 5, you also use the BUSINESS COMPONENTS module. In this module, you can store and manage test components created using SAP TAO. In the Test Plan module, these components are then grouped together to form test cases. Test cases created using the Process Flow Analyzer are also transferred to the Test Plan module.

▶ *SAP TAO* itself is an SAP product that can be installed locally as a standalone Windows application on the user's work station. The main task of the tool is to create test components at screen level by inspecting the system to be tested. Transactions and their screens within the repositories are then analyzed and test components are generated on this basis. You can create the components to be generated by entering the transactions or screens used in the processes to be tested. You can also use the Process Flow Analyzer, which records user interactions and uses this information to determine the required components and a test case design. To identify test cases affected by a change during test case maintenance, SAP TAO accesses the analysis results of the Business Process Change Analyzer in SAP Solution Manager and compares these with the test components you have created. Functions for exchanging data with SAP Quality Center and for optimizing automation scripts are also available. For this purpose, SAP TAO establishes connections to SAP Quality Center and to the target system to be tested.

▶ In Testing Option 2, *HP QuickTest Professional* is used as a test automation tool. SAP TAO requires a local installation of QuickTest Professional, which is used for the "UI Scanner" inspection mode if a transaction uses screens from other objects or contains screens with dynamically generated content. In addition, installation of HP QuickTest Professional is required for all users who execute automatic test scripts from within SAP Quality Center by HP.

▶ The *target system* used for the inspection by SAP TAO is an SAP R/3 or ERP system as of Version 4.6C. The system must have implemented the SAP Solution Tools Plug-In (ST-PI), which contains functions for interacting with SAP Solution Manager. For SAP TAO, in particular, it contains the current version of the TAO agent (TAO 2.0, TAOAGENT). SAP TAO 2.0 no longer supports the agent used for TAO 1.0 (TAO 1.0, TMW_TAOAGENT), which was previously a part of the SAP_BASIS layer, even if this agent is still available in the target system. Consequently, the SAP Solution Tools plug-in must always be available in the target system. For information about downloading and implementing this plug-in, see SAP Note 1404715.

Figure 6.1 shows an overview of the aforementioned components. For information about the detailed prerequisites for the individual tools as well as a description of the steps that you need to follow in order to install SAP TAO, see SAP Note 1404715.

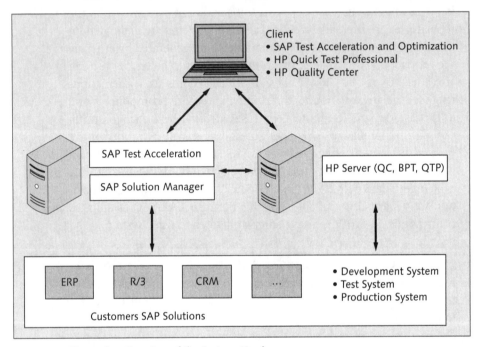

Figure 6.1 Overview of the Systems Used

Configuration

For information about configuring the SAP TAO front-end application and any connected systems, please refer to the latest version of the "Administrator's Guide SAP Test Acceleration and Optimization 2.0," which is available on SAP Service Marketplace (*http://service.sap.com/ instguides*). The administrator's guide describes the required system landscape and provides a detailed description of the SAP TAO configuration and the relevant configuration steps in the connected systems. These involve communicating with SAP Solution Manager, including retrieving the license and configuring SAP Quality Center by HP. Once you have completed the configuration, you can start a self-test, which checks the prerequisites required by SAP TAO 2.0. If an error occurs or if the system issues warning messages, you can call up additional information that will help you to resolve the error.

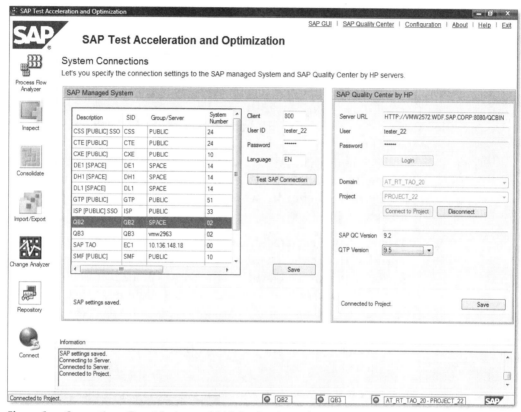

Figure 6.2 Connecting a Target System and SAP Quality Center by HP to the SAP TAO Front-End Application

6.3 Using SAP TAO to Create Test Cases

When you use SAP TAO 2.0, you can create automated test cases (for example, a process chain test as part of an integration test) in two different variants.

Process Flow Analyzer

You use SAP TAO Process Flow Analyzer to record the business process to be automated. The transactions used and their screen templates (screens) are recorded here. The sequence in which the elements and user actions are called is also stored here. The recording can then be used to automatically generate the required test components as well as a test-case design that takes account of the sequence and inputs. The test components are then transferred to the BUSINESS COMPONENTS module of SAP Quality Center by HP, while the test case design is transferred to the "Test Plan" module. The latter can be completed here.

Inspection

Alternatively, you can manually determine the components to be generated by selecting SAP GUI transactions and their screen templates. You do this by entering the transaction code and selecting the required templates. In a procedure known as an "inspection," test components can be automatically generated for the objects selected. The test components are then transferred to the BUSINESS COMPONENTS module of SAP Quality Center by HP, where they can be grouped together to form test cases.

Creating a test case

Once you have generated the required components, you can create the actual test case in the TEST PLAN module of SAP Quality Center by HP by connecting the generated components to predefined action components for a process flow. This includes the addition of check routines (for example, reading status messages) and test data. When you use the Process Flow Analyzer, a test-case design is already available to which you must add actions, data entries, and check routines, if these are required.

Consolidating the scripts

In the next step, you can consolidate the test scripts. Here, a test case that comprises several components is incorporated into a single component. This increases the execution speed of the test case because the test automation framework does not need to be initialized for each individual component but only for the entire test case.

Executing the test

Finally, you can use the relevant functions in SAP Quality Center by HP to schedule and execute the test scripts created and, if necessary, consolidated.

The steps outlined here will be described in detail below:

- Using the Process Flow Analyzer to create test components and test case designs

- Using the inspection procedure to create test components

- Composing test cases

- Defining test data

- Consolidating test scripts

- Planning and executing the tests

6.3.1 Using the Process Flow Analyzer to Create Test Components and Test-Case Designs

In real life, automated test cases are mostly created on the basis of existing manual test cases. Therefore, a useful precondition for working with automation tools is the presence of a sufficiently detailed test-case description. On the basis of this description, you can then use the Process Flow Analyzer in SAP TAO 2.0 to create a design for the automated test case (including the required components).

Prerequisite: test case description

In principle, the use of the Process Flow Analyzer to record a test case is the same as using a capture-and-replay tool to record a test case. While the user executes the test case or business process to be automated in a target system, the test automation tool executed in the background (in this case, the Process Flow Analyzer as a part of the SAP TAO front-end application) logs the work steps performed. Consequently, you must ensure that the test case works without terminations and error messages. Otherwise, these will also be recorded.

Principle of the Process Flow Analyzer

In the case of a capture-and-replay tool, the recording result is typically a static script, which makes it possible to replay the user actions in the target system. In the case of flexible test-case design through modularization, the Process Flow Analyzer delivers the following two work results:

- First, all of the transactions used or their individual screen templates (screens) are recorded and used to generate individual test components.

▶ At the same time, a test case design in which the newly created components are already referenced in the execution sequence is generated. This design also takes account of user actions and user inputs.

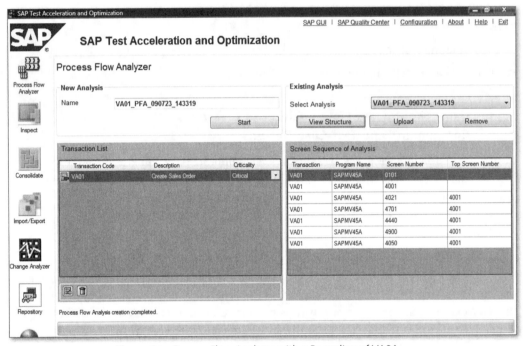

Figure 6.3 Process Flow Analyzer with a Recording of VA01

Recording test cases In technical terms, the recording process is as follows: Within the SAP TAO 2.0 front-end application, transactions that represent the initial screen for a test case or business process to be automated can be added to a list in the PROCESS FLOW ANALYZER view.

After you have chosen START, the selected transaction is called in the target system. At the same time, an additional window in which you can use the Process Flow Analyzer to control the recording is started.

In the target system, you can now perform the process to be automated. In the background, the Process Flow Analyzer records user activities in the system. These include:

1. Transactions used,

2. Individual screens for the transactions,

3. Inputs in data fields, and

4. User actions (for example, pressing buttons or keys)

Once the recording is complete, you can use the relevant function in the control window to stop the Process Flow Analyzer. The system then generates a report that groups together the recorded activities.

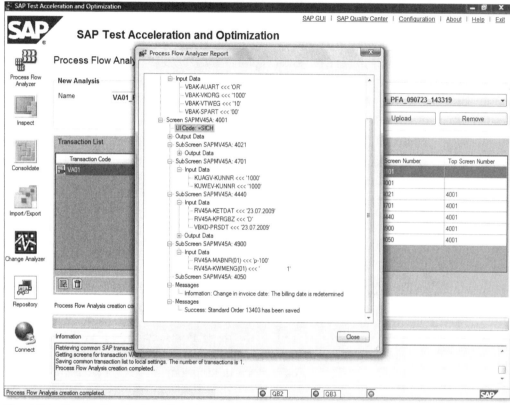

Figure 6.4 Process Flow Analyzer Report

For analyses created in this way, you can display the recorded screen sequence again in the Process Flow Analyzer view.

You also can choose to transfer a recording to SAP Quality Center by HP. Both the components for the recorded screens and a test-case design are created here. The latter contains the components in the recorded sequence, the recorded user actions, and the required components from the SAP TAO library (for example, for script initialization and a logon). The user actions registered by SAP TAO are also mapped using modules from the library. Furthermore, a Microsoft Excel document is created, which contains the data fields used by the user as parameters. You can use this document to define test data for a test. You can specify the storage path for this document in the settings for the SAP TAO application.

SAP TAO will let you know if you transfer components that are already referenced in consolidated components (see Section 6.3.5, *Consolidating Test Scripts*).

When you use the Process Flow Analyzer, selection of components to be inspected is automated. This was not possible in earlier versions of SAP TAO, where only manual selections were possible. Similarly, the creation of the automated test case as a subsequent step is accelerated by the test-case design generated during the recording. In the past, test cases had to be composed manually from the components available.

6.3.2 Using the Inspection Procedure to Create Test Components

Inspection

Alternatively, you can continue to generate test components via manual selection, which was the case in earlier versions of SAP TAO. This inspection procedure is suitable, for example, if you want to update existing components or if you want to create a library of frequently used components that will be used as a basis for the test-case design.

Prerequisite: test case description

One prerequisite for using the inspection sensibly is having a clear idea of the business processes to be automated; ideally this will take the form of adequately detailed test case descriptions. You can then use the inspection procedure to create individual test components that are based on these descriptions. If you choose not to use the Process Flow Analyzer, you can manually determine the screens used in a test case.

Determining the screens used

In the SAP Help, you can choose the TECHNICAL INFORMATION button to obtain the relevant screen numbers, which will also be used later to generate the relevant test components. When determining the screen numbers, please note that a template displayed in the system may comprise several individual screens. In particular, the screen displayed on a tab may have its own screen number.

Test case elements (screens) identified in this way can now be inspected using SAP TAO in order to create components. In the SAP TAO application, you will find the INSPECT function with the following two variants: INSPECTION and UI SCANNER (see Figure 6.5).

You can use INSPECTION to enter the relevant transaction codes. SAP TAO then automatically displays a list of screen templates (screens) that belong to the transaction. In SAP TAO, a list of all transactions and screens from which test modules can be generated is compiled in this way.

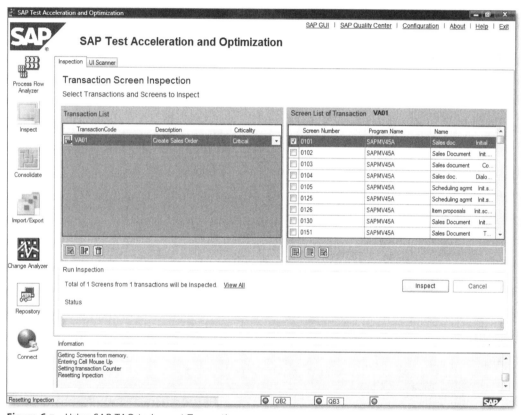

Figure 6.5 Using SAP TAO to Inspect Transactions

The selected elements are then inspected. For this procedure, the selected elements are analyzed in the system and created from these test components. Depending on the configuration selected, these elements are stored locally or transferred to SAP Quality Center. You can use the inspection to create test components without executing the application. In the current version of SAP TAO, the inspection cannot create any test components from dynamically generated screen content.

UI Scanner   If a screen cannot be read using the regular inspection, you can use the UI SCANNER, which is used in conjunction with HP QuickTest Professional and is less restrictive and able to read most screen elements, including dynamically created screens. Working with the UI SCANNER requires you to manually navigate to the screen to be inspected. Here, you also require HP QuickTest Professional so that you can create a test component.

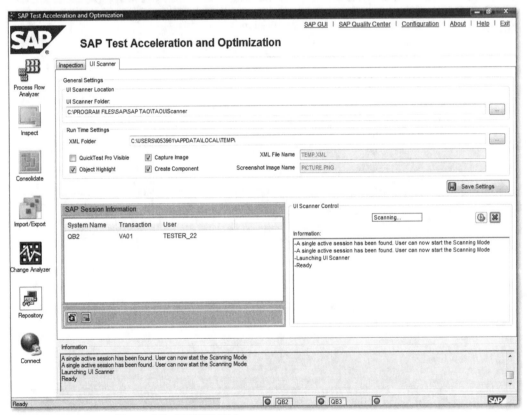

Figure 6.6   SAP TAO UI Scanner

The UI SCANNER is also controlled from the INSPECT function in the SAP TAO application (see Figure 6.6). It recognizes open SAP GUI windows and displays these in SAP TAO. In contrast to the inspection, the scanner, when used in conjunction with HP QuickTest Professional, can record and read all of the screens currently displayed in a SAP GUI. A component created in this way can also be transferred to SAP Quality Center by HP.

6.3.3 Composing Test Cases

After you have created and transferred the test components to SAP Quality Center by HP, the individual modules are available there and can be viewed and processed in the BUSINESS COMPONENTS module. Components predefined by SAP TAO are also provided. Such components must be transferred only once to SAP Quality Center by HP. The predefined components provide functions for dynpro transitions and for the extraction of values from the dynpros. Here, for example, you will find the click events for standard SAP GUI functions or functions for implementing checks (for example, for reading system messages).

Business Components

Test cases are composed in the TEST PLAN module (see Figure 6.7). Similar to the procedure for creating manual test cases (see Section 5.3.3, *Creating Test Cases*), new test cases of the BUSINESS PROCESS type are created here in a freely definable folder structure.

Composing and editing test cases

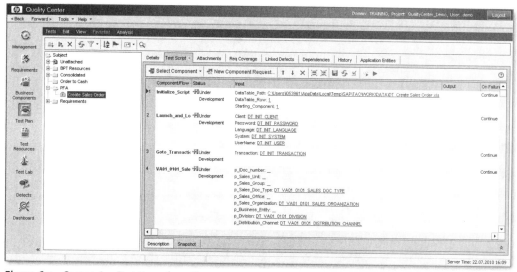

Figure 6.7 Composing Test Cases from Components

If you use the Process Flow Analyzer to create components and test-case designs, the generated test cases are stored here and can be processed further.

A test case created using SAP TAO always comprises the components defined under BUSINESS COMPONENTS. You can select the test components you require for the test case and then make them available in the required sequence. Typically, the components created by SAP TAO (the individual screens of the test case) are connected to predefined actions that control the test case process. For this purpose, SAP TAO makes the aforementioned selection of components available, namely standard SAP GUI buttons, menu entries, and functions (dynpro transition functions; see Figure 6.8).

Figure 6.8 Examples of Standard Components in SAP TAO

6.3.4 Defining Test Data

If an executable test case is available, you can start to parameterize it in the next step. This enables you to execute the test with test data from an external source or to output results for use in other components.

Parameterization

To create these parameters, SAP TAO uses Microsoft Excel files that contain the input and output parameters of a test case. Each table includes a header line whose columns contain the names of the relevant variables. The subsequent lines contain the input or output data for the test iterations to be performed.

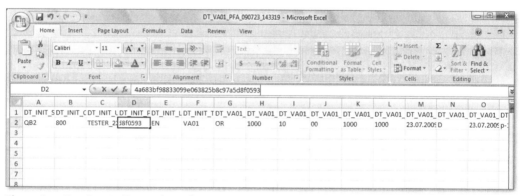

Figure 6.9 Test Data in Microsoft Excel

The components recorded using SAP TAO already contain an input parameter for each input field in the relevant screen. You can edit these parameters in the Test Plan by clicking the relevant component (see Figure 6.10). The values entered in this window are used each time you execute the test case. Variables that are to be referenced in the Excel file contain, instead of the value, a variable name with a specific prefix ("DT_ [Name]") by default; they are freely definable in the SAP TAO configuration.

The "Initialize Script" component, which you must use to start each SAP TAO test case, specifies the name of the Excel file used. You must ensure that this file is available on the relevant front end at execution time. Otherwise, execution of the test case will fail.

"Initialize Script" component

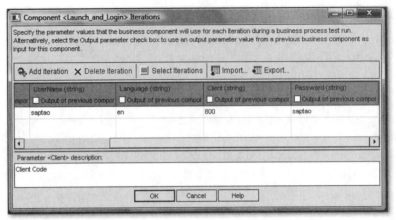

Figure 6.10 Parameterization of Components

6.3.5 Consolidating Test Scripts

As soon as the test case is complete, you can execute it using HP Quick-Test Professional. You can check the status of the automation script execution in the TEST PLAN module at any time. When you execute the test, the components are executed in the sequence specified. This means that Business Process Testing or the SAP TAO Framework must be reinitialized for each component, thus affecting the time it takes to execute scripts with HP QuickTest Pro. To avoid this and to significantly shorten the time required to execute complex process tests, you can consolidate test scripts. This procedure collects all objects and data associated with a test script developed from components and then generates a single test case in the form of a new component.

"Consolidate" function

Consolidation starts in the local SAP TAO application. The CONSOLIDATE function (see Figure 6.11) enables you to select the test cases to be consolidated via the folder structure of SAP Quality Center or by using the component involved. The latter method also enables you to recompose all test cases that contain an updated component. After you have selected a component, SAP TAO displays all test cases that use this component. In both selection modes, you can select test cases and transfer them to a consolidation list. The interaction between the current product versions of SAP TAO and SAP Quality Center by HP does not allow you to use versioning.

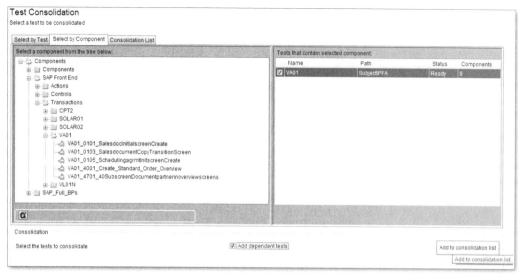

Figure 6.11 Consolidating Test Scripts

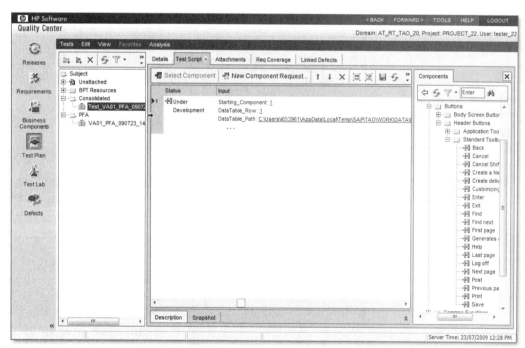

Figure 6.12 Consolidated Test Case in SAP Quality Center by HP

For each test case selected, the function creates a new, consolidated component in SAP Quality Center (see Figure 6.12). In the SAP TAO settings, you then can define the folder in which the components will be stored. Here, you can also specify that a test case is automatically created for each consolidated component.

6.3.6 Planning and Executing the Tests

You plan and execute tests using the methods described in Section 5.3.3, *Creating Test Cases*. In the TEST LAB module, you can group test cases into executable test runs. You can group them together with manual test cases or with automatic test cases created in HP QuickTest Professional. Test cases created using SAP TAO are also executed using the test automation tool HP QuickTest Professional, which must be available on the executing system. In addition to the test status defined in SAP Quality Center by HP, you can also display the test results in the result overview of HP QuickTest Professional or as an XML file generated by SAP TAO.

The resulting overview enables automation experts who are experienced users of HP QuickTest Professional to perform a fast error analysis. You can also use the XML generated by SAP TAO to analyze the components executed. Test managers use the status analysis of test plans in SAP Quality Center by HP.

6.4 Using SAP TAO to Maintain Test Cases

Flexible handling of components

The principle of using previously generated components to compose automatic test cases affects the way in which you maintain test cases. The basic principle behind dividing test cases into individual, independent modules is that these components can be reused and updated flexibly.

In the case of test cases recorded using eCATT or HP QuickTest Pro, the relevant automation experts determine the complexity of the script. Usually, such a script comprises a sequence of actions and check steps and can represent a complete business process (for example, a procurement process). The tool expert can choose the extent to which he or she will consistently implement the principle of modularization during automation. If one part of the process changes (for example, if you want new input fields to be taken into account), the process may have to be fully or partly recorded again. At the very least, it has to be adjusted. The same procedure applies to all test cases affected by this change.

When you adjust test cases that were created using SAP TAO, you can process the individual components irrespective of the test cases in which they are called. Changed components can be replaced or repaired. Updated components are immediately available in all affected, non-consolidated test cases.

Test cases are usually maintained after a system change has been successfully implemented and tested. In other words, test cases that cause an error must be adjusted to the new system conditions.

You can manually execute this process. To do this, use SAP TAO to reinspect the components of the test cases that failed when executing the test set. Components updated in this way are then transferred to SAP Quality Center by HP. Consequently, all non-consolidated test cases that use these components are updated. This step may be all you need to adjust test scripts to system changes.

Manually updating components

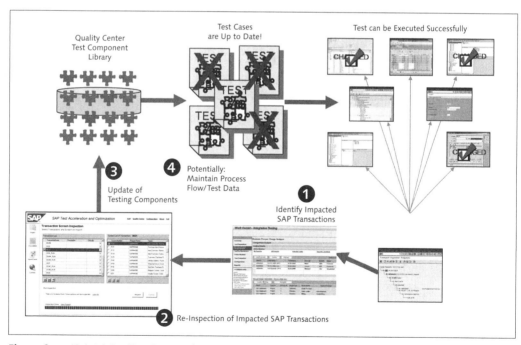

Figure 6.13 Maintaining Test Cases with SAP TAO When Using the Business Process Change Analyzer

In practice, you must also check the affected test cases in terms of the test data used (for example, if input fields were added or omitted). Similarly, you must adjust test cases for which the process flow or execution sequence of the individual components changes. In a final step, you can manually consolidate the updated test cases again in order to improve performance. Updated, executable test cases are then available after a change.

Using the Business Process Change Analyzer You can use SAP TAO 2.0 to automate the identification of components that potentially have changed. For this purpose, you use the Business Process Change Analyzer in SAP Solution Manager to assess the impact that a change will have on components created using SAP TAO and on the resulting test cases.

This presupposes that the necessary prerequisites are available and that upstream work steps have been performed in SAP Solution Manager (see Section 4.4.5, *Extended Functionality for Creating Test Plans and Packages*). In particular, these include:

1. Mapping or documenting the business processes in the form of a Business Blueprint (including the transactions used)

2. Recording the Technical Bills of Material (T-BOMs) for each business process or process step to be analyzed

3. Performing an analysis whereby the T-BOMs of a project are compared with a change event (for example, a transport request)

When assessing components, SAP TAO accesses the analysis results of the Business Process Change Analyzer, which are already available in SAP Solution Manager. These results contain information about the technical objects that were manipulated by the selected change. You can use the CHANGE ANALYZER function to select an existing analysis result from SAP Solution Manager on the basis of the assigned project and its unique ID. SAP TAO then compares this analysis result with the test components that have been created. Remember that you can only perform the analysis for a system currently connected to SAP TAO. You must therefore perform the change analysis successively for a cross-system test case.

A list of components affected by the change is then displayed. An assessment of the impact associated with the change is also shown for each component. The list also takes account of consolidated components.

You can now select the listed elements and assign a repair task that can then be started. The selected components are inspected again, while the consolidated components are automatically reconsolidated.

Components created using the UI Scanner must be manually created again using this scanner. You can then manually change their status to "checked" if, for example, you have successfully executed the relevant test cases and no negative effects result from the change.

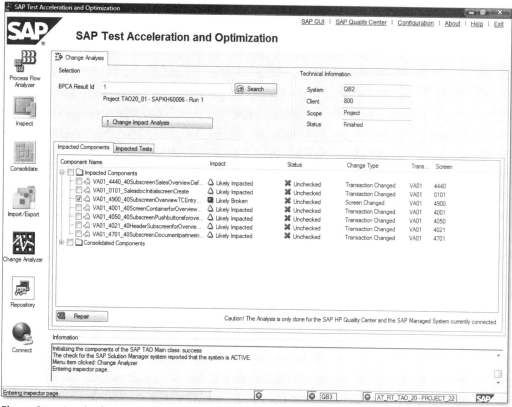

Figure 6.14 Result of a Change Analysis in SAP TAO

As in the case of a manual selection, note that a re-inspection of affected components may be enough to "repair" test cases that were not executable previously. However, you should also check the test case itself, especially to see if you need new test data or changes in the script flow; these will not be considered by a purely technical reinspection of the components.

Postprocessing

6.5 Summary

The new SAP product SAP TAO takes an innovative approach to test automation within the context of Testing Option 2, namely test case composition. The main feature of this procedure is a reduction in the effort associated with creating test cases. In the case of the capture-and-replay approach, the main efforts associated with automation are a (technically) correct recording and subsequent postprocessing of a script. The component-based composition of test cases, on the other hand, places the emphasis on mapping processes from individual, reusable components that are based on screen templates and user actions. There is also a shift in terms of the requirements profile of the test experts who create and maintain automated test cases.

By integrating the Business Process Change Analyzer in SAP Solution Manager, you can make it easier to identify test cases or individual modules that are no longer executable after a change and, for that reason, need to be updated. This means that, in addition to being able to automatically update these components, you can reduce the effort associated with maintaining test cases.

While the technical and the financial benefits of using an auto-mated approach to testing are obvious, the financial benefits are rarely quantified. ROI analyses allow us to determine the scope and limitations of the significant potential benefits of test automation.

7 Economic Aspects of Test Automation

Software testing is always associated with some degree of effort in terms of time (planning, execution, and post-processing) and of cost (systems, space, and, if necessary, installation and license fees for test tools). This effort must be weighed against the potential benefits of greater applica-tion stability and thus greater availability of the system landscape.

Effort and benefits associated with software testing

Software specifications are written by humans, and humans design and implement software. This means that software, by its very nature, always contains errors. Some of these errors will be detected if a certain amount of effort is invested in software testing. Doubling this effort, however, does not mean that twice as many errors will be uncovered. When increasing system stability and the degree to which software is free of errors, the costs involved increase at a much more dramatic rate. Total reliability—in other words, software that is completely free of errors and a completely failsafe system—can never be achieved. Software reliability can nonetheless be brought closer to this ideal.

All of this applies equally to proprietary software solutions and to the implementation of standard software and the adjustment, enhancement, and operation of this software. Test automation allows you to minimize the effort associated with striving to increase reliability over the useful life of your software.

This chapter first presents the benefits of automated testing, and then discusses the factors that have to be taken into account when costing both manual and automated software tests.

Benefits of
automated testing

The most important benefit of automated testing over conventional manual testing is surely the minimization of effort for repeated tests. However, several other factors also speak in favor of automated testing.

▶ The testing process is triggered with practically no need for personnel action, which means that valuable resources are freed up in business departments and specialist areas.

▶ The testing period is shortened dramatically, and the presence of errors is detected immediately.

▶ Thanks to defined checks and check steps, the results of an automated test case are completely clear and unambiguous (OK or not OK). Ambiguities due to incomplete or misleading test documentation are avoided.

▶ In practice, very complex business transactions must also be tested. Preparing, executing, and testing these may involve many different steps whereby the person performing the test may become a source of error. With an automated test script, correct execution does not present a challenge and a completely reliable test of the test objective is ensured. This also applies to situations where people tend to be negligent, for example, on Monday mornings or Friday afternoons when repeating a test for the nth time within a short period, or when the workload is extremely heavy. Automated testing ensures a greater degree of reliability than manual testing.

▶ Today's test automation tools normally generate detailed test logs that provide very good support for subsequent troubleshooting. The log can help you replicate the exact steps taken by the test script in the application in order to see which data was used and to understand the provisional and final results of the test run. The possibility of generating screenshots automatically (in varying degrees of granularity if you use eCATT) significantly increases the informational value of the log.

▶ Automated tests can be repeated under completely stable conditions to pinpoint errors or verify change effects.

▶ The time saved by automated testing can be put to good use by having testers perform additional manual spot checks, thereby providing coverage that exceeds the scope of the original testing plan.

▶ An existing set of automated test cases can be reused in many different ways, not just for testing purposes. Individual script modules, which generate master data and transaction data, can be grouped together and used specifically for data generation. This enables efficient support for the preparation of data in new training or demo clients. If the scripts cover entire business processes, they can be used during orientation of new employees or when teaching process flow to employees.

Because the implementation of automated testing is associated with a significant initial investment, you must determine whether and to what degree this investment can be made and how quickly it will pay for itself.

7.1 Cost Model for Software Testing

To assess the benefits of automated testing compared with manual testing, a cost model for software testing must be developed. The actual figures depend to a great degree on the individual system landscape and the processes used within the enterprise.

Automated testing requires carefully thought-out planning and modeling of a test. A review of test planning by a person or institution that has already successfully developed a similar testing procedure and maintained it on a permanent basis is strongly recommended. It is particularly important that professional support is always provided for the selection of the test tool.

The remainder of this section demonstrates how to calculate the various types of costs that have to be taken into account.

7.1.1 Cost of Designing Test Cases

ROI analyses must take account of the fact that some degree of effort is always associated with designing and creating test cases and documentation, whether testing is manual or automated. In both cases, documentation must be provided to help the testers and script developers do their job.

Level of detail in test case design

With manual testing, the test case descriptions for a very experienced group of testers can be generic because the testers can fill in any missing details based on their knowledge of the process. If, on the other hand, the group of testers have very little experience of the application or indeed of testing, a greater level of detail is required.

With automated testing, the test case documentation is aimed at script developers who generally have a limited knowledge of the application or process. The description of the test cases must therefore be very detailed. As a general rule, the cost of designing test cases is estimated to be slightly higher for automated testing than for manual.

Prerequisites for automated testing

However, the idea of setting up automated testing as an initial testing method and comparing its costs directly with those of manual testing is more of a theoretical consideration than a practical one. The automation of regression tests, for example, always represents a follow-up or supplementary step in the testing process; based on our experience, preparation and implementation of this automation would not necessarily require any additional materials.

An enterprise that does not possess an effective manual regression test set will not test more effectively with an automated approach. However, its desired level of reliability could still be achieved more efficiently. Implementing a tool does not eliminate the underlying lack of a meaningful collection of test cases. In other words: "Automating the chaos runs the chaos faster."[1]

7.1.2   Cost of Test Tools

License and maintenance fees

The manual testing process is often supported by test administration software. Approaches supported by MS Excel lists or Lotus Notes are becoming increasingly rare. This is partly because SAP Solution Manager with its integrated test tools can be used without additional license fees. In order to objectively compare the costs of the tools required by the two approaches, you must take into account the current support for manual testing activities (for example, as a share of the license fees or as maintenance fees). Current test administration products are frequently run on a separate PC or server and also require a special database application. When an enterprise embarks on the process of test automation, Initial investment in a software license for an automation tool is gener-

---

1   Fewster, Mark; Graham, Dorothy: *Software Test Automation: Effective use of test execution tools.* Addison-Wesley Professional 2000.

ally required. In addition to this initial license fee, annual maintenance fees also have to be paid.

Within the context of license and maintenance fees for test automation tools, you also must consider the entire tool landscape in the actual testing environment. For a seamlessly integrated testing process, you must ensure that the test *administration* tool you use supports not only the manual testing activities but also your choice of test *automation* tool. To implement an integrated testing process, you must integrate both of these tools. The test results of automated testing should always be forwarded to the test administration tool in order to achieve central and uniform reporting on the test run and its success.

Integrated use of test administration tools

Further integration into the system landscape enables you to create test automation scripts centrally and to store them together with the relevant manual test cases or in the context of the associated business processes. This also benefits operational test preparation because any change to manual test cases often requires the test scripts to be modified. Integrating these two work steps makes it easier to establish change management practice for automation scripts. That way, automation experts can see changes to manual test cases early on and can then modify the scripts accordingly. The process for accepting modified scripts can also be simplified in this way.

Because a test administration tool usually also controls the assignment of test cases to individual testers, this tool should make it possible for manual and automated test cases to be available to testers. In this way, automated regression test cases, for example, can be grouped together and substeps can be automated (see also the customer report by Hamm-Reno-Group GmbH & Co. KG in Sections 4.12, *Customer Report by Reno Fashion & Shoes GmbH,* and 4.13, *Update of the Customer Report by Hamm-Reno-Group GmbH & Co. KG*). Alternatively, automated procedures can ensure the basic prerequisites for the test; for example, creating test data or creating the necessary preconditions.

Time-based scheduling of automated test cases is a useful test planning function that is partly implemented using the test administration tool. In this way, for example, scripts can be executed at night so that they do not adversely affect manual testing activities. You can also execute test scripts on a regular basis in order to identify unexpected system changes early on. Please note that you must provide infrastructure for whichever test automation tool and methods you choose to use (for example, a client PC that executes GUI-driven test cases). When you use eCATT's TCD driver, server-side execution is also possible.

The test documentation should also be integrated, especially in terms of the obligation to provide supporting documentation. Because test automation tools generally produce extremely detailed technical logs, it makes sense to immediately integrate these documents into the existing test documentation so that they can be viewed during test reporting. You also should consider versioning the test results. In other words, each time you execute a test script, the test result should be documented again in the form of a complete log. Today's test automation tools also make it possible for you to document the test run by means of screenshots, which can be processed further in order to provide supporting documentation. Similarly, an error in a test automation script should also produce an error message in the error management tool being used. Integration scenarios also make sense here.

Considerations when selecting a tool
Such integrated use requires accurate coordination in order to develop the test administration tool and test automation tool. In real life, manufacturers have various product combinations that promise a high level of integration among tools, or interface scenarios that make it possible to exchange data between test tools. These capabilities deserves special attention when selecting a tool or assessing the costs of an automation solution. Your choice of test automation tool may determine how you use a specific test administration tool in order to implement the above integration scenarios and integrate test automation into the entire testing process in the best way without any integration gaps.

Typically, test administration tools are implemented first. In the case of an increasingly controlled testing process, automated test cases (for example, a regression test set) can be identified in a logical manner. Here, you must bear in mind that the tools used previously can influence your choice of test automation tool if correspondingly tight integration is required.

Other dependencies
Dependencies in the test automation environment must also be considered outside of test administration, in combination with other tools. Depending on the range of functions within the test administration tool and the other tools used, you have to take a look at integration in the context of other programs or functions. These include, for example:

- Document management for manual test cases that have been assigned and their test results

- Management of requirements for test cases, especially given an enterprise's internal or external obligation to provide supporting documentation

- Release management or sufficient versioning of test cases and test results

- Error management or Service Desk

- If necessary, the provision and forwarding of test data

During the project, automated test cases can also be used to identify performance bottlenecks or they can be used during performance analyses (in the sense of a single user performance test). Here you also find dependencies or a corresponding function that is provided by the test automation tool. In addition to evaluating the corresponding functions, it may also be necessary to check how the monitoring solutions used interact with each other.

Test automation and performance tests

The same applies to tools that support test automation or enhance existing approaches. In the SAP environment, this includes the creation of component-based test cases whereby, for example, SAP TAO can be used to create test automation components as a result of analyzing the relevant screens. In addition to the analysis tool, you usually require a specific test administration tool, which you can use to manage these modules and compose test cases by means of a specific procedure. Such test cases must also be executed using a test automation tool.

Dependencies when creating component-based test cases

When selecting a tool, such dependencies must be considered because they may significantly affect license and maintenance fees. Please note that test tools that require separate systems have specific hardware and software requirements that must also be fulfilled. In this case, it is necessary to implement a separate server, including an operating system, SAP NetWeaver Application Server, and a database. In addition to the initial costs including the time and effort required for the installation and, if necessary, training for administrators, you must also calculate the effort associated with production operation or system maintenance when selecting your tool.

Selecting test automation tools

Such considerations always arise against the backdrop of the test tools used, especially in the context of the enterprise's individual testing process when selecting the tool. The issues outlined here and in Section 2.8, *Selecting Test Tools*, should provide a foundation when creating an individual criteria catalog.

Qualification

If you do not want to outsource the implementation and maintenance of test automation, you must train some of your own staff in the use of the test automation tool. The quality, content, and scope of the training provided, as well as the quality and experience of the trainer or coach, will determine how soon your employees will be able to use the test tool correctly and efficiently.

Installation and upgrades

Today's automation tools normally have to be installed on the relevant clients. The effort involved in doing so must be taken into account, as must the effort associated with upgrading this installation when software patches or correction versions are delivered.

Clearly, then, this type of cost encompasses both one-off costs and ongoing costs. Once again, SAP Solution Manager is an exception to the rule because eCATT can be used from this central application management platform. When a regression test is enhanced to include process components that must be run on non-SAP systems, a third-party tool must be used in addition to eCATT to cover the third-party applications.

Using automation to garner initial experiences

If, today, an enterprise wants to embark on an automation project, we recommend that it should first acquire some expertise, either with a proof of concept or by making a minimal investment in tools.

Naturally, one alternative is to start with eCATT within your SAP solution. At a later stage, you can decide which third-party software you want to use to automate your non-SAP applications or whether to dispense with testing the third-party systems behind the interfaces. One alternative would be to use eCATT to trigger the import of fixed values in order to test the interface itself.

The option of using eCATT, supplemented by a third-party tool, also minimizes the number of software licenses required for the third-party tool, in particular if its scripts can be fully managed in SAP Solution Manager. We always recommend this approach to customers whose critical business processes are predominantly mapped by SAP applications.

Another way to garner initial experience with test automation is to execute a proof of concept for a solution that is subject to a license fee and to do this on the basis of a demo licensing contract. In such an approach, you can, with a reasonable amount of effort, assess the many functional options of the tool or tool suite in the application prototype. It is appropriate to use external support in order to support the installation, configuration, initialization of integration connections, and creation of demo scenarios within a limited period of time.

Demo scenarios

We recommend this approach to customers who have not deployed many SAP solutions in their landscape, those who, for training or standardization reasons, want to use only one automation tool, or those who want to reap the benefits of the "Testing by Composition" approach. For more information, see Section 7.1.6, *Testing Costs When Creating Component-Based Test Cases.*

7.1.3 Costs of Implementing Test Automation

The following general principles must be taken into account when automating testing.

General principles

▶ It is not essential to automate all test cases. A test case that will not be repeated does not have to be automated.

▶ The more a test script can be reused, the more worthwhile the investment in its design will prove to be.

▶ Test automation is a means to an end and not an end in itself. If automation of the last five percent of test cases has been too costly in terms of both time and money, these tests should be implemented manually instead.

In any case, there are many good examples of how both approaches to testing can be usefully combined. For example, complicated preparations (for data retrieval, for example) could be automated, while the actual testing is done manually.

The effort associated with implementing test automation essentially consists of the time required to create and parameterize the scripts and the time required to supplement semantic checks, if needed. One example of a semantic check is the export of a value from a database table for a comparison of target and actual results. These steps are accompanied by

Script creation and formal acceptance

ongoing, formal executability tests. Scripts that have been developed should always be formally approved by a person with an appropriate level of expertise.

Modularization and reutilization By developing generic automation modules to generate master data, you can ensure that your scripts are essentially recyclable. These can then be combined with other automation modules to map various process chains. Constant adherence to the principles of modularization and reuse accelerates the implementation and, in particular, the maintenance of test sets.

It must be noted, however, that the test scripts may be time-consuming to create, depending on the SAP transaction used and on the check logic to be implemented. In addition, real challenges may present themselves that can only be overcome by using a flexible and powerful tool. For example, certain transactions can store different user contexts in different sessions. You can solve this problem very efficiently with eCATT by using the `Inline ABAP` command with a short ABAP sequence. The integration of ABAP source code represents one of the unique features of eCATT (see also Section 8.12, *Further Steps*).

Defining automation goals In most cases, automation is technically only possible in cases where clear and correct programming is used. Once this is ensured, testing can be automated as much or as little as you want. Based on our experience, the test objective for an automated regression test set is usually verification of the functional correctness and resulting availability of the critical business processes in an enterprise. The testing of roles and authorizations can also be automated. Even if you combine these two test objectives, you still never will reach 100% automation, but you will achieve a sound level of reliability with minimal effort.

7.1.4 Costs of Maintaining Test Cases

In the past, when the costs of manual and automated testing were compared, the cost of maintaining scripts was always cited as an argument against automation. Certainly this cost is real and should not be ignored in any financial analysis. The actual costs are largely determined by the frequency with which changes are made, as well as the scope of those changes.

After changes are made in the system—for example, after you import a Support Package or change a process by integrating an additional screen—the test scripts must normally be adjusted in accordance with the changed software. These adjustments are required so that an up-do-date test set is always available and can then be used at any time for quick and reliable diagnostics. However, the automated test set itself indicates, by means of test logs, where the solution has changed. This corresponds to the original thinking behind a regression test and makes the entire adjustment process very efficient.

How up-to-date are automated test sets?

Many enterprises regularly use automated test sets, with which they naturally strive, first and foremost, to safeguard application stability and availability. Any changes that have to be made to the automated test scripts are thus evenly distributed.

The ideal approach to automated testing of a Support Package implementation would be to run all test scripts beforehand. Scripts that produce errors or terminate must then be analyzed and adjusted. After this adjustment, all scripts should run without terminating and without errors.

Automated testing of Support Packages

The Support Package can then be imported. In just a few hours, the automated test scripts return clear results, indicating which processes in the company are still stable and which were affected by the changes in the system. Mapping of the processes in the system requires adjustment activities that must also be performed for the parts of the test scripts that identified the problems. The "Implementation of Support Packages" project ends when both the solution and the test scripts run without errors.

To be accurate, however, the costs of adjusting and changing the manual test case descriptions must be added to the costs of adjusting and maintaining the automated test scripts. These must also be adjusted when changes are made to the system, in particular to individual functions or business processes. Naturally, it may be much more time-consuming in this case to pinpoint exactly where the adjustments should be made. With long process chains in particular, the effects of changes often cannot be foreseen. Actual maintenance may be completed in just a few minutes.

Maintenance requirements for manual test cases

7.1.5 Costs of Implementing a Test Cycle

The costs of implementing a test always involve the effort associated with planning, coordinating, monitoring, and reporting, as well as the execution times for the relevant test cases. In the case of manual tests, these execution times make up the greatest portion of the overall costs. Even if with the same group of testers, the execution times will remain largely the same.

With automated tests, on the other hand, the human effort involved in executing the test is limited to starting the scripts and evaluating the test logs. Compared with manual tests, the execution times are practically negligible, and they remain that way even when the tests are repeated.

The costs of implementing a test cycle are particularly significant because the costs are incurred each time testing is repeated. In the case of regression tests in particular, the automated approach is therefore associated with huge potential savings.

7.1.6 Testing Costs When Creating Component-Based Test Cases

Testing by
Composition

Creating component-based test cases is an alternative or supplementary approach to implementing test automation. The basic idea behind this concept is to compose test cases from individual components that can be used repeatedly in different contexts. Here, a component can be regarded as a module that executes a work step in the target system (for example, filling a screen template or screen). These modules can be used to compose a modular test case (a method known as "Testing by Composition"). Your parameters can then be filled with different test data.

The components from SAP transactions or for individual screens are created using a tool that analyzes the repository of an SAP system. In addition, predefined components are used that execute actions in the SAP system, such as activating standard control elements or reading displayed values. You can then use a test automation tool to execute the components themselves or the completed test cases.

Cost model

It is clear that the basic aspects of test automation (tool costs, the implementation effort, and test case maintenance), which were listed in the preceding chapters, also apply to this principle. We will discuss some factors that, in addition to our general observations, highlight the differences associated with this procedure from the perspective of testing costs. We do not claim that these descriptions are exhaustive. Rather, they provide information about designing an assessment matrix for the development of an individual cost model or a decision-making aid when selecting a different test automation procedure. Selecting a tool and establishing a cost model or ROI model must always occur on an enterprise or project basis. The same applies to assessing test automation approaches. The enterprise's own testing process should always be at the forefront of the assessment. Therefore, an assessment of which test automation approach brings benefits and a high ROI for a specific enterprise must include individual requirements and expectations as well as considerations from real-life test automation.

One key element when evaluating the "Testing by Composition" procedure for a specific enterprise is the aforementioned considerations of individual tools and tool components. There are dependencies here that must be considered in real life (depending on the test tools used previously) and that may significantly influence the license and maintenance fees associated with the required software. Especially when dealing with server-based products, you must also observe additional hardware and software requirements.

Tool selection and tool costs

At first it seems difficult to make a direct comparison between the "Testing by Composition" approach and the classical creation procedure. For the latter, a test automation expert creates a test case or a test case module within the selected automation tool. The result is an executable automation script that must be enhanced to include specific check steps and check instructions and that can be linked with other modules.

Implementing test automation

In the case of the "Testing by Composition" approach, the time and effort associated with script development (that is, recording and parameterizing a test script) gives way to the following two work steps: An analysis tool is used to create screen-based components, which are then used to compose a test case. The primary reason for recording the process is to identify the necessary components and specify their sequence in a test case. A test case design created in this way comprises individual components that can be used in a graphical interface to compose a test case. Alternatively, you can manually create the test components by selecting the transaction names and the screens called within a transaction.

Identifying and generating test components

In this case, the test case to be created is also composed of individual modules.

By composing test cases from reusable components, the "Testing by Composition" approach promises to significantly reduce the complexity associated with creating executable test cases, when compared with capture-and-replay approaches. The larger the existing module library, the faster you can create or enhance new test cases.

Please note that a script recording in the "Testing by Composition" approach represents a concatenation of individual components (for example, screen templates and user interactions). In every case, you must also check the executability of or need for other required components. When manually creating or modifying component-based scripts, you must also consider the effort involved in searching for suitable components or, if these are not available, identifying (for example, by screen used) or creating them. Significant efforts made in this way can reduce the speed advantage associated with automated component creation.

Creating test cases from test components

Test cases created from the components generated are used to compose complete test cases in a user interface. The requirements profile of users who compose the test cases must be checked beforehand. Although this approach seems easier when compared to classical script development, you must decide on a case-by-case basis whether, for example, key users or employees in user departments can assume responsibility for composing test cases. In addition to the visual creation of test cases, you need to have a solid basic understanding of test automation in order to validate the test cases, insert check routines, and use test data. As part of the qualification initiatives, employee training must be provided here. A cost analysis should take account of the time and effort associated with training employees and creating test cases by composing modules.

Check logic and semantic checks

In this phase, each individual project must be checked to learn how extensively check logic and semantic checks are required for automated test scripts and the degree of complexity with which these can be implemented. For example, reading a status message is much easier than direct access to a database table. However, the quality achieved when reading the database table is much higher than when reading the status message. Therefore, when selecting a tool, you should evaluate the extent to which you can use the relevant tool to implement the required flow logic and checks. Similarly, you need to evaluate the time and effort associated with using test data; in other words, how easy or time-consuming it is to define a list of values that can be used by component-based test cases. Fundamentally, parameterization, sequence control, checks, and pass-by values always require additional manual effort, irrespective of the automation approach used.

Similarly, during a tool analysis or cost-benefit assessment, you should compare the test objects to be automated with the functionality of the selected tool. Irrespective of the automation procedure that you actually use, it makes sense to identify the technologies to be automated (for example, SAP GUI, web interfaces, or web services) and to compare them to the functional scope of the test automation tools. When assessing effort and cost, you must consider an approach that is based on several test tools or different procedures. Issues to consider include additional license and maintenance fees, hardware and training costs, and a more time-consuming process for creating, adjusting, and accepting test cases.

Sometimes, particularly in the case of new test automation tools, you must also consider specific technological limitations. Answering the following questions may suggest that additional time and effort is required.

► For which technologies can you use a tool, for example, to create test components?

► What limitations exist here? Can all types of transactions in the SAP environment be entered or are certain technologies not taken into consideration (for example, program logic executed on the front end, or dynamic content)?

► Are there alternative methods for generating components for these non-analyzable technologies? If so, how much additional effort is required (for example, the amount of time needed to create a test case or to obtain the necessary expertise for test automation experts)?

The basic idea behind component-based testing is that you can edit individual components and therefore repair them (for example, after changes), irrespective of the test cases in which they are referenced. Within the context of a theoretical cost analysis, this significantly reduces the effort associated with maintaining test cases. If, for example, you use a component such as a system logon in several hundred test cases, you must only modify the component, not each individual test case.

Maintaining test cases

Furthermore, if components are not recorded but are automatically generated by the analysis of the system to be tested, the time and effort associated with maintaining cases falls even further. It is therefore conceivable that a set of test cases can be fully used again after regenerating components that can no longer run.

You can use these assumptions in a theoretical cost model in order to obtain an overview of the potential and possible reduction in effort associated with a component-based approach. However, you should always combine these considerations with other real-life factors.

In real life, you probably do not always achieve the ideal scenario—the complete repair of test cases after change events without significant effort—for each test case. The use of test data and changes in the process flow of a test case, for example, always require subsequent manual corrections and adjustments. In the case of the former, you should check how the regeneration of components affects the defined test data. Process changes also require an adjustment to the flow logic of the test case. Within the context of an effort and cost analysis, you must critically examine the extent to which this is relevant for customized test cases and typical change events.

Implementing a test cycle
The information provided in Section 7.1.5, *Costs of Implementing a Test Cycle,* in relation to implementing a test also applies, without any changes, to component-based approaches. An additional aspect that you must consider when composing test cases from individual components (irrespective of the tool used) is the speed at which the test is executed. Sometimes, you have to restart the test framework for each individual component, which results in a low execution speed. Measures to reduce this effect (for example, consolidating the individual steps) increase the complexity of the testing process. A corresponding consolidation step must also be scheduled when creating test cases. This step requires additional time for test preparation and test case maintenance. If necessary, you must also adjust the assignment of test cases to individual test sets or testers. Such efforts must be considered within the context of a cost analysis. You should also check the extent to which summarizing components can affect the use of test data that has already been defined.

7.1.7 Individual Test Cost Model

On the basis of these various cost types, you can create your own cost model for your test items, which will clearly show you the benefits of test automation for the life cycle of your software solution.

We have deliberately avoided using formulas or graphics here. Experience has shown that the full picture cannot be represented in models. However, the following key considerations can be derived on the basis of the information specified above and on your individual cost model.

▶ First, test automation incurs costs initially, but dramatic savings can **Key considerations** then be made in comparison with manual testing periods over the longer term. Valuable resources remain in the user departments.

▶ Because implementation of test automation represents an enhancement to an individual testing process, it must be integrated into each testing process in a logical manner. Product combinations that comprise test administration tools and test automation tools can support you here. Your selection of a suitable automation tool depends, in particular, on the planned or existing test tool environment and on the technologies to be automated. Your choice of tool may result in costs such as license fees, hardware and software costs, and training costs.

▶ The profitability of automated testing depends both on how long and how frequently the testing procedure is to be used during this time.

▶ When performing a cost-benefit analysis, you should also take into account the options for reusing your test scripts in other application scenarios (for example, test data generation).

▶ In practice, the effort associated with maintaining your automated test scripts is essentially determined by the number of tests to be performed and, in particular, how frequently changes are made in your system.

▶ If you have an automated regression test set, you should test at regular intervals (for example, once a week). This measure will not reduce your testing costs. However, it will increase the attainable benefits of the approach by helping you protect your solutions from unwanted changes.

▶ Automation approaches such as component-based test case creation can also contribute to a further reduction in costs and effort, especially when creating and maintaining test cases. In individual cases, you must check the extent to which the theoretically achievable potential benefits can actually be achieved for a specific project.

▶ Experience has shown (see also the INVISTA customer report in Section 7.5, *Customer Report by INVISTA Resins & Fibers GmbH*, and its update in Section 7.6) that, as a rule, significant and quantifiable savings can be made by implementing an automated regression test compared with manual testing. In most cases, the investment will have fully paid for itself by the time the initial project is completed and the first Support Package test is conducted.

This quantitative effect is easier to demonstrate than the increase in application stability and security that can also be achieved with automation. Message statistics from your Service Desk may shed some light on this. Look at the total number of errors that occurred in your production system over a given period. How critical were these errors?

Additional criteria, such as the cost of eliminating errors, as well as the costs in terms of profits lost during system downtime, are also helpful during your assessment. We describe this assessment in the next section.

7.2   Cost Model for Software Errors

The first part of this chapter concerned itself with the costs involved in software testing. We will now turn our attention to the benefits. Software testing is essentially used to detect errors before the software is used in production. In order to assess the benefits of software testing, it is necessary to consider the costs associated with software errors. We can distinguish between two different categories of errors:

▶ Errors not detected during software testing

▶ Errors detected during software testing

7.2.1 Errors Not Detected During Software Testing

If an error is not detected during software testing and it finds its way into the live system, this may result in disruptions to the system. A process for dealing with such situations is explained below in accordance with the ITIL standard (*IT Infrastructure Library*).

According to ITIL, a user reports a disruption in production operation to the Service Desk as an *incident*. The incident is recorded and forwarded to *Incident Management*. Incident Management finds a workaround and restores production operation as quickly as possible. The *Problem Management* process attempts to isolate the cause of the incident and to record it as a problem. If a problem is found, it is recorded and forwarded to *Change Management*. In Change Management, a change to eliminate the error is authorized. The error is then localized by developers at code level as a separate project, and is eliminated. The corrected version of the software is sent to *Release Management*, where it undergoes the standard *release process*, including software testing.

ITIL process for correcting errors

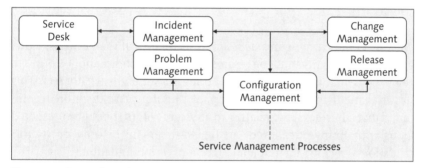

Figure 7.1 Extract from the ITIL Process Overview—Service Support Processes and ITIL Function Service Desk

The costs associated with an error not detected during testing are as follows.

Error costs

Error costs =   *Costs incurred by disruption of production operation*
      + Costs for Service Desk and workaround
      + Costs for detecting the cause of the problem
      + Costs for correcting the error
      + Costs for the release process

The critical point here is the costs incurred as a result of production operation being disrupted. If a business-critical core process in a company is affected or disrupted by an error, the potential costs are huge (for example, lost sales and profits). Therefore, regression tests normally focus on these processes at a minimum.

Business case One of our customers who used the services of SAP Consulting designed a business case for the occurrence of a fatal error in the live system and assessed the resulting costs. This helped the customer decide whether to implement test automation. This business case was created as part of the research into whether it would make sense to implement an upgrade project with test automation. The customer assumed that a fatal error could result in system downtime lasting a maximum of three days. After three days, a replacement system would be procured and installed. In this scenario, the costs would be as follows.

Financial implications of system downtime	€1,340,000
IT costs for troubleshooting	€57,500
Total costs	**€1,397,500**

Of course, the exact figures depend on the nature of the business. However, if sales orders cannot be created or delivery notes cannot be printed, this means that an enterprise can no longer supply its customers. This has an immediate effect on the company's liquidity. We therefore recommend that a business case relating to a system failure should be presented along with an investigation of the financial benefits before a decision is made for or against the implementation of test automation.

Costs of correcting an error Undetected errors may result in costs if they result in production downtime. The costs of providing support for users through the Service Desk, producing a workaround, identifying the cause of the problem, and eliminating the error are all unavoidable. However, they can be easily calculated and are relatively small. The costs of releasing the corrected software are high, however, because the entire release process, including testing, must be repeated. If a non-critical error occurs, these costs can be avoided if the corrections can be rolled out with the next scheduled release.

The actual costs of an error that is not detected during software testing depend on the company, the application, the processes, and other factors. According to Fewster and Graham,[2] these costs are likely to be in the order of €1,000—or approximately $1,400—on average. However, this figure is not based specifically on an SAP environment.

7.2.2 Errors Detected During Software Testing

If an error is found in the software before the start of production operation, the outlook is obviously much improved. Adverse effects on production can be avoided in this case. The costs of formulating a workaround and providing user support through the Service Desk do not apply. Instead of a complete release process for the corrected software version, a new test is simply conducted. The costs of a detected error are as follows.

Error costs = Costs for detecting the cause of the problem
+ Costs for correcting the error
+ Costs for testing the software again

The ratios between the various cost types may differ significantly depending on the exact nature of the error scenario.

This model applies to both manual and automated testing. If an error is detected with a test script, the cause must be isolated, the error eliminated, and the solution verified by testing the software again. Naturally, the costs and/or time and effort involved in actually eliminating the error are the same in both cases. On closer inspection, however, two advantages of using automated test scripts become obvious:

Automated software testing

▶ The log function that is available when you use a test automation tool provides considerable support for troubleshooting. The eCATT log, for example, not only records all of the relevant system messages, but also allows you to replicate all of the steps and data processing executed by the script in the application.

▶ If necessary, the error can easily be reproduced by starting the test script again. The time and effort associated with reproducing and accurately isolating the error are thus significantly reduced.

If the error detected is due to a deliberate change, the script can be adjusted and then repeated in order to verify the change and ensure

---

2 Fewster, Mark; Graham, Dorothy: *Software Test Automation: Effective use of test execution tools*. Addison-Wesley 1999.

that the script has been modified correctly. If, on the other hand, the error detected results from a change that was made unknowingly, in other words, if the error is a real error, the application itself must be modified.

7.3 Overall View

If we now juxtapose the costs of software testing with the costs of software errors, it becomes clear that the benefits of automated testing heavily outweigh those of manual testing.

Automation of regression tests

Automated tests can significantly reduce the time and effort associated with manual testing. The benefits increase in direct proportion to the frequency with which the test set is used, and in inverse proportion to the frequency with which the system to be tested is affected by changes. In practice, the most common application scenario for test automation is the regression test. In this scenario, significant savings can be made compared with manual testing.

The benefits are not as great in other scenarios, such as tests in the development system or module tests in a customer-specific development. It is often helpful to use automated tests here also, but the value added is significantly less than in the case of a regression test. This is because the cost of maintaining the test scripts is greater due to frequent changes to the system.

Regular execution of test sets

As well as reducing the time and effort associated with manual testing, test automation also generates benefits in another way. Because the costs of executing a test cycle are much less, the test scripts can be run more frequently and at regular intervals. Regular execution of the test scripts protects the system from unwanted changes and thus helps prevent errors from creeping into the live system. As a result, the risk of production downtime is reduced, and the costs of error handling avoided.

Faster troubleshooting

A final point to be considered relates to the costs of the actual error correction. The logs generated by automated test scripts are technically very detailed in the case of eCATT. They thus provide an ideal starting point for localizing and correcting the errors identified. Automated testing therefore reduces both the number of errors in a live system and the costs of correcting any errors detected.

7.4   Summary

Test automation is not an end in itself. It offers tangible and verifiable benefits in the form of reduced effort compared with manual testing, reduced use of specialist personnel and key users in testing, as provides a high level of application stability and availability. Errors can be quickly identified, localized, and analyzed.

In order to weigh the costs and benefits of automation, we must use a cost model to calculate the absolute profitability and the payback period compared with manual testing over the life cycle of a solution. The cost analysis must also take account of the costs involved in eliminating errors, as well the cost of profits lost in the event of system downtime. This analysis will produce the clearest results in the case of regression test automation. Other scenarios must be analyzed in more detail.

Weighing up the costs/benefits

We recommend that you obtain professional support from a source that has a proven track record in the successful development of an automated testing procedure and maintenance of the procedure over the long term.

7.5   Customer Report by INVISTA Resins & Fibers GmbH

> **Note**
>
> This customer report was published in the first edition of this book. The company profile has been updated at the request of the customer. However, the report itself remains unchanged. At the end of the chapter, you will find a sustainability report that describes the long-term effects of methods, tool use, consulting support, and current customer developments or projects and also updates the ROI study.

"With eCATT test automation, we can confidently reduce the risks to our business-critical business processes. Once the test scripts run without errors, we know we can rely on our SAP system to operate smoothly."

Lothar Hafner
INVISTA Resins & Fibers GmbH, SAP Cluster Lead

INVISTA Resins & Fibers GmbH

INVISTA is one of the world's largest integrated producers of polymers and fibers, primarily for nylon, spandex, and polyester applications. INVISTA operates in more than 20 countries across North America, South America, Europe, and the Asia-Pacific region. The company's global business areas deliver exceptional value to customers through its technological innovations, market insight, and powerful portfolio of globally recognized trademarks such as LYCRA® fiber, ANTRON® carpet fiber, and POLYSHIELD® resin. INVISTA products find many applications in everyday life, for example, home furnishings and bedding, as well as in sports and leisure equipment. INVISTA also supplies various technical products, such as furnishings for passenger compartments in cars, technical fabrics for transportation systems, safety belts, tents, silos, tarps, and airbags.

The first SAP rollout at INVISTA Resins & Fibers GmbH took place in Germany in 1998. The IT infrastructure at the company is characterized by an extremely high level of outsourcing. A total of approximately 520 SAP users are supported by a small team of in-house consultants, who also coordinate approximately 10 key user groups, and manage the SAP R/3 Enterprise system, in which around 75% of the available SAP functions and components are used (see Figure 7.2).

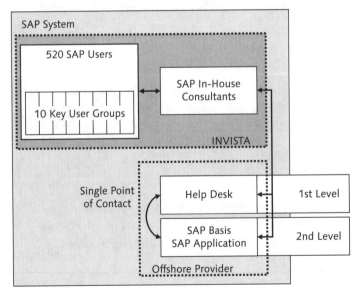

Figure 7.2 Organizational Structure of the SAP System at INVISTA Resins & Fibers GmbH

INVISTA saw the impending discontinuation of maintenance for its R/3 4.0B system as an ideal opportunity to upgrade to SAP R/3 Enterprise. The migration was largely defined as a technical upgrade. It was essential to ensure that the company's critical business processes were available after the upgrade without any major changes. The risks involved in the upgrade project also had to be minimized. An established manual testing process was already in place at INVISTA Resins & Fibers GmbH at this time. Detailed lists with test cases were developed in collaboration with the company that was INVISTA's outsourcing provider at the time. All test steps for all business transactions were documented in great detail in Word documents and with screenshots.

Manual testing represented a considerable cost, while documentation of the test results generated very large volumes of data. This situation provided the motivation for minimizing the recurring manual testing activities. Implementing automation as part of the upgrade project seemed to be a realistic objective because the benefits of doing so would be very quickly realized in this case because of the costs incurred by testing.

Lothar Hafner, Lead Project Manager and contact person for this reference customer, regards the systematic and structured documentation of all business transactions as a key factor in the success of the test automation project:

> *"We were very fortunate in that we had already organized our test cases in a very structured way according to component area. This gave us a huge head start when it came to setting up the SAP Test Workbench and automation. I would advise anyone embarking on a similar project that this preparatory will work really pay off. Once you have done this, it is much easier to answer the question: 'What exactly do I need to test?'"*

A tendering process involving 11 vendors had to be completed before the company involved any external partners in this complex system conversion. The project objective was to complete the upgrade within a short time frame and on a tight budget, while simultaneously providing intensive training for all users and automating testing for the subsequent regression test sets. In 2004, SAP Consulting Germany won the tender by offering a "one-stop package." As well as the SAP consultants and

Upgrade to R/3 Enterprise

Decision to use SAP Consulting

INVISTA's in-house consultants, team members from the then outsourcing provider were also involved in the project. A manageable project team meant that coordination problems and misunderstandings were avoided, while the central project space provided allowed for short communication channels.

A decision also had to be made about which automation tool to use. SAP's test automation tool was quickly chosen, thanks to the tight integration of eCATT with the SAP NetWeaver Application Server. It can be used without incurring additional license costs due to its availability as a component of SAP Basis.

Task sharing The sharing of tasks among the in-house and external consultants followed a clear strategy. SAP's consultants brought with them technical expertise and experience of developing automated test scripts and implementing the tool. The in-house consultants, meanwhile, provided business process expertise. Looking back, Lothar Hafner believes that this clear distinction still makes sense:

> *"This was the key to the project's success. The business expertise was provided by INVISTA Resins & Fibers GmbH, while the expertise in tools and technologies was supplied by SAP Test Management Consulting. This approach worked very well."*

Level of automation INVISTA Resins & Fibers GmbH initially envisioned starting several test steps with the automated solution as part of the project. Specifically, the plan was to automate some 300 test cases. However, once the project had started, and on the advice of the SAP consultants, it was decided that one complete business process, the plant maintenance process, would be used as a pilot as part of an integration test.

This very complex process chain incorporates several different application components. Automating the entire process chain using eCATT scripts that were linked allowed us both to test the individual transactions, and to check their interaction with one another and their interfaces.

"Preliminary products" process The "preliminary products" process was by far the most complex process in terms of automation because it incorporated two levels of production plus the sales process (see Figure 7.3). The script first generates the required master data and transaction data. Next, the materials, inspection plan, planned recipe, certification profile, and control cycle are created.

The raw materials are then purchased and released, the goods receipt generated, and the process order created. A batch is created with an INVISTA-specific transaction called ZACK, and an inspection lot is generated. Access is then simulated via the PMS (Production Management System) interface.

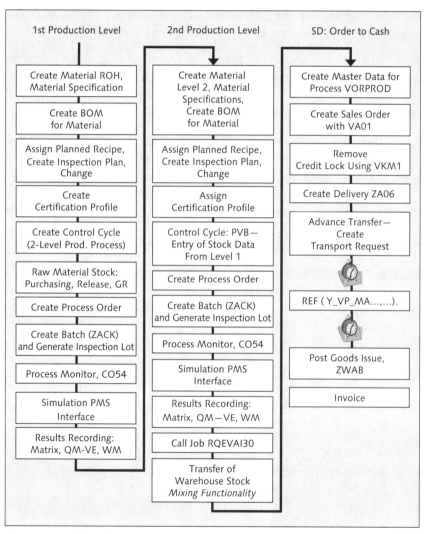

Figure 7.3 Outline of the "Preliminary Products" Process as an Example of a Fully Integrated Test Automation Solution with Linked eCATT Scripts

As soon as both transaction processes have been completed, the script tests the order-to-cash process. Master data, a sales order, and a delivery schedule are created, the credit lock is removed, and an advance transfer is created. Because posting of the documents is processed asynchronously in a background job for performance reasons, a script to verify this posting is triggered. The script then waits a certain length of time (20 seconds) to give the background job enough time to complete the posting. The goods issue is then posted, and the process ends with the invoice.

The automated test script for this complex business process has a runtime of just 26 minutes. Previously, nine testers from different business departments had been required to test this same process manually, which involved a total effort of approximately two and a half full-time equivalents.

Prototype produces a fresh approach With the creation of the prototype described above, INVISTA realized that the potential benefits of automation could best be realized by ensuring that business processes were mapped in an integrated manner. Instead of viewing individual transactions and business transactions in isolation, the focus of the automation project now shifted to the integrated mapping of business processes. The project specifications changed accordingly, and the objective became one of covering all business-critical processes.

By covering all business-critical processes, a test automation level of approximately 75% was achieved based on all individual transactions used. The key point here, however, is not the number of transactions covered, but rather the seamless coverage of business-critical processes.

The current level of test automation could now only be enhanced by automated testing of authorizations and the integration of external components. These options have so far been deliberately ruled out because the functional correctness of the current regression test set was defined as the primary test objective.

In the next upgrade project, however, SAP SRM-EBP is to be integrated into the automated regression tests, following the template provided by the upgrade to R/3 Enterprise.

Modular scripts The business processes are tested by scripts that are linked to each other across several hierarchy levels. Test data is firstly generated, and is reused as master data and transaction data while the script is running. The generation of new test data each time the script is run eliminates problems caused by deleted or obsolete data from previous runs.

A range of individual scripts are called by a *master script*. Because these script modules can be used for more than one process, this modular structure offers considerable potential for saving time and effort.

Furthermore, because the individual script modules can be reused for different test data, such as materials, the number of eCATT scripts required to cover the documented test cases can be significantly reduced.

INVISTA Resins & Fibers GmbH has been implementing a key user concept for quite some time. The objective of this concept is to create a community of experienced users and in-house consultants, who exchange process-related information and build up relevant expertise. The key users themselves belong to the business departments. With the support of the IT department, they form permanent process teams that strive continuously to improve business processes.

Key user concept

It is the task of the IT department to bring together the team members, who may come from different business units, different company codes, or even different countries. The communities discuss such key questions as "How is this business process used?", "Where do problems occur when using various SAP functions?", and "What are the unique features of this process?"

Lothar Hafner regards the creation of a key user structure as a crucial step that has benefits above and beyond the scope of testing:

> *"These communities allow us to build up extensive process expertise. We were then able to apply this expertise to the upgrade project in various ways; for example, as part of the process definition, user training, and, of course, testing."*

There is, however, one difficulty associated with the key user concept. As a rule, key users are employees who are normally very busy with their day-to-day work and who lack time to devote to other tasks. This is where test automation comes full circle. Because the involvement of key users in automated testing is much less than in manual testing, these internal resources can be freed up to a significant degree.

The project team took a fresh approach to transferring process knowledge. Based on the existing test case descriptions, all critical processes were defined by key users and recorded in the SAP Tutor tool. The recordings developed in SAP Tutor have an edge over Word documents

SAP Tutor

in many ways. They take much less time to create, for one thing, and they normally are self-contained and self-explanatory, which means that they provide eCATT script developers with an ideal template for automation.

Their use in test automation is an example of the synergies that are created when SAP Tutor is used. The tool was used primarily to transfer expert knowledge to INVISTA. Enhancements with the upgrade meant that the new software differed considerably from the existing user interfaces and process sequences in the SAP applications. Therefore, every effort had to be made to ensure that the users felt comfortable with the new system from day one. To supplement the existing training program, numerous tutorials were developed in order to train all 520 INVISTA users within the short time frame. These company-specific electronic instruction manuals mirror the processes used in the company right down to the very last input field.

While the tailor-made tutorials are primarily intended to help end users refresh their knowledge on-the-job, to quickly fill in any knowledge gaps, or to train new employees, Lothar Hafner believes that they also have the potential for other applications. In Hafner's view, the tutorials also provide ideal demonstration tools that can be used to give personnel in other INVISTA regions an insight into the integrated business processes supported by SAP. The training concept and its implementation (for example, classroom training) were provided by SAP Education.

ROI study An ROI study was conducted to assess the benefits of test automation. Its starting point was a calculation of the costs incurred by the previously used manual testing procedure. A total of 100 full-time equivalents (FTEs) were allowed for each of the three systems (sandbox, development, and consolidation system). This figure was an estimate based on experience and was then compared with the actual figures from the project.

The actual effort involved 20 FTEs for the initial development of the SAP tutorials by key users. Next came the 118 FTEs it took the SAP consultants to create the test scripts, and 30 additional FTEs for additional manual testing activities by key users (in the consolidation system only). This produced a total actual effort of 168 FTEs for the automated test, compared with the estimated 300 FTEs for manual testing (see Table 7.1).

Estimated Effort for Manual Testing (in FTEs)		Actual Effort for Automated Testing (in FTEs)	
Sandbox system	100	One-off creation of SAP tutorials (test cases)	20
Development system	100	Test management and automation	118
Consolidation system	100	Additional manual testing activities by key users	30
Total	**300**	**Total**	**168**

Table 7.1 Comparison of Estimated and Actual Effort

Thanks to the continuous enhancement of the automated test scripts across all applications and interfaces, as well as consistent use of these scripts, the additional manual testing activities by the key users served only to detect authorization problems. All functional problems had already been identified by eCATT.

In this case, test automation yielded a saving of 44%, a result that speaks for itself! However, the results of the regression tests run as part of a Support Package implementation (see Figure 7.4) were even more clear-cut.

Savings of 44%

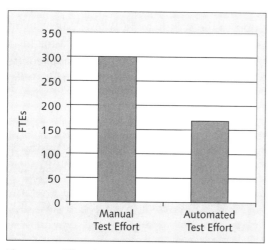

Figure 7.4 Effort Comparison for Testing Activities as Part of the Upgrade Project at INVISTA

From April to November 2004, changes were made to the system as part of the Change Management process. The test scripts had to be updated during the preparation phase for the Support Package implementation. The time taken to modify the scripts accounted for just three and a half FTEs out of a total period of seven months.

Script modification The scripts had to be modified as follows before the Support Packages were imported.

▶ New RFC connections were added.

▶ New printer names were added.

▶ A new screen was integrated into the business process.

According to Christian Koch, in-house consultant at INVISTA:

"Because we always used existing scripts, we were able to complete testing in the Change Management area in a quarter of the time it would have taken otherwise."

The scripts had to be modified again after the Support Packages had been imported because errors were detected in the critical business processes and in the print programs.

These modifications amounted to five FTEs for the script developers, plus half a FTE for support from the in-house consultants (see Table 7.2).

Maintenance and modification of the scripts by SAP Test Management Consulting personnel helped the project run very efficiently for both sides. This meant that INVISTA Resins & Fibers GmbH did not require additional eCATT expertise in order to start the scripts and interpret the log.

Estimated Effort for Manual Testing (in FTEs)		Actual Effort for Automated Testing (in FTEs)	
Development system	25	Adjusting scripts to the new SP level	5
Consolidation system	25	Hours for in-house consultants	0.5
Total	**50**	**Total**	**5.5**

Table 7.2 Comparison of Estimated and Actual Effort

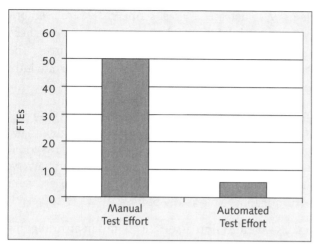

Figure 7.5 Effort Associated with Testing Activities when Importing Support Packages

The regression test for the Support Packages was completed without the involvement of key users. This unusual step posed a definite risk, says Christian Koch: **[Support Package upgrade without key users]**

> *"We took a small risk by not involving key users in this testing activity. However, we proved that Support Packages can be imported without key users and that using eCATT test scripts reduces the risk to production rollout. A key factor is the huge saving in terms of resources, and the reliability of the test script results."*

Because this experiment proved successful, key users are now only involved in tests that fall outside the scope of the current level of automation. These are limited to tests for authorizations and, in particular, additional spot checks.

In most cases, the performance of the Support Packages increased dramatically, with the result that INVISTA is currently considering importing more than one Support Package per year. **[Support Package performance]**

Due to a change of provider, the hardware was changed and the system migrated to the US in the third quarter of 2005. This change naturally posed a risk to application stability, which was countered by automated regression tests using an approach that has since become established at the company. **[Project: system migration and change of provider]**

Performance problems were detected by test scripts that were used primarily to ensure the functional stability of the system. The cause of these problems was easily identified as inadequate network resources. The provider reacted promptly and provided greatly increased bandwidth, quickly eliminating the threat.

As well as detecting this limitation (a positive secondary effect of test automation), an extensive regression test served to verify the functional correctness of the business processes mapped in the development and consolidation systems. The stability of the business processes on the new hardware was ensured with an effort of just 11.5 FTEs. Key users were not required to perform manual tests at any point.

Lothar Hafner estimates that the effort associated with safeguarding this type of system migration manually would amount to a total of 40 FTEs. This estimate is based on the assumption that business-critical transactions are tested with manual spot checks (see Table 7.3).

Estimated Effort for Manual Testing (in FTEs)		Actual Effort for Automated Testing (in FTEs)	
Development system	15	Adjusting scripts to the new SP level	9.5
Consolidation system	25	Hours for in-house consultants	2
Total	**40**	**Total**	**11.5**

Table 7.3 Comparison of Estimated and Actual Effort

The effort comparison indicates a saving of 28.5 FTEs, or approximately 70%. More important than this saving, however, was the guaranteed application stability thanks to the seamless coverage of business-critical processes, something not provided by spot checks.

Project: change of application provider
After the hardware provider was changed, the application provider was also changed, to one located offshore. This posed the question of how the employees of the offshore provider could be trained and their progress evaluated. The test cases defined in the SAP Test Workbench also proved to be a useful tool here. Business process-oriented management of the test cases facilitated the transfer of knowledge. Meanwhile, monitoring

and evaluation of training progress was supported by the personalized work lists of individual employees of the provider in the SAP Test Workbench. Lothar Hafner believes that main objective at this point was to ensure that the quality of support was the best it possibly could be:

> *"The defined structures within the SAP Test Workbench allowed us to train the employees of our application provider in all of our business processes, and to then evaluate what they had learned. The savings were huge, although it is difficult to put an exact figure on them."*

The final testing activities at INVISTA in 2005 were used to safeguard the restructuring of material groups as part of regional consolidation. With this restructuring, the two European SAP systems were merged and all documents in the systems converted.

Project: restructuring the material groups

The restructuring was successfully safeguarded using the automated test scripts, with an effort of just two FTEs. A point of comparison was provided by the other European cluster, where manual testing alone was used. In this case, the development system remained untested, while testing activities in the consolidation system consumed eight FTEs.

A closing analysis of ROI with automated test scripts yields very clear results (see Table 7.4).

Overall assessment of ROI

Year	Effort for Manual Testing (in FTEs)	Effort for Automated Testing (in FTEs)
2004	350	177
2005	48	13.5
Total	**398**	**190.5**

Table 7.4 Overall Assessment of ROI

The initial costs of creating the test scripts are considerable but they pay for themselves almost immediately if test automation is implemented within a testing-intensive project. Ongoing maintenance costs arise once the test scripts are available. However, these are negligible in comparison with the potential benefits to be reaped by reusing the scripts for other applications. After just under two years, INVISTA Resins & Fibers GmbH had managed to reduce the effort associated with testing activities by key users by 207.5 FTEs, or approximately 52%. Readers can calculate for themselves what the financial benefits would be for their company based on their own figures.

Application
stability

While these figures may speak for themselves, the benefits of test automation cannot simply be calculated on the basis of potential savings alone. At least as important is the contribution it can make to application stability, although this contribution is much harder to pin down.

The number of messages generated in the error management system within a defined period is often used as a measure of application stability. In this case, the cluster of all SAP systems within the INVISTA Group generated the fewest messages.

In addition, there have been no high-priority incidents in the live system since the production rollout of the new release and the associated implementation of automated regression test sets.

Information value
of the scripts

Informative scripts, which guarantee the correct functioning of business-critical processes, are the most important prerequisites for deriving any benefit from test automation. Lothar Hafner warns:

> *"The worst possible project outcome would be for the scripts we created to cover the wrong business transactions and processes. This could easily happen if the wrong processes are selected initially. Test cases may then be automated, which provide no information about the functioning and stability of your business processes. The benefits of the entire automation project will stand and fall on the information value of the scripts. This, in turn, depends on the selection of the right process chains."*

Conclusion

The test automation project was completed on time and within the set budget. The ROI study provided evidence of its benefits. The sharing of tasks between the in-house consultants and SAP consultants allowed the project to be implemented efficiently and without risk. The process expertise acquired by INVISTA's key users was transferred with the help of SAP Tutor, and provided the script developers with essential input. At the end of the day, Lothar Hafner views the outcome of the project as follows:

> *"Automation of the regression test sets is initially time-consuming, but the figures from the ROI analysis speak for themselves. INVISTA*

achieved a positive outcome the first time we used the automated solution. However, you must ask the following questions: 'What is the information value of the tests?', 'What is the quality of the testing activities?' In our case, the answer to both is 'very high,' which is something we were not fully aware of at the start of the project.

We are part of the chemical industry, and the greatest risk to us is production downtime caused by non-availability of the SAP system. The goal of testing is to minimize this risk. The scripts developed mean that the system is much more reliable. Once the scripts run without errors, we can be almost certain that our business-critical process will work properly."

What can you learn from the experience of INVISTA?

Lessons learned

- ▸ Test automation yields significant and quantifiable savings in the testing process.

- ▸ Test automation demonstrably increases application stability.

- ▸ If you have limited in-house resources, you should focus these on providing process knowledge, while procuring the required technical expertise from outside.

- ▸ SAP Tutor is an ideal tool for documenting test cases. These can then be reused as e-learning materials.

7.6 Update to Customer Report by INVISTA Resins & Fibers GmbH

"Both the concept and use of our automation concept are still valid."

Christian Koch
SAP Cluster Lead INVISTA Resins & Fibers

INVISTA has been able to further extend its market presence as a global player in the production of polymers, fibers and raw materials, and various intermediate products. A subsidiary of privately owned Koch Industries, Inc., the company is divided into four business areas with responsibility for developing apparel, intermediate products, surface materials, and polymer and fiber products. In 2006, the sale of the Technical Fibers business unit resulted in a business change that considerably

INVISTA Resins
& Fibers GmbH

affected INVISTA's IT organization and system landscape. As a result of removing this business area from the corporate structure, the European system was reduced by three plants.

In-house consultants

Overall, the IT organization was more closely aligned with the company's business processes. Unlike an approach that is more oriented towards system technology, this facilitates more efficient project implementation and a more targeted support of individual enterprise areas and user groups. The concept of in-house consultants was retained. Their core competencies continue to reside in direct support for user departments or process-related support for IT support.

When "carving out" the unit, INVISTA's in-house consultants were available to support the European systems. In the transition phase, they also assisted the new owner of the Technical Fibers business area. INVISTA's internal consultants also supported quality assurance in terms of the system separation required within the context of the "carve-out." In particular, the tried-and-trusted testing procedure was used here (while using eCATT).

System landscape

A European system and a system for the European and Asian markets are in operation at present. A total of eight in-house consultants are used to support the system landscape, three from Germany, three from Great Britain, and two professional contacts in Asia. A central system is in operation for North and South America. There is also a system for North America and one for Mexico. The support organization for these systems is global but with regional modifications. Here, the employees of the Center of Excellence in North America, which is responsible for providing support, are assigned to business units. INVISTA's in-house consultants not only perform administrative tasks but also track and manage service messages.

Process documentation and test management

Overall, INVISTA's test organization had already achieved a very high level of maturity. As the ROI study demonstrated in the first customer report, this applies to test automation in particular. In order to optimize the procedure model and the use of existing Solution Manager tools for process documentation, test documentation, and test management, a two-day strategy workshop was held in conjunction with SAP Test Management Consulting. This included an analysis of the use of SAP Solution Manager. During the workshop, both established and new functions within the application management solution were presented and suggestions for their use within the INVISTA IT organization were discussed.

Here, the use of project administration and business process documentation, including the prior development of a Business Blueprint for a global SRM project, was considered and a roadmap for using the functions was developed. It was determined that the Test Workbench for test management, the Service Desk for recording error messages in the test, and go-live support should also be used during the project. For the project implemented in the US, test management coordinated 45 main testers from various user departments, which processed approximately 16,400 test cases in seven languages and five different back-end systems. The Test Workbench was used to perform the tests in their entire scope. A total of three integration tests were implemented, each with an increasing degree of integration. Furthermore, the unit tests for custom developments were already documented in SAP Solution Manager.

SRM implementation with SAP Solution Manager

In order to document the development activities themselves, the corresponding SAP Solution Manager functions are used in the Business Blueprint environment. Here, the DOCUMENTATION tab is used to centrally document customer developments in various development systems and to track their progress. SAP Solution Manager enables developers to immediately navigate to the relevant development object in the ABAP Development Workbench in the target system.

Documenting custom developments centrally

At INVISTA, numerous different documentation objects are used to document projects. In addition to tracking custom developments and storing e-learning materials, SAP Solution Manager is also used to manage additional project-relevant documents (for example, process descriptions). INVISTA uses status profiles, which make it possible to flexibly control document releases for each document type and, if necessary, set a digital signature. In particular, the procedure was used to agree the status of the documentation of custom developments with local contact persons, offshore developers, and external consultants. According to Christian Koch:

Process documentation

> "We required storage that could be accessed by everyone involved in the project; in other words, internal key users worldwide, external offshore developers, and external consultants. We therefore established central document management for custom developments."

Document management has also proven itself in terms of the high fluctuation among project members in the SRM project. For example, numerous project members were replaced in the implementation phase. The storage of project documentation in the context of the relevant processes enables new employees to be trained quickly and easily find the documents they need. As a key criterion for accepting SAP Solution Manager as the main document management system in the project, it is advisable to always keep the Business Blueprint up-to-date and to uphold the discipline of maintaining the process structure and documents, advises Christian Koch. He stresses that such efforts make a significant contribution to the success of the project:

> *"If we had not deployed SAP Solution Manager as the central backbone to the project, testing with offshore support and testers located all over the world would not have been possible."*

The uniform structure of the Business Blueprint for the SRM implementation project includes not only the documentation but also the definition of transactions in the business process structure. These are used, for example, in test management to enable testers to directly access test objects in the quality assurance system.

Status information system and reporting

The status information system in SAP Solution Manager facilitates a differentiated analysis of the document status. Consequently, it is possible to monitor the progress of documents and associated customer developments. Although INVISTA essentially uses this function to quickly obtain an overview of the status of the selected developments, the in-house consultants met with a lack of acceptance of SAP Solution Manager by the implementation partner, according to Christian Koch. Here, it was necessary to do additional translation work for the integrated documentation approach, which shows documents and their statuses in the context of the business processes to be implemented.

Test management

The Test Workbench was used to implement test management for the SRM project. Here, INVISTA used tried-and-trusted test management processes from previous projects. Within the SRM project, test cases were saved in the context of the Business Blueprint and could then be used to compose test plans for the integration tests. The option to create individual test packages for individual testers or test teams in a flexible manner met with very positive feedback from American colleagues. Christian Koch summarizes:

> "With process-oriented document management (including test cases), I can now compose test plans and test packages much faster. User acceptance of SAP Solution Manager was high among our American colleagues as a result of assigning a personal work list (test packages)."

In the run-up to the integration tests, consultants from SAP Test Management Consulting configured the Service Desk of SAP Solution Manager so that an error recording and troubleshooting process could be mapped in accordance with INVISTA's specifications. Christian Koch regards the mail notification function that was implemented, which informs developers about open messages or testers about a request for a retest, as an essential user-friendly feature. Establishing this asynchronous communication path was an essential requirement, primarily because of the global presence of the testers and the offshore development in India. At the same time, the Service Desk makes it possible to document each troubleshooting step in the relevant messages. Christian Koch sees an optimization potential in establishing a link between an error message and a test case. At present, there is no way to navigate from a message directly to the referenced or causal test case. | Service Desk

Testing took place without a dedicated test manager. Christian Koch, together with another employee, planned the test in the run-up to the testing activities. During the test phase, Christian Koch, as a member of the project management team, assumed responsibility for monitoring and daily status reporting of the integration tests. He was supported by the project office, which maintained not only the standard reporting functions of the Test Workbench but also a project dashboard in Microsoft Excel. This dashboard was composed of raw data exported from the Test Workbench. With the availability of SAP Solution Manager 7.0 EhP 1, integrated BW reporting, which is part of SAP Solution Manager, will be used in future projects. This will make it possible to prepare key performance indicators in the testing environment and display them in a web interface. In particular, reporting that uses BW integrated into SAP Solution Manager makes it easier to analyze test results and error messages over time. Consequently, additional manual preparation of the relevant data will no longer be necessary in the future. | Testing and test reporting

Replacing SAP Tutor INVISTA used SAP Tutor to transfer process knowledge within the company. This tool was used to develop self-running or interactive tutorials for the purpose of training end users (in addition to classroom training). In addition to successfully using recordings as learning materials that end users can retrieve at any time, SAP Tutor videos were also used to demonstrate business processes and their interdependencies for other INVISTA regions. However, high acceptance of this medium sparked the desire for more functionality and flexibility.

SAP ProductivityPak by RWD After comparing the documentation tools available on the market, INVISTA opted in favor of SAP ProductivityPak by RWD. This tool can also be used to create self-running or interactive demonstration videos that can be provided in various formats (for example, as an Adobe Flash video). The tool can also be used to create adequate documentation in Word format on the basis of recorded user interactions. By selecting various target formats, both interactive training and documented process flow descriptions can be created from a recording.

ROI study: test automation The test automation procedure presented in the first customer report was continuously applied and optimized. Similarly, the ROI study was updated for all larger or more complex change events, which will be described below.

Sale of the "Technical Fibers" business unit The sale of the Technical Fibers business unit in 2006 required the complete removal of the unit from the existing systems and therefore the separation of this unit from its former business areas. The opening balances (for example, all assets in this area) had to be reevaluated. With the exception of financial data, all historical data for this business area was made available. This was achieved using a complete copy of all historical data from which the financial data, and not the data associated with the business area, was selectively deleted.

Technically, one of the greatest challenges associated with the "carve-out" was the need to ensure that existing business processes would work properly in the new environment. Another difficulty was the narrow time frame for the implementation, which required the business unit to be removed within a period of just seven weeks.

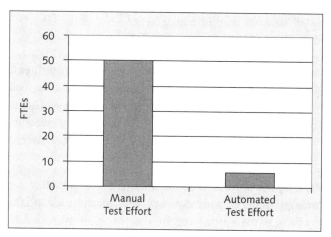

Figure 7.6 Effort Associated with Testing Activities when Carving out the "Technical Fibers" Business Unit

Because the required test scripts were immediately available via the regression test set, it was possible to quickly validate the function of business-critical processes. First, the scripts had to be adjusted to the system's new data environment. It was necessary to ensure that the scripts in previous regression test sets could also run in the context of the new system environment. This work step took approximately six FTEs. Then, the test cases in the development and quality assurance systems could be executed in the new environment. On the basis of empirical values obtained for past projects, manual testing of a similar nature would have required approximately 50 FTEs. This equates to a savings of 44 FTEs or 88% of the effort associated with the test. Test automation secured the go-live of the new system and resulted in a successful "carve-out."

For a period of one year, INVISTA provided support to the new owner of the business area.

Changing the fiscal year

In November 2006, the fiscal year changed for the now standalone business unit. Consultants from SAP Test Management Consulting provided support for the testing activities within this project.

Existing eCATT scripts were copied and modified to the objective associated with the testing activities. All in all, it took less than one and half FTEs to modify the scripts.

Automated scripts ensure application stability under the new strategy and are therefore an essential step for minimizing risk. When INVISTA was creating or modifying the relevant automation scripts, supplementary manual testing activities were only required in the Finance environment. In particular, it was necessary to check the month-end closing as well as the structure of custom-developed reports and the accuracy of their content. The effort required here was four FTEs. Furthermore, no further manual activities were required. Automation for this change event resulted in a savings of 14.5 FTEs or 72.5%.

Occurrence of an SQL error

In October, INVISTA put the effectiveness of the regression test set to the test. Recurring, irregular update errors and dumps in standard transactions such as the payment run and invoice creation mystified IT Support initially. Since the effects of the error could not be reproduced, an exact diagnosis was not possible. However, further observation and analysis of the effects helped us to identify two symptoms. Two of the SAP applications used, which ran on different instances, lost connection to the database at irregular intervals. The only indication that the connection had terminated was a "Connection Lost" message in the Oracle database.

The second symptom was an additional interface problem in an instance. Status confirmations for faxes that had been sent as well as the transfer of data from the barcode system terminated at regular intervals. In both cases, however, a unique, detailed analysis was not possible as a result of undifferentiated error messages.

The automated regression test set was used to identify the error within the system. By continuously executing the scripts in different combinations, it was possible to provoke the error in both the development and quality assurance system. Consequently, a network error was increasingly likely as the cause of the second symptom. In a subsequent network load test, it was possible to identify an incorrect router. For the first symptom (the occurrence of irregular connection terminations), it was possible to rule out a network error by continuously using the eCATT scripts and subsequently analyzing the test execution logs. It was therefore clear that the problem was the responsibility of the database manufacturer. After identifying this possible cause, INVISTA consulted with the manufacturer, who provided a repair patch that had not been released yet. Consequently, INVISTA implemented the repair patch at its own risk.

Similarly to the error search, determining whether the problem was resolved by a database patch was made more difficult by the fact that the errors occurred only sporadically and diffusely. However, by constantly executing selected eCATT scripts that reproduced the connection termination during the error search, it was possible to ensure that this error no longer occurred. Consequently, the eCATT scripts were actively used to identify a stability problem with the database and verify the resolution of this problem. Christian Koch, who has been working as an in-house consultant since 2006, confirms that detecting the error and using manual tests to examine whether the error had been resolved was impossible in the short term and would have been associated with very high costs:

> "With manual testing, we would not have been able to act so promptly and effectively. It would have been inconceivable to involve a large number of key users in manual testing over a period of 14 days."

Similarly, the use of automated regression test sets established security during the final implementation of the unreleased database patches in the production system. This ensured that the patch removed the error without harming system operation. Lothar Hafner, INVISTA Cluster Lead, confirms the above and recommends keeping existing automated regression tests up-to-date and executable at all times in order to be prepared for such situations:

> "Without eCATT scripts, this would have been similar to open-heart surgery. Under no circumstances would we have been able to import an unreleased patch into our production system without prior verification. It is therefore advisable to keep existing test scripts up-to-date at all times."

In July 2007, INVISTA migrated selected systems to new hardware. It was also able to use existing test scripts here. INVISTA did not require any involvement by SAP Consulting in order to ensure that the change in infrastructure did not harm the migrated SAP applications. Nor was it necessary to modify the scripts extensively. All in all, it was possible to verify the successful migration within four hours. For manual testing activities with a more limited scope (only business-critical processes within the scope of the test), INVISTA would have had to allow approximately 16 FTEs (see Figure 7.7).

Hardware refresh

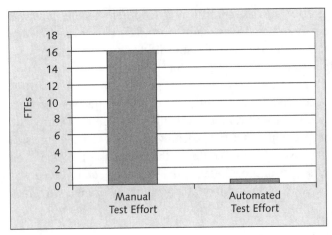

Figure 7.7 Effort Associated with Testing Activities During Hardware Refresh

Harmonizing the
material group
structure

2008 was also the year in which some significant change events occurred. As a condition of this project, it was necessary to harmonize the material group structure of five SAP systems globally. For this purpose, the groups were converted into the Universal Standard Products and Services Classification (UNSPSC). The testing procedure proved to be highly efficient, not least because the necessary testing activities were planned and implemented in the same way as the change of material group structure in 2006. Accordingly, the testing activities could be concluded within two days through the use of automated scripts. For comparable manual tests, it would have been necessary to schedule at least eight days. This resulted in an overall reduction in effort that equates to six days or approximately 75%.

Harmonizing units
of measure in the
SRM environment

Another essential harmonization project in 2008 was aimed at implementing standardized units of measure in five back-end systems that communicated with one common SRM system. Here, eCATT was used to safeguard the operation of the European systems. Automated testing demonstrated the proper functioning of the systems and the accuracy of the conversion within a period of just one day. Based on empirical values from previous test runs, Christian Koch estimated that it would have taken 12 FTEs to perform manual testing activities of a comparable scope. The actual manual testing effort in the North-American cluster of INVISTA was 34 FTEs. According to Christian Koch, this can be explained with the much higher degree of maturity in the testing environment in the European cluster. Based on Europe's experience, test automation here equates to a savings of eleven FTEs or a reduction by 91.67%.

Thanks to the tried-and-trusted test automation procedure, testing activities are now a routine part of importing Support Packages. Additional Support Packages were imported into the system in May 2007 and December 2008. After the importing, it was possible to schedule the continuously up-to-date library of automated test cases as a complete test run. The test manager, Christian Koch, started the test cases in 2007. In December 2008, INVISTA's offshore provider started the scripts. Following a successful execution of the regression test set, INVISTA was able to confirm that the system was running properly and/or identify changes. Manual testing activities by in-house consultants were only planned in the event that the automated scripts would detect errors. In May 2007, two application errors were identified as a result of executing the scripts. After resolving the errors and modifying the relevant scripts, a retest was performed. It took approximately two-and-a-half FTEs to execute the test cases and maintain the scripts. The technical side of both of these activities was supported by SAP Test Management Consulting. The in-house consultants who delivered the input for the process-related changes in the application required half a day. In December 2008, extensive automated testing did not detect any errors, thus verifying the stable and reliable operation of the business processes. There were no indications that additional manual testing was required. As expected, the system did not issue any error messages after INVISTA imported the Support Packages, thus confirming the quality of the regression test set.

Importing Support Packages

In 2009, INVISTA also used regression test scripts to test Support Package implementations and a simultaneous change of database. As a result of closing a plant, INVISTA had to modify some of the scripts in order to adjust plant-specific processes or remove references to the plant. Since 2009, the scripts have been managed centrally in SAP Solution Manager. From there, they are scheduled or executed whenever change events occur. All in all, such activities required a manual effort of four FTEs. Compared with the effort associated with manual testing (16 days), this amounts to a savings of 75% for 2009.

A comparative assessment of the individual change events shows a clear overall picture of the savings potential associated with test automation.

Overall assessment of ROI

Table 7.5 shows the overall assessment of the ROI study for the years 2004 to 2009. For the testing activities performed over a period of four years, test automation achieved a savings of 339 FTEs or approximately 61%.

Year	Effort for Manual Testing (in FTEs)	Effort for Automated Testing (in FTEs)
2004	350	177
2005	48	13.5
2006	70	11.5
2007	32	3
2008	36	4
2009	16	4
Total	552	213

Table 7.5 Overall Assessment of ROI 2004 – 2009

The ROI study does *not* include smaller change events (for example, importing SAP Notes). These are also safeguarded through the use of automated test cases. Similarly, selected test scripts can be used to prove the benefit of any performance optimizations that have been made. Furthermore, continuous test runs, which can be executed with little effort, result in very high application quality because errors are detected early on and can be reproduced, and the impact of system changes can also be assessed at an early stage.

Conclusion

Today, test automation supports all complex and far-reaching system changes. The savings that INVISTA was able to implement as part of the aforementioned change events clearly prove the practical value of automation. Furthermore, a carefully structured automated regression test set can be used for many years. The more such a solution is used, the greater its ROI.

In addition to test automation, test management also continued to be developed through the use of SAP Solution Manager and the Test Workbench within the SRM implementation project. Today, the use of the Business Blueprint (including the project documentation and the process-oriented storage of test cases) is an integral part of the project. INVISTA's test management is based on established best practices. In addition to the accurate assignment of test cases, this approach permits cross-country testing and comprehensive reporting.

What can you learn from the experiences of INVISTA?   Lessons learned

▶ The Test Workbench provides options to compose individual work packages for testers. The tester worklist facilitates "time-delayed working," irrespective of national borders and time zones.

▶ The email notification function within the Service Desk is a powerful utility for coordinating troubleshooting worldwide.

▶ The SAP ProductivityPak by RWD solution makes it possible to create interactive e-learning materials and documentation from recorded user interactions.

▶ The significant and quantifiable savings in the testing process will increase significantly over time. INVISTA's ROI study provides impressive proof of this.

▶ A carefully structured set of automated regression test cases that cover all business-critical processes can be used for all change events in the life cycle of an SAP solution landscape.

▶ If error effects occur unexpectedly, an automated regression test set makes it possible to efficiently detect errors. In comparison to manual testing, resource use is not extensive.

eCATT gives you many new options for automating the testing of SAP solutions. By automating user behavior, it enables both component-based functional tests and integration tests based on process chains. Because of its integration with the SAP system, eCATT offers comprehensive functionality for automating regression tests in the SAP environment.

8   Test Automation with eCATT

This chapter primarily addresses the needs of a hands-on IT employee who requires detailed technical information about the use of eCATT (extended Computer Aided Test Tool).

eCATT is a powerful test tool that is included in the basic delivery of SAP applications. As of Web AS Release AS 6.20, eCATT is tightly integrated with the SAP Basis and provides flexible possibilities for accessing a system to be tested. This chapter describes eCATT in SAP NetWeaver Release 7.02, the version that was current when the book went to press. Where necessary, the chapter references the difference with lower release versions or higher release versions that are still in the planning stage.

Part of the SAP Basis

eCATT is not only used by numerous SAP customers, but also by SAP itself during development and maintenance of new and old products. At SAP, more than 300,000 eCATT-based tests are implemented on average every month. These tests contribute to a significant reduction of the manual testing requirement and thus result in considerable savings. Thanks to the very active internal usage of eCATT, the eCATT development team continuously receives qualified feedback. Over the last few years, this has led to some significant further developments of the very stable test automation tool—also to the benefit of SAP customers. Several additional enhancements are currently being developed.

Using eCATT

eCATT is appropriate for both component-wise functional tests and process-oriented integration tests. In the simpler component testing, it is primarily used as a developer test for quickly finding errors during

Area of use

the implementation. Integration tests, however, are more interesting. In this case, a test is executed automatically across application components and system boundaries, along a business process. A typical test scenario is the automated regression test, which is performed after extending the system or installing support packages, for example. Later chapters describe the numerous further developments in progress.

8.1 Implementation and Prerequisites

eCATT offers many ways to create, manage, and perform automated test cases in the SAP environment. This section describes the basic functioning, the structure of eCATT scripts, as well as the technical prerequisites of the test automation tool.

8.1.1 Architecture of the Test Landscape and eCATT Fundamentals

Central test system
eCATT was designed to be operated via a central test system. SAP recommends implementing SAP Solution Manager 7.0 for both manual and automated tests. This means that eCATT itself is maintained on the central test administration system and accesses the application to be tested via RFC or HTTP connections (see Figure 8.1). The application to be tested can reside on any standalone system of the system landscape. It can consist of a variety of components, each of which is addressed via an appropriate test driver. Integration testing—that is, testing several components on different systems in an integrated way—is supported by eCATT as well. The requirements for operating eCATT as a central test administration system are described in Section 8.1.3, *Technical Requirements*.

All created test objects, such as test-case descriptions, test scripts with test logic, as well as test and system data that are stored in the central test administration system. The test documentation (that is, the evidence of test performances) is managed in the central system.

Test coverage
eCATT covers not only your entire test landscape, but you can also integrate test runs with all layers of the system: presentation layer, application layer, and database (see Figure 8.2). While all external test tools

test an SAP system by addressing the front end and treating the SAP GUI as a standalone application, eCATT can access the application server and the database and thus reflect the entire multilayered nature of the SAP system in tests.

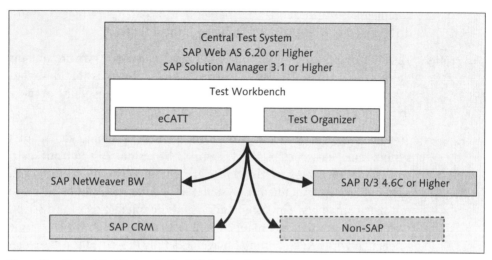

Figure 8.1 Central Test System in the SAP Application Landscape

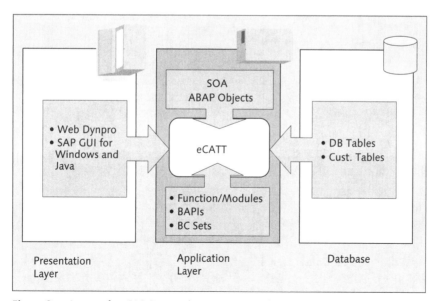

Figure 8.2 Layers of an SAP System that Can Be Tested

To be able to test different types of SAP applications, eCATT includes various test drivers that are specialized in their respective requirements. For example, there are different drivers for testing transactions in SAP GUI, with or without using the control framework, Web Dynpro applications, web services, and BAPIs. Furthermore, eCATT can use a set of commands to read and check the content of database tables. The test driver to be used is provided along with the test script.

Test objects   The basic object for working with eCATT is the test script, which contains the flow logic. A test script is a sequence of commands that describes the test flow. For example, it can consist of the recording of one or more transactions and the associated checks and calculations.

To ensure that the test can run on the relevant systems, you require system data that specifies the systems to be tested. Last but not least, you require test data records which can be used to execute the test case. System data is maintained in system data containers, and test data in test data containers. The combination and the interaction of test script, system, and test data are mapped in a test configuration which can be integrated with SAP Solution Manager as a fully described test case. Figure 8.3 shows the interaction of the test objects.

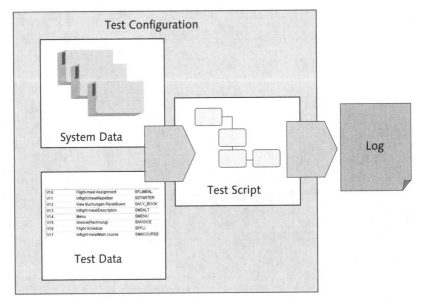

Figure 8.3 Interaction of Test Objects

The test configuration presents the executable test case in eCATT as it is displayed in the worklist of SAP Solution Manager (found in the test management work center). It comprises the following:

▶ A set of test instructions that describe the test case

▶ One or more data records with which the test case is executed

▶ A description of the system landscape in which the test case is executed

The result of executing a test configuration is summarized in a status (Passed/Failed/Not executed/Precondition not fulfilled). Further details of the test execution are documented in a log that contains detailed information on the test environment, the commands executed, which data was used, and the results returned by the application.

Test configuration

A central aspect of testing using eCATT is the modularity achieved by separating test logic (test script), test data, and system data. Both test and system data can thus be used in more than one test configuration. This information is managed in test data or system data containers. As a result, this data can be access from every test configuration. The test logic can also have a modular structure so that individual modules of the test logic call each other and can be implemented in several test configurations.

Modularity

To execute eCATT tests on different systems (for example when the system landscape has changed), it is necessary to encapsulate the system-specific aspects of the test. This encapsulation ensures that the information about the systems in which tests are to be run can be exchanged very easily.

System data containers and logical targets

eCATT provides a very simple and effective mechanism for this encapsulation. In a system data container (see Figure 8.4), a number of target systems (logical targets) within the test landscape are defined. A target system describes the role of an application instance in the solution landscape. In the system data container, every logical target can be assigned exactly one RFC and one HTTP connection that reference the system to be tested. In eCATT scripts, only the logical target specifications are used.

Encapsulation

Thus, in case of changes in the test landscape, only the system data container needs to be exchanged within the test configuration. Both for a temporary change and for the execution of tests against a second test system landscape, a different system data container can be specified before starting the test run.

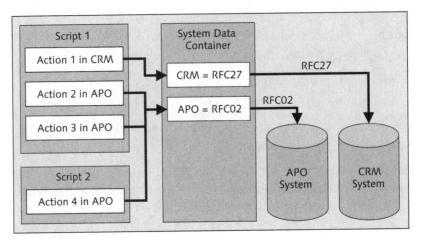

Figure 8.4 Function of the System Data Container

Test driver

To flexibly interact with the system to be tested, eCATT uses test drivers. These adapters are interlinked on different levels with the system to be tested, and thus enable you to directly check the different application components.

By implementing the appropriate driver, you can test both function-like objects (such as BAPIs), function modules, and web services, as well as transactions and Web Dynpro applications, depending on the implementation purpose and release of SAP NetWeaver Application Server. Figure 8.5 shows the decision path to select the right test driver.

Using a test driver, the SAP system to be tested can be addressed at different levels. The following drivers are provided for selection.

- ► **TCD driver**
  The TCD driver is appropriate for conventional transactions (without controls). An advantage is that the TCD mode is based on batch input technology. Therefore it is possible to process the recorded transactions in the background (that is, without a GUI), which allows for very efficient tests.

  Additionally, the TCD driver enables you to make small adaptations in finalized scripts. This driver is therefore particularly easy to maintain.

  Section 8.2.1, *Testing Transactions without Controls (TCD)*, provides more details about the TCD driver.

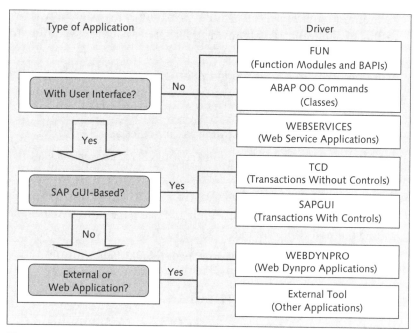

Figure 8.5 Decision Path to the Right Test Driver

▶ **SAPGUI driver**

The SAPGUI driver enables you to test transactions in SAP GUI that use controls. It is handled differently than the TCD driver because the recording directly refers to the user interaction with SAP GUI. The driver exclusively works with and via the SAP GUI for Windows.

Section 8.2.2, *Testing Transactions with Controls (SAPGUI)*, provides more details about the SAPGUI driver.

▶ **Web Dynpro driver**

Web Dynpro applications on the Java stack of SAP NetWeaver AS are supported by a separate driver as of Release 6.40. With Release 7.02 and as of SAP NetWeaver 7.20, Web Dynpro applications are also supported on the ABAP stack.

More information can be found in Section 8.2.3, *Testing Web Dynpro Applications*.

▶ **Web service driver**

From SAP NetWeaver 7.0, web services can be tested in a way similar to that used for function modules. Only the establishment of a connection requires special handling. An interesting possibility is the testing of applications that provide their services both as Web Dynpro applications and as web services.

More information can be found in Section 8.4, *Creating Tests for Web Services*.

▶ **FUN driver**
The FUN driver is used to test function modules and BAPIs.

More information can be found in Section 8.3.2, *Function Modules and BAPIs*.

▶ **ABAP OO driver**
This driver provides numerous commands for generating instances or calling methods (for example, CREATEOBJ, CALLMETHOD).

More information can be found in Section 8.3.3, *Inline ABAP*.

8.1.2   Structure of the eCATT Test Scripts

The logic of a test is contained in the test script. The structure of an eCATT test script is similar to that of an ABAP function module. It consists of attributes, parameters, and commands (see Figure 8.6).

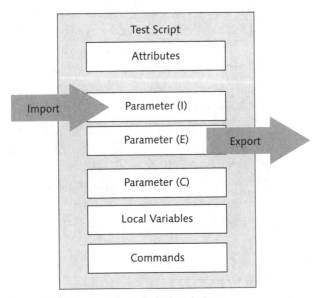

Figure 8.6 Structure of an eCATT Test Script

In addition to management information such as title, package, person responsible, and component, the attributes of a test script also include keywords and versioning information that are used by the system for supporting script management. The keywords enable you to search specifically for scripts. Versioning data enables the system to automatically select the correct script version if there are several versions.

Attributes

Parameters are divided into four classes, according to their function and visibility.

Parameters

▶ Import parameters are used for importing test data from variants or other scripts. They are the input interface of the script and contain the input values at runtime.

▶ Results of the script can be forwarded using export parameters, which are the output interface.

▶ Local variables are parameters, the values of which are only available within the script. They are used as additional storage space for interim results.

▶ As of SAP NetWeaver 7.1, runtime data containers are included in the standard delivery and provide data areas outside the test scripts that can be written to and read by test scripts. Runtime data containers are used to provide shared data areas for various interacting test scripts. When there are many test parameters, using runtime data containers can enable a more efficient test processing than using import and export parameters. A parameter with visibility "C" manages a reference to the runtime data containers described here.

A runtime data container is an instance of a data record (variant) of a test data container (TDC). At runtime, a runtime data container contains parameters that are defined and named exactly like those in the underlying test data container. At the beginning, the parameter values of the runtime data container are initial and can be filled through assignments or dedicated commands (FILL_RDC) for the runtime data container in the course of the test script.

Every parameter has a unique name that is valid only within the script. Different scripts can therefore contain parameters of the same name.

Using this name, the test data is assigned to the parameters. You should therefore make sure to give parameters in different scripts the same names if they are used for fields with matching contents. A parameter used for entering a customer number, for example, could be named I_CUSTOMER_NO throughout all scripts.

These and other conventions should be documented in an automation manual that is mandatory for your organization.

Complex parameters

In addition to its name, a parameter has a type reference. eCATT parameters can use references to ABAP Dictionary as well as to class-based type definitions as of SAP NetWeaver Release 7.11. Using such a reference to a structured data type from the ABAP Dictionary, a structured or tabular parameter is created. Structured parameters correspond to a row in a table, and they consist of several fields identifiable by names, like the columns in a table. Tabular parameters are made up of a sequence of structured parameters; they are comparable to tables.

Commands

The test steps and check logic of eCATT scripts can be supported by a wide range of commands. Typically, an eCATT script consists of two blocks. First, a test driver is called. It transfers the control flow (execution management) to the test object, which is a transaction, a function module, or a BAPI. The import parameters of the script are thus passed to the input interface of the test object. This procedure is called "parameterization." It is essential for a successful script because the parameterization links the test logic of the test drivers to the test data. As soon as the test object has been executed, the eCATT script can perform calculations and comparisons in a second step to compare the result returned by the test object to an expected value. These comparisons are mainly performed using the messages and values returned by the tested system. In individual cases, however, you may need to directly search a database table in the tested system for the existence of data records or characteristics of values of individual fields.

Recommended modularization procedure

Generally, several transactions can be recorded in a test script. These more complex script structures should be avoided, though, because they prevent the script from being reused and require a lot of maintenance effort due to redundancies. In more complex test cases, it is preferable to divide the test case into several partial scripts and have them called by a top script (see Figure 8.7).

In this example, the business process was initially split into its basic parts, and a script was created for each part. Because an eCATT script can call other scripts, it is possible to create an entire script collection of reusable scripts. They are reused in a main script.

More information on this topic can be found in Section 8.8, *Modularizing Test Scripts*.

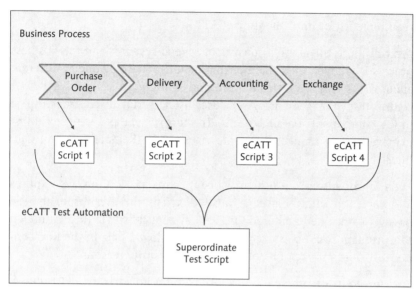

Figure 8.7 Modularization of a Business Process

When an eCATT script is executed, the system first assigns the corresponding system and test data, then calls the test driver, and checks the results. In parallel, logging occurs for all steps (see Figure 8.8).

Flow of the eCATT script

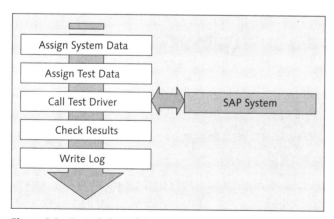

Figure 8.8 Typical Flow of the eCATT Script

8.1.3   Technical Requirements

In addition to the requirements for the test organization that have been described in detail in the previous chapters, there are some technical requirements for implementing eCATT.

Typically, a test landscape consists of several systems, and the business process is mapped by a chain of transactions. These belong to different applications that are distributed to and running on several systems. A central test management system uses a test script to control the test of the components on all systems. The test system and the central test management system communicate via the RFC (Remote Function Call) interface.

Even for an automated test run, a connection via RFC always requires an interaction with the user because the client, the user name, and the password must be re-entered for every system called via RFC. Although this problem could be solved by storing the logon data in the RFC connection, doing so is not recommended for security reasons.

The procedure recommended by SAP is to set up a trusted RFC connection. That way, no manual logon is needed and logon data does not need to be stored anywhere. SAP Note 128447 provides exact instruction for setting up a trusted RFC connection.

The systems to be tested that are connected via (trusted) RFC must fulfill specific minimum requirements regarding the installed support-package levels of the SAP basis if their basis release is lower than 6.20.

Basis Release	Basis Support Package Level
Web AS 6.20 or higher	No requirements
4.6D	At least 21
4.6C	At least 32

Table 8.1 Minimum Requirements Regarding the Support-Package Level According to Installed Release

You can also find more information about required release and support levels in SAP Note 519858.

An explicit permission must be set for every client in which an automated test is to be executed via eCATT. The clients are adapted in Transaction SCC4. The corresponding client can be selected via the transaction. Several options are available under CATT AND ECATT RESTRICTIONS. The following selection is available:

▶ **eCATT and CATT Not Allowed**
Prevents test scripts to be started in the client. This option may not be set for any client in which automated tests are to be run.

▶ **eCATT and CATT Allowed**
Enables you to implement eCATT and CATT without restrictions. Using inline ABAP and function modules, any code can be run on the target system (security). Therefore, this is a security-relevant setting.

▶ **eCATT and CATT Only Allowed for Trusted RFC**
Automated test cases can be started only if the target system has been addressed via a trusted RFC connection. In this case, the full range of functions can be implemented for tests on this client.

▶ **eCATT Allowed, but FUN/ABAP and CATT not Allowed**
With this setting, only transactions can be executed in the target client. They must be addressed via eCATT.

▶ **eCATT Allowed, but FUN/ABAP and CATT only for Trusted RFC**
This protection level allows calling function modules and executing inline ABAP, provided that the connection to the target system is established via a trusted RFC.

In addition to the actual execution of eCATT scripts, cross-client customizing must also be permitted. This setting is maintained via Transaction SCC4 as well.

If you want to record transactions with controls using the SAPGUI driver, both the central test system and all target systems must have SAP GUI scripting enabled. The setting of the scripting permission on the server is maintained via Transaction RZ11. The corresponding profile parameter is `sapgui/user_scripting`, which must be set to `TRUE` (note: uppercase letters).

Enabling SAP GUI scripting

Additionally, you need to install and enable scripting on the front-end during the SAP GUI setup. Scripting is enabled via the menu CUSTOMIZING OF LOCAL LAYOUT (ALT-F12) • OPTIONS. You can enable the SAP GUI scripting in the corresponding dialog box (see Figure 8.9). However, please note that the settings in this dialog box are client-specific. If you change your work center, you must verify this setting and may need to adjust it.

We recommend disabling the NOTIFY WHEN A SCRIPT ATTACHES TO A RUNNING GUI option because, although it is relevant to security, it disturbs the automatic script execution. The second message, NOTIFY WHEN A SCRIPT OPENS A CONNECTION, should remain enabled because eCATT does not establish any connections via scripts.

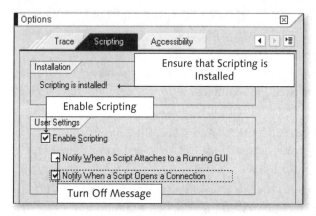

Figure 8.9 Customizing of Local Layout—Options

Parameter pre-assignment via Transaction SU3

Another necessary preparation step is to remove the existing parameter pre-assignments. Transaction SU3 enables you to make user-specific pre-assignments to parameters. These predefined values are then automatically completed in the dynpro, if necessary. This option is very easy for the user but can lead to errors in two ways when eCATT is used. If the pre-assignments are changed between recording and processing the script, the changed assignment can produce errors. The same happens if the script is to be processed by a different user (SAP user).

You should therefore ensure that no user-specific parameters are predefined when you record scripts. For this purpose, you can create a new user, for example, TESTRECORD, and use it exclusively for recording. Alternatively, you can use Transaction SU3 to delete the parameter pre-assignments for your user before recording (see Figure 8.10), if you need to document the creator of the automatic test case for verification management.

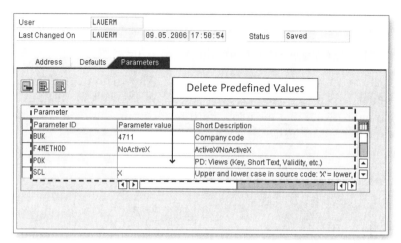

Parameter ID	Parameter value	Short Description
BUK	4711	Company code
F4METHOD	NoActiveX	ActiveX/NoActiveX
POK		PD: Views (Key, Short Text, Validity, etc.)
SCL	X	Upper and lower case in source code: 'X' = lower,

Figure 8.10 Deleting All User-Specific Parameter Pre-assignments

8.1.4   Summary

eCATT was designed to be operated via a central test system that accesses the systems or applications to be tested via RFC or HTTP connections. eCATT comprises different test drivers to test the different types of SAP applications.

The test script is the basic object for working with eCATT. An eCATT script consists of attributes, commands, and parameters. The attributes are management information for organizing the scripts. The commands support the mapping of test scripts and check logic. They are used for addressing a test driver and for checking results. The parameters are the interface of the script to the outside. They link commands to test data.

The test data can be recorded in test data containers. You also can define system data in system data containers to specify the systems to be tested. The interaction of test script, system data container, and test data container is mapped in a test configuration that can be defined as a completely automated test case in the business blueprint of SAP Solution Manager.

8.2   Creating and Running UI-Driven Tests

Using eCATT, you can test the following UI-based applications: transactions with and without controls as well as Web Dynpro applications.

8.2.1   Testing Transactions without Controls (TCD)

To create an eCATT script, first start eCATT (Transaction SECATT). In the initial screen (see Figure 8.11), select the Test Script item, and enter a name. Note that the name must reside in the customer-specific namespace.

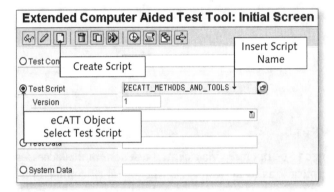

Figure 8.11   eCATT Initial Screen

Script editor   The script editor is the central tool for creating eCATT scripts. Its interface is divided into three areas (see Figure 8.12). The lower area is occupied by the command editor. There you edit the script logic that is composed of the different commands.

The upper area provides an input possibility for creating the parameters of a script. If you want to edit a command interface, the structure editor is opened to the right. It can be enabled by double-clicking on the name of a command interface in the command editor.

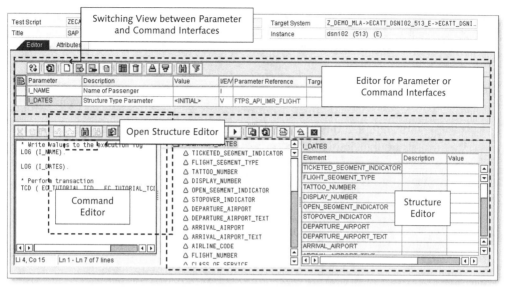

Figure 8.12 Script Editor

The first step in creating the script logic is recording a transaction. Use the RECORDER function of the script editor for this purpose.

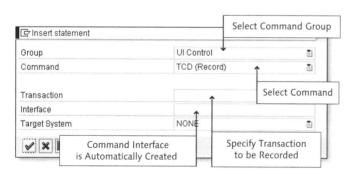

Figure 8.13 "Start recording" Dialog

To start recording, in the script editor select the PATTERN button. A dialog   Start recording is displayed where you can specify the necessary settings for the recording (see Figure 8.13). The available commands are sorted by functions and divided into groups. First select the desired UI ADDRESSING function group and then the test driver. In the following description, we assume that you use the TCD driver for recording transactions without controls. As soon as you select the driver, you can select the transaction to be tested. An appropriate interface is then automatically created by the script editor.

eCATT now opens the transaction. Perform the transaction as usual and then close the transaction window F12. eCATT asks you if you want to accept the data. If you confirm with OK, a new command line with the TCD command is displayed in the editor. The entire recorded transaction is now included in the corresponding command interface.

"TCD" Command

The TCD command is designed for addressing the TCD driver. It has the following format:

```
TCD ( <transaction code>, <command interface>,
      [<target system>] ).
```

A TCD command must always be created via a recording.

Command interface

When a TCD driver is used, the command interface records all dynpros with all fields that have been displayed in the transaction (see Figure 8.14). The data you entered and the default values for fields you did not fill in are recorded.

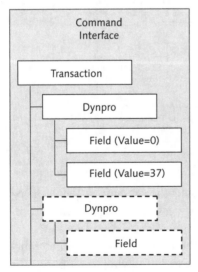

Figure 8.14 Structure of the Command Interface

The values you entered are displayed as fixed values in the command interface. You can use the search function later to find these fixed values during parameterization. No fixed values are recorded for fields you kept at their preset default values. During parameterization, you therefore you might have difficulties with identifying these fields. When recording, ensure that you enter input values for all fields that are relevant to the test case.

If the test case is to be executed with values other than those used during the recording, the corresponding fixed values need to be replaced with parameters (see Figure 8.15). During execution of the test script, the parameter value is then inserted in the appropriate place. This procedure links a part of the command interface of the TCD command to parameters that are visible from the outside. In other words, fields of the command interface can be linked to parameters to return results of the TCD command. Use import parameters to transfer values to input fields. Use export parameters or local variables to process results from the command interface.

Script parameterization

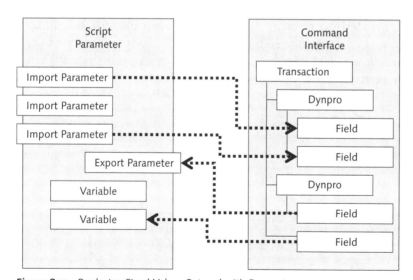

Figure 8.15 Replacing Fixed Values Entered with Parameters

The automatic creation of parameters is supported as of SAP Web AS Release 6.40. You can also manually create the parameters required. For this purpose, complete a row in the parameter editor to add a parameter (see Figure 8.16).

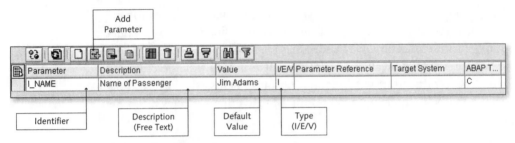

Figure 8.16 Adding a Parameter

Recommended
procedure
for naming
conventions Every parameter has a unique name for identification. To improve the readability of the scripts, we recommend keeping a consistent notation. A well-established procedure is to have all import parameters start with "I_," all export parameters with "E_," and all local variables with "V_."

Parameter types Once the names of the parameters have been defined, you specify their visibility. In the parameter editor, specify "I" for import or "E" for export parameters. If you need local variables you can create them now as well. Set the type to "V."

To parameterize a recorded `TCD` command, open the related command interface in the structure editor (double-click). Look for the entered fixed values. When you have found the corresponding field, replace the value with the name of the parameter (see Figure 8.17).

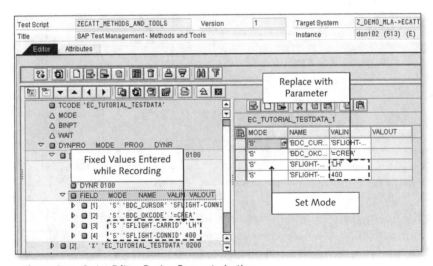

Figure 8.17 Script Editor During Parameterization

eCATT supports different kinds of parameterization. We distinguish between three actions. Two passive modes are also available. In the MODE column, you can set the appropriate mode:

Parameter mode

1. **S (set value)**

   This mode is used for transferring import parameters or local variables to transaction fields. If you select this mode, the parameter value is transferred to the corresponding dynpro field during script execution, just like user input.

2. **G (get value)**

   This mode is designed for exporting values from the command interface. A value calculated by the transaction is transferred to an export parameter or a local variable after the TCD command has been executed.

3. **C (check value)**

   The third mode permits a simple verification of the results. The value returned by the TCD command is compared to the specified parameter. If the comparison fails, the test case is regarded as faulty. Note that the possibilities of this test are rather limited. For more complex conditions, you should use the "G" mode to first read the field value and then check it later using the CHEVAR command. More information on this topic can be found in Section 8.8, *Modularizing Test Scripts*.

4. **I/O (passive)**

   The "I" mode refers to an input field that is not changed by eCATT. Via user parameters, the application can predefine the field with values, though.

   The "O" refers to an output field that is neither read nor checked by the eCATT script.

The dynpro simulator is an alternative to the value maintenance in the field lists. To open the simulator, select the desired dynpro in the list of recorded dynpros and then the SIMULATE DYNPRO function.

Dynpro simulator

The dynpro of the application is simulated on the screen and provided with eCATT-specific functions; for instance, INSERT PARAMETER. You can also navigate between the recorded dynpros so that you can edit the entire recording.

The relevant values, parameters, and mode entries are copied to the field list when you exit the dynpro simulator.

The TCD driver enables you to re-record driver calls that have already been parameterized. This option is used if the test script encounters an error after the underlying transaction has been changed; for example, after installing a support package. Such an error can have two causes. The obvious cause is that the change has caused an error in the application logic. In this case, the error must be corrected in the application. Although the joy at a successful test—testing is always successful when errors are found—is usually muted by the awareness of difficulties for the operation or the project, valuable insights can still be gained.

The second possible error source consists of an incompatible change in the structure of the recorded transaction for the existing test script. Because the structure of a transaction changes more frequently than its fields (a field can be assigned to a different dynpro or another group but is hardly ever renamed or deleted), you can re-record an existing TCD driver call while maintaining the parameterization.

Double-click on the command to open the CHANGE COMMAND dialog (see Figure 8.18). Trigger the re-recording of the transaction, and record the transaction as usual. Fields that have already been parameterized are taken over from the old command interface according to their field names. In most cases, the transaction is already fully parameterized immediately after the recording. Only newly added fields must be completed during the parameterization. This functionality is exclusively available in the TCD driver and makes the recordings performed using this driver extremely easy to maintain.

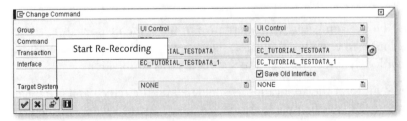

Figure 8.18 "Change Command" Dialog Window

For processing a script, you are provided with various start options for selection. The options relevant to the TCD driver can be found under the UI CONTROL tab in the TCD area (see Figure 8.19).

Start options for the TCD driver

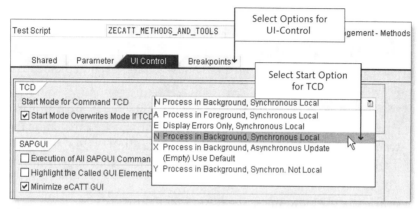

Figure 8.19 Start Options for Processing a TCD Recording

Start options are selected before a script is processed. You have the following options:

▶ **Process in Foreground, Synchronous Local**
The script is processed in the foreground; that is, with a user interface. All actions of the script can be observed on screen. The database is updated synchronously. This option ensures that all input values have been updated in the database before the next step in the script is executed. For tests using eCATT, you should always select one of the options with synchronous update for the reason mentioned above.

▶ **Display Errors Only, Synchronous Local**
This option processes the script in the background; that is, without a user interface. If an error occurs during the execution, the corresponding position is displayed in the user interface. The error can now be manually corrected. The script is then continued in the background until another error occurs or the test case has been completed. The database is updated synchronously.

▶ **Process in Background, Synchronous Local**
This option processes the script completely in the background. There is no output to the screen. Errors are not reported immediately, but they can be viewed in the automatically created log of the eCATT run

433

after the script has been executed. The database is updated synchronously.

▶ **Process in Background, Asynchronous Update**
This option processes the script completely in the background. The database is updated asynchronously. This means that the control flow might return to the script before the updater has changed all values in the database. For a subsequent step of the script, therefore, there is no guarantee that a change from a previous step has been implemented in the database.

The option can be used when eCATT is implemented to provide mass data in the system. This can happen either during a data migration or when test data is created for preparing manual tests or trainings. By disabling a synchronous update, you can often considerably increase the speed.

▶ **Process in Background, Synchronous Not Local**
The script is processed in the background, and the update takes place synchronously but via a different work process than the transaction. This option is obsolete and is only supported for downward compatibility.

▶ **Use Default**
The option stored in the command interface of the command is used.

Regarding the message handling within the TCD driver, please refer to Section 8.6.3, *Message Handling*.

8.2.2 Testing Transactions with Controls (SAP GUI)

Starting with SAP basis Release 4.5B, transactions are able to present more complex and user-friendly graphical user interfaces via SAP GUI controls. One characteristic of this way of programming is the requirement that a part of the application logic is run on the front end.

Because the TCD driver immediately interferes with the application server, application parts running on the front end are outside its reach. Therefore, eCATT provides its own test driver for recording transactions with controls. The SAPGUI driver works with the SAP GUI for Windows and interferes with the SAP system at a different level than does the

TCD driver. An important difference is that the SAPGUI driver does not connect to the application server but to the front end.

> **"SAPGUI" Command**
>
> The SAPGUI command is designed for addressing the SAPGUI driver. It has the following format:
>
> SAPGUI (<command interface>, [<target system>]).
>
> In contrast to the TCD command, the SAPGUI command only allows the transfer of values to the application. There are separate commands for reading and testing values.

While the TCD driver records the result of the input in the record fields, the SAPGUI driver registers events. These events refer to changes of the state of screen elements; for instance, the selection of a value in a listbox, the input of text in a text field, or the expansion of a branch in a tree control. In particular, this means that the SAPGUI driver only records information about the fields that the user actually changes during recording. Another difference is that the SAPGUI driver uses different commands for reading and querying screen elements while the TCD driver serves all actions of the TCD command (see Table 8.2).

Events

Function	TCD Driver	SAPGUI Driver
Parameterizing	TCD (mode S)	SAPGUI
Reading	TCD (mode G)	GETGUI (as of SAP Web AS 6.40)
Check	TCD (mode C)	CHEGUI (as of SAP Web AS 6.40)
Passive (output)	TCD (mode O)	
Passive (input)	TCD (mode I)	

Table 8.2 Commands for Parameterizing, Reading, and Checking Field Values

Because this type of recording generates many events for complex transactions you must specify the appropriate level of granularity prior to recording. This level of granularity determines the number of individual commands into which the script is subdivided. The higher the level of granularity for the recording, the better the overview, reusability, and maintainability of the script. It is also easier to insert descriptive comments between the individual steps. Figure 8.20 shows the different

Recording granularity

levels of granularity, with the level of granularity increasing the farther you go to the right.

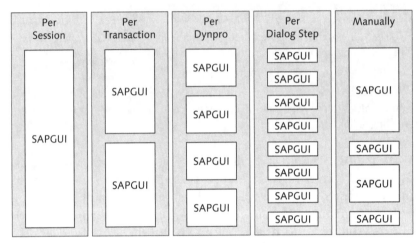

Figure 8.20 Granularity Levels of the SAP GUI Recording

The various granularity levels of the SAP GUI recording have the following meanings:

1. **Per dialog step**
   For every GUI event (every roundtrip between front end and back end), a separate row containing one SAPGUI command is inserted into the script.

2. **Per dynpro**
   Events referring to the same dynpro are joined to form one command.

3. **Per transaction**
   Events referring to the same transaction are joined, even if they span several dynpros.

4. **Per session**
   All events between starting and ending an SAP GUI session are joined to form one command.

5. **Manual**
   The creation of an SAPGUI command is explicitly triggered by the user, who activates an appropriate button during the recording. If you use

this option, you should add a comment to the creation of every command to maintain a better overview.

In general, the granularity level per dynpro as proven as the most appropriate solution for most requirements.

If you want to change the granularity of your script subsequently, you can join steps using the `Join` command or split them using `Split`. If it should become necessary to change the test script, for example, to adapt it to a new support package level, you can use the `SAPGUI (Attach)` command to re-record the affected part of the script, rather than the entire sequence. These commands are described in more detail in the course of this chapter.

To prepare recording of one or several `SAPGUI` commands, go to Transaction SECATT, create a new test script, and then select the PATTERN button. In the INSERT STATEMENT dialog window, select the UI CONTROL group and then the SAPGUI (RECORD) command. If you leave the [GENERATED] presetting in the INTERFACE field unchanged, eCATT generates a name for the command interface based on the selected granularity. For example, if you selected the granularity level per transaction, the generated name includes the transaction code followed by a number. If the generated name does not match your naming concept, you can enter the desired name in the INTERFACE field.

Prepare recording

When you confirm the entries, the system shows a dialog window in which you set the granularity of the recording (see Figure 8.21).

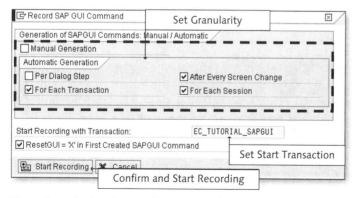

Figure 8.21 Setting the Granularity Levels of the SAP GUI Recording

With SAP Web AS Release 6.40, you must specify a start transaction. Then, the recording starts directly with the first screen of the transaction selected. In SAP Web AS Release 6.20, by contrast, you must start the transaction by entering the appropriate transaction code during recording.

ResetGUI

If you've selected the RESETGUI option, a `ResetGUI = 'X'` flag is generated in the first generated command interface of the recording. This means that the command has a similar effect during processing as an "/n" prefixed to the transaction code. To explain further: A correct processing of the SAP GUI commands is only ensured if every subsequent command starts precisely at the point where the previous command has stopped. This condition is met with everything that you're recording in one single step. But if you record a test script in several steps, this might not be the case. For this reason, you can select the `ResetGUI` flag in the first `SAPGUI` command of every transaction when you process an SAP GUI flow with several individual transaction changes.

After you've made your selection, click START RECORDING to confirm. The system displays the RECORD SAP GUI COMMAND window (see Figure 8.22).

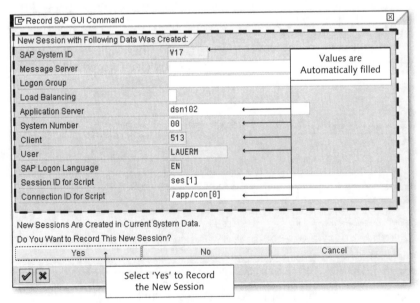

Figure 8.22 Dialog Window for Starting the Recording in a New Session

eCATT generates a new session when a recording is started. It automatically recognizes the values of this newly generated session and displays them in the dialog window. In most cases, it is therefore sufficient to confirm the preset values with YES. SAP Note 1307732 provides further information on exceptions.

Based on the *connection ID* and the *session ID*, the GUI sessions are uniquely identified during the recording of SAPGUI commands. By default, these different IDs are also used for processing to address different sessions. *Session* always refers to a mode and *connection* to a target system. If all SAPGUI commands are supposed to be run in the same session, all SAPGUI command interfaces must have the same session ID and connection ID. Different combinations, in turn, stand for different sessions. This is significant if you work in different modes in parallel for a recording; for instance, if you record an application in one mode and open another mode in which information is to be checked and recorded at the same time. During processing, eCATT determines which command must be executed in which session, based on the different session IDs.

Session ID and connection ID

You have two ways to override these ID values. You can change values for multiple commands in the script editor simultaneously by selecting EDIT • PARAMETER/COMMANDO INTERFACES • REPLACE IDS IN SAPGUI INTERFACES. Alternatively, you can select the EXECUTION OF ALL SAPGUI COMMANDS IN A SINGLE SESSION PER DESTINATION option in the start options for all commands of a destination (that is, a target system). With this option, the different IDs are ignored and all SAP GUI commands are executed in the same session.

If you confirm the values in the RECORD SAP GUI COMMAND window, the system displays the RECORDING RUNNING window (see Figure 8.23). In this window, you can implement different actions; for instance, inserting commands manually and stopping recording again. The functions of this window are described later on.

Run recording

In parallel to the RECORDING RUNNING window, the start transaction for recording is opened in another mode, the recording mode (not in SAP Web AS 6.20, where you must still start the transaction manually). Execute the transaction as usual. If you selected the manual mode, you must change back to the recording window (see Figure 8.23) and trigger the creation of SAPGUI commands using the appropriate button. After the transaction has finished, go back the RECORDING RUNNING window and terminate the recording.

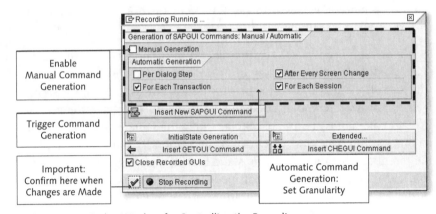

Figure 8.23 Dialog Window for Controlling the Recording

Using "CHEGUI" and "GETGUI"

In your scripts, you will often have to copy values from the screens or check contents. In eCATT, this is implemented with the commands, GETGUI and CHEGUI, which are available as of SAP Web AS 6.40. GETGUI reads the values of a GUI element, for instance, for a text field. CHEGUI reads and checks.

At the point where you want to determine a value, go back from the application mode to the recording dialog and select INSERT GETGUI COMMAND. If you want to additionally check the field content, select INSERT CHEGUI COMMAND (see Figure 8.24).

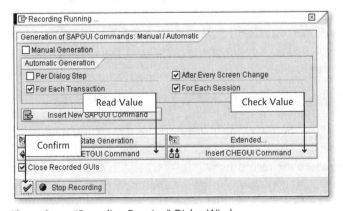

Figure 8.24 "Recording Running" Dialog Window

After you've selected the relevant option, the control returns to application mode. The subsequent steps are identical for the two commands.

You can use the mouse to select the area whose value you want to determine. Because SAP GUI is in selection mode, the selected area is indicated with a colored frame if you move the mouse over it. The selected area is copied using the left mouse button.

After you have selected the corresponding field, the system takes you to the dialog for editing the GETGUI/CHEGUI command (see Figure 8.25).

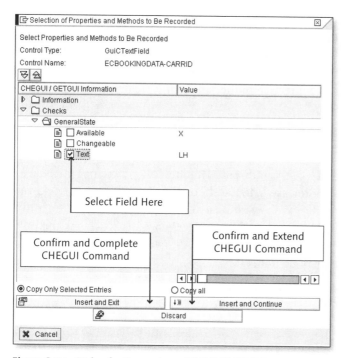

Figure 8.25 Dialog for Processing a "CHEGUI"/"GETGUI" Command

Because every screen element contains quite a number of properties, you must decide which of these properties you want to check. Usually this is the input value of the field. For text fields, this is the TEXT property to be found under GET/GENERALSTATE/TEXT. For some other screen elements, like list fields, for example, the input value is named VALUE and can be found in the same place.

Selecting properties

In some situations it might make sense to check the availability of a screen element before it is accessed. For this purpose, there is an AVAILABLE property. It always has the value "X" at the time of recording. For processing, it only has a value of "X" if the relevant screen element is accessible.

After you've selected the attribute that you want to read or want to read and check, you must select from the following options:

▶ **Insert and Exit**
Enters the attributes in the command interface of the GETGUI/CHEGUI command and returns to the recording.

▶ **Insert and Continue**
Enters the attributes in the command interface of the GETGUI/CHEGUI command and returns to the recording. You can insert additional fields in the command interface of the same GETGUI/CHEGUI command.

▶ **Reject**
You exit the dialog, and the GETGUI/CHEGUI command is not inserted into the script.

Initial state recording

Because the eCATT commands CHEGUI and GETGUI were not introduced until SAP Web AS Release 6.40, a different option of accessing field values has to be used in Web AS Release 6.20. For this purpose, the initial state recording is implemented. For SAP Web AS 6.20, this is the only option to read values. As of SAP Web AS 6.40, it is no longer recommended to use this function.

"Extended" button

Last but not least, the recording window also provides the EXTENDED button. If you select this option, you are provided with the following additional functions (see Figure 8.26):

▶ In the RECORDING MODE area, you can specify in FOR TREE CONTROLS whether the recording is supposed to be run via a key or path and in FOR CONTEXT MENUS whether the recording is supposed to be implemented based on a key, text, or position.

▶ In the INSERT COMMENT IN SCRIPT area, you can insert a comment which is inserted into the currently recorded script in the background.

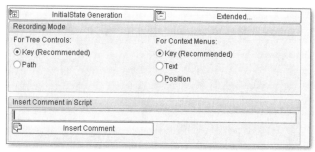

Figure 8.26 Dialog with Expanded Extension Functions

After recording, you can find all actions performed by the user in the relevant command interface with all details. This interface contains different nodes depending on the command used (SAPGUI, GETGUI, CHEGUI).

Command interfaces

The SAPGUI command interface comprises the following main nodes (see Figure 8.27):

"SAPGUI" command interface

▶ The first node below the main folder contains the system information. The CONNECTIONID and SESSIONID nodes specify the window in which the system runs the SAPGUI command. It is essential that all SAPGUI commands have exactly the same values here in order to execute them in the same window. You can directly change the values for connection ID and session ID here. For more details on the IDs, refer to the relevant sections in this chapter.

▶ Each PROCESSEDSCREEN node corresponds to an executed dynpro within the SAPGUI command.

▶ Below the PROCESSEDSCREEN node, you can view the USERCHANGED-STATE section which lists all actions at GUI element level executed by the user. At this point, you can parameterize the GUI elements; for instance, input fields. For example, the blue arrow pointing to the right just before the term "text" indicates that the user made an entry in an input field. These fields can be parameterized, or more precisely only those dynpro fields can be parameterized that you've changed via user entries during recording. This also means that F4 input helps are not recorded, but only the actually selected value. If in this example we assume that the name "Printer1" was entered as the value, then, a parameter (I_PRINTERNAME in this case) can be assigned to this value in the window on the right.

443

In the USER CHANGEDSTATE section, you can only set the values. With GETGUI and CHEGUI, you can read and check values of output fields.

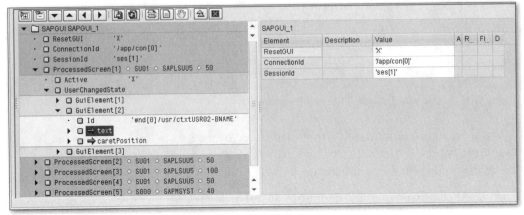

Figure 8.27 "SAPGUI" Command Interface

"GETGUI" command interface If you inserted a GETGUI command for the recording, you can parameterize the corresponding field in the command interface so that you can exchange the values at runtime.

For this purpose, expand the GUIELEMENT node that contains the selected field, and enter the parameter or variable to be used in the VALUE row (see Figure 8.28).

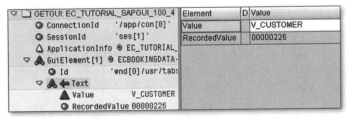

Figure 8.28 "GETGUI" Command Interface

"CHEGUI" command interface The command interface of CHEGUI is very similar to the GETGUI command interface (see Figure 8.29).

In line with your selection, a CHEGUI command is inserted into your script. To parameterize a field, expand the GUIELEMENT node that contains the selected field. Select a relational operation (=, <>,...) in the

444

CHECKACTION row, and enter the parameter or variable to be used for the check in the EXPECTEDVALUE row. You can also parameterize the VALUE field; there, you find the actual value at the time of execution.

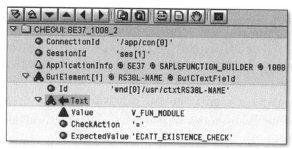

Figure 8.29 "CHEGUI" Command Interface

As of SAP Web AS Release 6.40, there are a number of functions for revising SAPGUI commands that have already been recorded. In addition to improving the usability, they primarily simplify the maintenance of the scripts.

Revising "SAPGUI" commands

An important aspect is that SAPGUI commands recorded as of SAP Web AS Release 6.40 can be extended at a later stage. To extend a script, you first need to ensure that you are at that point in the recorded session where you want to insert the extension. Then select PATTERN, and specify UI CONTROL as the group and SAPGUI (ATTACH) as the command. In the RECORD SAP GUI COMMAND WINDOW, define the granularity and whether the command is supposed to be recorded manually or automatically.

SAPGUI attach

After you've activated the ATTACH mode, the system displays a list of all sessions that you can record. This list contains all sessions on the local PC on which scripting is activated in the front end and the back end (except for the eCATT session). Choose the sessions to be recorded; you can activate multiple sessions at a time. Run the script recording as usual. The existing script is extended by adding the new steps.

If you want to use the extension function without working directly in the correct position in the application to be recorded, temporarily comment-out the commands not desired. Then execute the script. Ensure that the DO NOT CLOSE CREATED SESSIONS option has been selected in the script execution dialog. As soon as the session has reached the appropriate state (in other words, the end of the existing part of the script), return to the script editor. Select SAPGUI (ATTACH) from the pattern dialog.

The function of splitting or joining SAPGUI commands after recording has also been added to the SAP Web AS Release 6.40. This is very useful for inserting CHEGUI/GETGUI commands at a later stage and improving the readability of the script.

To join SAPGUI commands, highlight them in the script editor and open the context menu. From the menu, select the JOIN item. A new SAPGUI command is created, and its command interface comprises the actions of all highlighted commands. The commands marked are commented out.

Split functionality divides an SAPGUI command into several commands. This ensures a better overview, but is even more important in a re-recording when you want to split existing commands and insert new steps for re-recording. For example, if you forgot during a recording to fill a text field, you can split the command at the point where the text field needs to be filled. To split a long SAPGUI command, highlight the relevant command in the script editor. Open the context menu, and select the SPLITTING AT submenu. Then select the granularity. The following granularity levels are available:

- Transaction change
- Dynpro change
- Dialog step
- Methods/property

If you split a command in the script editor, the number of new commands depends on the granularity selected.

As of SAP NetWeaver 7.0, you can split in any place. If you split a command in the structure editor, two new commands are created for the resulting parts. Select the SPLIT COMMAND INTERFACE option from the context menu.

The original command is commented out, and the new commands are inserted with the new command interfaces. The original command interface is not lost. You can delete it if you are sure that you no longer require it.

There are several alternatives for flexibly designing SAPGUI commands. This flexibility enables you to cover several test variants with different details in a single test script. For example, you can set the editing of a dynpro to optional. In the command interface of the SAPGUI command, set the `ProcessedScreen[n]\Active` value from "X" to "O" for optional. The dynpro is edited only if it is displayed by the application. Otherwise, this part of the script is skipped. The common use of this option is to handle popup windows in the script that, depending on the input data or context, are either displayed or not.

Flexibility of the recording

You can create more complex constructs to cover alternative paths using a dynpro. For this purpose, select a fine granularity for the recording (for instance, METHOD) and then toggle between different SAPGUI commands using conditionals (see the IF command; Section 8.9, *Additional eCATT Commands*).

When processing a script using SAPGUI commands, you are provided with separate SAPGUI-specific start options (see Figure 8.30).

Start options for the SAPGUI driver

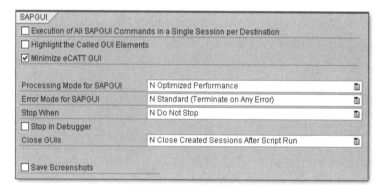

Figure 8.30 Start Options for Executing "SAPGUI" Commands

▶ The option EXECUTION OF ALL SAPGUI COMMANDS IN A SINGLE SESSION PER DESTINATION causes one session to be used per destination (target system). This is useful if you have different combinations of connection ID and session ID in your script or if you encounter difficulties with opening a new session due to a stored limitation of the number of sessions (default: 6).

▶ If the HIGHLIGHT THE CALLED GUI ELEMENTS option is enabled, the active screen element is highlighted with a red frame while the script is being executed. This option can be very useful for debugging scripts.

▶ The Minimize eCATT GUI option minimizes the SAP GUI window running eCATT to an icon on the task bar.

▶ The Processing Mode for SAPGUI option is a performance parameter. The following modes can be selected:

  ▶ **Optimized Performance**
  In this mode, the GUI updates are processed via the *automation queue*, which forwards them to the GUI. On the one hand, this improves the performance. On the other hand, a possible error in the script may not be displayed in the eCATT log directly where it occurs. Nevertheless, this is the recommended execution mode.

  ▶ **Synchronous GUI Control**
  Bypasses the automation queue and sends GUI updates directly to the front end. In this mode, GUI updates are sent to the GUI synchronously.

▶ The Error Mode for SAPGUI option controls the behavior of eCATT in the case of an error. The selections are self-explanatory.

▶ The Stop When option causes eCATT to interrupt the script execution in specific places. It is not continued until the user confirms it. This option is particularly useful during script development. In case of an interruption, the execution control operates via a popup window.

▶ If you additionally enable Stop in Debugger, the eCATT script switches to the debug mode whenever it is interrupted. In this case, the execution control is via the debugger and not via a popup window. More information can be found in Section 8.12, *Further Steps*.

▶ The Close GUIs option enables you to specify whether and when the modes that have been automatically created during the script execution are automatically closed again.

Screenshot
functionality

As of SAP NetWeaver Release 7.00, functionality for automatically creating and saving screenshots is provided (see Figure 8.31). This functionality was designed primarily for covering the documentation requirements in an environment where validation is mandatory. However, a sequence of screenshots can also be useful for tracing the individual steps of test runs for troubleshooting purposes.

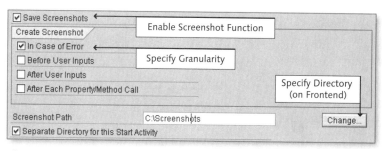

Figure 8.31 Screenshot Options in the Start Options

To enable the functions for automatically creating screenshots, select the SAVE SCREENSHOTS option in the start options. The screenshot options are displayed. Specify the granularity and a directory where the screenshots are to be stored. The specification of the granularity level defines the application events for which the screenshots are to be created. The screenshots are saved in .jpg format.

Because the functionality for automatically creating screenshots requires the availability of a user interface, it is only available for the SAPGUI driver. In an environment requiring validation, you should consider this when you select the test driver. It may make more sense in such a case to use the SAPGUI driver even for recording a transaction without controls, even though you would normally use the TCD driver due to its better maintainability and performance.

Regarding the message handling within the SAPGUI driver, please refer to Section 8.6.3, *Message Handling*.

8.2.3 Testing Web Dynpro Applications

As of SAP Web AS 6.40, eCATT supports the direct testing of Web Dynpro Java-based applications. For SAP NetWeaver 7.02 and as of SAP NetWeaver 7.20, the testing of Web Dynpro ABAP-based applications is also supported.

When recording a Web Dynpro application, the user operates it either in a Web Dynpro client (for Web Dynpro ABAP and Web Dynpro Java) or via the browser (only for Web Dynpro Java). Figure 8.32 shows the recording via the Web Dynpro Business Client.

Architecture

449

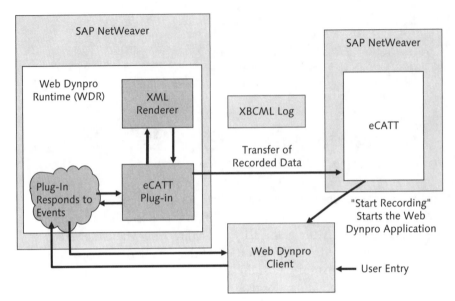

Figure 8.32 Recording Web Dynpro Commands

Communication
while recording

When you start the recording of a Web Dynpro in Web Dynpro ABAP, the Web Dynpro Client opens. In Web Dynpro Java, the user can select between the recording in the Web Dynpro Business Client and recording via the browser. The user operates the application in the Web Dynpro Client or in the browser. As soon as changes are made to the Web Dynpro context (back end) that is, if data change or actions are executed the plug-in is informed about this and then records the operations. In Web Dynpro, eCATT records the business logic of the application and not the events in the interface as in the SAP GUI with controls, for example. The data recorded is then sent to eCATT as an XML file in the background.

Communication
while processing

The processing of Web Dynpro applications is done in the background via HTTP without a browser.

During processing, the request is sent to the target system via HTTP in XML format. The request corresponds to an input in the UI plus the Web Dynpro action. An XML description of the next page to be displayed is returned as the response. The description contains the structure of the window or the subareas of a window as well as the data. If, for example, an input field is filled with values, this value is also part of the client's response. The processing usually occurs in the background. Using the simulator, you can trace the processing of the transactions on screen.

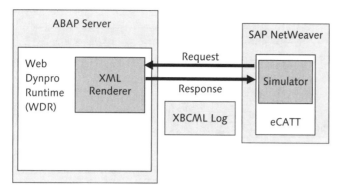

Figure 8.33 Processing a Web Dynpro Transaction

The URL for addressing the Web Dynpro application is structured as follows:

Structure of the URL

```
HTTP://<Server>:<Service>/<URL extension>/<Application>
```

The meanings of server (name or IP address) and service (port) are familiar. The URL extension looks different depending on whether the Web Dynpro runtime environment is based on the Java or the ABAP stack. If you are using the ABAP stack, the extension is:

```
<ABAP URL extension> = sap/bc/webdynpro
```

If the Web Dynpro runtime environment is based on Java, the extension has the following format:

```
<Java URL extension> = webdynpro/dispatcher
```

The first step for recording a Web Dynpro-based application is the creation of the targets for the HTTP connections. Use Transaction SM59 for this purpose. Java-based applications require an HTTP connection to an external server (connection type G). For ABAP applications, you should create an HTTP connection to the SAP system (connection type H).

Creating the connections

Enter host name and service (port) of the target system as shown in Figure 8.34.

As soon as you have created and successfully tested the HTTP connection, insert a logical target in the system data container. In the HTTP DESTINATION column, store the newly created connection for this target system.

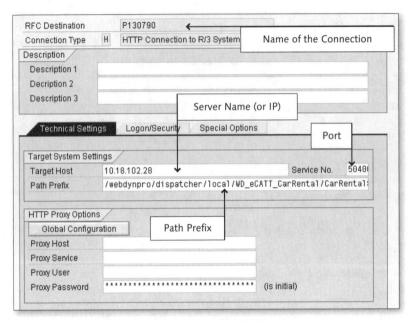

Figure 8.34 Creating a Connection Transaction SM59

Recording Web Dynpro transactions

To record a `WEBDYNPRO` command, go to the script editor. Select Pattern, and from the UI Control group select the WEBDYNPRO command. A dialog box for specifying the Web Dynpro application is displayed. This dialog box differs, depending on whether you want to record Web Dynpro ABAP or Java. In case of Web Dynpro Java, you have the option of starting the recording in the Web Dynpro Client or in the browser. In case of Web Dynpro ABAP, only the recording button is available, and the recording is started automatically in the Web Dynpro Business Client when you select this button. Select a target system (the target system with the HTTP connection you previously created; see Figure 8.35).

In the Application input field, complete the basis URL of the connection with an application-specific section. This section depends on the application to be recorded; for example, CarRental. The address sections are then merged by eCATT. Then, in the case of Web Dynpro Java, select the recording type (in the browser or Web Dynpro Business Client). Subsequently, click the Start Recording button. Note that the Web Dynpro Business Client must be installed to be able to start the recording in the Business Client (see SAP Note 773899).

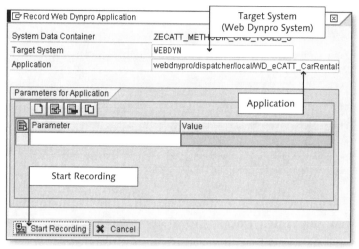

Figure 8.35 Starting the Web Dynpro Java Recording

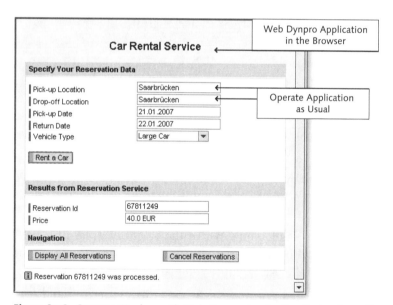

Figure 8.36 Browser Window with Web Dynpro Application During Recording

As soon as you start recording, eCATT automatically opens a browser window or Web Dynpro Business Client window containing the Web Dynpro application (see Figure 8.36). In this window, you operate the application as usual and populate the dialog elements with values. Your input is recorded and is later available in the command interface of the WEBDYNPRO command.

At the same time, another window opens in which you can stop recording again (see Figure 8.37).

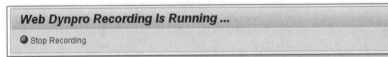

Web Dynpro Recording Is Running ...

 Stop Recording

Figure 8.37 Dialog Window for Stopping the Recording

As soon as you have stopped the interaction with the Web Dynpro application, use the task bar to change to this window and stop the recording. Now the WEBDYNPRO statement is displayed in the script editor.

> **"WEBDYNPRO" Command**
>
> The WEBDYNPRO command is designed for addressing the Web Dynpro driver. It has the following notation:
>
> WEBDYNRPO (<Command interface>, [<Target system>]).
>
> The target system must be an HTTP connection of the G type (for Java Server) or the H type (for ABAP Server).

Command interface

The command interface of the WEBDYNPRO command comprises the following nodes with recording details (see Figure 8.38):

▶ Under SCREEN • DATA, you can find the XML description of the page returned. This description is relevant if the pages are supposed to be displayed in the eCATT Web Dynpro simulator.

▶ Under DATACHANGES, you can find the values entered during the recording. Like with an SAPGUI command, you can parameterize the recording to link the Web Dynpro command to the test data.

▶ Under ACTION, you can find the actions that trigger a round trip. For example, data changes do not become effective until the relevant action triggers the round trip.

▶ Under GETS AND CHECKS, the system displays the details on checks or value determinations. This node is only visible if such checks/value determinations have been started from the simulator (see next section).

▶ Under PAGE • SCREEN • MESSAGES, you can find the messages sent during recording. You can process messages from Web Dynpro applications via a `MESSAGE ... ENDMESSAGE` block as well (see Section 8.6.3, *Message Handling*).

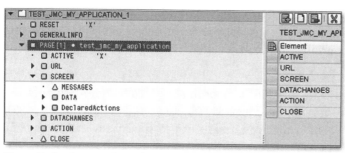

Figure 8.38 Command Interface of the Web Dynpro Command

The `WEBDYNPRO` command includes a page simulator which enables you to determine values from output fields or execute checks on their content. To start the simulator, open a `WEBDYNPRO` command interface in the structure editor, and select the magnifying glass button. In the simulation, select the field to be checked, and then choose INSERT CHECK. If you want to determine the value of a field, select INSERT GET instead. In both cases, a new node, GETS_AND_CHECKS, is inserted in the command interface. In this node, you can now determine or test the values of a page. The parameterization is similar to that from the `GETGUI` and `CHEGUI` commands.

Simulator

You can also directly go to the simulator display from the log if you double-click the PAGE node. This way, you can immediately determine to which screen a possible error refers. Even in the debugger, you go to the simulation if you press the F5 key. Note that the SAP NetWeaver Business Client must be installed to use the eCATT Web Dynpro simulator. SAP Note 773899 provides more detailed information.

When the Web Dynpro driver is used, you have the following start options:

Start options for the Web Dynpro driver

▶ If you select the PROCESS IN BACKGROUND option, the script is processed without being displayed in a user interface. The progress of the script cannot be traced on screen. However, this option ensures the best performance.

▶ If you select the PROCESS IN FOREGROUND option, the progress of the script is displayed in a user interface. The PROCESS IN FOREGROUND (DISPLAY RECORDED PAGE IN PARALLEL) option causes the progress of the test case in the application at the time of recording to be displayed in a second window in addition to the actual script. Because it enables comparison, this option is very helpful for the troubleshooting process during the script development. For both options for processing in the foreground, you can specify how long the respective screen is supposed to be displayed.

SE80 connection   You can also start the eCATT recording of a Web Dynpro application directly from the object navigator (Transaction SE80; see Figure 8.39). Here, the benefit is that you don't need to specifically call the eCATT Transaction SECATT. An XML file is returned.

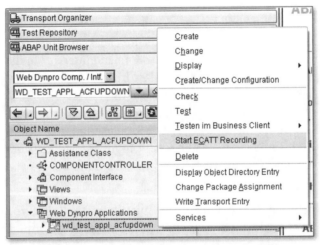

Figure 8.39 Starting the Recording from Transaction SE80

If you select the Pattern button in Transaction SECATT, two additional Web Dynpro commands are available for selection within the UI CONTROL group: WEBDYNPRO (attach) and WEBDYNPRO (import). The latter option refers to the Web Dynpro Java applications. If a Web Dynpro Java application is recorded in SAP NetWeaver Developer Studio, the system generates an XML file that can be uploaded to eCATT. Then, the corresponding Web Dynpro commands are generated in eCATT. WEBDYNPRO (attach) enables you to extend scripts from the Web Dynpro simulator.

8.2.4   Summary

UI-based applications can be tested with eCATT via different test drivers.

Transactions without controls can be recorded by the TCD driver: comparable to a macro recorder that you might know from Microsoft Excel. During parameterization, you replace the fixed values entered during the recording process with parameters and thus can create a flexible, usable script. Changing the assignment mode enables you to read and check the actual values of a parameter.

Transactions with controls can be recorded using the SAPGUI driver. The selection of the correct granularity is very important, although it can be corrected at a later stage in more recent eCATT versions. For reading and checking values, the GETGUI and CHEGUI commands are available. Moreover, you can join and split script commands using the JOIN and SPLIT commands.

Web Dynpro applications can be recorded just like SAP GUI transactions. The URL is opened automatically in the Web Dynpro Business Client or a browser. The recording takes place in parallel while the Web Dynpro client or the browser is being operated by the SAP application.

8.3   Creating Tests Via Direct Program Control

eCATT enables you to test the following program controls:

- ▸ Global ABAP object classes
- ▸ Function modules and BAPIs
- ▸ Inline ABAP
- ▸ Database accesses

8.3.1   Testing Global ABAP Object Classes

The eCATT command set comprises commands for testing global classes. You can find the set of commands if you open the desired test script in transaction SECATT, click the PATTERN button, and select the ABAP OBJECTS group.

To be able to access instance attributes and methods of a class, you must create an instance of the class. As a prerequisite, there must be a parameter of the type to which the object can be assigned. The parameter must contain the type of the class and a class or an interface from which the class inherits.

By default, an object is created using the CREATEOBJ command. However, you also can create an object by using a function module or a method that provides an object.

Instance attributes and static attributes
To access instance attributes, you first need to instantiate the object. The following table lists commands available for accessing instance attributes and static attributes of a class.

Command For Accessing Instance Attributes	Command For Accessing Static Attributes	Description
CHEATTR	CHESTATIC	Compares the current value of an attribute with the value specified.
GETATTR	GETSTATIC	Calls the current value of an attribute and assigns a parameter to this value.
SETATTR	SETSTATIC	Changes the current value of an attribute to a value specified.

Table 8.3 Commands for Accessing Instance and Static Attributes

Methods
You use CALLMETHOD to call an instance method of a class. For this purpose, you must first instantiate the object. To call a static method, use CALLSTATIC.

8.3.2 Function Modules and BAPIs

In the following cases, it could be necessary to test or use function modules:

▶ In a test in which you test an individual function module.

▶ In a background process in which you test a chain of function modules which represent a complete process by transferring results of a module to the next one. You can perform this work step in a single script or in several consecutive test scripts.

▶ As a utility within a script; for instance, to call data from the database which you want to use in transactions or to perform complex plausibility checks via already existing function modules.

"FUN" Command

The eCATT command required to call function modules is named FUN. After opening a test script in Transaction SECATT, you can select the PROGRAM CONTROL group via the Pattern button.

The command interface corresponds to the interface of the function module. In the structure editor, it is subdivided into areas for the different parameter types—import, export, change, and tables—with an additional area for exceptions. For the transfer to a function module, you assign the relevant literal or variable to the correct parameter in the command interface. To call a value from an export parameter of the function module, you assign a variable to the parameter.

8.3.3 Inline ABAP

Inline ABAP provides the option of inserting complex programming elements into an eCATT script. An inline ABAP block is initiated with the ABAP script statement and ends with ENDABAP. This statement can also be selected via the Pattern button in the PROGRAM CONTROL group.

Within the inline ABAP block, you can use (almost) any ABAP commands. Inline ABAP is particularly required for complex database accesses, but it can also be used for all calls of function modules and ABAP OO routines.

Note

When you use inline ABAP, you should avoid any user interactions as well as mode-generating or mode-ending operations (for instance, CALL FUNCTION STARTING NEW TASK) because otherwise an automatic test execution is no longer possible.

The connection to the eCATT script is established via the local variables (parameter type V). All local variables are automatically declared within inline ABAP and are provided with the current values from the script execution. After executing the inline ABAP block, all local variables are in turn provided with the values that were assigned within the inline ABAP.

Tip

You should outsource inline ABAP scripts to custom scripts in order to keep the number of local variables as low as possible. Transfer to and from inline ABAP can hurt performance when complex variables and large tables are used.

8.3.4   Database Accesses

CHETAB

> **"CHETAB" Command**
>
> The CHETAB command compares field values of a database table with values which you define in the command interface; the command interface has the same structure as the table.

Using the CHETAB command, you can check the following:

- Database updates after transactions
- The existence of specific table entries
- Entries in customizing tables

You maintain the values of fields in the command interface. For this purpose, you aren't limited to the key fields, and you don't need to specify the complete key either. However, you shouldn't leave any key field empty; we recommend entering an asterisk in each key field to which you don't assign a value.

If no data record is found that meets the search criteria, an error message is written to the log. If one or more data records are found, the check is entered as successful in the log.

You can specify the system in which the database table can be found. If you specify a target system, a corresponding system container must be assigned to the test script or the test configuration.

GETTAB

> **"GETTAB" Command**
>
> The GETTAB command reads a data record of a database table and assigns the values of the data record to the corresponding fields of a command interface. The command interface has the same structure as the table.

In general, the same conditions as apply to CHETAB apply to the maintenance of field values. For this reason, if you don't specify the full key, multiple data records can meet the selection criteria. GETTAB reads the first data record that meets the selection criteria.

8.3.5 Summary

Besides UI-based applications, you can use eCATT to test the following program-controlled applications: ABAP object classes, function modules and BAPIs, and inline ABAP, as well as database accesses.

8.4 Creating Tests for Web Services

The SAP NetWeaver Application Server enables enterprises to extend their solutions by integrating web services and providing them to their users. It supports the XML, SOAP (Stateless, Stateful, and Security), WSDL, and UDDI standards.

As of SAP NetWeaver 7.0, eCATT supports the automated testing of web services. A web service is then called in the same way as an internal ABAP function module. The necessary ABAP proxy classes are generated automatically.

Because the functionality of the eCATT web service driver is not limited to testing web services provided via the SAP NetWeaver Application Server, you indirectly gain an interesting alternative for testing third-party solutions. As long as the third-party system in your process chain has a web service interface, you can integrate it seamlessly in the test coverage via eCATT scripts.

Testing third-party solutions

To test a web service, first generate an HTTP connection using Transaction SM59. Then, in the eCATT script editor, click on the PATTERN button and from the ENTERPRISE SERVICES group select the WEBSERVICE command. Figure 8.40 shows the dialog field that is displayed.

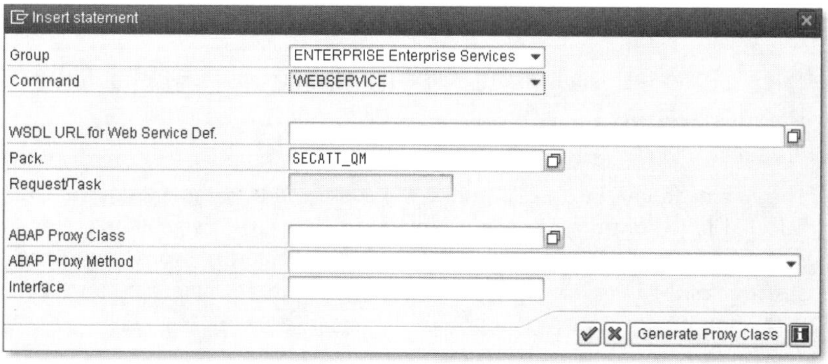

Figure 8.40 Inserting a Web Service Test

Because web services are function-like objects that do not allow for direct user communication, no recording occurs in this step. Instead, you specify a method call that is submitted to the web service.

If the web service is implemented on an SAP NetWeaver Application Server and you know the ABAP proxy class on which it is based, you can select the corresponding ABAP proxy class from the directory. Once you've confirmed your entries, the appropriate values are inserted in the fields, ABAP PROXY METHOD and INTERFACE.

If there is no appropriate ABAP proxy class yet, eCATT supports you by automatically creating an appropriate ABAP proxy class. In the WSDL URL FOR WEB SERVICE DEFINITION field, enter a URL where a web service description can be found. The WSDL description (Web Service Description Language) specifies the functions provided by the service. Usually, you will want to obtain the description directly from the used server. In that case, the URL normally uses the following format:

```
HTTP://<Server>:<Port>/<Web Service Name>/Config?wsdl
```

As soon as the correct address for the service description has been entered, click on the GENERATE PROXY CLASS button; eCATT queries the capabilities of the web service and generates an ABAP proxy class. This generated class is entered directly in the ABAP PROXY CLASS field. You need to assign the class to a package.

Once you have a functioning proxy class, you can select the visible methods of the class in the ABAP PROXY METHOD field. Select the wanted method from the list, and close the dialog box. eCATT then generates a WEB SERVICE command in the script editor.

"WEB SERVICE" Command

The WEB SERVICE command is used for addressing web services. It has the following format:

```
WEB SERVICE(<Command interface>, [<Target system>] ).
```

The command interface (see Figure 8.41) corresponds to the interface of the selected function from the ABAP proxy class. Usually, it is generated automatically from the WSDL. Therefore you do not need to worry about the structure of the transferred parameters. Just populate the command interface with appropriate values.

Figure 8.41 Command Interface of the "WEB SERVICE" Command

With SAP NetWeaver 7.1, you can upload web service test scenarios as XML files into eCATT to test WEB SERVICE commands with eCATT. For this purpose, you need the Composition Environment as of Release 7.1. Moreover, the Web Service Navigator must be configured accordingly. Prior to the uploading process, you can make presettings for parameterization. You can select which import or export parameters should be created.

Uploading web service test scenarios

The following upload options are available:

▶ Upload of the test scenario and simultaneous generation of eCATT objects (test configuration and test script). For this purpose, open Transaction SECATT, enter the name of the test script you want to create or overwrite, and select eCATT OBJECT • OTHER FEATURES • UPLOAD WEB SERVICE TEST SCENARIO DATA.

▶ Upload of the test scenario and simultaneous generation of a new web service command interface. For this purpose, open Transaction SECATT of the wanted test script, and select the PATTERN button. The INSERT PATTERN selection screen is displayed. In this screen, select ENTERPRISE SERVICES as the group and WEB SERVICE (UPLOAD) as the command.

▶ Upload of the test scenario in an already existing command interface. For this purpose, open in transaction SECATT the wanted test script, and double-click the web service command interface that is supposed to be uploaded to the file. The command structure is displayed in the subscreen on the right. Then select the UPLOAD WS TEST SCENARIO option.

▶ Upload of a test scenario to create test configuration variant(s). For this purpose, open the test script in Transaction SECATT and double-click the web service command interface that is supposed to be uploaded to the file. The command structure is displayed in the subscreen on the right. Then select the CREATE CONFIGURATION VARIANT option.

Except for the option to upload to an existing command interface, all upload variants are "capable of mass processing;" that is, multiple data records can be selected for processing.

After the upload process, the script editor displays a log including all originally selected settings and possible error messages. This enables you to reproduce the upload process.

Integration of Web Dynpros and web services

An interesting application scenario is created when web services are tested that are integrated with Web Dynpro-based transactions. For example, a data record can be entered via an automated Web Dynpro transaction to check the correct update of the data in the test system via an appropriate web-service call. This enables a continuous test of service-oriented solution landscapes.

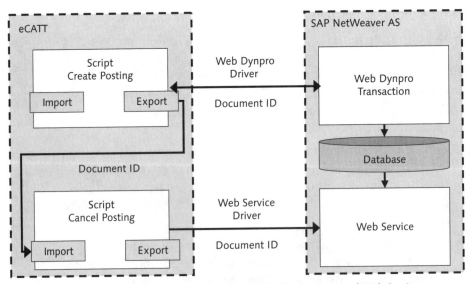

Figure 8.42 Example of a Test Scenario with Web Dynpros and Web Services

Conclusion

The web-services test is fully supported and integrated with eCATT as of SAP NetWeaver 7.0. Because ABAP proxy classes are generated automatically from WSDL descriptions, addressing a web service is just as simple and comfortable as calling a function module. In combination with Web Dynpros, this results in very elegant possibilities for testing modern service-oriented solution landscapes via different forms of access.

8.5   Integration with External Test Tools

The driver for external test tools plays a special role among the eCATT test drivers. An external tool is a program of a third-party provider that uses the implementation of the BC-eCATT interface to interact with eCATT. SAP can certify the successful interaction. Under *http://www.sap.com/ecosystem/customers/directories/SearchSolution.epx, you can find a list of the test tools certified by SAP for the* interaction with eCATT. Then select BC-ECATT 6.2WIN in the first dropdown list.

In heterogeneous solution landscapes, business processes can be effectively tested automatically with eCATT. The external test tool then covers those process steps that do not use a SAP GUI for Windows or Web Dynpro as a user interface.

Such an external test tool must be installed on the front end to be tested, and registered in the back end. The documentation of the external test tool contains information on the registration. In registration, the external program works as an adapter for the software to be tested. The work process—that is, the recording, editing, and processing—of user interactions is controlled via the external tool (see Figure 8.43). For this purpose, the tool is addressed by eCATT via the BC-eCATT interface. Recorded scripts are transferred via BC-eCATT and stored and managed in the central repository like native eCATT scripts. This ensures central, continuous, and consistent data storage even for the integration of external tools.

BC-eCATT

For recording, a distinction is made between two different processes. For the integrated recording scenario, eCATT is the driver that calls the external tool. In the standalone scenario, however, the recording is initially run in the external tool and then transferred to eCATT.

Recording

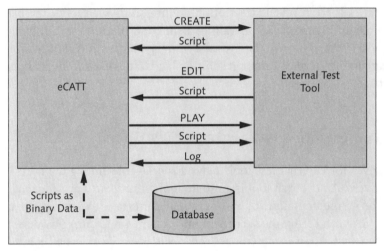

Figure 8.43 Integrating an External Tool with eCATT

Integrated
recording The procedure for integrated recording is as follows.

1. When you create the script in Transaction SECATT, enter the desired test script name and select the external tool to be used.

   The system takes you to an editor window whose functions are highly reduced because the recording itself takes place in the external test tool.

2. Click the SCRIPT button to start the recording in the external tool.

3. After the interaction with the application to be tested is completed, the user stops the recording, defines transfer parameters if required, and selects the save function of the respective external test tool.

4. The recorded script is transferred via BC-eCATT and stored in the database.

Standalone
recording For standalone recording, the recording takes place in the external test tool independent of eCATT. If you want to transfer the data to eCATT after recording, then—depending on the implementation in the used external test tool—you must save the data in such a way that it can be transferred to eCATT. You then create the corresponding test script and a test configuration in eCATT.

The script is edited and maintained in the external tool. For this purpose, eCATT sends the script back to the external tool. After it has been edited, the script can be uploaded again.

During the execution, eCATT interacts with the external tool in the same way, except that in this case no further user interaction is required other than starting the eCATT test configuration. eCATT sends the script to the external tool. The tool is then started by eCATT, receives the possibly transferred parameter from eCATT, and executes the script. After the script has run, result values can be returned to eCATT in the form of parameters and can then be further processed. Additionally, the log of the external tool is created, transferred to the SAP system via BC-eCATT, and stored by eCATT in the database. In contrast to the script format, the log format is defined by the BC-eCATT standard. These logs can thus be fully integrated in the log of the eCATT test configuration and be displayed, searched, and analyzed just like the logs of native eCATT scripts.

Depending on whether this function was implemented in your external test tool, you have the option in eCATT to define a Uniform Naming Convention (UNC) path to the log in the external tool. If you've defined a UNC path and a script is executed, the complete log is stored in the external tool at the location referenced by the UNC path. Additionally, a node is added to the eCATT log that specifies the UNC path as a link. If you follow this link, the log is displayed in the log viewer of the external tool. This functionality is beneficial, for example, if you store screenshots in the external system, together with the log, which are not supposed to be transferred to eCATT for performance reasons.

The actual user interaction is not stored in the command interface when an external test driver is called. Instead, every external driver call has its own script that is marked as external. Analogous to the REF command that references to another test script, the external script is referenced via the REFEXT command.

"REFEXT" Command

The REFEXT command serves for calling a test script recorded by an external tool:

```
REFEXT ( <external script>,
         <command interface>,
         <version> ).
```

467

Start options for
the external driver

When an external driver is implemented, you have the following start
options.

▶ **Normal**
The external tool is not visible during the execution. Only the test
execution, by interacting with the application to be tested, can be
watched on screen.

▶ **Debug mode**
The debugger of the external tool is started, and the test script stops
and remains in debug mode before the first statement. Depending on
the capabilities of the implemented external tool, the test script can
now be executed and analyzed step-by-step in the debugger.

▶ **With the interface of the external tool**
The external tool is visible during the test execution. The actual test
execution is the same as for the Normal start option.

Start options and
start profile

If the external test tool has its own authorization concept, you can store
a user name and a password in the start options. These are then used to
log on to the external tool. However, because you may forget to set these
entries in the start options, a storage alternative is available: the start
profile. If you then run a test from the Test Workbench, specify which
test configuration is supposed to be executed with which start profile. A
fast way to create a start profile is to copy the current settings in the start
page (Start Options • Save Start Profile).

"SENDEXT"
command

Let's assume that your script contains a REFEXT command with a DO loop,
and the external script is supposed to be run 100 times. Normally, the
REFEXT command would send the script to the external tool for every
single execution. To avoid this unnecessary data transfer, the REFEXT
command interface has the Do not send option. When you select this
option, a SENDEXT command is put at the start so that the data is transferred only once at the beginning.

External tools and
process chains

Let us now look at some implementation scenarios for the external tool
driver. A typical case is the integration of a web application with an SAP
system, such as the implementation of a third-party web shop as a part
of a front end for an ERP system.

The key aspect from the tester's point of view is that the browser-based
application of the web shop is not based on a user interface directly sup-

ported by eCATT. It is out of reach for the test drivers presented so far. Because most relevant business processes also affect the web shop as an integral component, it isn't useful to exclude it from the test.

Because complete business processes are to be tested end-to-end in the context of an integration test, a separate test of the web shop is not very useful either. You need to completely and automatically test the integration with the other components of the solution landscape as well. The objective of implementing the external test tool is to close the gap in the automated test chain.

One scenario assumes that we are dealing with an SAP-dominated system landscape with few foreign components. In this situation, an eCATT-based test using an external test tool is recommended. A major part of the testing then benefits from the deep integration of eCATT with the SAP applications; the gaps can then be elegantly closed by the external driver.

SAP-dominated solution landscape

If a system landscape is dominated by systems of one or several third-parties, SAP applications might only be used sporadically. The advantages of an eCATT-based automation solution seem less striking. Before making a decision, however, we should weigh the integration possibilities of SAP Solution Manager. In the sense of a holistic application management, it enables you to integrate steps of non-SAP applications with the Business Process Repository (BPR) and to build the test organization across systems in a process-oriented way. In addition to this organizational advantage, we should consider the chance to minimize the total cost of operation for the automation solution. For the non-integrated implementation of external test tools, in addition to the actual tool costs, there are usually costs for the infrastructure required by the tool, that is, databases, file services and their license and administration costs. With integration in eCATT, this cost can be avoided almost entirely. Even in this situation, you should always check the alternative of eCATT-based test automation.

Heterogeneous system landscape with SAP share

In the SAP Developer Network (SDN) on the certification page of BC-eCATT, you can obtain information on the BC-eCATT interface as well as the test tools that can be integrated. This page is available via the following link: *https://www.sdn.sap.com/irj/sdn/interface-certifications*.

Test tools that can be integrated

Conclusion

eCATT treats third-party programs implementing the BC-eCATT interface as external test tools. These external programs are addressed like native eCATT test drivers; however, they do not store the recorded information in command interfaces but in specific scripts. The external scripts themselves can be called from eCATT using the REFEXT command. For the standalone recording variant, the test scripts are a direct part of the test configuration. The scripts, their test data, and the execution logs are all managed within the SAP system.

8.6　Implementing Checks

An eCATT script typically consists of two logical blocks: the call of the test driver, and the subsequent checking of the results. The possibilities of recording, parameterizing, and revising commands for the various test drivers have been presented in the previous sections. We now look at the actual checking process: the comparison of the result returned by the driver and an expected value.

An important consideration is that scripts do not necessarily fail just because the recorded transaction returns an error. Conversely, a script is not necessarily successful just because the transaction returns a value. To clarify these statements, let's look at the following example:

In a transaction, a passenger is to be booked on a flight. The flight is determined by a flight number and a date. If a reservation on the specified flight is possible, it should be entered in the database, and a reservation number should be returned. The most obvious case is that a flight number and a date are entered and a reservation number is returned. However, there are a number of other possible outcomes.

Unexpected errors
1. The desired flight exists, and there is a seat available. In this case, the reservation is to be completed and a reservation number should be returned.

   If an error is still reported by the software, there might be a programming or customizing error. If this error is detected during the test, we refer to an unexpected error.

2. The desired flight does not exist because an invalid flight number has been entered. In this case, the error message "Invalid flight number" should be returned.

   This is obviously an error, or at least an error message is displayed. However, this is not a software error but an incorrect entry. Because our test refers to the SAP system and not to the users, this problem is outside our responsibility. We refer to this as an expected error. Expected errors or, more specifically, the proper handling of expected errors belong to the correct functioning of a software system. If expected errors occur during the execution of the test, the test case is regarded as successful.

3. The desired flight exists but is fully booked. In this case, the error message "Flight fully booked" should be returned.

   This is a problem as well. After all, the customer has still not received a boarding card. It is worth noting that the omission of this error message results in two or more passengers occupying the same seat.

   A missing expected error shows up in an unexpected error. Such an error must be found and exposed by the test.

It is helpful to view error messages as normal return values of an application. With this approach, it becomes clear that you do not need to check whether the software produces an error but whether the software returns an unexpected result, either a number, a text, or an error message. A test that checks the correct appearance of an expected error is often referred to as a negative test.

But how can you access the results of transactions for testing purposes? eCATT provides a broad range of possibilities, which are presented in the following section.

8.6.1 Testing Parameters

Values can be transferred via the command interface of a command to a parameter, for example. Then the parameters can be further processed and checked using the CHEVAR command. This is the most flexible way of testing values, and should be applied whenever you need to perform more complex tests than the direct comparison of two values.

> **"CHEVAR" Command**
>
> The CHEVAR statement serves for checking parameters. It has the following format:
>
> CHEVAR (<Logical expression>).
>
> The condition uses an operator to relate a parameter to another parameter or a fixed value. If the comparison fails, the script is regarded as faulty.

Relational
operators

The CHEVAR command relates the value of a parameter to a different value. The following operators are available for this purpose: equal to, not equal to, smaller than, greater than, lesser than/equal to, and greater than/equal to.

Operator	Description
A = B	equal to
A <> B	not equal to
A < B	lesser than
A > B	greater than
A <= B	lesser than or equal to
A >= B	greater than or equal to

Table 8.4 Relational Operators to be Used with "CHEVAR"

In all cases, the script fails if the comparison is not met. If you want the script to fail if the comparison is met, you can invert the comparison. For example, if a script should fail if two values are equal, you should test for not equal. However, please be careful: Comparisons are inverted according to the rules of Boolean algebra, which do not always match everyday language. The opposite of lesser than, for example, is not greater than but greater than/equal to.

Comparison	Inverted Comparison
A = B	A <> B
A < B	A >= B
A > B	A <= B

Table 8.5 Inverting Simple Relational Operators (Valid for Both Directions)

472

There are additional logical operators for building more complex comparisons. These are AND, OR, and NOT (see Table 8.5). They require some caution as well: In everyday life, "or" usually means "either a or b". An OR (logical or), however, means "a or b or both." This subtle difference often leads to unintended results if you do not pay attention.

Logical operators

Operator	Description
A AND B	A and B
A OR B	A or B
NOT A	not A

Table 8.6 Logical Operators

Composite expressions are simply inverted by a preceding NOT. You must, however, ensure that the following expression is enclosed in parentheses (see Table 8.7).

Comparison	Inverted Comparison
A = 2 OR A = 4	NOT (A = 2 OR A = 4) Corresponds to: A <> 2 AND A <> 4
A < 2 AND B = 0	NOT (A < 2 AND B = 0) Corresponds to: A >= 2 OR B <> 0
A <> 0	NOT (A <> 0) Corresponds to: A = 0

Table 8.7 Inverting Composite Relational Expressions (Examples)

8.6.2 Direct Testing of Values

For simple checks, it is not always necessary to first transfer a value to be checked to a parameter. The TCD command permits the parameterization of values in the "C" mode (C for check). In this case, a relational operator is selected in addition to the field. After the TCD command has been executed, the value in the corresponding field is compared to the parameter or a specified fixed value.

"TCD" command

A comparable functionality is provided by the CHEGUI command as a part of a block of SAPGUI commands. Instead of first reading the value using GETGUI and then checking the parameter via CHEVAR, the value can also be checked directly. Just use the CHEGUI command in the same way

SAPGUI/CHEGUI

you use GETGUI. After the recording has completed, open the command interface and parameterize the CHEGUI command, then specify a reference value (parameter or fixed value) and a relational operator.

It is possible to check more than one value in a single CHEGUI or TCD command; the tests are then implicitly joined with the AND operator. The command is successful if all included checks have been successful (see Figures 8.44 and 8.45).

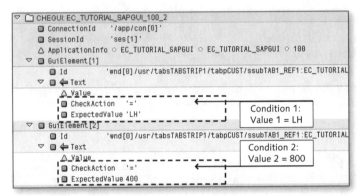

Figure 8.44 Command Interface of the "CHEGUI" Command (I)

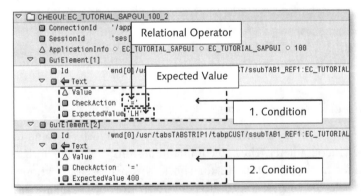

Figure 8.45 Command Interface of the "CHEGUI" Command (II)

8.6.3 Message Handling

Messages are used for returning data from transactions. For example, a transaction can produce a certain message if a specific state change or an error occurs. All occurring messages are generally reported in the log. If the script should react to messages, they can be intercepted by the test script and processed accordingly.

> **"MESSAGE ... ENDMESSAGE" Command**
>
> The MESSAGE ... ENDMESSAGE block is used for intercepting messages.
>
> ```
> MESSAGE (<Command interface 1>).
>    <Command 1>.
>    ...
> ENDMESSAGE (<Command interface 2>.
> ```
>
> The command interface of the MESSAGE command specifies a number of filters. These filters are used to determine the reactions to specific messages. After the block has terminated, all messages sent during the execution of the block reside in the command interface of the ENDMESSAGE command.

The command interface of the MESSAGE command specifies how to handle any messages. For this purpose, a filter is created that consists of a list of individual rules. Every rule first defines to which sort of messages it applies. You can specify any combination of message type (MSGTYP), message class (MSGID), and message number (MSGNR). The type of a message is its most general characteristic. The following six message types are available:

Message filter

Message Type	Event
A	Transaction aborted
E	Errors
I	Information
S	Status message (success)
W	Warning
X	Exit with short dump

Table 8.8 Message Types (MSGTYP)

The message class and message number define a specific message, they depend on the application and on customizing. Every one of these characteristics can be specified or not specified, where an empty characteristic is regarded as a wildcard. This applies to all messages.

When a message occurs, one rule after another is applied until a match occurs. If a matching rule is found, downstream rules are no longer applied. The order of the rules therefore plays an important role (see Figure 8.46).

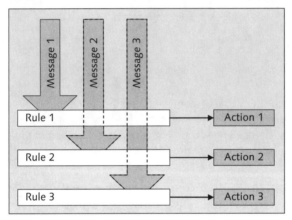

Figure 8.46 Structure of a Message Filter

The structure of a message filter is comparable to a sieve: At first you look for specific messages using specific rules (coarsely meshed sieves); later, more general rules (finely meshed sieves) are applied in order to include the remaining potential messages.

Message mode Every filter rule has an action—also called a mode—that specifies what to do with a recorded message. eCATT provides four different actions:

1. Every message marked with "R" is required. The MESSAGE ... ENDMESSAGE block is successful if all messages identified with "R" have occurred (conjunctive link).

2. From the group of all messages marked with an "E" (expected), at least one must occur for the MESSAGE ... ENDMESSAGE block to be regarded as successful. If exactly one rule of all defined filter rules has a mode of "E," this rule behaves like a rule with the "R" mode.

3. The occurrence of a message marked with "A" (allow) is ignored. The MESSAGE ... ENDMESSAGE block is successful, irrespective of the messages marked with "A." This option can be used to explicitly tolerate a message that would normally lead to an error.

4. A message marked with "F" (fail) is illegal. The MESSAGE ... ENDMESSAGE block is error-free if none of the messages marked with "F" occurs.

   This option can be used to regard messages not planned for in the test case as errors, even though they would normally be regarded as success messages. See also the explanations about negative tests in Section 8.6, *Implementing Checks*.

5. In addition to the actions "R," "E," "A," or "F," a rule can be marked with "X" (exit). A rule marked with "X" terminates the MESSAGE ... ENDMESSAGE block. As soon as a message occurs that meets a rule marked with "X" the control flow immediately jumps to ENDMESSAGE.

Table 8.9 shows some examples of message rules.

Mode	Exit	Type	ID/No.	Effect
R		S		Requires any status message. If the message does not occur this is regarded as an error.
E	X	E	DH/803	Requires an error message of the DH or DA group.
E		E	DH	
E		E	DA	The MESSAGE block is terminated if this is the DH/803 message.
A		E	DH/803	Permits the error message DH/803. If the message does not occur this is regarded as a success as well.
F		S	DH/802	Prohibits the DH/802 status message. (Normally a status message would not be regarded as an error).

Table 8.9 Examples of Message Rules

Standard rules   In addition to the rules that are defined in the command interface of the
MESSAGE command, there are also a number of standard rules (see Table
8.10).

Mode	Exit	Type	ID/No.	Effect
F	X	E		Type E is always regarded as an error.
A		I		Types I and W are ignored.
A		W		
E		S		Type S is always regarded as a success.

Table 8.10 Standard Rules for Messages

These rules are always applied but they follow the rules in the command
interface of the MESSAGE command. The standard rules therefore apply to
messages that are not handled by any self-defined rule.

Creating   To include message handling in your script, proceed as follows. First,
message filters   use the PATTERN button to select the MESSAGE command (with the basis
release of the Web AS 6.40 in the SCRIPT CONTROL group). Use cut-and-
paste to insert the commands the messages of which you want to process
between the MESSAGE command and the ENDMESSAGE part.

Next, you create the message filter. Double-click to open the command
interface of the MESSAGE command.

The structure editor displays the overview of the filter. Insert a rule by
clicking on the appropriate button (see Figure 8.48). Now you can click
through the structure of the rule and populate the relevant fields with
values. Continue by adding more rules. If necessary, change the order of
the rules via drag-and-drop.

Handling messages   Even after you leave the ENDMESSAGE block, the message handling is not
individually   always completed. All messages that have been sent within the MESSAGE
... ENDMESSAGE block are saved in a table in the command interface of
the ENDMESSAGE command. By iterating through these tables, messages
can be treated individually after leaving the MESSAGE ... ENDMESSAGE
block and edited with specific actions. However, this requires a deeper
knowledge of the programming of eCATT scripts.

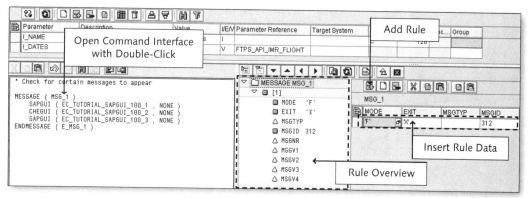

Figure 8.47 Creating a Message Filter in the Command Interface of the "MESSAGE" Command

A typical scenario for adding commands in the script editor involves reading, checking, and processing values from the ENDMESSAGE interface.

Reading the "ENDMESSAGE" interface

The command interface of the ENDMESSAGE command has a table-like structure and is organized as follows:

Field	Description
TFILL	The first row contains the total number of messages in the field, followed by the index of the respective message.
MSGTYP	Message Type
MSGID	Message ID
MSGNR	Message number
MSGV1 .. MSGV4	Message parameter. Depending on the message, these fields are populated differently. Not all of the four fields must be populated.

Table 8.11 Structure of a Command Interface Row of an "ENDMESSAGE" Command

To iterate through the messages you first need to determine the number of messages. After a command editing a table, the eCATT system parameter TFILL contains the number of entries in this table. In this case, this is the number of messages in the command interface of the ENDMESSAGE

Determining messages

command. In the following example, an actual message is searched and its first variable part taken into the log.

```
MESSAGE ( MSG_1 ).
   SAPGUI ( S000_1 ).
ENDMESSAGE ( E_MSG_1 ).
DO &TFILL.
   IF E_MSG_1[&LPC]-MSGNR = 24.
      LOG ( E_MSG_1[&LPC]-MSGV1 ).
   ENDIF.
ENDDO.
```

8.6.4 Parameterization of Message Handling

A typical reason for manually working with the message table is the parameterization of the message handling. This statement is required if a test case is to be checked in several variants. Some of these variants are expected to function without errors, while others are expected to produce errors, for example by exceeding a threshold (negative test).

The difficulty of this test is that the script should show a different behavior depending on the variant. This demanding task can be solved by handling the messages variably. The script is therefore completed by an import parameter I_ERROR_EXPECTED. It has a value of "YES" if an error message is expected in a variant. For variants to run without errors, the parameter has a value of "NO".

Encapsulating the commands

Encapsulate the commands in a MESSAGE ... ENDMESSAGE block where all messages are permitted at first. This can be achieved by inserting a generic rule that accepts (mode "A") error messages (type "E"):

```
MESSAGE ( MSG_1 ).
   SAPGUI ( SESSION_MANAGER_100_STEP_1 ).
   SAPGUI ( DYNPRO_STEP_1 ).
ENDMESSAGE ( E_MSG_1 ).
```

After leaving the MESSAGE ... ENDMESSAGE block, all messages that occurred reside in the command interface of the ENDMESSAGE command. They can now be searched via a loop. A variable (V_ERROR) records whether a specific error message has occurred:

```
V_ERROR = 'NO'.
DO &TFILL.
    IF (E_MSG_1[&LPC]-MSGTYP = 'E').
        V_ERROR = 'YES'.
    ENDIF.
ENDDO.
```

After running through the loop, the V_ERROR variable is set to the value "YES" if an error message occurred; it has the value "NO" if there was no error message. Now you can determine whether an error was expected for a specific variant to the actual occurrence or absence of the message. If the obtained result deviates from the expected value, the script is set to "error" and we know that a problem exists. This is achieved by writing an error message to the log using the LOGMSG command:

Logging an error message

```
IF ( (V_ERROR = 'NO') AND (I_ERROR_EXPECTED = 'YES') ).
    LOGMSG( I_ERROR ).
ENDIF.
IF ( (V_ERROR = 'JA') AND (I_ERROR_EXPECTED = 'NO') ).
    LOGMSG( I_ERROR ).
ENDIF.
```

"LOGMSG" Command

The LOGMSG command writes a message to the test log. In the case of an error message (type "E"), the script decides to return the status "error." The most important application of this command is to have the test script fail when an unexpected error occurs.

```
LOGMSG ( <Parameter> ).
```

The LOGMSG command is available in eCATT with the basis release 6.40.

If you operate eCATT in the basis release 6.20, you can use a CHEVAR command to specifically set the script to "error." In this case, the exact reason for the script failure is incomprehensible, so you should add to the test log a line with a more detailed explanation of the error cause.

```
IF ( (V_ERROR = 'NO') AND (I_ERRO_EXPECTED = 'YES') ).
    V_ERROR = 'Script failed. Reason: ... '.
    LOG ( V_ERROR ).
    CHEVAR( V_ERROR = 'YES').
ENDIF.
```

8.6.5 Checking Tables

In addition to sending messages, there is another way for transactions to interact with their environment. A transaction typically accesses specific tables of the SAP system. These tables are the environment in which the transaction is executed. By querying the tables, a transaction can read data. In other words, a transaction can write data to the table via the update task or directly.

In a production operation, working via the database is the typical scenario for the communication of different transactions and matches of the workflow. An agent creates a process using a transaction and writes it to the database. At a later stage, this created object is then taken up by another agent and further processed using a different transaction.

Communication between transactions

An eCATT script could directly test the communication between two transactions. This works when you want to make sure before calling a transaction that the previous transaction really transferred the correct result. In this case it can make sense to access the database directly from the eCATT script.

The GETTAB and CHETAB commands are available for this purpose.

> **"GETTAB" Command**
>
> The GETTAB command is used for reading a value from a table in the database.
>
> ```
> GETTAB ( <Table> , <Command interface>,
>         [<Target system>] ).
> ```
>
> The structure of the command interface corresponds to that of the queried table. The data record to be read is narrowed down by populating some of the fields with values. Key fields must be populated either with a value or a wildcard "*". The command finds the first row of the table where all fields match the specified values and transfers these fields to the parameters that have been specified in the command interface.

CHETAB works like GETTAB and is used for checking values.

"CHETAB" Command

The CHETAB command is used for directly checking values in a database table.

```
CHETAB ( <Table> , <Command interface>,
         [,<Target system>] ).
```

The structure of the command interface corresponds to that of the queried table. The CHETAB command checks if a row exists where all fields match the specified values. If this is not the case, the script fails.

8.6.6 Summary

Checks in an eCATT script can be performed via testing parameters and values, querying message handling, and checking tables. For the first kind of implementation, the GETGUI and CHEGUI commands are among the resources available.

Using filter rules, individual messages or message groups can be specifically filtered from the stream of messages and handled in a different way than stipulated in the standard rules. Filter actions enable you to influence the success or failure of a script depending on the messages. In addition, the Exit flag permits an intervention in the control flow.

The communication between transactions takes place indirectly via the database. eCATT scripts can use the GETTAB and CHETAB commands to directly access the database and test the interim and end results.

8.7   Managing Test Data

A test case is mapped in eCATT via a test configuration. A configuration consists of test data, system data, and a test script. The test data and its handling in eCATT are introduced in the following section. We must first have a look at the test configuration.

8.7.1   Test Configuration

Here's how to create a test configuration. In. In the eCATT startup screen, first select the TEST CONFIGURATION item. Enter a name, and create the configuration by pressing F5 (see Figure 8.48).

Creating a test configuration

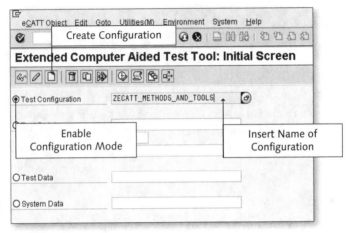

Figure 8.48 Creating or Opening Configurations

After you have entered attributes such as title and component name, compose the configuration. First, select a test script you created previously as well as an appropriate system data container (see Figure 8.50).

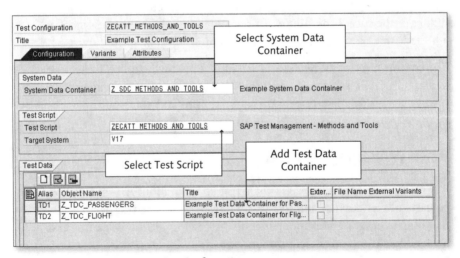

Figure 8.49 Creating a Test Configuration

You can also have these steps run automatically. For this purpose, open the desired test script in the test script editor, and select UTILITIES • TEST

CONFIGURATION • CREATE. All attributes previously mentioned are copied from the test script to the test configuration.

8.7.2 Variants

The next step is the input of the test data. You have two options, the first of which is entering test data directly in the configuration by means of a manual variant. This procedure allows for a quick entry and is helpful for creating smaller tests.

Manual variant

In a manual variant, you create a table directly in the test configuration. This table contains one column per import parameter of the script. A table row corresponds to a variant to be tested. To create a manual variant just populate one row of this table (see Figure 8.50). Manual variants have one decisive drawback: The test data is tightly linked to the configuration. This complicates maintenance and prevents the data from being reused in other variants and with other test scripts.

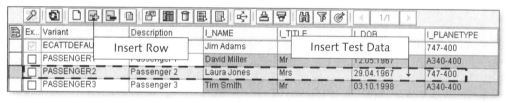

Figure 8.50 Adding a Variant

8.7.3 Test Data Container

To avoid the complex maintenance imposed by manual variants, there is another option to manage test data which should be used in most cases: storing the test data in a test data container. With this procedure, the test data is stored separately from the test script and the configuration in one or more separate test data containers. These containers are then merged in the configuration, and a subset of the test data contained therein is then selected for and referenced in the test run.

There are several options for distributing test data to containers. The most obvious choice is to use one container per test configuration (see Figure 8.51). Because some redundancy results from replication of the same data when creating a separate test data container per test configuration, this

One test data container per test configuration

form of test data management greatly impairs maintainability. If the test data is to be changed, you need to find out where specific data is used in order to then change all affected test data containers. Not only is this tedious, but also error-prone. In fact, this form of test data management does not provide any advantage over the test data storage in the form of manual variants, as described above. Still, in real life, this procedure represents the first step on the way to optimal test-data management.

A central test data container An advanced alternative is to create one test data container per application. This container stores the data for all test configurations of this application, thus minimizing redundancy (see Figure 8.52). Such a consolidated container has the disadvantage that it might become unmanageable for large test projects, making it more difficult to handle test data.

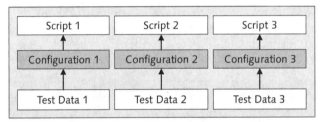

Figure 8.51   One Test Data Container per Test Configuration

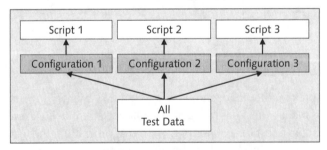

Figure 8.52   A Central Test Data Container

Recommended procedure: several test data containers separated by contents The best possibility for managing test data is the distribution of test data to several containers. The data is divided by content (see Figure 8.53). Data that belongs together from the application's point of view or is connected to the same business object is put together in one test data container. This division enables you to select the subset of test data

486

containers that is required to execute a specific test configuration. By logically grouping the data, these sets remain manageable.

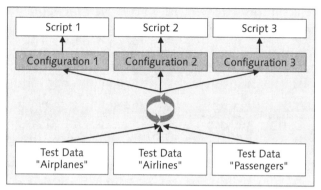

Figure 8.53 Groupings Divided by Content

To create a test data container, first select the TEST DATA item from the initial eCATT screen. Enter a name and create the container by pressing F5. Note that test data containers must reside in the customer's namespace.

Creating a test data container

Once the test data container has been created, you can start creating parameters. Select the PARAMETERS tab and insert one row per parameter (see Figure 8.54). The rows you create in the PARAMETERS tab are later shown as columns in the VARIANTS tab.

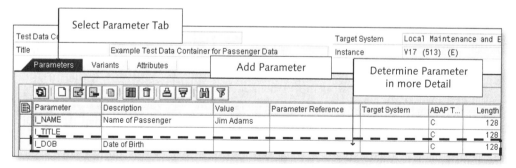

Figure 8.54 Manual Creation of the Parameters in the Test Data Container

Instead of creating parameters manually, you can also import parameters already created in other eCATT objects. Select the menu EDIT • IMPORT

Importing parameters

487

PARAMETERS. The import screen for parameters is displayed (see Figure 8.55). You can import parameters from test scripts or other test data containers. First select a source. All import parameters existing in the specified eCATT object are displayed in a list. You can mark the appropriate parameters and add them to the new test data container.

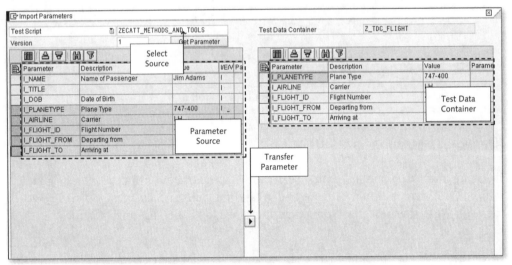

Figure 8.55 Creating Parameters in the Test Data Container via Import

Creating variants   Then enter the data records; that is, the variants. A variant consists of an actual value for each parameter. To create the variants, select the VARIANTS tab and create one row per variant (see Figure 8.56).

Downloading/ uploading variants   Instead of manually entering variants, you can also exchange data with external programs. The typical procedure is as follows. At first you import the desired parameters from a script to the test data container. Then you export the (still empty) variant. You receive a text file with appropriate column titles for the parameters. In this file, you edit the test data using an application such as Microsoft Excel. Finally, you upload the text file to populate the variants in the test data container.

To download a variant, select the EDIT • VARIANTS • DOWNLOAD menu and enter the file to be created. You will find it in a tab-separated TXT format that can be directly imported in Excel using drag-and-drop and then further processed.

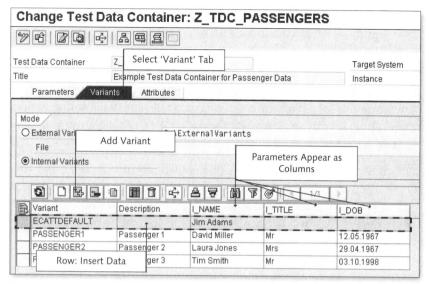

Figure 8.56 Maintaining Variants in the Test Data Container

To upload variants, select the EDIT • VARIANTS • UPLOAD menu and again select the file. You are asked if you want to delete the variants existing in the container. Select YES to replace the data, NO to append to the existing variants.

Another option to storing the data directly in a test data container is linking an external file. In the VARIANTS tab select the EXTERNAL VARIANTS • PATH item, and enter a text file created in an application such as Microsoft Excel that meets the eCATT formatting rules. This can be easily ensured by exporting existing variants and modifying that file.

External variants

However, there are several things to watch for when using external variant files. First, such an external file is stored outside of the SAP system. This has the obvious disadvantage that another user who wants to use the test data must have access to the storage location. Conceptually, this contradicts the principle of the SAP system keeping all data ready in a central database. We needn't go into detail about the difficulties this involves for the administrator who needs to guarantee data security, if the data required for the test resides in different storage systems.

Frequently, the upload of data to an internal variant is preferable to the linking of an external variant. An exception would be a scenario where the user department provides the test data in the form of a frequently updated Excel sheet.

Variants with test data container

The last step for using the test data containers is to actually implement them in the test configurations. The test data containers to be used are first selected in the test configuration. From the resulting set of parameters you can then filter the set of test data relevant to the configuration. You can make this selection per parameter, per variant, or in any combination of the two.

To add test data containers to a test configuration, first open the configuration editor. In the CONFIGURATION tab add test data containers. Then switch to the VARIANTS tab and open the VARIANT MAINTENANCE ASSISTANT. In the following dialog you can use the variant assistant to compose your variants (see Figure 8.57).

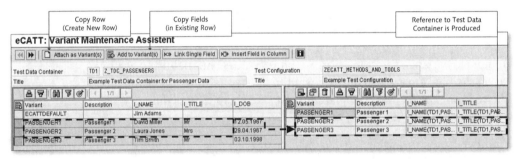

Figure 8.57 Assistant for Editing Variants

Using the Variant Maintenance Assistant

In the left part of the window, navigate through the various test data containers attached to the test configuration. Mark the variants by row. Use the ATTACH AS VARIANT(S) button to transfer the variants to the configuration. For every selected variant, a new row is created. The parameters (columns) are identified by their names and assigned accordingly.

Combining data

To combine data from different test data containers, first insert the data from the first test-data container as a new line, as described above. Then switch to the second test data container, and mark the rows you want to add. Then mark the rows in the test configuration that should be amended. Use the ADD TO VARIANT(S) button to link the fields from the test data container to the variant. In the corresponding rows in the right part of the dialog you can see that the variant now contains links to data from different test-data containers.

In such an amendment, be sure to set the data order. The first marked row from the test data container is merged with the first marked row in the configuration and so on. You may first need to change the displayed order to make sure that the data is merged correctly.

8.7.4   Runtime Data Container (RDC)

The Runtime Data Container (RDC) that is available as of SAP NetWeaver 7.1 enables you to provide an instance of a test data container as a runtime object. With the FILL_RDC command, you can directly access a variant.

"FILL_RDC" command

The FILL_RDC command fills a Runtime Data Container (RDC) with values.

```
FILL_RDC  ( <RDC_Parameter>, <Commando interface>
          [, <Target system>] ).
```

In the command interface you can specify the source to be read in more detail. It is possible to specify a variant, a test data container with variant, or a variant from an external file.

For this purpose, the command is only given information about the variant which is supposed to be read from the test data container. Subsequently, you are provided with a structure that contains all parameters of the test data container, including all values of this variant. These may also be complex values, for instance, structures, and tables.

In contrast to the standard procedure for integrating a test-data container via a configuration, the advantage of using the RDC is that you do not have to execute a new script each time a new variant of the test configuration is started. Within the runtime of a script, you can reload data variants.

A runtime variable of the runtime data container type that refers to a test data container is provided with initial values. As a result, a complete variant is loaded when the script is started, via a single parameter that must be transferred.

Note that the runtime data container is not remote-enabled. But you can manipulate the runtime object. It is available in the same way as a local eCATT variable. It is not possible to write back to the database when you use a runtime data container. To do this, you must use the test data container API which is described in the following section.

8.7.5 Test Data Container Programming Interface (TDC-API)

Unit tests showed that there is demand for globally available, centrally maintained data which you can access directly from the ABAP development environment. The option to have read and write access to a test data container independent of the test environment was implemented with the TDC-API.

To access a test data container from a program, the test data container must be loaded and prepared by the statistic method, GET_INSTANCE. The test data container usually resides in the same system, but GET_INSTANCE also enables the processing of an RFC destination.

Methods   After the runtime objects have been created, the object methods can be called. The methods can be subdivided into the following categories.

- General read access; GET_PARAM_LIST, for example, returns the table of the defined parameters.
- Read access to content; GET_VALUE, for example, reads a value from the test data container in a variable.
- General write access; CREATE_PARAMETER, for example, creates a new parameter.
- Write access to content; SET_VALUE, for example, transfers the value from a variable to the test data container.

Note that the read-API is available as of SAP NetWeaver 7.10. The methods for write access are partly available as of 7.11 (only for values and variants) and partly as of SAP NetWeaver 7.20 (create parameter, create TDC).

Exception handling   Furthermore, the TDC-API provides comprehensive exception handling. The GET_INSTANCE method can be provided with a mode (I_EXEPTION_MODE) that specifies the type of exception handling to be performed. You can select, for example, whether the exceptions are triggered directly, collected, or ignored.

8.7.6 Summary

SAP offers a test configuration to cover an automatic test case if eCATT is used. A test configuration consists of a script, a system data container, and test data. The test data is divided into content groups, stored in test data containers, and selected and combined in the test configuration according to the script. This reduces test data redundancies to a minimum and ensures manageability and maintainability.

8.8 Modularizing Test Scripts

An important capability of eCATT scripts is the property that allows them to call other scripts. This enables you to split a business process into a combination of individual business events and cover every one of them with a separate script.

> **"REF" Command**
>
> The REF command is used for calling other scripts.
>
> ```
> REF ( <Script> , <Command interface>,
>       [<Target system>] ).
> ```
>
> The specified script is executed on the target system. The import parameters are transferred via the command interface. After this command has been successfully executed, the export parameters of the called script remain in the command interface and can be used by the calling script. Messages sent during the REF command can be handled via the MESSAGE command as of basis release 6.40.

The function of the REF command is quite simple but requires planning. Because REF enables you to divide a script into several pieces that call one another, you face the question of how such a script system can be organized.

The simplest form of organization is to do without modularization. In this case, only one script is created per test case. Branches are implemented only via IF ... ENDIF blocks. This is, however, the worst organizational option. Due to its size, the script becomes unmanageable, and there is not much chance that it will be usable with another test case. Because all individual steps are grouped into one script, it is not possible to reuse individual steps in other test cases.

Single script

493

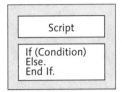

Figure 8.58   Single Long Test Script with Possibly Complex "IF ... ENDIF" Blocks

Script sequence   If you use a sequence of scripts, the process of the test case is split into a sequence of smaller scripts. The last command of every script calls the next script (see Figure 8.59).

This possibility is only slightly better than using one central script. Although readability is improved with the shorter scripts, there is no chance of reusing parts of them. The reason is that the REF command stores the continuation of the process at the end of the scripting part.

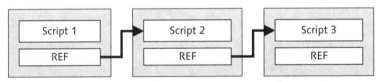

Figure 8.59   Sequence of eCATT Scripts

Sequence of scripts   The best method is a sequence of scripts that are called from a common
in a top script   top script. The test case is split into a sequence of scripts. These scripts do not call each other, though. Instead, a top script is created that is responsible for calling the individual test scripts in the correct order and with the correct parameters. The top script itself does not perform any tests but only calls the other scripts in the appropriate order (see Figure 8.60).

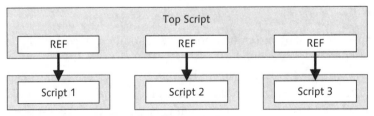

Figure 8.60   Sequence of Scripts in a Top Script

If the results of a called script are required in a subsequent script, you proceed as follows. In the command interface of the first script, the export parameter is assigned to a local variable of the top script. The same variable is then used to populate the import parameter in the command interface of the subsequent script. The value can thus be transferred between two scripts (see Figure 8.61).

Value transfer between two scripts

The command interface of the REF command consists of the import and export parameters of the called script. Therefore, it is worth thinking a little more about the design of this interface when creating the script. Particularly, it makes sense to parameterize fixed values as well (see Figure 8.62). By replacing a fixed value with a parameter, you gain the option of exchanging the fixed value when the script is later used in the context of a different test case. To prevent such parameters from requiring a correct value for each call, they can be assigned default values.

Design of command interfaces

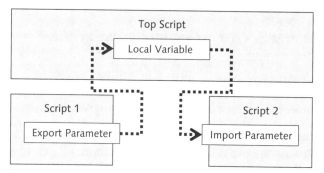

Figure 8.61 Transferring a Value Between Two Scripts via a Local Variable in the Top Script

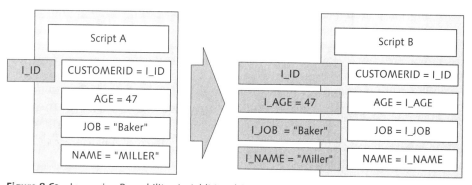

Figure 8.62 Improving Reusability via Additional Parameterization of Fixed Values

Introducing additional import parameters increases reusability because you can transfer values to the script in a more flexible way. For the same reason, as many interim results as possible should be exposed as export parameters.

CATT integration   There already may be CATT scripts for testing specific processes. For calling CATT scripts from eCATT, the REFCATT command is available. It enables you to integrate existing CATT scripts.

"REFCATT" Command

The REFCATT command is used for calling scripts from the CATT.

```
REFCATT ( <Script>, <Command interface>,
         [<Target system>] ).
```

The system executes the specified CATT script. The input parameters are transferred via the command interface. The command is comparable to the REF command for eCATT scripts.

When dealing with existing CATT scripts, keep in mind that SAP has clearly decided in favor of using eCATT. In addition to the protection of investments in eCATT due to its upward compatibility, this involves a gradual abandoning of CATT support. With the basis release of Web AS 6.40, CATT scripts can still be called but no longer changed.

Migration of   Instead of integrating existing CATT scripts, you should consider perform-
CATT scripts   ing a migration. This is supported by eCATT and can in many cases be carried out fully automatically using the RECURSIVE MIGRATION function. In specific cases, however, it requires a post-processing that can extend to a fully manual re-recording of the scripts. In this case, we recommend that you contact a consultant who is familiar with this migration task at an early stage in the testing.

Conclusion

The REF command enables scripts to call one another. This improves maintainability and reusability of script modules. To take advantage of this, be sure to expose all relevant values as parameters. The script structure that has proven most useful is a sequence of small units that are called by a top script.

8.9   Additional eCATT Commands

The previous sections already discussed some eCATT commands. The following pages contain additional important commands for working with eCATT.

> **Note**
>
> A reference list of all eCATT commands is available in the SAP Help Portal (*http://help.sap.com*).

The IF ... ENDIF conditional is used for switching between the execution of different commands.   **IF ... ENDIF**

```
IF ( <Condition 1> ).
   <Command 1>.
ELSEIF (<Condition 2>).
   <Command 2>.
...
ELSE.
   <Command 3>.
ENDIF.
```

The system validates the conditions one after the other and executes the first command block whose condition is met. If no condition is met, the command linked to ELSE is executed.

The conditional must have exactly one IF part, can contain any number of ELSEIF parts, and may include a maximum of one ELSE part.

Example:

```
IF ( A > 0 ).
   LOG ( A ).
ELSE.
   LOG ( V_ERROR ).
ENDIF.
```

Another important statement is the DO ... ENDDO loop.   **DO ... ENDDO**

A loop serves for executing commands several times, for example once per table row.

```
DO ( <Parameter> ).
   <Command>.
```

```
  . . .
ENDDO.
```

The system validates the parameter. The number of executions of the command block corresponds to the parameter value. Within the loop a special variable, &LPC. &LPC refers to *loop counter* and indicates the number of the current loop run at any time. The count begins at 1.

LOOP ...
ENDLOOP

LOOP ... ENDLOOP is better suited for running loops in table parameters than DO ... ENDDO. This command is typically used for activities that only involve a few table rows and where the content of the table fields is relevant. The use of LOOP avoids complex expressions that are typical for DO ... ENDDO.

The command interface enables you to specify WHERE conditions. The loop only runs through those rows of tables that meet these conditions. If you don't specify any conditions in the command interface or if no command interface exists, the loop runs through all rows of the table.

The alias parameter must have the same structure as the row type of the table parameter. Activate the ALIAS PARAMETER checkbox in the parameter list.

Within the loop, the alias parameter refers to the current row of the table. If changes are made to the parameter, for instance, a value is assigned to a field. These changes immediately affect the table parameter.

Nesting

LOOP ... ENDLOOP loops can be nested. Nesting could be used, for example, in a field of a row that is also a table.

Command
interface

The command interface contains a SELECTION field in which you can define a table with WHERE conditions.

Field	Description
FIELD	Only elementary, but no structured fields of the row can be used.
VALUE	If you enter a value, the WHERE condition corresponds to this value. If you don't enter any value, this field is ignored; other conditions can be defined in RANGES.
RANGES	You can specify complex conditions, for instance, SIGN 'I', OPTION 'BT', LOW 'AA', HIGH 'LH'.

Table 8.12 Command Interface

Examples of LOOP ... ENDLOOP and DO ... ENDDO with the same function:

```
LOOP ( SPFLI_TABLE , SPFLI_ROW ).
LOG ( SPFLI_ROW-CARRID ).
ENDLOOP.

GETLEN ( SPFLI_TABLE , LEN ).
DO ( LEN ).
LOG ( SPFLI_TABLE[&LPC]-CARRID ).
ENDDO.
```

You can use the EXIT (<Condition>) command to conditionally abort a DO/LOOP loop or a test case.

EXIT

If the EXIT condition is not met, the following statement is executed. If the condition is met within a loop, the statement is executed that follows ENDDO/ENDLOOP. If the condition

▶ is met within a test case called by the REF command, the statement is executed that follows the REF statement in the calling test case.

▶ is met within the test case itself; the test case is terminated.

To formulate conditions, you can use the following operators:

Conditions

Operator	Description
=	equal to
<>	not equal to
<	lesser than
<=	lesser than or equal to
>	greater than
>=	greater than or equal to
AND	Boolean AND
OR	Boolean OR
NOT	Boolean NOT

Table 8.13 Conditions

For simple conditions, the following syntax applies:

```
<Parameter1> <Relational operator> <Parameter2>
```

You can combine multiple logical expressions in one logical link. In order for the logical expression to be met, the following applies:

▸ If only all combined expressions are true, link them using AND.

▸ If at least one of the combined expressions is true, link them using OR.

To reverse the result of a logical expression, you can prefix the NOT operator.

NOT has priority over the AND operator. AND has priority over OR. However, you can use parentheses to specify the sequence of processing.

Example:

```
EXIT ( NOT ( A < B AND A > D ) ).
```

LOG The LOG command is used to document parameter contents before and after the execution of other eCATT commands:

```
LOG ( <Parameter> ).
```

This command writes entries to the log. The current data of the object defined by `<Parameter>` is entered in the log whereas `<Parameter>` can be a simple parameter, a structured parameter, or a command interface.

LOGTEXT The LOGTEXT command writes a text to the log. The text can be specified directly as a character string or through a parameter that contains a character string:

```
LOGTEXT ( <Transfer/failure> , <character string> ).
```

You can use this command to simulate a situation during the script execution in which the script fails.

The value of `<Transfer/failure>` determines whether the command triggers a failure of the script. `<Transfer/failure>` can be a fixed value or a parameter. Only 0, '0', or an empty parameter causes a transfer. All other values cause a failure.

Example:

```
LOGTEXT ( 0 , 'Transfer with value 0' ).
PASS_FAIL = 1.
V_STRING = 'Not equal to zero causes failure'.
LOGTEXT ( PASS_FAIL , V_STRING ).
STORE
```

The command

```
STORE ( <Parameter> ).
```

writes an entry to the log similar to the LOG command; however, the parameter contents can be read by the log in a subsequent test script execution using the RETRIEVE command. This is useful if test steps depend on data that was created in previous test steps.

The parameter can be a simple parameter, a structured parameter, or a table parameter.

The RETRIEVE command reads data that was written to a log during the previous test script execution using the STORE command and assigns it to a parameter. The parameter name doesn't need to be the same as the one used for the STORE command. The parameter can be a simple parameter, a structured parameter, or a table parameter.

RETRIEVE

```
RETRIEVE ( <Parameter> , <Command interface> ).
```

The data values are displayed in the log similar to the display in the LOG command. However, the selection criteria you've specified in the command interface (for the log search that contains the STORE command) and the used selection values are also added.

RESCON resets the RFC connection to the target system specified:

RESCON

```
RESCON ( <Target system> ).
```

Depending on the release and the patch level of the target system, this can be relevant when working with function modules and inline ABAP. You can use the forced reset of the connection to bypass restrictions that are caused by a limitation of the number of subroutine pools that can be generated (36).

The DELSTORE command deletes the index entries that refer to data created using the STORE command.

DELSTORE

```
DELSTORE ( <Command interface> ).
```

DELSTORE doesn't delete data in the original logs, but in case of missing index entries the RETRIEVE command cannot read the data.

For example, after a successful execution of RETRIEVE you can use the DELSTORE command to prevent that the same data is found by another RETRIEVE. You specify the selection criteria in the command interface. All data that meets the selection criteria is deleted.

If you haven't made any specifications in the command interface, no data is deleted.

BCSET   The BCSET command is used for testing Business Configuration Sets (BC Sets) that are available in the target system.

```
BCSET (BCSET, <Command interface>, <Target system>).
```

BC Sets provide a basic function that enables the automatic transfer of customizing settings. Using this functionality, you can document customizing settings in the sense of a snapshot in separate objects, whereas these BC Sets represent transportable objects of a repository and can thus also be transported to target systems.

The procedure with regard to BC Sets is subdivided as follows:

1. Creating the BC Set in the source system, including assignment of a transport request

2. Transferring customizing settings to the BC Set

3. If required, transporting the BC Set to a target system

4. Checking the contents of the BC Set against the underlying tables in the target system (what changes after transfer?)

5. Activating the BC Set in the target system (transfer of the customizing settings to the target system)

Within the scope of test automation, you can now use eCATT to run various tests on BC Sets of the target system. Among other things, this enables you to answer the following questions:

▶ Existence check: Is the BC Set available in the target system?

▶ Comparison of BC Set and current customizing settings: Do the entries of the BC Set correspond to the entries of the underlying customizing tables?

▸ Simulation: Do the current system settings enable activation of a BC Set?

▸ Activation: Do your automatic test cases also run after the customizing settings defined in the BC Set have been transferred?

8.10   Starting, Logging, and Analyzing Test Executions

Successfully implementing automated test scripts includes their start as well as the subsequent interpretation of the test results stored in the scripts' log. It also includes the finding of any errors in the script. A performance analysis is also possible using eCATT.

8.10.1   Running eCATT Scripts

You have four ways to run eCATT scripts.

1. First, you can start the script directly from the script editor. In this case, just select the button for running the script. If necessary, specify a system data container and a target system. If you don't enter any values in the PARAMETERS tab of the start options, the input parameter keeps its default values. The script is run exactly once. This procedure is recommended during script development to implement first test runs with minimum effort.

   Script editor

2. As soon as you have created a test configuration you can start the test execution from the configuration editor. In this case, the system data container stored in the test configuration is used. The input parameters take on the values stored in the configuration. References to test data containers are resolved at runtime. The script execution is repeated once for every stored variant; one row in the variant editor corresponds to one script run. The automatic version finding is implemented to find the appropriate test script version for the target system.

   Configuration editor

3. A third option is the restart option from the log. This is particularly suitable if changes were made to your test scenario and you want to re-run the test with the parameter values and the start conditions of a previous test run. You can then restart the test or parts of the test from the corresponding log and thus run it under the same conditions.

   Log

4. For the execution of eCATT scripts within larger test projects, you will probably select a fourth procedure: the organization of test configurations within test plans. If you use SAP Solution Manager for administering tests, you can group several test configurations in a test plan. This allows for integration tests that test business processes in the sense of an end-to-end coverage. More information about implementing test plans can be found in Chapter 4, *Test Management with SAP Solution Manager*.

Start Options

Depending on which of the above methods you use to start eCATT scripts, you can choose among several start options for influencing the script execution.

The following options are available for the behavior in the case of an error:

- ▶ Termination, continue with next variant
- ▶ Termination, continue with next test configuration
- ▶ Termination of start process
- ▶ No termination, continue with next script command

These options control the way you proceed in case an unexpected error occurs. Remember that eCATT assumes an unexpected error in the following situations:

- ▶ The condition in a CHETAB, CHEVAR, or CHEGUI command is not met.
- ▶ An error message occurs outside of a MESSAGE block.
- ▶ None of the messages marked as "Expected" occur within a message block, a message marked as "Required" is missing, or a message marked with "Fail" is displayed.
- ▶ The recorded interaction sequence does not match the interaction sequence at the time of execution.

If one of these cases occurs, the procedure specified in the appropriate option above is followed.

You can specify a system container and a target system under SYSTEM DATA. If this option is used, the specified data overwrites the values stored in the eCATT script or in the test configuration. This option is helpful when you want to run an available test case in a different system environment with minimal effort.

Under Log, you can display or archive the eCATT log. An archived log is stored as an object in the SAP database and can later be loaded from the archive and displayed. Moreover, you can specify the scope of logging. More information on this topic can be found in Section 8.10.2, *Logging eCATT Tests*.

Log options

In the PARAMETERS tab, you can store test data. All import parameters of the script are displayed, and you can change the stored default values once for this specific execution.

The various options for controlling the user interface are driver-specific. Therefore, you can find the options explained in the previous descriptions on the respective drivers.

UI control options

Versioning

Every piece of software has its own lifecycle. Due to the further development and elimination of errors, different software versions arise in the course of time. In the case of SAP solutions, these involve releases and support packages. An enterprise or organization can simultaneously operate multiple instances of a software solution in different versions.

Motivation

Test automation's scope would be limited if there was only one version of an automated test for a software solution. One version of a test could only test one version of the software. To support the regression testing of SAP systems, eCATT therefore offers ways to simultaneously provide multiple versions of an automatic test.

The basic idea is the versioning of objects of the automatic test, analogous to the versioning of the software to be tested. This ensures that a test exists for every version of the application to be tested.

Even so, development of automatic tests always involves some effort. To minimize the maintenance effort for test objects and to ensure reusability, it makes sense to version only those parts that must be different with regard to the application to be tested, rather than an entire automated test.

Versions in eCATT For eCATT, the term *versioning* refers to the ability to keep several versions of a script or a test data container (the latter with SAP NetWeaver 7.11) ready for testing of different development statuses, releases, and support packages of an application to be tested.

For example, after a support package implementation, an adaptation of a test script may be required if the functionality of the tested application has changed because of the support package. In this case it often makes sense to generate a new version of the test script and not overwrite the old one, instead keeping it for regression tests against other target systems that lack the specific support package implementation.

Version finding An essential feature of eCATT is that at test runtime the test tool automatically selects the version of the test script that matches the application to be tested. The correct version is selected by comparing the software release information of the system to be tested with the attribution of the test script versions.

Every SAP system to be tested contains information about its current version per software component (version = release + patch level). This data is available via the SAP GUI and the System • Status • SAP System Data menu. eCATT collects this data in the target system and also records it in the test log.

For every version of an eCATT test script (and a test data container with SAP NetWeaver 7.11), an assignment of a software component, a release version, and a patch level version can be made an attribute. With Release 7.11, eCATT versions can also be linked/attributed with switches of the switch framework.

For finding the version, only those versions are used for which the additional attribute, BACKUP, has not been set. When test script versions are copied within a test script, the BACKUP attribute is set by the tool if more than one version with the same versioning attributes occurs after the copy process.

Creating versions To create a new version of a script, start eCATT and enter the name of an existing script. Then select CREATE NEW SCRIPT [F5]. Because there already is a script of the same name, you are asked if you want to create a new version or edit the existing script.

If you use more than one version of the script, you need to store the versioning information in the attribute view. This information is used by eCATT to automatically select the appropriate script version for the target system whenever the script is called.

The script version is re-selected based on the target system before every call of the script. If you use a REF command to call the same script twice on different target systems, the appropriate script version for the respective target system is determined and executed.

The following additional functions are available in the context of versioning.

Additional functions

▶ **Versioning editor**
While the test script editor generally shows a version of a test script, the versioning editor offers a cross-version view and maintenance options for all versions of a script (UTILITIES • VERSION MANAGEMENT).

▶ **Simulation of version finding**
The test script editor includes an option to simulate the version finding, which is otherwise run only at test runtime, and to thus check the effect of attribution using versioning data without having to run the test script (UTILITIES • SIMULATE VERSION FINDING).

8.10.2 Logging eCATT Tests

A log is used to check the process and the results of a script execution while it runs or shortly after its start. Moreover, a log can later be used as a proof for executed tests. You should therefore archive logs from test measures and not delete them, so that you can access them later on.

A log is generated for every execution of a test script or a test configuration. It is displayed as a hierarchical structure with nodes which depends on the respective individually designed test script.

Displaying logs

By default, the test log is displayed immediately after a test has been executed. You can deactivate this function in the start options or restrict it via the LOG DETAILS dialog window. For example, you can specify that only in case of an error is a high-level log supposed to be displayed, including information on the test configuration and the associated script.

You have a variety of options to access logs.

1. You can select the log icon in the toolbar in the eCATT initial screen (Transaction SECATT). The selection screen LOG SELECTION is displayed in which you can set appropriate filter criteria.

2. You can display the log for the last executed test run of a script by opening the script and selecting EXECUTE. The system then takes you to the start options. When you click the log icon, the system displays the log of the last test run of this script executed with your user ID.

3. All "associated" applications, for instance, the Test Workbench, have a navigation option to reach the eCATT logs.

Restarting logs   If you've made changes to your test scenario, but want to re-run the test with the parameter values and the start conditions of a previous test run, you can restart the test or parts of the test from the relevant log and thus run it under the same conditions. For a restart in the log, right-click an executable node (for instance, the test configuration or the test script), and start the test from this point via the context menu (see Figure 8.63). You can choose whether the test is supposed to be started with or without displaying the start options. It makes sense to display the start options if the parameter values are supposed to be checked again prior to execution.

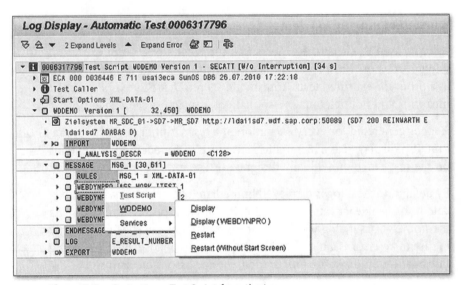

Figure 8.63 Restarting a Test Script from the Log

The test is executed starting at the point selected in the log. If you select a tree element via which the restart is not possible (for instance, a command), the system automatically offers the next higher executable element as the starting point of the re-execution of the test (for instance, the test script).

You have two options if a test takes a long time and you want feedback while the test is being executed. You can open a mode in parallel and view the development of the log, or you start execution control (see Figure 8.64). As the name *execution control* already implies, you not only receive feedback on the execution, but you can also control events.

Execution control

You start the execution control either prior to the test run via the start options or at a later point in time via UTILITIES • EXECUTION CONTROL.

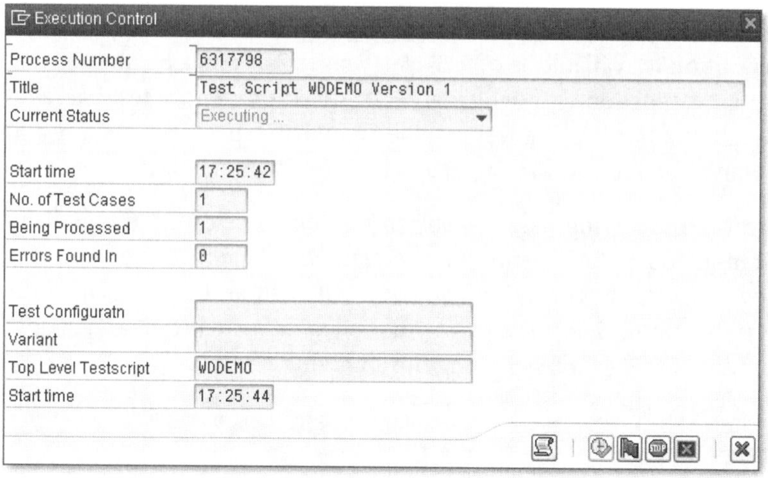

Figure 8.64 Displaying the Execution Control

When execution control is started, the system first displays an overview of the most important management data; for instance, process number, title, current status, and start time. You can use the buttons in the lower screen area to select various functions. You can directly go to the log to view the current status of the test run. You can also stop the execution, go to the debugger, or terminate the execution completely. The execution of these functions is also written to the log.

Naturally, execution control is only useful if the test takes long enough. For short tests, it would be closed immediately. In this case, you should take a look at the status bar, which also outputs different status messages.

8.10.3 Log Archiving

In order to reduce strain on the database, you should archive logs which you don't need now but might want or need to access again later on. The logs are written to archive files and are then deleted from the system in a background process. The corresponding archiving and deletion jobs must be scheduled in the archive administration (Transaction SARA). The object name is ECATT_LOG.

You have two options for archiving logs: Set the archiving flag either directly for selected logs or in the Test Organizer for entire test plans. The latter option is available as of SAP NetWeaver 7.11. Its advantage is that it is a mass function with which you can specify for entire test packages that only the last log of a test case be archived respectively. As a result, you don't need to set this flag manually for individual logs.

Setting the archiving flag directly in the log
You can set archiving flags directly in the log by selecting the log icon in Transaction SECATT, entering the wanted selection conditions, and choosing EXECUTE. The system shows a list with all logs that meet the selection criteria. Select the row with the log to be archived, and choose ARCHIVING ON/OFF for switching the archiving flag.

> **Note**
>
> Only those logs are archived that have the (X) flag and whose expiry date has not reached the current system date yet.

Setting the archiving flag in the Test Workbench or Test Organizer
To be able to use the archiving function, you need the authorization for the authorization object S_ECATTADM. Note that only the log of the respective last test run is archived when you set this flag.

You have two options to set the archiving flag for a test package:

1. Select the test package management or the status overview in the test plan management (Transaction STWB_2). There, choose the test

package for which you want to set the archiving flag, and then select GOTO • AUTOMATIC TEST.

2. Set the flag in the status info system of the Test Organizer (Transaction STWB_INFO). Then choose the test package, and click GOTO • AUTOMATIC TEST.

The system takes you to the dialog window in which you can set the flag for archiving the current logs. In this window, you have the following options:

▶ TEST MODE
Only a simulation takes place. No changes are made to the database.

▶ SUMMARY
After you've confirmed your entries, an ALV grid is displayed including the changes made.

The archiving flag for archiving logs of the respective last test runs can be set or removed.

Depending on where you are in the hierarchy, the system activates or deactivates the archiving setting for this and the underlying nodes.

8.10.4 Automated Performance Analysis

To manually run performance analysis for a specific part of an application, all preceding steps must first be implemented manually until the trace-relevant position is reached. For example, if you want to measure how long an update takes on the database, only the last step "Save" is trace-relevant. However, all preceding steps must still be performed manually to generate the required data quantity. Only then is the trace switched on and off manually and the data analyzed. If changes are made later on, for example during system optimization, the transaction must be implemented manually again to obtain the desired measuring data. You also must ensure that the scope of the computing operation is identical.

Benefit of automation

If you use eCATT, these manual steps are omitted for the performance analysis. For this purpose, the test is recorded using eCATT and assigned to a test configuration. This way, you obtain a self-contained test that can also be implemented against remote systems.

The performance tests implemented by the global performance analysis (Transaction ST30) in the tested systems are saved in a central database. You can access this data at any time for analysis purposes, such as running long-term comparisons or statistical evaluations (including scalability or regression tests).

The individual steps for using the global performance analysis are as follows.

1. Open Transaction ST30 to perform performance analyses automatically.

2. Enter the log ID. The log ID serves as a grouping criterion and has the task of joining related or similar tests in one shared node so that the test can easily be found later on and be displayed in a list. This way, you can compare or correlate current and previous traces. You must either enter an existing log ID or create and save a new log ID. Creating a new log ID requires a transport request in order to transport log ID entries to other systems. You create new log IDs via EDIT LOG IDs.

3. Then enter the name of the test configuration.

4. Enter the number of eCATT preprocesses in the NUMBER OF ECATT PRE-PROCESSES field. We recommend you enter at least five pre-processes to fill the system buffers.

   eCATT pre-processes run before the main processes, from which the performance statistics are generated. The pre-processes must provide the resources (program buffer, table buffer, and so on) with a defined status for the run before the performance of the following eCATT runs is measured.

   Set the number of main runs in the NUMBER OF ECATT MAIN RUNS field; we recommend at least 10. These are the runs whose performance is to be measured. They run after the eCATT preprocesses.

   If you set the WITH RUN FOR SQL TRACE flag, the system runs the test configuration once more to create an SQL trace. This is supposed to prevent the SQL trace from influencing the measurement in the main run.

5. In the DATA COMPARISON group box, you can compare the statistics of two performance tests. Enter the names of the tests to be compared as well as the parameters required.

6. Then, in the TEST CONTROL group box, select the execution type, for instance, ECATT TEST ONLY or ECATT TEST + DATA COMPARISON.

7. When the test runs are finished, check the log for possible error messages in the AUTOMATIC TEST: LOG TAB.

Figure 8.65 summarizes this procedure.

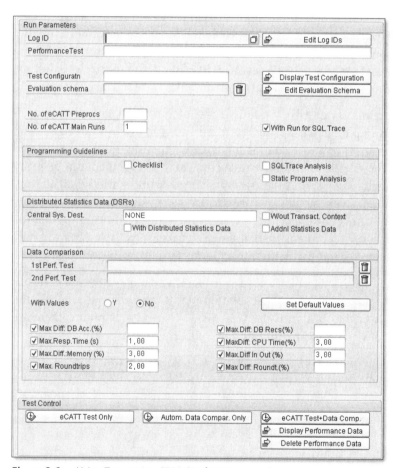

Figure 8.65 Using Transaction ST30 (Performance Analysis)

After you've run a performance test using Transaction ST30, you can view the test result in the DATA OVERVIEW tab. In the ANALYSIS tab, you are provided with additional information from the analysis of the test results.

HTTP connections present a special case. If you run SAP GUI tests, for example, they are usually implemented via RFC which provides direct access to the session and target machine. For HTTP requests of web services or Web Dynpro applications, there is no such direct access to the session through which you could activate or deactivate an analysis.

An RFC connection to the target system is established in parallel to the HTTP connection to solve this problem. This RFC connection is used to switch the performance trace on or off for the relevant user. This feature is available as of SAP NetWeaver 7.0. It is important that an RFC destination be specified for the target system in the system data container.

The previously described standard case of automatic performance analysis is implemented per driver command (for instance, SAPGUI, TCD). However, in certain scenarios the trace is supposed to be implemented only for a certain part of the test script. In this case, there can be many preparatory steps, and the trace would not to be started until the relevant call. To enable this "partial tracing," a language construct—the PERF block—can be inserted in the test script. With the PERF ... ENDPERF command, you can ensure that the performance analysis is started only for the test script part within this block.

To indicate that a test includes a PERF block, you must activate the MODULAR PERFORMANCE MEASUREMENTS option. If this option is selected, the trace is enabled only for the PERF block. In the start options, there are additional ways to fine-tune and override the PERF block.

"PERF ... ENDPERF" Command

The purpose of the PERF ... ENDPERF command is to execute the automatic performance test only for parts of a test scripts:

```
PERF ( <Block name> , <Commando interface> ).
ENDPERF.
```

The block name enables you to identify the block. PERF blocks can be nested.

8.10.5 Error Analysis for eCATT Scripts

The creation of test scripts is a development-oriented activity that itself can be fraught with errors. If you encounter difficulties while you are handling eCATT scripts, there are a number of established procedures and tools to support you.

As with any debugging activity, the first and most important step is to identify the cause of the error. First, you need to clarify if the error lies in the script or the tested application. The easiest way to do this is to run through the application manually. Select exactly that path through the transaction that the script should take. If you can reproduce the error with manual operation, the error will not be found in the script but in the application to be tested.

Faulty application

Another error cause might be the script logic (semantic error), which can occur for many reasons. eCATT supports you with appropriate tools to find these errors.

Error in the script logic

While looking for the error, you should first process the scripts in the foreground so that you can observe the way that the script runs the application. A typical error in a dynpro-based application that can be found using this method, for example, is the display of an optional popup window that is missing in the recording. If you've used the recording of the script via the SAPGUI driver, it must be supplemented with a dynpro for the popup (using `Attach`). The dynpro can then be set to "optional."

The step-by-step execution of the commands can be as helpful as using the option Highlight the Called GUI Elements for finding errors in recordings via the eCATT SAPGUI driver.

An indispensable means of troubleshooting eCATT scripts is the automatically created log. It provides you with an exact documentation of the script process. You can understand the values of every parameter and every variable and trace the scripting process step-by-step. Errors are highlighted in red and can be identified immediately. More information on this topic can be found in Section 8.10.2, *Logging eCATT Tests*.

Troubleshooting using the log

While logs only list the errors of an individual script execution, the errors of multiple eCATT runs can be displayed in an error list as of SAP NetWeaver 7.10 EhP 1. The sorting and filter functions of the error list are particularly helpful in getting a better overview of repeatedly occur-

Troubleshooting using the error list

ring errors. The ERROR LIST function enables you, for example, to have the system display an overview of all erroneous test runs within a specific period of time or for a selected starter.

The error list display is available both from the initial screen of transaction SECATT (GOTO • DISPLAY ERROR LIST) and from the log views. If you call the error list from one of the log views, a log of the list must be marked in the eCATT log selection. The selection screen is displayed in a shortened form, and the PROCEDURE NUMBER input field is pre-populated accordingly.

Because the table for listing errors of a test run contains a great deal of information, the individual columns are grouped; for instance, the "key" group including key fields, error path, and command. From the error list, you can directly create a corresponding support message (see Figure 8.66).

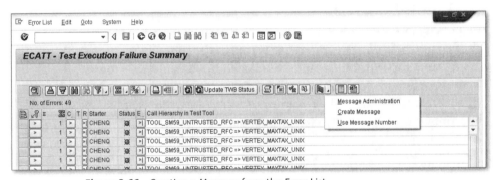

Figure 8.66 Creating a Message from the Error List

Troubleshooting using the debugger If these simple measures do not help, you can execute the debugger. The main idea of the debugger is the option of setting breakpoints (see Figure 8.67). Breakpoints can be set directly both in the test script and in the debugger.

Breakpoints determine places in the script where execution is interrupted. This enables you to execute the script up to a specific command and then deliberately interrupt the process. eCATT displays the script in debug mode (see Figure 8.68).

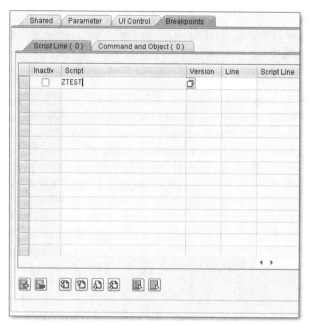

Figure 8.67 Setting Breakpoints in the Start Options

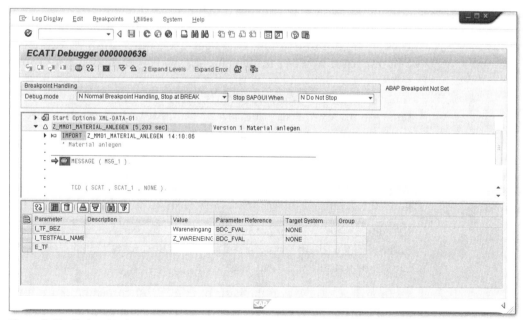

Figure 8.68 Debug Mode

In debug mode, you can control the individual steps of the script execution even between set breakpoints. For this purpose, there are buttons for controlling the script process.

In this mode, you can view the current values of all parameters and variables. As well as running scripts step-by-step, you can trace the script process in a very detailed way. Set the parameter view so that the values of all relevant variables are visible at a glance and execute the next step in the script. Changes to the parameter values are then visible immediately.

8.10.6 Summary

There are different options for starting a test: starting from the test script (script editor), from the test configuration (configuration editor), or from the log with the values used for creating the log, as well as within the scope of major test projects from SAP Solution Manager.

eCATT allows you to keep separate versions of a script ready for different versions of an application. The selection of the correct version is made automatically based on the stored versioning information whenever the script is called.

Logs are used for the result checks and are created for every execution of a test script or a test configuration. If you've made changes to your test scenario, but want to re-run the test with the values of a previous run, you can restart the test or parts of the test from the log under the same conditions. You also can view a log already while it is being created. For this purpose, you either can open a new mode in parallel to the test execution to view the development of the log or you can start the execution control. In the second method, you not only can go to the log to view the current status of the test, but you can also stop the execution, go to the debugger, or terminate the execution completely.

Because logs are the proof of implemented tests, you should archive them and not delete them. You can choose to set the archiving flag directly in the log or in the Test Organizer.

Performance analyses on the basis of eCATT test configurations can be run automatically using Transaction ST30. This standard form of automatic performance analysis is implemented per driver command (for instance, SAPGUI or TCD). If the trace is to be run only for a certain part of a test script, you can insert the PERF block into the test script. The purpose of the PERF ... ENDPERF command is to start the performance analysis for the part of the test script within this block.

When an error occurs in an eCATT script, you should first run through the transaction to be tested manually to exclude it as a source of error. If you are sure that the error is to be found in the script, a preliminary look at the log or the error list can give you valuable information.

If the error cannot be identified in this way, use the debugger. It gives you very comprehensive technical support when troubleshooting scripts. The debugger enables you to process scripts step-by-step and at the same time observe the values of parameters and variables.

8.11   Overview of the eCATT Versions

At the end of this chapter, we give you an overview of the different eCATT versions in the basis release of SAP NetWeaver Application Server.

With the SAP basis release 6.20 of Web Application Server, eCATT is included in the SAP system delivery. Web AS 6.20 is the basis release for SAP R/3 Enterprise as well as for versions 3.1 and 3.2 of SAP Solution Manager. A completely new architecture has been created with the development of eCATT. Furthermore, eCATT includes the functionality that has not been covered by CATT: testing transactions with controls, modularization capabilities, exceeding system boundaries, integration of third-party tools, and a better test data management in test data containers. You are also provided with a script migration option from CATT to eCATT.

Web AS 6.20

The version in Web AS 6.40 is part of the delivery of SAP NetWeaver 04 and SAP ERP 2004. From a technical point of view, this basis release contains a number of innovations and enhancements. The Web Dynpro Java driver is an essential innovation (Web Dynpro ABAP is supported as of SAP NetWeaver 7.02 and 7.20). Furthermore, the operation of the tool is clearly improved by comprehensive enhancements of the SAPGUI driver support as well as numerous details in the user interface. Examples of this are the possibility of changing the granularity of SAPGUI commands at a later stage as well as directly creating parameters during

Web AS 6.40

parameterization. The simple access to values via the `CHEGUI` and `GETGUI` commands, as well as a more comprehensive drag-and-drop functionality, further improves the usability.

Further innovations include the use of BC Sets, debugging, and the option of testing global ABAP object classes. Moreover, you can create external variants as an alternative for saving data directly in a test data container. For this purpose, you link an external file with the test data container. The new functions for the where-used list, version management, and version simulator are also very helpful.

At the time this book was printed, the current release SAP NetWeaver 7.02 was the basis of SAP Solution Manager 7.0 and was implemented in SAP ERP 6.0. Technically, the version included in SAP NetWeaver AS 7.0 has fewer differences from its predecessor. The driver selection has been extended by a driver for web services and Web Dynpro ABAP. New functions in this release are the variant wizard and Pretty Printer. The introduction of a function for searching references rounds this version off.

The successor release SAP NetWeaver 7.20 was still being developed as this book went to press. New options in this release include the start profile, the test data container versioning, the error list, the Runtime Data Container (RDC), the performance analysis, and the `LOOP` command.

Drivers	6.20	6.40	7.02	7.20
TCD	Yes	Yes	Yes	Yes
SAPGUI Record	Yes	Yes	Yes	Yes
SAPGUI Attach	No	Yes	Yes	Yes
GETGUI/CHEGUI	No	Yes	Yes	Yes
Web Dynpro Java	No	Yes	Yes	Yes
Web Dynpro ABAP	No	No	Yes	Yes
Web services	No	No	Yes	Yes
REFCATT	Yes	Yes	Yes	Yes
REFEXT	Yes	Yes	Yes	Yes

Table 8.14 Availability of Test Drivers According to Releases

Drivers	6.20	6.40	7.02	7.20
BC Sets	No	Yes	Yes	Yes
ABAP Objects	No	Yes	Yes	Yes
RDC	No	No	No	Yes

Table 8.14 Availability of Test Drivers According to Releases (Cont.)

8.12 Further Steps

eCATT is a powerful test tool that is included in the delivery of the SAP application. However, we stress that eCATT—just like any other test automation tool—is not a tool for end users. A good background in software development is indispensable for successfully implementing it in real life, even though the first steps might work without this comprehensive knowledge.

If you decide to implement eCATT, we highly recommend the three-day course CA611, *Test Management Using the New eCATT*. This book cannot replace training. The course is included in the official portfolio of SAP Education. The course covers the version included in SAP NetWeaver AS 7.0.

Training CA611

In this context, SAP Test Management Consulting offers a 10-day qualification and coaching program that takes place on your site and on your systems. The coach guides your employees step-by-step through the implementation of enterprise-specific test cases in production: a proven and much-demanded exercise.

For more information on eCATT refer to the SAP Developer Network (SDN) at *https://www.sdn.sap.com/irj/sdn/ecatt*.

8.13 Summary: Advantages of the Integration of eCATT in the SAP System

With eCATT, the most powerful test automation tool by far in the SAP environment is available as part of your SAP application. You may want to evaluate commercial products by other vendors as well when you are selecting your test automation tool. The following list of unique eCATT attributes can serve as a basis for a comparison.

▸ eCATT is included for free as part of your SAP application. For the implementation of eCATT there are no additional license and main-tenance costs.

▸ eCATT is ready to use: There is no additional installation effort neces-sary for eCATT. It can be used directly without any customizing activi-ties. It is not necessary to build and maintain a separate (additional) tool infrastructure. Related additional administration costs do not occur either.

▸ eCATT is fully integrated in the usage concept of SAP applications. All objects are transported and stored centrally in the SAP system. The access to these objects is reliably controlled via the SAP authorization system.

▸ eCATT provides security. In eCATT test cases, no user-related logon information such as user name or password is stored anywhere.

▸ eCATT offers direct access to all layers of the SAP system. The pre-sentation layer, application layer, and the database can be included in test runs and thus enable end-to-end test scenarios as well as the checking of provisional and final results and value updates.

▸ eCATT enables you to directly access the SAP database, function mod-ules, BAPIs, BC Sets, and web services as well as the direct integration of ABAP code. Because you can access these objects without a UI, the transaction chain is not violated. Despite comprehensive and complex checks, you are thus still able to run through the exact transaction sequence between the steps that a manual tester would go through when performing the test.

▸ eCATT makes customizing work more flexible. By integrating BC sets, you can securely and reliably specify at the beginning of the test the customizing settings necessary for running the test, and to consis-tently reset them after the test has been completed.

▸ eCATT is language-independent: It accesses the application to be tested exclusively using the technical field names. The technical test execu-tion is therefore completely independent of the logon language to the system. For example, a test can be created using a logon language of "French" and then run in the logon language "Italian" without further processing. Particularly in international rollout projects, the language independence of the (automated) test cases is an issue that is frequently underestimated. With eCATT, you can reuse the script logic, which allows you to achieve enormous cost saving potential in rollout projects.

▶ eCATT is modular. The native eCATT concept of test configurations results in a consequent separation of system data, test logic, and test data. The advantages of this separation are a minimum of redundancy and a maximum of flexibility, reusability, and maintainability of the test cases.

▶ eCATT's version-finding is automated. The test case versioning solution integrated in eCATT is characterized by an automated version-finding of the test script depending on the target system. Particularly for version transitions in the application landscape, this enables continuation of test automation during the entire transition phase.

▶ eCATT's message handling lets you specify for test scripts to respond to specific classes of messages or even specific messages during test script execution.

▶ eCATT offers investment protection. The eCATT product development is synchronized with the development of the SAP basis technology. eCATT thus can immediately cover new technologies as soon as they are released.

▶ eCATT can be integrated with external tools. You can integrate programs of a third-party provider with eCATT via the BC eCATT interface that can be certified. In heterogeneous solution landscapes, the external test tool covers those process steps whose UI is not a SAP GUI for Windows or a Web Dynpro.

▶ eCATT is suitable for automated mass tests.

▶ eCATT is integrated in SAP Solution Manager. The application management solution SAP Solution Manager enables you to store manual test case descriptions and automated test cases (eCATT test configurations) along with the business process structures of a project. In addition to the requirements (what is to be implemented) you can, for example, integrate jumps to the relevant customizing and development objects (what has actually been implemented) at the process or process-step level. This enables a continuous understanding of the respective testing activities. This integration is exclusively available with eCATT and accelerates the troubleshooting process through direct access to all relevant information about the respective process step.

▸ eCATT supports PI runtime testing. Using inline ABAP, you can call the PI outbound proxy from eCATT and thus perform a test of the PI runtime environment. For example, you can check if a message reaches the recipient using the given configuration.

8.14 Customer Report by Zürcher Kantonalbank

> **Note**
>
> This customer report originates from the first edition of this book and is still applicable today. The enterprise figures have been updated; otherwise the report is unchanged.

Within the complex project "Migration of Money Inventory Management," the account management of all current and savings accounts was migrated from a third-party system to an SAP-based solution. By consequently implementing automated test scripts, the project could be completed successfully and with a relatively limited testing effort. In order to secure development activities, very detailed functional tests were performed. The extremely heterogeneous system landscape was accounted for with comprehensive integration tests.

Zürcher Kantonalbank

With the founding of the Zürcher Kantonalbank (ZKB) in 1870, the canton put in practice at an early stage the idea of a bank that is close to the people. Following governmental request, the credit institution first offered mortgage credits and met the capital requirements of workmen, craftsmen, employees, and small to medium-sized companies.

With its transition from a mortgage to a universal bank the ZKB opened up new business areas and thus achieved strong growth between 1960 and 1988. With a balance sheet total of 113 billion CHF and client assets of 122 billion CHF in 2008, the ZKB is among the five largest financial asset- management organizations in Switzerland today. The Zürcher Kantonalbank currently has about 4,685 employees in 103 offices.[1]

---

1 Refer to *http://www.zkb.ch/de/center_worlds/ueber_uns/portraet/auf_einen_blick. html*.

The IT organization of the ZKB is divided into infrastructure, operations, and support, as well as applications engineering. These areas are supplemented by supporting functions such as project management or IT architecture. The test-automation activities belong to the applications engineering area.

IT department

Due to its versatile and very specific requirements, the application landscape of the ZKB is extremely heterogeneous. The implemented SAP systems are divided into different tracks. In a back-office track, in addition to FI, PS, CO, MM, SD, RE, and CFM (Treasury), the investment management is implemented as well. The PS module is mainly used for ZKB-internal projects.

In a second track, the SAP Business Information Warehouse is used, in a third one the SAP HR, and in a fourth one the Deposits Management.

The project called Migration of Money Inventory Management is intended to migrate account management from a third-party system to SAP. After the project was completed, the entire account management of the current and savings accounts takes place via the "SAP Deposits Management" module.

Migration of Money Inventory Management

Due to its great complexity, the migration is carried out in three releases. The number of accounts to be migrated is continuously growing. Release 1 went live in November 2004. The technical requirements for installing the software were fulfilled and all vostro bank accounts were migrated. In Release 2, the savings inventory was migrated (about 800,000 accounts). The main part of the migration, the customer current accounts and all remaining positions (foreign currencies, internal accounts, metal accounts, investment target accounts, fixed and call deposits for CHF and foreign currency, contingent commitments) followed in Release 3.

This comprehensive project included various testing tasks. In the scope of the release change, both module and integration tests had to be performed. Especially the module tests were tightly coupled to the development activities and thus to be considered as particularly critical.

Because of the sensitive data in the production system, the decision was made to establish a test environment with synthetic test data. To make the test data available, the SAP test tool eCATT was used among others.

eCATT for test data generation

Development-
oriented
functional tests With such a new development, the risk of an error—which would involve extensive consequences for the added value of the organization—is much higher than with the implementation of a proven standard solution. This risk was of great importance. The development activities within the project were therefore accompanied and secured by a set of automated functional tests.

eCATT scripts with
semantic check The automated test cases checked more than whether a transaction worked correctly or produced an error. Using special eCATT functions they were supplemented by a number of semantic checks that also tested the accuracy of the contents of the business events at various levels. Database access allowed checking to see if the data displayed by the transaction was actually updated and whether the calculated results made sense from a business perspective.

Technically, this was mainly implemented by the eCATT commands CHE-VAR and CHETAB. Particularly the CHETAB function, which enables you to select updated values from the database, proved to be an indispensable tool and represents one of the central benefits of eCATT as opposed to third-party tools. These can only interact with the SAP user interface and do not provide any deeper diagnosis functionality. Because the SAP test tool is integrated in the application server, eCATT can check results at various levels. Messages can be received and analyzed, pulled or calculated field values can be checked directly in the GUI, and–what might be most important–direct access to tables enables you to check the correct update of results in the database without interrupting the transaction flow of the test sequence.

Heidemarie Brenner, who is the responsible test manager at the Zürcher Kantonalbank, attaches great importance to the possibility of checking results at more than one technical level:

> *"Accounting is one of the most sensitive areas of a bank. Therefore it is obvious that we do not only want to check whether a transaction provides a correct result but also whether this result has really been updated in the database."*

For technical reasons, this possibility is not provided by user interface-oriented automation tools. Such application-independent or non-specific tools offered on the market by several third-party providers directly access the user interface and can thus only check the displayed results of a transaction. A direct access to the database is not possible with these tools.

In a second test step, the coverage of relevant business processes was tested in an automated way in the form of continuous integration tests.

Automation of the integration tests

Due to the heterogeneous structure of the system landscape, numerous interfaces between SAP and third-party systems are implemented in the ZKB. These are mainly IM3 and file interfaces.

A test of the third-party systems behind the interfaces was intentionally omitted. Although such a test would have been possible via the eCATT REFEXT driver, the decision was made that the additional value would not justify the effort, particularly since the ZKB would have had to invest in licenses for integrating a tool for covering the third-party systems. Instead, eCATT triggered the reading of fixed values. These values were provided in the forefront and regarded as a part of the test data. The interfaces themselves could thus be tested without getting lost in the automation of third-party systems.

A special case was presented by the test of a number of functionalities without any GUI. The ZKB primarily uses the Deposit Management as a back-office system. Only few transactions are processed via the SAP GUI. Most data is received and outsourced via interfaces. To ensure the continuity of the tests, function modules were implemented as adapters. The function modules could be controlled via the eCATT FUN driver so that the pure back-end functionality could also be covered using automated test cases.

Direct call of function modules

In the end, this combined procedure proved the right way to go: The interfaces and the interaction of the modules could be tested successfully. The script creation effort still remained manageable.

Particularly in the field of banking applications, there are serious security concerns against the use of real data from the production system for testing purposes. As one solution, ZKB considered anonymizing or garbling the original data via a scrambling procedure before importing it to the test system. Alternatively, the test system could be built with fully synthetic test data.

Structure of a test system with synthetic test data

Because roughly the same effort was involved in both methods, Heidemarie Brenner decided to take the safe option and create the test data synthetically.

Creating synthetic test data

Synthetic test data was easily created by the user departments, which were supported by the test teams. Unfortunately, it turned out that there was no packaged solution for providing test data. For simply structured test data, eCATT proved to be the best solution, creating the test data by recording and executing SAP transactions in the system. The stored update logic could thus be used and master-data consistency could be ensured effortlessly.

For creating complex master data with many views, like the creation of material, eCATT was used only sporadically. The creation of the eCATT scripts were regarded as too laborious by the customer because the numerous views to be populated had to be recorded initially. From the ZKB's point of view, the usage of the update logic did not justify the effort involved in creating and parameterizing the scripts.

LSMW

As an alternative solution, the Legacy System Migration Workbench (LSMW) was used. In a data transfer via the LSMW, the update logic used in the transaction is not implemented. However, the recording of scripts, which would be laborious in this case, can be avoided because the data is transferred to the test system via the batch input technology.

In retrospect, Heidemarie Brenner is satisfied with this mixed approach:

> "We were very satisfied with eCATT as a test tool. For building the master data in a test system, however, it was suitable to only a limited extent. Depending on the kind of master data to be captured, the recording of the scripts presented a disproportional effort. In individual cases, it is quicker to manage with LSMW. However, we will closely observe the new possibilities provided by the Test Data Migration Server for future projects. Possibly there is further potential for improvement, particularly if a standardized data scrambling solution is provided for the banking industry."

Consulting support

The team of the subproject for test automation was made up of various parties. Consultants of SAP Test Management Consulting participated primarily in the design phase, in the methodical planning as well as in specific technical issues. The test scripts were created by internal personnel (mostly system engineers of the ZKB), SAP consultants, and freelancers who were hired as script developers for the test project.

A special difficulty resulted from the fact that the eCATT of version 6.20 was not able to read test data from Excel files. This possibility had been intensely used during the automated tests using the predecessor CATT and resulted in a considerable simplification of the workflow.

> **Note**
>
> With the basis release of Web AS 6.40, the functionality of uploading external files is standard. The consulting solution described below, however, still has its right to exist despite of the availability of the external file upload in the standard version. This is because it can be used to read data directly from Excel without having to save the file to a different format first (CSV).

SAP Test Management Consulting could provide a consulting solution in this case. It was already known that there was no functionality for uploading Excel files, which has been bypassed by many customers by implementing a consulting solution. The tool developed for this purpose converts Excel files to an XML file that meets the formatting requirements of a test data container. Via the upload functionality in eCATT, this file can be loaded to the SAP system and is then available as a test data container. A nice side benefit of this solution is that the XML converter is more flexible than the Excel upload regarding the structure of the data to be imported.

Consulting solution

Conclusion

The Zürcher Kantonalbank implements automated tests for a broader range of application scenarios. For development-oriented functional tests, it is necessary to enter deeply into the system in order to verify interim results and check the update of values in the database. Integration tests focus on the interaction among transactions and on the interface test. In part, process steps without user interface had to be tested to ensure the continuity of business processes.

To meet the security concerns in the banking area, a test system was set up with purely synthetic data. eCATT scripts were successfully used for providing simple test data, while LSMW was implemented for creating more complex master data.

What can you learn from the experience of Zürcher Kantonalbank?

▸ In the scope of functional tests, you can include semantic checks in the automatic test cases to ensure that results are updated in a way that is correct from a business perspective.

▸ However, the development of such detailed test cases with contents checks is clearly more difficult than creating pure process descriptions. Presumably the user departments need more support in the development of test cases.

▸ In heterogeneous system landscapes, it requires a lot of experience and sure instincts to determine reasonable test coverage for an automated test approach. If critical business processes are not adequately covered, there is a risk that errors with massive consequences will remain undetected. Clinging to a full coverage of the automation—even within the third-party systems—can easily make the script creation effort escalate so that it becomes unmanageable. Regarding test economy, support by experienced consulted makes especially good sense during the design phase.

▸ eCATT can also test transactions without user interface: a unique attribute. For testing function modules or BAPIs, the FUN driver can be used.

▸ With the simulation of interfaces to third-party systems, you can avoid having to use external test tools. Provided that third-party systems deliver correct data to the interface, you can implement a continuous integration test of SAP applications exclusively using eCATT.

▸ Considering the cost-value ratio and the amount of data to be produced, eCATT can be implemented for generating test data. A clear plus for the use of eCATT in this application scenario, however, is the creation of data via the update logic of the SAP transactions; this ensures the best data quality.

The quality of data-driven software testing largely depends on the quality of the available test data. In contrast to the commonly used process of creating a copy of the production database, the SAP Test Data Migration Server enables you to migrate a reduced set of data from the production system into a non-production system with minimal effort. At the same time, SAP TDMS supports you in anonymizing business-critical information and personal data.

9 SAP Test Data Migration Server

Software tests that are carried out in the context of quality assurance on the customer's side, such as integration and regression tests, are usually black-box tests. The test data used in these data-driven tests is of primary importance. This holds true whether the testing activities are performed on implementation of new components, upgrades, or a custom development.

The test data is subject to different, sometimes even contradictory, requirements:

Requirements of test data

▶ The available quantity of suitable test data must be sufficient to test all critical business processes and as many variants of business transactions as possible. However, the test systems should be kept as small as possible in order to minimize storage space and administrative work, to reduce the hardware costs, and to ensure good performance of the test systems on hardware that is as small as possible.

▶ The test data should be as up-to-date and representative as possible, and the recognition factor should be high with regard to the data used in the production system. However, because the work involved in providing test systems with data can be intensive, compromises are often regarded as inevitable in practice.

▶ If test cases require sensitive data, such as personal details of employees or confidential accounting data, you must make sure that the testers do not have access to this information. However, the tests must be carried out using data records that must be as similar as possible to the original datasets; otherwise, the test results would be useless.

These requirements must be weighted differently from case to case. For example, if you test the performance of a new mass-transfer process or of a portal, you need a larger quantity of data of the same type than you would for the functional test of a specific application function. For the functional tests, you can use a comparatively small selection of data records.

Production system copy

A commonly used method is to create a full copy of the production system and to customize this copy afterwards in order to set up a test system. This method presents several disadvantages. For example, a full copy of a production system involves a high memory-space requirement of the target systems. Besides the high hardware costs of the non-production systems created this way, you must also consider an increased administration effort for the systems due to high data quantities. The follow-up work after a copy of the production system has been made is also very extensive. For example, you must change or close interfaces, create test users with appropriate authorizations, and re-import backed-up objects in the target systems after the copy has been made. Some routine tasks, such as use of eCATT scripts, can be automated; however, copying the production system is always associated with manual effort, in addition to the runtime of the copy in project planning.

Irrespective of the technical procedure, you must take another central aspect into account: When copying the production master and transaction data to non-production systems, it is possible that personal data and business-sensitive data will be made available to a broader group of users or that it is much easier to access this data because the authorization concept in these systems is usually less restrictive.

SAP Test Data Migration Server

Historically, only a few procedures were available to simplify the creation of a production system copy. They covered only individual aspects and were specific to certain customers. With its SAP Test Data Migration Server (SAP TDMS), SAP now offers a product that enables you to structure test systems per your requirements and to supply the test systems with current data from the production systems with considerably less effort. SAP TDMS supports SAP Enterprise Resource Planning,

SAP Human Capital Management, SAP NetWeaver Business Warehouse, and SAP Customer Relationship Management.

The following sections discuss the basic functioning as well as the core functionality of the SAP Test Data Migration Server based on SAP TDMS 3.0 for SAP ERP and SAP TDMS for HCM. You first learn about the process types of SAP TDMS. These enable you to create a reduced copy of a production database using various methods, and they thus represent the basic idea of SAP TDMS. This is followed by an overview of the system architecture as well as an outline of a typical system landscape that enables the data transfer from a sender system to a receiver system. Subsequently, you learn how SAP TDMS supports you in the creation of new test systems and in the data refresh of an existing test system.

Against the background of data privacy, particularly in the HR environment, the focus of this chapter is on the presentation of the functions of SAP TDMS for SAP HCM.

9.1   Data Privacy for Test Data Collection

Data privacy is an essential aspect of the task of collecting test data by copying existing production data. Besides the safeguarding of business-critical information, this term particularly refers to the privacy of personal data. For this much-discussed topic, there are numerous specifications and regulations that must all be taken into account for creating test data.

Protection of business-critical and personal data

Various challenges and risks arise from use of data records from a production system as the basis for the test data of non-production systems. For instance, the EU has adopted Directive 95/46/EC to protect the privacy of natural persons in the processing of personal data. Article 6 of the directive requires that personal data answers the purpose for which it is collected and/or further processed and its use may not exceed this purpose. From this principle of data being committed to a specific purpose, we can assume that real personal data must not be used for testing purposes.

Privacy directives

Not only EU directives, but also the Sarbanes-Oxley Act and other laws intensify regulation of data privacy and security measures. ISO/IEC 27002, an international standard, which comprises a variety of control mechanisms for information security, includes similar specifications for the use of personal data.

Such directives and the associated considerations are intended to protect personal data for the HR environment. To follow the directives mentioned, personal data must not leave the production system unchanged.

The concern about the privacy of personal data is absolutely justified. Studies of market analysts as well as regular reports in the IT press with regard to cases of data misuse and the theft of personal data clearly indicate the importance of this subject.

The unchanged transfer of production data to the development and quality assurance systems therefore always presents a risk factor. Sensitive data is made available to a wide group of users; furthermore, the security measures—for instance, roles and authorizations—in non-production systems are often incomparably lower than in a production system. Appropriate protection of data must be ensured, especially if test cases are processed and implemented beyond enterprise business departments, for example by testers of an external service provider.

Advantages of test data close to production The use of production data nevertheless offers many advantages and often presents the only workable method in real life. The entire span of testing activities requires a considerable amount of test data. Data, such as sets, is consumed and can no longer be used due to the repeated execution of business processes. This particularly applies to the load and performance tests. Because several hundreds of virtual users are deployed within the framework of a load test, the data is changed to the appropriate extent. A dataset that is close to production also emphasizes the significance of load tests.

Software testers, particularly the testers from the business departments, benefit from test data that is as close to reality as possible; for example, when they implement integration tests. Real-life experience has shown that the number of errors found within the scope of tests is much higher if the testing users of business departments implement the business processes to be tested using known and practical data. You can also use a known data environment or high-quality test and sample data to increase the acceptance of new software; for instance, for trainings or during acceptance tests.

When you use test data from production systems, you must be sure that all data privacy aspects are taken into account while the flexibility, high quality, and genuineness of test data is retained. One method to achieve this is to anonymize data in non-production systems to avoid the risk of data misuse and data loss.

To enable enterprises to fulfill the complex requirements of data privacy, SAP TDMS comprises various functions for the anonymization of production data. SAP has developed SAP TDMS for SAP Human Capital Management, particularly for the high requirements of protecting personal data in the HR environment. Besides various HR specifics, SAP TDMS specifically considers the mentioned directives concerning the privacy of personal data. The SAP TDMS for HCM includes predefined anonymization rules. In accordance with the requirements of various data-privacy guidelines, production data is anonymized, for example, already before it leaves the production system (see Figure 9.1). This enables you to quickly and efficiently build non-production environments in compliance with the relevant regulations in the HR area.

Anonymization of test data

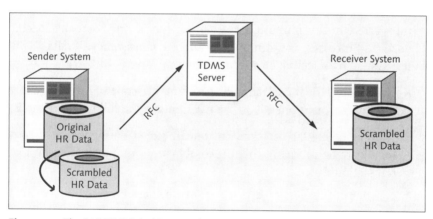

Figure 9.1 The SAP TDMS Architecture for HCM

9.2 Process Types

SAP TDMS allows you to create a downsized copy of the production database. To this end, the data quantity is specifically reduced according

Data reduction through defined criteria

to defined criteria. The goal is to avoid inconsistencies. By default, the current version of SAP TDMS for ERP supports the following methods that allow you to restrict the dataset to be used for setting up the new non-production system.

▶ Transfer of repository and client-independent customizing (shell-creation functionality)

▶ Transfer of master data and customizing data without transaction data

▶ Transfer of master data and customizing data plus transaction data as of a defined key date (from-date)

Of course, the selection of the key date directly affects the size of the test system to be set up: The further back the required from-date lies, the more data is transferred to the test system. You should select a from-date that enables you to transfer all document flows completely into the test system.

SAP TDMS contains rules to ensure consistency of document flows for standard cases even if data from the period before the from-date must be transferred for this purpose. However, for special and company-specific business processes, you can only ensure the consistency of data in the test system by selecting an appropriate from-date.

Criteria for data selection Among the criteria for selecting data within the scope of the data reduction processes mentioned, you can differentiate the following methods:

▶ Transfer of master data and customizing data plus transaction data for a specific company code in combination with a time excerpt of transaction data

▶ Transfer of business objects using the Business Process Library (BPL) to extract a subset of objects with their entire data environment

Business Process Library The Business Process Library (BPL) has been available since October 2007. Using the BPL you can select individual business objects and filter them specifically from the SAP production systems. This enables you to provide SAP test systems with data that is close to production for defined test scenarios. The Business Process Library provides predefined business object and process data scenarios for:

▸ Master data only

▸ Selected transaction data with dependent master data

▸ Entire business processes

This way, you can extract sales orders with all associated data from the production system and migrate them to the non-production system to implement an integration test of a business process. According to the logic defined in the Business Process Library, the data recorded together with the sales orders includes sales documents, customers, materials, and conditions.

The data extraction is based on the dependency provided in the Business Process Library. This dependency can be supplemented with customer-specific data; the individual entities of the BPL can be extended with custom elements using the drag-and-drop function.

Data extraction

The default version of the Business Process Library comprises the core areas of SAP ERP and additionally covers industry solutions. Table 9.1 shows an overview of the business contexts that are currently available in the Business Process Library. Moreover, the BPL contains empty scenarios for customer-specific objects.

Master Data	Transaction Data	Process Data
Business partner	Accounting document	Purchase order
Material	Purchase requisition	Sales order
Salesperson	Purchase order	Insurance object (FS-CD)
Customer	Sales order	Contract (FS-CD)
G/L account	Material document	Loan contract
Fixed assets	Billing document	Contract (IS-U)
Functional location	Bill document	Investment (IS-U)
Structure	Quality notification	Device (IS-U)
Internal order	Maintenance order	Production order
Project	Assignment table (retail)	Process order

Table 9.1 Overview of Available Business Contexts in the Business Process Library (BPL)

Master Data	Transaction Data	Process Data
Article (retail)	FI-CA document	Investment (CFM)
Insurance object (FS-CD)	Transaction (CFM)	Bank account (BCA)
Contract (FS-CD)	Controlling document	Investment (IS-U)
Loan contract (CML)		Business partner (IS-U)
Investment (CFM)		
User		
Cost center		
Work center		
Purchasing info record		
Material BOM		

Table 9.1 Overview of Available Business Contexts in the Business Process Library (BPL) (Cont.)

Product-specific data reduction

In addition to the data-reduction procedures provided in the standard version, the product-specific versions of the SAP TDMS contain further scenarios which consider the specific features of the dataset and its structure in the respective target systems. This includes the SAP TDMS versions for SAP Human Capital Management, SAP Customer Relationship Management, and SAP NetWeaver Business Warehouse.

SAP TDMS for SAP Human Capital Management

SAP TDMS for SAP Human Capital Management (SAP HCM) offers the following procedures for data transfer:

▸ Data selection from the personnel administration perspective

▸ Structural data selection, for instance, via the organizational management

▸ Data selection via the expert mode

Data selection via personnel administration

For the data selection from the personnel administration perspective (PA, see Figure 9.2), only data from the PA area is selected using the logical database PNPCE. The ad-hoc query is integrated for extended data selection. In particular, you can select all infotypes, all cluster data, country-specific additions, and custom tables. This type of data selection makes sense for enterprises that don't have any organizational management.

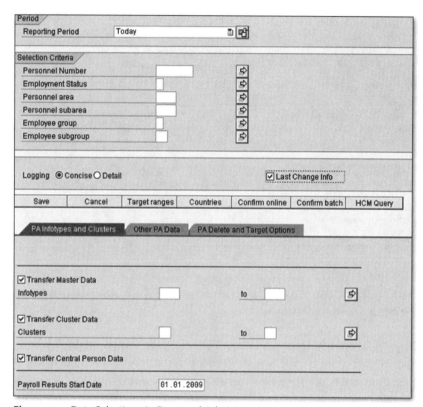

Figure 9.2 Data Selection via Personnel Administration

The structural selection of organizational data (objects and links, see Figure 9.3) can be done using the logical database PCH. Here, the evaluation path determines which object types and links are selected. Moreover, you have the option to also select data of personnel administration. This selection can be fully identical to the pure PA transfer. The structural data selection is particularly suited for enterprises that use organizational management.

Structural data selection

539

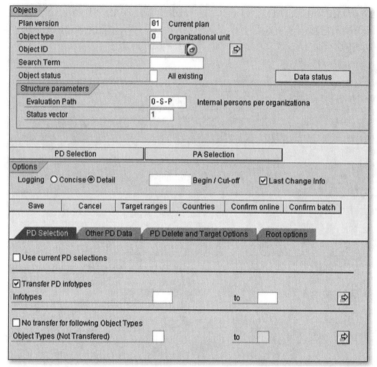

Figure 9.3 Structural Data Selection

Data selection via expert mode The third variant, data selection via the expert mode, enables you to transfer mass data to the non-production system. A structural data selection does not occur for performance reasons. This kind of data selection requires expert knowledge and makes sense for enterprises that want to transfer a considerable amount of (master) data.

Anonymization of personnel data The core functionality of SAP TDMS for SAP Human Capital Management involves scrambling; in other words, the anonymization of production personnel data. In the standard configuration, SAP TDMS for HCM can anonymize all personnel data based on predefined rules and consider content dependencies at the same time. The anonymization rules include overwriting of data fields with fixed values or the random selection using a value table. SAP TDMS for HCM is delivered with predefined (out-of-the-box) anonymization rules (scrambling rules). The anonymization can be made flexible by selecting scrambling groups, scrambling sets, and field sets as shown in Figure 9.4.

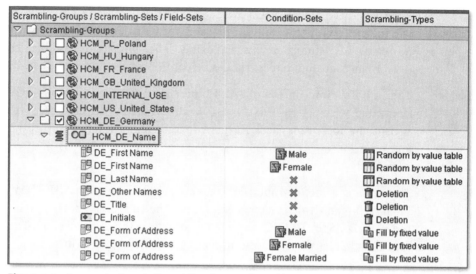

Figure 9.4 Anonymization via Scrambling Groups, Scrambling Sets, and Field Sets

The individual fields can be anonymized using predefined scrambling types (see Figure 9.5).

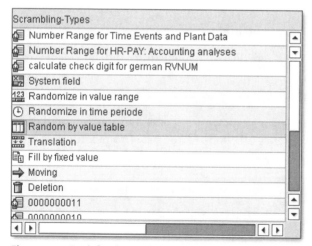

Figure 9.5 Predefined Scrambling Types

SAP TDMS for HCM provides many customizing settings. For example, you can set target number ranges per user or define upper limits for objects per user. You can also exclude from transfer specific object types and infotypes via a table and specific persons via a defined characteristic. Moreover, in customizing you can flexibly define which clusters or tables (for instance, custom tables) should be considered for transfer.

SAP HCM authorization concept
The authorization concept of SAP Human Capital Managements is fully integrated with SAP TDMS for HCM. But you can reduce a comprehensive authorization check for performance reasons; for example, the authorization check can only take place at object level or is omitted completely.

This product therefore rounds off the functional scope of the SAP TDMS for the Human Capital Management area. The specific process types of the SAP TDMS for HCM ensure high flexibility in the data selection. The tool also enables the simple addition of custom tables and clusters.

SAP TDMS for SAP Customer Relationship Management
Besides a product component that takes into account the specific features of Human Capital Management, SAP TDMS supports SAP Customer Relationship Management (SAP CRM) and SAP NetWeaver Business Warehouse (BW), and offers a variety of procedures for data reduction which consider the respective product-specific dependencies in the dataset.

With SAP TDMS for CRM you can use the following process types:

▶ Transfer of repository and client-independent customizing (shell creation)

▶ Transfer of master data and customizing data

▶ Transfer of master data and customizing data plus transaction data in the form of a time slot as of a defined key date (from-date)

SAP TDMS for SAP NetWeaver BW
If you use SAP TDMS for BW, the following process types apply:

▶ Transfer of repository and client-independent customizing (shell creation)

▶ The transfer of master data and transaction data as of a defined key date (from-date)

The selected restriction procedure only refers to the transaction data. Master data and client-dependent customizing data are always transferred completely. Client-independent customizing, administration and repository data are preserved in the (non-productive) target system and are not overwritten by the SAP TDMS.

Additional process types for SAP TDMS for SAP ERP, SAP HCM, SAP NetWeaver BW, and SAP CRM can be implemented within the scope of a supplementing consulting support. Furthermore, a partner platform enables SAP TDMS experts to develop additional functionality for specific industries and application cases and to offer this functionality to their customers.

Additional process types

9.3   Architecture and System Landscape

The system landscape for an SAP TDMS installation consists of the following components (see Figure 9.6):

System landscape of the SAP TDMS installation

▶ **Sender system**
This is a system from which the data for the non-production system is copied. Typically, this is the production system or a mirror system of the production system. You can also use a quality assurance system that has been created as a full copy of the production system as a sender system.

▶ **SAP TDMS**
The SAP TDMS system assumes the following functions.

   ▶ It is the central system that stores the settings and customizing for the structure of the non-production system.

   ▶ It acts as a process monitoring system that uses the monitoring functions of the TDMS in order to monitor the progress of the data transfer and the access to the log files of the TDMS.

▶ **Receiver system**
This is the non-production system to be set up, such as a development, test, quality assurance, or training system.

The SAP TDMS can therefore be implemented in a separate system or also in SAP Solution Manager. This system transfers data from the sender to the receiver system.

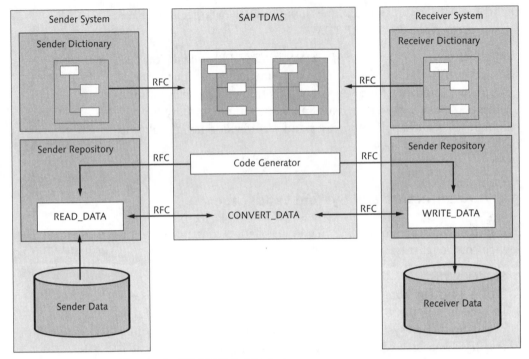

Figure 9.6 SAP TDMS Architecture

Connections
Both the sender and receiver systems are connected to the SAP TDMS via remote function calls (RFCs). With the exception of some minor extra work, all activities in the different systems are started and monitored exclusively from TDMS. For security reasons, a specific user of the COMMUNICATION DATA type is used to carry out the activities related to the SAP TDMS. A user of this type can access the remote systems (sender and receiver) exclusively via RFC and is not authorized to carry out any activities in dialog mode in the remote systems.

The SAP TDMS is set up in a separate instance. You can choose to install the SAP TDMS on a machine that also runs a development system, or in an SAP Solution Manager system.

Hardware requirements
The central system, hence the SAP TDMS, must meet the following requirements:

▶ ERP system with Basis AS 6.20, 6.40, or 7.00 (SAP ABA)

▶ 4,000 SAPS

▶ Required disk space of approximately 20 GB

There are no specific requirements for installing the SAP TDMS at the patch level. The sender and receiver systems must have the same release status.

SAP TDMS for SAP ERP currently supports the Releases SAP R/3 4.6C and 4.7 as well as SAP ERP 5.0 and 6.0. SAP TDMS for SAP HCM is currently available for Release 4.7. SAP TDMS for SAP NetWeaver BW supports the product versions 3.5 and 7.0. SAP Test Data Migration Server for SAP CRM works with Releases 4.0, 5.0, and 6.0.

The software for the SAP TDMS must be installed in all involved systems.

9.4 Data Transfer and Extraction

The Migration Workbench, a stable migration technology that has been tested over many years is used to transfer data from the sender to the receiver system. The Migration Workbench that is operated on the basis of the SAP NetWeaver technology (Web Application Server 6.20 or higher) establishes the connection between the production system and the non-production environment, and it controls the migration of the business objects. The actual migration of data occurs in four steps:

1. Definition of the sender structure (production environment) and the receiver structure (non-production environment) by determining the relevant data tables including their hierarchical relationships. At this point, no relationships exist between the two structures. The Migration Workbench reads and stores all field information for all selected tables.

2. Definition of the relationships between the production landscape and the non-production landscape. In this context, the data tables are linked with each other and rules enable you to control with precision how the dataset will be reduced. By reducing the dataset, you will obtain a more compact, easier-to-handle, and more efficient test system.

545

3. Automatic creation of the code for the data migration using the Migration Workbench.

4. Migration: During the migration process, the Migration Workbench reads the data, converts it, and writes it to the receiver structure in the non-production system.

Data extraction using the Business Process Library of the SAP TDMS requires additional steps and offers enhanced options for defining the data to be transferred. A typical process for extracting production data based on information of BPL involves eight steps:

1. Perform setup, if not available yet, or maintenance of RFC connections to sender and receiver system. When using extraction scenarios that are based on the usage of the Business Process Library, you can also connect the systems via RFC or qRFC connections.

2. Select the "ERP Initial Package for Business Process Library" process type.

3. Select the relevant business contexts, for instance, "sales order."

4. Start the table crawler, which subsequently determines a table histogram of the sender system and uses this as the basis to identify customer-specific tables and table relations that deviate from the standard content of the BPL.

5. Define and activate of selections.

6. Start simulation.

7. Optionally, you can start a deletion run whose purpose is to ensure data consistency in the receiver system. Currently, there are two different deletion modes. In the standard mode, the contents of the tables contained in the scenario are deleted completely in the receiver system. The intelligent mode additionally considers dependencies; here, only a subset of the table entries is deleted.

8. Start data transfer.

If a test system has been provided with data from the production landscape using the SAP TDMS, it can easily be refreshed with current data from that landscape on a regular basis, as the existing configuration can be reused here.

9.5   Creation and Refresh of Test Systems

The following sections describe the details of the work processes involved in the creation of a test system.

First you must make sure that the Data Dictionary (DDIC) and cross-client customizing of the receiver system match their counterparts in the associated sender system. Although the SAP TDMS provides consistency checks for the most important parameters, it is useful to ensure the consistency of the data in question right at the beginning.

Data Dictionary

For this reason you should create a copy of the sender system that can be used as a basis for the non-production system. Alternatively, you can also use an existing copy, such as a test system. If a snapshot technology is used, you can use a snapshot instead of a system copy.

Snapshot Technology

The *Snapshot* concept is used for different situations in IT. It therefore makes sense to describe it in the context of SAP TDMS, where it is used with reference to data storages. A snapshot function is provided by many storage providers (for instance, IBM, HP, EMC, Netapp, and so on), partly with different names.

The basic idea of this technology is to freeze data of one or more SAP systems at a specific point in time. The frozen dataset is available for further processing without affecting the source of the data and without restricting its further usage. This process can be compared with a copy of an SAP system without requiring downtime and without doubling the data quantity. You don't require additional storage for this virtual copy process (snapshot); the downtime only consumes a few seconds and is therefore negligible.

SAP TDMS uses the properties of snapshot technology. The time period of the system copy is highly significant, particularly with regard to consistent copying of data within multiple interconnected systems. Using the snapshot functionality of the storage systems, the dataset of the sender systems is frozen within a short period of time so that SAP TDMS can consistently read the data of the systems. This reading process takes some time, but doesn't affect the sender system. Work can be continued without any interference. Once the data is read, the snapshot—the frozen dataset—is released again at the touch of a button.

For many SAP users, the downtime of the receiver system is also a decisive factor for setting up non-production systems. Here, it is also possible to use the snapshot technology. For example, the receiver system (for instance, a quality assurance system) can be frozen so that users can continue their work without being interrupted by the rebuild. SAP TDMS then builds the new receiver system. After the activities have been completed, you can delete the "old" receiver system, and the users can continue their work using the "new" receiver system. This procedure doesn't involve any benefit with regard to memory space savings; instead, additional memory space is temporarily required. The benefit of this procedure is that downtime is avoided. This can be a decisive advantage, particularly during the test phases.

Shell creation A system shell is then generated by deleting the client-dependent data from the system copy. This functionality meets the frequent requirement for generating a current copy of the production system that only contains repository objects and client-independent customizing.

In contrast to the common manual procedure of first creating a full copy of the production system and then deleting its clients, shell creation is able to select repository objects and the client-independent customizing from a source system and use these to build a new system. Whereas the manual procedure would require you to double the database size, shell creation only requires additional memory space for the size of the selected data. In many cases, this is only a fraction of the entire system size.

Once the shell has been created, you can use the other SAP TDMS functions to transfer the desired set of business data to the clients for setup.

If you want to provide other non-production systems, such as a quality assurance system or a training system, with data from the same sender system, it makes sense to store a ready-to-use system shell. SAP TDMS provides the following options for this task.

▶ **Save Shell**
This option enables you to save a copy of the system shell. However, if you want to create a new system based on this shell at a later stage, you must import into the shell all transports that have been imported into the production system in the meantime.

▶ **Master Shell**

This option also enables you to save a copy of the system shell. However, this copy is integrated into the transport processes so that all transports for the production system also go into the master shell. This way, you can make sure that the DDIC and cross-client customizing are always up-to-date in the master shell, and you can create a new system based on the master shell without any additional transports at any time.

Once the required software has been installed in all involved systems, you can carry out the technical preparations. The SAP TDMS contains a flow structure that guides users through those preparations and all other steps.

Next, you must analyze the sender system. If you want to copy only master data and customizing data, this phase is primarily used to analyze the existing customer-specific tables in order to determine if those tables are relevant in this context. If you want to copy transaction data as well, you must determine the reduction criterion you want to use, such as the from-date, and which tables you can copy in reduced form. The actual data transfer from the sender to the receiver system then takes place. Then you must carry out only some small tasks, such as resetting the buffers. Once this step has been completed, the non-production system contains data and can be used right away.

Analyzing the sender system

You can refresh the test system at any time based on the defined configuration. Because the existing settings can be drawn upon, the flow structure here is much shorter and simpler than that used when setting up the system for the first time. During a refresh, the table structures in the sender and receiver systems are reconciled with each other. If new tables or fields have been added to the sender system, they are also transferred to the receiver system. This ensures the consistency for the systems even if the test system is not part of the transport path. Thus, changes to table structures in the DDIC are not automatically made in the test system.

Refresh

In the context of the refresh process "Transfer of master data and customizing data plus transaction data as of a defined key date (from-date)," you must define a new from-date in order to adapt the dataset to be transferred to current requirements. The existing client-dependent data is deleted from the test system during the preparation of the refresh process. For this purpose, the corresponding functions in the SAP TDMS are used.

Other applications of the SAP TDMS

In addition to the actual test systems, other non-production systems, such as training systems for end users, are usually needed in the environment of software tests. You can use SAP TDMS to install and update those systems.

In practice, SAP TDMS is also often used to directly create a separate test client in the development system so that the developers can perform initial tests using current data in the development system. This enables them to identify and correct program errors early on.

Product-specific variants

Using the product-specific variants of SAP TDMS, you can similarly provide non-production HCM, CRM, and BW systems with test data from the production systems. The data structures and the specific requirements of the respective areas, such as the anonymization of personnel data, are taken into account and provided in the form of scenarios for data extraction or through enhanced functionality.

A look ahead

The next SAP TDMS release is being designed to supplement the Business Process Library with additional business contexts. Further industry solutions are supposed to be considered as well. Plans also include the extension of the functionality for data anonymization as well as the support of a central test data management. Within the scope of SAP TDMS, other solutions are supposed to be provided for the SAP Business Suite components. An execution manager is to be made available by default for successor versions. This execution manager can be used to automatically trigger individual activities in the process tree of SAP TDMS so that additional manual steps are omitted and the operation of the tool is accelerated.

9.6 Summary

SAP Test Data Migration Server (TDMS) provides functionality that allows you to extract a subset of the data from a production system and to transfer this subset to a non-production system. Here, various process types contribute to data reduction and are available in the standard configuration of the SAP TDMS. The data to be extracted can be selected, for example, via a defined period of time or using the Business Process Library based on the business process logic.

The scrambling platform in SAP TDMS enables the customers to flexibly define their rules within the scope of SAP ERP. The SAP TDMS for HCM provides customers with predefined rules for anonymizing production data.

The SAP TDMS is a tool that enables you to retrieve up-to-date and consistent test data. This particularly applies to testing activities within the scope of customer-specific quality assurance of SAP solutions. Similarly, test data can also be transferred to non-production systems. For example, the use of data close to production in the development system improves the quality of the testing activities in the software development. Training systems can also be provided with production data. The refresh function allows you to update non-production system at any time with new data from the production system, with very little setup work.

The SAP Test Data Migration Server can be used in the entire system landscape. The tool is available for the SAP solutions SAP ERP, SAP NetWeaver BW, SAP CRM, and SAP HCM, and supports product-specific data elements and procedures where required.

9.7   Customer Report by Behr GmbH & Co. KG

> **Note**
>
> This customer report originates from the first edition of this book and is still applicable today. The enterprise figures have been updated; otherwise the report is unchanged.

By using SAP Test Data Migration Server (SAP TDMS), Behr GmbH & Co. KG has again been able to provide test clients with productive data, even in the development system. It is possible to generate up-to-date and consistent data for sandbox or test systems without any production system downtime. The memory capacity required has been reduced by around 70% compared with the production system, with hardware costs and preparation efforts being significantly reduced.

Behr GmbH & Co. KG As a major automotive supplier, Behr GmbH & Co. KG specializes in environmentally friendly vehicle climate control and engine cooling. Behr numbers among the leading manufacturers and suppliers of original equipment in the private and commercial vehicle sector and is the number one in Europe. The Behr brand has become synonymous with the field of thermo-management for modern engines. Behr technology provides safe, healthy driving comfort in approximately 30% of all European vehicles equipped with air conditioning.

With global sales of approximately €3.3 billion (as of 2008), Behr employs about 15,000 people.[1]

IT department As the leading SAP system, Behr uses an ERP system based on Basis Release Web Application Server 6.20. This widely used automotive industry solution is applied in Release 4.71. The SAP systems currently have approximately 2,800 users, of whom as many as 1,000 are active at the same time.

Allocation of test systems A recurring problem for Behr's IT department was the allocation of test systems. This was because seemingly contradictory requirements had to be met.

On the one hand, there is an ongoing requirement to provide up-to-date and consistent test data. On the other hand, given the Behr system's total system volume of over a terabyte, substantial hardware costs are incurred for redundant memory and backup capacity for the development and test systems. Alexander Angermann, SAP Basis Manager, Behr GmbH & Co. KG:

> *"Currently our database totals around 1.2 terabytes in size. Prior to the implementation of the SAP Test Data Migration Server, we were unable to supply the desired number of test systems with up-to-date production data. While the Q system was regularly newly built as a system copy by the production system, the copy required the full memory. A rebuild with a system copy is not possible for providing productive data in the development system, and the SAP tool, the client copy, reaches its limits with these database sizes. We had to take action!"*

---

1 Also see *http://behr.de/Internet/behrcms.nsf/pages/uberbehr.html.*

System copies were made to regularly rebuild the Q system. In each case, a backup of the production system is then restored into the Q system (see Figure 9.7).

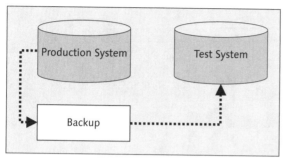

Figure 9.7 Generating a Test System by Restoring a Backup

This method can no longer be used if there are multiple clients in the Q system, of which only one has to be rebuilt.

The alternative was to produce a flash copy of the database using the option FLASH-COPY (NOCOPY). This database function would also have allowed Behr to obtain a system copy without or with minimal production system downtime.

Flash-Copy

The flash copy method creates a copy of the entire production system that is almost instantly available. This is done by creating a so-called logical copy of the source system (production system) at the time the copy is made. Instead of physically transferring the entire system, the current version of the production system is "frozen." The test system refers to the production data using file system pointers. If data is now changed in the production system, the old version is first copied into the test system (see Figure 9.8). If you make changes in the test system, the referred data is read in the production system but the changes are stored in the test system. The great advantage of this approach is the immediate availability of the copy.

Nevertheless, with this procedure, the test system remains linked to the production system during the entire procedure. Because obsolete or missing parts of the copy must constantly be copied, resource consumption on the production system cannot be ruled out during reloading. This approach was also rejected.

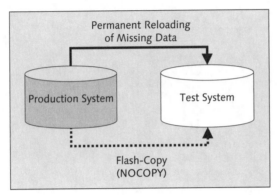

Figure 9.8 Generating a Test System by Using the Flash-Copy Function

Ramp-up of the SAP Test Data Migration Server

A convincing solution did not present itself until the ramp-up of SAP TDMS in the first quarter of 2006. Behr decided to participate as a ramp-up customer in the rollout of SAP TDMS. With SAP TDMS, SAP provides its customers with a data migration tool for supplying non-production systems with a subset of the data from the production system. Alexander Angermann:

> *"We had already been trying to find a solution to our problem for two years. SAP Test Data Migration Server provided the most sensible solution. Since this product is so new, at first we were not sure if it would fulfill all of our requirements. But even as we took part in the ramp-up, our expectations were already surpassed."*

Solution design

The chosen solution appeared as follows: SAP TDMS was installed on an instance of SAP Solution Manager 3.2, which performs the data reduction and then supplies the non-productive systems with data. The data extract is made from a temporary system that is created from the production system with FLASH-COPY (NOCOPY), with minimal downtime of the production system (see Figure 9.9). The advantage over working with a simple system copy using FLASH-COPY (NOCOPY) is this: When the target system is built, no further connection is required between the production system and the copy (temporary system).

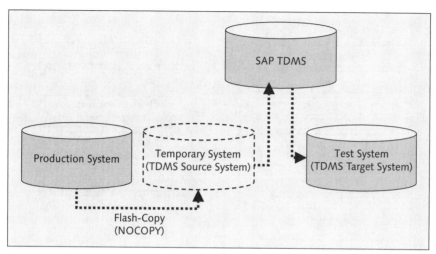

Figure 9.9 Final Structure for the Data Supply of Test Systems

Ultimately, a total of four systems were involved in the data supply of the test system at Behr: The production system was copied into a temporary system using the option FLASH-COPY (NOCOPY). The central SAP TDMS used this temporary system as a source system and then performed the data reduction and the data supply of the test system.

The use of SAP Test Data Migration Server had a huge impact on the entire development and testing process at Behr. With the previous procedure, the rebuilding of the Q system using a system copy of the production system required a lot of manual follow-up work. This is because when a system copy is created, all objects from the production system, including master and transaction data, the customizing settings, and the customer's own developments, are always taken into account. This applies r whether the copy was created from a backup or by using a flash copy.

Reduction of the required transports

In practice, this has the considerable disadvantage that the test system will then exist at the same level as the development version of the production system. The differences that must be tested—in particular all in-house developments that have been made in the meantime—must be transported from the development system (see Figure 9.10).

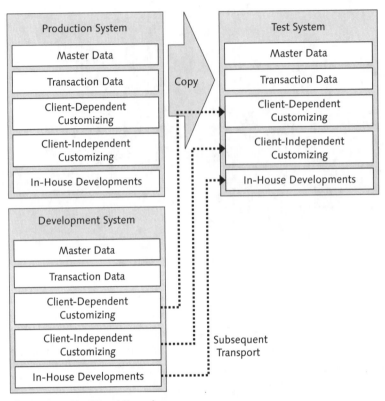

Figure 9.10 Traditional Procedure

For the testing process, this means that the schedule for creating a new test system is pushed back as far as possible, so that as many as possible of the changes to be tested are included in the transport. However, because the operation is time-consuming, including both the copy and transport runtimes and significant effort on the part of the Basis employees, this method was considered unsatisfactory.

This procedure has been significantly improved through use of SAP TDMS: Now specific data is copied from the production system into the development system (see Figure 9.11).

The possibility of using a simple refresh allows specific master data, a usable subset of the transaction data, and the client-dependent customizing to be copied from the production system into the development system using SAP TDMS. Customizing and development objects are preserved in the target system.

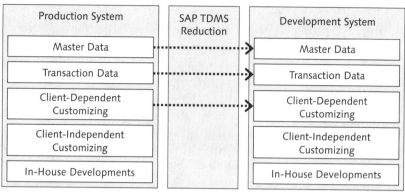

Figure 9.11 Procedure Using SAP TDMS

This small technical difference has enormous implications for the procedure in development projects. The possibility of performing quick tests directly in the development system with data from the production system has substantially shortened development cycle times. At the same time, it was possible to noticeably improve the quality of the development at the beginning of the test phase.

Improving the development process

All in all, Alexander Angermann is quite satisfied with this new procedure:

> *"Our development work is no longer interrupted by permanent transports, since we can perform functional tests directly in the development system. This has helped us immensely to improve the efficiency and quality of our in-house developments. We can now test changes one phase earlier than it was usually the case. This saves time and assists in ensuring the seamless integration of business processes at an early stage."*

Thanks to SAP TDMS, it is possible to refresh the test system without halting development or without any downtime. It was also possible to greatly improve the planning of testing activities. Previously, a successful refresh on the test system was delayed for as long as possible, to avoid any impact on the development process. If a refresh was not possible at a particular time, sometimes tester requirements had to remain unmet. Alexander Angermann sees this conflict as having now been overcome through the use of SAP TDMS:

"Thanks to SAP TDMS, today we are in a position to refresh a test system at any time. We can plan test system requirements for the entire year and beyond. Test weeks are appointed for roll-out projects. For these weeks, test systems are then supplied with data from the production systems."

Conclusion

Thanks to the SAP Test Data Migration Server, Behr was able to reduce the volume of test systems by around 70%. As well as reducing hardware costs, this brought about an enormous time saving when building a test system.

The option of copying master and transaction data separately from customizing and development objects means that it is possible to perform functional testing early, and do so directly in the development system. As a result, development cycles can be shortened and the quality of in-house developments can be noticeably improved before entering the test phase. The number of transports required has been drastically reduced.

Because SAP TDMS allows the test systems to be refreshed without disturbing development or production operation, test systems can be resupplied at any time. This massively boosts the ability to plan testing activities.

Lessons Learned What can you learn from the experience of Behr GmbH & Co. KG?

▶ The use of the SAP Test Data Migration Server allows us to provide consistent test data that requires a much reduced dataset in comparison with the production system.

▶ A temporary system created using FLASH-COPY (NOCOPY) is an optimal source system for SAP TDMS.

▶ SAP TDMS allows current transaction data to be copied again through a refresh, with minimal setup input required. This means that you can supply not only test systems, but also additional systems, such as a development system. This allows functional testing to be performed early with data from the production system, directly in the development system.

▶ SAP TDMS also supports the independent organization of IT projects run in parallel by selectively refreshing individual clients in different systems.

9.8   Customer Report by Infineon Technologies AG

"The usage of SAP TDMS has already paid off with the first application, and we expect further positive effects in future."

Helmut Schneider,
Infineon Technologies AG

Infineon Technologies AG is a high-technology enterprise which emerged in 1999 when Siemens AG outsourced its semiconductor business. The enterprise develops semiconductor and system solutions for the core application areas of energy efficiency, communication, and security. The subsidiary Qimonda offers storage products. The target markets and applications include the automotive environment (including safety, drive control, telematics), industry and multimarket (including control of industrial facilities, domestic appliances, and consumer electronics), chip cards and security, as well as wired and wireless communication solutions. Approximately 21,600 patents document the enterprise's versatile technology portfolio. With about 28,000 employees at 58 locations around the globe, Infineon Technologies AG generated a turnover of €4.321 billion in 2008.

Infineon Technologies AG

The IT organization of the enterprise is subdivided into the areas of Corporate Business Services, Supply Chain Management, Governance, Processes & Services, Operational Services, and Enterprise Application Platform. Infineon uses nine SAP ERP solutions as well as three SAP Business Suite solutions: in Europe, the United States, and in the Asia/Pacific region. A myriad of different modules are used in the SAP ERP systems; the Business Suite solutions used include Customer Relationship Management, Product Lifecycle Management, and Supplier Relationship Management. SAP Human Capital Management is used in the HR area. About 90% of the system maintenance work is performed by external service providers.

IT organization

The multilayered system landscape is characterized by various rapidly growing production systems. At Infineon, virtually every SAP application faces the requirement to set up new quality assurance systems for quality assurance and software development or to create appropriate client copies. In the past, these activities consumed more and more resources due to the size of the production systems. Besides the increasing memory space requirement of the production copies, the runtime of the system

Challenges in the test data management

copies was also considered a critical aspect; for example, these had to be integrated at specific times and be implemented on weekends. After the copy had been made—for creation of a new quality assurance system, for example—it often required complex post-processing with corresponding employee engagement. At the same time, various target groups had to be provided with suitable and high-quality test data that allowed the enterprise's business department to run practical tests with a realistic dataset.

Selection of SAP TDMS

Against this background, the enterprise actively searched for solutions to simplify the creation of test systems as well as the regular refresh of its test data. The company quickly decided to use SAP Test Data Migration Server. After a workshop held by SAP Consulting, the opportunity arose to participate in the ramp-up of the enhancement of SAP TDMS 3.0 for Human Capital Management (HCM). The initiative to deploy SAP TDMS at Infineon and initially use it in a pilot project within the scope of a selected solution was developed by the employees of the software architecture and the SAP platform groups of the IT organization. The goal was to deploy SAP TDMS for all SAP ERP systems on a global scale after the tool had been used successfully in the pilot project.

Pilot project in the HR environment

The initial project to evaluate the functionality and the benefit of SAP TDMS was implemented in the environment of the SAP HCM solution. This was coordinated within IT via the software architecture and the SAP Basis teams. Thanks to the pilot project in the HR area it was possible to also test specific functions of SAP TDMS for the SAP HCM environment.

Use of SAP TDMS was transferred to a sub-unit of the Corporate Business Services area that provides basic activities and IT support for the global HR systems. The department deploys five internal and two external employees for this purpose. Helmut Schneider, responsible for all interfaces with the global HR system and the technical advisor in the HR environment, was given the task of implementing and initially applying SAP TDMS. As the central contact for the implementation and use of the tool, he mainly supervised the topical range of test data creation and test data management.

Installation and configuration of SAP TDMS

The installation and implementation of SAP TDMS itself was not scheduled as a separate project, but was performed in addition to the daily amount of work and running IT projects in the HR environment. This meant more work for Helmut Schneider and his co-workers, particularly during the implementation and the first configuration of the tool, because no additional resources could be made available. Helmut Schneider therefore recommends planning implementation of SAP TDMS as a separate project.

The installation, basic configuration, and subsequent training of SAP TDMS users were done within approximately two weeks. The individual steps were performed with the support of SAP Consulting as part of the ramp-up.

Helmut Schneider notes that some initial difficulties had to be mastered because of the new features of Version 3.0 of SAP TDMS. These were remedied by SAP's TDMS experts during the ramp-up. For example, various additional patches and objects had to be imported initially; then the application could be used without difficulty.

Following the installation, SAP Consulting held a workshop to train the future SAP TDMS users. The first day of the training was also used for the final configuration of SAP TDMS. Beyond that, additional workshops were held to transfer knowledge. The goal of these workshops was to raise awareness of the tool's functionality among various target groups, such as IT management and SAP Basis, in order to identify further applications in the medium term. In addition, Helmut Schneider's project team was supported by ramp-up coaches of SAP Consulting, who were available for technical questions and who exchanged error messages and improvement suggestions with the developers of SAP TDMS.

Workshops and coaching

Following the workshops, SAP TDMS was ready for use. The basic functionality of the system was at first made accessible in a "trial phase" by transferring some organizational elements and selective data records from the production system to quality assurance or development systems. At the same time, the implementation of a new payroll procedure for the Asian region was identified as the project for which SAP TDMS was supposed to be used in production for the first time. Within the scope of this project, SAP TDMS was primarily used for two different application scenarios.

For all testing activities during the implementation phases of the payroll project, SAP TDMS was used for regular creation of client copies. Up to that point, these had always been created manually, which resulted in

Creating client copies

downtime of the systems concerned as well as numerous post-processing steps. The client copies ensure that a client is always available for the individual test cycles and that this client corresponds to the production environment with regard to customizing and transported developments. With each client copy, approximately 16,500 person master records, 500 organizational units, 9,000 positions, and about 7,000 jobs are transferred in total in the HR environment.

This also ensured that the testers have current test data from the production environment at hand. During the implementation phase, the team evaluated how much SAP TDMS simplified the creation of new systems and the provision of test data. The results of the pilot project were then analyzed, and a roadmap was created for use of SAP TDMS in all other SAP systems.

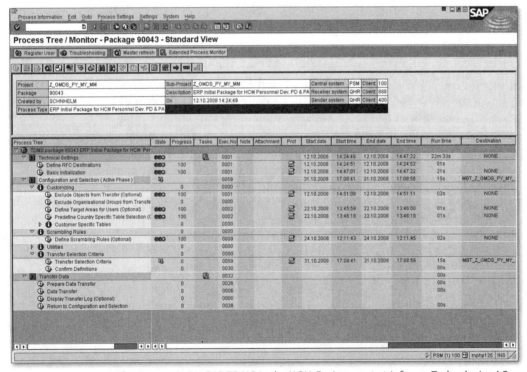

Figure 9.12 Using SAP TDMS in the HCM Environment at Infineon Technologies AG

Creating sandbox systems for troubleshooting

SAP TDMS was used in another application scenario to set up sandbox systems for identifying and correcting errors in the production operation. This procedure is used if error situations in the production systems require a thorough analysis of the error cause and a subsequent test of the implemented troubleshooting. Here, a solution must be provided as fast as possible for the problems that occurred; at the same time the procedure must ensure that the production operation is not jeopardized through changes or testing activities. According to Helmut Schneider, the structure of a system for troubleshooting meets exactly this goal.

> "If, for example, a problem occurs in payroll and a quick solution is required, the data of the production system must be transferred to the development or quality assurance system under high time pressure to simulate the error and then remedy it quickly."

In the past, a particular challenge was the time consumed for creating the system copy and the necessary post-processing. This could be reduced considerably by using SAP TDMS.

The challenges that were identified during the first use of SAP TDMS included the performance of the system installed. For example, the project team determined that it took several hours to copy an organizational unit with more than 50 persons. This was a critical factor for a possible system copy, due to the size of the production systems as well as the time window. As a result, the transfer of data was scheduled at night due to the initially longer runtime, so that the resource consumption in the production system was non-critical for the daily business. The performance problem was analyzed with the support of SAP Consulting, and an update of SAP TDMS was provided. Thanks to new program coding, it was possible to considerably reduce the copy runtime. Helmut Schneider is satisfied with the current system performance. He emphasizes that in the near future a changeover or update of the installed SAP TDMS system's hardware is required, independent of the software performance, to ensure sufficient performance for the extended future use of the tool.

SAP TDMS
Performance

At the beginning of the ramp-up, the system copies had to be made in the online mode. The required activities could not be scheduled as background jobs in this case. A corresponding development suggestion was forwarded to SAP and has been implemented. The same applies to the users used by SAP TDMS. During the ramp-up phase, the users, with whom SAP TDMS works in the sender and receiver systems, still had to be declared as dialog users; now they can also be created as background users for security reasons so that they cannot work via the SAP GUI.

Optimization
during ramp-up

Furthermore, some optimizations for the operability of the tool were identified during trainings and in the daily use of SAP TDMS. These were forwarded to SAP and implemented there. Helmut Schneider thinks that there is optimization potential in the project management of the TDMS. At the moment, all users who have access to SAP TDMS can view all projects and—provided that they have appropriate authorization—execute work steps within the projects.

Furthermore, the current version doesn't allow for the deletion of projects. Although this makes sense in light of possible obligation to provide documentation, it can lead to confusion, particularly if SAP TDMS system is also used for demonstration and training.

Accelerating the client copy

Overall, using SAP TDMS could significantly contribute to the success of the payroll project. This way, it was possible to accelerate the creation of new clients for the software quality assurance by approximately 50%. The one-time preparation time to set up corresponding selection scenarios for transferring data took about half a day. Helmut Schneider confirms that the required test data was available in time in the quality assurance system, thanks the use of SAP TDMS. Other than using SAP TDMS, no system settings such as adaptation of RFC connections and interfaces, were necessary in order to use the new clients. Comprehensive post-processing, which previously took about one workday and comprised numerous, error-prone work steps, was omitted completely. Direct comparison with previous work efforts was not possible because the implementation of the Asian payroll system was a completely new implementation. Even so the creation of a system shell with subsequent selective data migration was more efficient than the manual creation of a client copy with subsequent implementation of all necessary post-processing work. The selective transfer of data also allows for the reduction of the development and test systems' size. Helmut Schneider summarizes the benefits that are decisive in daily use:

> "With SAP TDMS, we can definitely reduce our preparation time by 50%. This is due to the fact that the system settings no longer need to be updated, comprehensive post-processing work is therefore omitted completely. Particularly for the client copy—as experience has shown— we usually need more than one day to provide a quality assurance system like the one we had before. Here, important configuration settings

were often forgotten in particular for interfaces. I no longer have this problem with SAP TDMS for HCM."

Already, the creation of a new quality assurance system or a client within the system is significantly simplified with SAP TDMS. In the medium term, Helmut Schneider wants to keep the dataset in the test systems up-to-date by using periodic refreshes. This way, the number of client copies, which have been made about once per quarter so far, is supposed to be reduced so that they need to be created not more than once a year.

Refresh of test data

In real life, says Helmut Schneider, the occasional new creation of test systems cannot be avoided completely because the transports of systems must be coordinated with those of the production system and because redundant transports from the development systems occasionally remain in the test systems. These effects can only be corrected by creating a new client copy, he says. Thanks to the TDMS option to update test data via the refresh functionality, the number of complete client copies can be reduced significantly.

Another benefit emerged independent of using SAP TDMS in the payroll project: Selected test data from the production systems could be provided for the software development of the portal environment.

Developer test with production data

Up to now, portal developers used to test their programs exclusively with synthetic, custom test data. The manually created dataset did not have the scope and characteristics of real system data, which meant that some errors were not identified until the integration tests.

By using SAP TDMS, Helmut Schneider was able to provide developers with test data from selected organizational units in a development system. Additionally, SAP TDMS was used to anonymize test data before transfer.

This way, it was possible to test new developments with real data in the portal area as soon as possible. The availability of real data not only makes the developer test more convenient, but also enables the detection of errors which used to remain undetected due to the use of generic test data. This results in a much better application quality, and as a result costs for troubleshooting can be avoided in subsequent project phases such as integration tests.

Conclusion

The payroll system for the Asian region went live successfully. The holistic approach shows that the use of SAP TDMS within the scope of the project has led to a considerably accelerated creation of quality assurance systems. SAP TDMS was used to create systems and clients for integration tests of the SAP HCM solution and update them periodically. Furthermore, SAP TDMS was deployed to copy current production data from a test system to reproduce error effects that occur in this system. This made it possible to analyze and correct errors in the production operation quickly and without interruption in a controlled environment. Moreover, selected test data from production systems were provided to developers to enable a practically oriented test of custom development at the earliest possible point in time.

Medium-term planning calls for reducing the number of client copies and thus the effort required for those through regular data refreshes using SAP TDMS. In future, SAP TDMS is supposed to be gradually deployed for further SAP applications at Infineon beyond the HR environment.

Lessons Learned   What can you learn from the experience of Infineon?

▶ After the implementation of SAP TDMS, target group-specific workshops impart know-how and raise awareness for the functions of the tool.

▶ Use of SAP TDMS greatly reduces the effort in making client copies. Particularly extensive and error-prone manual post-processing is omitted.

▶ The use of system refreshs allows for a time-saving synchronization of the target system with the data from the production system.

▶ Besides the creation of quality assurance systems, SAP TDMS can also provide test data to other non-production systems. These include development systems or, as shown in this report, sandbox systems for error analysis.

▶ Thanks to the use of test data from the production environment already for the software development and thanks to practically oriented developer tests, high troubleshooting costs can be avoided in subsequent project phases.

PART III
Performance Tests

A test that evaluates the time-related behavior of several business transactions that take place at the same time is referred to as a performance test. Depending on the size of the load the test is based on, we distinguish between load tests and stress tests. Although those tests reveal various critical risks for production operations, they are often neglected in real life, which sometimes causes severe damage. This should be reason enough to dedicate Part III of this book to the subject of performance tests.

10 Project Outline of a Performance Test

The term performance test generally refers to a test that checks non-technical requirements of a system both in single-user operation and under multi-user load. Depending on the goal of the test, we must distinguish between different variants.

Definition

The goal of the single-user measurement is to obtain a "best case" impression of the system performance, because it can be assumed that the response times in parallel operation can never be better than with a single user. If the system behavior observed is "too poor" already—that is, it doesn't meet the defined key performance indicators (KPIs)—the system must be optimized before a load test is implemented.

The goal of a load test is the simulation of realistic operating conditions. In this respect, a load test differs from a stress test. In the latter, the system is also put under a load, but this is done in order to purposely exceed the realistic operating conditions and in this way to determine the limits of the system.

If the focus of the performance test is on processing large quantities of data—that is, on background processing—this is referred to as mass data or volume test.

Successful completion of the functional tests ensures that a single business transaction can run correctly through the entire process chain. Although this is an extremely important step during the project execution, it neglects an essential dimension of the system: the non-functional behavior of the system. This is particularly important in processing of multiple simultaneous business transactions and simultaneous interaction of multiple users.

Risks covered The next step therefore consists of testing the system under performance conditions. Such a performance test captures numerous risks that cannot be covered by functional tests:

▸ **System failure caused by overload**
In a system whose resources are not sufficient, the total system throughput can be too small for the existing load. Possible causes can be insufficiently sized hardware or network bandwidth, incorrectly sized software resources, or inefficient programming. This can result in reduced availability, the termination of transactions, and—in a worst case scenario—system downtime. You can realistically identify such errors only by means of load simulation.

▸ **Time-critical processes**
Time restrictions exist for some processes. For example, let's suppose that all period-end closing data for a specific customer must be loaded into the SAP SEM-BCS system within n hours. You must make sure that this time-critical process will be completed within the permitted period of time so that downstream processes can begin without delay.

▸ **Service-Level Agreements (SLAs)**
Performance goals are often contractually guaranteed in service-level agreements. Thus, for example, an average response time of less than one second could be guaranteed for all transactions or a specific minimum throughput of mass data could be agreed upon. If service-level agreements exist, adherence to them is always part of the goals of a performance test.

▸ **User acceptance**
A factor that is often neglected is that the actual response times of the system are central to user acceptance. For this reason, it is important to define acceptable response times and also to consider the subjec-

tive perceptions of the users in addition to hard factors such as an interruption of the work process caused by wait times.

The test goals for the performance test can be directly derived from those risks:

- ▸ System availability under load
- ▸ Functional stability under load
- ▸ Response times that are acceptable for the user
- ▸ Adherence to time restrictions and service level agreements for business processes
- ▸ Identifying bottlenecks in both infrastructure and application

10.1   Load Test—Stress Test—Volume Test

Depending on the test goal, you can subdivide performance tests into the following variants: load tests, stress tests, and volume tests.

Single-user tests can precede a load test to obtain a general impression of performance. The benefit of the single-user test is that it can be implemented manually with the appropriate tools and can therefore be used at an early stage in the development cycle.

A load test represents the test of a system against the expected maximum load. A successful load test makes sure that a system works with acceptable performance under the conditions that can realistically be expected. The test identifies both bottlenecks in the application and the incorrect sizing of system components (oversizing and undersizing).

A stress test is a test in which the load put on the system exceeds the maximum load that can realistically be expected. In such a test, the forecast maximum load is increased step by step up to the point at which KPIs can no longer be met. For example, if a maximum load of 180 simultaneously working employees was forecast, corresponding to 100%, a stress test could increase the load to 130%, 160%, and 190%. The load is then continuously increased until it reaches a number of users at which the response times become significantly longer, the processing terminates, or the system fails. A stress test allows you to forecast the system behavior in the case of increased requirements, for instance when the organization grows. Based on this information, you can create investment plans, such as those for future hardware extensions.

Volume test
The volume test represents the third variant of the performance test. Whereas load tests and stress tests are intended to simulate all the constraints of a live operation as realistically as possible, a mass test focuses on the data throughput. Volume tests are often carried out without the simulation of dialog users and can serve either as benchmarks for the comparison of different systems or as preparatory steps for load tests.

10.2 Roles in the Performance Test Project

An important aspect of planning and implementing a performance test project is the definition and assignment of project roles. Note that the actual characteristics of the roles depend on the respective project situation. Depending on the structure and number of people involved in the project, a role can be assigned to a person or a team. In smaller projects, one person may be assigned several roles.

There are several standard roles that should be assigned in every performance test project. All the role descriptions provided in this section are based on our many years of experience. The roles can be assigned to customers as well as external persons.

Customer
The *customer* must approve various project steps. These steps include the definition of the test goals, the project plan, and the test result. The customer primarily communicates with the test lead. In the case of an externally assigned performance test project, the customer represents the interests of the sold-to party in the project team. In addition, the customer often acts as the linking element between the key users and external team members. The role of the customer is always assigned to an internal employee of the sold-to party.

Test lead
The *performance test coordinator* is responsible for managing the performance test project. He or she coordinates and controls the project flow. Usually, the test lead defines the test goals and test-end criteria in cooperation with key users or the system operation, designs the project plan, and creates the final report. The customer holds the test lead responsible for those documents as well as for intermediate and final results. Other tasks of the test lead include process and data analyses in collaboration

with key users, and the planning of resources such as test systems, load injectors, performance test tools (including licenses), and premises.

The role of the test lead can be assigned to an internal or external employee, and both assignments are common. In any case, we recommend releasing the respective person from all other responsibilities for the project period.

The job of the *script developers* consists of implementing the specifications from the load analysis technically and mapping the load profile determined in this way as realistically as possible using the selected performance test tool. For this purpose, they record test scripts according to the specifications laid down in the test case descriptions. The responsibility of the script developers also includes the parameterization and the composition of the scripts into test scenarios. Script developers also integrate application monitoring into the execution control of the load test tool.

Script developer

The work of a script developer primarily requires technological knowhow with regard to tools. For this reason, the role of a script developer is frequently assigned to external specialists.

The *key users* are responsible for transporting the business knowledge from the user departments into the project team. They are essentially responsible for creation of the load profile, the process analysis, and the determination and retrieval of the necessary test data.

Key user

Key users are always experienced internal employees from the user departments on the customer's side or in-house consultants with corresponding knowledge of the business.

The employees of the *SAP Basis team* are responsible for providing technical support to the project team. They provide the appropriate test systems, users, and authorizations, and prepare the environment for integrating the load test tool into the system landscape. It often becomes necessary to make changes to the test system during the course of a performance test project. The Basis employees check the feasibility of those changes and, if possible, implement them.

SAP Basis

The purpose of *technical system monitoring* is to monitor the performance-relevant system key figures during the load test run and to use the findings as a basis for the technical input for the intermediate and final reports.

Technical system monitoring

To identify optimization potential and to make recommendations for taking actions, technical system monitoring also considers the results of application monitoring.

It is thus an indispensable requirement to have the corresponding know-how in optimizing the performance of SAP applications to perform this role.

10.3   Phase Model of a Performance Test

Ideally, you should carry out a performance test as a separate project or sub-project. Experience has shown that the prospects of retroactively integrating a performance test as an additional activity in a rollout or upgrade project are rather dismal. There are several reasons for this:

Budget

First, a performance test project needs a budget for hardware, software, consulting services if necessary, and access to internal employees. To finance the budget for a performance test from the budget of an upgrade or implementation project without prior planning is not realistic in most cases.

Completion period

Moreover, a performance test requires a block of time in which to be carried out. As you will see later on, this test consists of an iterative process that may have to run several times through the *execution → analysis → optimization* cycle. For this reason, you must reserve an appropriate time frame for the testing and optimization activities. Here too, it is rather unrealistic to accommodate a performance test "on the side" in the schedule of another project.

The most important aspect, however, is the clear definition of the scope, goals, tasks, and responsibilities in the project plan. To support you in planning your performance test project, we have designed a project outline that you can use as a starting point for your individual planning activities.

Project phases

A performance test project is subdivided into four phases:

▶ Planning

▶ Performing the load test

- ▸ Performing the stress test (optional)
- ▸ Completing

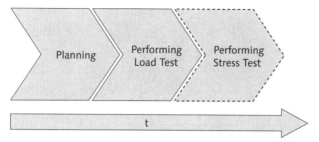

Figure 10.1 Performance Test Project Phases

The planning phase consists of analyzing the processes to be mapped and the required data and selecting the load test tool. During this planning phase, a load profile is created that serves as a basis for all other activities once it has been formally approved.

Planning

The execution of the load test comprises the provision of data and system as well as test runs with different system loads. The tests are followed by an analysis of the results and, if necessary, an optimization phase. This means that it may be necessary to run through the *execution → analysis → optimization* cycle several times.

Performing the load test

Optionally, a stress test can be carried out after the load test. The stress test is used to further measure the system in order to obtain information on system reserves and boundaries.

Performing the stress test

Comprehensive documentation in the form of a detailed report is created within the completion phase of the performance test project. The documentation ensures that the test can be repeated and contains a catalog of recommendations for actions to be taken based on the test results.

10.4 Planning

The first phase of the performance test project comprises a process analysis, a data analysis, and the selection of the load test tool (see Figure 10.2). These three activities can run in parallel. In any case, you should do the process analysis first because its results can be used to derive information for the data analysis and tool selection.

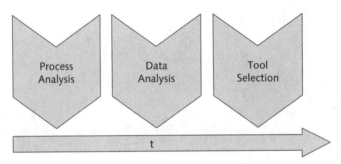

Figure 10.2 Steps of the Planning Phase

10.4.1 Process Analysis

During the process analysis, you must identify and prioritize the key processes of the enterprise. After that, you must define performance goals for each relevant process or process step. For example, the performance goals for dialog transactions are the average response times for the end user. For background processes, you must usually define a minimum and an average throughput and, if necessary, specific processing periods.

Rule of thumb As a rule of thumb, you can say that a load test should not examine more than 10 processes. This means that the five most frequently used processes should be tested first because they have the biggest influence on the generated load. In this context, you should also take into account reports that are known to greatly affect the overall performance because of their architecture or the data volume to be expected, even if the reports are rarely called. You should always involve customer-specific transactions and new developments in the load test because no past values are available for them.

In addition to the five most frequently used processes, you should also include the five most business-critical processes in order to ensure their performance.

Factors influencing the load profile While the number of simultaneously active users is the most obvious factor, the time-based distribution of the load also has a major influence on the runtime behavior of the individual transactions. Likewise, background processes affect the system behavior and should therefore also be considered.

Above all, you must distinguish between load that is caused by dialog users and load caused by background processes. The load that actually occurs in the system primarily consists of those two types of load. It is often quite useful to assume that the two load types occur at different times. Dialog users mainly work during typical office hours between 8 a.m. and 6 p.m., whereas background processes usually run outside of that period; that is, from approximately 10 p.m. until 6 a.m. If such a clear differentiation exists, you can consider each load type separately. The advantage of doing this is that the load profile is significantly simplified by that and that the load generation is less complex.

However, there are factors that make it hard to separate these load types. If a system is used from several different time zones, the dialog user load will probably be distributed more equally and overlap with the background processes.

To analyze the dialog load, you must first estimate as realistically as possible which transactions are called how often by how many users in a given period of time (usually per hour). In doing so, you must pay particular attention to the time-based progression of the load during the course of the day for each transaction to be considered.

Load profile

If a system that was used for a similar purpose already existed prior to the implementation of an SAP application, you can use the statistical data from that system as a basis for the load analysis. This can be done without problems if the legacy system is an SAP system. If that system is a third-party system, you must check whether the data can be read and transferred to the new system without a problem. The availability of a legacy system presents the ideal scenario for creating the load profile: It makes it much easier to make your estimate because you can base your calculations on real company data.

Legacy system

If no comparable legacy system is available, you must make an estimate based on the organizational model. Here are the most important steps involved in this process:

Estimate

1. **Identification of core processes**
   Which transactions are called most frequently, at what times, and to what extent?

2. **Assignment of user groups to applications**
   Who is going to use which application (for example, SD/MM/FI), at what times, and how often?

3. **Refinement of user groups**
   Who will execute which function, at what times, and to what extent (for example, the person who enters invoices, person who approves invoices, and so on)?

In this process it is very important that the different activities be carefully synchronized with the implementation project and the employees in the user departments. Questions such as "How often is Transaction X processed on a typical Friday?" are generally answered most reliably by the users in the various departments. The same holds true for information about load peaks; for instance at the end of a quarter or at weekends, before public holidays, and so on. This information is usually available from the user base in rather detailed form, but you should ask for it.

Peak load
A typical method for determining the peak load is to overlap different load curves. For example, a user department could provide information showing that the number of postings increases mostly on Fridays, towards the end of a quarter, and before public holidays. This information allows you to determine the peak load based on the overlapping of load curves (Fridays at the end of a quarter; when the following Monday is a public holiday). But again you should be sure to communicate with the user department and consult with the specific users! Under certain circumstances there can be other, very different influencing factors that are specific to the industry or the company in question and that can only be described by the users.

SAP Quick Sizer
It can be a useful first step to base the creation of a load forecast on the information provided by SAP Quick Sizer. This tool allows you to forecast what hardware will be required on the basis of data retrieved from live operations or based on data that is available for a new application. Although the data recorded by SAP Quick Sizer is insufficient for a complete load analysis, it can provide useful support.

Note that the Quick Sizer data is usually recorded at a very early stage within the project, which means that it may no longer be up-to-date at the time of the load test. Checking the data provided by SAP Quick Sizer can generally provide useful information for the creation of the load profile.

At this point we would like to do away with a common misapprehension: In no way does an SAP Quick Sizer analysis replace a performance test! Although SAP Quick Sizer enables you to roughly assess the required hardware, its functionality does not allow you to take into account various factors. Thus, it considers neither customer-specific customizing settings nor the interaction with (non-SAP) applications on the customers' side. The effects of custom developments and transactions as well as of background processes cannot be considered either. But the most important consideration is that SAP Quick Sizer assesses the hardware requirements for an *optimally configured system*. One of the main purposes of a performance test, after all, is to make sure that errors in the system configuration are uncovered.

No substitute for performance tests!

At the end of the process analysis, you must have a list of load-relevant processes sorted by their priority. In the following example, we examined a process step that maps email functionality through a portal.

Load profile documentation

The following information should be provided in order to ensure a sufficient consideration in the context of a load profile.

▶ **Role**
Who will execute this process? This piece of information enables you to make a first assessment of how many users will be involved and it indicates the contact persons who can be used as sources of information for the process and data analyses.

▶ **Navigation**
Where exactly is the function located in the menu?

▶ **Page/iViews**
Which steps are executed? To prepare a list of iViews (or pages), you can use the test case and process description as a basis. Make sure that all required steps are actually considered.

▶ **Response time**
You must document both the expected and permitted maximum response times. The first value describes the permitted average response time, while the second value indicates the still acceptable response time for the slowest case.

▶ **Number of users in role**

The total number of users must be specified for each role as well as the number of concurrent users at peak times. The first value simply lists all users that are authorized to execute the transaction. The second value indicates how many users execute the transaction simultaneously (thus representing peak load).

▶ **Data throughput/frequency**

This value specifies how many of the operations considered are carried out by each active user in total and during the peak load. Along with the number of USERS IN ROLE, you can use this value to determine the total system load.

▶ **Repetition**

This value specifies how often the function is executed or how often the load peak occurs in the respective transaction (daily/weekly/per month/per quarter/per year).

▶ **Peak load**

This value indicates the period in which the peak load is expected, as well as its share in the total load of the transaction under consideration.

Table 10.1 shows an example for the result of a process analysis:

Role	All	
Navigation	Work center/ overview	
Page/iView	**Inbox**	**Double-click on mail**
Expected response time	5 sec	3 sec
Maximum response time	8 sec	6 sec
Number of users in role (total)	300	300
Duration/frequency (peak)	30/hour	15/hour
Number of concurrent users in role (peak)	20	20
Peak load	8:00 – 10:00 (75%)	8:00 – 10:00 (75%)

Table 10.1 Sample Result of a Process Analysis

Figure 10.3 illustrates the time-based progress of each process use con- Illustration
sidered within the load profile during the course of a day. In the example
shown here (incoming email) it is obvious that a peak exists between
8 a.m. and 10 a.m., which is when most employees check their email
inboxes in order to organize their work and to answer the first emails.

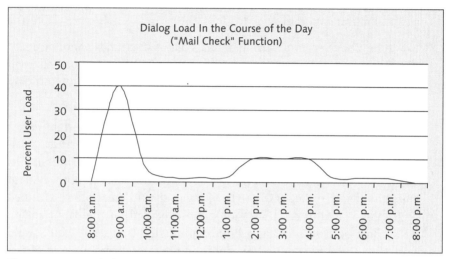

Figure 10.3 Example for the Load Forecast (Time-Based Distribution) of a Process

To analyze the background processes, you must retrieve existing informa- Background
tion from the project team. Scheduling information about background processes
processes should usually be available as job schedules. SAP does not
provide any predefined processes to implement this information technically, and it often happens that the relevant information is maintained
in Excel sheets or similar documents.

If the information about when a background job should be executed
is not available, the only way to obtain it is to ask the respective user
departments and to create the required overview manually.

10.4.2 Data Analysis

The process analysis is followed by the data analysis. Here, the data Determining
structures required by the relevant processes are identified so that the data structures
necessary consumption data, such as materials, can be determined.

Based on the relevant processes and the number of registered users, you must then estimate the required data volume. In doing so, keep in mind that performance tests "consume" large quantities of test data.

For example, if an order is triggered, the available material stock is automatically reduced. A typical problem that often occurs during performance tests is that the system is understocked because insufficient consumption data is provided.

If, in the above example, the material is out of stock and cannot be delivered, the planned process cannot be executed so that the load test will fail. To avoid this situation, you must make sure as early as the test-data retrieval that, a sufficient quantity of materials is available.

Test data quantity This possible lack of test data is the downfall of many performance test projects. Whereas the goal of a functional test is to cover all critical business processes with a quantity of test data that's as small as possible, a performance test requires large quantities of test data. The process that transfers the test data into the test system should therefore be planned early on and sufficient time should be scheduled for the data transfer. Note that each system has a limited throughput rate, and you should calculate the time required for importing the necessary quantity of test data caused by the actual technical restrictions.

Verifying test data In addition to the type and scope of test data, you should also specify the process used to generate this data. In many cases a suitable set of test data is already available in legacy systems or Excel worksheets. This data must then be migrated into the test system. If that's not the case, you must provide appropriate test data. In any case, you must verify the test data prior to using it, using these criteria:

▶ Can the test data be used for the selected processes?

▶ Is the set of test data consistent? Do batch numbers match the orders; customer numbers match the documents, and so on?

▶ Is a sufficient quantity of test data available in order to iteratively run the test for optimization verifications and also to perform a complete stress test, if necessary?

▶ Is the structure of the test data suitable for the load test? Does the purchase order, for example, contain a sufficient number of individual items? Do too many trivial cases such as empty purchase orders exist?

Once you have verified the test data, you can transfer it to the test system.

10.4.3 Selecting the Load Test Tool

In parallel to the process and data analyses, you should start selecting an appropriate load test tool.

Frequently, load tests have been carried out in previous projects, and the relevant tools are still available. If so, you must check whether the licenses purchased at that time are still valid and if you are still entitled to maintenance support from the manufacturer. Furthermore, you should determine whether the existing licenses meet the current requirements with regard to both the number of users to be simulated and the systems to be tested.

Using existing tools

If you need to purchase a new tool or want to test a new technology using the existing tool in the coming load test, you should examine the eligible tools for suitability in the context of a proof-of-concept procedure. This way you can make sure that the success of your test is not endangered by an insufficient functionality of the load test tool.

Selecting new tools

In any case, it is advisable to involve experienced personnel, such as SAP consultants, when selecting and checking a suitable load test tool.

10.4.4 The Load Profile

The essential result of the test preparation is the load profile. It is useful to have the user departments formally approve this document, as it will serve as a basis for all other activities later on. The load profile describes the most important processes, prioritizes them, specifies the load progress to be expected over a specific period of time, and defines the performance goals for the processes under peak load. The load profile should at least answer these questions:

- ▶ Which processes are executed most frequently?
- ▶ When does the peak load occur for each process?
- ▶ How many concurrent users work in the process during peak load?

▸ How often are these processes executed at peak load?

▸ Which data objects are required for each process?

▸ To what extent does this data have to be available?

▸ How is the data retrieved for the test?

▸ Which relevant background processes run when?

▸ How many resources are required by the background processes?

▸ Which data structures must be available for the background processes?

▸ Which tool should be used to generate the load?

▸ How is system and application monitoring carried out during the load run?

10.5 Performing the Load Test

The main phase of the test project consists of four steps. It starts with the preparation of data and the system. This is followed by a single-user test, and then by a multi-user test in which the number of users increases gradually (see Figure 10.4). The final step of the test consists of a result analysis. If necessary, an optimization phase follows, including another test to verify the optimization measures. The *execution → analysis → optimization* cycle creates an iterative process.

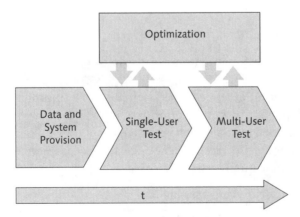

Figure 10.4 Load Test Execution Steps

10.5.1 Data and System Preparation

The first step in the execution phase consists of preparing the data and system. This step involves the provisioning hardware for the test system as well as suitable test data. Theoretically, the test hardware for the load system should be the same as the hardware that will be used for the production system. However, the reality is much different. For cost reasons, the system used for the load test is rarely identical to the one used for live operation.

The following scenario comes closest to meeting the requirement for providing identical systems, and occurs when an implementation project is accompanied by performance tests at an early stage. You can begin carrying out the first tests once the first transactions have been completed and can be combined into scenarios that make sense. In this case, for instance, you can carry out tests on the future live system during a rollout project until just before the actual go-live.

Load test accompanying the implementation

> **Warning!**
>
> In no case should you carry out a performance test in the production system after the go-live, because the following can happen:
>
> ▶ The system can be impeded and eventually fail.
> ▶ Created and updated data can be removed only with great difficulty from the production system later on, and possibly you won't be able to remove the data completely.

To prepare the test system for the performance test, you must first check the availability and functional integrity of the relevant processes. To do that, you can use process analysis. If the processes are available, make sure the test data is available as well. For this, you can use the data analysis you created during the project preparation phase.

Functional integrity of the test system

In addition to the test system, you may need other systems to generate the load. Note, however, that these requirements can vary from tool to tool. Further information is available in Chapter 11, *SAP LoadRunner by HP*.

The installation of the test tool within the IT infrastructure of a customer can entail a great deal of synchronization work. You should therefore include a corresponding time buffer in your schedule. In any case, you should consult with expert personnel regarding the tool you want to use.

Creating the test scripts

The final step involved in providing the system consists of creating the test scripts. Again, the exact method depends on the tool being used. After all, this is often done by recording a transaction and linking it to the test data with parameterization. This recording process is similar to the process of using a macro recorder. In this context, you must consider the time needed by the tester to get familiar with the load test tools. On top of this, the solution of complex scenarios requires a high degree of expertise in the use of the tool. For this reason, it is useful to have a tool specialist record the test scripts.

10.5.2 Single-User Test

The first test run should be a single-user test. To set it up, you should execute all identified processes both manually and using the load test tool, based on the simulation of only one active user. The single-user test first ensures the functional integrity of the test system and test scripts. The test data is checked by taking samples. In this process, the first problems may be uncovered because the system used for the performance test usually does not correspond to the consolidation system on which the functional tests have been carried out. Once the single-user tests have been completed, you have made sure that all test scripts can be executed correctly and that the test data is consistent.

Individual analysis of process performance

A first analysis of the process performance has already been carried out during the single-user test. Although the result doesn't tell you much about the data throughput, it identifies response-time problems with particularly slow processes. For this reason, individual analysis of the process performance must be carried out. This analysis records the response time for each process step with an otherwise unloaded system.

If necessary, you should make adjustments to specific transactions before the next phase starts, in order to avoid further performance problems. If that is the case, you must once again verify the modification in an individual analysis before you can continue with the next step.

10.5.3 Multi-User Tests

The next step consists of the simulation of a few concurrent users. As a rule of thumb, you should start with the simulation of approximately 20% of the number of users that has been forecast for the maximum load. If this test is successful, increase the load step by step. It is a good idea to increase the load by 20% in each step, but you can also use larger steps at the beginning if the first test with 20% provides satisfying results. You must carry out the load test up to and including the forecast maximum load.

Gradual load increase

The gradual increase of the system load allows you to determine the scalability. You can thus identify slow processes and accelerate them by making adjustments to the system.

Poor performance of transactions is often caused by the following problems.

▶ **Poorly formulated SQL statements**
If the database is the limiting factor, this might be caused by a poorly formulated SQL command. Among other things, you should check the sequence of complex `JOIN` clauses.

▶ **Missing database indices**
High database load and poor response times can also be caused by the lack of indices on tables.

▶ **Unresolved data locks**
If you find that your system has very poor response times although the workload is low, it might be that a data lock has not been resolved. In that case, you should check the locks that have been set.

▶ **Errors in the system infrastructure**
Incorrectly configured network adapters can also be at fault for the poor response behavior of a system if they delay the database access.

Of course, there are numerous other and often much less trivial problems. To familiarize yourself with this topic, take a look at the book *SAP Performance Optimization Guide*, Schneider, SAP PRESS, 6th edition 2011).

10.5.4 Result Analysis

Once the performance test run has been completed, you must analyze the results. To this end, the performance values measured must be compared with the requirements from the load profile. If there are no deviations, you can continue with the subsequent test step. If the test goal has been reached (100%), you can carry out the stress test if you choose to.

Optimization step
If some of the requirements are not met, an optimization step must be performed after the result analysis. You must always verify the success of an optimization step by repeating a test run.

10.5.5 Optimization

Based on the results obtained in the load test, the optimization step enables you to identify the system bottleneck and to take the necessary action to optimize it. Optimization measures can include the following activities.

▶ **Extending or reconfiguring the hardware**
If the performance bottlenecks are caused by insufficiently sized hardware, you must either extend specific system components or replace the entire system.

Because undersized hardware is a possibility you must always take into account, you should agree on delivery times for subsequent orders with the hardware provider before the testing activities begin. Your test plan should then provide for a sufficient time after the performance test so that the additional hardware can be made available on time before the go-live phase.

▶ **Adjusting customizing or database settings**
Optimizations outside of the program logic can usually be carried out rather quickly. In this context, the largest part of time is required by the repeated execution of the *test execution → result analysis* sequence after each optimization action.

▶ **Optimizing customer-specific transactions**
If custom developments are identified as non-performing at all during the performance test, they must be returned to development in order to have performance optimized. However, a code review should be

carried out only by experienced developers. SAP Consulting provides this service, which is also tool-based.

A performance test project should never end with an optimization that hasn't been verified. If the test results require adjustments to be made, you must definitely repeat the test after the optimization step. Note that you do not necessarily have to carry out the entire test again. Usually it is enough to repeat the test step that verifies the optimization.

Optimizations must be tested as well!

If, for example, the single-user test was successful but the system failed during the multi-user test at a load of approximately 60% due to insufficient memory in the application server, you can repeat the test with a load of 60% immediately after solving the problem. You then can continue the test with gradual load increases. If, however, the programming has been changed, you should start re-testing at a lower level, such as 40% of the maximum load, after the optimization step. If, in the above example, a poorly programmed transaction rather than insufficient memory was at fault, you should first make sure after optimization that the system can handle 40% of system load before you increase the load to 60%. This way, you can avoid new problems caused by the adjustment of the programming code.

10.6 Performing the Stress Test

If the load test with 100% of the forecast maximum load does not identify any problems, you can be sure that the required performance can be reached in production operations. Thus, the main goal of the load test has been attained. Optionally, you can now carry out another test phase: the stress test.

A stress test is primarily useful for companies that expect growth in the near future. Stress tests are supposed to identify system bottlenecks that occur beyond known load values. The test answers questions such as the following.

When are stress tests useful?

▶ How many additional users can the system handle?

▶ Which is the first component to cause a problem when the system load increases?

▶ Which actions would I have to take in order to enable x additional users to work in the system?

▶ To what extent can the transaction volume grow in the existing configuration before the system falls below the performance goals defined in the load test?

However, you face other issues when performing a stress test. First of all, the license costs for the majority of load test tools are primarily determined by the number of simulated users. This means that a stress test may cause additional license costs.

Moreover, when providing the test data you must make sure that the data quantities made available are sufficient.

Additional findings — The reward for added investments for a stress test shows up in additional findings from this extra system analyses and in additional planning security. You should make use of the existing testing landscape: Never again will you get this information as cost-efficiently as with a stress test immediately after a load test.

10.7   Completing

Report — The final phase of the performance test project consists of creating a final report. This report is usually created by the persons who execute the test (load test coordinator and monitoring expert), and it should be formally approved by the customer. According to SAP Best Practices, the performance test report is divided into the following parts.

▶ Executive Summary

▶ Action Plan

▶ Description of the Test Structure

▶ Description of Test Goals

▶ Documentation of the Test Execution

▶ Lessons learned

10.7.1   Executive Summary

The purpose of the executive summary is to provide a brief description of the essential results of the final report. It should contain the following items.

- Summary of test goals

- Total evaluation of results, Go/No-go recommendation

- Identification and prioritization of problems resolved in load test

- Additional recommended action

10.7.2 Action Plan

The action plan suggests measures to be taken in order to implement the recommended actions. For each measure, the following aspects should be specified.

- **Problem**
  To which problem does the measure refer?

- **Priority**
  What should be the priority of the measure? The different priority levels are:

  - *Very high*: If this action is not taken, the system availability or functional integrity is endangered.

  - *High*: If this action is not taken, the performance goals cannot be attained in various respects.

  - *Medium*: If this action is not taken, the system can be operated although performance goals may be missed in individual cases.

  - *Low*: The action can be taken at a later stage in order to avoid problems the next time the system is extended.

- **Action description**
  A summary of the suggested action; for example, extending the hardware, importing a support package, or analyzing and optimizing a custom development with poor performance.

10.7.3 Description of the Test Structure

Once the summary and action plan have been created, a detailed description of the test execution should follow. The description should contain details of the system landscape and the structure of the test. The main purpose of the test documentation is to describe the test in such a way that it can be reproduced whenever it becomes necessary to repeat it. For this purpose, it is also useful to archive the test scripts.

System landscape

The best way to document the structure of the tested system landscape is to use a graphic. You should document the hardware used in each system as well as the installed software, including its version and patch level. Moreover, the graphic should document the network infrastructure including firewalls and the places at which the load was "injected" into the system.

The load test tool being used should also be mentioned including the associated hardware equipment.

10.7.4 Description of the Test Goals

You can copy the detailed description of the test goals from the process analysis.

10.7.5 Documentation of the Test Execution

The documentation of the test execution makes up the largest part of the final report. It documents the execution of the different load levels (number of simulated users) and lists different performance indicators, such as the CPU utilization, memory use, and response times. This data basis originates from the monitoring of the load test runs and is provided by suitable load test tools.

10.7.6 Lessons Learned

Load tests are often implemented together with the project. If additional iterations of a load test are supposed to be run within the scope of the same project or other projects, we recommended holding a workshop for reviewing the tests.

The goal of this workshop is to challenge the effectiveness and efficiency of the test implementation. In this context, it is particularly important to consider and evaluate the performance test objectively to identify improvement potential and transfer proven procedures to best practices.

10.8   Summary

The importance of performance tests is often underestimated. Performance tests capture substantial risks for system availability that cannot be covered by functional tests. In addition, by checking and optimizing the response times these tests ensure that the solution is accepted by the users.

A load test represents the test of a system against the expected maximum load. If a load that exceeds the forecast maximum is purposely used, the test becomes a stress test. A volume test is a test that examines the throughput of (synthetic) mass data.

The assignment of the different project roles represents an important step in the preparation of the performance test. We recommend you carry out this step as early as possible in order to clarify the different responsibilities and to avoid misunderstanding.

A performance test should be carried out in the form of a project. You can gear the project planning towards the project outline provided here, which subdivides the performance test into the four phases of *planning*, *performing the load test*, (optionally) *performing the stress test*, and *completing*.

A performance test project starts with the analysis of the processes. To do that, you should use the five most frequently used processes as well as the five most important processes, which add up to a maximum of 10 processes.

To identify and describe these processes, you should either use statistical data from a legacy system or carry out the analysis manually based on the organizational model.

The process analysis involves the following activities.

▶ Identification and prioritization of the relevant processes
▶ Creation of a load forecast for relevant processes
▶ Definition of formal performance goals

The data analysis involves the following activities.

▶ Determining data structures

- ▸ Specifying the test data creation
- ▸ Verifying the test data (quality and quantity)

The final step of the test preparation consists of selecting an appropriate test tool.

Project execution starts with the provision of data and the system. Keep in mind that because of the large number of test cases to be carried out, a performance test also requires a corresponding quantity of test data.

The actual execution of the tests begins with a single-user test followed by a multi-user test in which the system load is gradually increased. The execution of the test is then followed by a result analysis and, if necessary, an optimization phase. The *execution* → *analysis* → *optimization* cycle represents an iterative process that may have to be run through several times.

After a load test, you can choose to carry out a stress test in order to obtain additional information on the limits of the system as a basis for future investment plans.

The load test project concludes with the creation of the final report. The document can be regarded as the counterpart to the load profile and should be formally approved. It is useful to create the performance test report according to a firmly defined schema in order to ensure the repeatability and transparency of the tests. A consistently used control loop helps to challenge and improve the currently selected procedures.

SAP and HP have teamed up to jointly offer the SAP LoadRunner by HP and SAP Performance Center by HP applications, both of which provide extensive support to companies that wish to execute and analyze performance tests. SAP LoadRunner by HP creates a system load through automated user interactions whereby hundreds or even thousands of simultaneous user accesses can be simulated. Different protocols enable end-to-end business processes to be recorded in a heterogeneous environment. Such business processes are executed on different systems or user interfaces. SAP Performance Center by HP provides advanced functions for enterprisewide coordination of load test activities.

11   SAP LoadRunner by HP

SAP LoadRunner by HP is a comprehensive solution for executing performance tests on different platforms. Consequently, the performance and scalability of end-to-end business processes can be checked and optimized, whether they are executed on SAP or non-SAP systems. This application is jointly offered by SAP and HP and is available from SAP as a price-list component. The licensing model for the software is primarily based on the number of virtual users used in the load test.

SAP LoadRunner by HP can be used to minimize risk in implementation and upgrade projects and to safeguard extensive changes within the system landscape. The methodology for executing a load test, the general project flow, and the SAP LoadRunner by HP architecture used to create a load are largely identical to the approach described in Section 10.1, *Project Outline of a Performance Test*.

Load test architecture

Performance tests executed using SAP LoadRunner by HP are essentially based on user interactions that are recorded and then automated (similarly to test automation). Such scripts are modified for parallel execution and can be executed repeatedly and simultaneously in a load test, thus making it possible to simulate thousands of virtual users who create a corresponding load on the target systems. Because this load can be controlled accurately, you can execute performance tests repeatedly in a tactical manner.

Protocols SAP LoadRunner by HP supports performance tests in many applications through the use of *protocols*. The most commonly used end-user programs in the SAP environment are SAP GUI and a web browser, both of which are predominantly covered by the SAPGUI, Web (HTTP/HTML), and SAP-Web protocols. In addition, several protocols that are not directly relevant to SAP are supported and can be used in addition to the aforementioned protocols in order to facilitate a performance test in heterogeneous system environments. Because SAP LoadRunner by HP is independent of certain platforms, it is possible to test end-to-end business processes across system boundaries.

When creating the load, SAP LoadRunner by HP records response and performance times (for example, response times from the perspective of end users or performance times for individual system components). This tool allows you to create complex analyses on the basis of the test results. For this purpose, SAP LoadRunner by HP provides extensive analysis options that enable load test experts to identify performance bottlenecks.

In addition to a method for creating a load, SAP LoadRunner by HP provides an integrated environment for script development as well as the aforementioned analysis options. Various monitoring values from the application and infrastructure can be integrated directly into the results log of a load test, for example.

Components The following SAP LoadRunner by HP components are used to execute activities within a performance test.

▶ LoadRunner Virtual User Generator

▶ LoadRunner Controller und LoadRunner Agent

▶ LoadRunner Analysis

We will now introduce you to each component.

11.1 LoadRunner Virtual User Generator

In the script development phase, LoadRunner Virtual User Generator (*VuGen* for short) is used to create load test scripts based on established test case descriptions. It runs through the following work steps: *recording, modification,* and *validation*.

First, the required user behavior (for example, executing a business process) is recorded using SAP GUI or the browser. Actions in SAP GUI are recorded in such a way that when the script is executed later the SAP GUI scripting interface in SAP GUI is used to control the user interface remotely. In contrast, only network communication is logged for test cases recorded using the web (HTTP/HTML) protocol. As an alternative to this protocol, it may also be necessary to select the Web(Click and Script) or SAP(Click and Script) protocol, whereby the user actions are fully recorded and can be played again later (in the same way as the SAPGUI protocol).

Script recording

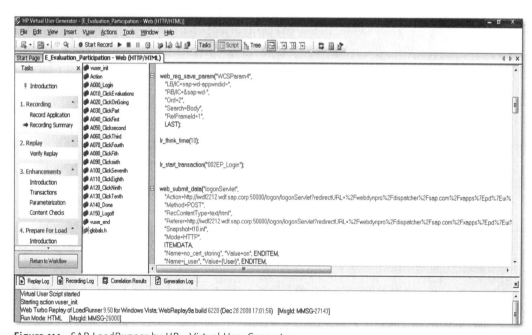

Figure 11.1 SAP LoadRunner by HP—Virtual User Generator

Parameterization   Because user behavior among the users of the system to be tested is not identical in reality, you now need to give the recorded load scripts some more variance. In the case of a "Create purchase order" test case, for example, this could be achieved with varying customers and materials. Here, SAP LoadRunner by HP can select the required testing data, such as a test data file, at random. Another variance can be implemented by incorporating central user management into the test. For example, you can assign varying user IDs to virtual users. This can also be achieved by reading the relevant data from a file. To avoid overlaps, you should choose the "unique" selection type over the "random" selection type when selecting data, so that each test data record is used by one virtual user only.

Content check   To ensure that the scripts will work correctly, the content of the elements controlled by the script must be checked to ensure that it is correct. SAP LoadRunner by HP provides various commands for this, including the `web_reg_find` and `sapgui_is_object_available` functions.

Time measurement and think times   The scripts themselves can be edited in the programming language C. Together with an extensive library of commands, it is possible to influence and if necessary correct script behavior.

Once you have ensured that the script reflects the behavior of an end user, you can set measuring points for response-time measurement, if this has not been done yet. The relevant commands are `lr_start_transaction` and `lr_end_transaction`. You can also insert think times and wait times in order to map, for example, navigation operations and breaks taken by a real user. The relevant command here is `lr_think_time`.

Comparing SAP GUI with browser-based load tests   There is one central difference between the way in which performance tests are executed in SAP GUI-based applications and in browser-based applications. While scripts for SAP GUI-based scenarios directly access the user interface installed on the client side and control it remotely, this detour is not necessary for browser-based applications.

When automating web-based applications that handle end users via a browser, only the HTTP requests recorded when creating a script are transferred directly to the application to be tested (see Figure 11.2). You can then play the recorded user interaction without a detour via the browser (see Figure 11.3). From the application's perspective, there is no difference between this procedure and the way in which a real user interacts with a browser. Another advantage of this procedure is that the hardware requirements of the load generators are relatively small even if there are many virtual users.

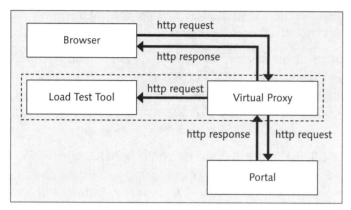

Figure 11.2 Using the Load Test Tool to Record HTTP Requests

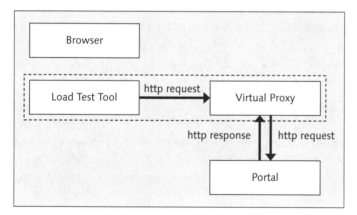

Figure 11.3 Playing the Scripts — No Browser Involvement

For this reason, you can execute a performance test for a browser-based application with much fewer hardware resources than for a comparable test for an SAP application used via SAP GUI for Windows. This is relevant when testing portal applications (for example, SAP NetWeaver Portal).

Performance test for browser-based applications

The properties of the HTTP protocol are used here. By definition, the protocol is stateless. This means that it can only be used with restrictions for many portal-specific applications, such as a shopping-cart process in a web purchasing site. For this reason, sessions are often used in response to the demand for user-friendliness. These sessions can store user-specific information that is obtained during the interaction with a user. In the aforementioned example, a session could save the content of a shopping cart for each active portal user, for example.

Session IDs   The identification of the sessions and hence the separation of different concurrent users is made possible by using session IDs. These IDs are assigned by the portal and are used to identify the different users. For this purpose, the session IDs are transferred to the portal with each request, either as cookies or as URL extensions.

The resulting challenge in the load test is that the portal assigns a different session ID to each user. In order to correctly handle the session ID in subsequent requests, the load test tool must be able to identify and read an assigned session ID in the reply. For this purpose, SAP LoadRunner by HP provides the option of entering rules during parameterization of the script. Based on these rules, the transferred HTML pages can be searched for character strings in order to extract the relevant ID. The ID can then be used in the subsequent request via a parameter. This ensures that the actions of different virtual users can be clearly separated and consistently handled.

Care when assigning session IDs is vitally important in having the performance test work correctly. If these IDs are handled incorrectly by the load test tool, a portal usually creates a large number of new sessions in a continuous manner. The resulting memory consumption is considerable and will significantly distort system performance, significantly affecting the test result. Therefore, in case of doubt, an experienced script developer should be consulted in order to safeguard the test project.

11.2   LoadRunner Controller and LoadRunner Agent

Executing the test   After recording, processing, and verifying individual scripts, the load test configuration to be tested is transferred to LoadRunner Controller (see Figure 11.4). Here, all basic settings are made centrally, especially those that include assigning the load test scripts to the virtual users and load generators as well determining the test runtime. Furthermore, you can specify numerous optional settings that enable you to accurately control the test run and its analysis. For example, by monitoring the systems involved in the test, you can perform an initial analysis of the load test centrally from the controller at runtime. For this purpose, numerous monitor interfaces and options are available for selection.

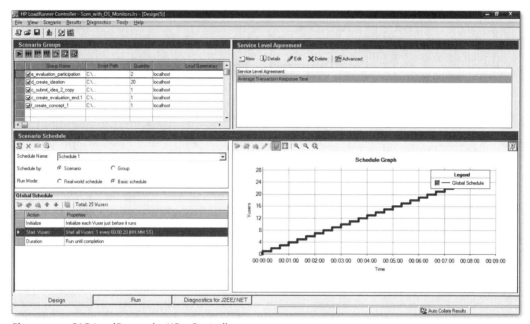

Figure 11.4 SAP LoadRunner by HP—Controller

Because you can save a test configuration defined in this way, you can use the same parameters to re-execute a test at a later time. Once you have defined a testing activity, you can reuse it as often as you wish, with stable results. Similarly, if you re-execute a performance test that has already been executed, this verifies system optimizations that have been made in the meantime, thus making it possible to quantify their success immediately.

Reusability

LoadRunner Agent is used for the actual emulation of virtual users, while LoadRunner Controller is used to control the emulation. It also queries measurement results so that they can be displayed.

Generating a system load

Distributed load
generation A hardware key exclusively links the license for SAP LoadRunner by HP to LoadRunner Controller. A decisive advantage here is that load script development and the results analysis can be installed on other PCs. Because you do not require a separate license key to install SAP LoadRunner by HP agents and load generators, you can create loads in a flexible manner in different locations within the company and then collect the measurement results. Nonetheless, a corresponding license for using load generators must be available in LoadRunner Controller.

11.3   LoadRunner Analysis

Analyzing
measurements You use the LoadRunner Analysis program to perform a detailed analysis of the measurements collected in the load test. This tool is used to prepare and display the copious amounts of data collected during testing, thus facilitating a more in-depth interpretation of this data. In this way, you can derive meaningful results from the test run and diagnose performance bottlenecks and causes of error.

Predefined graphs and reports can be used for the analysis (see Figure 11.5). You can also add custom analyses. Such custom analyses may contain load test measurements that were entered during testing. Graphs can be created using any measurements. Useful examples here include the "response time" in relation to "processor utilization" or the "error frequency" in conjunction with the "number of virtual users," both of which can be displayed in graphs.

Comparing
test results Especially in the case of implementation and upgrade projects with planned changes in infrastructure (for example, hardware renewal or a change in database), we recommend that, prior to the go-live, you test different configurations in a load test and then use the results to identify optimal conditions for the customer. The analysis functions of SAP LoadRunner by HP also support you here by bringing together the results of several load tests and displaying them in a graph. After you have selected or created the graphs, diagrams, and reports, you can create a results report in HTML format or as a Microsoft Word document.

Naturally, use of this function is not limited to implementation and upgrade projects. Before-and-after comparison, in particular, immediately shows the effect of system changes and optimizations. In addition to displaying optimization effects within a load test, you can also use the analysis to minimize risk and assure quality in projects that have continuous development cycles.

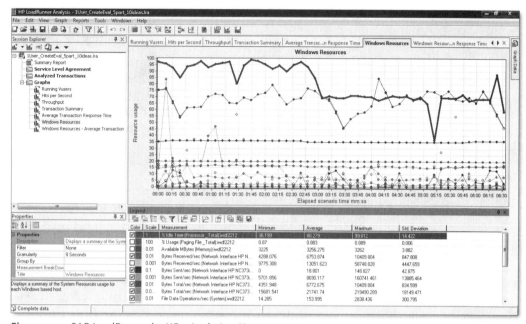

Figure 11.5 SAP LoadRunner by HP—Analyzing Measurements

11.4   SAP Performance Center by HP

SAP LoadRunner by HP is a complete suite of tools that provides extensive options for creating scripts as well as planning, executing, and analyzing load tests and performance tests. The application focuses on implementing individual load test projects.

Groupwide control of load test initiatives

SAP Performance Center by HP is a tool that facilitates the enterprisewide coordination of load tests while using SAP LoadRunner by HP to avoid redundancies and achieve synergy effects.

Multiple load tests and performance tests are often planned in global companies. However, they are mostly restricted to local sites or individual projects. Depending on the level of maturity and the structure of the test organization, this may lead to various problems in real life.

Technical challenges   Technically speaking, individual SAP LoadRunner by HP installations are frequently used and can have different versions, patch levels, and upgrade strategies. Consequently, the SAP LoadRunner by HP versions used may not be compatible with each other. As a result, it may not be possible to reuse work results (for example, the results of load test scripts) across projects; even if it is possible, there are limitations. Frequently, the hardware on which the load tests and performance tests are executed cannot be divided flexibly between different projects.

Licensing aspects   Separate installations have separate licensing agreements. Virtual users (VUsers) can only be used for specific purposes. They cannot be used in other projects, market units, or regions. Consequently, virtual users may need multiple licenses. It is also conceivable that, following the completion of a project, an SAP LoadRunner by HP installation is not used to its full potential and therefore some virtual users are not always used. At the same time, another project performed using a second SAP LoadRunner by HP installation requires additional virtual users as a result of the load test currently being performed. However, this installation would have to be licensed again even though appropriate licenses from other projects would be available elsewhere in the enterprise.

Organizational challenges   Often of a more serious nature, but more difficult to quantify, are costs resulting from organizational deficits associated with failure to standardize load test projects. A key aspect here is a lack of collaboration or inadequate interaction between projects, especially if there is no cross-project instance for planning and coordinating the relevant activities. Because standards are lacking, a much greater effort is required. For example, project elements such as procedures, test concepts, quality standards, reporting requirements, or load test scripts for scenarios that apply elsewhere in the enterprise are developed again for each individual project, thus limiting the cross-project comparability of load test projects. The same applies to personnel and their qualifications. While some projects have dedicated load test experts, other quality assurance initiatives may not be sufficiently prepared for load tests and performance tests.

As is also the case with functional tests, the challenge is to retain an overview of all quality assurance initiatives and to coordinate these accordingly from both a technical and organizational perspective. In order to avoid the negative effects outlined above, a sensible objective is to centralize the load test and performance test activities or, at the very least, to coordinate them centrally. By controlling the testing activities centrally and establishing consistent standards, it is possible to achieve faster speeds, cost savings, and improved quality. Such an organizational unit can be implemented in the form of a test center (see Chapter 13, *Test Center*).

Centralizing load test activities

SAP Performance Center by HP facilitates the central coordination of enterprisewide load test activities and performance test activities that are executed using SAP LoadRunner by HP, thus effectively supporting the activity of a central load test organization or its implementation. The advanced functions for cross-enterprise use address technical, licensing, and organizational issues.

SAP Performance Center by HP

The SAP LoadRunner by HP functions described above are the basis of SAP Performance Center by HP. In addition, the Performance Center provides a web-based platform that can be used to manage and distribute resources and, in particular, licenses for load test activities across the enterprise.

Components of SAP Performance Center by HP

Optionally, HP Diagnostics also facilitates the central monitoring of servers or standard architectures during a load test. SAP R/3, J2EE, and .NET are some of the technologies it supports. Analysis results can be applied to the relevant load test activity or the business processes executed during the tests.

At the heart of SAP Performance Center by HP is the Performance Center application, which provides a central interface for the enterprisewide, cross-project planning and execution of load tests. The Performance Center permits the management of load test projects and their resources. The current resource requirement of each project can also be displayed here. The users assigned to the projects can also plan and execute the load tests themselves via a web interface. Cross-project reporting is also possible.

Central management of load tests

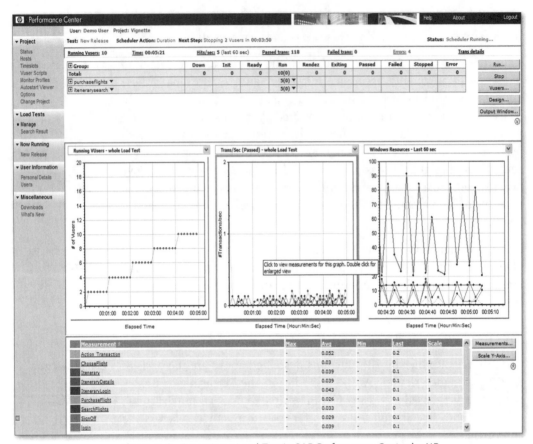

Figure 11.6 Executing a Load Test in SAP Performance Center by HP

License administration

Performance Center supports the central administration of licenses for virtual users. In contrast to SAP LoadRunner by HP, which uses exclusive licenses, these licenses are not limited to one controller. Instead, they can be freely distributed to different controllers (for cross-project use). Licenses can therefore be distributed arbitrarily in order to further optimize the licenses available, for example, in different time zones or regions. A central organizational unit such as a Test Center or Center of Excellence can use these functions to plan and control multi-user performance tests.

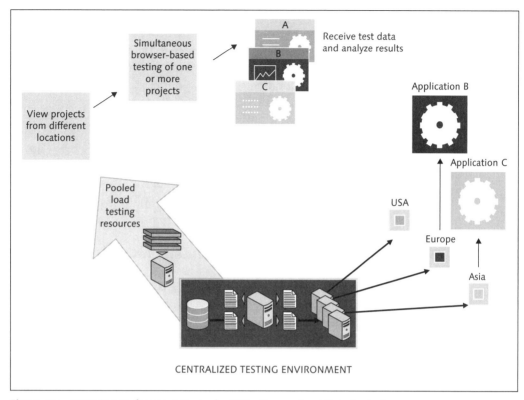

Figure 11.7 Using SAP Performance Center by HP to Manage Load Tests Centrally

11.5   Summary

SAP LoadRunner by HP is a comprehensive suite of tools for executing performance tests in SAP and non-SAP systems. Thanks to the efficient way in which it handles load generation for web-based applications, SAP LoadRunner by HP is also particularly suited to SAP NetWeaver Portal performance tests. When used in implementation and upgrade projects, SAP LoadRunner by HP minimizes the risks that result from adhering to expected or requested system performance. Furthermore, the response times and scalability of a solution (and therefore its perceived quality) can be checked in detail.

Despite all the support provided by the tool, executing a load test requires a considerable amount of tool expertise and know-how with regard to the structure and functionality of the complex system infrastructure. In particular, the handling of dynamic content (for example, session IDs) requires special attention. Similarly, you need to interpret the large volume of data generated during a performance test in order to be able to determine the corresponding actions for optimizing the tested business processes or systems.

The same applies to the structure of a central organization that executes load test projects or provides support in terms of methodology, knowledge, and resources. Here, SAP Performance Center by HP can deliver added value by bundling resources (including licenses) and providing standardization and reuse options.

11.6   Customer Report by HeidelbergCement AG

"SAP Test Management Consulting helped us to achieve our project goals. We executed a load test that not only verified that we could achieve the system performance we required but also showed potential for optimization, thus wholly justifying our investment."

Andreas Heid,
Head of Business Intelligence, HeidelbergCement AG

Heidelberg Cement AG

With approximately 60,000 employees in more than 2,600 locations across five continents and leadership in many international markets, HeidelbergCement is one of the world's leading manufacturers of building materials. The company's core activities include the production and sale of cement and aggregates, the two essential raw materials for concrete. The company supplements its product range with downstream activities such as the production of ready-mixed concrete, concrete products, and concrete elements, as well as other related products and services. The company is active in approximately 50 countries. In 2008, the group achieved total sales of approximately €14 billion.

Founded in 1873, the company was active solely in Southern Germany until the end of the 1960s. It first dipped its toes in international waters at the end of the 1970s through joint ventures and acquisitions. In the 1980s and 1990s, the company's international expansion accelerated. In

2007, HeidelbergCement greatly expanded its market position in North America, Australia, and Great Britain through the acquisition of Hanson, a British manufacturer of building materials. The company is currently expanding its commitments, especially in growth markets such as China, India, Kazakhstan, Georgia, and Russia. HeidelbergCement is geographically divided into the following group areas: Europe, North America, and Asia-Australia-Africa. The company's trading activities belong to the group service area.

In Germany, HeidelbergCement employs approximately 4,000 employees. It sells and distributes cement, ready-mixed concrete, sand and gravel, concrete products, and paving stones as well as sand-lime bricks and lime right across the country.

HeidelbergCement AG is a long-standing customer of SAP and uses various different SAP R/3 and SAP ERP systems worldwide. In addition to its existing systems, it installed SAP NetWeaver Business Warehouse in order to implement an enterprise reporting platform. When it came to implementing a solution for its cross-enterprise financial statements, HeidelbergCement chose SAP SEM, a component of SAP ERP.

SAP system landscape

On the basis of these products, a central consolidation system was implemented for the HeidelbergCement group within the "COMET" project. Consolidated financial statements would now be created centrally for the entire company. The new solution replaces a series of legacy systems and be used as part of an enterprise initiative to harmonize consolidation processes. Thanks to the company's many good experiences with SAP products in the past, implementing new products within the project was a logical step, explains Andreas Heid, Head of Business Intelligence at HeidelbergCement AG. He summarizes the project goal as follows:

Central consolidation system

> "Up to now, we used smaller, decentralized systems for consolidation purposes. The individual locations preconsolidated their financial results before forwarding them to company headquarters for final processing. The new solution will enable us to perform all of these tasks in one system."

Changing over to central consolidation facilitated the worldwide harmonization of consolidation processes and therefore standardized the procedure for consolidated financial statements in all group areas and countries, thus significantly reducing the time and effort required, particularly for quarterly and annual financial statements.

Challenges associated with the central solution

However, renouncing decentralized solutions in favor of a centralized system brought with it a new set of challenges. In particular, the performance requirements of the central consolidation system rose considerably. This was particularly true of the aforementioned quarterly and annual financial statements, which represent a critical period in which the activity within the new system rises significantly. Andreas Heid identified the very high number of reporting units as a major challenge here.

Load test

In order to guarantee stable, high-performing, and smooth production operation in the new system, it was necessary to ensure that this system could withstand the expected load. During the project, this was done by executing a load test. In particular, a check was performed to see whether the system was sufficiently sized for the annual financial statement and the peak loads that would occur during this time. It was also necessary to check the system's hardware and software configurations to see if there was any potential for optimization.

These requirements resulted in a unique objective for the load test. According to Andreas Heid:

> "The load test verifies the initial planning in order to ensure that the system is sufficiently sized to cope with the expected load. Since it would be completely unacceptable for such a critical system to fail, we needed an experienced partner who could confirm that our solution was sufficiently sized and had the best possible configuration for peak load times."

Decision in favor of SAP Test Management Consulting

After carefully examining various offers to execute a load test, HeidelbergCement decided in favor of the load test and performance optimization service provided by SAP Test Management Consulting. According to Andreas Heid, the added value of SAP's offer lay in the extensive knowledge of its consultants who, in addition to having a wealth of practical experience in planning and executing load tests, could also demonstrate comprehensive expert knowledge about SAP NetWeaver Business Warehouse and the SAP SEM-BCS solution. Having direct contact with the product development team was also a deciding factor. In addition, the company expected that any optimization recommendations made by the product manufacturer would be much clearer than those made by another consulting firm. Furthermore, the services provided by SAP's implementation partner for the project, namely the international management and IT consultancy firm Capgemini, came highly recommended. They had already successfully collaborated with the load test experts from SAP Test Management Consulting.

Thomas Schröder, Managing Consultant of Finance Transformation Business Intelligence Solutions at Capgemini Deutschland GmbH, stresses that collaboration made sense for this project:

> *"We had already successfully collaborated with SAP Test Management Consulting on a similar project. Our core competencies are design, implementation, and our in-depth knowledge of financial consolidation and business intelligence solutions. It made sense to leave the actual load test in the hands of the experts at SAP Test Management Consulting."*

At the start of the load test, both partners reached agreement on the project plan and test plan prepared by Capgemini. This initially called for the preparation of a load test within which the key processes to be tested and the test data to be used would be identified. A total of 12 end-to-end test cases were defined for the load test. These represented the processes that are most frequently used in consolidation and would also have the greatest impact on system performance. They included data inputs, uploads, and validations within SAP SEM-BCS, and data imports for planning and reporting in SAP NetWeaver BW via BEx Analyzer Query.

Preparing the load test

The data used by the identified processes was then analyzed and the required consumption data determined. Consequently, it was possible to prepare a test system that would mirror the production system by generating or duplicating the required data, thus ensuring that a sufficient amount of consumption data was available for multiple test runs.

Another step during test preparation was the installation of the load test tool SAP LoadRunner by HP. This tool makes it possible to simulate a defined number of virtual users who create a load on the target system by executing test scripts that were created earlier. One of the strengths of

SAP LoadRunner by HP

this tool is its detailed monitoring and reporting functions, which permit comprehensive load test analysis.

Load profile · A comprehensive load profile was then created from these preparation steps. This mirrored the expected production load and formed the basis for subsequently executing the load test. The load profile showed, among other things, the peak load of individual processes over time, the frequency with which they were executed, and the type and volume of test data used for each process.

Collaboration between load test experts and implementation partners · When creating test cases for the load profile, the consultants from SAP Test Management Consulting and Capgemini collaborated closely with the user departments in HeidelbergCement. The consultants held regular coordination meetings. Within the company, Alexander Ziegler, Senior Business Intelligence Consultant at HeidelbergCement, headed up this project. He regards open communication and flexibility by everyone involved in the project as a key success factor for the scheduled completion of the project:

> *"The SAP and Capgemini consultants worked very well together and ensured that the load test was completed within the required time."*

Executing the load test · Once the preparations were complete, the consultants from SAP Test Management Consulting began to create the test scripts for the end-to-end test cases that had been identified. After assigning the load profile, SAP LoadRunner by HP was used to schedule and execute the finished scripts in different load test runs. Numerous different load scenarios were defined in the load profile, each of which could be differentiated by the number of users and the activities of the individual users logged on to the system at defined times. Using these specifications, 55 different load test runs were executed in this way, each of which comprised various combinations of the 12 end-to-end test cases, thereby insuring that all conceivable process-flow constellations were considered during a consolidation run.

The way in which the test runs were executed was based on the real-life environment. This was a basic prerequisite for achieving a successful load test with meaningful results. Consequently, all test runs were executed on the hardware of the production system that would be used later. The test runs ranged from initial single-user tests to assess the performance of the business-critical consolidation activities to simulation of the activities of more than 100 reporting units that were in operation simultaneously. The fact that users in local sites could only access the system via a Citrix environment was also taken into consideration.

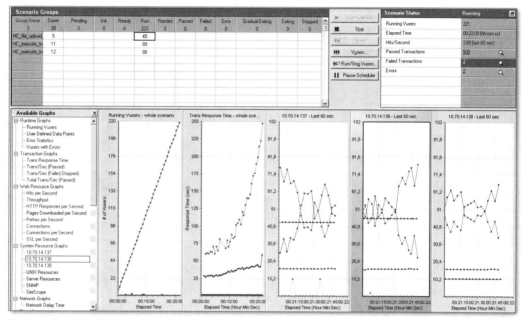

Figure 11.8 Using SAP LoadRunner by HP to Execute the Load Test

SAP Test Management Consulting executed the tests at the customer location. It also used off-site resources that supported the monitoring and analysis of the load test and checked the settings of the load test system. The on-site SAP consultants forwarded the corresponding work packages directly to their remote colleagues. These work packages accompanied the performance test runs and checked the system load via monitoring and analyses by SAP LoadRunner by HP, as well as via central system monitoring by SAP Solution Manager.

The flexible availability of the remote employees made it possible to quickly execute the individual test cycles. Furthermore, an SEM expert from SAP accompanied the testing activities via remote access. This made it possible to analyze and—following consultation with the SEM expert—resolve any errors that occurred in the system or any performance bottlenecks that arose. Alexander Ziegler confirms the efficiency of the collaboration:

Sort: Server

Server Name	No.	Type	PID	Status	Reason	Sem	Start	Error	CPU	Time	User Names	Report	Action	Table
grpsgheid937_HCT_35	0	DIA	8340	Running			Yes			300	VIRTUSR056	CL_RSR_DB_WORKBOOK============CP	Wait for DB lock	RSRWBINDEX
grpsgheid937_HCT_35	1	DIA	5904	Running			Yes			216	VIRTUSR002	CL_RSR_DB_WORKBOOK============CP	Wait for DB lock	RSRWBINDEX
grpsgheid937_HCT_35	2	DIA	5304	Running			Yes			467	VIRTUSR022	CL_RSR_DB_WORKBOOK============CP	Wait for DB lock	RSRWBINDEX
grpsgheid937_HCT_35	3	DIA	6148	Running			Yes			469	VIRTUSR021	CL_RSR_DB_WORKBOOK============CP	Wait for DB lock	RSRWBINDEX
grpsgheid937_HCT_35	4	DIA	8096	Running			Yes			433	VIRTUSR052	CL_RSR_DB_WORKBOOK============CP	Wait for DB lock	RSRWBINDEX
grpsgheid937_HCT_35	5	DIA	8900	Running			Yes			281	VIRTUSR001	CL_RSR_DB_WORKBOOK============CP	Wait for DB lock	RSRWBINDEX
grpsgheid937_HCT_35	6	DIA	5224	Running			Yes			400	VIRTUSR055	CL_RSR_DB_WORKBOOK============CP	Wait for DB lock	RSRWBINDEX
grpsgheid937_HCT_35	7	DIA	9124	Running			Yes			281	VIRTUSR031	CL_RSR_DB_WORKBOOK============CP	Wait for DB lock	RSRWBINDEX
grpsgheid937_HCT_35	8	DIA	3800	Running			Yes			488	VIRTUSR082	CL_RSR_DB_WORKBOOK============CP	Wait for DB lock	RSRWBINDEX
grpsgheid937_HCT_35	9	DIA	8068	Running			Yes			511	VIRTUSR019	CL_RSR_DB_WORKBOOK============CP	Wait for DB lock	RSRWBINDEX
grpsgheid937_HCT_35	10	DIA	7988	Running			Yes			399	VIRTUSR088	CL_RSR_DB_WORKBOOK============CP	Wait for DB lock	RSRWBINDEX
grpsgheid937_HCT_35	11	DIA	4348	Running			Yes			352	VIRTUSR090	CL_RSR_DB_WORKBOOK============CP	Wait for DB lock	RSRWBINDEX
grpsgheid937_HCT_35	12	DIA	1936	Running			Yes			138	VIRTUSR030	CL_RSR_DB_WORKBOOK============CP	Wait for DB lock	RSRWBINDEX
grpsgheid937_HCT_35	13	DIA	600	Running			Yes			539	VIRTUSR018	CL_RSR_DB_WORKBOOK============CP	Wait for DB lock	RSRWBINDEX
grpsgheid937_HCT_35	15	DIA	5576	Running			Yes			512	VIRTUSR048	CL_RSR_DB_WORKBOOK============CP	Wait for DB lock	RSRWBINDEX
grpsgheid937_HCT_35	16	DIA	5812	Running			Yes			129	VIRTUSR060	CL_RSR_DB_WORKBOOK============CP	Wait for DB lock	RSRWBINDEX
grpsgheid937_HCT_35	17	DIA	4840	Running			Yes			349	VIRTUSR057	CL_RSR_DB_WORKBOOK============CP	Wait for DB lock	RSRWBINDEX
grpsgheid937_HCT_35	18	DIA	4360	Running		17	Yes				SAPSYS	<BUFFER SYNC>	Sequential Read	DDLOG
grpsgheid937_HCT_35	19	DIA	5884	Running			Yes			284	VIRTUSR003	CL_RSR_DB_WORKBOOK============CP	Wait for DB lock	RSRWBINDEX
grpsgheid937_HCT_35	20	DIA	3988	Running			Yes			505	VIRTUSR020	CL_RSR_DB_WORKBOOK============CP	Wait for DB lock	RSRWBINDEX
grpsgheid937_HCT_35	21	DIA	3404	Running			Yes			554	VIRTUSR017	CL_RSR_DB_WORKBOOK============CP	Wait for DB lock	RSRWBINDEX
grpsgheid937_HCT_35	22	DIA	5048	Running			Yes			568	VIRTUSR077	CL_RSR_OLAP===================CP	Owning DB lock	RSRWBINDEX
grpsgheid937_HCT_35	23	DIA	5816	Running			Yes			504	VIRTUSR081	CL_RSR_DB_WORKBOOK============CP	Wait for DB lock	RSRWBINDEX

Figure 11.9 Monitoring During the Load Test—Database Lock in the Global Work Process Overview

> *"The collaboration between the on-site and off-site experts from SAP was excellent. Any challenges that arose were always resolved quickly."*

The use of on-site load test experts, experienced Basis consultants for monitoring purposes, and the involvement of product experts laid a solid foundation for executing the load test and ensured that the load test results were analyzed in detail. Furthermore, concrete measures were recommended for resolving or improving problems discovered during the load test.

Load test result

Thanks to the highly experienced load test experts and the effective collaboration between SAP Test Management Consulting, the implementation partner Capgemini, and those HeidelbergCement AG employees involved in the project, the load tests were executed successfully within the required time. Based on the test results, the load test experts from SAP Test Management Consulting suggested a wide range of optimization recommendations in a detailed report.

Alexander Ziegler points out that, based on discussions with management and the user departments, a key objective of the load test was a successful implementation project. Much more important, however, was the knowledge acquired and the way in which optimization was subsequently implemented:

> *"The consultants from SAP Test Management Consulting identified possible bottlenecks and optimization potentials in system performance. All in all, the load test showed us how the consolidation system works under real conditions."*

The optimization suggestions comprised not only changes to the system configuration but also the recommendation to adjust the hardware sizing in order to catch peak loads.

Optimization suggestions

In the data-input area for consolidation, the consultants discovered a critical performance bottleneck under certain conditions. When a large number of parallel users entered data, the hardware used was not able to process all of the data entered. Andreas Heid describes the criticality of this effect:

> *"If the problems in the data input area had not been recognized in good time, this would have lead to major problems, at the very latest, during the first consolidation. The recommendations by SAP Test Management Consulting helped us to proactively solve this problem and therefore avoid the risks associated with such a problem."*

SAP's recommendations for eliminating the bottleneck in the data-input area, including hardware adjustments and changes to the system architecture, were implemented in subsequent months up to the go-live in July 2009. The optimizations implemented after the load test removed the performance bottlenecks that had been identified. During the test, the company verified that the processing time frame currently available for a consolidation run is not critical for HeidelbergCement AG.

Conclusion

It was possible to execute the load test within the pre-assigned time. Looking back, Andreas Heid regards the effective collaboration between HeidelbergCement AG, Capgemini, and SAP Test Management Consulting as well as the clearly defined roles and responsibilities as the main factors in project success from the outset. The load test results verified the expectations of the consolidation solution and paved the way for a smooth go-live. The optimization potentials identified and their subsequent implementation prevented incidents from occurring during production operation. Andreas Heid therefore believes that the company's investment in the load test service has been fully justified. Furthermore, the company fulfilled its expectation that—in addition to planning, executing, and analyzing the load test the advice of the product manufacturer would determine the solutions offered (SEM-BCS) and that the company would benefit from direct contact with the relevant product development teams.

The central consolidation system is now equipped for the next quarterly and annual financial statements. Harmonization and centralization of additional processes in the Logistics environment are planned for the near future.

Lessons learned What can you learn from the experiences of HeidelbergCement AG?

- A load test confirms that a system can withstand the expected production load and minimize performance risks in the production system used later.

- Load tests should always be performed as independent (sub)projects with separate schedules and budgets.

- Roles and responsibilities should be clarified early on because they form the basis for effective collaboration. This is particularly true if different external parties are involved in the project.

- Use the services and experiences (best practices) of SAP Consulting in the load test environment. Direct contact with the manufacturer's product development team gives additional security and makes it possible to achieve product-specific optimization of the tested solution.

11.7 Customer Report by Sanofi-Aventis

> **Note**
>
> This customer report was published in the first edition of this book and its content continues to remain valid. Key company figures have been updated. Apart from this, the report is unchanged.

"Only the performance test opened up the portal to us in its entirety. We learned many things about the system: about the portal itself, the back ends, and the interaction. Some pieces of information were rather surprising."

Thilo Reichenberger
Head, Center of Competence, Sanofi-Aventis

Sanofi-Aventis is the leading pharmaceutical company in Germany and France, the number one in Europe, and the third-biggest drug manufacturer in the world. The company is the world leader in its medical core areas: drugs for the treatment of cardiovascular diseases, thromboses, and the central nervous system, as well as for diabetes and metabolic diseases. Moreover, it specializes in oncology, internal medicine, and vaccines.

Sanofi-Aventis

With 17,000 scientists and 100,000 other employees, the company is active in more than 100 countries,[1] the subsidiaries in Germany and France being the largest Sanofi-Aventis sites with a total of approximately 40,000 employees.

The company's IT area is divided into a functionally structured global unit located in Paris and local units that are part of the regional subsidiaries. In recent years, the IT strategy has significantly changed: Whereas outsourcing used to be the main principle, today the company tries to have projects handled by its own employees, to keep competencies within the company, and to reduce the dependency on external partners.

IT area

The implementation of SAP NetWeaver Portal 6.0 at the beginning of 2004 represented a long-term strategic decision. At that time, Sanofi-Aventis used three legacy systems that had been configured on different platforms and were integrated only to a very small extent. With the implementation of SAP NetWeaver Portal 6.0, these legacy systems were supposed to be replaced by a flexible, powerful, and future-proof platform.

Implementation of SAP NetWeaver Portal

As no previous experience with the new technology was available within the company, extensive tests were scheduled right from the start.

---

1 See *http://www.sanofi-aventis.de*.

In cooperation with the consultants of the SAP Consulting division, a performance test concept was developed that consisted of two phases. In a first step, the company performed a sizing of the system and technical network infrastructure in collaboration with an external service provider. The actual performance test was then carried out in cooperation with the SAP Consulting employees. During this test, the behavior of dialog users was simulated in order to obtain a realistic load profile that could be used as a basis for forecasting the performance behavior of the entire system.

For Thilo Reichenberger, the manager who was responsible for the portal project at Sanofi-Aventis, a performance test had always been out of the question:

"It would be very counterproductive if we had performance problems in our system operations. Just imagine the following: We set up such a strategic platform and it fails ... In light of this scenario, it becomes obvious why our steering committee expected a straightforward answer: Will the architecture provide the required performance or not? To answer this question, a performance test was inevitable!"

Project scope and future-proof platform
The implementation of the portal was a strategic decision. Today the portal serves 18,000 users worldwide, whereas the plan had allowed for 12,000 users at the time of the implementation. If the Employee Self-Service is extended to France in the future, the portal would have to serve another 30,000 employees.

This means that the best interests of the company lay not in meeting the requirements of the portal as cost-efficiently as possible, but rather in providing a future-proof platform that could be adapted to growing requirements. The budget was used to the full although this wouldn't have been necessary for the originally planned 12,000 users. Surplus capacities were deliberately provided for in order to have some room for maneuver when new users and applications would be added in the future. Thilo Reichenberger draws a comparison with cheaper projects:

"I have seen portals that cost only a fraction of our budget. But a portal is a strategic platform that will be further developed and has enormous potential. This requires strategic planning. If a portal project merely meets the requirements of today, its future developments will cause problems."

As the implementation of the new portal represented a strategy-driven technology leap, the functionality was supposed to match that of the legacy systems in the first step. The gradual extension of the portal by integrating new systems was planned for subsequent projects.

This situation facilitated the first step in the creation of a load profile and the definition of the performance goals. The load test team assumed that, at first, the new portal would have to handle the same load of dialog users as the legacy systems. The monitoring tools that existed in the legacy systems could be used to quickly derive a load profile. This load profile was then applied unchanged to the new portal. This procedure guaranteed a much more reliable load profile than the use of estimates.

The definition of the performance goals was carried out in a similar manner. In the first expansion phase, the new platform did not provide any new functionality, which is why Thilo Reichenberger assumed that no tolerance for performance losses would exist. The following guideline was defined for the performance test: We will be happy if we reach at least the performance of the legacy systems in all situations.

The performance test enabled the team to avoid drawing the wrong conclusions because of experience gained with the legacy systems. The monitoring data from the legacy portals provided the team with detailed information on the user behavior. This information contained exact details on the frequency with which certain functions were executed and how many users worked concurrently, for example at a specific time on Fridays.

However, the one thing that was missing was information on the system behavior of the portal caused by those conditions. At first, the limits of the new technology were hardly known, as were the differences to the legacy systems: Which iViews run faster than before; which ones are slower?

During the course of the performance test, it became obvious that the first expansion phase of the portal merely consisted of administrating the back end. The portal contained almost no proprietary, native functionality, so that the existing user load had to be processed almost completely by the back end. It also became clear that the performance of the Employee Self-Service application was primarily restricted by the Internet Transaction Servers (see Figure 11.10).

Load profile and performance goals

Avoiding risks

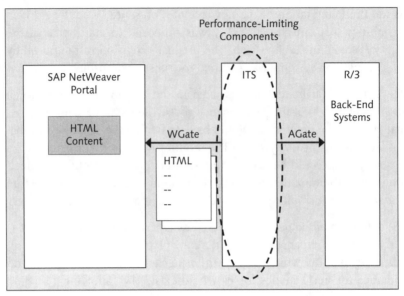

Figure 11.10 ITS Identified as a Performance Bottleneck for the Employee Self-Service

This meant that the portal was sufficiently sized even if the application grew significantly, so that no further investment in additional hardware and administrators was needed in this respect. The following concrete findings could be derived from the performance test.

Findings from the performance test

▸ Planned investments in additional hardware for the portal can be avoided.

▸ The back end should soon be optimized. The ITS, in particular, limits the performance of the Employee Self-Service.

Thilo Reichenberger draws a positive conclusion from this result:

> *"The information about the ITS alone is almost worth 25 days of testing. That's a fast ROI..."*

Load test tool With regard to the test tool to be used, the decision was made in favor of LoadRunner by Mercury Interactive.[2] There were several reasons. SAP Consulting did not provide its own solution that was able to communicate with web interfaces as well. Thus, the only options available

---

2 HP acquired Mercury Interactive in 2006. This product is now available on the market as *HP LoadRunner* or, when sold by SAP, as *SAP LoadRunner by HP.*

were tools such as QALoad by Compuware, and LoadRunner by Mercury Interactive. Because Sanofi-Aventis already owned Mercury LoadRunner licenses, including a number of virtual users, the company decided to use the existing tool. The missing licenses for the additionally required users were purchased for the period of the test project.

The configuration of the testing landscape involved certain obstacles. The first attempts in this direction were made by Sanofi-Aventis employees in the US without any external support. However, they had to overcome numerous problems, from issues regarding the network administration to very simple aspects that had to do with the load test tool.   Test system

The first decision to be made was to specify the location from which the load test should be performed. Executing the test from the office in the US was not a good idea as, first because the available network bandwidth in the office would have become a bottleneck and second because network administrators were concerned that the network within the building would be negatively affected.

A minor difficulty arose during the load test for reports as those were displayed by the system in PDF format. Opening hundreds of PDF files soon became a problem because the system resource requirements of Adobe Acrobat Reader. The laptop that was used as a test system was not able to handle that and became a bottleneck, so that the test results were useless.

It thus became clear to Thilo Reichenberger that external specialists should be consulted in order to carry out the test. The consultants were supported by network and architecture experts of Sanofi-Aventis in-house IT.   Consultants

More important than a performance forecast for the portal implementation project was the need to provide fast feedback to the implementation consultants. This feedback requirement was the main reason the decision to have both the load test and the implementation handled by only *one* provider, which usually cannot be taken for granted. Thilo Reichenberger speaks about the pros and cons of that one-stop-shop concept:

> *"Providing feedback to implementation consulting becomes easier if there's only one party to be provided with feedback. Of course, the downside of this concept is the potential risk that exists if those who implement the system also do the testing. If that is the case, you must*

try to ensure the highest possible degree of objectivity and make sure that the performance is increased by optimization measures and not just made a little nicer. SAP Test Management Consulting represented a good compromise in this respect. They are close enough to implementation consulting so that smooth feedback is guaranteed and, at the same time, they are far enough away so that I could be sure: 'Here they are touching a sore point'."

Project planning and timeframe When the project was planned, a distinction was made between the areas of Human Resources (HR) and Corporate Financials/Industrial Operations (FI/CO and IO). The reason was that the developments for the HR area did not allow for a go-live on the scheduled date. For this reason, two separate go-live dates were scheduled. Figure 11.11 shows that the go-live for the FI/IO departments was scheduled for calendar week (CW) 0, whereas the go-live for HR occurred five weeks later (see Figure 11.13 further below).

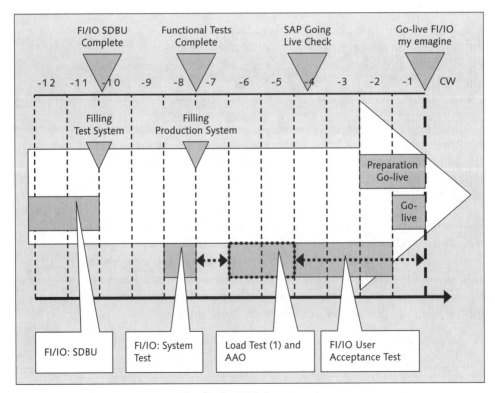

Figure 11.11 Project Plan for the FI/IO Department

Let us first take a look at the planning for the FI/IO department (see Figure 11.11). The development phase (solution definition, design, build, and unit test) was completed approximately 10 weeks before the go-live. After that, the test system was available.

The technical system test for the FI/IO area was carried out eight weeks before the go-live. After that, the production system was available. One week later, that is, in CW –6 and CW –5, the first performance tests were executed. This approach created a period of four weeks prior to the go-live date when several runs through the *test → analysis → optimization* cycle would have been possible, if necessary.

Planning for FI/IO

In the HR area, the developments took place until week –7. For this reason, the system test could not be executed until four weeks before the go-live date of the FI/IO area. Moreover, the SAP GoingLive Check was also carried out in the context of this first system test (see below). This service identified the problem that a specific support package had not been installed, which is why the traffic lights were set to yellow. While the problem was examined, the go-live of the FI/IO area could be carried out without any problem. The team then found out that the missing support package only affected a few parameter settings, but not the entire system. Thus, the traffic lights could be set back to green.

> **SAP GoingLive Check**
>
> The SAP GoingLive Check is a one-day standard service to safeguard the go-live process (see Figure 11.12). The service is part of several selected safeguarding services provided free of charge by SAP Standard Support. The check consists of three parts:
>
> ▶ Analysis
> ▶ Optimization
> ▶ Verification
>
> We recommend carrying out the SAP GoingLive Check for all implementations or extensions of an SAP system that involve a significant extension of the data quantity or the number of users.

The HR system test was followed by a user acceptance test in weeks –3 and –2. After that a break of two weeks followed, caused by the go-live phase in the FI/IO area. The load test for the HR area was carried out three weeks after the go-live of the FI/IO area.

User acceptance test

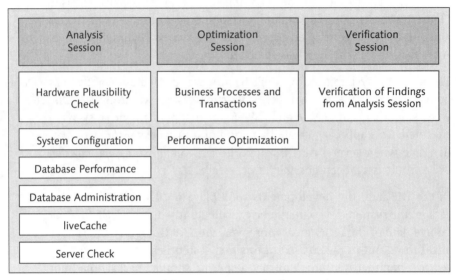

Figure 11.12 Overview of the SAP GoingLive Check

Load test in the
production system

At that time, a decision was made to carry out the second load test in the production system over a weekend. This meant that no additional test system had to be configured. Consequently, distortions caused by differences between the production and test systems could be avoided.

Furthermore, such a procedure requires special care so that the live operations are not affected by the performance test. The fact that the test was scheduled for a weekend took care of that. In addition, only the HR area was tested, which hadn't gone live yet at the time. Thus, it was impossible for test data to be inadvertently transferred to live operation.

This plan provided for two additional weeks between the second load test and the go-live of the HR area. Of course, it depends on the application to be tested to decide how much available time is useful in such a case. Thilo Reichenberger summarizes his impressions:

"If your solution is close to the standard version, you often have to reset a parameter or change a path if a problem occurs. This can be done on the side, as it were. However, many portals are integrated with custom developments. And those developments are usually tested consistently

*in a performance test. If performance bottlenecks arise, you must get
to grips with Java or ABAP code. In that case, two weeks of buffer as a
period for making corrections are definitely not enough."*

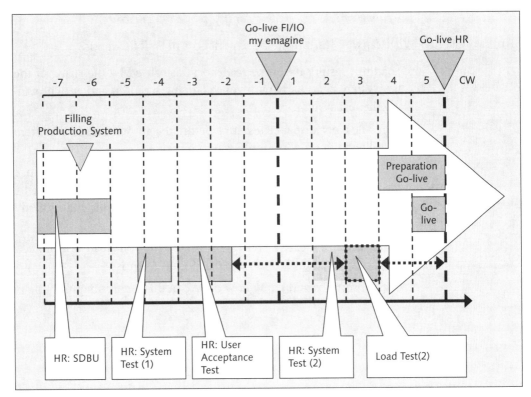

Figure 11.13 Project Plan for the HR Area

Conclusion

The portal went live in two steps within the scheduled period and budget, not least thanks to the performance tests. Today, SAP NetWeaver Portal acts as a reliable, high-performance, and above all strategic platform and will be gradually extended as planned. But despite the very positive project completion, Thilo Reichenberger still sees potential for optimization, particularly with regard to the technical aspects of the performance test:

"It was not at all easy to get the licenses for LoadRunner and use them. The installation of the test environment required some know-how too. All this only worked because both the SAP Consulting and Sanofi-Aventis employees were very involved. Today I would start earlier with the plan creation, especially regarding the test architecture."

Lessons learned | What can you learn from the experiences of Sanofi-Aventis?

- ▶ Load test results are prone to distortions caused by the sizing of the test system. Start early with your planning activities and with providing the test system.

- ▶ Schedule a performance test long before the go-live date so that there is still enough time for optimization measures.

- ▶ Act with caution about drawing conclusions based on experience made with legacy systems: The user behavior (load profile) can be transferred without a problem, but the system behavior will certainly be much different!

- ▶ If you want to create a concrete schedule for your load test project, you can base your plans on those of Sanofi-Aventis.

- ▶ Use the services and know-how of SAP in this environment.

Finding and identifying performance problems is one of the most demanding tasks within a performance test project. The goal of monitoring activities is to pin down the symptoms of insufficient system performance to such an extent that other experts can be consulted for more in-depth analyses and effective problem solving.

12   Monitoring a Performance Test

The goal of performance tests is to verify the defined performance goals: acceptable overall load behavior, on-time background processing, and response times that can be tolerated by the end users. To achieve this goal, the SAP system provides you with a number of effective monitors.

This chapter is not intended as a comprehensive treatise on the performance analysis and optimization of an SAP system. If you want to get more detailed information on this topic, we recommend the books *SAP Performance Optimization Guide* (Schneider, SAP PRESS, 6th edition 2011) and *ABAP Performance Tuning* (Gahm, SAP PRESS 2009). A description of using SAP Solution Manager for performance analysis in system landscapes with multiple systems is available in the SAP PRESS Essentials *Performing End-to-End Root Cause Analysis Using SAP Solution Manager* (Klöffer/Thier, SAP PRESS 2008). The goal of this chapter is rather to enable you to narrow down an identified performance problem in such a way that you can bring in an expert for further analysis and troubleshooting.

The following sections first describe a sample process in to follow in case performance problems occur. In this context we'd like to point out that the search for performance problems is a process that's barely standardized and requires a high degree of experience and intuition. The process described here is based on experience and should be regarded only as one possible way to reach the goal. In any case, it makes a great deal of sense to assign the monitoring role within the performance test project to

Experience and intuition

an experienced person whose know-how is ideally complemented with technical expertise about the solution to be tested. This concentration of knowledge makes it possible to deliver optimization recommendations for the configuration of the SAP application being used.

The description of the sample process for analyzing performance problems is followed by descriptions of the individual monitoring transactions.

12.1 Sample Process In Case Performance Problems Occur

The execution phase of a performance test consists of several steps. Once the data and system have been provided, load generation begins. A single-user test is followed by a multi-user test in several steps until the maximum load has been reached. The load generation is then followed by an analysis phase, in which the collected load creation results are analyzed.

Monitoring concepts
When monitoring the test, you must distinguish between two separate monitoring concepts, both of which are commonly used and which complement each other:

▸ **Real-time monitoring**
Real-time monitoring means the manual monitoring of the running load tests using appropriate monitoring transactions. In addition to monitoring load tests using the CCMS performance monitors, the currently available load test tools also provide options for real-time monitoring and for the collection of performance data. The available options differ from tool to tool. For example, SAP LoadRunner by HP provides correlation of response times, CPU utilization, script errors, and the test progress.

▸ **Retroactive analysis**
The *retroactive analysis* evaluates automatically collected information after the end of test execution. This also includes the (manual) correlation of values from the execution log of the load test tool with the values collected in the real-time monitoring process.

Real-time monitoring fulfills an important function in that it allows you to intervene in the testing process at an early stage in order to directly obtain first-hand information. Moreover, you can use the information provided by the current monitoring process in order to configure the data collection for the more detailed retroactive analysis. This retroactive analysis is used to narrow down performance problems and to provide general information on the system behavior. Table 12.1 provides a list of transactions for real-time monitoring and the retroactive analysis.

Transaction for the current monitoring process	Transaction for the retroactive analysis
AL08—List of all Users Logged on	SM21—Display System Log
SM04—User List	ST04—Database Monitor
SM12—Lock Entry List	ST05—Performance Analysis
SM66—Global Work Process Overview	ST06—OS Monitor
ST05—Performance Analysis	ST22—ABAP Runtime Error
ST06—OS Monitor	STAD—Display Statistical Records
STAD—Display Statistical Records	

Table 12.1 Transactions for Real-Time Monitoring and Retroactive Analysis

Let's take a look at an example in which the runtime monitors of a load test tool indicate unusually long response times. The following actions are taken already during the running load test generation.

Application example

▶ **Use of the operating system analysis of the database server via Transaction ST06 in order to check hardware utilization of the database server (CPU, memory, network, disks)**
The analysis reveals a high degree of CPU utilization of the database server.

▶ **Use of Transaction STAD**
The analysis shows that the database time represents a large portion of the total runtime.

▶ **Recording an SQL trace using Transaction ST05**
To be able to run a more detailed analysis of database access, the database accesses are recorded for a specific period of time.

Once the load generation has finished, these measures are taken for a more exact analysis.

▶ **Database analysis**
The status of the database is checked and analyzed using ST04.

▶ **Program analysis using the SQL trace**
A more detailed analysis of the database access is run using Transaction ST05, based on the traces that have been previously created. An SQL trace is used to identify and analyze the performance-limiting database accesses at SQL level. In this way, you can obtain first information on the cause of the performance problem; for instance, a missing index.

▶ **Further program analysis**
In addition, you can retroactively create traces of individual transactions. This process does not consider the load profile for the individual trace, but it still plays a very important role in the detailed analysis of individual transactions.

12.2 Localization of Performance Bottlenecks

As a classical client-server application, the SAP system consists of three layers (see Figure 12.1): client (usually SAP GUI), application server, and database server. Each of those layers could contain the cause for the long response times we observed.

Analyzing the
load injectors

The first step is to rule out the load injectors as the source of the problem. Because each front end processes only the requests of a single user, the SAP GUI is responsible for performance problems in the least of all cases. For this reason, however, the load test employs load injectors instead of real front ends. These load injectors process several SAP GUI instances simultaneously. In order to guarantee a correct execution of the performance tests, you must make sure that the load injectors themselves won't become the performance bottleneck. For this reason you should first check the utilization of the machines that are used as load injectors. To do that, you must observe the CPU utilization of the load injectors. Single short-term CPU peaks of 100% give no cause for concern; however, plateaus at 100% indicate the overload of an injector. In this case you must reduce the number of virtual users on the injector. In cases of doubt, you must use additional load injectors.

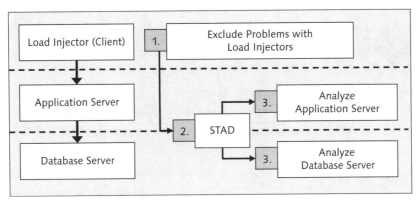

Figure 12.1 Client-Server Layer

If you were able to rule out the load injectors as sources of error, you should use the next step to find out whether the response time is primarily used within the application server or by the database. The most efficient way to do that is to use the SAP Workload Monitor (Transaction STAD, see Section 12.3.6, *STAD: Transaction Analysis*). This transaction enables you to analyze the response time of a transaction separated by database response time and processing time. If the response times of the database exceed an acceptable limit, you should continue with an analysis of the database.

If the response times of the database are acceptable, you can rule out the database server as the performance-limiting component. The next step then consists of analyzing the application server.

If, however, you have identified the database server as the performance-limiting component, you can use a number of additional options for diagnosis. First you should use the database monitor ST04 and, if possible, the operating system monitor ST06 to check whether the hardware of the database server is overloaded. The relevant parameters in this context are primarily the CPU utilization, memory use, and hard disk activity. Transaction ST06 additionally provides a history which enables you to analyze the utilization over several days (see Section 12.3.10, *ST06: OS Monitor*). You can use Transaction SM66 to find out whether only one transaction or all transactions within the determined load profile are affected.

Analysis of the database server

This results in the following decision matrix.

Observation	Symptom	
	Database server overloaded	**Database server not overloaded**
Only one transaction is affected	Assumption: Inefficient or expensive SQL programming → consult with SQL developer	Assumption: Problem with DB locks, indices, or I/O problem → consult with database expert
All transactions are affected	Assumption: Insufficient hardware capacity of the database server → consult with database and Basis expert	Assumption: I/O problem or faulty configuration of the database server → consult with database expert

Table 12.2 Decision Matrix for Analyzing the Database Server

The matrix described here contains typical suspicious factors and the related recommendations for taking action.

Although this matrix does not provide enough information to locate the cause of the problem or even to remove it entirely, it is often sufficient to identify the right person to contact when a problem occurs.

Analysis of the application server

The analysis of the application server should start with a check for a possible overload of the application server. To do that, you must use the operating system monitor ST06. Then you should try to find out whether the long response times are a general problem of the system; that is, whether all transactions specified in the load profile are affected, or whether it is only one transaction that causes the problem. To do that, you can use Transaction SM66.

If you use the operating system monitor ST06 and find out that the application servers are overloaded, due to a high CPU utilization or insufficient memory, the next actions to be taken are clear. If the problem involves only one transaction, it is very likely that this transaction has been programmed inefficiently. In this case the possible symptoms would be that the largest part of the CPU time or of the memory is occupied by a single transaction. If that is the case, you should involve the development team. However, if the system load is equally generated by several transactions, you can usually solve the problem by adding more hardware in the application servers. Here you should involve employees from SAP Basis and members of the project management team to indicate and discuss an extension of the hardware. If, however, the analysis using ST06 does not indicate any OS-side overload of the application servers, the next steps to be taken are somewhat more complicated. If only one transaction shows longer response times, it may be possible that locks are the cause of the problem. To verify this, you should use Transaction SM12. If the assumption is correct, you should involve the development team.

Observation	Symptom	
	Application server overloaded	**Application server not overloaded**
Only one transaction is affected	Assumption: Inefficient or poorly performing ABAP programming → consult with ABAP developer	Assumption: Problem with locks queues, and the like → consult with development department
All transactions are affected	Assumption: Insufficient hardware capacity of the application server → consult with Basis employees	Many problems possible; for example, network problems, locks, incorrectly configured work processes, or another configuration problem → further investigation required; consult with Basis and IT employees

Table 12.3 Decision Matrix for Analyzing the Application Server

If the performance of all transactions in the load profile is unsatisfactory, there can be several possible causes that you should investigate sequentially.

You can either use appropriate network diagnosis tools or reduce the available bandwidth in order to prove an overload of the network. To do that, you should consult with an expert from the SAP Basis team.

Network diagnosis

When a number of work processes have been configured too small, this typically causes long dispatcher queues for waiting transactions. This can be checked using Transaction SM51. Another possible cause may be incorrect size of the various buffers in the SAP system; in other words, the buffers are too small. Use Transaction ST02 to check the buffers. If you suspect a configuration problem in the application server to be the cause of the trouble, you should definitely consult with an expert from the SAP Basis team.

12.3 Transactions for Technical Monitoring

The following sections describe the transactions introduced in the previous methodological section. The sequence of the descriptions used here is based on the alphabetical order of the technical transaction names.

12.3.1 AL08: List of all Users Logged On

Effectiveness of load balancing

Transaction AL08 provides an overview of the distribution of users across all instances available. You can, for instance, assess the effectiveness of a load balancing process.

Among other things, Transaction AL08 (see Figure 12.2) provides the following options:

▶ Display of the number of test users already logged on

▶ Check whether test users are still logged on but are no longer active, for example between two test runs

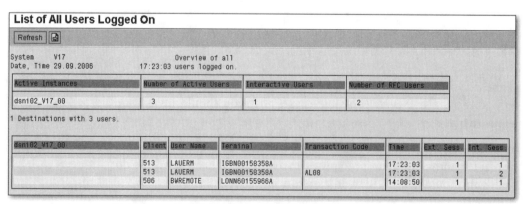

Figure 12.2 List of all Users Logged On

▸ Identification of unwanted users in the system who represent a risk because they distort the test results and must therefore be avoided

As an example, consider a configuration in which the dialog users should not work on the central instance, but on the dialog instances. Transaction AL08 enables you to check during a load test whether the load balancing process regulates this accordingly. It is advisable to update Transaction AL08 regularly during the test, and also to use the transaction before the test begins. Depending on the configuration being used, a load balancing process can itself become a problem during the load test. Usually, this happens if the period of time that elapses between the logon of new users is significantly shorter than the time interval on which the load balancer bases its checks of distribution.

Example

> **Note**
>
> If the application servers are suddenly overloaded, and you cannot explain this on the basis of the test run up so far, you should check whether users foreign to the performance test are active in the system. Unfortunately, it frequently happens in practice that, in spite of early announcements of the performance test, the system is still used for other purposes during the test run. The result is that the performance test becomes distorted and useless.

12.3.2 SM04: User List

Transaction SM04 (User List) provides an overview of logged-on users for an instance as well as of their cumulative memory usage (Figure 12.3). The transaction also allows you to monitor the memory usage of a user in real time. This way, you can easily identify the originator of a memory bottleneck.

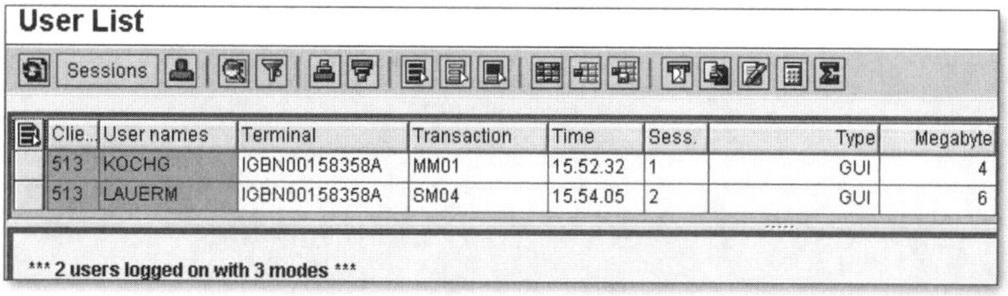

Clie..	User names	Terminal	Transaction	Time	Sess.	Type	Megabyte
513	KOCHG	IGBN00158358A	MM01	15.52.32	1	GUI	4
513	LAUERM	IGBN00158358A	SM04	15.54.05	2	GUI	6

*** 2 users logged on with 3 modes ***

Figure 12.3 Viewing the User List Using Transaction SM04

Modes per user   In addition, you can use a terminal identification in order to find out how many modes are currently in use by a single user, and where exactly in the SAP system that user has logged on (see Figure 12.3). As with Transaction AL08, you can also identify the point in time at which the last end-user interaction with the SAP system occurred.

If the front end being used is UNIX-based, the terminal name matches the display variable of the front-end process. In the case of a Windows front end, the terminal name matches the name of the machine on which the front end was started.

> **Note**
>
> When setting up the test scenarios, make sure that the test users are not arbitrarily distributed across processes or transactions to be tested. Instead, bundle them into groups of users. This makes it easier to identify performance problems with individual transactions or programs.

12.3.3   SM12: Lock Entry List

If you suspect locks in system to be the cause of the problems, you should use Transaction SM12 to check the locks that have been set (see Figure 12.4). If your suspicion turns out to be true, you should consult with the development team.

Cl.	User	Time	Mode	Table	Lock argument
001	C5041571	09.05.2006	X	BCSM10	01200314690000113834920006
001	C5041571	09.05.2006	X	BCSM10	01200314690000114046920006
001	C5072055	02.06.2006	X	BCSM10	01200314690000159636220006
001	C5072055	02.06.2006	X	BCSM10	01200314690000170971020006
001	I802596	02.06.2006	X	BCSM10	01200314690000167047520006
001	I802596	02.06.2006	X	BCSM10	01200314690000167047920006
001	D031457	03:14:37	X	BCSM10	01200252310000059533020006
001	I025366	04:50:12	E	USR04	001I025366
001	C5078764	04:56:42	X	BCSM10	01200615320001708523200006
001	C5078764	04:56:42	X	BCSM10	01200615320001708529200006
001	C5070447	04:57:28	X	BCSM10	01200314690000206757320006
001	C5070447	04:57:28	X	BCSM10	01200314690000207953820006
001	C5070447	04:57:28	X	BCSM10	01200314690000209987120006
001	C5070447	04:57:28	X	BCSM10	01200314690000210164620006
001	C5070447	04:57:28	X	BCSM10	01200314690000211448420006

Figure 12.4   Overview of Locks Set in the Lock Entry List

Transaction SM12 provides an overview of active locks in the system. For   **Active locks**
each lock the following information is displayed:

▸ Client and user that set the lock

▸ Start time of the transaction that set the lock

You should check the lock entry list whenever you think that performance problems are caused by locks that haven't been deactivated. This can happen if a specific transaction has long response times in the application server whose hardware is not overloaded.

In that case, you must check the locks using Transaction SM12. If the locks are indeed the cause of the problem, the locks are probably set on the tables required by the slow process. If so, you should involve the development team.

12.3.4 SM21: System Log

Transaction SM21 (System Log) allows you to analyze system or error messages during or after a test run (see Figure 12.5).

```
                    System Log: Local Analysis of dsni02              2

Date : 01.10.2006

Time    |Type|Nr |Clt|User  |TCode|Priority|Grp|N|Text
06:51:31|DIA |001|000|SAPSYS|     |    O   |EJ |F|Could not find or load print parameters for step 1, job SWWDHEX/06513103
06:51:31|BTC |017|000|SAPSYS|     |    O   |EJ |F|Could not find or load print parameters for step 1, job SWWDHEX/06483104
06:51:31|DIA |001|000|SAPSYS|     |    O   |EJ |F|Could not find or load print parameters for step 1, job SWWDHEX/06513104
06:52:31|DIA |001|000|SAPSYS|     |    O   |EJ |F|Could not find or load print parameters for step 1, job SWWERRE/06523101
06:52:31|DIA |001|000|SAPSYS|     |    O   |EJ |F|Could not find or load print parameters for step 1, job SWWCOND/06523101
06:52:31|BTC |014|000|SAPSYS|     |    O   |EJ |F|Could not find or load print parameters for step 1, job SWWERRE/06313102
06:52:31|BTC |016|000|SAPSYS|     |    O   |EJ |F|Could not find or load print parameters for step 1, job SWWCOND/06223101
06:53:31|BTC |015|000|SAPSYS|     |    ▣   |EB |F|Failed to activate authorization check for user MARSTON
06:53:31|BTC |015|000|SAPSYS|     |    ▨   |D0 |1|Transaction Canceled 00 560 ( MARSTON 506 )
06:53:31|BTC |015|000|SAPSYS|     |    △   |R6 |8|Perform rollback
06:54:31|DIA |001|000|SAPSYS|     |    O   |EJ |F|Could not find or load print parameters for step 1, job SWWDHEX/06543101
06:54:31|DIA |001|000|SAPSYS|     |    O   |EJ |F|Could not find or load print parameters for step 1, job SWWDHEX/06543102
06:54:31|BTC |014|000|SAPSYS|     |    O   |EJ |F|Could not find or load print parameters for step 1, job SWWDHEX/06513101
06:54:31|BTC |016|000|SAPSYS|     |    O   |EJ |F|Could not find or load print parameters for step 1, job SWWDHEX/06513103
06:54:31|DIA |001|000|SAPSYS|     |    O   |EJ |F|Could not find or load print parameters for step 1, job SWWDHEX/06543103
06:54:31|BTC |015|000|SAPSYS|     |    O   |EJ |F|Could not find or load print parameters for step 1, job SWWDHEX/06513102
06:54:31|BTC |017|000|SAPSYS|     |    O   |EJ |F|Could not find or load print parameters for step 1, job SWWDHEX/06513104
```

Figure 12.5 Displaying the Message List in the Syslog

You can use the input fields in the SELECTION group to define a filter   **Filter**
(see Figure 12.6). The most frequently used filters restrict the period in which a message occurred (FROM DATE/TIME and TO DATE/TIME). Other filter criteria refer to the user, the transaction code, and the SAP process.

In order to have a change to the filter settings take effect, you must use the REREAD SYSTEM LOG view.

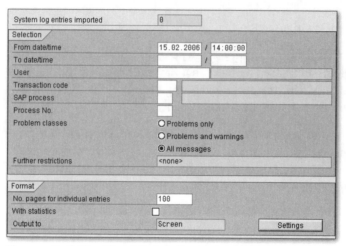

Figure 12.6 Setting Filter Criteria in Transaction SM21

12.3.5 SM66: Global Work Process Overview

Transaction SM66 (Global Work Process Overview) provides you with all the relevant information on the active work processes of all instances in your SAP system. You can use this information to gain early insight into problems with locks and in order to check which transactions are affected by performance problems.

The global work process overview provides the following options:

▶ Monitoring the load of the work processes for all active instances across the entire system

▶ Identifying locks in the database

▶ Determining transactions that cause long system response times

Available information

The following information is displayed in the global work process overview (see Figure 12.7):

▶ **Type of a process**
Dialog process: DIA, update: UPD, enqueue: ENQ, batch: BTC, spool: SPO, V2 update: UP2

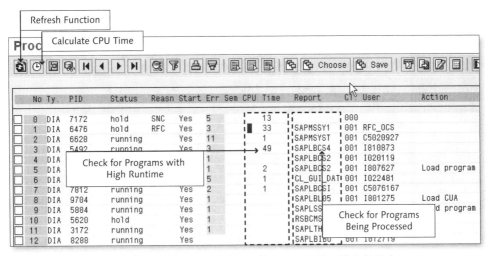

Figure 12.7 Monitoring of Use and Status of Various Processes in the Global Work Process Overview

▶ **Status of the individual application servers**
Here, the HOLD (wait) status is especially important. If a process is in HOLD status, the reason is specified in the subsequent row.

▶ **CPU time and execution time**
Both times provide you with information about how long the process has already been busy with its current task. You can use this information to determine whether an identified performance problem affects only one or several programs.

12.3.6 STAD: Transaction Analysis

In most cases, the call of the transaction analysis (Transaction STAD) represents the first step in narrowing down a performance problem. You can use the transaction analysis to identify programs with long runtimes. Transaction STAD also subdivides the total response time into its CPU time and database time subcomponents and can therefore be used to narrow down causes of long response times on the application servers or the database server (see Figure 12.8).

Identifying problems

You should use Transaction STAD to assign a performance problem to an application server or the database server. Moreover, the transaction provides the first details about the programs affected by the performance problem.

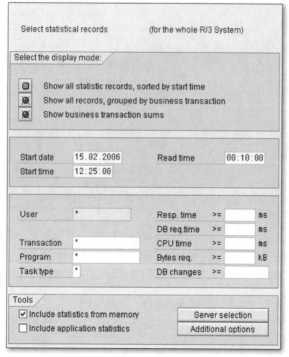

Figure 12.8 Evaluating the Response Time of a Transaction—Split by CPU Time and Database Time

Programs with long response times

Apart from assigning a long response time to an application or database server, you can also use Transaction STAD to obtain an overview of the programs affected by a performance problem. To do that, you must check the program names (NAME column) of the programs with long response times. This way, you can learn whether the performance bottlenecks are caused by one or several programs.

12.3.7 ST02: Overview of SAP Buffers

Transaction ST02 displays an overview of the different buffers of the application server (see Figure 12.9). The buffers and buffer directories need to be large enough to allow reloading of objects without deleting existing objects and those objects that are still needed from the buffer. If the buffers or the buffer directories are too small, the number of reloads from the database increases, which in turn affects system performance.

```
System: dsni02_V17_00                        Tune summary
Date & time of snapshot: 10.01.2006  12:37:22  Startup: 07.01.2006  15:24:58


    SAP memory           Current use    Max. use  In memory  On disk      SAP cursor cache    Hitrat
                          [%]    [kB]      [kB]       [kB]       [kB]                             [%]

  Roll area              0,17     452     1.256     262.144        0       IDs                   99,9
  Paging area            0,03      84    28.440     128.000  134.144       Statements            94,0
  Extended Memory       38,22  74.752   167.936     195.584
  Heap Memory                       0         0


    Call statistics     Hitratio  ABAP/4  Processor                  Database
    794 tables buffered   [%]    Requests   Fails   Total calls  AvgTime[ms] Rows affected

  Select single         99,40  1.161.763  404.934     24.303       0,000     756.829
  Select                75,17    721.615        0    434.387       0,000     409.803
  Insert                          5.224    3.719      5.579       0,000      11.966
  Update                            495      375        556       0,000       1.548
  Delete                          9.148    5.769      9.221       0,000      11.471

  Total                 87,29  1.898.245  414.797    474.046                1.191.617
```

Figure 12.9 Buffer Overview Using ST02 (Lower Part)

As a rule of thumb, two limits must be observed (see Figure 12.10): One way to measure the effectiveness of the buffer sizing is to determine the HIT RATIO. In general, the hit ratio should be at least 98%. SWAPS should not occur. An exception is the program buffer, in which up to 10,000 swaps can be accepted per day.

Limits

```
System: dsni02_V17_00                        Tune summary
Date & time of snapshot: 27.02.2006  13:52:31  Startup: 25.02.2006  15:51:44


   Buffer          Hitratio  Allocated    Free space      Dir. size    Swaps   Database
                     [%]       [kB]      [kB]     [%]      Entries                accesses

Nametab (NTAB)
  Table definition   99,63     7.593     5.826   89,82     35.332         0       4.111
  Field description  99,41    54.546    42.187   79,56     35.332         0       4.207
  Short NTAB         99,45     5.890     5.105   96,27      8.833         0         872
  Initial records    99,80    11.193     9.943   93,75      8.833         0       2.123

Program              99,87   500.000   187.721   38,74    125.000         0      15.060
CUA                  99,94    10.000     8.186   93,37      5.000         0         127
Screen               99,85    20.000    15.991   80,43      2.000         0         413
Calendar            100,00       488       369   77,20        200         0         146
OTR                 100,00     4.096     3.603  100,00      2.000         0           0

Tables
  Generic key        99,85    60.000    40.103   68,95     10.000         0       4.275
  Single record      95,72    20.000    13.399   67,35        500         0      10.776

Export/import        88,42     4.096     3.198   88,76      2.000         0           0
Exp./Imp. SHM        81,48     4.096     3.577   99,28      2.000         0           0
```

Figure 12.10 Buffer Overview Using ST02 (Upper Part)

You should use Transaction ST02 if you suspect an incorrect configuration of the buffer sizes to be the cause of the problem. If that is true, you should consult with an SAP Basis expert in order to optimize the buffer configuration.

Also observe the use of the SAP memory (ROLL AREA, PAGING AREA, and EXTENDED MEMORY; see Figure 12.9). Check whether the majority of the memory used for the page and roll area is located in the shared memory and not on the disk. If necessary, consult with an SAP Basis expert.

12.3.8 ST04: Database Overview

Transaction ST04 provides an overview of the database status (see Figure 12.11). ST04 is a database-specific transaction. The basic appearance has been designed over time for all available databases.

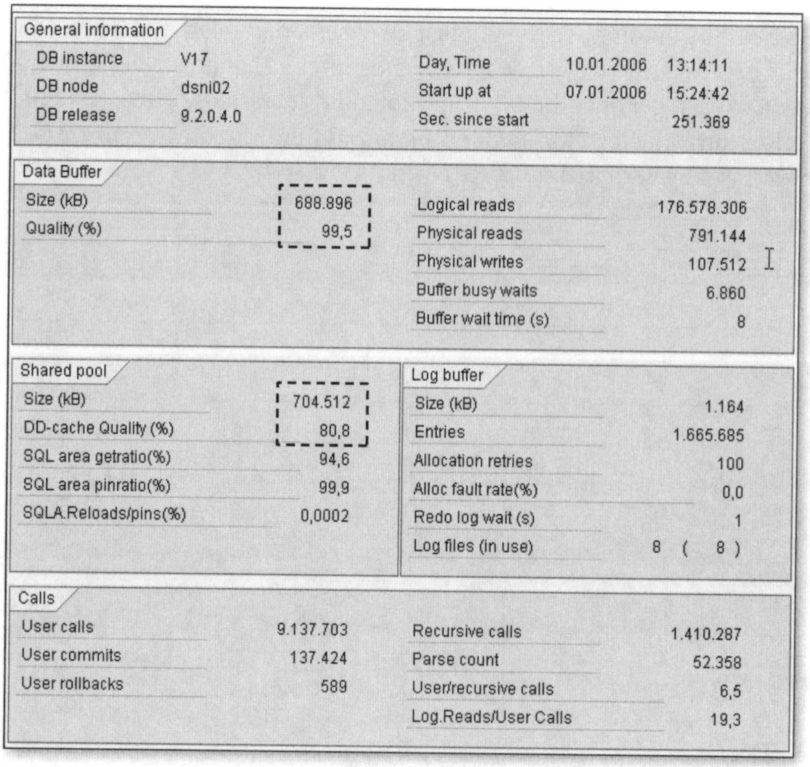

General information				
DB instance	V17	Day, Time	10.01.2006	13:14:11
DB node	dsni02	Start up at	07.01.2006	15:24:42
DB release	9.2.0.4.0	Sec. since start		251.369

Data Buffer			
Size (kB)	688.896	Logical reads	176.578.306
Quality (%)	99,5	Physical reads	791.144
		Physical writes	107.512
		Buffer busy waits	6.860
		Buffer wait time (s)	8

Shared pool		Log buffer	
Size (kB)	704.512	Size (kB)	1.164
DD-cache Quality (%)	80,8	Entries	1.665.685
SQL area getratio(%)	94,6	Allocation retries	100
SQL area pinratio(%)	99,9	Alloc fault rate(%)	0,0
SQLA.Reloads/pins(%)	0,0002	Redo log wait (s)	1
		Log files (in use)	8 (8)

Calls			
User calls	9.137.703	Recursive calls	1.410.287
User commits	137.424	Parse count	52.358
User rollbacks	589	User/recursive calls	6,5
		Log.Reads/User Calls	19,3

Figure 12.11 Database Overview with ST04

The database overview allows you to view the status of the database. Here, details on the cache size and quality of the data buffers and of the shared pool are of particular interest. If these values range below the reference values recommended by the vendor, you should consult with a database expert in order to adjust the configuration. Because these values depend on the database being used, reference values cannot be provided.

Vendor-dependent values

12.3.9 ST05: SQL Trace Analysis

The SQL trace analysis (ST05) enables you to evaluate the communication between the application server and database server. Specifically, you can use the option to jump directly to the generating ABAP code in order to clarify whether an SQL statement with a long runtime was created by a custom development. This question represents an important step towards optimization of database access by the development team. Thus, Transaction ST05 is a valuable utility that allows you to carry out first steps in the analysis of a performance problem on the database server.

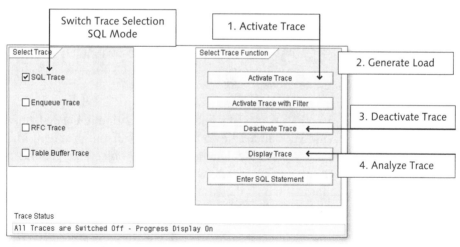

Figure 12.12 Menu for Trace Selection (ST05)

An SQL trace process consists of the following four steps (Figure 12.12):

Process

1. Start SQL trace using ST05

2. Generate load

3. Stop SQL trace

4. Analyze the SQL trace

The analysis of the SQL trace provides a lot of interesting information. First, you can view the response times of the individual queries in the DURATION column (see Figure 12.13), which enables you to identify particularly slow queries. The overview of individual response times usually helps you to determine whether a performance problem exists within the database.

Transaction SU3	Work process no 1	Proc. Type	DIA	Client 513	User	LAUERM

Duration	Obj. name	Op.	Recs.	RC	Statement
10	USR02	REOPEN		0	SELECT WHERE "MANDT" = '513' AND "E
637	USR02	FETCH	1	0	
10	USR21	REOPEN		0	SELECT WHERE "MANDT" = '513' AND "E
442	USR21	FETCH	1	0	
11	TPARAT	REOPEN		0	SELECT WHERE "PARAMID" IN ('WLC' ,
541	TPARAT	FETCH	5	1403	
8	TPARAT	REOPEN		0	SELECT WHERE "PARAMID" IN ('TWB_CH
423	TPARAT	FETCH	5	1403	
6	TPARAT	REOPEN		0	SELECT WHERE "PARAMID" IN ('POK' ,
392	TPARAT	FETCH	3	1403	

Figure 12.13 Analyzing the Response Times of the Database

If that is the case, the analysis of additional information in the SQL trace can then provide your first clue to the location of the problem. The PROGRAM column displays the name of the ABAP object that generated the SQL call. Use this to determine whether all slow queries are caused by the same transaction or if they are distributed across several transactions.

It is also useful to aggregate the trace after SQL statements using the TRACE LIST menu item. This way, similar SQL statements are joined and can be analyzed accordingly.

Jump to the source code For further analysis, you can jump directly from a selected query into the ABAP source code. This is particularly useful if you want to check whether the query in question was generated by a custom development or by a component of the standard SAP version.

12.3.10 ST06: OS Monitor

Transaction ST06 represents a good starting point for the analysis of performance problems. For this purpose, OS-specific performance parameters are queried without using generic tools of the operating system. You can analyze all systems of your instance from every server. To do so, first select the instance that you want to analyze. By default, you first consider the data of the server which you are logged on.

Use Transaction ST06 to check whether the hardware of the individual servers of your SAP system is overloaded. Figure 12.14 shows a selection list. The most important indicators are the CPU use, memory use, and hard disk activity (see Figure 12.15).

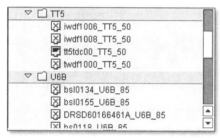

Figure 12.14 Selecting the Application Server

The transaction provides you with information on various resources made available by the operating system. These resources comprise the following:

Start with Transaction ST06

▶ Virtual memory

▶ Physical memory

▶ CPU time

▶ Storage space in the file systems of the hard disks

The OS monitor helps you identify bottlenecks in these resources. For this purpose, it displays a number of performance indicators:

▶ Average load and utilization of the CPU

▶ Memory use

▶ Hard disk use

▶ Network activity

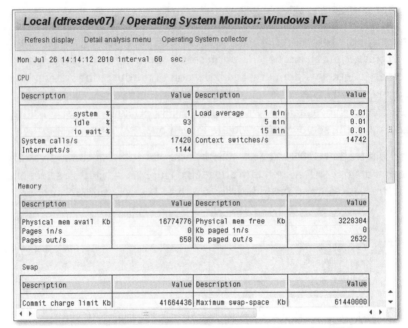

Figure 12.15 Querying the Operating System Status via Transaction ST06

Also use the option to analyze the history of the individual resources. Here, you obtain a comprehensive overview of the resource use in the past.

You should compare the displayed values with the values you've seen in your own experience. CPU use (CPU UTILIZATION USER) should not constantly range above 60% to 70% per CPU. If the range is higher, it is very likely that the application server is overloaded. You should then try to identify the process that causes the load.

Swap memory | The swap memory on the hard disk should not be overtaxed. If the system shows a high activity of virtual memory management (MEMORY PAGES IN/S on Windows systems, MEMORY PAGES OUT/S on UNIX systems), the application server has insufficient memory. As a rule of thumb, not more than 20% of the physical main memory should be swapped per hour (*SAP Performance Optimization Guide*, Schneider, SAP PRESS, 6th edition 2011). The less swap memory is used, the better this is for the system.

Use of the slowest hard disk (DISK WITH HIGHEST RESPONSE TIME value in the RESPONSE TIME group) should remain below 50%. If that is not the case, the hard disk may be overloaded.

The network should not receive any erroneous packets (LAN ERRORS IN/S and LAN ERRORS OUT/S = 0). If this is the case, there can be a problem in the network hardware. In this case, you should consult with your network administrators in order to further narrow down and analyze the cause of the problem. The same goes for packet collisions (LAN COLLISIONS > 0).

Network

12.3.11 ST22: ABAP Runtime Error

Transaction ST22 enables you to analyze shortdumps that have occurred (see Figure 12.16). Shortdumps are frequently caused by:

Causes of shortdumps

▶ ABAP exceptions

▶ Time-out dumps for dialog processes that have a longer runtime than the permitted maximum response time

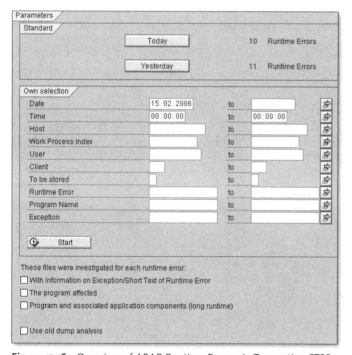

Figure 12.16 Overview of ABAP Runtime Errors via Transaction ST22

You can use Transaction ST22 to identify and display the section of the programming code in which the exception occurred. The transaction provides analysis and correction recommendations, but these are rather generic. For this reason, it is advisable to search for additional information in SAP Service Marketplace.

12.4 Summary

The most demanding step within a performance test consists of narrowing down performance problems and then finding out their causes. To do this, you should use the diagnostic tools provided by your SAP systems.

The first step to take when analyzing a performance problem is to narrow down the components that limit the performance. You must determine whether it is the application, the database, the hardware, or another component that causes the long response times.

Once you have identified the performance-limiting component, you must further isolate the possible cause within the component and finally consult an expert to locate, analyze, and eliminate the cause.

The monitoring tools contained in CCMS provide you with the information needed to narrow down, locate, and analyze performance problems. You can use these tools during a test run in order to monitor the load behavior of the system. In addition, the tools provide monitors for retroactive analysis. No other tool provides more information on the status of your SAP system. All currently available monitoring and load test tools access a subset of this information.

PART IV
Test Center

A Test Center is a centrally organized approach that provides defined services in a testing environment. Such services are suitable for use in all projects and create synergies through standardized structure and process organization. The Test Center supports a high level of application quality through formal correctness and stability in the availability and performance of solutions. The approach can be scaled flexibly and expanded to include outsourcing models in order to achieve additional cost savings. This chapter will introduce you to the wide range of services available with a Test Center as well as the many support options provided by SAP. Finally, a customer report will demonstrate how a Test Center can be implemented and used extensively in an SOA project.

13   Test Center

By having an efficient test organization, you can ensure that any solution you want to test achieves a defined level of quality at a reasonable cost. The level of success achieved with testing depends on many factors, which we have already described in detail in earlier chapters. The following are some basic requirements for setting up a successful Test Center.

Success factors

▶ **The theoretical foundation for organizing testing activities in a structured manner and for executing them efficiently**
This includes not only international standards and training programs such as ITIL or ISTQB (*International Software Testing Qualifications Board*), but also SAP-specific processes and procedures that are documented in the ASAP Roadmaps and Run SAP Roadmap, among other resources. Knowledge of these standards and best practices paves the way for suitably qualified and experienced employees participating in a test (for example, the tester, test coordinator, or test manager).

> ‣ **A controlled testing process that considers company-specific and project-specific requirements (for example, a validated environment)**
> This is closely linked to overall project planning and project management and is typically implemented using a test management tool. Throughout the testing process, numerous procedures are developed and many documents are produced, most of which are based on standards and best practices. These work results and empirical values support the entire life cycle of an application. Often, many elements can be reused in other projects within the enterprise.

> ‣ **Extensive knowledge of test tools**
> In the planning phase, this primarily concerns the tools that you select in order to best support the testing process and ensure that the tools used for technical system tests are optimally adapted to the system landscape used. During testing, knowledge of the test tools used applies specifically to test management, test automation, and performance tests. Having suitably qualified employees is also a critical factor for success here.

Nature of the test   You also need to consider the nature of the testing activities. These might include extensive integration tests when implementing an SAP solution, performance tests in order to safeguard a planned go-live, or continuous regression tests in order to safeguard the operation of a productive solution. Each test type, each test level, and each phase in the application life cycle demands specific procedures. Testing occurs throughout the entire project life cycle. In addition to a concept for testing activities in the implementation and upgrade phases of solutions, there must also be a methodology for testing changes during productive operation; for example, during change management.

These challenges go hand-in-hand with increasingly complex system and project landscapes. This goes beyond the technical aspects, such as knowledge of the applications, user interfaces, and interfaces used within a testing environment. The complexity of the business processes to be tested, most of which are cross-system business processes, also creates challenges in creating case, planning, and executing a test.

Such a complex environment does not forgive weaknesses in the testing process. Unstructured testing activities lead to gaps in test coverage and therefore to quality lapses which inevitably lead to critical situations in production operation. An ineffective testing process can lead to a disproportionate use of resources, an inefficient use of test tools, and low information value in terms of test coverage, test progress, and the success of a test.

With this in mind, the importance of conducting testing activities with a structured testing process quickly becomes apparent. However, the complex parameters also show that the initial stages of setting up a test organization are both resource-intensive and costly. In order to satisfy the above criteria and cope with the aforementioned complexity, enterprises increasingly rely on centralized approaches, which coordinate all testing activities within one central organization that will plan and execute testing activities as a service. Expertise in the testing environment is therefore bundled. The reusability of procedure models, standards, and best practices, the best possible assignment of available resources, and continuous optimization of processes are all fostered here. Synergy effects achieved in this way result in cost savings that can be expanded through outsourcing. In some enterprises, such a Test Center model is also known as a *Test Lab* or *Test Factory*.

Central test organization

13.1   Setting Up a Test Center

With its Test Center approach, SAP offers a service portfolio that provides flexible support when setting up and operating such an organization. The services range from initial planning services to the complete implementation and operation of a Test Center. They include its organizational structure, the necessary processes, tool selection, knowledge transfer, and the setup and maintenance of the technical infrastructure.

Essentially, a Test Center is a separate organizational unit in which software quality assurance activities are centralized. This organization creates a standardized methodical framework for supporting the testing activities of programs and projects within an enterprise. A Test Center can also perform testing tasks while solutions are operating in production, thereby planning and executing regression tests, in particular. The Test Center provides a defined and documented set of services (typically all of the testing activities and test types required by an enterprise), which can be retrieved in a flexible and calculable manner with defined service levels. Centralizing the activities ensures that methods, processes, and standards can be reused. Control cycles can also be run to ensure that they improve on an ongoing basis. In this way, reviews and project debriefings, for example, can be established on the basis of testing activities. Optimization has a direct effect on all test projects that are conducted and on all services that are rendered in the future. The central approach also makes trained personnel available for the services offered by the Test Center or for appropriate training to be given to employees in terms of their roles, the methods used, and the tools deployed. Standardization also permits reduction in setup times. Thanks to the empirical values available, testing activities can be prepared quickly and therefore planned more accurately in terms of the effort required and the implementation periods.

Potential cost savings can also be achieved on the software side. By having a central test organization, an organization can bundle the use of software licenses for test tools that are subject to license fees. This is possible because, for one thing, the number of user licenses required simultaneously can be optimized as a result of centrally planning and controlling testing activities.

All in all, this approach makes it possible to make optimal use of the resources available (personnel, systems, and tool licenses). In addition, specific testing models (for example, out-tasking manual testing activities or test automation) can permanently reduce the workload of employees in the user departments within an enterprise.

In addition to the aforementioned benefits in speed and cost achieved as a result of standardization and specialization effects, establishing a Test Center brings about a lasting improvement in the quality of the testing activities, thanks to controlled and continuously optimized processes. Figure 13.1 provides an overview of the key benefits associated with setting up a Test Center.

Implementing a Test Center

There are different ways to operate a Test Center. It can be wholly operated by an external consulting firm, or it can be fully established and operated by the customer except when external support is requested for specific issues only. The latter approach demands extensive expertise in the field of software quality assurance, detailed knowledge and experience in the areas addressed by a Test Center, and in organizational development.

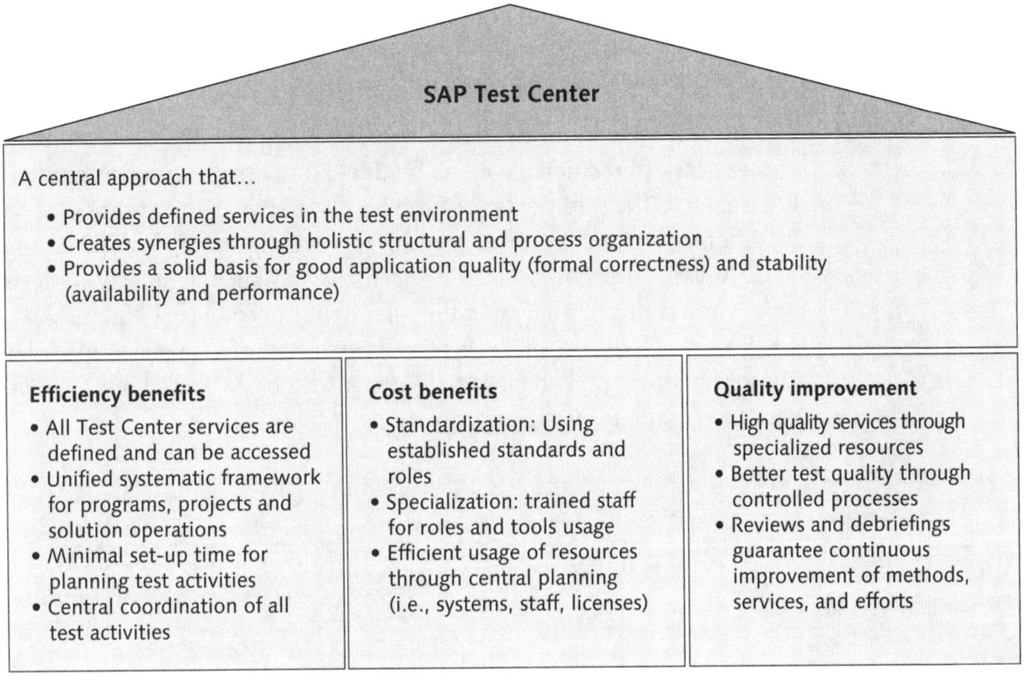

A central approach that...

- Provides defined services in the test environment
- Creates synergies through holistic structural and process organization
- Provides a solid basis for good application quality (formal correctness) and stability (availability and performance)

SAP Test Center

Efficiency benefits	Cost benefits	Quality improvement
• All Test Center services are defined and can be accessed • Unified systematic framework for programs, projects and solution operations • Minimal set-up time for planning test activities • Central coordination of all test activities	• Standardization: Using established standards and roles • Specialization: trained staff for roles and tools usage • Efficient usage of resources through central planning (i.e., systems, staff, licenses)	• High quality services through specialized resources • Better test quality through controlled processes • Reviews and debriefings guarantee continuous improvement of methods, services, and efforts

Figure 13.1 Overview of the SAP Test Center

In either case, SAP Consulting can provide extensive support to the project. SAP Consulting can undertake to fully plan the Test Center approach. Here, organizational key roles are occupied by consultants who understand the necessary basic principles and have a wealth of experience. Alternatively, consulting support can compensate for a lack of in-house know-how, or help to build that expertise.

Support by SAP Consulting

Initially, SAP Consulting provides support when analyzing the customer-specific requirements for a Test Center and its subsequent conceptual design. The setup of the Test Center, its workflows, the roles used, and the range of test services implemented are defined according to specific requirements. Furthermore, a model is developed for collaboration between test management, user departments, and the Test Center.

13.2   Test Center Services

Whether building or supporting a Test Center approach, SAP provides very flexible services that can be used when implementing and operating a Test Center. These can be planned with the customer and then combined to achieve the overarching goal, namely the successful use of a Test Center.

The services offered here cover all fields of competence in software quality assurance. The services range from basic test management support (via test automation) and performance tests to selecting, using, and qualifying tools. Advanced services include specific issues such as managing testing environments or analyzing the quality of the code (see Figure 13.2). For the individual service categories, there are various service modules whose elements range from initial services and basic workshops ("Quick Start") to complete support for the issue at hand.

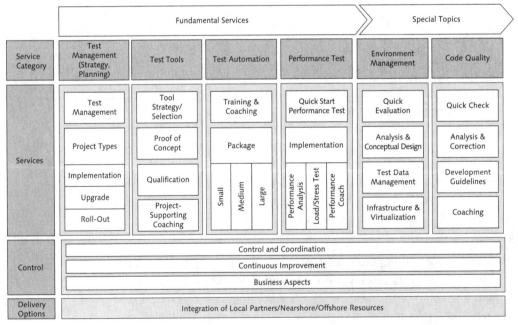

Figure 13.2 Overview of Test Center Services Provided by SAP Consulting

The Test Management area includes consulting support when establishing or enhancing a test strategy and its implementation in the form of a testing process. In this area, support can be requested for implementation, upgrade, and roll-out projects. This includes all test types required within this project type (including future regression tests).

Depending on the range of services, this involves support when setting up and implementing the necessary processes. Such support might include a testing process, defect management, and change management, along with the monitoring and reporting services required in each case. Test Management also involves creating the necessary concepts and standards, such as test strategy, test concept, document templates for test cases, and tester documentation.

The Test Tools service category contains consulting services in the field of tool selection and tool use. Within the context of a diversified tool strategy, for example, SAP offers a workshop that deals with the initial selection of test tools used within the Test Center or during a project. In that workshop, the tools offered by SAP are described as they are used within specific enterprises or in the context of an actual project. The result of a tool selection can be validated using a proof-of-concept exercise whereby initial experiences with the new tool can be gained and assessed. The roll-out of test tools (including the suitable qualification of the key employees) can also be supported, for example, within the context of test automation projects.

Services for the Test Automation area include qualifying measures that range from initial workshops and individual training to fully support coaching measures. Depending on the objective (for example, the required level of automation), test automation can be achieved using standard packages with various services. These include the analysis of the test case descriptions available and the selection of processes or test cases to be automated. After creating and implementing an automation concept, the test cases are created on the basis of the existing test case descriptions. Optional components include training a test automation team in the methods and tools used, and providing support when adjusting test cases after system changes have been made.

Performance test
With the "Quick Start performance test," the Performance Test area also includes an initial workshop that provides information about the basic methods for executing performance tests and presents a roadmap for their implementation in an actual project scenario. SAP Consulting can fully undertake the task of executing testing activities (for example, load tests and stress tests) or these can be controlled as part of the Test Center approach. Additional services include the use of monitoring tools to analyze system performance as well as coaching programs, such as one in which an experienced load test expert supports the performance test team assigned to the customer's Test Center.

Enhancement options
In addition to the aforementioned basic service categories and their services, other categories dedicated to supporting and implementing specific topics are available. These include management of testing environments (including test data management) or implementation and operation of the required test infrastructure (including the application to be tested, if necessary). The range of services provided by a Test Center can also include the setup and maintenance of test systems. Virtualizing non-production systems and selectively migrating test data (for example, using SAP Test Data Migration Server—SAP TDMS) can actively help reduce costs.

Another service category includes the analysis and optimization of program code. This can be offered as a consulting service, in the form of coaching, or the implementation of development guidelines by SAP Consulting. Particularly in the case of projects that have a great deal of custom code, it is extremely useful to deploy this service either as a support service or, if necessary, while performing quality assurance on the code. This service has proven to be very successful in real life.

Of course, the services of the customer-specific Test Center are defined individually and can be extended beyond the range of services outlined here. If software quality is measured in terms of performance and error-free operation or fast error analysis during production operation, the option of managing a Test Center can also be addressed. As part of its advanced services, SAP Consulting can also provide support here in the form of appropriate consulting modules.

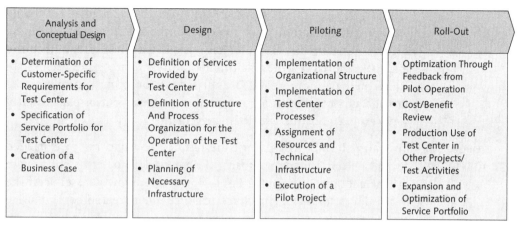

Figure 13.3 Implementing a Test Center

Typically, a phased model is used to fully set up a Test Center with the support of SAP Consulting (see Figure 13.3). The customer-specific requirements for the test organization are defined in the analysis and conceptual design phase. These are based on an earlier testing procedure, which was the basis for developing a test strategy for the Test Center model. In the subsequent Design phase, the required services and the steps needed to set up the Test Center are defined in a roadmap, which can be used as a guide for further implementation from now on. This also includes the organizational setup of a Test Center (for example, planning the necessary infrastructure). It also forms the basis for estimating the effort required for the entire implementation. Alternatively, these services can be performed as independent consulting services. During planning, a pilot project for first-time use of the Test Center is also identified.

Implementation support by SAP Consulting

The previously defined organizational structure and processes of the Test Center, the resources, along with the technical infrastructure, are then set up in the subsequent Pilot phase. The pilot project is performed using the procedures and tools implemented here. Once it has been successfully completed, the Test Center is optimized on the basis of the findings from the pilot operation. In the subsequent Roll-Out phase or the go-live of the Test Center, the services of the Test Center are used in additional projects. The service portfolio is continuously expanded and optimized.

If at first the Test Center is primarily operated by an external consulting partner, a medium-term goal should be for the customer to take over the organizational unit as soon as it has reached a defined level of maturity and the required roles for controlling the Test Center have been established on the customer side. Of course, SAP Consulting can continue to provide support during the continuous improvement or expansion of services, including the issue of management.

Outsourcing approaches
To achieve further cost savings, the Test Center model can be expanded to include outsourcing approaches. Here, various delivery options are available for operation of the Test Center and for individual services. The basic idea is to always outsource resource-intensive and cost-intensive testing activities to an external provider. SAP Consulting can build a corresponding model with its own nearshore and offshore resources (SAP Global Delivery) and with local consulting partners.

13.3 Summary

A Test Center can be established as a service organization that provides some or all aspects of software quality assurance across all projects in an enterprise. Resources and technical expertise can be bundled together. As a result of centralizing and standardizing testing activities, it is possible to achieve savings goals and even extend them through the use of outsourcing models.

With its flexible service model, SAP Consulting provides extensive support implementing a separate organizational unit for software quality assurance. Here, the services range from selective services to the complete implementation and operation of a Test Center. Moreover, SAP Consulting, in conjunction with SAP Global Delivery, provides support during implementation of outsourcing.

13.4 Customer Report by Deutsche Telekom AG

"Within the scope of the TeSSA project, our accounting processes were centralized in accordance with the Service-Oriented Architecture for business applications. Consistent testing of the individual layers was a prerequisite for project success. This was particularly true for the

Financials environment, because business-critical data was always in operation here and, as a result, testing played a key role. The Test Center that we set up for the duration of the project fully satisfied these requirements. The Test Center not only undertook to design and implement all of the testing activities but it also supported the management of already productive processes through extensive monitoring and reporting. In the TeSSA project, SAP Solution Manager was successfully used for these issues and much more."

Dr. Sascha Dawo,
Project Manager IT

Deutsche Telekom AG is one of the world's leading telecommunications and information technology service companies. It offers its customers a comprehensive range of telecommunications and IT services, including fixed network telephony, broadband internet, cellular mobile telephony as well as Information and Communication Technology solutions (ICT) for business customers.

Deutsche Telekom AG has established itself on the market with the brands T-Home, T-Mobile, and T-Systems. T-Home is aimed at the fast-growing broadband market and comprises all private customer offerings for the home. The voice and data communication services include broadband services such as IPTV offerings. T-Mobile bundles Deutsche Telekom's cellular mobile telephony activities. The T-Mobile International AG unit of Deutsche Telekom is one of the world's leading providers of cellular mobile telephony with more than 110 million customers in Europe and the U.S. Mobile broadband services with innovative voice and data solutions are at the heart of further development. T-Systems, the business customer brand of Deutsche Telekom, provides integrated ICT solutions to multinational groups and approximately 160,000 large and medium-sized enterprises in Germany.

Deutsche Telekom AG, an international group of companies, is represented in approximately 50 countries and employs approximately 235,000 people worldwide. In 2008, the company achieved sales of €61.7 billion. Half of the group's sales were generated outside of Germany. The group is committed to the principles of sustainable development and bases its business operations on economic, social, and ecological criteria. Deutsche

Deutsche
Telekom AG

Telekom AG regularly ranks highly in international sustainability ratings, based on its environmental and social performance.

Telekom Shared Service Accounting (TeSSA)

To harmonize accounting for the core brands T-Home, T-Mobile, T-Systems, and other business units, and to operate it centrally, the Telekom Shared Service Accounting (TeSSA) project was initiated and the new company—Deutsche Telekom Accounting—was founded as part of the project. The goal of the project was to implement modern, efficient accounting in the form of a Shared Service Center. The central service organization became responsible for all accounting throughout the enterprise.

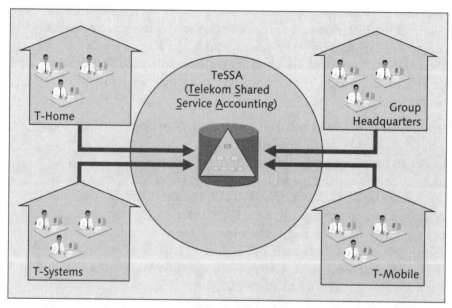

Figure 13.4 Telekom Shared Service Accounting (TeSSA)

Standardizing the processes

One significant benefit associated with centralized accounting in the form of a Shared Service Center was the cost savings that could be achieved by standardizing processes and automating previously manual procedures. As part of the redesign, existing processes were optimized and simplified. Bundling the systems and harmonizing the processes facilitated reorganization of all accounting activities within the organization group and created the conditions for rendering flexible services through a central contact partner (one-stop service).

Approximately 200 employees were involved in the project. The project team came from relevant user departments and contact persons from the IT organization.

Project scope

The implementation of a strategically important project brought with it a number of challenges. Setting up a new organization demanded the harmonization of existing processes or the complete redesign and implementation of centralized processes. This was accompanied by the gradual removal of existing business processes from the field of accounting in the enterprise areas of the various companies within Deutsche Telekom. In addition to the technical requirements, it was also necessary to add a service-oriented architecture to the existing system landscape. This included SAP and non-SAP systems that had to be implemented again within the project.

Challenges

In order to establish a basis for rollouts to various companies within Deutsche Telekom with a flexible, definable range of services, and to also ensure that the services offered to the entire enterprise would have the highest level of flexibility in future, the implementation was, from the very outset, designed using Service-Oriented Architecture (SOA) methods and technologies.

Service-Oriented Architecture (SOA)

Essentially, the functions and services of the project were to be established in SOA so that numerous services could be provided in the form of web services. Applications that implement business processes were to be composed from specific functions. In addition to the high level of flexibility, a significant goal of the architecture concept was to achieve the highest possible reusability of these services in different contexts or business processes.

In real life, this essentially meant a greater decoupling of the business logic from individual back-end systems. The combination of individual services to form process chains and their subsequent use by end users were therefore simplified because the complexity of the IT components (for example, servers, databases, and software in the back-end systems) was hidden behind a standardized architecture with defined interfaces. It was possible to use encapsulated services without any knowledge of the underlying processes in the back-end systems. Technically speaking, portal applications were used to implement the project. The services implemented in the sense of the SOA principle were largely based on web services.

Both the consistent use of the SOA approach and of appropriate web technologies had an immediate effect on the procedure implemented during software development and afterwards when executing testing activities. The software and system architecture resulting from the SOA concept demanded a range of specific procedures for software development and therefore also for planning and executing software tests.

The high level of technical integration for individual components gave rise to challenges in terms of designing and implementing the test strategy. Fundamentally, it was necessary to test developed services, interfaces, and front ends as early as possible while taking account of the usual prototype-oriented development in the web environment. Both test management and testing in this area demanded that the employees involved in the test had extensive experience in the relevant test levels, from developer tests in individual modules and web service tests to complete integration tests. For each test level, it was necessary to consider development specifications within the context of the SOA methodology. This also applied to test automation. On the technical side, automation in the SOA environment demanded test automation tools that facilitated creation of automated test cases for web applications and individual web services. This was accompanied by corresponding specialist knowledge of the test automation experts in the area of web technologies. What was especially needed, however, was a dedicated procedure model that took account of the architecture and development cycles in the field of the SOA application to be implemented. In addition to the functional testing activities, the SOA concept and the strong reference to web technologies also affected the performance test performed on the system; for example, when executing a load test.

The system landscape of the TeSSA project was aligned with the web-based service orientation and involved three-layer system architecture. The users of the business processes implemented by the project connected to the Accounting portal via their front-end computers. This portal was implemented on the basis of SAP NetWeaver Portal. On this portal, the users executed the processes implemented there. Access to the processes and functions offered occurred solely in the form of web pages. Here, users accessed the portal with a browser.

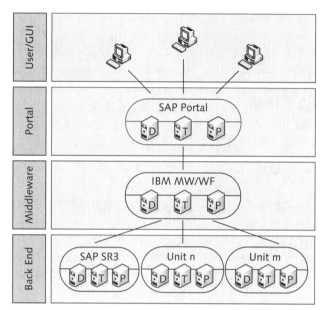

Figure 13.5 Schematic Diagram of the Telekom Shared Service Accounting System Landscape

The portal, in turn, communicated with web services that were implemented on an IBM WebSphere Application Server, which acted as middleware that accessed back-end systems for the purposes of data procurement and posting. These back ends included SAP systems that focused on ERP or HR. Similarly, other systems used within Deutsche Telekom were encapsulated via the services. The middleware communicated with the SAP back end primarily via remote-enabled function module calls (BAPIs).

In addition, an Accounting Interaction Center based on SAP CRM (SAP CRM AIC) was implemented for service management. Moreover, an SAP NetWeaver Business Warehouse was set up for reporting within the Service Center.

Software quality assurance for such a comprehensive and technically very challenging business project required a holistic approach that would support the project in every phase of the life cycle. This was particularly

Test management

true because of its implementation in SOA. Those involved in testing, especially test coordinators, test case designers, and automation experts, had to have specialist knowledge of the SOA approach from the very outset. Therefore, testing was already extremely important in the conceptual design phase. Due to the demand for high quality within the extensive project, the decision to establish a separate "Testing" work package was made early on. SAP Test Management Consulting, in collaboration with T-Systems, was responsible for the conceptual design of this work package. This package was designed as a service provider for the project, covering all activities in the field of software quality assurance within the TeSSA project.

Setting up the Test Center

The Test Center established within the scope of the work package was divided into two activity areas. In the first activity area, the manual test organization planned and coordinated functional testing activities during the project. These were designed in collaboration with the user departments and then, depending on the test level, executed within the Test Center or by the user departments. The second activity area controlled technical system tests, which included various performance tests and load tests as well as low-level testing activities, among other things. This area also automated test cases for use in regression tests, for example. Furthermore, during the course of the testing activities, additional application areas were developed in the field of management and were also assigned to the Test Center for integrated management of the newly implemented solution. In particular, this included business-process-oriented monitoring of the solution landscape as well as the detection of defects in testing activities.

Procedure model

A separate organization for software testing within the project demanded a solid conceptual foundation. Therefore, a separate procedure model based on market standards, best practices, and project experiences was developed for the testing process. The basic testing procedure in the TeSSA project is based on a V model that describes the major development phases as well as the corresponding test phases. The phases of the V model and the related validation steps were defined and adjusted to the project specifications. The requirements and results of the respective phase were then formulated. The entire procedure model was recorded in a cross-project testing manual. The methodology, the definition of individual phases, and the related task packages within the project were presented and coordinated among all those involved.

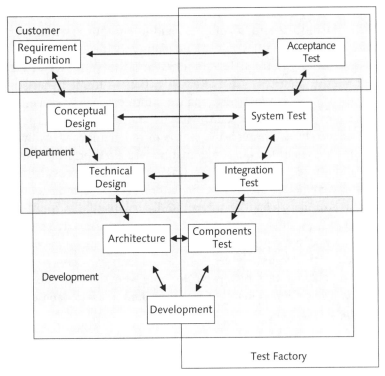

Figure 13.6 V Model with the Test Center Scope

The V model itself represents the basic project phases and related validation steps while serving as an overview of Test Center activity related to the testing process. The left branch of the V model describes the conceptual design of the processes for the Shared Service Center through to their implementation in the project. Detailed roles and responsibilities as well as the documents and work results to be delivered are defined for the individual steps. Figure 13.6 shows the V model for the TeSSA project, including the main participating groups.

The right branch of the V model describes the corresponding test levels. Services in this area are rendered by the Test Center. At the first level, in order to check the quality of the new modules, the Test Center employees execute previously defined end-to-end test cases during the development phase and as part of the developer integration tests. Successful execution of these testing activities was the prerequisite for completing the development phase and therefore for the transition to the check performed by the departments. Here, with support from the Test Center, extensive

Test levels and range of services provided by the Test Center

667

integration tests were performed to check the quality of the entire solution. Such tests also recorded complete end-to-end processes in each case and were supposed to execute all previously defined test scenarios and test cases without errors. Technical system tests were executed in addition to integration tests. Technical system tests included checking the adherence to system key performance indicators (KPIs), executing single user performance tests, and planning and executing load tests and performance tests. Through the efforts of the employees involved in the technical system tests, test automation was also performed. In a final validation stage, an acceptance test was defined, which provided for the formal acceptance of the contract by the respective customers once the previous test phases had been successfully completed. In the steps that needed to be validated within the V model, the respective parties involved, the necessary prerequisites, and the documents and results were defined so that accurately defined requirements and service levels would be available for each test level. Not only were the dependencies between the levels defined here but also the communication and coordination interfaces.

Selecting the test management tool For the global planning, control, and execution of testing activities within the TeSSA project, the use of a test management tool was planned and a requirements catalog created when designing and implementing the testing process. Various subject areas that summarized the main requirements for the functionality of such a tool were identified here.

Basic requirements Essentially, the test management tool was intended to facilitate the entire testing process, including the process of planning testing activities, assigning testers to test cases, and reporting. The flexible management of error messages during testing was also to be an integral part of the tool. It was also necessary to record the testing activities and related documents; for example, specifications and requirements for services and entire business processes, in a structured manner. Ideally this would be done in the context of existing process structures that were modeled using the ARIS tool.

Accessibility and usability The accessibility and usability of the tool were essential criteria here. All project team members in all roles had to be able to access the procedures mapped in the tool and the information defined there at any time. Ideally, different user groups were to have their own access to those functions that are relevant for them. In user management, the access and authorizations of individual users and user groups were to be mapped using a sophisticated authorization concept. Furthermore, tool management was to be independent and only possible by those users who had the necessary authorization. It would be possible to retrieve key functions and documents created during the project in the portal or via a web application.

Another set of criteria described the requirement for document management in the testing environment. In addition to some basic criteria (for example, the central storage of all test cases as well as the documentation for all test scenarios), it was necessary to ensure the standardized recording of all test results and test logs. A key requirement in this context was the versioning and release of those documents relating to the test. For auditing reasons and as a result of the auditing-relevant specification in accordance with the Sarbanes-Oxley Act (SOX), this requirement was given a lot of attention.

Reproducibility

Reporting in the testing environment was another major issue. Extensive reporting of the test status and test run, along with the status of the error messages recorded, was to be possible for all testing activities in the TeSSA project. In addition to the requirement for ad-hoc reporting that displays all relevant information in real time, there were extensive requirements for management reporting. It was also intended that reporting would present the graphical display of aggregated data over the course of time in individual test phases. Consequently, it was possible to display trends, the test progress, and their correlation with error processing so that a forecast of the test run could be done and project risks detected early on. All analyses were also to be available for further processing.

Test reporting

Furthermore, it was necessary to create a subsequent report on the test phases that had occurred. This report contained all details about the test run and therefore served as a document for the respective test phase.

Other recording requirements included potential license and maintenance fees for a tool, the implementation effort, future viability, and added value by other functions.

Deutsche Telekom quickly decided in favor of SAP Solution Manager, which almost fully satisfied the aforementioned requirements and also fulfilled additional requirements in the project environment. The use of SAP's application management solution permitted the use of test management and test automation tools without additional license fees. Application scenarios as well as testing activities could be integrated

SAP Solution Manager

into the management of the entire project life cycle in a logical manner. In this context, a key benefit of SAP Solution Manager was consistent process orientation. In earlier project phases, it was possible to provide all of the project documentation via a business process view known as the Business Blueprint, which was also derived from the process models created using ARIS. Within test management, SAP Solution Manager uses this structure to implement process-oriented testing activities. Here, SAP Solution Manager also permits the use of the test automation tool eCATT (without additional license fees), which permits the immediate integration of test automation scripts into test planning when preparing for testing. In production operation, the system can also be monitored on the basis of the processes documented initially.

Along with the test management and test automation scenarios, additional use cases were identified in this early project phase. In the medium term, these use cases were very significant for the project; for example, the option to implement central business process monitoring for all connected systems. Under the keyword "future viability," additional SAP Solution Manager 7.0 EhP 1 functions were evaluated during the project and then implemented so that significant testing process optimization and resource savings could be achieved. These included the use of BW Reporting.

Test planning and testing The organization that was established in the TeSSA project comprises four areas: general ledger accounting, accounts receivable accounting, accounts payable accounting, and asset accounting. Numerous processes were to be implemented from each of these areas but only one complete process occurs simultaneously for each area. This is also true for testing activities. Tests in the four areas frequently occur in parallel. Here, a comprehensive core process is tested for each area. Within the project, testing activities were planned and executed in accordance with the aforementioned procedure model or the specifications in the test manual. During the project run, the individual work steps and activities were mapped and integrated in SAP Solution Manager or in the Test Workbench.

Central roles in the test Project-specific roles are essential for test planning and testing. In particular, these include a *key accounter* who is the mediator between IT and the user departments and the *test coordinator* who is responsible for all testing activities and therefore the successful implementation of a complete business process test.

Each process area has a key accounter who acts as a central contact person between IT and the user department. The relevant employees have a deep knowledge of the process and also establish contact with the user departments in order to address detailed questions about the process flows and other issues. The key accounters are involved in all decisions in the field of process design and testing activities and must reach final agreement before releasing process-relevant documents.

Key accounter

Within the Test Center, each of the testing activities in the individual accounting areas is controlled by a test coordinator. In the case of complex processes, two coordinators are involved. This role is a central construct of the TeSSA Test Center with a wide range of tasks. The tasks of the test coordinators include controlling the creation of test cases, coordinating test preparation and testing, and continuously monitoring and subsequently reporting testing activities. The test coordinator therefore supports the testing activities for a complete process test throughout its entire life cycle. The procedure used to establish a central contact person who provides end-to-end support for each process has proven itself, according to Ralf van Koll, the Head of the Test Center on the customer side.

Test coordinator

> *"This structure demands a high level of social and technical skills from the test coordinators because continuous communication occurs with all stakeholders. Since our customers have only one contact person for their issues, there is a high level of acceptance for test management."*

In the TeSSA project, the process-oriented planning and execution of testing activities began at the discussion on requirements. Even in this early phase, which involved modeling and specifying the new business processes, the test coordinators were involved and delivered feedback on the pending testing activities. Such input included proposals in relation to criticality and test coverage for individual process steps.

Process-oriented test case creation

During the project, business processes were modeled in ARIS (see Figure 13.7). In the SAP Solution Manager interface provided by the modeling tool, the relevant process information was sent to a project in SAP Solution Manager whereby a Business Blueprint was created. All of this occurred after process modeling was complete. Consequently, it was possible to quickly establish a process structure that would be used in all project phases and numerous work steps. This basic construct was

Creating the Business Blueprint

initially used for the requirements definition and the documentation for the entire TeSSA project.

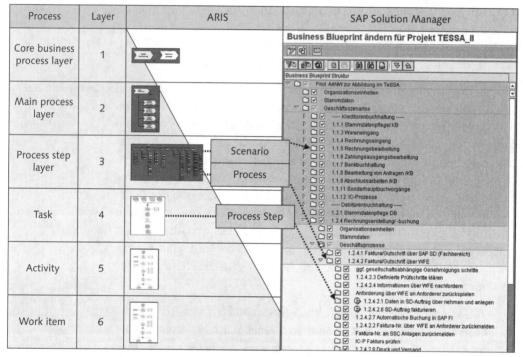

Figure 13.7 Creating the Business Blueprint from ARIS Models in Business Processes

The document management functions of SAP Solution Manager permit the holistic and audit-proof documentation of the project with the Business Blueprint. This also includes the creation of manual and automated test cases for all test phases, from developer tests to complete integration tests.

Roll-out of processes

The Business Blueprint created in this way (including the relevant process documentation and all test cases) served as a template for the roll-out of the TeSSA processes to the individual companies within Deutsche Telekom.

Creating test case documents

Test cases are primarily created by the user departments. Here, the test coordinators or the Test Center employees assigned by these coordinators provided support through specifications and templates for the conceptual design of test cases, methodical approaches, and reviews of test cases that had been created. In addition, the process models defined in ARIS were used as a technical basis for the test cases, thus ensuring that they covered all possible process paths. The possibility of external employees executing test cases during testing was already discussed at the start of the project. Therefore, a fundamental objective when creating test cases was a very high level of detail in order to design these test cases in such a way that they could be understood without requiring any technical knowledge of the relevant process. Accordingly, the test cases were created with extensive textual documentation and screenshots while using a standardized template. This procedure was fully mapped in SAP Solution Manager. The relevant document templates were stored centrally and equipped with a status profile that provides for a review cycle by test coordinators. Therefore, early on, the test coordinator gained an insight into the creation of test cases, assessed their quality, and, if necessary, made adjustments to ensure that the quality of the test cases met the required standard. This also made it possible to provide adequate test data early on. Test coordinators are responsible for the coordination and timely delivery of each test case (in its entirety) for a business process. At the same time, the high demand for test cases justifies subsequent test automation because automation experts do not require further input from the user departments in order to create scripts based on this template.

At the start of the test phase, the coordinators undertook the organizational and system-side preparations for the testing activities. The organizational preparations included scheduling of the test phases as well as the planning and organization of downstream steps such as training the testers and other project team members. On the technical side, it was necessary to ensure the availability of the test systems and to coordinate their preparation; for example, through provision of test users and their authorizations and test data. Selecting the relevant test cases and assigning them to individual testers took place within the Test Workbench in SAP Solution Manager (see Figure 13.8). At time, all of the required test cases were already available and of suitably high quality. In the context of the Business Blueprint, they were used to compose test plans for the relevant business processes in order to facilitate process-oriented testing. In particular, integration tests for processes chains were quickly created in this way. The test cases were then assigned via test packages to the software testers.

Test planning

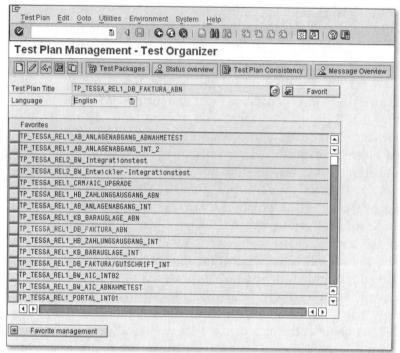

Figure 13.8 Test Plans in the Test Workbench

Testing The manual integration test cases were primarily executed by the project test team. Temporary workers were used who could work on a daily or weekly basis in accordance with the capacity requirement. Such use of external personnel is only possible if the previously created test cases have the aforementioned high level of quality. This is also ensured by the test coordinator. The testers executed the manual test cases in accordance with the test case description, they recorded error messages, and they provided support when reconstructing the effects of an error. Furthermore, the external employees were instrumental in the quality assurance of the test cases or gave feedback on the quality and clarity of the test case descriptions. The procedure for executing tests in this way has proven beneficial. As many as 12 external employees were deployed at peak times; for example, during parallel testing for all accounting areas. The subsequent acceptance tests were executed by employees from the user departments. Successful completion of these testing activities was the prerequisite for releasing the transport of new or changed objects into the production systems.

The testers accessed the tester worklist in SAP Solution Manager, executed the test cases assigned to them, and assigned a status in accordance with the test run. Each test execution was also documented here. The tester documentation served as proof that testing had taken place. Furthermore, it became permanently available in subsequent reporting for verification purposes.

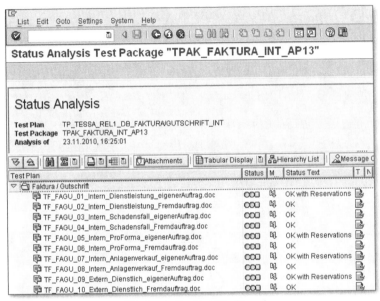

Figure 13.9 Overview of Testing in the Test Workbench

If a defect has been identified, the testers used the Service Desk in SAP Solution Manager (see Figure 13.10) to open a message that was then forwarded to the relevant developer. Contact persons from IT Basis or Development were available during testing. They were involved in the testing activities at an early stage and they reported on the current status of development or troubleshooting in regular status meetings. They also informed the test coordinator of any potential risks that would affect testing.

Error management

Testing was controlled by the test coordinator. In addition to the personnel capacity planning for testers and the assignment of test cases, the execution phase also involved continuous monitoring of the test status as well as the status and criticality of error messages. The monitoring results were discussed with the testers and developers in regular status meetings, and any necessary measures for achieving the test goals were

Monitoring and reporting

implemented or the possible risks communicated to project management. The test coordinator was also responsible for regularly communicating the test status to the relevant project stakeholders, especially project management and the user departments. The coordinator also created the necessary reports for status meetings and mails.

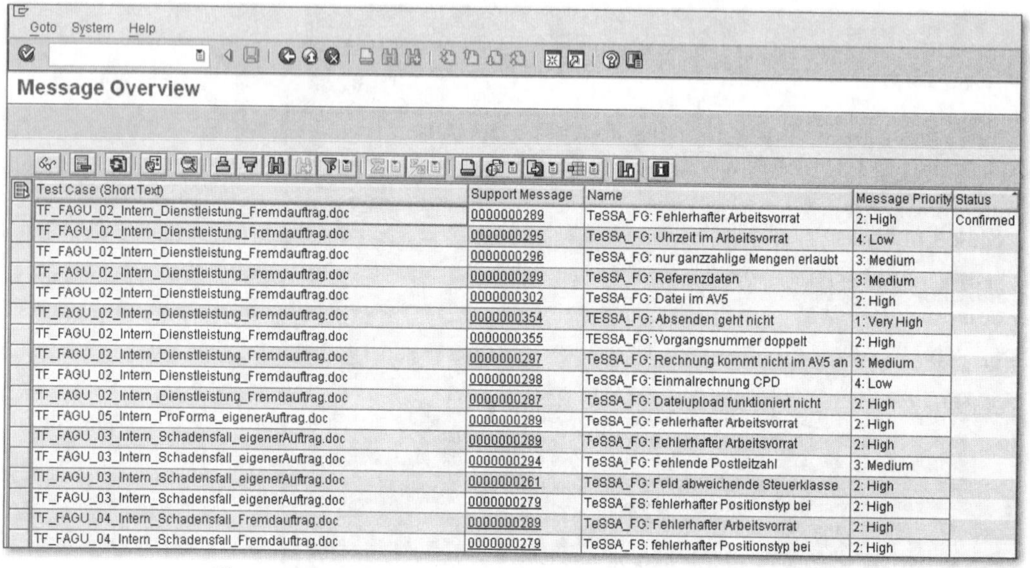

Test Case (Short Text)	Support Message	Name	Message Priority	Status
TF_FAGU_02_Intern_Dienstleistung_Fremdauftrag.doc	0000000289	TeSSA_FG: Fehlerhafter Arbeitsvorrat	2: High	Confirmed
TF_FAGU_02_Intern_Dienstleistung_Fremdauftrag.doc	0000000295	TeSSA_FG: Uhrzeit im Arbeitsvorrat	4: Low	
TF_FAGU_02_Intern_Dienstleistung_Fremdauftrag.doc	0000000296	TeSSA_FG: nur ganzzahlige Mengen erlaubt	3: Medium	
TF_FAGU_02_Intern_Dienstleistung_Fremdauftrag.doc	0000000299	TeSSA_FG: Referenzdaten	3: Medium	
TF_FAGU_02_Intern_Dienstleistung_Fremdauftrag.doc	0000000302	TeSSA_FG: Datei im AV5	2: High	
TF_FAGU_02_Intern_Dienstleistung_Fremdauftrag.doc	0000000354	TESSA_FG: Absenden geht nicht	1: Very High	
TF_FAGU_02_Intern_Dienstleistung_Fremdauftrag.doc	0000000355	TESSA_FG: Vorgangsnummer doppelt	2: High	
TF_FAGU_02_Intern_Dienstleistung_Fremdauftrag.doc	0000000297	TeSSA_FG: Rechnung kommt nicht im AV5 an	3: Medium	
TF_FAGU_02_Intern_Dienstleistung_Fremdauftrag.doc	0000000298	TeSSA_FG: Einmalrechnung CPD	4: Low	
TF_FAGU_02_Intern_Dienstleistung_Fremdauftrag.doc	0000000287	TeSSA_FG: Dateiupload funktioniert nicht	2: High	
TF_FAGU_05_Intern_ProForma_eigenerAuftrag.doc	0000000289	TeSSA_FG: Fehlerhafter Arbeitsvorrat	2: High	
TF_FAGU_03_Intern_Schadensfall_eigenerAuftrag.doc	0000000289	TeSSA_FG: Fehlerhafter Arbeitsvorrat	2: High	
TF_FAGU_03_Intern_Schadensfall_eigenerAuftrag.doc	0000000294	TeSSA_FG: Fehlende Postleitzahl	3: Medium	
TF_FAGU_03_Intern_Schadensfall_eigenerAuftrag.doc	0000000261	TeSSA_FG: Feld abweichende Steuerklasse	2: High	
TF_FAGU_03_Intern_Schadensfall_eigenerAuftrag.doc	0000000279	TeSSA_FS: fehlerhafter Positionstyp bei	2: High	
TF_FAGU_04_Intern_Schadensfall_Fremdauftrag.doc	0000000289	TeSSA_FG: Fehlerhafter Arbeitsvorrat	2: High	
TF_FAGU_04_Intern_Schadensfall_Fremdauftrag.doc	0000000279	TeSSA_FS: fehlerhafter Positionstyp bei	2: High	

Figure 13.10 Error Messages Entered and Completed in the Service Desk

Reporting in the Test Workbench

At the start of the project, reporting took place solely by means of the standard functionality in the Test Workbench. The reports that were defined in the test concept and made available to the various different project stakeholders were exported from the status overview in the Test Workbench and formatted in tabular or graphical form. They were then being forwarded as tables or presentations to the relevant target groups or used in status meetings. The regular reports included visual displays of test case status or open messages over the course of a testing activity as well as the graphical display of the test cases and messages that were processed daily.

BW Reporting

Quickly, the manual creation of time series and graphics via the circuitous route of a spreadsheet was replaced with BW reporting for test management. With the upgrade to SAP Solution Manager 7.0 EhP 1, it was possible to use the new functions without additional license fees. Following the basic configuration of reporting, the standard system contained numerous reports that satisfied the majority of reporting requirements, especially in relation to test statuses and message statuses over time. Here, reporting was based on the typical BW web interface; in addition to graphics, this has a drilldown function in the dataset and the option to filter results according to all attributes. This type of intuitive reporting is available via the *Test Management* work center in SAP Solution Manager and supports both proactive and risk-based decisions.

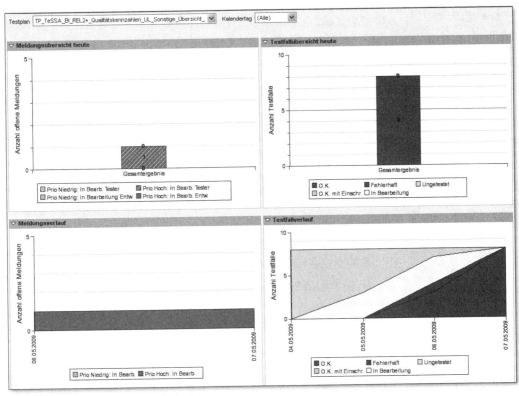

Figure 13.11 Test Management Cockpit

In addition to the reports that were supplied, the reporting function was enhanced in the TeSSA project. This was done in collaboration with SAP Test Management Consulting. As part of a consulting solution, a test management cockpit was designed for the project. Within a web interface, this cockpit displays all relevant testing activity analysis at a glance (see Figure 13.11). This cockpit can be called as a web page. Furthermore,

Test management cockpit

it can be viewed by test managers, project managers, and management at any time. Other reports were created that map the reporting requirements of the project. Furthermore, the layout and color of the reports were adjusted to the project requirements and corporate identity of Deutsche Telekom. The reports created manually at the start could now be called at the click of a mouse. Up-to-date reporting in accordance with the requirements defined initially is now available any time without the need for any manual post-processing.

Completing the testing activities
After a test run, the coordinator completed the test and then documented the final test result in a test report in the Test Workbench, which listed all of the testing activities, their statuses, and documentation as well as any related metadata in detail. Any further changes to the plan were prevented by setting the relevant status profile in the test plan. Following an acceptance test, the test coordinator prepared the acceptance documents and obtained the necessary approvals.

All in all, using SAP Solution Manager has greatly improved the speed and transparency of testing activities, thus ensuring that deadlines are adhered to and any solutions tested are of a sufficiently high quality. So says Jörg Olliger, who was responsible for setting up the Test Center in the implementation phase and who played a key role in the implementation of SAP Solution Manager. Within the application management solution, the functions used in the area of documentation, test management, and error management enjoyed a high level of acceptance.

The Service Desk allowed those involved in the test and the relevant developers to efficiently communicate with each other. It also accelerated troubleshooting and error resolution. Using email notifications that were based on status changes meant that no time was lost during communication between testers, test owners, and developers. For management reporting, maximum transparency was achieved across the entire test run. In particular, BW reporting and the Test Center management cockpit based on BW reporting provided extensive graphical formatting of all data, thus supporting well-informed decisions.

Training effort
Testers needed just a few hours of training on document management, the Test Workbench and, in particular, the tester work center. The numerous support options available when documenting executed test cases were positively received. These permit exact reproduction of the test run at

any time and also fully reproduce the testing activities in the long term as part of the obligation to provide supporting documentation.

All in all, Jörg Olliger praises the highly integrated and central concept of the solution. All of the functions interact with each other and, as a result, there are no integration gaps between the individual application areas. Within the TeSSA project, SAP Solution Manager is an important platform that forms the basis for future phases of the project and for productive operation.

Alongside the functions already available in the standard system, SAP Solution Manager was specifically enhanced to include minor custom developments in order to implement project-specific and enterprise-specific requirements. In addition to the aforementioned cockpit for BW reporting, a web interface for displaying the Business Blueprint and all project documents was implemented in the SAP portal. The initial requirement for document management assumed that everyone involved in the project would be able to view central information at any time, including specifications, process descriptions, manuals, procedure models, and other documentation. This also included users who do not have direct access to SAP Solution Manager or who can only access the individual functions of SAP Solution Manager via the work center. To satisfy this requirement, a web interface was developed that accesses a project in SAP Solution Manager by means of a system user and then displays the relevant documents in a Business Blueprint on a portal page (see Figure 13.12). Authorized portal users with read access can call any document stored there.

Project-specific enhancements

In addition to manually executing functional test cases, the project focused on test automation in order to improve efficiencies and save resources during roll-outs and for regression tests. End-to-end test cases that correspond to the perspective of the end user were automated.

Automation strategy in the SOA project

The procedure for end-to-end automation is primarily used for web applications composed of existing web services and function modules. For this strategy, an application that meets the specification or is initially available as a prototype design is directly tested via the user interface in the portal. A major benefit of this approach is automation from the perspective of the end user who accesses the user interface. This automation can easily be implemented by adopting the capture-and-replay approach. The test object is considered here from the user interface perspective.

End-to-end automation

Access of the web application to services or functions in the back end is initially handled as a black box.

Dokumentenmanagement im Solution Manager							
Dokumentenstruktur	Link	Status	Geändert am	Geändert durch	ausgecheckt	ausgecheckt durch	
▶ **Service Manual AM INES**							
▼ **Dokumentation für AP14**							
· **Konfiguration**							
· **Organisationseinheiten**							
· **Stammdaten**							
▼ **Geschäftsszenarios**							
▼ Projekt							
· Organisationseinheiten							
· Stammdaten							
▼ Geschäftsprozesse							
▶ Präsentationen							
▶ Ziele und Aufgaben							
▶ Customizing Dokumentation							
▶ x500							
▶ IMAGEMASTER							
▼ Betrieb							
· Organisationseinheiten							
· Stammdaten							
▼ Geschäftsprozesse							
▼ BPM							
▼ Projektdokumentation	Dokumentenordner						
· Prozess-Monitoring Servicemanagement - Konzept.ppt	Dokument	In Bearbeitung	24.02.2009	X13841			
· TP IT_AP14_BPM_ Payment Factory.doc	Dokument	Copy-Editing	03.12.2008	X13701			
· TP IT_AP14_BPM_Servicemanagement.DOC	Dokument	Copy-Editing	03.12.2008	X13701			
· 20091802_BW-Prozess_Überblick.ppt	Dokument	Copy-Editing	19.02.2009	X13701			
· WebServices/views TeSSA Prozesse (von J.Krumnow)	Dokument	Copy-Editing	24.02.2009	VKLOSE			
· Kopie von Schnittstelle MWWF PortalRelease2V1.1	Dokument	In Bearbeitung	24.02.2009	VKLOSE			
· BPM TeSSA-Prozesse.xls	Dokument	Copy-Editing	06.05.2009	X13701			
· Webservices_J2EEApps_FAK.xls	Dokument	Copy-Editing	07.05.2009	X13701			
· Diagnostics							

Figure 13.12 Displaying the Documents in SAP Solution Manager Within the SAP Portal

This procedure requires a high stability of the test objects or all of the technical objects used by the test object. This is not always possible for the prototype-development approach frequently used in the web environment or in services under development, as a result of high dynamics. Consequently, the strategy of end-to-end automation is primarily used for test objects that are largely based on standardized functions or functions that are already stable.

Test automation in the roll-out The test automation procedure is also linked to the roll-out of the central template of the TeSSA project. In an effort to verify the re-implementation of processes in a company as quickly as possible, automated test cases are increasingly used in integration tests. The manual test effort associated with the roll-outs is significantly reduced in this way so that only a manual sample test and an acceptance test for critical business processes are executed in the meantime. In the roll-out phases, both the test duration and the effort required in terms of personnel were reduced considerably.

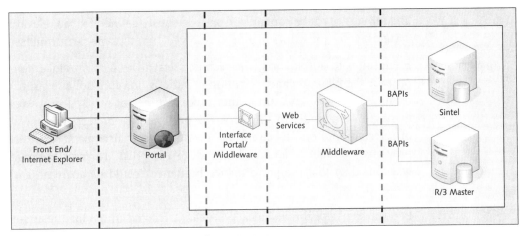

Figure 13.13 End-to-End Automation in the TeSSA Project

The use of test automation for any web interfaces based on the Hypertext Transfer Protocol (HTTP) is not part of eCATT's range of services. For this purpose, Borland SilkPerformer, which facilitates the automation of web interfaces by means of the capture-and-replay approach, was used when testing end-to-end processes. User inputs were initially recorded in the web browser before being parameterized and equipped with check routines. Because Borland's test automation tool was already in use at T-Systems, Deutsche Telekom already had extensive knowledge of the tool.

Another reason for using this tool is that it can be integrated into eCATT. Borland SilkPerformer is certified for use with the eCATT interface defined by SAP. Here, eCATT assumes control of SilkPerformer. Scripts created using SilkPerformer are uploaded into SAP Solution Manager and can also be managed there. Scripts are downloaded from SAP Solution Manager and subsequently executed using Borland SilkPerformer. Because this tool can be integrated into eCATT, it is also possible to assign

Integration into SAP Solution Manager

input parameters to the scripts and to make recorded output values available for follow-up steps. Thanks to this option, eCATT can be combined arbitrarily with SilkPerformer scripts in order to automate testing of end-to-end processes.

Defect management in test automation

Similar to the manual testing activities, a defect management process was implemented for automated testing. Any errors that occurred in the test were documented in the Service Desk within SAP Solution Manager and forwarded to the contact persons previously defined for the relevant systems. Once the errors had been resolved, a re-test was performed.

Non-functional tests

In addition to automation, the technical test team also provided support for the planning and execution of various non-functional tests; for example, regularly measuring the response times of selected processes in single user mode. In this way, the performance or response speed of selected applications could be assessed from a user perspective. If previously defined tolerance limits were exceeded, an error message was issued so that the performance bottleneck could be analyzed and resolved.

Load test

In a further step, the technical test team executed initial load tests for individual systems and processes in accordance with the tried-and-trusted procedure model from SAP Test Management Consulting. The main activities associated with preparing the load test were the creation of a load profile, the creation of an appropriate test dataset, and use of the selected load test tool to implement the load profile. Once again, Borland SilkPerformer was used to execute the load test. Because numerous automated test scripts for critical business processes were already available thanks to previous automation endeavors, Deutsche Telekom was able to significantly reduce the time and effort associated with preparing for the load test. After the test, the findings were summarized in the form of extensive reporting and presented to the project team members. In addition, optimization measures were identified on the software side that could subsequently be implemented with support from the technical test team.

Backup and recovery tests

The technical team also provided support for backup and recovery tests in the TeSSA system by creating schedules and coordinating any other testing activities.

In addition to the testing process, the consultants from SAP Test Management Consulting provided support to the Test Center or project during activities in the testing activity environment, such as when managing the solution after the go-live. In particular, this included monitoring of the solution landscape. Comprehensive monitoring had already been established in the context of load tests. The experience gained here was used to implement monitoring of the production systems and processes.

Other activities in the Test Center environment

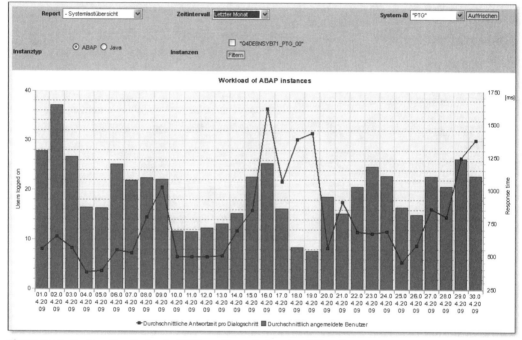

Figure 13.14 System Monitoring in BW Reporting – System Load Overview

In addition to test management, BW Reporting within SAP Solution Manager is also used for the graphical formatting and reporting of monitoring data. In particular, peak loads and long-term trends can be analyzed in this way, thus making it possible to anticipate potential risks. The web interface used in reporting facilitates intuitive navigation by means of a comprehensive dataset. Furthermore, key reports on the system status, for example, a system load overview (see Figure 13.14) or use of the memory of the satellite systems connected to SAP Solution Manager (see Figure 13.15) are provided in the standard system. BW Reporting

BW Reporting for monitoring

for monitoring essentially permits the analysis and graphical display of all values provided in Computing Center Management System (CCMS) via agents of the respective target systems.

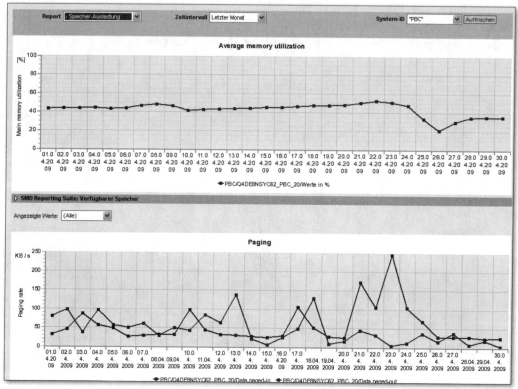

Figure 13.15 System Monitoring in BW Reporting—Memory Utilization

Monitoring the
IBM WebSphere
Application Server

During the project, a separate agent was developed for the IBM WebSphere Application Server. This agent permits analysis of the server's many key performance indicators. The BW system contained in SAP Solution Manager was filled with user-defined information that records selected metrics associated with the WebSphere server. In this way, SAP Solution Manager was used in the project to monitor a central non-SAP system, to display the resulting data ad hoc, and to also make it available as a trend analysis.

BW Reporting for monitoring was used productively. The reports established here made it possible to obtain an overview of the status of each system at any time and therefore facilitated prompt response to variances. As a result of using BW Reporting extensively for monitoring in the entire system landscape and involving non-SAP systems in particular, Deutsche Telekom is leading the field in the use of SAP Solution Manager as a central monitoring and analysis platform.

In addition to technical system monitoring, the project team implemented business process monitoring in order to check critical business processes. This is based on the process flows already documented in the implementation and mapped in the Business Blueprint. During production operation, the business processes defined here are linked with appropriate monitoring attributes that permit a direct statement as to whether a process can run smoothly without any incidents or whether error effects that occur within the system landscape interfere with the business process.

Business Process Monitoring

Monitoring data includes both technical and business key performance indicators, both of which are displayed in the context of the associated process step or related interface. In the TeSSA project, proactive monitoring of all core business processes was established in this way, thus making it possible to detect problems and risks in the process flow early on and therefore ensure smooth production operation.

In terms of managing the project, the ROOT CAUSE ANALYSIS function in SAP Solution Manager was used to facilitate a systematic cause analysis of errors in the entire system landscape. This function is available in SAP Solution Manager Diagnostics. Here, root cause analysis provides a central interface for error diagnosis, which permits access to all diagnostic data. This includes system load, error messages, configuration, and change information, all the way through to logs and traces in the systems connected within the solution landscape. This function is based on an open infrastructure that facilitates the comprehensive diagnosis of SAP systems and selected third-party systems.

Root cause analysis

In the TeSSA project, causes of error in back-end systems were determined in this way. For example, the trace analysis shown in Figure 13.16 provides information as to whether performance losses occur when calling a function from the front end, the network, or the back-end systems. Thanks to a structured methodology and versatile analysis options, root-cause analysis helps detect error causes during testing and in production and therefore helps accelerate the entire error resolution process.

E2E trace analysis

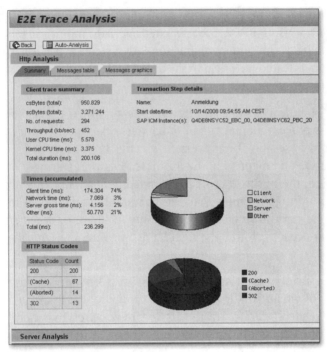

Figure 13.16 E2E Trace Analysis

Application
Lifecycle
Management

Key functions in SAP Solution Manager were already used extensively in the TeSSA project. Consequently, Deutsche Telekom was able to significantly improve the efficiency of project implementation and the management of solutions in the project environment. Continuous expansion in the use of SAP Solution Manager is planned in the future. Because key constructs already exist—for example, the Business Blueprint of the project, test plans, and data in the field of management—these can also be used for additional application scenarios and functions.

Each of the test levels shown, the test automation, as well as the additional activities performed place very different demands on the Test Center employees and on the tools used. In addition to controlling the testing activities globally—which requires methodological knowledge—it was also necessary to address those technical issues that demand specialist technical knowledge. Similarly, the context of SOA always had to be considered, which demanded specialist knowledge of the resulting web architecture from those technically oriented individuals involved in testing.

Ralf van Koll attributes a major part of the success of the Test Center to experts from SAP Test Management Consulting. Those consultants deployed as test coordinators and technical experts demonstrated a high level of control expertise. Thanks to a high level of technology expertise in relation to the tools used and methodical specialist knowledge in the testing environment, the consultants acted as drivers of innovation and continuously applied their specialist knowledge and experience to the setup and operation of the Test Center. In many cases, the basic design setup and the continuous optimizations in the Test Center processes can be traced back to the input of the consultants, who also act with a high level of problem-solving expertise and can therefore push the further development of the Test Center in all areas. This is especially true for the integrated use of SAP Solution Manager as an application management solution for the entire project and the development of potentials for improving transparency and efficiency beyond test management. Furthermore, Deutsche Telekom was able to incorporate new developments in SAP Solution Manager 7.0 (for example, BW Reporting) into the project in a timely manner so that the Test Center now relies on the most up-to-date strategic tools within SAP Solution Manager and is therefore leading the field in the use of these tools.

SAP Test Management Consulting

In the future, the Test Center will be available as a central contact partner for testing activities as well as the technical management of Telekom Shared Service Accounting, and also for projects other than TeSSA. In future, both the project and the operation will be more strongly aligned with business processes because the concept of process orientation has proven itself in the context of implementation, testing, and management within the framework of business process monitoring. Consequently, business process monitoring will be continuously expanded in order to record all processes in the project. To control the individual sub-projects and their changes in production operation, further implementation is planned of the transport management in CTS+, which enhances functionality in the standard transport management system within SAP Solution Manager. In this way, all transports associated with all connected systems can be planned and executed centrally. In this context, change request management, which permits the scheduling and execution of transports in the context of change requests, is currently being implemented.

A look ahead

In test automation, Deutsche Telekom also plans to steadily improve the level of automation. In particular, it is pushing ahead with the further automation of regression tests in order to be able to quickly test the necessary changes in production automation without needing many resources.

Conclusion

The Test Center established with the help of SAP Test Management Consulting enabled the TeSSA project to use extensive services for all aspects of software quality assurance. This approach has proven itself, and the Test Center has been positively received at group level. The high degree of standardization not only facilitated the efficient planning and execution of tests and activities based on these tests in the TeSSA project but also allowed methods and tools to be reused in other projects.

Using SAP Solution Manager in all phases of the project ensured maximum transparency across the broad range of project statuses and activities. The extensive reproducibility of process information, changes, testing activities, and monitoring data as well as the use of status profiles and digital signatures satisfied the project's strict auditing requirements.

The use of SAP Solution Manager in the coordination of manual testing activities in test management already has produced a greater degree of efficiency among testing activities while at the same time increasing transparency. This is particularly true for BW Reporting, which delivers up-to-date information about the status of the tests and error messages at any time in the form of a management dashboard without any additional effort.

In test automation, the test cases for roll-outs and future regressions tests were automated by using procedure models that took account of the specifications in the SOA environment, thus reducing the manual test effort significantly. As a result of the web architecture, eCATT and Borland SilkPerformer were used to automate testing of back-end systems, web services, and the portal from an end user perspective. Functional test cases were also re-used for load tests.

In addition to test management, the Test Center mainly focused on management, business process monitoring, and the analysis of defects. Because process-oriented reporting was based on the process descriptions established in the downstream project phases, the organization was able to implement it with very little effort. The reporting tools support monitoring of essential critical business processes.

Thanks to the aforementioned methods and tools, Deutsche Telekom also successfully uses the latest functions of SAP Solution Manager EhP 1 and is therefore leading the field in the integrated use of SAP Solution Manager in the entire application lifecycle. The innovative procedures are enhanced in a logical manner to include custom configurations and developments.

Today, the Test Center supports the TeSSA project throughout its entire project lifecycle. With the above integrated procedure, Deutsche Telekom is leading the field in process orientation and management reporting in the IT environment. By using SAP Solution Manager and especially by using its new functions, it is possible to achieve a very high degree of automation in the area of IT reporting. Status reports that were previously created manually (for example, for test management, technical system monitoring, and the status of productive business processes) can now be retrieved directly and are always up-to-date.

Thanks to its broad and successful use in the TeSSA project across different application scenarios, SAP Solution Manager has established itself as a strategic platform that will also play a central role in future projects. The test automation and management procedures have already been requested for additional productive solutions.

What can you learn from the experiences of Deutsche Telekom?   Lessons learned

▶ You can set up a Test Center as a comprehensive service organization that is available for all aspects of software quality assurance within a project or an entire enterprise. Expert knowledge of test methods and technical procedures can be bundled and expanded through the involvement of external resources. As a result of centralizing and standardizing testing activities, significant savings (cost and speed benefits) can be achieved and further intensified by out-tasking testing and test automation. Established procedure models can be fine-tuned gradually through feedback and experience, and can make a decisive contribution towards achieving a high-quality solution.

▶ Thanks to its proximity from a content perspective, a Test Center is not only able to plan and execute testing activities but it can also tackle operations issues such as monitoring and troubleshooting.

The Test Center therefore becomes a central service provider with responsibility for the comprehensive and qualitative safeguarding of solutions.

▶ Test automation in SOA projects can be implemented in accordance with an end-to-end strategy whereby a capture-and-replay approach is used to automate testing of complete business processes via the front end. Depending on the procedure model used in software development, the relevant tools (for example, eCATT) can also be used to test function modules, BAPIs, and web services in earlier test levels.

▶ SAP Solution Manager permits the development of extensive IT reporting, which can be used to analyze and display project-relevant key performance indicators and monitoring data at any time in a flexible manner. Because reporting can be adjusted to the requirements of the enterprise, it can replace manual reporting.

Appendices

A SAP Solution Manager Test Workbench vs. SAP Test Organizer

To safeguard projects in the SAP environment and to minimize the costs of testing activities, many customers have been successfully using the SAP Test Organizer, the predecessor of the SAP Test Workbench that is contained in SAP Basis, for several years now. This tool supports efficient test management as well as methodological procedures, It also supports the implementation of automated testing using CATT or eCATT, which is important with regard to its high cost-saving potential (see also Section 7.5, *Customer Report of INVISTA Resins & Fibers GmbH*). This part of the appendix shows the differences between SAP Test Organizer and the integrated Test Workbench of SAP Solution Manager.

The SAP Test Workbench was already included in early SAP R/3 releases. CATT was made available with SAP R/3 Release 3.0. The fact that the SAP Test Workbench is included among SAP Basis components enables customers to use it without any additional licensing costs.

In contrast to SAP Solution Manager, the test organization concept can be regarded as classical. It is based on the assumption that test case descriptions and automated test scripts or test configurations are managed in a freely definable hypertext structure, the test catalogs. The test objects are stored in the SAP Repository; the test case descriptions can be created, attached, or referenced using the SAP Editor.

Test catalogs

Based on those test catalogs, you then can copy test case descriptions into the plans, which in turn can be made available to the testers as part of test packages. At that level, the integration of the SAP Test Workbench with SAP Solution Manager begins (see Figure A.1). In this context as well, test plans are generated on the basis of test case descriptions, the test cases being stored in a project structure.

Although SAP Solution Manager is also available at no additional licensing cost in the SAP environment, customers sometimes still tend to avoid migrating to SAP's Application Management platform. They often refer to existing investments that have already been made and consider the value added by using SAP Solution Manager as being insignificant.

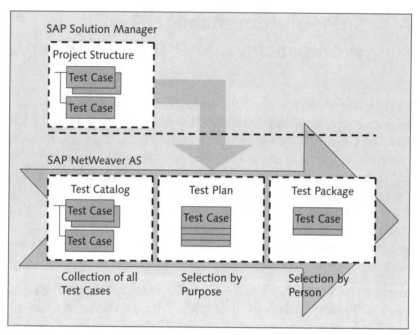

Figure A.1 Integrating SAP Solution Manager and the SAP Test Workbench

For customers who have primarily used the basic test functionality of the Test Workbench so far, SAP Solution Manager 7.0, particularly as of Enhancement Package 1, offers a significant added value through additional functionality in the test management field. This is true especially when considering specific requirements, such as the requirement of comprehensive reporting, obligation to produce documentation in the validated environment, or support for test case selection in the regression test. Essential aspects are outlined in the following paragraphs; for more detailed descriptions of the individual functions you should refer to Chapter 4, *Test Management with SAP Solution Manager*.

Complete transparency SAP Solution Manager supports the customer in setting up structured, central storage for all information that is created during the different project phases. The user can find, for instance, the requirements of a mapped business process based on at a central location as well as the implementation that's based on the business process (such as jumps to customizing and development objects), the test cases, and training documents. This enables you to interpret test results in direct relation to the provided information and to subsequently process error messages promptly on the basis of comprehensive information.

The fact that test-specific activities can be consistently reproduced is a feature the SAP Test Workbench provides only to a limited extent without using it in conjunction with SAP Solution Manager.

SAP Solution Manager integrates the SAP Knowledge Warehouse functionality that is contained in the scope of the standard delivery of SAP Basis. This means that you can create, edit, and release test case descriptions using a document management tool. Each processing history is directly available via the document attributes. In addition, all document versions can be reconstructed.

Document management

The functional scope of SAP Test Workbench when used alone is rather limited with regard to reproducing changes to test cases.

The digital signature can be used in SAP Solution Manager to safeguard status changes to KW documents with regard to authorizations (for instance in release scenarios). Appropriate status schemas allow you to restrict change authorizations to specific groups of users.

Digital signature

The digital signature is not available for the SAP Test Workbench.

A test plan that has been created on the basis of test catalogs (in the classical sense) can merely inherit the relevant test case descriptions. The test cases (repository objects) contained in those descriptions can be assigned test objects such as transactions, reports, or function modules. However, this data is only informational in character.

User guidance

By using SAP Solution Manager, you can generate test plans on the basis of a project within the project-relevant system landscape. This enables the tester to access the test case description and the relevant transaction (maintenance via the TEST OBJECT field) through his or her test package. The transaction can then be directly started in the associated test system at the click of the mouse.

Referencing relevant transactions in the business blueprint of a project is also the prerequisite for using Business Process Change Analyzer, which is also only available in SAP Solution Manager. It performs a change analysis by comparing technical bills of material (TBOM) with transport requests and can use the results of this analysis to suggest a test plan with relevant test cases for a regression test (see Section 4.5, *Extended Functionality for Creating Test Plans and Packages*).

In general, the user guidance has been greatly improved in SAP Solution Manager. This involves using the test management work center, which provides a web-based introduction to the functionality of test management.

BW reporting   Besides the classic reporting functionality of the Test Workbench, the work center also offers integrated BW reporting, which enables comprehensive evaluations of testing activities and their graphical processing (see Section 4.7, *Status Analysis*).

Conclusion

SAP Solution Manager is far more than just a tool to support the test management activities in customer projects. Because of its additional test-management functionality and particularly given the new functions of Enhancement Package 1, it should always be preferred to the classic SAP Test Organizer if high requirements are set for the testing process (for instance, obligation to produce documentation) and for reporting.

Compared to SAP Solution Manager, the SAP Test Organizer pursues a somewhat narrower approach. Depending on the project situation, it can make sense for customers to start with that approach in order to achieve short-term results. However, in the medium term even those customers will find it advisable to migrate to SAP Solution Manager, as this is the only way to benefit from the aforementioned synergy effects with other application scenarios.

B SAP NetWeaver Knowledge Warehouse—Functionality in SAP Solution Manager

SAP Solution Manager uses numerous basic functions that come with SAP NetWeaver Application Server by integrating them into its own functional scope. In particular, SAP Solution Manager makes use of the functionality of SAP NetWeaver Knowledge Warehouse (KW) that is provided in the standard delivery of SAP Basis.

When creating or storing a KW document in the structure of an SAP Solution Manager project, documents can be newly created based on a specific project template, and existing documents can be reused. To this end, documents can be uploaded into SAP KW and references within SAP Solution Manager or references to an external storage can be integrated.

By default, documents are stored in the SAP database. However, you also can store documents on a separate content server and reference them in SAP Solution Manager. A migration at a later stage is possible at any time. The settings required to do that are described in great detail in the SAP Reference IMG. To access these descriptions in the SAP Reference IMG, select the following path: SAP SOLUTION MANAGER • SCENARIO-SPECIFIC SETTINGS • IMPLEMENTATION • OPTIONAL ACTIVITIES • DOCUMENT MANAGEMENT.

Content server

When a project is created in SAP Solution Manager, the context of the project-specific objects of the SAP KW is defined. You must define the project language in the GENERAL DATA tab (see Figure B.1); however, the user is queried for document enhancements when saving the project for the first time. This context allows you to protect the authorizations for document access.

The document attributes provide the user with an overview of important organizational aspects of an object. The GENERAL DATA tab, in particular, enables you to enter information on responsibilities and about the type of documentation being used (in the sense of a document template). Here you can also enter details regarding the priority, the status, and search

Document attributes

terms. Note that in this context the value selection can be manipulated via project standards (see Section 4.1, *Creating a Project*).

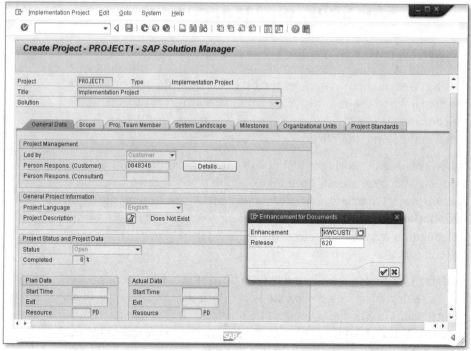

Figure B.1 Enhancement for Project-Specific SAP KW Documents

During testing you can use the document attributes; for example when enhancing the selection options for the generation of test plans. Experience has shown that the default options can be efficiently complemented via search terms.

The document attributes also enable you to integrate comments and cross-references to other documents within and outside of SAP Solution Manager. The HISTORY tab (see Figure B.2) gives you access to the current status of the document as well as to all previous statuses.

Customer-specific attributes for KW documents

The document attributes made available by the standard SAP version can be complemented with customer-specific attributes in the Document Modeling Workbench. Here you can add attributes to the standard document classes.

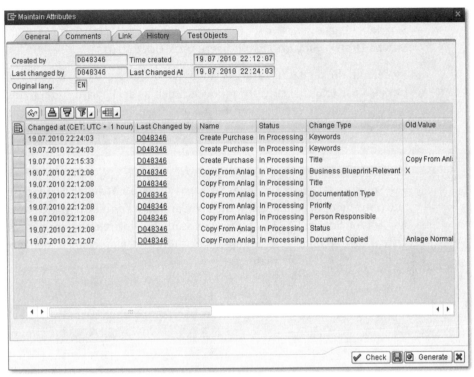

Figure B.2   History of a Project-Specific SAP KW Document

In this context, we refer you to SAP Notes 350535, 436430, and 805477. These notes describe the necessary technical requirements.

A digital signature can be used in SAP Solution Manager to safeguard status changes to KW documents with regard to authorizations (for instance in release scenarios). Appropriate status schemas allow you to restrict change authorizations to specific groups of users. This guarantees the authenticity of test cases and test notes and protects the test cases and test notes against unauthorized changes.

Digital signature

When creating a digital signature, you must define authorization objects and assign authorization groups to them. Moreover, you must define individual signatures and integrate these into signature strategies. You can link the signatures to the document types by using the document status schema in Transaction SOLAR_PROJECT_ADMIN. You can find a comprehensive description of setting up digital signatures in the SAP Reference IMG. To access these descriptions in the SAP Reference IMG, select the following path: SAP Solution Manager • Scenario-Specific Settings • Implementation • Optional Activities • Document Management • Digital Signature and Status for Documents.

By default, the digital signature is generated by the system itself, but you can also use external security products, such as an ID card. Integrating external products can become relevant if legal requirements must be fulfilled.

Conclusion

SAP Solution Manager integrates SAP NetWeaver Knowledge Warehouse functions that are contained in the standard delivery of SAP NetWeaver Application Server. SAP KW represents a suitable document management system that enables you, among other things, to map change management in a reproducible manner.

C   Recommended Reading

Performance Monitoring

▶ Thomas Schneider: *SAP Performance Optimization Guide.* 6th edition, Boston, SAP PRESS 2011.
The standard work on performance optimization, it helps to identify and analyze performance problems as well as tuning of ABAP and Java applications.

▶ Hermann Gahm: *ABAP Performance Tuning.* Boston, SAP PRESS 2009.
This book describes the available methods of performance analysis (analysis during design, ad-hoc analysis, traces, and post-mortem analysis) as well as the tools used, for instance, ABAP and performance trace, Code Inspector, and Memory Inspector. It then outlines the details of programming. Particularly SQL processing, data buffering, internal tables, and data transfer are discussed.

▶ Michael Klöffer, Marc Thier: *Performing End-to-End Root Cause Analysis Using SAP Solution Manager.* Boston, SAP PRESS 2008.
In this SAP PRESS Essentials guide, the authors describe all scenarios and tools for end-to-end analysis.

SAP Solution Manager Enterprise Edition

▶ Marc O. Schäfer, Matthias Melich: *SAP Solution Manager Enterprise Edition.* 2nd edition. Boston, SAP PRESS 2009.
This book provides administrators, consultants, and IT managers with a comprehensive description of the functionality and use of SAP Solution Manager. It describes all scenarios where this system management solution provides support: from roadmaps of the design phase, to testing and operation (administration, monitoring, reporting, service desk, diagnostics, and much more), to optimization using change management and upgrades.

▶ SAP Help Portal (*http://help.sap.com*).
This information offer is available on the Internet free of charge. Here, readers can find an online help documentation of SAP Solution Manager.

▶ SAP Service Marketplace (SMP) (*http://service.sap.com*).
This information offer is available after registration for SMP. The required user IDs can be requested on the initial screen of SMP.

  ▶ Quicklink */solutionmanager*
  General information offer of SMP on the SAP Solution Manager topic.

  ▶ Quicklink */enterpriseedition*
  Special information offer of SMP on the SAP Solution Manager Enterprise Edition.

  ▶ Quicklink */testing*
  Special information offer of SMP on the E2E Integration Testing topic.

  ▶ Quicklink */tmc*
  Information on SAP Test Management Consulting, which provides customer reports, presentations on tools and services, as well as useful links.

  ▶ Quicklink */rkt-solman*
  Online learning material on the SAP Solution Manager topics (among others, SAP Tutors and screencams).

  ▶ Quicklink */instguides*
  Via SAP COMPONENTS - SAP SOLUTION MANAGER, you can find the official guides on the SAP Solution Manager topic (among others, master guide, security guide, operations guide).

▶ SAP Developer Network (SDN) (*http://sdn.sap.com*).
SDN is continuously developing into a valuable source of information about SAP Solution Manager. Relevant blogs, wikis, and so on offer a myriad of tips and tricks developed in the respective communities.

D   The Authors

Markus Helfen is Consulting Director of the SAP Test Management Consulting unit of SAP Deutschland AG & Co. KG. He joined SAP in 1994 and was recently involved in developing the SAP test-tool strategy, building a global consulting organization for SAP Testing Services, and the related service portfolio. With his team, he drove many topics and standardized services successfully in the market, such as IT Reporting with SAP Solution Manager and SAP BusinessObjects Xcelsius, or data anonymization with SAP Test Data Migration Server. He is also involved in a constantly growing number of Test Center implementations. Currently, Markus Helfen is responsible for building the SAP Application Lifecycle Management capability. He has many years of experience in the corporate and customer environment, dealing with quality assurance and with testing in particular.

Today, **Hans Martin Trauthwein** is a member of the executive board of Sofis AG, a consulting service provider specializing in Application Life Cycle Management with SAP Solution Manager. Before he joined Sofis AG, he was Principal Consultant of the SAP Test Management Consulting unit of SAP Deutschland AG & Co. KG. He led the SAP-internal SAP Solution Manager focus group, an EMEA-wide union of consulting experts who cover all phases of SAP Application Lifecycle Management. Since 1996, he has gained wide-ranging experience, both within the group and with customers, in the areas of quality assurance, test management, test automation, basis technologies, and SAP Solution Manager (e.g., incident management, change request management, global roll-out). He has put this know-how to good use in his project activities.

Index

X

Shows how to install and activate enhancement packages via the switch framework

Explains how to successfully use all related EHP tools

Covers best practices for planning and running EHP projects

Martina Kaplan, Christian Oehler

Implementing SAP Enhancement Packages

With SAP NetWeaver 7.0 or SAP ERP 6.0, SAP has fundamentally changed the method of how you can import new functions to your running systems: Enhancement packages (EHP) can be activated in a more target-oriented, faster, and controllable way in the SAP system, via the switch framework. This book offers project guidelines for administrators on the use of SAP enhancement packages, including topics such as areas of use, planning, installation, project specifications, and best practices. It explains the planning of EHP projects (compared to common upgrade projects), provides details on the implementation of enhancement packages, and offers tips and tricks based on the authors' experiences.

220 pp., 2010, 69,95 Euro / US$ 84.95
ISBN 978-1-59229-351-3

>> www.sap-press.com

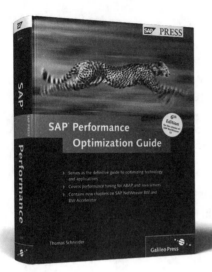

Serves as the definitive guide to optimizing technology and applications

Covers performance tuning for ABAP and Java servers

Contains new chapters on SAP NetWeaver BW and BW Accelerator

Thomas Schneider

SAP Performance Optimization Guide

This book explains the fundamentals of analyzing and optimizing SAP system performance, covers performance-critical architectural aspects of all important SAP backend servers, and describes tools and hints for analyzing and tuning performance. Revised and updated, the new edition includes new chapters on SAP NetWeaver BW and BW Accelerator (TREX), and is updated for SAP NetWeaver 7.1 throughout.

798 pp., 6. edition 2011, 79,95 Euro / US$ 79.95
ISBN 978-1-59229-368-1

>> www.sap-press.com

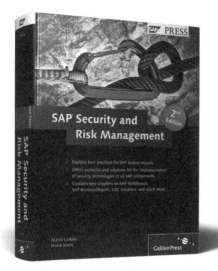

Describes system security for all SAP components

Contains new chapters on SAP GRC, SAP NetWeaver, SOA, J-SOX, and much more

Revised and updated with approximately 200 pages of brand new material

Mario Linkies, Horst Karin

SAP Security and Risk Management

With step-by-step instructions and numerous examples of proven methods, this book teaches you how to technically implement security in SAP NetWeaver. For all SAP applications, you'll learn where and how you can secure processes or improve the security of existing systems. To this end, you will learn the best practices of an SAP security strategy, as well as international standards. You will also learn how to integrate new technologies with your risk analysis. For this second edition, all parts of this book are updated to expand the description of new SAP products.

742 pp., 2. edition 2010, 69,95 Euro / US$ 69.95
ISBN 978-1-59229-355-1

>> www.sap-press.com